THE ROUTLEDGE HANDBOOK OF CONTEMPORARY ITALY

History, Politics, Society

Edited by
Andrea Mammone, Ercole Giap Parini, and Giuseppe A. Veltri

LONDON AND NEW YORK

First published in paperback 2018

First published 2015
by Routledge
2 Park Square, Milton Park, Abingdon, Oxon OX14 4RN

and by Routledge
711 Third Avenue, New York, NY 10017

Routledge is an imprint of the Taylor & Francis Group, an informa business

British Library Cataloguing in Publication Data
A catalogue record for this book is available from the British Library

Library of Congress Cataloging in Publication Data
The Routledge handbook of contemporary Italy: history, politics, society / edited by Andrea Mammone, Ercole Giap Parini and Giuseppe A. Veltri.
pages cm
Includes bibliographical references and index.
ISBN 978-0-415-60417-8 (alk. paper) – ISBN 978-1-315-70997-0 (alk. paper) 1. Italy – History – Handbooks, manuals, etc. 2. Italy – Politics and government – Handbooks, manuals, etc. 3. Italy – Social life and customs – Handbooks, manuals, etc. I. Mammone, Andrea. II. Parini, Ercole Giap, 1968– III. Veltri, Giuseppe A.
DG417.R68 2014
945.092 – dc23
2014042156

ISBN: 978-0-415-60417-8 (hbk)
ISBN: 978-1-138-58957-5 (pbk)
ISBN: 978-1-315-70997-0 (ebk)

Typeset in Bembo and Stone Sans
by Florence Production Ltd, Stoodleigh, Devon, UK

CONTENTS

FIGURES

TABLES

CONTRIBUTORS

Editors

Andrea Mammone is Lecturer in Modern European History at Royal Holloway, University of London, UK.

Ercole Giap Parini, Associate Professor in Sociology at the Università della Calabria, Italy.

Giuseppe A. Veltri, Associate Professor in Cognitive Sociology and Research Methods, University of Trento, Italy.

Contributors

John Agnew, Distinguished Professor of Geography at UCLA, USA.

Gianluca Argentin, Researcher in Sociology at the Università Cattolica del Sacro Cuore, Milano.

Jean-Louis Briquet, Research Professor in Politics at the Centre européen de sociologie et de science politique (CESSP), CNRS-EHESS_Université Paris 1 Panthéon-Sorbonne, France.

Martin J. Bull, Professor of Politics at the University of Salford, UK.

Anna Cento Bull, Professor of Italian History and Politics at the University of Bath, UK.

Peter Ceretti, MSc in Political Economy of Europe from the London School of Economics and Political Science, UK.

Iain Chambers, Professor of Cultural and Postcolonial Studies at the Università degli Studi di Napoli "L'Orientale," Italy.

Michele Colucci, researcher at the Istituto di studi sulle società del Mediterraneo, CNR, Naples, Italy.

Nicolò Conti, Associate Professor of Political Science at the Unitelma Sapienza University of Rome, Italy.

Philip Cooke, Professor of Italian History at the University of Strathclyde, UK.

Mario Diani, Professor of Sociology at the Università degli Studi di Trento, Italy and Research Professor of Social Sciences at ICREA at the Universitat Pompeu Fabra, Barcelona, Spain.

Mark Donovan, Senior Lecturer in Politics at Cardiff University, UK.

Maria Fabbri, researcher at the Sociolab, Florence, Italy.

Alessandro Giovannini, PhD researcher in Economics at Sciences Po, Paris, France.

Lilia Giugni, PhD candidate in Politics at the University of Cambridge, UK.

Annarita Gori, postdoctoral researcher at the Instituto da Ciências Sociais, University of Lisbon, Portugal.

Alfonsina Iona, Senior Lecturer in Economics and Finance at the Università di Messina and Senior Lecturer in Economics and Finance at Queen Mary, University of London, UK.

Paolo Jedlowski, Professor of Sociology at the Università della Calabria, Italy.

Marc Lazar, Professor of History and Political Sociology at Sciences Po, Paris, France and President of the School of Government at Luiss Guido Carli, Rome, Italy.

Leone Leonida, Senior Lecturer in Economics and Finance at the Università di Messina and Senior Lecturer in Economics and Finance at Queen Mary, University of London, UK.

Carl Levy, Professor of Politics at Goldsmiths, University of London, UK.

Donatella Loprieno, Assistant Professor of Public Law at the Università della Calabria, Italy.

Julia Lynch, Associate Professor of Political Science at the University of Pennsylvania, USA.

Dario Maimone Ansaldo Patti, Assistant Professor of Public Economics at the Università di Messina, Italy.

Raoul Minetti, Professor of Economics at Michigan State University, USA.

Pietro Navarra, Professor of Public Economics at the Università di Messina, Italy and Visiting Professor of Economics at the University of Pennsylvania, USA.

James L. Newell, Professor of Politics at the University of Salford, UK.

Cinzia Padovani, Associate Professor of Media Studies at Southern Illinois University Carbondale, USA.

Roberta Pergher, Assistant Professor of History at Indiana University, USA.

Francesco Raniolo, Professor in Political Science at the Università della Calabria, Italy

Elisabetta Ruspini, Associate Professor of Sociology at the Università di Milano Bicocca, Italy.

Damiano Bruno Silipo, Professor of Economics at the Università della Calabria, Italy.

Marco Tarchi, Professor of Political Science at the Università di Firenze, Italy.

Guido Tintori, Senior Research Associate, FIERI.

Luca Verzichelli, Professor of Public Policy Analysis and Italian Politics at the Università di Siena, Italy.

INTRODUCTION

Notes on Italy in recent decades and the Handbook

Andrea Mammone, Ercole Giap Parini, and Giuseppe A. Veltri

Writing on Italy

Traditionally, a foreign reader always finds a good number of books dedicated to Italy. A great emphasis is usually given to the artistic heritage of the nation, cuisine, travel guides, and its significant past, from ancient Rome to Mussolini and fascism. For social scientists, the usual attempts to analyze Italian society have instead regularly focused on Italy's politics and institutions. In other fields, Italian culture, literature, and arts are continuously attracting the attention of scholars. In many ways, Italy matters, and this Handbook wants therefore to reinforce this belief, and it is grounded on the acceptance of the geopolitical, intellectual, social, and economic significance of the Italian peninsula for the Western world. For example, the experience of the "Berlusconi years," the so-called Second Republic, and the advent of a new wave of political and social actors have been, and are going to be, at the center of attention. In truth, many recent works especially, though not exclusively, in Italy seem to be devoted to the "Italian case," its somewhat bizarre democracy, and the various examples of corruption, bribes, and waste of public funding. They, at times, provide some generic (if not sensationalist) journalistic accounts of Italian society and politics (whilst the scholarly production tends to be narrower). This has inflated the market for more scientific overviews.

Some of these books, naturally, relate to the analysis of the controversial experience of "Berlusconismo," the particular political style that has characterized the Italian agenda, system, and external image in recent decades. There are, of course, exceptions to some of the non-academic accounts of this political phenomenon. The controversial figure of Silvio Berlusconi, in fact, attracted writers, readers, and the international media. Yet, besides some space in this introduction and in a limited number of chapters, we have usually resisted the temptation to focus on all this, and, given the wider aims of our book, on the quality of Italy's democracy. We are well aware how studies have often described the nation as a specific example of Western democracy (and this would, at least partially, explain the rise of Berlusconi's political agenda and his enduring appeal). Some of the contributors to this Handbook have also participated in this debate by calling Italy a "sick man of Europe," and wondering how normal the nation has been recently. Others took a diverse approach, though not many works have been able to focus on Italy in a really broad framework as we have done with this edited volume.

Not many books offer, for example, a collection of essays about the social and cultural transformations and continuities of contemporary Italy. In this Handbook, we aim to fill this gap by publishing contributions that analyze contemporary Italy from a sociological and cultural point of view, and they have been organized for this purpose into five parts. This goes along with discussions on memory, reflections on politics, an overview of the economy, and the role played by some institutions. *The Routledge Handbook of Contemporary Italy* has the goal, and perhaps the ambition, of becoming a fundamental tool of support to scholars and readers interested in understanding Italy in recent decades. It tries to provide a panoramic view of Italian society and its related narratives, policies, and Italian culture that, although not complete (as this would be impossible to achieve), is as wide and diverse as possible.

As we mentioned before, a very large number of books have a very journalistic tone, whereas others suffer from the editorial and thematic constraints which very often limit discussion. Some of them do, nonetheless, offer interesting perspectives (though they are narrow in their aims), and students of Italy might wish to find out more about them. Journalist Bill Emmott, for example, recently published *Good Italy, Bad Italy* (2012). Emmott's work is based on a number of interviews, and essentially compares some reasons that contributed to Italy's downward turn with the "positive" sides of the country. Maurizio Viroli published a more intellectually complex book on contemporary Italy. His *The Liberty of Servants* (2011) is based on the assumption that Italy, under Berlusconi, became a land of humble servants and courtiers. Whilst we share some of the frame brightly provided by Viroli, the *Routledge Handbook* aims to add some further dimensions. There is the necessity to broaden the understanding of the implications of Berlusconism (this latter perceived as a sort of culture and worldview) and the functioning of Italian society, politics, and mentalities, which is probably larger than a modern Middle-Ages-like court. Other quite successful books include David Gilmour's *The Pursuit of Italy* (2011), which provided, on the other hand, another long-term history of Italy. In addition, his book devoted a few pages to the recent era. The beautifully written *The Force of Destiny* (2007) by Christopher Duggan similarly devotes only some sections to the postwar years, and this book mostly deals with the building of modern Italy.

Another interesting recent work is Silvana Patriarca's *Italian Vices: Nation and Character from the Risorgimento to the Republic* (2013). It analyzes the public rhetoric about the "national character" that became a favorite explanation for a good number of Italy's problems. Such debate about the remedies for transforming Italians from being undisciplined and inefficient into almost heroic people shaped the country's political and social discourses. This also permeated culture in the 1950s and 1960s (particularly popular culture), and it was present in the 1990s. Another fine book on the cultural aspects of Italy is Emanuela Scarpellini's *Material Nation: A Consumer's History of Modern Italy* (2011). This is an exploration of the evolution of consumer culture in which an underlying contradiction is in the background: Italians' capacity for aesthetic beauty and commercial success and, at the same time, the presence of difficult living conditions. Scarpellini observes that it was Italian, rather than American or French, craftsmanship that truly democratized luxury. Yet, according to the author, many contemporary Italians, who are now glued to television sets and shopping in supermarkets, have sunk to the culturally and aesthetically lowest common denominator. These books are examples of a social and cultural perspective that would be, at times, useful for understanding Italy. The Handbook also offers some contribution to this.

Interestingly, in the last few years, Italian nonfiction literature has also been revamped by neo-Southerner revisionism, which is an attempt to rewrite the history of the unification process. It believes that, essentially, the Savoia family and patriots like Cavour and Garibaldi (and, generally, Northern Italian ruling groups), (allegedly) subjugated Southern people, during and after the

Risorgimento era, to exploit their resources and start a process of underdevelopment in favor of industrial growth in the regions of the North. The most representative book is *Terroni. Tutto quello che è stato fatto perché gli italiani del Sud diventassero Meridionali*, which was written by journalist Pino Aprile (2010) and which sold hundreds of thousands of copies. This trend, though based on controversial documentation also overestimating Southern regions' wealth before 1861, feeds an inveterate sense of discontent. For historian Salvatore Lupo, this is "a 'simplistic revisionism' which stems from the political attempts to find into the past what does not exist in it, a recriminatory mentality which looks in the history for the responsibilities of contemporary disease" (Petti, 2012).[1] However, as we suggest in Parts I and V of the Handbook, this shows the role played by political movements, media, and other vectors, the legacy of some historical developments, and the relevance of historical interpretations in shaping national society and local cultures in recent years in Italy.

Static and fluid Italy

Interest in Italy is generally due to the fact that this country really represents a fascinating case, as this Mediterranean nation might look like a land in a state of long-term emergency, and surely relevant for the developments of modern democracies and societies. However, all this, along with some of the things mentioned above, and including the challenge after more than 150 years to national unification, might give the related impression (and this is often a well-accepted opinion, at least amongst some Italian people) that many things change in Italy, though with no huge transformation in the general set-up of society and the political setting. As we all know, a century ago, Italian writer Giuseppe Tomasi di Lampedusa stated, in his masterpiece *Il gattopardo*, how "all changes so that nothing changes." It is therefore believed that this involves other sectors, from the economy to elites, from family models to religious institutions, and from labor relations to the inner features of capitalism. In other words, one may say that many changes take place, but they do not often actually materialize (at least in the long term), and this gives the, at times, false belief in a static Italy. At the same time, and as the Handbook shows, it is evident that there is an increasing recognition that Italy has been transformed from the late 1980s until today. For a while, and as suggested before, this was labeled as a decline of the country not only economically (as we will mention briefly, in respect of globalization, the financial crisis, EU-led austerity, the loss of competitiveness, and the public debt), but also in its political, cultural, and social life.

Under the influence of global transformations, the Italian social fabric has, in fact, greatly changed in recent decades. Italy, for example, used to be characterized by a system of permanent jobs. This fact assured, for a long time, social stability. It represented a genuine support for a society based on stable nuclear families and ties, and, in other words, with a familiar structure consistently linked with the typical values of the Catholic Church. Starting from the 1980s, the diffusion of more "atypical" forms of job contracts, which have decreased job security, together with the scaling down of the welfare system, has strongly influenced people's perspectives on their lives. Young people delay their decision to marry and have children, and keep living with their parents, in many cases until their forties. The Istat 2013 Report tells us that the average age for getting married in 2012 was almost 31 for women and 34 for men, and this trend seems destined to rise. In 2013, there were fewer than 200,000 marriages, which represents the lowest level in Italian history (Istat, 2014). This led to a significant reduction in the birth rate. Even if this represents a diffused trend in the industrialized Western world, in Italy, it has reached alarming levels: for an Italian woman the average number of children is less than 1.3, and this is hardly balanced by immigrants living in Italy, since their birth rate is similarly decreasing (according to the Istat 2014 Report in 2013 it was 2.20). At the same time, and in a way that is variably connected to the trend we have mentioned, the decay of traditional values and calls for new model of life organization (and a positive approach toward diversity) seem to have strongly influenced family models. At least since the 1990s, different family models have been developing, in particular, the so-called *more uxorio* unions, the majority of which are constituted by people coming from a previous marriage. Same-sex couples who decide to live together are also growing and pushing for formal recognition. The strict connection of cultural changes with the economic situation is revealed by the fact that many people who are living *more uxorio* are young couples waiting for better conditions in order to get married and to have children.

In the background of these cultural, economic, and structural transformations, there is the process of the secularization of religion, especially with reference to the Catholic Church, which is traditionally assimilated to Italian culture and history. The weakening of traditional religious authority in people's daily life, the decrease in the number of people – even amongst those who consider themselves believers – who attend religious services, in short, "privatization" (religion as a more intimate fact), seem to be the most important aspects of secularization in Italy. Besides that, sociologist Vincenzo Bova has identified an inner process regarding the Catholic Church: the pluralization of the ways individuals or even groups interpret and put into practice their religious beliefs (Bova, 2013). Another sociologist, Enzo Pace, rightly mentioned how "though religious practice is decreasing, together with belief in religion [la credenza religiosa] and adherence to Catholic doctrine, Italians, in the majority, continue to think of themselves as not 'against the Church'" (Giorda).

Significantly, Italy is also becoming a multicultural country, though much more slowly than other European nations, and even if migratory flows toward Italy have been decreasing in recent years (for example 307,000 in 2013, as opposed to 350,000 in 2012: Istat, 2014). Second- and third-generation immigrants living in Italy are making a series of requests in terms of citizenship, and access to and quality of the education system. In particular, it is difficult to satisfy this with an education system characterized by high levels of bureaucratization. In recent years, Italy has also suffered from relatively indiscriminate spending cuts because of the Italian and the international economic crises.

A new wave of immigration from the southern regions to Northern Italy and Europe is, once more, taking place. It involves, especially, people who are highly educated. This is further reducing the number of well-educated workers in some historically disadvantaged geographical areas. It is, in fact, worth remembering that Italy's overall economy has faced a very difficult period. As we know, it was initially the challenges of globalization that posed a major threat to the national manufacturing sector with increasing competition from developing nations (and their less expensive labor costs). This had specific effects on the economic environment because of the dominant presence of small and medium-sized firms, often family-owned. Once praised as a model of flexibility and, in some cases, of innovation, the nature of Italy's industrial actors opened up a wider discussion about the status of national capitalism and governance (Minetti, 2010). Indeed, the long-standing issue of political and governmental influence in many sectors persisted, and with additional costs also for the inefficient bureaucracy and the lack of infrastructure. Another unresolved issue, as mentioned before, is the complex and nowadays dualist labor market, with a core of "old" workers who tend to be well protected, whilst "new" (and usually young) workers have experienced extremely volatile and precarious contractual conditions. The macroeconomic picture of the country has been shaky for the past few years with steady negative or low growth and high youth unemployment, which, as we have suggested, has had an influence on people's lives, family structures, and, therefore, society at large.

This long "winter" of Italy's economy endured even after the first difficulties of globalization and entry into the Eurozone. It is still debated whether Italian firms were more penalized than helped by the adoption of the Euro. The financial and economic crisis which started in 2007–8 hit Italy hard precisely because it was struggling with some previous and ongoing challenges. At the same time, the Italian banking sector, though not greatly exposed (initially and at least compared with some foreign banks), did reduce what was already difficult access to credit for firms and families. In sum, the Italian economy was not really helped nationally. Indeed, it was also greatly affected by the range of (poor) actions by the governments (when, in truth, they were not characterized by immobility). The political economy of the country, then, has been dictated by national contingencies, the international environment, and European constraints (like the absolute respect of European economic targets for member states' public finances). All this helped the rhetoric and success of anti-European movements.

The overall picture of the Italian economy is, once more, mixed, with reasons for optimism and other more negative issues. The gap between northern and southern areas, as mentioned before, is very large. The increasing presence of the organized mafia, which has expanded its economic and financial influence to the central and northern regions thanks to the huge amounts of cash it has available, often has effects on (lack of) growth. The north-eastern regions, moreover, which have been for years the strong driving economic force of the country as a whole, suffered terribly from worldwide competition, difficult access to credit, and limited innovation. Yet, unsystematic spots of modernization emerged. A number of companies have found a way to be competitive again in the global market, particularly those that managed to increase their exports. Clusters of innovation have emerged also in the South (for example, in Sicily, and Apulia's renewable energy and the ICT technology sector). Somehow, the Italian economy has regained a few signs of vitality, but it is too early to say whether these will stabilize and become something more. Because of the political instability but also the lack of comprehensive and long-term goals, this economy is, at times, like a patient trying to recover at home without a doctor. Economic, political, and social reforms are, nonetheless, very difficult in Italy because of the enormous number of vested interests and lobbies that have a rather good record of resistance to change. However, as we suggested earlier, the Italian economic sector is not fully static. It might also be dynamic, especially when supported by politics, innovation, and, of course, meritocracy.

It is evident that some of these transformations do not often find a political manifestation and the space they need in public opinion debates. This does not mean that Italian politics has not evolved in recent decades. It is easy to play with the usual (and real) historical feature of "trasformismo," from Liberal Italy to today, with politicians, deputies, and their followers changing political sides merely for personal interests. We all know how the nation was affected by the above-mentioned *Berlusconismo*, the crisis in political representation, the transformation of parties into electoral machines, the mediatization of the political discourse, and, recently, the appearance of novel forms of political mobilization. What we find even here is possibly another mixture of innovations and continuities, adaptation of old features, and other types of political socialization. If one, for example, looks at it from an international media standpoint (which is how a number of foreign students initially approach Italy), there is, then, a never boring Italian political merry-go-round. In their view, Italy's politics is indeed exciting, innovative, and backward-looking, at times unintelligible, and surely full of surprises. One example is what happened with the latest change in leadership, namely the downfall of Enrico Letta's government and the rise of the center-left leader Matteo Renzi, the mayor of Florence, and the secretary of the Democratic Party.

Renzi is young, appealing for the media, and very straightforward. His meetings with world leaders were greeted with enthusiasm by some international newspapers. He is also Europe's youngest prime minister (and this is very surprising in an Italian politician). All this led, nonetheless, people in Italy and abroad to overlook a significant anniversary. In 1994, a successful businessman officially announced the start of a political enterprise which would later generate consternation, admiration, and also hilarity in much of the Western world. This was the day that media tycoon Berlusconi decided to enter the political arena with a newly born movement. Much ink has already been spilled on his political trajectory, one that ended with sexual and financial scandals and an uncomfortable, not to mention unpleasant, ban from public office. Yet, not even this has deterred one of Europe's longest-serving political leaders. He has been, in fact, discussing the implementation of reforms in Italy with Renzi. The government, moreover, needs votes for key laws, and Berlusconi's movement plays an important part in this game. The media tycoon wants his voice to be heard. Was his political trajectory an innovation in a somewhat "static" Italian political life?

To answer some of this, one has to start by looking back at Italy's past and the European sociopolitical environment. Berlusconi, as we are all aware, won because there was a vacuum in the political system. A number of traditional parties collapsed under trials and judicial investigations in the last decade of the last century. Bribes and illegal party funding were the rule rather than the exception, and magistrates became venerated as almost divine beings. The Christian Democrats, the leading political actors in postwar Italy, quickly disappeared. The Socialists were completely pulverized. Suspicion of the traditional ruling elites was very strong. This led, for example, to a series of victories for local mayors with roots outside the political world, though they were often left-leaning.

This was, however, not enough for the center-left to take control of Italian politics after historically leading some of the best-organized regions (Emilia Romagna and Tuscany, amongst others). The parties generated from the once powerful Italian Communist Party were often not able to elaborate significant and dynamic policies, and, most importantly, a shared agenda. In sum, they suffered, like other fellow European movements, as a result of the decline of international communism. In Italy, since at least the 1980s (if we ignore the tumult of 1968, and the communists' refusal to understand the demands of Italian youth and intellectual innovations), the leftist world had also abandoned some of its key reference points. In the decades following, the prominent role of high political and scholarly culture in shaping society and generating policies was no longer in place. "Pop" and "low-profile" values, including those backed by Berlusconi's commercial television stations, became exciting magnets (though leftists showed an evident incapacity to make use of the media as a powerful outlet and spread its political and social vision). Once they got Berlusconi, with his strong media expertise and almost unlimited funding, they encountered an unknown world. Imagine Dante alone, without a guide like Virgil. This left the tycoon with virtually no realistic opponents. There was almost no comparison with other European nations.

The center-left was also unable to maintain power when it did win elections. Romano Prodi, a moderate and internationally respected figure, beat Berlusconi twice but was failed by his coalition, which eventually dispensed with his services. The left was a quarrelling galaxy of disparate voices, whilst Berlusconi was often able to keep control of his allies and govern for longer than any other postwar Italian leader. The left was not even immune from scandals, and this had a negative influence on its usually loyal voters. Berlusconi, for his part, managed to tell people "his" own stories, promising the earth, accusing the now disappeared communists and existing elites and judges for the decline of Italy, and spreading clear, simple, and demagogic messages through the TV channels he controlled. This mediatization of politics is, however, not peculiar to Italy, and, in some ways, placed the country in a wider Western framework.

As the above-mentioned economic troubles started to hit the nation in the wake of the global financial crisis, and it appeared that traditional politics was ineffective, some citizens understood that not even a miracle-working king like Berlusconi had magic powers. Yet, rather than voting for the left, the solution for many was found in the Five Stars Movement, initially an online network of citizens led by the comedian Beppe Grillo. This represented the complete rejection of most Italian politicians, and a call for innovation and, above all, novelty. They gained, in fact, millions of votes in 2013. They entered parliament and promoted the moralization of politics, society, and the nation (although this theme was not novel in historical terms). This was unique in modern Italian history, and there are, so far, not many similar examples in the West.

It is open to discussion whether this is really helping to improve Italy's political life. How Grillo managed all this is yet another story. The style of the message rather than its content might have been, nonetheless, once more significant. His movement, however, started to be observed with curiosity abroad, taken as a role model by other European movements, and its EU parliamentary alliance with UKIP ensured more articles in foreign media. Is Italy, then, in this sense, an innovator in some forms of political socialization and citizens' mobilization?

Renzi is, in some ways, in line with this Western tradition, along with the low quality of the Italian public debate. He is naturally different from many other left-leaning politicians (though some notice in him the style of the socialist leader Bettino Craxi). He likes to foresee a better Italy. He also looks abroad for inspiration (and this is quite common for the Italian moderate left in recent times), and particularly at Tony Blair (bizarrely, given the evolution of Blairism, even if this might show some limited knowledge of international politics).

His enthusiasm, rhetoric, and decisiveness look exciting to many disillusioned voters (as this almost never happened before), even if he has yet to explain fully how he can turn Italy into a wealthy nation, find resources for the reforms, and, above all, decrease pressure from the Euro elites, who show little flexibility. Moreover, the traditional elites of his own movement are opposing him. The vote in May 2014 for the EU parliament showed how appealing this politician may be. However, and most interestingly, this vote put Italy politically in a better place compared with other nations where anti-EU, protest, and anti-establishment forces won the election. What it is evident here is that Italy offers an interesting platform for Western democracies, and some of its historical developments appear old and new at the same time.

Outline

It is true that all these Italian developments may hardly be covered in a single volume (and the Handbook discusses some of them). Instead of giving a whole picture of what Italy is today, the aim of this Handbook is to provide readers with a framework for and an overview of some of the key factors in Italian history, politics, economy, memory, and society in order to understand the main developments. Connections between chapters flow throughout the book, but there is not a common thread: that is not the aim of this work. Instead, each chapter aims to perform the double function of informing the reader about contemporary Italy and, at the same time, being a starting point for further research and investigation. It will be up to the reader to navigate through the sections and explore the common threads and interlinkages that are sometimes highlighted by the authors and in other instances are implicit.

The first section contains sociological contributions that analyze a number of aspects of contemporary Italian society. Chambers discusses one of the most resilient and pervasive of social issues, which is the Southern Question (and how it may be perceived today). Veltri explores the validity of another very vigorous trope about the cultural differences between Italian geographical areas, and in particular, between the macro-regions of the North, Centre, and South. Tintori and Colucci analyze an old plague of Italian society, notably emigration and its recent developments. Levy examines xenophobia in a nation which has never before experienced a large presence of immigrants. Ruspini considers the role of women in society after many years of lagging behind other European countries. Argentin, for his part, focuses on another relevant story in contemporary Italy, namely the social and economic conditions of young Italians. Parini's contribution concludes Part I, analyzing the mafia, and removing some conceptual and geographical misconceptions.

Part II focuses on democratic life and political institutions. Bull gives an account of the functioning of Italian democracy and the many attempts at institutional reform that often resulted in unsuccessful outcomes. Verzichelli discusses the nature and quality of the political class and its strong resistance to renewal. Padovani tackles another peculiar feature of national democracy, which is the relationship between the mass media, politics, and society. Conti adds the European variable in our understanding of contemporary Italy, as this has become an increasingly important dimension of domestic life. Loprieno looks at another feature of Italian society, in particular the relationship between the state, religion, and the Vatican.

Part III aims at providing an overview of the most recent political actors and developments. Agnew starts with an analysis of a political geography of the country, and discusses regional differences in terms of political traditions and voting behavior. Raniolo and Tarchi discuss the right-wing end of the Italian spectrum, an environment usually mostly known for Berlusconi's leadership. Lazar and Giugni examine the often quarreling left-wing parties, which have intermittently led the nation in recent decades. Donovan then scrutinizes what is left of the once dominant Italian Christian Democrats, the leading force for a very long period of time. Cento Bull presents a detailed account of the Northern League's political trajectory, and, therefore, how it may be better understood. Newell considers the relationship between magistrates and politics, discussing the example of Antonio Di Pietro and his (almost disappeared) political party. Diani and Fabbri shed light on the nature of the above-mentioned very recent political development represented by Grillo's Five Stars Movement.

Part IV contains contributions on the sociopolitical environment. Lynch and Ceretti analyze the trajectory of (often not fully implemented) welfare reforms in Italy, and also the lack of long-term planning. Briquet discusses the costs and consequences of corruption and clientelism, two key pervasive problems in Italy. Leonida, Maimone, and Navarra examine the relationship between economic growth and political competition. Giovannini and Minetti offer an analysis of the nature of Italian firms, from their governance structures to their capacity for innovation and exports. Iona, Leonida, and Silipo examine the Italian banking sector, often considered a critical aspect of capitalism.

Part V contains essays on some cultural themes that have a relevance, which should not be left out, also for their significance in public discourses, politics, and society. Jedlowski discusses the role of the Italian filmmaking industry in shaping the cultural identity and memory of the country. Gori examines the Risorgimento in the political and cultural debate, including its uses. Cooke analyzes anti-fascism, once very powerful, and its place in recent history. Pergher, for her part, examines Italy's overlooked colonial past and its influence on national identity.

In sum, this might therefore be considered as a kind of open handbook, at times more oriented toward posing questions than giving full answers, whilst covering many aspects of Italy. This means also being attentive to the historical, political, and social processes taking place. We are convinced that, in order to understand this nation, it is necessary to construct a new way of looking at it, possibly an interdisciplinary one.

Note

1 Two books are very different in tone, though they were probably not successful like some of the anti-unification literature. One is *L'unificazione italiana* (2011), also by Lupo, in which the entry of Southern Italy into the Italian nation is mainly a social and political fight and at the same time a clash between different patriotisms. The other is *Borbonia felix. Il regno delle due Sicilie alla vigilia del crollo* (2013) by Renata De Lorenzo, which tries to get over the anti-Risorgimento rhetoric through an insightful analysis of the social, economic, and political conditions of Southern Italy before 1861.

Bibliography

Bova, E. (2013) *Cattolicesimi d'Italia. Un'identità religiosa*, Rome: Carocci.

De Lorenzo, S. (2013) *Borbonia felix. Il regno delle due Sicilie alla vigilia del crollo*, Rome: Salerno Editrice.

Duggan, C. (2007) *The Force of Destiny*, London: Allen Lane.

Emmott, B. (2012) *Good Italy, Bad Italy*, Yale, CT: Yale University Press.

Gilmour, D. (2011) *The Pursuit of Italy*, New York: Farrar, Straus, and Giroux.

Giorda, M. 'Il fenomeno religioso nell'Italia contemporanea. Intervista a Enzo Pace', *Sei Idr*. Available online at www.idr.seieditrice.com/interviste/intervista/il-fenomeno-religioso-nellitalia-contemporanea (accessed 24 August 2013).

Istat (2013) *Statistiche Report 26 giugno – Indicatori demografici*, Rome: Istat.

Istat (2014) *Statistiche Report 13 novembre – Indicatori demografici*, Rome: Istat.

Lupo, S. (2011) *L'unificazione italiana*, Rome: Donzelli.

Minetti, R. (2010) 'The Crisis of Family Firms and the Decline of Italian Capitalism', in A. Mammone and G. A. Veltri, eds., *Italy Today: The Sick Man of Europe*, London: Routledge.

Patriarca, S. (2010) *Italian Vices: Nation and Character from the Risorgimento to the Republic*, Cambridge: Cambridge University Press.

Petti, E. (2012) 'Contro il Risorgimento è in atto un revisionismo spicciolo', *Linkiesta*, 8 August. Available online at www.linkiesta.it/risorgimento-revisionismo-terroni-salvatore-lupo (accessed 17 August 2013).

Scarpellini, E. (2011) *Material Nation: A Consumer's History of Modern Italy*, Oxford: Oxford University Press.

Viroli, M. (2011) *The Liberty of Servants*, Princeton, NJ: Princeton University Press.

PART I

Old and new tensions in contemporary Italian society

1

THE 'SOUTHERN QUESTION' . . . AGAIN

Iain Chambers

Viewed from London, Los Angeles, New York, Berlin, Paris and Milan, the south of the world is invariably considered in terms of lacks and absences. It is not yet modern; it has still to catch up. It remains, as Dipesh Chakrabarty would put it, an inadequate place (Chakrabarty, 2000). The south is spatially and temporally located elsewhere, at the edge of the map. Of course, as we know from Edward Said, and through him from Antonio Gramsci, this is a geography of power. It is about being placed and systematised in a manner not of your own choosing. It is about being rendered subordinate and subaltern to other forces, and being exploited, not only economically, but also politically and culturally, in order for that subalternity to be reproduced and reinforced. The south of the world is framed, not only conceptually enclosed, but also falsely accused of failing to respect a modernity being triumphantly pursued elsewhere. To return to the south as a critical, political and historical problem is, ultimately, to return to the north and its hegemonic management of the planet. The ills, failures and breakdowns that are located down there, across the border, are precisely the products of a northern will to make the world over in its image and interests. This is the political economy of location. Here the south, of Italy, of Europe, of the Mediterranean, of the world, is rendered both marginal but paradoxically central to the reproduction of that economy. If the whole world were equally modern, then modernity as we know it would collapse. The cancellation of the inequalities, property and differences that drive the planetary machinery of capitalist accumulation would render what we today call modernity superfluous. The subversion of linearity and the lateral redistribution of 'progress' and development would undo historical time as it is currently understood. The 'south' is a political question and also a historical one; in both cases, it is about the power and the exploitation of those held in its definitions.

Brigands, lazy peasants, mafia and corruption

If by the end of the nineteenth century a stereotypical image of southern Italy had already been established as a land inhabited by brigands, lazy peasants and corruption, we need, as a minimum, to understand the historical processes that led to this state of affairs. But then history provides us with an ambiguous archive. Irreducible to simple causality and a transparent rationality, the 'south' emerges as a category, a construction, an invention (Petrusewicz, 1998). Its definition reveals the semiotics of power. The 'south' is always destined to experience that combination of repression and refusal that is the foreclosure of hegemony seeking to negate the trauma of its violent affirmation (Mellino and Curcio, 2012).

It is within this matrix that we might turn to the unification and the creation of the modern nation of Italy, engineered on the back of the conquest of one sovereign state (the Bourbon kingdom of the Two Sicilies) by another (the Piedmont monarchy of the House of Savoy). Behind the offensive labelling of its inhabitants, and the reduction of rebellion against, resistance to and refusal of that conquest as 'brigandage', there existed an altogether more complex social and political world. This was characterised by the brutal exercise of feudal powers, whose representatives willing allied themselves with the new national Parliament and political order in order to continue their rule over the land and its peasantry. In brokering hegemonic interests, agricultural reform was deliberately avoided by the new unitary state. This recycling of change in order to sustain the status quo, what the Neapolitan historian Vincenzo Cuoco and Antonio Gramsci referred to as 'passive revolution', might be considered one of the central subtexts of Giuseppe Tomasi di Lampedusa's *Il Gattopardo*, also well caught in Luchino Visconti's film of the novel. It is really only after the conclusion of the Second World War that a certain degree of post-feudal land reform occurs in Italy. In the terrible conditions of agricultural life and labour, the fact that the 'bosses' live in Naples or Turin, and state authority shifts from Naples to Rome, makes little difference. Reading Carlo Levi's *Cristo si è fermato a Eboli* (*Christ Stopped at Eboli*), published in 1955, and registering the nuanced critique of Italian unification in Mario Martone's recent film *Noi Credevamo* (based on Anna Banti's beautiful novel of 1967), one stumbles across the persistent repression and exclusion of a subaltern peasantry from the national narrative. This, of course, is the key motif in Gramsci's analysis of the 'failure' of Italian unification.

Here it would be hypocrisy to talk in terms of historical progress directly attributable to the transit to the modern nation. The military occupation and juridical enforcement of unification in southern Italy, in the wake of military operations that witnessed the deployment of 120,000 troops and resulted in at least 30,000 dead, was followed by mass migration from rural poverty to the Americas. Subsequent colonial adventures in east Africa and Libya (home at one time to 150,000 Italians) were also considered a potential safety valve for relieving the pressure of southern destitution. There is no linear progress here but rather a contorted spiral of development in which the resources of southern Italy often fuelled northern interests and advancement. If the feudal regime of the Bourbons was suppressed and forcefully incorporated into the modern Italian state, the latter tended to govern this southern acquisition through the biopolitical grammar of alterity. The Mezzogiorno was inferiorised as the racialised object of anthropological and biological categories. It was considered closer to Africa and the Arab world in its customs and culture than to Europe (Moe, 2002). Forms of social opposition, political resistance and alternative modalities of government were reduced to questions of criminality, public order and corrupt practices inherited from the *ancien régime*. These were persistently contrasted with the industrious modernity of the north.

The responsibilities that a centralised national government should have exercised in economic and cultural, and not just political, terms were both conceptually and structurally evaded. This inferiorisation of the south affirms that its subordination to northern concerns was not a historical accident but a power relationship. It was justified in the languages of colonialism and racism, and it rendered the south inferior, less European, inherently underdeveloped. This, of course, was a particular instance of the far wider appropriation of the Mediterranean and the south of Europe (Spain, Italy, Greece and the Balkans), not to speak of the extra-European world, when viewed and framed from London, Paris, Berlin, Turin and, later, Rome. The south is relegated to the margins of the national epic; its existing conditions are considered an impediment to the realisation of 'progress'; its history is yet to come. In this sense, Carlo Levi's *Christ Stopped at Eboli* becomes a profoundly instructive political text.

The long national debate on the 'Southern Question' that accompanies the history of modern Italy and the incorporation of the ex-kingdom of the two Sicilies into the new nation constantly veers between outcries against an aggressive northern act of deliberate colonisation and the more academic discussion of national and international cycles and rhythms evidencing uneven development. If, on the one hand, the north apparently robbed the south of its financial assets in order to establish its industrial base, and in the process waged a war on the population in order to exercise this right, this was counterbalanced by a liberal paternalism that saw its task of dragging the south out of decadent government and feudal inefficiency in order to make it modern. If the colonising imperative that saw in the south an exotic world of disturbing alterity still remains very much in play today in internal racisms (and the Northern League is symptomatic of that virulent syntax), the liberal insistence on educating the south through a programmed 'progress' also continued to dominate the state policy of post-1945 Italy. The clearest manifestation of the latter approach was the creation in 1950 of a national fund – Cassa del Mezzogiorno – for financing the development of southern Italy. This was to launch the era of the notorious 'cathedrals in the desert': industrial plant parachuted into rural southern Italy that was supposed to kick-start the local economy. Despite the massive amounts of money involved it was a historical failure; or, rather, its economic and social aims were largely side-tracked into the machinery of sustaining and reproducing political power. In this sense, it was by no means an exclusively 'Southern Question', but rather a component in the composition and management of a national mosaic of powers, interests and political groups.

One of the more obvious examples of this mechanism is that of the complex interweaving of national and local powers which witnessed political party machinery and organised crime allied in the creation and reproduction of political and cultural hegemony. This had already been encouraged by the Allied war authorities in their conquest of Sicily and southern Italy from Fascism after 1943. Such an alliance stretched from the maintenance of everyday local consensus through political patronage and organised crime to domestic Cold War containment of political unrest and the subsequent crisis management of national emergencies and disasters (the 1980 earthquake in Campania is here emblematic: massive state funding simultaneously consolidated and extended political power and organised crime, both locally and nationally). The details, of course, are complicated, but I think that it is once again clear that the seemingly separate specificity of the 'Southern Question' has consistently played a fundamental role in the political and economic arrangements that compose the national (and international) picture.

The continuing twentieth mass migration of the reserve army of labour of southern Italians to northern Italy and northern Europe, on the back of migration to the Americas and North Africa, also alerts us to this structural reality. It touches the essential dimension of alterity and the periphery in composing and reaffirming the 'centre'. This needs to be consistently borne in mind if we want to avoid being dragged into an endless and fruitless debate overdetermined by stereotypical language, racialising prejudices, and a biopolitics passing for common sense. Migration also reminds us of the shifting conditions of international labour. While migration from the south of the world has serviced the north, the Italian south itself is today clearly destined never to be industrialised – today that nineteenth-century model of 'progress' has literally migrated elsewhere, to be charted in the megapolises of China, India and Brazil. The labour pool has been outsourced along global networks that draw upon capital gains and infrastructures that the Mezzogiorno will never have. It is now necessary to change perspective and seek to reformulate the 'Southern Question'. To do this, I suggest we need to adopt another series of coordinates and maps.

The dead end of localism

I believe that Antonio Gramsci helps us to identify a series of elements that pull the question out of its immediate historical and critical coordinates in post-unification Italy and allows us to better consider its contemporary implications. Here we will discover that it is no longer possible to talk of a 'Southern Question' within the boundaries of the Italian nation state, and perhaps, despite all the immediate peculiarities of the 'Mezzogiorno', it never was. Without anticipating the argument, there lies here the suggestion that the 'Southern Question', identified as a political problem, and as a historical and cultural question, was not external to the modernity that it was presumed could resolve it. It was, and is, *internal* to modern Europe and the formation of its nation states. In an important sense, seeking to respond to the 'Southern Question' ultimately implies replying to the structural inequalities and distribution of power that accompany the formation of nation building and Occidental modernity. I feel, as Gramsci himself once put it, that this 'thinking globally' is of significance in casting what seems an almost unresolvable historical, cultural and political dilemma into an altogether more extensive critical space that throws a suggestive critical light back into the specificities of the Italian case.

So, it seems to me imperative to acknowledge wider landmarks when referencing the 'Southern Question'. To avoid remaining trapped in a tangle of historical and cultural debate that reconstructs and deconstructs the question, it is perhaps time to apply a critical cut. A local inheritance can never be cancelled, but it can be exposed to other questions, examined with new critical coordinates. To step beyond the south's location in existing knowledge–power relationships, and follow Edward Said's proposal to de-orientalise the logic that reconfirms subordination in a self-perpetuating discourse, is to adopt a postcolonial approach that insists that the colonisation and construction of the 'periphery' is essential for the sustenance and extension of metropolitan power. The rest of the world is not simply an accessory and witness to Occidental progress but is deeply stitched into its fabric of production and reproduction. It does not simply absorb and consume modernity; in its labour power, cultural forces and political antagonisms, it produces modernity. It is not simply where modernity recycles and dumps the refuse of 'progress'; it provides the very matrix of a modernity that requires the world, and not simply the West, in order to extract, circulate and accumulate its riches and authority (Mezzadra and Neilson, 2013),

Beyond the pertinent provocation of Franco Cassano's 'southern thought' refusing a subaltern status, a postcolonial engagement allows us to promote an understanding of the Southern Question from the south itself (Cassano, 2011). This is not simply to overturn prevailing accounts that tend to reduce the Mezzogiorno of Italy to a stable and homogeneous object of analysis, robbing it of subjective agency. It also permits a wider exercise in challenging the premises and protocols of the critical machinery that believes that its version of 'modernity' and 'progress' is unique and hence universal. At the same time, this also allows us to relocate the Italian 'Southern Question' on a wider map, beginning in immediate terms with the Mediterranean. Here we are forced to annotate the annexation of southern Italy and subsequent national unification within the same temporal frame of the French conquest of Algeria and the British takeover of Egypt. Modalities of appropriation were different, the combination of histories never the same, although there was always the constancy of military might, death and destruction to back up and enforce the enterprise. In the extension of one rule and law over another we find ourselves in the common nineteenth-century matrix of colonialism that extends, without request, the civilising mission of the west to the rest. As a minimum, this establishes the Italian 'Southern Question' in a colonial framework, not too dissimilar to the experiences of Scotland and Ireland and their political, administrative, cultural and military subordination to London and the unification of Great Britain.

In *The Southern Question* (1926), the Sardinian intellectual Antonio Gramsci offered a lucid analysis of the structural impoverishment of southern Italy in terms of existing economic, political and cultural forces. He spoke of stagnation characterised by the mass of peasantry in the economic and political clutches of large, often absentee, landowners. He also spoke of southern intellectuals supplying the administrative personnel of the Italian state, both locally and nationally, and of the role of such intellectuals (he was referring in particular to Benedetto Croce) in reproducing the status quo. Ten years later, incarcerated in a Fascist prison, he was to observe:

> The poverty of the Mezzogiorno was historically incomprehensible for the popular masses of the North; they could not comprehend that national unity was not achieved on the basis of equality, but as the result of the hegemony of the North on the Mezzogiorno and the territorial relationship of the city to the countryside; the North was an 'octopus' that enriched itself at the cost of the South, its industrial and economic progress was in a direct relationship to the impoverishment of southern industry and agriculture.
>
> *(Gramsci 1975: 2021–2)*

Much of what Gramsci had to say then continues to echo within the existing political economy of the south and in its one-time capital, Naples. Yet the 'sources' of this malaise perhaps lie not only in local coordinates, but also in a deep-seated inheritance that today would be considered part and parcel of the processes of 'globalization' (Chambers, 2008).

Naples, unlike Genoa and Venice, was never a major port and commercial centre in the manner of its northern cousins. Up to the end of the sixteenth century Venice and Genoa were 'world ports', central to a trading system that stretched from Beijing to Lima. The port of Naples served mainly for the importation of foodstuffs from Sicily and Puglia to feed its metropolitan population and immediate hinterland. In 1615 Naples was buying pepper from Livorno that had arrived from London. By then it was no longer the Mediterranean that sold spices to England and northern Europe, but spices arriving from London and Amsterdam that were now sold to the Mediterranean in the ports of Livorno, Naples and Istanbul. By the end of the seventeenth century virtually all of the seaborne commercial traffic of the Kingdom of Naples was transported on English merchant ships. In the second half of the century the hegemony of English commerce in the Mediterranean, reinforced by the regular presence of the Royal Navy, supervised the structural undoing of the relationship between a commercial and industrial northern Italy and its complementary relationship to the agricultural south (Pagano de Divitiis, 1997). Both the north, with its own commerce, cloth and silk industries subordinated to the needs of London and the emerging English textile industry, and the agricultural south were equally transformed into sources for primary materials for the markets and merchandising of northern Europe and the Atlantic seaboard. By 1680 the conditions of the 'Southern Question' – economic underdevelopment, social backwardness and cultural isolation from northern Italy – had been established, not so much through Spanish domination of the Kingdom of Naples, or northern Italian 'progress', where capital once invested in seagoing ventures was now conserved in the security of land and revenue, as by English mercantile hegemony in the Mediterranean.

These historical observations might provide one way to reopen the 'Southern Question'. They serve, above all, to insist on the critical necessity of adopting a diverse cartography in order to step out of the straightjacket of a debate, overwhelmingly shaped by regional and national concerns, that urgently needs to be 'provincialized' (Chakrabarty, 2000). The pauperisation of the peasantry in the rural fringes of an emerging modern Europe – both in Calabria and in the Highlands of Scotland – are as interconnected as the price of pepper on the London Stock

Exchange and in the markets of Naples and Istanbul. In the following century, the nascent Neapolitan Republic, directly inspired by the French Revolution, will be crushed in May 1799 by a peasant army overseen by the presence of the British fleet in the Bay of Naples. Part of that fleet, together with its commander Admiral Horatio Nelson, had the previous year destroyed French naval forces in Egyptian waters in the Battle of Aboukir Bay. In the very same period, republican France was refusing the demands of the slaves in revolt to extend the terms of the French Revolution to its Caribbean colony Saint-Dominique. Freedom, equality and brotherhood were denied until the 'Black Jacobins' successfully expunged French control and established the black republic of Haiti in 1804.

These wider coordinates are not intended to stifle the local narrative. If anything they serve to deepen and extend that account in the belief that they help us to grasp the historical and cultural density of the question in the context of the 'global colonial archive' (Conelli, 2013). What holds this particular picture together in the first instance is the struggle for world hegemony between Britain and France, waged in the many corners of Europe from Spain and Italy to the steppes of Russia, as well as across the seas and islands of the world. This exercise of power, its administrative, military, economic and cultural organisation – frequently outsourced to non-nationals (Polish troops deployed in the unsuccessful French attempts to reconquer Saint-Dominique, black African sailors in the British fleet) – was in the last instance about the control of resources, riches and markets required in order to command the world and ensure the planetary reproduction of its political economy.

With this in mind we could now move back to the 'Southern Question' with a further set of concerns. One of the central features that emerges from the incorporation of the ex-Kingdom of the Two Sicilies into the new Italian state in 1861 is that of the systematic racialisation of the south (Moe, 2002). The evidence – drawn from Piedmont officers and government officials involved in the 'pacification' of the Mezzogiorno, to subsequent endorsement by sociologists, anthropologists and criminologists – is overwhelming. Southern Italy, whether explained in biological or historical terms, is populated by an inferior 'race'. As we have already noted, the racialisation of southern Italy was an essential part of its subordination to colonisation by the nascent national state that in turn applied verdicts already rehearsed by visitors in English, German and French. Anthropological generalisations quickly flowed into a more precise institutional regime of knowledge through the criminalisation of dissent and revolt. It produced a pathology to be catalogued, studied and defined, and the figure of Cesare Lombroso is central to this project and its becoming 'common sense'. Historical and cultural differences were transformed into arbitrary distinctions. These acquired the legislative force to incorporate, discipline and educate the captured, subordinated body. Once defined, catalogued and located, that body reconfirmed the manner and procedures of its objectification. Even if we might want today to consign such perspectives to the closed chapter of European positivism, such practices seeped down into the practices of everyday life and cast long historical shadows. In the opening sequences of Luchino Visconti's film *Rocco and His Brothers* (1960), the arrival from Lucania of the Parondi family in a Milanese housing estate is simply greeted with the exclamation 'Africa'.

The transference of landed property to financial gain and commercial profit, of the revenue of rural estates to industrial and financial capital and urban life styles, accompanied by the passage from peasantry to the national and international labour market, is a constant rhythm in the formation of the modern political economy since 1500. In the planetary processes induced by capitalist accumulation there is obviously much regional differentiation, within the nation as well as beyond its frontiers. Some would call them time lags and apply the terminology of backwardness and underdevelopment to explain their presence. Here history is a train called

Progress that carries us into the future. However, when slavery coexists with the foundation of republican democracy, as in the Atlantic world of the eighteenth and nineteenth centuries, and feudal land ties with the establishment of modern industrial plant, as in Italy in the first half of the twentieth century, it is perhaps critically more instructive to consider their political interaction and historical complementarity. Rather than assuming that one dimension (modern, democratic and industrial) is separate and superior to the negative survival of the seemingly archaic histories of slavery and feudalism, we need to consider their being coeval. And if we are understanding these to be planetary, and not merely national, conditions and forces, then we are required to recognise this dissonant and heterogeneous history to be integral to modernity, that is, to be *the* history of modernity itself.

The violent accumulation of capital does not simply lie back there with slave labour, colonialism and racialised hegemony, or with expropriation of the commons, the expulsion of peasantry from the land and its subsequent enclosure by a landowning class seeking to invest its gains elsewhere (in the colonies, in industry, in buildings, transport and cultural goods). It continues. There is no simple passage from an original or primitive accumulation to a subsequently more civil and ordered one. Eighteenth-century Scottish crofters dispatched to Canada after the crushing of the 1745 Rebellion, peasants moving from Lucania to Milan and the Alfa Romeo factory in the 1950s and 1960s (the subject of Visconti's *Rocco and His Brothers*) and present-day Chinese labour migrating in millions from rural areas to the high-tech belts of Guangdong, Shaanxi, Qingdao and Shenzhen, are part of a shared temporality. In other words, the creative destruction of territory and time by capital that produces a mobile constellation of effects on a planetary level is not to be explained in terms of the linear succession of circles of development radiating out from a primary centre in Europe. The resources that went into European development, as the history of modern racial slavery so powerfully portrays – both in its labour and in its abolition and compensatory payments – always depended on a planetary network of conquest, exploitation and management (Hall, 2013). Dispossession, expropriation and unilateral control of land, law and political licence are not simply the prerogative of seventeenth-century England and life in the North American colonies; they are very much part of our world today. That 'original' violence persists – from seeking to patent medicinal plants to bulldozing villages and towns into dams. It is part, as Kalyan Sanyal has argued, of the very reproduction of capital: it is not a trace of the past, but is a constant and unstable universalism oriented to the future (Sanyal, 2007). Rather than localised transitions to accumulation, registered in the linear fashioning of time, there are transformations that reach through a mosaic of temporal and spatial scales and coordinates, sometimes subtle and with subterfuge, more usually brutal, violent and without redress.

These considerations throw a very different light onto the 'Southern Question'. Here we discover not pockets of underdevelopment, inhabited by those who apparently live outside the measured time of modernity and who have not yet been invested by progress, but 'traces of autonomous initiatives' as Gramsci referred to them. These signal the multiple contours of the modern world where a hegemonic pulse is folded into local performances, crossed by translation and mixed by tradition, sounded and sourced in the ongoing construction of place and belonging. The blueprint and template are dirtied and deviated, punctuated by the dense grammars of cultural immediacies, by a resistance to a singular will (Chambers, 2013).

What lies 'south of the border' in the undisciplined excess of life that seemingly does not respect the rules is clearly a threat to the disciplined productivity of the linear accumulation of a capitalist and cultural redemption. These other, southern, spaces, however, are not merely decadent and unruly peripheries, expelled from the motor of modernity. They propose the challenge of heterotopia. Although constantly seeking to establish borders, set limits, monitor unrest and patrol confines, modernity is unable to produce a distinct exterior, a not yet modern or still primitive elsewhere. What is maintained at a distance, transformed into a separable 'other' and then rendered subaltern and subordinate within the institutions and practices of 'advanced' capitalist culture is at the same time structurally integral to the very production and reproduction of dominance and subordination. The negated, feared and despised 'native', black, Arab, Muslim, Rom, and migrant other is inside the modernity that seeks to define, discipline and decide his or her place. No matter how objectified and anonymously rendered, the subaltern is nevertheless a historical actor, a subjectivising force *within* a shared but differentiated modernity (Guha, 2003). It is this negated conviviality that sets the terms for unrecognised communalities. The chains of power are here tested (and not simply suffered), stretched and sometimes snap. If, then, there is no absolute outside to house the excluded and the damned, there is also no untouched or pure alternative to the historical network and assemblage in which these political and cultural relations are inscribed. It is precisely in this sense, that the 'Southern Question' irrupts within the midst of a modernity still to be registered and recognised.

Exemplified in Carlo Levi's *Christ Stopped at Eboli*, Ernesto De Martino's ethnographic field research in the Mezzogiorno of Italy in the 1950s and the cinema of Pier Paolo Pasolini, seemingly pre-modern practices, beliefs and customs are not 'back there', in an abjured or primitive past, but are 'in here', part of the stratified and subaltern complexities of the present. Through rendering the familiar unhomely and out of joint, the present becomes plural and incomplete, that is, irreducible to a single point of view or manner of narration. Along this critical path lies the injunction to think less *of* the south and rather *with* the south. Here, where historical, cultural and structural conditions have been formed in subordination to the needs of the north of the world, the predictable critical frame is decentred and destabilised. The powerful lessons of the Subaltern Studies group in India, of the lengthy tradition of Black Atlantic intellectuals and artists, of the critical constellation of radical Latin American thought and political practices clearly confirm this point. The abstract universalisms of 'progress', 'humanism' and 'democracy' unwind in the cruel insistence of their being historically embedded in power, exploitation and unjust cultural detail. This observation, most obviously drawn from Fanon's *The Wretched of the Earth*, allows us to register the structural inequalities of economic, political, social and cultural justice that characterise the souths of the planet while at the same time harvesting the specificities of a precise elaboration of space and time that distinguishes one place from another.

Radical rurality

To return to the rural south of Italy again also allows us to continue to cultivate further lines of flight from conventional accounts of this region as a political problem. I, personally, have had some involvement in projects that have sought in abandoned mountain areas to encourage a radical revaluation of contemporary rurality in the light of modern memories of migration (Chambers *et al.*, 2007). Associated with this involvement is the ethno-literature and proposed 'ruralogy' (*paesologia*) of the writer Franco Arminio, who poetically reworks a received inheritance into a modality of modern connections (Arminio, 2011). In a form of psychogeography, Armino's words drift in rural landscapes that actively query their subaltern location in the mappings of modernity. What comes to be registered is an impossible set of roots: village life is neither autonomous nor separated from the modernity that produces it as its alterity. There emerges the awareness that belonging simultaneously draws upon a series of locations: from a high mountain village in Matese to a suburb of New York. It is a process impossible to confine to a single place. This provides another critical compass with which to navigate the multiple spaces of modernity. Perhaps this is a lesson that was first learnt by rural folk. If their lives were subordinated to the demands of the metropolis, they experienced migration, social upheaval and transformation under the sign of the city long before the inhabitants of the city began querying their own assumed stability. In the same manner, the rest of the world has experienced precarious livelihood, structural unemployment and the violence of capital in a colonial condition for many decades prior to the ingression of these coordinates into the heartlands of the metropolitan West.

The seemingly external rural interruption is, of course, not really external, only repressed and negated, consigned to the margins. Today's metropolis is the modern world. And if the city does not fully absorb the surrounding world, it does, however, profoundly discipline its horizons of expectancy. In this sense, the rural scene provides one of the places and temporalities of modernity. It is not on the outside. It circulates within as a potential critical seed. It proposes another rurality that lies both beyond the placid Romantic framing of the sublime or the brutal vitalism of imposed economic 'progress'. Its very hybridity – after all, today hardly anyone simply lives in the countryside, whether in Irpinia in southern Italy or in rural Bangladesh, without the presence of television, mobile phones, computers and the Internet – suggests an altogether more extensive critical cartography. In a truly political and poetical sense this renewed sense of rurality promotes a subaltern and minor history able to challenge and deviate hegemonic versions of a unilateral modernity. Defending seed banks in rural India against Occidental monopolies or contesting economically and ecologically unviable high-speed trains in the Alpine valleys of northern Italy is, in however ragged and unsystematic a fashion, to express local democracies that are witness to a modernity that is not simply authorized by the existing institutions of political and economic power.

Here the rural world is no longer something left over from yesterday, an appendage to today's urban life, providing foodstuffs, recreation and relics of superseded lifestyles, but rather reveals the potential of a critical interrogation. A seemingly 'lost' world actually proposes new points of departure. The elaboration of the 'loss' can lead to the proposal of beginnings for those seeking to escape both the claustrophobic localism of blood and soil and the terrible costs of earlier rural life. To elaborate that inheritance and work it through is also to re-elaborate modernity itself. Emigration, exploitation and poverty, both yesterday and today, are woven together along global axes. The abandoned village in the Apennines is not merely the sign of a local drama; it is the also the symptom of the processes of a planetary political economy. The question, then, is how to narrate this complex suturing of time and place, of modernity and rurality, in a manner that leads to a new, critical sense of 'place' and temporality that simultaneously exists along multiple scales of belonging: from the local bar to the Internet.

At this point, where do a place, a locality, a village and territory conclude, and something else commence? Perhaps the limited linearity of this reasoning suggests another configuration in which 'place' and belonging are simultaneously proposed and lived in multiple sites. These propose other narrative forms. In an altogether more fluid topography, specificities such as poverty, organised crime, structural unemployment, migration and peripheral 'underdevelopment' are charted on multiple maps that simultaneously conjoin the local with those wider, transnational conditions that also produce the local. Modernity at this point is opened up to interpretations that challenge a unitary logic. And alterity, as both the past that has never passed and the presence of the extra-European world, radically interrupts the present. Such proximities invite us, as a minimum, not so much to speak for these negated matters, and thereby reproduce our authority, as to speak in their vicinity in a manner that leads precisely to the undoing of that authority (Djebar, 1999).

The south of the world

Borrowing this suggestion from the Algerian writer Assia Djebar, I would like to propose a final perspective that consists in considering the interruption of the structures that produces the 'south' as a delimited space (Bhambra, 2007). This obviously extends the Italian 'Southern Question' through a geography of powers onto a planetary scale. It also fruitfully intersects a growing intent to rethink modernity outside the geopolitical structures and ethnographic dividends of European colonialism and their installation in the assumed methodological 'neutrality' of the social sciences (Connell, 2007). Brought into the multiple folds of a postcolonial revaluation, such a critical configuration permits us to reopen the archive in order to expose the present-day coordinates of a multilayered modernity: the latter now emerges as a global networked formation in historical process, rather than as a conceptual bloc or place (the Occident). If this is to world the west, it is also to re-engage with the 'Southern Question', and with it the south of Europe and the south of the world, with a very different set of critical languages and questions.

Bibliography

Arminio, F. (2011). *Terracarne. Viaggio nei paesi invisibili e nei paesi giganti del Sud Italia*. Milan: Mondadori.

Bhambra, G. R. (2007). *Rethinking Modernity. Postcolonialism and the Sociological Imagination*. Basingstoke: Palgrave.

Cassano, F. (2011). *Southern Thought and Other Essays on the Mediterranean*. New York: Fordham University Press.

Chakrabarty, D. (2000). *Provincializing Europe. Postcolonial Thought and Historical Difference*. Princeton, NJ: Princeton University Press.

Chambers, I. (2008). *Mediterranean Crossings. The Politics of an Interrupted Modernity*. Durham, NC: Duke University Press.

Chambers, I. (2013). Lessons from the south. *UniNomade 2.0*. Available online at www.uninomade.org/lessons-from-the-south/ (accessed 15 January 2015).

Chambers, I., Calabritto, C., Carmen, M., Esposito, R., Festa, M., Izzo, R. and Lanza, O. (2007). Landscapes, parks, art and cultural change. *Third Text* 21 (3): 315–26.

Conelli, C. (2013). *Per una storia postcoloniale del Mezzogiorno d'Italia*. Unpublished MA thesis, University of Naples, 'Orientale'.

Connell, R. (2007). *Southern Theory. The Global Dynamics of Knowledge in Social Science*. Cambridge: Polity.

Djebar, A. (1999). *Women of Algiers in their Apartments*. Charlottesville, VA: University of Virginia Press.

Fanon, F. (2001). *The Wretched of the Earth*. London: Penguin.

Gramsci, A. (1975). *Quaderni del Carcere*. Turin: Einaudi.

Guha, R. (2003). *History at the Limit of World-History*. New York: Columbia University Press.

Hall, C. (2013). *Legacies of British Slave-ownership*. Available online at www.ucl.ac.uk/lbs/ (accessed 15 January 2015).

Levi, C. (1955). *Cristo si è fermato a Eboli*. Turin: Einaudi.

Mellino, M. and Curcio, A. (2012). *La razza al lavoro*. Rome: Manifestolibri.

Mezzadra, S. and Neilson, B. (2013). Extraction, logistics, finance: Global crisis and the politics of operations. *Radical Philosophy* 178: 8–18.

Moe, N. (2002). *The View from Vesuvius. Italian Culture and the Southern Question*. Berkeley, CA: University of California Press.

Pagano de Divitiis, P. (1997). *English Merchants in Seventeenth-Century Italy*. Cambridge: Cambridge University Press.

Petrusewicz, M. (1998). *Come il Meridione divenne una questione. Rappresentazioni del Sud prima e dopo il Quarantotto*. Cosenza: Rubbettino.

Sanyal, K. (2007). *Rethinking Capitalist Development: Primitive Accumulation, Governmentality and Post-Colonial Capitalism*. New Delhi: Routledge.

Tomasi di Lampedusa, G. (1958) *Il gattopardo*. Milano: Feltrinelli.

2

FRATELLI D'ITALIA

Differences and similarities in social values between Italian macro-regions

Giuseppe A. Veltri

Introduction: a divided country

According to many scholars, politicians and opinion makers, the social, economic and cultural differences within Italy are of such magnitude to speak of 'three Italies': the North, the Centre and the South. For example, the GDP per capita of the South is around 58 per cent of that of the North and Centre, with 36 per cent of the Italian population (Malanima and Zamagni, 2010).

Debates about the disparity between the North and South have been present almost from Italy's creation as a unified state in the nineteenth century. A hundred and fifty years later, during the national celebrations of 2011, the presumed cultural differences remain at the core of the public debate on Italian national identity. The later distinction between the North, Centre and South introduced the idea of 'three Italies'. Surprisingly, since the publication of Edward Banfield's famous 'The moral basis of backward societies' (1965) and Robert Putman's *Making Democracy Work* (1993), there has been a lack of recent research on the nature and extent of these cultural differences. There have been some historical studies on the stereotypes of the South in Italian history and culture (Dickie, 1999; Lumley and Morris, 1997; McCrae *et al.*, 2007), but most studies are from the social capital literature (Leonardi, 1995; Girlando *et al.*, 2005) and little else has been published on the topic of cultural difference within Italy using more complete and larger sets of cultural indicators beside 'social capital' proxies. Recently, Tabellini (2010) investigated the role of cultural factors for economic development in European regions, including Italy, which he analysed at a regional level using the NUTS-2 classification. Similarly, De Blasio and Nuzzo (2009) studied the role of social capital on local economic development indicators, finding the presence of an effect. Yet, whilst there is a great deal of research on the differences in the economic performance and social structures of the Italian 'macro-regions', there are very few recent studies available on the issue of cultural differences that are based on more than one or two indicators.

Over 20 years after Putnam's work, the differences within Italy continue to be exploited by political parties – in particular the Lega Nord (Northern League) – and have therefore assumed an even more central role in the political and cultural arena. The ostensible cultural differences between the North and South have become so politically charged that some scholars describe these as a form of 'internal orientalism' (Schneider, 1998). However, the attribution of regional characteristics to individuals is problematic and runs the risk of falling into the trap of the ecological fallacy (Robinson, 1950; Hofstede, 1980, 2001).

This study will analyse carefully the cultural differences between the Italian macro-regions within the context of 'social values'. The most important step is to identify suitable definitions of cultural differences that can be used to identify and compare supposed geographical clusters. In this sense, the conceptualization of 'culture' is defined by the psychological and social construct of 'values'. In the social sciences, values are conceptualized in different ways (Hitlin and Piliavin, 2004). Tsirogianni and Gaskell (2011) define social values as 'socially collective beliefs and systems of beliefs that operate as guiding principles in life' (p. 2). The sociological perspectives on social values follow the example of Zerubavel (1997) and his proposed cognitive sociology. The next section describes in more detail the theoretical aspects underpinning each set of indicators.

The aim of this study is twofold: first, to determine and assess the differences in social values between macro-regions in Italy, exploring the existence of culturally homogeneous areas distinguishable among them; second, to contribute to the debate in sociology about culture as a 'latent variable'. Data from the European Value Studies (EVS) will be used to carry out a multilevel variance components analysis to identify and determine regional differences.

Social values as cultural indicators

What constitutes 'culture' is a long-standing debate in the social sciences, and the use of this term outside academia appears to be even more vague and equivocal. However, when the aim is to compare different cultures, the emphasis is given to cultural traits that are trans-situational, long-standing and social. The notion of 'values' – and of social values, in particular – points precisely in this direction. It refers to the more abstract beliefs that are immune to sudden change and has a solid research tradition in the fields of social and cross-cultural psychology and sociology. At the same time, the choice of theoretical approaches is limited by the availability of empirical data specifically collected to measure dimensions of social values. This chapter applies different conceptualizations of the notion of 'values' drawn from the literature on cultural sociology, which implement differently the notion of 'values' as a way to measure ideological dimensions: economic conservatism-liberalism (Middendorp, 1978); a democratic/authoritarian dimension (Eckstein, 1966); generalized trust as the foundation of civic participation; and social capital (Uslaner, 2002; Putnam, 1993).

Economic attitudes are measured in the EVS (2008) in terms of economic liberalism and conservatism versus a progressive economic agenda (Middendorp, 1978). The items are designed to capture individual preferences regarding welfare, unemployment, competition, commercial freedom and income inequality. This set of indicators is of particular interest given the significant differences in GDP per capita between Italian regions and the differences in economic development between the more advanced 'North' and the rest of Italy (Malanima and Zamagni, 2010). Cultural 'compatibility' is often considered an independent variable of economic performance (Huntington and Harrison, 2000).

The set of indicators in the EVS (2008) that relate to the attitudes of Italian citizens towards political systems and democracy includes items on leadership, the role of experts, democracy as a system, democracy and the economy, and democracy and law and order. These indicators represent the conceptual legacy of Harry Eckstein's congruence theory (Eckstein, 1966), which argues, in essence, that political systems tend to be based on authority patterns that are congruent with the authority patterns of other units of society. Two classic studies rooted in this approach are Almond and Verba's *The Civic Culture* (1963) and Putnam's *Making Democracy Work* (1993).

The fourth set of indicators of social values applied in this study concern the notion of 'generalized trust'. Individual actors do something for the general good not because they know other actors but because they trust that their own action will be 'rewarded' by the positive development of communal relations. Trust is necessary when role expectations and family relationships no longer help us to anticipate the reactions of our individual or collective interaction partners. Generalized trust in a society is inextricably linked to the generalized trustworthiness of that particular society (Uslaner, 2002); and, unfortunately, to be trusting among a gallery of rogues is to be gullible (Ostrom and Walker, 2003; Cook *et al.*, 2005). Naturally, trust is neither individually rational nor socially beneficial if betrayal is likely: 'social trust is a valuable community asset if – but only if – it is warranted' (Putnam, 2000: 135). Moreover, 'generalized trust' has the capacity to create positive feedback: trust creates reciprocity and voluntary associations, and reciprocity and associations both strengthen and generate trust (see Putnam, 1993: 163–85).

In summary, the sets of indicators include different approaches to social values: economic conservatism, a pro-democracy/authoritarian dimension and generalized trust, which have been used in the vast sociological literature on social capital and cultural variables to explain differences in economic development. Applying all sets, this study aims to address the following research questions:

1. What are the macro-regional differences in Italy in terms of social values measured by four different sets of conceptual and empirical constructs?
2. Given the large differences that exist in terms of socio-economic conditions, do the five Italian macro-regions represent distinct cultural entities in terms of social values endorsement?

Data and methodology

The analysis uses one data set: the European Value Studies (EVS) 2008 data on Italy. Social values indicators come from the 2008 EVS. Several preparatory steps on the data were needed before the main analysis.

The first step was to recode the regional classification of respondents to create a variable for macro-region classification that is the same for both data sets. Data were nested and analysed using the software MLwIN 2.27 (Rasbash *et al.*, 2009). The second step is to identify the controlling variables to perform between-groups comparisons. Two demographic characteristics were selected as control variables: age and education. Initially the variable 'income' was also selected, but it was discarded because of the high number of missing values in both data sets, which reduced considerably the size of the samples for the subsequent analysis. Age and education were selected as control variables because of their impact on social values (Ferssizidis *et al.*, 2010; for education, albeit in the context of social capital (including generalized trust), see Huang *et al.*, 2009).

The third step is to compute a baseline two-level model (with the two controlling variables) to determine variances at both levels. The fourth is to perform a multilevel variance components analysis calculating the variance partition coefficient[1] that is the proportion of total variance due to level-2 (in this case macro-regional) differences. A VPC equal to 1 would tell us that all the people in a particular macro-region have an identical level of endorsement of a specific cultural indicator (that is, 100 per cent of the total individual differences are at the macro-regional level); a VPC equal to zero would indicate that the people do not share any macro-regional-related common level of endorsement. A high VPC value informs us that macro-regions are very important for understanding individual differences in social values. On the other hand, a VPC of zero would suggest that the macro-regions are similar to random samples taken from any location and would suggest that macro-regions are not relevant for understanding cultural differences.[2]

Analysis

The sets of indicators from the EVS survey have been analysed to determine and quantify macro-regional differences. The Italian macro-regions used in this analysis are: the North-West or 'NW' (EVS, $N = 406$) which includes Piedmont, the Aosta Valley, Liguria and Lombardy; the North-East or 'NE' (EVS, $N = 302$) including the Veneto, Friuli Venezia Giulia, Trentino Aldo Adige (composed of the 'Province Autonome of Trento and Bolzano') and Emilia Romagna; the Centre or 'C' (EVS, $N = 282$) comprising Tuscany, Umbria, the Marche and Lazio; the South or 'S' (EVS, $N = 358$) consisting of Abruzzo, Molise, Campania, Apulia and Calabria; and the Islands ('I'): Sardinia and Sicily (EVS, $N = 171$). This particular configuration of regions in macro-regions is that adopted by the Italian Statistical Office (ISTAT) and EUROSTAT. The analysis begins with the evaluation of economic conservatism, followed by authoritarianism and generalized trust.

This section presents the analysis carried out on four sets of survey items from the European Values Survey 2008, covering economic conservatism, authoritarianism, democratic values and generalized trust.

Economic conservatism and macro-regions

The first set, shown in Table 2.1, regards the dimension of economic conservatism measured by six indicators: individual responsibility (1) vs state responsibility (10); the unemployed should not refuse jobs (1) vs unemployed have a right to refuse jobs (10); competition is good for people (1) vs. competition harmful (10); state should give freedom to firms (1) vs. state should control firms (10); equalize incomes (1) vs. incentives for individual efforts (10); private ownership should be increased (1) vs. state ownership increased (10). Table 2.1 presents the mean scores of economic conservatism by macro-region. The Islands and the South, followed by the Centre, are the most supportive of the state having responsibility for ensuring that everyone is provided for. These regions are followed by the North-West and North-East respectively.

Regarding the next indicator on the 'unemployed having the right to accept or refuse any job', there are almost no differences in the mean scores of the macro-regions: all the macro-regions lean towards the statement that the unemployed should accept any job available. The same can be said about the item 'competition is good or harmful for people': there is very little difference in the mean scores and all the macro-regions endorse the idea that competition is good for stimulating people to work hard and encouraging the development of new ideas.

The next item in the economic conservatism set concerns the freedom of firms and the regulatory role of the state. This topic offers a rather mixed picture: the South and the Centre were the most in favour of the state controlling firms, while the Islands, the North-West and North-East – the latter being the most entrepreneurial region of Italy – endorsed this the least. However, all the macro-regions leant towards endorsing more state control. The next item regards the polarities of a more equal vs a more meritocratic society. All the macro-regions are

Table 2.1 Means and standard deviations of economic conservatism indicators across macro-regions

Italian 5 Macro-regions		*individual vs state responsibility for providing for people (Q58A)*	*take any job vs right to refuse job when unemployed (Q58B)*	*competition good vs harmful for people (Q58C)*	*state to give more freedom to firms vs to control firms more effectively (Q58D)*	*equalize incomes vs incentives for individual effort (Q58E)*	*private vs state ownership of business (Q58F)*
NW	Mean	5.51	3.65	4.60	5.74	6.07	4.60
	N	393	395	391	380	392	361
	Std. Deviation	2.533	2.561	2.480	2.708	2.709	2.220
NE	Mean	5.14	3.23	4.52	5.67	5.96	4.08
	N	293	294	297	287	293	276
	Std. Deviation	2.515	2.157	2.524	2.740	2.691	2.037
C	Mean	5.90	3.46	4.39	6.02	6.14	4.81
	N	268	263	257	252	263	235
	Std. Deviation	2.564	2.542	2.644	2.719	2.739	2.413
S	Mean	6.20	3.75	4.37	6.28	5.63	5.15
	N	345	338	331	319	343	298
	Std. Deviation	2.545	2.497	2.633	2.857	2.895	2.593
I	Mean	6.25	3.52	4.23	5.80	5.34	4.96
	N	166	163	149	138	161	118
	Std. Deviation	2.851	2.559	2.560	2.838	3.138	2.543
Total	Mean	5.75	3.54	4.45	5.91	5.87	4.69
	N	1465	1453	1425	1376	1452	1288
	Std. Deviation	2.605	2.469	2.563	2.771	2.815	2.368

Table 2.2 Multilevel variance components analysis for each cultural set by macro-regions

Values	*Macro-regional level variance* (σ_u^2)	*Individual level variance* (σ_e^2)	*VPC*	*VPC %*	*N*
Individual vs state responsibility for providing for people	0.27	6.393	0.0405	4.05	1465
Take any job vs right to refuse job when unemployed	0.331	5.492	0.0568	5.68	1453
Competition good vs harmful for people	0.262	6.322	0.0397	3.97	1425
State to give more freedom to firms vs to control firms more effectively	0.26	7.372	0.0340	3.40	1376
Equalize incomes vs incentives for individual efforts	0.406	7.394	0.0520	5.20	1452
Private vs state ownership of business	0.291	5.334	0.0517	5.17	1288
Factor 1 Dissatisfaction towards democracy	0.037	0.886	0.0400	4.00	1054
Factor 2 Authoritarianism	0.005	0.965	0.0051	0.51	1054
Trust: People can be trusted vs you can't be too careful	0.01	0.197	0.0483	4.83	1456
Trust: Most people try to take advantage of you vs try to be fair	0.284	4.754	0.0563	5.63	1481
People mostly look out for themselves vs mostly try to be helpful	0.377	4.644	0.0750	7.50	1500

slightly inclined towards support for a meritocracy, with differences in the intensity of their endorsement. Differences between the macro-regions are not significant, as proved by the MANOVA analysis presented later. The last item concerns the role of the state in owning businesses and industry. The least supportive of state ownership and instead endorsing more private ownership is the North-East followed by the North-West and the Centre (M = 4.81, SD = 2.41). The South and the Islands are more supportive of state ownership.

Results were analysed using a one-way MANOVA between-groups design controlled for the respondents' age and education. This analysis revealed a significant multivariate effect of macro-regional identity on values scores, $F(23, 4166) = 3.254$, $p < 0.0001$, Wilks' λ 0.937. Subsequent univariate ANOVA of the response variables showed significance at the $p < .05$ differences between groups for several variables of economic conservatism values: 'individual vs state responsibility', $F(4, 1201) = 7.706$, $p < 0.000$; 'take any job vs right to refuse when unemployed', $F(4, 1201) = 2.592$, $p < 0.05$; 'private vs state ownership of business', $F(4, 1201) = 7.262$, $p < 0.000$. Differences were not statistically significant at the $p < .05$ for 'competition is good vs harmful for people', 'more freedom vs control for firms' and 'equalize incomes vs incentives for individual efforts'.

Table 2.2 presents the amount of variance at the macro-regions level σ_u^2 and at an individual level. The VPC quantifies the proportion of variance at macro-regional level (or level-2) for each of the six indicators in the economic conservatism set. The proportion of variance due to differences at the macro-regional level for the first indicator – 'individual vs state responsibility for providing for people' – is 4 per cent. The second indicator regarding the right to refuse a job when unemployed has a 5.7 per cent variance due to differences between macro-regions. For the third indicator, regarding competition being helpful vs harmful for people, the level-2 variance amounts to 4 per cent. The fourth item, on having more freedom for firms or more state control, has a 3.4 per cent variance due to differences between macro-regions. The fifth item on the choice between a more equal vs a more meritocratic society has a level of variance at the macro-region level of 5 per cent. Similarly, the last indicator on the larger or smaller role of the state in the economy has a 5 per cent variance due to differences between macro-regions. Overall, the multilevel variance components analysis of the economic conservatism indicators has, on average, a 4.5 per cent variance due to differences between macro-regions.

Authoritarianism and pro-democracy values

The second and third sets[3] of indicators aim to capture the degree of authoritarianism and the support for a democratic system, and all the indicators of these two sets are analysed in terms of latent variables or factors. A first group of indicators concerns 'leadership' or preference for a strong leader (and therefore a reduced role for parliament and elections), the role of experts in decision-making, and a general endorsement of the overall merits of a democratic political system. Table 2.3 reports the mean scores and standard deviations of the three items by the five macro-regions.

Regarding the first item, there are no statistically significant differences in the mean scores across the five macro-regions. The second indicator on 'having experts making decisions, not the government', reveals some minor differences, with the North-East, the South and the Islands finding the role of experts to be more negative in comparison with the Centre and the North-West, which is the least sceptical. The last item in this group is an evaluation of democracy as a political system: citizens of all the macro-regions consider democracy to be beneficial and there are only very marginal differences in that regard. Results were analysed using a one-way MANOVA between-groups design controlled for age and education. This analysis revealed a significant multivariate effect of regional identity on values scores using macro-regions, $F(11, 3328) = 2.057$, $p < 0.05$, Wilks' λ 0.981. Subsequent ANOVA of the response variables showed that differences in two items – the role of leaders and the overall appraisal of democracy – were not statistically significant at $p < .05$. Differences in attitudes towards the role of experts across macro-regions were statistically significant $F(4, 1262) = 2.542$, $p < 0.05$.

Table 2.4 reports the means and standard deviations for the third set[4] of indicators on the endorsement of democracy. The first item concerns democracy as the best possible political system (although not without its pitfalls) and there are almost no differences in the mean scores: all respondents agree democracy to be the best possible system. The second item regards democracy as bad for the economy. Similarly, there are no large differences between the macro-regional mean scores and all of them tend to disagree with this statement, with the South and Islands disagreeing to a slightly lesser extent. The next item describes democracies as 'indecisive and hav[ing] too much squabbling'; there are similar mean scores for all the macro-regions without any significant difference: all respondents mildly disagree with this statement. The last indicator states that 'democracies aren't good at maintaining order'. On this statement, once again, there

Table 2.3 Means and standard deviations of authoritarianism indicators across macro-regions

Italian 5 Macro-regions		*political system: strong leader (Q66A)*	*political system: experts making decisions (Q66B)*	*political system: army ruling (Q66C)*	*political system: democratic (Q66D)*
NW	Mean	3.42	2.56	3.68	1.38
	N	382	372	384	383
	Std. Deviation	.815	.916	.626	.580
NE	Mean	3.42	2.72	3.68	1.43
	N	286	268	284	291
	Std. Deviation	.807	.919	.557	.609
C	Mean	3.43	2.63	3.68	1.34
	N	255	251	256	259
	Std. Deviation	.871	.905	.619	.564
S	Mean	3.27	2.72	3.63	1.40
	N	329	305	316	325
	Std. Deviation	.963	.951	.611	.567
I	Mean	3.41	2.73	3.69	1.47
	N	162	142	156	159
	Std. Deviation	.903	.981	.528	.549
Total	Mean	3.39	2.66	2.66	1.40
	N	1414	1338	1338	1417
	Std. Deviation	.871	.931	.928	.577

are no large differences among Italian citizens from the five macro-regions. All of them tend to disagree with this statement; the South alone was slightly less in disagreement.

Results were analysed using a one-way MANOVA between-groups design controlled for age and education. This analysis revealed a significant multivariate effect of macro-regional identity on values scores $F(15, 3419) = 1.914$, $p < 0.05$, Wilks' λ 0.973. Subsequent ANOVA of the response variables showed that differences in all four items on democracy were not statistically significant at $p < .05$.

Both sets of indicators were analysed using a factor analysis. A Principal Components Analysis (PCP) with a Varimax (orthogonal) rotation of the previous 7 Likert scale questions was conducted on data gathered from 1,054 participants. An examination of the Kaiser-Meyer Olkin measure of sampling adequacy suggested that the sample was factorable (KMO = 0.803). The results of an orthogonal rotation of the solution are shown in Table 2.5. When loadings of less than 0.25 were excluded, the analysis yielded a two-factor solution with a simple structure (factor loadings = > 0.25).

The two-factor solution is interpreted as follows: four items are loaded mainly into one factor and it is clear from Table 2.5 that all the items – especially the first three – relate to a dimension of dissatisfaction with democracy; three items define a second factor and all relate to a form of authoritarianism. Two items – 'democracy cannot maintain order' and the preference for strong leaders – contributed to both factors.

Results were analysed using a one-way MANOVA between-groups design controlled for age and education. This analysis revealed a significant multivariate effect of macro-regional identity

Table 2.4 Mean scores of three items measuring attitudes towards democracy across macro-regions

Italian 5 Macro-regions		*democracy: best political system (Q67A)*	*democracy: causes bad economy (Q67B)*	*democracy: is indecisive (Q67C)*	*democracy: cannot maintain order (Q67D)*
NW	Mean	1.52	2.81	2.50	3.02
	N	376	362	370	372
	Std. Deviation	.589	.649	.730	.684
NE	Mean	1.56	2.86	2.48	3.01
	N	286	256	276	275
	Std. Deviation	.628	.623	.690	.678
C	Mean	1.51	2.86	2.61	3.14
	N	255	223	248	241
	Std. Deviation	.560	.696	.817	.709
S	Mean	1.53	2.77	2.52	2.98
	N	326	268	302	300
	Std. Deviation	.541	.669	.768	.715
I	Mean	1.56	2.61	2.47	3.02
	N	153	125	131	133
	Std. Deviation	.572	.792	.871	.707
Total	Mean	1.53	2.80	2.52	3.03
	N	1396	1234	1327	1321
	Std. Deviation	.579	.675	.763	.698

Table 2.5 PCP: rotated two-factor solution

	Rotated Component Matrix[a]	
	Component	
	1	*2*
democracy: is indecisive (Q67C)	.836	
democracy: causes bad economy (Q67B)	.781	
democracy: cannot maintain order (Q67D)	.690	.282
political system: experts making decisions (Q66B)	.262	
political system: democratic (Q66D)		–.751
democracy: best political system (Q67A)		–.737
political system: the army ruling (Q66C)		.664
political system: strong leader (Q66A)	.429	.480

Extraction Method: Principal Component Analysis.
Rotation Method: Varimax with Kaiser Normalization.
a. Rotation converged in 3 iterations.

on the factor scores $F(4, 2092) = 2.365$, $p < 0.05$, Wilks' λ 0.989. Subsequent ANOVA of the response variables showed that only in one factor – the authoritarianism dimension – are the macro-regional differences statistically significant at the level of $p < .05$.

Table 2.2 shows the amount of variance of both factors due at the macro-regions level σ_u^2 and the variance at the individual level. The proportion of variance due to differences at the macro-regional level for the first factor – 'dissatisfaction towards democracy' – amounts to 4 per cent. In the second factor on the dimension of authoritarianism, level-2 variance is at 0.5 per cent and this is confirmed by the fact that a level-two model is not statistically superior to a one level solution, 'Factor 2 Authoritarianism' (χ^2, N = 1482) = 0.942, $p = 0.331$.

Generalized trust and macro-regions

The fourth set of indicators concerns one of the most heavily debated aspects of cultural differences between the macro-regions in Italy: 'generalized trust'. As discussed previously, generalized trust has often been associated with economic development as a precondition of healthy economic transactions and relationships reducing their costs. Table 2.6 shows the mean scores and standard deviations.

The first item is about choosing the endorsement between the binary choices 'most people can be trusted' and 'you can't be too careful in dealing with people'. All respondents leaned towards the second option. The South and the Islands are stronger endorsers of the 'not trusting' option compared with the Centre and the North-East. The strongest endorser of generalized

Table 2.6 Means and standard deviations of generalized trust items across macro-regions

Italian 5 Macro-regions		*people can be trusted vs you can't be too careful (Q7)*	*most people try to take advantage of you vs try to be fair (Q8)*	*people mostly look out for themselves vs mostly try to be helpful (Q9)*
NW	Mean	1.59	5.57	4.36
	N	396	403	403
	Std. Deviation	.492	2.154	2.171
NE	Mean	1.67	6.00	4.38
	N	283	294	298
	Std. Deviation	.469	2.119	2.167
C	Mean	1.67	5.36	4.06
	N	272	273	278
	Std. Deviation	.473	2.311	2.248
S	Mean	1.79	4.94	4.05
	N	344	345	352
	Std. Deviation	.407	2.356	2.346
I	Mean	1.80	4.69	3.67
	N	161	166	169
	Std. Deviation	.400	2.253	2.211
Total	Mean	1.69	5.37	4.16
	N	1456	1481	1500
	Std. Deviation	.462	2.274	2.240

trust for this item was the North-West. The second trust indicator is constituted by two polarities: 'most people try to take advantage of you' and 'most people try to be fair'.[5] Similarly, the Islands and the South mostly leaned towards the cynical pole compared with the more trusting Centre and North-West. The most trusting macro-region was the North-East. The third trust indicator concerns the choice between the two polarities 'people mostly look out for themselves' and 'people mostly try to be helpful'. All respondents leaned towards the cynical pole. As with the previous item, the Islands and the South are the two macro-regions that are the least trusting, closely followed by the Centre. The most trusting respondents were from the North-West and the North-East.

Differences in scores were analysed using a one-way MANOVA between-groups design controlled for age and education. This analysis revealed a significant multivariate effect of regional identity on values scores using macro-regions, $F(11, 3672) = 5.375$, $p < 0.000$, Wilks' λ 0.955. Subsequent ANOVA of the response variables showed that differences in all three items were statistically significant at the $p < .05$: 'people can be trusted/you can't be too careful' $F(4, 1392) = 9.110$, $p < 0.000$; 'most people try to take advantage/try to be fair' $F(4, 1392) = 9.615$, $p < 0.000$; 'people mostly look out for themselves/mostly try to be helpful' $F(4, 1392) = 2.629$, $p < 0.05$.

Table 2.2 also shows the amount of variance for the political system values set of indicators at the macro-regional level and at an individual level. The proportion of variance due to differences at the macro-regional level for the first indicator, 'people can be trusted/you can't be too careful', amounts to 4.8 per cent. The second indicator of generalized trust, 'most people try to take advantage of you/try to be fair' has a level-2 variance of 5.6 per cent. The third item or 'people mostly look out for themselves/mostly try to be helpful', has 7.5 per cent variance due to macro-regional differences. Overall, the average proportion of variance due to differences between the macro-regions for this set was 6 per cent.

Discussion

In the dimension of 'economic conservatism', the five Italian macro-regions are extremely similar without considerable differences. The same can be said of the factorial dimensions of authoritarianism vs support of democracy. Regarding the 'generalized trust' dimension, the South and the Islands are only slightly more distrustful than the North and, in particular, the North-East – which is the area in which respondents are the most willing to trust others.

A small regional cultural variance is in line with a recent study by Tabellini (2010), which found that the regional dummy variables for most of his cultural indicators explained around 6 per cent of the variance and that 'regional distributions are clearly different, but the range of variation within each region remains large' (p. 687). Tabellini interpreted this finding as ambiguous because of the small number of respondents in some regions and therefore questioned the representativeness of the samples. In this study, the analysis of five macro-regions indicated the same low proportion of variance explained at macro-regional level, although much larger samples were used.

Overall, however, the findings reveal the existence of small differences between the Italian macro-regions analysed. There are several potential interpretations and explanations for such findings but two aspects are particularly important: one is historical and one is related to social and psychological theory.

First, an interpretation of these results should consider Italian history and in particular the relationships between Northern, Central and Southern Italy. Following the unification of the Italian kingdom (in 1861), there was an almost continuous flow of migration from Southern

Italy to the rest of the country, particularly after the Second World War (during the 1950s and 1960s), when an enormous number of people left the South to live in the Centre and the North of Italy. In other words, internal migration in Italy has been (and continues to be) a notable phenomenon. Hence, regional cultures have undergone many years of mutual contamination and influence.

Second, people implement and combine relational models depending on their values, position in society, groups, institutional and cultural contexts, historical processes, and relations to others, etc. In other words, people maintain distinctive and inconsistent action frames that are invoked in response to particular contextual cues (DiMaggio, 1997). For example, social values also compete strongly with social norms (Bardi and Schwartz, 2003) and may not be used as much by individuals who value conformity to the social context (Lönnqvist *et al.*, 2006; Mellema and Bassili, 1995). In conclusion, the existing differences in collective behaviour between the Italian macro-regions should be explained more accurately considering the combined effect of the situational and ecological factors, rather than in terms of a coherent cultural expression.

Conclusions

The analysis indicates that cultural differences between macro-regions do exist but the situation is complex with some noticeable differences and many surprising similarities. However, it is difficult to judge whether such differences should be considered significant and what effects they might have. Ideally, a comparison with other European countries and their internal diversity would provide a reference point; for example Steel and Taras (2010) consider a variance of between 3 and 18 per cent at country level as small, highlighting the danger of using national averages to make assumptions about individual cultural values.

In general, the proportion of variance explained at the individual level (or differences between individuals) is much larger than that due to the differences at the macro-regional level for the large majority of indicators. Overall, macro-regions are not homogeneous and distinct cultural areas. It follows that there is little evidence of clearly dissimilar cultural macro-areas in terms of large differences in social values among Italian citizens.

The results presented in this study challenge the notion of fundamentally culturally diverse – in terms of individual social values – macro-areas in Italy. In other words, they reveal the ecological fallacy of the application of regional characteristics to individuals without distinguishing between individual correlations and ecological correlations (Robinson, 1950).

There are several other potential analytical routes for future research to follow in order to measure cultural differences in Italy and therefore the evidence is not conclusive. However, this analysis takes an important first step towards debunking a dangerous simplification in the study of Italian society with the hope that other scholars will complement it in the near future.

Notes

1 The formula for the VPC is:

$$VPC = \frac{\sigma_u^2}{\sigma_u^2 + \sigma_e^2}$$

For example, the level-two baseline model for one indicator with the controlling variables is:

$$\nu 295_{ij} \sim N(XB, \Omega)$$

$$\nu 295_{ij} = \beta_{0ij}\text{cons} + \beta_1 \nu 303_{ij} + \beta_2 \nu 336_{ij}$$

$$\beta_{0ij} = \beta_0 + u_{0j} + e_{0ij}$$
$$\left[u_{0j}\right] \sim N\left(0, \Omega_u\right) : \Omega_u = \left[\sigma^2_{u0}\right]$$
$$\left[e_{0ij}\right] \sim N\left(0, \Omega_e\right) : \Omega_e = \left[\sigma^2_{e0}\right]$$

2 For quantifying explained variance, R^2 analogs are defined at each level as the difference between the variance components for the baseline (i.e. intercepts only) model and the variance component for the current model divided by the variance component for the baseline model (Kreft and DeLeeuw, 1998). For testing the significance of the variance between the macro-regions, the log likelihood of the model that includes σ^2_u can be compared with the log likelihood of the almost identical model that does not include σ^2_u. If the χ^2 test with 1 degree of freedom rejects the null hypothesis of no difference at 0.05, then σ^2_u is statistically significant. If p is noticeably larger than 0.05, say $p > 0.10$, then σ^2_u is not statistically significant. All reported level-two models are significant compared with a level-one solution, unless stated otherwise.

3 In the second set, all items were measured with the following scale: -5 other missing; -4 question not asked; -3 nap; -2 na; -1 dk; 1 very good; 2 fairly good; 3 fairly bad; 4 very bad.

4 In the second set, all items were measured with the following scale: -5 other missing; -4 question not asked; -3 nap; -2 na; -1 dk; 1 very good; 2 fairly good; 3 fairly bad; 4 very bad.

5 'Most people would try to take advantage of me' was 1 and 'most people would try to be fair' was 10, variable 63 Q8, EVS 2008. Similarly, for the following item ' people mostly look out for themselves' had value 1 and 'people mostly try to be helpful' had value 10, v64 Q9, EVS 2008.

References

Almond, G. A. and Verba, S. (1963). *The civic culture: Political attitudes and democracy in five nations*. Princeton, NJ: Princeton University Press.

Bardi, A. and Schwartz, S. H. (2003). Values and behavior: Strength and structure of relations. *Personality and Social Psychology Bulletin*, 29(10): 1207–20.

Cook, K. S., Hardin, R. and Levi, M. (2005). *Cooperation without trust?* New York: Russell Sage Foundation.

De Blasio, G. and Nuzzo, G. (2009). Historical traditions of civicness and local economic development. *Journal of Regional Science*, 50(4): 833–57.

Dickie, J. (1999). *Darkest Italy: The nation and stereotypes of the Mezzogiorno, 1860–1900*. New York: St. Martin's Press.

DiMaggio, P. (1997). Culture and cognition. *Annual Review of Sociology*, 23: 263–87.

Eckstein, H. (1966). *Division and cohesion in democracy: A study of Norway*. Princeton, NJ: Princeton University Press.

European Values Study (EVS) (2008) Integrated Dataset. GESIS Data Archive, Cologne. ZA4800 Data file version 3.0.0, doi:10.4232/1.11004.

Ferssizidis, P., Adams, L. M., Kashdan, T. B., Plummer, C., Mishra, A. and Ciarrochi, J. (2010). Motivation for and commitment to social values: The roles of age and gender. *Motivation and Emotion*, 34(4): 354–62.

Girlando, A. P., Anderson, C. J. and Zerillo, J. W. (2005). An examination of Hofstede's paradigm of national culture and its malleability. *Journal of Transnational Management*, 10(1): 23–36.

Hitlin, S. and Piliavin, J. A. (2004). Values: Reviving a dormant concept. *Annual Review of Sociology*, 30(1): 359–93.

Hofstede, G. H. (1980). *Culture's consequences: International differences in work-related values*. Newbury Park, CA: Sage.

Hofstede, G. H. (2001). *Culture's consequences: comparing values, behaviors, institutions, and organizations across nations*. Thousand Oaks, CA: Sage.

Huang, J., Maassen van den Brink, H. and Groot, W. (2009). A meta-analysis of the effect of education on social capital. *Economics of Education Review*, 28: 454–64.

Huntington, S. P. and Harrison, L. E. (2000). *Culture matters: How values shape human progress*. New York: Basic Books.

Kreft, I. and DeLeeuw, J. (1998). *Introducing multilevel modeling*. Thousand Oaks, CA: Sage.

Leonardi, R. (1995). Regional development in Italy: Social capital and the Mezzogiorno. *Oxford Review of Economic Policy*, 11(2): 165–79.

Lönnqvist, J., Leikas, S., Paunonen, S., Nissinen, V. and Verkasalo, M. (2006). Conformism moderates the relations between values, anticipated regret, and behavior. *Personality and Social Psychology Bulletin*, 32: 1469–81.

Lumley, R. and Morris, J. (1997). *The new history of the Italian south: The Mezzogiorno revisited*. Exeter: University of Exeter Press.

McCrae, R. R., Terracciano, A., Realo, A. and Allik, J. (2007). Climatic warmth and national wealth: Some culture-level determinants of national character stereotypes. *European Journal of Personality*, 21(8): 953–76.

Malanima, P. and Zamagni, V. (2010). 150 years of the Italian economy, 1861–2010. *Journal of Modern Italian Studies*, 15(1): 1–20.

Mellema, A. and Bassili, J. N. (1995). On the relationship between attitudes and values: Exploring the moderating effects of self-monitoring and self-monitoring schematicity. *Personality and Social Psychology Bulletin*, 21: 885–92.

Middendorp, C. P. (1978). *Progressiveness and conservatism: The fundamental dimensions of ideological controversy and their relationship to social class*. The Hague: Mouton.

Ostrom, E. and Walker, J. (2003). *Trust and reciprocity: Interdisciplinary lessons from experimental research*. New York: Russell Sage Foundation.

Putnam, R. D. (2000). *Bowling alone: The collapse and revival of American community*. New York: Simon & Schuster.

Putnam, R. D., Leonardi, R. and Nanetti, R. (1993). *Making democracy work: Civic traditions in modern Italy*. Princeton, NJ: Princeton University Press.

Rasbash, J., Charlton, C., Browne, W. J., Healy, M. and Cameron, B. (2009). *MLwiN Version 2.1*. Bristol: Centre for Multilevel Modelling, University of Bristol.

Robinson, W. S. (1950). Ecological correlations and the behavior of individuals. *American Sociological Review*, 15(3): 351–7.

Schneider, J. (1998). *Italy's 'Southern question': Orientalism in one country*. Oxford: Berg.

Steel, P. and Taras, V. (2010). Culture as a consequence: A multi-level multivariate meta-analysis of the effects of individual and country characteristics on work-related cultural values. *Journal of International Management*, 16(3): 211–33.

Tabellini, G. (2010). Culture and institutions: Economic development in the regions of Europe. *Journal of the European Economic Association*, 8(4): 677–716.

Tsirogianni, S. and Gaskell, G. (2011). The role of plurality and context in social values. *Journal for the Theory of Social Behaviour*, 41(4): 441–65.

Uslaner, E. M. (2002). *The moral foundation of trust*. Cambridge and New York: Cambridge University Press.

Zerubavel, E. (1997). *Social mindscapes: An invitation to cognitive sociology*. Cambridge, MA: Harvard University Press.

3

FROM MANPOWER TO BRAIN DRAIN?

Emigration and the Italian state, between past and present

Guido Tintori and Michele Colucci

Emigration[1] from Italy has been thoroughly analysed in particular with reference to the large contribution that Italians made to the mass migrations from and within Europe between 1815 and 1939 (Baines, 1995; Hatton and Williamson, 1998; Bade, 2003). The country experienced a second wave of mass emigration after the Second World War, which has only recently caught scholarly attention (Colucci, 2008; De Clementi, 2010; Bonifazi, 2013).[2] In addition, even though Italy has almost constantly had a positive net migration since 1974, thus becoming a country of immigration, there have always been relatively significant numbers of people leaving, up to the so-called *nuove mobilità* ('new mobility') of the 2000–10s (Bonifazi and Heins, 2009; Tintori, forthcoming).

Official statistics tell us that roughly 28,500,000 citizens left Italy between 1869 and 2005, with an arithmetic mean of 211,000 people per year. The periods with the highest intensity of mobility out of the country were 1869–1931, with more than 18,500,000 expatriates, and 1946–74, with over 7,500,000 people leaving. The peak of emigration took place in 1913, when more than 872,500 Italians left.[3] Even though we lack reliable data on return migrations, it is estimated that backflows from European countries reached almost 80 per cent of the total, while roughly 50 per cent of those who left for the Americas or Australia went back (Foerster, 1919: 23–43; Gould, 1980: 86; Baines, 1995: 35–8; Cerase, 2001: 115–16).

The latest official data show that, in 2012, 67,998 citizens moved their residency abroad, the highest figure in the last ten years, with a 35.8 per cent increase on the previous year. The majority of the expatriates came from the northern regions and went to European countries, with Germany, Switzerland and the UK as their main destinations. The average age was around 33 and there was a slight prevalence of males (54.6 per cent) over females (ISTAT, 2014). These trends and features are confirmed by the most recent data of the AIRE (Registry of Italian citizens residing abroad), with the number of Italian citizens officially residing abroad up from 4,341,156 at the end of 2012 to 4,482,115 at the end of 2013.

It is important to underline that these statistics should be taken with a grain of salt: they are essentially useful for indicating a trend and the numbers of non-temporary emigrants. In fact, not all Italian citizens who emigrate register with their consulates. According to the law, Italians moving overseas should register with the AIRE at consulates if they intend to stay abroad for at least one year. Since failure to comply with the law is not punished, most people typically register only when they are in need of a service from the consulate. Thus, ISTAT and AIRE data certainly underestimate the actual number of current expatriates from the country, especially because they do not detect temporary and circular migrants. On the other hand, though, the AIRE registry is not an accurate tool for counting Italians who have left the country, since it contains sizeable numbers of people who were born outside Italy and obtained citizenship by descent. According to the latest available data, between 1998 and 2010 at least 1,003,403 individuals got Italian citizenship by descent at Italian consulates abroad and were automatically added to the AIRE registry. Of total new Italian/EU passports, 73.3 per cent were released in Argentina, Brazil and Uruguay alone (Tintori, 2009, 2012a).

Determinants, processes and patterns of Italian emigration are complex. The same complexity applies to the causes behind Italy's 'continuing history of emigration' (Tintori, 2013). Push-and-pull models, based on a cost-benefit analysis applied to wage differentials and core–periphery segmented labour markets, offer insufficient explanations. Demographic pressure, social upheavals, differences in the process of industrialisation between Italy and the destination countries, the development of an increasingly interdependent international labour market, the perpetuation of migration chains, and personal reasons have all contributed to determining emigration from Italy.

In this chapter, we aim to investigate how the Italian state discursively framed expatriation at various points in time and how these institutional perceptions were translated into policies; to what extent the conventional narrative that describes past emigration as mainly formed by labourers, often unskilled, and the more recent one as a 'brain drain' is empirically grounded; to what extent the international dimension, in terms of participation in the development of an international economy, played a role in defining Italy's emigration policies.

A brief digression on the so-called 'Great Emigration' of the 1860s–1930s will set the proper background for our analysis. Not only will it provide a historical perspective, but more importantly, it will offer the opportunity to look at the larger picture and point out continuities and breaks throughout the whole history of the unified Italian state.

The foundation of Italy's emigration policies: 1861–1945

Soon after the unification of the country in 1861, emigration became a major social and economic issue the state had to cope with, simply because of its sheer scale. At first, the liberal ruling classes addressed the question with administrative provisions. All these acts dealt with mass migration essentially as a matter of public order and were aimed at avoiding the state's finances incurring the costs of repatriations (Sori, 1979: 255–9; Ostuni, 2001: 309–11). Prime Minister Francesco Crispi, who saw mass migration as a safety valve to ease the pressure of unemployment and social tensions, promoted the first organic law on emigration in 1888 (no. 5866, 30 January). The legal protection of emigrants was kept at a minimal level. Yet, the 1888 Act marked the beginning of an increasing interventionism by the state in emigration.

In an age of mounting nationalism, a more proactive attitude developed with the evolution of a strategic plan that not only viewed emigration positively as a safety valve, but most of all aimed at transforming Italian emigrants abroad into a tool for Italy's export and colonial expansion (Tintori, 2006; Choate, 2008). As a consequence, even though Italian emigration had been characterised as being mainly 'circular' and 'temporary', the state directed its efforts towards that strategic goal and concentrated its actions on the 'settlers', especially in those countries that were deemed crucial for Italy's interests in the international economy, such as the United States and, to a lesser degree, Argentina and Brazil.

More consistently, Act no. 23 of 31 January 1901 – the Emigration Law – set up the *Commissariato generale dell'emigrazione* (Cge) [General Emigration Agency], a branch of the ministry of Foreign affairs, and an Emigration Fund, to finance several programmes of assistance for emigrants and strengthen their chances of success. The 1901 law marked what was described as the 'golden period' of Italian emigration legislation (Cometti, 1958: 822) and inaugurated a tradition of commitment in assisting Italian emigrants, provided they were compatible with the international interests of the country. The Cge was established as a central institutional body with the sole purpose of regulating and managing emigration from Italy. Among its tasks, it would ideally rationalise the outflows and improve the emigrants' human capital, through targeted training programmes.

The aim was to 'outsource' as much as possible the social and moral protection of emigrants, through the Emigration Fund's subsidising of mutual aid, and religious and migrant associations. Most of the bureaucratic resources were to be dedicated to the strategic plan of establishing 'free colonies' of Italians.

When the fascist movement seized power in 1922, at first the rationales behind emigration policies remained substantially identical. For example, Mussolini replaced the *Istituto Nazionale per la Colonizzazione e le Imprese dei Lavori all'estero* (INCILE), founded in 1920, with the *Istituto di Credito per il Lavoro Italiano all'estero* (ICLE or Credit Institute for Italian Labour Abroad). But its functions remained to provide financial support for 'colonization projects abroad' (Cannistraro and Rosoli, 1979: 681–92). It was rather the adoption of increasingly restrictive measures towards international immigration by the main destination countries during the 1920s and throughout the 1930s, which practically ended the era of free mass migration, that prompted a change in the regime's emigration policies. Initially, the regime tried to negotiate a higher quota for Italians, especially with the US, and extended the policy of 'selective emigration' already started by the Liberal governments, that is training programmes for prospective emigrants specifically tailor-made to match the needs of the destination country's labour market. When it became clear that restrictionism in the Americas was due to economic as much as ideological reasons, in 1927 Mussolini suspended all governmental subsidies to private associations, dismantled the Cge and replaced it with the *Direzione Generale degli Italiani all'estero* (Dgie or General Bureau of Italians Abroad, still a branch of the Ministry of Foreign Affairs). In parallel, he announced a new demographic policy whose goal was to increase Italy's population, by means of both higher birth rates and return migration. The new regime of international migration put an end to temporary and circular mobility and accelerated the process of settlement for those who were abroad. In this light, the regime's emigration policies consistently carried on what had been started by the Liberal state. It just turned the 'free colonies' into 'fascist colonies'.

Already at this early stage, especially if we place our analysis in comparative perspective with other countries producing emigrants (Dufoix *et al.*, 2010; Collyer, 2013), the Italian state displayed a great deal of proactive commitment towards the expatriates, in terms of both resources and governmental agencies.

To answer the question of what sort of citizens the country was exporting, we should break the analysis down according to specific destinations and years. Skilled workers and even elite emigrants were represented throughout the whole period (Foerster, 1919; Sori, 1979; Incisa di Camerana, 2003). But unskilled male labourers were by far the largest group. This fact, though, must be placed in the proper historical context. First of all, that was the profile of the European, not only the Italian, mobile workforce at the time. Second, according to Italian census data, 77 per cent of the population was illiterate in 1861 and still more than 35 per cent in 1921.

Third, and most importantly, this supply of manual labour 'caused by the declining numbers of workers employed in agriculture and the collapse of rural industry' (Hanagan, 1977: 29) was met, on the demand side, by the expanding system of manufacturing under new mechanised methods of production that were characterising the international economy.

The resumption of mass emigration: 1945–73

At the end of the Second World War the economic and social situation was particularly critical. The scenario that confronted contemporary observers was that of a country scarred by conflict: its infrastructure destroyed, its avenues of communication barely usable and its industrial apparatus badly damaged. It was a scenario that was inevitably reflected in the everyday life of the people: the difficulty in procuring adequate food supplies, the unhealthy and precarious living situations, and the hygienic and sanitary conditions that were growing notably worse. In order to understand the characteristics of the resumption of emigration in the aftermath of the Second World War one must inevitably start here.

The choice to emigrate was initially an inevitable response to unemployment and to the dashed hopes for the reconstruction following liberation (Pugliese and Rebeggiani, 2003; Colucci, 2008; Rinauro, 2009). The most tangible consequence of the negative economic circumstances in the immediate post-war period was precisely the presence of widespread unemployment throughout all of the country's productive sectors, a situation that was destined to worsen in the two-year period between 1945 and 1946 while at the same time social and political tensions increased. In 1946 the offices of the Ministry of Labour and Social Policy registered the presence of 2,098,257 unemployed persons, especially in the construction and agriculture sectors (*Ministero per la Costituente*, 1946). From the return of veterans to assistance for war victims, from layoffs to social assistance, the causes and consequences of unemployment constituted the heart of political confrontations and debate among social forces. Once again, one of the most immediate solutions to confronting the relationship between the economic crisis and unemployment was emigration.

After the Second World War, however, that solution was shown to be much less practicable than it had been in the past. Those governments interested in Italian manpower (among which figured many continental European ones taken up with reconstruction) had every intention of rigidly controlling their respective national labour markets, while other states which in the past had accepted Italian immigrants in large numbers had already erected barriers between the two world wars. With laws impeding the long-term residency of foreigners, provisions limiting family reunions and instruments controlling the labour market that considered foreigners' presence as transitory and rotational only, the direction the immigration policies of many European countries assumed (like Switzerland, Belgium and Germany) was of a restrictive type. In countries like France and Great Britain as well – in which the ruling classes' prevalent orientation was favourable toward an increase in immigration – this was notably contingent on and related to the strictest demands of the national labour markets.

One important change of these immediate post-war years, however, was the behaviour of the Italian government, which more than ever insisted on supporting the continuation of emigration at all costs, signing cooperation accords with interested countries and explicitly encouraging emigration among the unemployed. From the government point of view, the objective was twofold: on the one hand, to relieve pressure on the Italian labour market and, on the other, to attempt to ease the social tensions that could easily have erupted with such a large number of unemployed.

Another significant change was the presence of women workers – primarily recruited by Switzerland and Great Britain – who moved on their own, that is, without family members – a migratory phenomenon that had been much less common in previous decades. A less new, but extremely significant, characteristic was the existence of widespread clandestine emigration – above all to France – due precisely to the rigidity of the rules and the policies of certain states and certain companies that encouraged illegal recruitment (Rinauro, 2009).

What were the concrete results of this post-war trend? We can distinguish them as follows: first, mass emigration resumed but to a lesser degree than the Italian governments would have wanted. Between 1945 and 1957 3,157,269 persons left Italy, 1,745,089 of them to European countries. In the same period, however, 1,216,203 persons were repatriated, 904,835 of whom came from Europe (Prencipe and Nicosia, 2010). Already in 1949 a Ministry of Foreign affairs report (*Direzione generale emigrazione*, 1949) pointed out that it would have been impossible to allow more than two or three hundred thousand people to leave per year as the demand from destination countries was not so high; ministers in charge in 1945 still forecast and hoped for, however, at least one million emigrants per year. Second, the European states and the new non-European states interested in Italian labour (Australia, Canada and later Venezuela, countries that prior to 1945 had absorbed little Italian manpower) above all sought qualified personnel and opened recruitment offices in Italy themselves. Only a fraction of the unemployed eligible for expatriation managed to pass the selection process and therefore mainly qualified workers or those who could guarantee previous experience were selected.

Third, emigration became a terrain of extreme political conflict. The departure of qualified workers, who should have had a primary role in the reconstruction of Italy, became the object of heated debate and animated discussions.

Controversy also arose from the living and working conditions that Italians encountered abroad. Having been encouraged to leave, once abroad they frequently found themselves in situations that glaringly violated the accords signed with Italian governments. Yet no one – if one excludes the trade unions and religious organisations and only very rarely the consular structures – attempted to improve those conditions. The mining disaster of Marcinelle in 1956 (137 Italian dead) opened the eyes of the entire country to this reality, but in the preceding ten years 520 Italians had died in Belgian mines.

In spite of the improvement in Italy's economic conditions in the early 1950s, emigration continued to represent a structural voice for the Italian economy. Money sent back by migrants, for example, amounted to 397.5 million US dollars; in 1970 it surpassed the symbolic number of a billion US dollars to reach 1004.6 million US dollars. Considering the effect of remittances on familial finances, from the immediate post-war period onwards they were an important factor in providing a support to income. In 1949, for example, Italian miners in France on average sent 9,476 lire a month back to their families. In the same period the salary of a specialised worker at FIAT was around 30,000 lire; therefore, the sum that a family of a miner working abroad received was equivalent to about a third of the salary of a specialised worker.

In the period of reconstruction emigration once more began to be a customary presence for the working classes of the country who moved primarily to Europe and who, over time, even managed to take advantage of the process of European integration. Beginning with the Treaty of Rome in 1957, the European Common Market in fact envisaged the free movement of workers among its member countries.

In the course of the 1960s, the Italian migratory context was modified. Already at the end of the 1950s the 'economic miracle' had contributed to directing the flows not only abroad, but, increasingly, to the industrialised areas of the central-north, in particular to Piedmont, Lombardy and Liguria. In the 1960s the number of people leaving Italy declined, even though emigration remained significant: 383,908 citizens emigrated in 1960, 151,854 in 1970.[4] A new geography of mobility was taking over: many returnees did not, in fact, go back to their places of origin, but to the major cities of central Italy (Fofi, 1964).

European countries remained the preferred destination of Italian emigrants throughout the whole period. The country that statistically recorded the most arrivals of Italians was the Federal Republic of Germany. The takeoff of mass Italian emigration to Germany dates to the period from 1959 to 1960 when the annual number of emigrations rose from 28,394 to 100,544.

It is important to underline that Italians shared their migratory experience with a growing number of communities, not only from southern Europe, but from the rest of the world as well. In Germany in 1964 Italians made up 31 per cent of all foreigners, in 1966 30.3 per cent, in 1968 28.3 per cent and in 1973 16.7 per cent. In the 1960s – after the 1955 migration accord with Italy – Germany in fact signed similar agreements with Spain and Greece (1960), Turkey (1961), Morocco (1963), Portugal (1964), Tunisia (1965) and Yugoslavia (1968) (Collinson, 1993). Outside Europe the most significant data relates to the decline in departures for South America. The countries that showed a persistence of Italian emigration were in fact Canada, the United States and Australia; only Venezuela in the early part of the 1960s was anywhere close. Throughout the 1960s Italy even enjoyed a positive migratory balance with Argentina, the symbolic country of Italian migration par excellence; only in the years 1967 and 1969 were departures for Argentina lower than returns from Argentina.

The typology of the outflows from Italy remained particularly tied to the migratory policies of the host countries. Switzerland undertook a redefinition of its immigration laws, which found a direct application in the new accord signed with Italy in 1964. In any event, working conditions remained rather precarious: in 1965 the Mattmark Dam disaster occurred when half a million metric cubes of ice fell on workers building the dam. This resulted in 83 deaths, 57 of which were Italian. The catastrophe is still remembered by the Italian community today. In Switzerland from the mid-1960s onwards the campaign against the so-called 'forestation' of the country – initially culminating in 1969 with the Schwarzenbach proposal – or, in other words, the progressive reduction of the country's foreign population, took place. That proposal, however, was struck down by a 1970 referendum in which a 55.5 per cent majority voted 'no' (Niederberger, 2004; Ricciardi, 2013).

Up until 1967 the majority of Italians who arrived in Canada in the post-war period had entered the country through the channel of 'sponsorship' which, having been introduced in 1948, was, however, abolished in 1967. The mechanism forecast that one Italian could legally enter Canada if a relative was already a resident and open to guaranteeing and covering the costs of the initial period of settlement. Among the foreign communities present in Canada, Italians were the major beneficiaries of this provision, which up until 1967 allowed many of a low professional level to immigrate. The mechanism of sponsorship had in fact not envisaged any type of professional standard and the new arrivals, in terms of their work-related assimilation, had the possibility of becoming clerks in sectors connected to ethnic businesses or in other fields where specific competences were not required. As we have stated, the practice of sponsoring ended in 1967: for entry by new immigrants the Canadian authorities – instead of sponsorship – established criteria based on professional qualifications (Akbari, 1999). Thus the final phase of emigration to Canada – which ended in the middle of the 1970s – was characterized by the arrival of specialised workers who were already assimilated into the Italian labour market or into that of other countries accepting emigration (such as the United States). In the United States, the abolition in 1965 of national entry quotas for the years following had a bearing on the increase of Italian emigration to the country, which remained in any case at a fairly low level (Maffioletti, 2004).

Over the course of the 1960s, the actions of the Italian government were centred mainly on social and moral assistance to emigrants, amending and supplementing what was ratified in the bilateral agreements signed since the end of the war. For example, Law 1115 of 27 July 1962 gave Italian workers affected by silicosis in Belgium a series of indemnities and Law 302 of 10 March 1968 guaranteed medical assistance to Italian workers in Switzerland, including their families, and to cross-border workers (Zanetti Polzi, 2007).

The 1960s represent a decade of profound transformations in the evolution of Italian communities abroad. In this respect, the pathways of the associations to which Italian emigrants belonged represent a meaningful lens. In fact, new social and cultural organisations aligned themselves with traditional mutual aid groups. Sponsorship, trade unions, Catholic and lay groups, and political parties without a doubt still represented important points of reference, but together with them grew the importance of associations organised along regional or provincial lines which founded their membership on geographical origin. As we shall explain in the next section, this tendency was notably reinforced in the 1970s, as a consequence of the devolution of power to the *Regioni*. Commercial ties, import-export channels, and initiatives connected to tourism multiplied between the zones of departure and the zones of arrival: it was the emergence of the transformation of the emigrant communities into *business communities* (Guidotti, 2002; Devoto, 2007).

From the turn of the twentieth century onwards, associations filled in for the state. As we have already mentioned, Italian governments did their best to promote 'emigration', but when Italians had started living abroad as 'immigrants', they were often ignored by Italian government institutions.

From working class to elite emigration? 1974–2010s

Just like the Great Depression following the stock market crash of 1929, the 1973 oil crisis had a great impact on international migrations, with a restructuring of the global division of labour and states' regulations on the mobility of migrant workers. The age of assisted migration and bilateral agreements on the expatriation of Italian workers was over. As we have already mentioned, this was a turning point for Italy, whose net migration rate has been quite constantly positive from 1974 to the present day. Initially, this inverted trend was also due to the high proportion of Italian returnees, but from the 1980s inflows of foreign workers became its main cause (Pugliese, 1996). Between 1974 and 2011, emigration of Italian citizens from the country waned, with an arithmetic mean of 58,700 people per year for the whole period and 41,680 for the years 2000–11.[5] Not even quite high unemployment rates, constantly at between 9.1 and 12 per cent from 1982 to 2001,[6] contributed to emigration resuming in numbers comparable with the immediate and more distant past.

Yet, it is exactly during these decades that emigration gained great visibility in the national narrative and momentum in the public discourse. The strategic salience of Italian emigrants for the country was already noted at the turn of the twentieth century. In 1900, Luigi Einaudi, future president of the Italian republic (1948–55), published the short essay *Un principe mercante: studio sulla espansione coloniale italiana*, celebrating the entrepreneurial skills of Enrico Dell'Acqua and the Italian expatriates in South America. Two Congresses of Italians Abroad were held in Rome in 1908 and 1911 on the initiative of Italian institutions. But substantial steps towards the pursuit of business strategies and the formal inclusion of extraterritorial citizens in the political life of the nation were taken just when mass emigrations ended.

As we mentioned in the previous section, in 1970, with the devolution of power to the *Regioni*, the regional administrations took over most of the social and economic responsibility for emigrants. Basically all twenty Italian regions established an Emigration Department and developed specific programmes dedicated to these communities abroad, ranging from social subsidies to vocational training and co-development projects. Regions have since increasingly invested human resources, together with Italian and European taxpayers' money, to create permanent business opportunities and networks, import-export channels, return programmes for prospective investors and potential employees for local companies, often relying on the collaboration of regionally based private associations.

These efforts have often been intended to replace immigrants who arrive in Italy from all over the world with 'co-ethnic' ones, i.e. the descendants of former expatriates. Programmes providing financial incentives for the 'return' of ethnic descendants have been run at least since the early 1990s by both conservative and progressive local administrations. The Veneto region's 'Project Return' has invested several million euros since 2001 to help Argentine and Brazilian descendants of Italian emigrants to work for local industries. The programme has not been able so far to achieve any of the planned targets. Both the Liguria and Piedmont regions have traditionally allocated funds to support the return, especially from Argentina, of descendants of emigrants. Trentino Alto-Adige and Friuli Venezia Giulia have implemented a combination of co-development and return programmes in Latin America (Tintori, 2009: 50–60). As recently as 30 December 2010, Umbria approved a measure (Law 238), based on the Regional Law 37 of 1997 and funded by the European Social Fund, that grants tax incentives to 'return employees/workers' who are hired or start business activities in Italy. The programme is tellingly called 'Brain Back Umbria'.[7]

The Italian state has, on the one hand, bureaucratically conflated expatriates and emigrant stock, the latter being mainly 'ethnic' descendants, while on the other, it has created a narrative where those loosely termed 'Italians abroad' are transformed into an asset. Both the Ministry of Foreign affairs and the Ministry of Labour have recently developed several action plans, often coordinated with local administrations, to support the creation of new transnational businesses. *Italia internazionale – Sei Regioni per cinque Continenti*, active since 2000, the *Osservatorio sul lavoro e la formazione degli italiani all'estero* (formerly known as ITENETs), the agency *Italia Lavoro SpA* and its project *Occupazione e sviluppo della comunità degli italiani all'estero* (ITES) are all endeavours to turn the Italian diaspora into an integrated global labour and trade market (Tintori, 2013: 140–1).

This perspective provides a possible explanation of why Italy has consistently favoured a self-perception as a country of emigration, despite official figures showing the opposite. It also accounts for the rationales behind the Italian state's intense activities of symbolic and political incorporation of the Italian diaspora during these decades: three more Congresses of Italians Abroad were organized in 1975, 1988 and 2000 (CNE, 1975; CNE, 1990–1) and a Congress of Parliamentarians of Italian Origin in 2000; the *Museo nazionale dell'emigrazione italiana* (National Museum of Italian Emigration) was inaugurated in Rome in 2009; non-parliamentary forms of institutional representation of the Italians abroad, such as the *Comitato consultivo degli italiani all'estero* (Ccie) in 1967, the Committees of Italians Abroad (Comites) in 1985 and the General Council of Italians Abroad (CGIE) in 1989, paved the way for the Acts of 2000 and 2001 which granted voting rights and special representation to citizens abroad (Colucci, 2002; Tintori, 2012b). All of this contributed to the notion that the Italian diaspora is mainly formed by individuals with high human and social capital, or 'brains', instead of 'workers'. This was perfectly epitomized by the initiative of Mario Monti's government in 2012, when the Ministries of the Interior and Education cooperated in setting up an online 'platform', called *Innovitalia*, whose goal is to 'maximise the impact of human capital' of Italian 'brains' abroad and 'promote research and business opportunities' in partnership with the motherland.[8]

To what extent, though, is this true? If we look at the composition of the emigrant population in the whole period, despite all the government rhetoric, those who were unemployed at the moment of leaving between 1974 and 1990 ranged from a minimum of 23.6 per cent to a maximum of 45.8 per cent of the total.[9] In addition, if we focus on the years 2000–13, when both Italian institutions and media reports have particularly stressed the presence of graduates among the new emigrants, the data show that the percentage of those with not even secondary school qualifications (diploma) is constantly over 60 per cent. The percentage of graduates in the emigrant population above 25 years of age has increased from 11.9 per cent in 2002 to 27.6 in 2012.[10] Thus, even though there is a clear growing trend of graduates leaving the country, the sheer numbers tell that 'brains' are still by far a minority in the emigrant population. In addition, the increase in graduates among the emigrants mirrors a similar trend in the population at home.[11] Even in comparative terms, then, Italy does not export more graduates than, say, Germany, France or the UK. The problem is instead twofold: Italy is not able to participate in 'brain circulations' or 'exchanges', in that the country does not attract a number of educated foreigners equal to that of educated Italians leaving. The main cause is that the recruitment system for high-ranking jobs is scarcely transparent and meritocratic (Becker *et al.*, 2004; Beltrame, 2007; *Economist*, 2011). Lastly, Italian graduates choose the United Kingdom as their first destination, where they find employment mainly in the financial sectors and academia. The UK comes only third, though, after Germany and Switzerland when we consider the whole emigrant population. Without downplaying the importance of the academic and financial sectors in the latter countries, the main demand from Germany and Switzerland's labour markets is for workers for their manufacturing and industrial sectors. Once again, it seems that the Italian ruling classes are disregarding the actual composition of the emigrant population.

Conclusion

In this review of emigration and the Italian state, we have tried to offer a synthetic representation of the main continuities and changes, features and rationales of Italy's emigration policies and emigrant population. Determinants and patterns of Italian emigration are tremendously complex and should be addressed at deeply disaggregated levels. Yet we can extend to the whole period what Faini and Venturini (2005) showed in their analysis of the determinants of Italian emigration between 1876 and 1913. Interactions among demographic transitions, income differentials, labour market conditions, better transportation links, perpetuation of migration chains, and transformations in the production system and in society, all played a role according to specific cases and different points in time and contributed to generate outflows from the country. But labour demand in destination countries and the effect of income growth in Italy, which spreads better levels of education and living conditions, and therefore higher expectations about employment and social status especially among young adults, have been more critical in prompting people to migrate.

To that we should add the responsibility of the state or rather its political leadership. There is in fact a recurrent pattern in the Italian governing classes' attitude towards emigration over time: concentrating the main resources and efforts on the strategic assets that the presence of Italian citizens abroad might secure, while reducing to a minimum any commitments in the social and moral sphere as well as addressing the economic and structural causes behind this continuing history of emigration. As pointed out by Fenoaltea (2011: Ch. 4) in his reinterpretation of Italy's economic history from the Unification to the Great War, the economic strategies of the Liberal state, based on protectionism and centred on productive sectors that were not labour-intensive, caused the Italian diaspora and stunted development.

Emigration is a fundamental feature of contemporary Italy that observers ought take into account to better understand the social, economic and political developments of the country.

Notes

1 Michele Colucci wrote the section 'The resumption of mass emigration 1945–73'; Guido Tintori wrote all the other sections.

2 An important exception is Cometti (1958).

3 ISTAT, *Espatriati e rimpatriati per destinazione e provenienza europea o extraeuropea – Anni 1869–2005.* Available online at http://seriestoriche.istat.it/index.php?id=7&user_100ind_pi1[id_pagina]=45&cHash=a4fa14cbf3bdc927952e25cacbf64e5b (accessed 25 March 2013).

4 ISTAT, *Espatriati e rimpatriati per destinazione e provenienza europea o extraeuropea – Anni 1869–2005.* Available online at http://seriestoriche.istat.it/index.php?id=7&user_100ind_pi1[id_pagina]=45&cHash=a4fa14cbf3bdc927952e25cacbf64e5b (accessed 25 March 2013).

5 ISTAT, *Espatriati e rimpatriati per destinazione e provenienza europea o extraeuropea – Anni 1869–2005.* Available online at http://seriestoriche.istat.it/index.php?id=7&user_100ind_pi1[id_pagina]=45&cHash=a4fa14cbf3bdc927952e25cacbf64e5b (accessed 25 March 2013); ISTAT *Indagine sugli italiani residenti all'estero – 13 June 2012 – Allegato statistico.* Available online at www.istat.it/it/archivio/64737 (accessed 25 March 2013).

6 ISTAT, *Serie storiche, Tassi di occupazione, di disoccupazione e di attività per classe di età e ripartizione geografica – Anni 1977–2011.* Available online at http://seriestoriche.istat.it/index.php?id=7&user_100ind_pi1[id_pagina]=76&cHash=c255f48159e3c338760577586eaab610 (accessed 25 March 2013).

7 Available online at www.brainbackumbria.eu/index.php (accessed 25 March 2013).

8 Available online at www.innovitalia.net/crowdforce/product/index.html (accessed 25 March 2013).

9 ISTAT, *Espatriati per sesso e condizione professionale – Anni 1876–1990.* Available online at http://seriestoriche.istat.it/index.php?id=7&user_100ind_pi1[id_pagina]=45&cHash=a4fa14cbf3bdc927952e25cacbf64e5b (accessed 25 March 2013).

10 ISTAT, *Indagine sugli italiani residenti all'estero – 13 June 2012 – Allegato statistico.* Available online at www.istat.it/it/archivio/64737 (accessed 25 March 2013), where the data on the levels of education also include minors. The percentages in the text are taken from ISTAT, *Migrazioni internazionali e interne della popolazione residente*, 28 December 2012, and ISTAT, *Migrazioni internazionali e interne della popolazione residente*, 27 January 2014. The share of those with no degree ranges from a maximum of 56.4 per cent in 2004 to a minimum of 37.9 per cent in 2011

11 ISTAT, *Popolazione residente in età da 6 anni in poi per grado di istruzione, regione e ripartizione geografica ai censimenti – Censimenti 1951–2001 (valori assoluti in migliaia e composizione percentuale).* Available online at http://seriestoriche.istat.it/index.php?id=7&user_100ind_pi1[id_pagina]=9&cHash=b327bf3eae2185defcfbc1066e1756be (accessed 25 March 2013).

References

Akbari, A. H. (1999). Immigrant 'quality' in Canada: more direct evidence of human capital content, 1956–94. *International Migration Review*, 33 (1): 156–75.

Bade, K. (2003). *Migration in European History*. Oxford: Blackwell.

Baines, D. (1995 [1991]). *Emigration from Europe 1815–1930.* Cambridge: Cambridge University Press.

Becker, S. O., Ichino A. and Peri G. (2004). How large is the 'brain drain' from Italy?, *Giornale degli Economisti e Annali di Economia*, 63: 1–32.

Beltrame, L. (2007). Realtà e retorica del *brain drain* in Italia. Stime statistiche, definizioni pubbliche e interventi politici. Trento, Università di Trento, Dipartimento di sociologia e ricerca sociale: *Quaderno* 35.

Bonifazi, C. (2013). *L'Italia delle migrazioni*. Bologna: Il Mulino.

Bonifazi, C. and Heins, F. (2009). Ancora migranti. La nuova mobilità degli italiani. In P. Corti and M. Sanfilippo (eds). *Storia d'Italia. Annali 24. Migrazioni*. Turin: Einaudi: 505–28.

Cannistraro, P. V. and Rosoli, G. (1979). Fascist emigration policy in the 1920s. An interpretative framework. *International Migration Review*, 13 (4): 673–92.

Cerase, F. P. (2001). L'onda di ritorno: i rimpatri. In P. Bevilacqua, A. De Clementi and E. Franzina (eds). *Storia dell'emigrazione italiana: vol. 1*. Rome: Donzelli: 113–25.

Choate, M. I. (2008). *Emigrant Nation. The Making of Italy Abroad*. Cambridge, MA: Harvard University Press.
CNE (Conferenza nazionale dell'emigrazione) (1975). *L' emigrazione italiana nelle prospettive degli anni Ottanta: Atti della Conferenza nazionale dell'emigrazione, Roma, 24 febbraio–1 marzo 1975*, 5 vols. Rome: Rinascimento.
CNE (Conferenza nazionale dell'emigrazione) (1990–1). *Atti della seconda Conferenza nazionale dell'emigrazione, Roma 1988*, 3 vols. Milan: Franco Angeli.
Collinson, S. (1993). *Europe and International Migration*. London: Royal Institute of International Affairs.
Collyer, M. (2013). *Emigration Nations. Policies and Ideologies of Emigrant Engagement*. Basingstoke: Palgrave Macmillan.
Colucci, M. (2002). Il voto degli italiani all'estero. In P. Bevilacqua, A. De Clementi and E. Franzina (eds). *Storia dell'emigrazione italiana: vol. 2*. Rome: Donzelli: 597–609.
Colucci, M. (2008). *Lavoro in movimento*. Rome: Donzelli.
Cometti, E. (1958). Trends in Italian emigration. *The Western Political Quarterly*, 11 (4): 820–34.
De Clementi, A. (2010). *Il prezzo della ricostruzione. L'emigrazione italiana nel secondo dopoguerra*. Rome-Bari: Laterza.
Devoto, F. J. (2007). *Storia degli italiani in Argentina*. Rome: Donzelli.
Direzione generale emigrazione, Ministero affari esteri (1949). *Emigrazione italiana (situazione – prospettive – problemi), 31 marzo 1949*. Rome: Tipografia riservata del Ministero degli Affari Esteri.
Dufoix, S., Guerassimoff, C. and De Tinguy, A. (eds) (2010). *Loin des yeux, près du Cœur. Les États et leurs expatriés*. Paris: Presses de Sciences-Po.
Economist (2011). No Italian jobs. Why Italian graduates cannot wait to emigrate. *The Economist*, 6 January. Available online at www.economist.com/node/17862256?story_id=17862256 (accessed 14 January 2015).
Faini, R. and Venturini, A. (2005 [1994]). Italian emigration in the pre-war period. In T. J. Hatton and J. G. Williamson (eds). *Migration and the International Labor Market, 1850–1939*. London and New York: Routledge: 69–87.
Fenoaltea, S. (2011). *The Reinterpretation of Italian Economic History from Unification to the Great War*. Cambridge: Cambridge University Press.
Foerster, R. F. (1919). *The Italian Emigration of Our Times*. Cambridge, MA: Harvard University Press.
Fofi, G. (1964). *L'immigrazione meridionale a Torino*. Milan: Feltrinelli.
Gould, J. D. (1980). European inter-continental emigration, 1815–1914. The road home: return migration from the USA. *Journal of European Economic History*, 9: 41–112.
Guidotti, M. (2002). La risorsa emigrazione. *Studi Emigrazione*, 146: 489–502.
Hanagan, M. (1977). Artisan and skilled worker: the problem of definition. *International Labor and Working-Class History*, 12: 28–31.
Hatton, T. J. and Williamson, J. G. (1998). *The Age of Mass Migrations. Causes and Economic Impact*. Oxford: Oxford University Press.
Incisa di Camerana, L. (2003). *Il grande esodo. Storia delle migrazioni italiane nel mondo*. Milan: Corbaccio.
ISTAT (2014). *Migrazioni internazionali e interne della popolazione residente, Annual report 2012*, 27 January. Available online at www.istat.it/it/archivio/110521 (accessed 14 January 2015).
Maffioletti, G. (2004). Gli Italiani negli USA. *Studi Emigrazione*, 154: 449–75.
Ministero per la Costituente (1946). *Atti della Commissione per lo studio dei problemi del lavoro*. Roma: Uesisa.
Niederberger, J. M. (2004). La politica di integrazione della Svizzera dopo la seconda guerra mondiale. In E. Halter (ed.). *Gli italiani in Svizzera. Un secolo di emigrazione*. Bellinzona: Casagrande: 93–107.
Ostuni, M. R. (2001). Leggi e politiche di governo nell'Italia liberale e fascista. In in P. Bevilacqua, A. De Clementi and E. Franzina (eds). *Storia dell'emigrazione italiana: vol. 1*. Rome: Donzelli: 309–19.
Prencipe, L. and Nicosia, A. (2010). *Museo nazionale dell'emigrazione italiana*. Rome: Gangemi.
Pugliese, E. (1996). Italy between emigration and immigration and the problems of citizenship. In D. Cesarani and M. Fulbrook (eds). *Citizenship, Nationality and Migration in Europe*. New York: Routledge: 106–24.
Pugliese, E. and Rebeggiani, E. (2003). *Occupazione e disoccupazione in Italia dal dopoguerra ai nostri giorni*. Rome: Edizioni Lavoro.
Ricciardi, T. (2013). *Associazionismo ed emigrazione. Storia delle Colonie Libere e degli Italiani in Svizzera*. Rome-Bari: Laterza.
Rinauro, S. (2009). *Il cammino della speranza. L'emigrazione clandestina degli italiani nel secondo dopoguerra*. Turin: Einaudi.

Sori, E. (1979). *L'emigrazione italiana dall'unità alla seconda guerra mondiale.* Bologna: Il Mulino.

Tintori, G. (2006). Cittadinanza e politiche di emigrazione nell'Italia liberale e fascista. Un approfondimento storico. In G. Zincone (ed.). *Familismo legale. Come (non) diventare cittadini italiani.* Rome-Bari: Laterza: 52–106.

Tintori, G. (2009). *Fardelli d'Italia? Conseguenze nazionali e transnazionali delle politiche di cittadinanza italiane.* Rome: Carocci.

Tintori, G. (2012a). More than one million individuals got Italian citizenship abroad in twelve years (1998–2010). *EUDO Citizenship News*, 21 November. Available online at http://eudo-citizenship.eu/news/citizenship-news/748-more-than-one-million-individuals-got-italian-citizenship-abroad-in-the-twelve-years-1998–2010%3E (accessed 14 January 2015).

Tintori, G. (ed.) (2012b). *Il voto degli altri. Rappresentanza e scelte elettorali degli italiani all'estero.* Turin: Rosenberg and Sellier.

Tintori, G. (2013). Italy: the continuing history of emigrant relations. In M. Collyer (ed.). *Emigration Nations. Policies and Ideologies of Emigrant Engagement.* Basingstoke: Palgrave Macmillan: 126–52.

Tintori, G. (forthcoming). *Nuove mobilità.* State Discourses and Policies in Italian Emigration, 2000s–2010s. Paper presented at the International Conference 'ÉMIGRÉ', University of Cork, 27–28 September 2013.

Zanetti Polzi, P. (2007). *Lavoro straniero. Cgil e questione migratoria dal 1945 a oggi.* Sesto San Giovanni: Archivio del lavoro.

4

RACISM, IMMIGRATION AND NEW IDENTITIES IN ITALY

Carl Levy

Introduction

It has often been said that the Italians have never had a racist tradition. But the myth of the 'brava gente' (Bidussa, 1994; Ben-Ghiat, 2004; Focardi and Klinkhammer, 2004; Favero, 2010; Meret et al., 2013), the good Italians who ignored or sabotaged the anti-Semitic policies of the Fascist regime after 1938 or lived in open contradiction to an Italian form of apartheid in the African colonies, has been undermined by the research of historians over the past thirty years (see Pergher in this volume). More recently the display of openly xenophobic and racist politics in Italy since the 1980s has also undermined another assumption. Since the late 1970s Italy has been transformed from a nation which exported emigrants to the four corners of the globe to an immigrant-receiving nation (on the overall theme of emigration, see Tintori and Colucci in this volume). In the course of this process Italy has become a multicultural country in which over one million Muslims are now residents and/or citizens. The foreign resident population of Italy increased fivefold from 1992 to 2008, and naturalised and second-generation 'New Italians' and the 'host community' have forged hybrid cultures which have undermined the prevalent ethnic basis of Italian citizenship; indeed the extension of voting rights to overseas Italians and the liberalisation of citizenship laws for the descendants of Italian migrants in the global diaspora confused the issue even further (Pastore, 2004; Battison and Mascitelli, 2008; Bigot and Fella, 2008; Tintori, 2009; Finotelli, 2009; Finotelli and Sciortino, 2009; Clough Marinaro and Walston, 2010: 13; Thomassen, 2010; Gilmour, 2011: 21).

In 2012, the proportion of the population of foreign origin was close to 10 per cent, the immigrant population of Lombardy was one million out of a total of nine million, while 24 per cent of this dynamic region's schoolchildren did not possess Italian citizenship (Gilardoni, 2011: 450–1). There were over 600,000 Romanians living in Italy; Prato had a large and dynamic population of Chinese traders, small industrialists and shopkeepers; and Rome's Esquilino and Monti districts hosted a growing South Asian population (Mudu, 2006; Cingolani, 2009; Johanson et al., 2009; Chang, 2010). Nevertheless, the default position of many Italians was to self-identify Italy as white and Catholic (Clough Marinaro and Walston, 2010: 14–16; Bianchi, 2011: 331; Saitta and Cole, 2011).

In the 1980s and 1990s the half-forgotten Empire struck back. Italian armed forces were once again involved in Somalia and Albania, no longer as imperialist conquerors but as peace keepers and peace enforcers under the flag of the United Nations. However, several incidents involving violence and sexual abuse tarnished this new remit. The ramifications of the Ethiopian/Eritrean Wars spilt over into the peninsula (Del Boca, 1994a; Del Boca, 1994b; Triulzi, 2002). Waves of Albanian refugees in the early and late 1990s caused major political crises in Italy (King and Mai, 2008). The break-up of Yugoslavia briefly reopened the question of Istria, when the National Alliance in the first Berlusconi government (1994) lobbied for the rights of Istrians in Slovenia, reawakening anti-Slavic sentiments (Ballinger, 2003: 104–5). The unprecedented rise of the populist and regionalist Northern League saw the stoking of long-term prejudice against the South. The saloon bar commonplaces of its charismatic leader, Umberto Bossi, were disseminated on television, radio, newspapers and the Internet, and by the 2000s, the outrageous behaviour of representatives of the Northern League (see Anna Cento Bull's chapter in this volume) and others on the Far Right, indeed in a broader spectrum of the political world, was commonplace: a government minister demanded that cannon fire be directed on boatloads of refugees (Geddes, 2008), another suggested that the grounds of a mosque be polluted with the corpses of pigs (Moore, 2008), and a local politician proposed having 'Milanese' only underground carriages on that city's lines (Duff, 2009), while the inevitable linkage of violent crime with *extracomunitari* by the broader media saw a disconnect with the 'Italian' violence of the lethal Camorra and the 'Ndrangheta (except perhaps by those *leghisti* who had forgotten that their script had been altered: the target had moved from the Southern Italian to the global Southern or Eastern 'Others') (Sciortino and Colombo, 2004; Hanretty and Hermanin, 2010); and there were the provocative 'White Christmases' of certain Northern mayors (Hooper, 2009). Italy's first black government minister, Cécile Kyenge, named minister for integration in April 2013, had bananas thrown at her, and she sustained a barrage of racist insults including one from the Lega Nord senator, Roberto Calderoli, who compared her to an orang-utan. (Kington, 2013a; BBC, 2013). Behaviour which would have led to prosecution for provoking racial and religious hatred in some of Italy's neighbours was ignored or sloughed off as 'folkloric' and practitioners of this dirty art on the streets of Italy's towns and cities were careful to remain peaceful; the stress was on innocuous-looking middle-aged citizens of the 'Green Patrols' rather than muscular, shaven-headed, sullen young men (Squires, 2009; Avanza, 2010).

With the end of the so-called First Republic in the early 1990s, debates on the fate of the Italian nation and 'Italian character' stimulated by revisionist historians argued that the nation state and patriotism had for too long been suppressed or ignored by a joint 'conspiracy' of the Cold War Christian Democratic regime and the politically correct, 'anti-Italian' Italian Left (Rusconi, 1993; Gentile, 1997; Galli della Loggia, 1999). When did the Italian nation start to die and how could one revive it? The antidote for the revisionists was the celebration of Italian achievements, and with careful, but increasingly rather haphazard surgery, Fascism was reappraised and contrasted with the supposedly postnational Cold War 'consociational regime' (Levy, 1999; Mammone, 2006; Ventresca, 2006; Cento Bull, 2008). Wishful thinking or exercises in serial anachronism characterized these instant history books (Patriarca, 2001; Patriarca, 2010). But the reinvention of the Italian past (Cossu, 2010) was allied to the demand for the reinstatement of the ethno-linguistic basis of Italy and/or the North, just when legislation was being passed to allow the teaching of other languages in schools and just when immigrants, refugees and asylum seekers were turning the great Italian cities into cosmopolitan urban centres (Lepschy et al., 1996; King, 1999; Moss, 2000; Colombo and Sciortino, 2004; Clough Marinaro and Thomassen, 2014).

Rising tensions for nearly two decades culminated during the general election in 2008, which, was fought when anti-immigrant sentiment was at a fever pitch, indeed a fever induced by the media and the knee-jerk reaction of politicians on the Left and Right to a series of violent and murderous incidents involving Roma Romanians (Sigona, 2010). In what then seemed the last hurrah of the Northern League, working-class voters in northern suburbs and small towns rallied to Umberto Bossi's party. The headlines shouted that Italy was ageing, Italy was falling down the economic pecking order (indeed it was predicted that Romania would surpass Italy in a decade or so), while a series of public opinion surveys showed that Italians felt like aliens in their 'own' piazzas. Fear of crime was mixed uneasily and incoherently with fear of newcomers from Albania, Romania, North Africa or China, while the image of Italians being swamped by more fecund newcomers flooded the media. By the late 2000s unconscious reflex racism was widespread. The commonplace term *extracomunitari* was employed as a blanket term not for all non-EU citizens resident in Italy but those from the Global South and East, echoing and reinforcing earlier terms of exclusion such as *marocchino*, *zingaro*, *meridonale*, and, for the far right, *ebreo*. This hysteria culminated in a pogrom of Roma in the outskirts of Naples (such events had happened earlier too), which caused the UNHCR to draw comparisons with ethnic cleansing in the Balkans. In 2008, the newly installed Berlusconi government announced a fingerprint census of Roma during the seventieth anniversary of the census of the Jews by Mussolini's regime in 1938. The incoming government may have confronted a budget deficit but it seemed also to suffer from an irony deficit (Clough Marinaro and Daniele, 2011; Clough Marinaro and Sigona, 2011; Sigona, 2011).

Academia was not slow to detect new fields of study. In 1999 the Centre for the Study of the History and Theory of Italian Racism was established at the University of Bologna. Italians embraced postcolonial studies from the middle of the 1990s onwards (Burgio, 2000: 9). Thus studies of Antonio Gramsci, moribund since the decline of Eurocommunism in the early 1980s, were revived. This comatose 'Gramsci' was revived through the interaction of his thought with Michel Foucault, Edward Said, Stuart Hall and the British School of Cultural Studies and perhaps most importantly, the Indian School of Subaltern Studies. In turn engagement with this 'postcolonial Gramsci' stimulated discussions of cultural hybridity and liminality, postnational citizenship and cosmopolitanism (Lombardi-Diop and Romeo, 2012; Srivastava and Bhattacharya, 2012). But the concerns of the postcolonialists were not alien to the growing debates over the place of first-, second- and even third-generation immigrants in Italy, 'New or hyphenated' Italians, modes of Italian citizenship (*jus sanguinis*, *jus soli*, multiculturalism), and dimensions of religious tolerance (and the ambiguous position of the Catholic Church). However the alarms, concerns, prejudices and neuroses of the Italians were not that different from their neighbours' reactions. The context, the timing and the historical legacies of the peninsula merely produced a variation on a troubling European theme (Janoski, 2010). Thus on many different levels, questions of race and racism had become major concerns for Italians and the residents of Italy in the late twentieth and early twenty-first centuries.

Racisms in Italy from the 1990s to 2013

In other work I have traced the byways of Italian racism from 1861 though the post-war 'First Republic': 'Orientalism' and the *Mezzogiorno* (see also Schneider, 1998), colonialism and the colonial subject, the North-East, Trieste and the Slavic 'Other', anti-Semitism and the Shoah, the more complex, dominant/submissive relationship with the Habsburg Austrians, French and Germans, and Italian-Americans as not quite 'white' in the USA's racialized culture. I have argued that anti-Southern stereotyping in the late nineteenth century foreshadowed the skin-colour and anti-Semitic biological racism of the Fascist regime of the 1930s. In a similar fashion the anti-Southern rhetoric of the Northern League in the 1980s and 1990s slides easily into xenophobic reactions to asylum seekers, refugees, Roma, and immigrants from the Global South and East (Levy, forthcoming).

Racial discourse became widespread via the media presence of the Lega Nord. The Lega Nord set the pace of Italian politics in the nineties and first decade of the twenty-first century. At every crucial step in the transition of Italian politics over twenty years, the League was the catalyst or active agent, as Anna Cento Bull demonstrates in her chapter in this volume.

Thus, by the early 2000s Bossi was the kingmaker and regicide of Italian national politics and his anti-Southern and xenophobic pronouncements became commonplace, acceptable parts of the discourse of politics and social life in Italy (just as concurrently the sexist language and images of Berlusconi and his media outlets became the common sense of quotidian life of Italy).

By the 2000s, the Lega Nord had been transformed from a free-market, regionalist European and anti-Southern party into a xenophobic, Islamophobic, antiglobalist, protectionist political formation (see Cento Bull in this volume). It peddled a *Volksgemeinschaft* welfare state for 'Padanian' workers. This populist racist proletarian turn alienated a part of the League's original free-market constituency, especially in the Veneto, where many businesses had met the challenges of globalisation by massive outsourcing in Eastern Europe, particularly in Romania, and whose trade association complained about the League's 'excess ideology', which seemed to threaten their business plans (Messina, 2001). But despite these contretemps, the League helped shape or at least limit the flexibility of the immigration and citizenship policies of the Berlusconi governments (although Bossi and his son received their comeuppance by going 'native' in the most spectacular fashion when they were brought down in a scandal involving the Calabrian Mafia).

As Cento Bull explains in her chapter, the Northern League was and is a regionalist variation on the neo-populist conservative or Far Right party, common throughout Europe since the 1980s.

However, the League's variety of racist neo-populism must be placed within the shifting parameters of both historical context and the effects of human agency (Bossi and Matteo Salvini). Like other neo-populist conservative or Far Right parties, outright classical racist discourse and open anti-Semitism have been banished from public consumption. Adapted from the strategy of the French New Right of the 1980s, racism was transformed into cultural difference (Bar-On, 2007; Bar-On, 2013). Thus the right of cultural difference (a strange but clever inversion of postmodern anti-racist discourse) and the proclamation of ethnic exclusivity for Italians (for the Far Right) and 'Padanians' (for the Lega Nord) were joined with the right of cultural exclusivity for the migrants in their original homes. Foreign aid should be targeted at immigrant-producing countries on the proviso that they keep their own people home. Some of these policies were not too dissimilar to those of the mainstream European Centre-Left and Centre-Right, and indeed some had been pioneered by the Centre-Right in Germany, for example, and thus they could then be used as camouflage or as an electoral bridge by neo-populists throughout Europe for their more radical plans (Bale, 2003).

However, the Italian case has had its unique characteristics. The Lega Nord started as an anti-fascist but racist party because it originally opposed the MSI/Alleanza Nazionale as a manifestation of Southernism: against all historical evidence Fascism was considered a Southern product, the North was the home of the Resistance; so went the rhetoric of the 1980s and early 1990s. But in due course the Lega Nord ended up as a devolutionist and racist party, more racist than (at least) the leadership and particularly Gianfranco Fini of the (traditionally Fascist) Alleanza Nazionale, as Fini and elements of his party journeyed to the Centre with policies on citizenship and voting rights that were on the left of Berlusconi's coalition governments, and caused a variety of Extreme Right breakaways, although the Roma 'crisis' of 2008 revived older and more menacing tones in Fini. Eventually Fini was outmanoeuvred by Berlusconi (he came to see him as a political rival for the leadership of the Centre-Right) and some of the previously more racist and fascist formations ended up in Berlusconi's electoral vehicle *Il Popolo della Libertà* (Mammone, forthcoming). The end result was that it was not always clear where on the Right one found the most racist remarks: a cacophony of insults was not always easily mapped onto the same political formations. As for Berlusconi himself, just like Umberto Bossi, the billionaire employed the same sort of banter but in a more jokey, homespun style than *Il Lumbard*; thus the notorious remark about the then recently elected President Obama's sun tan (which one year later was followed by vulgar, sexist remarks and gestures on meeting the First Lady, Michelle Obama) (Glendinning, 2008; Leonard, 2009). However, in terms of policy on immigration and citizenship in the 2000s, Berlusconi through much of his time in power in this period let Fini, Roberto Maroni of the Lega Nord and Christian Democrat politicians fight it out: much in the manner of the Veneto industrialists mentioned previously, Berlusconi's globalising and European market instincts made him wary of 'excess ideology'. He was much more comfortable with 'dog-whistle' politics, unpleasant but insubstantial noise, catering to the populist vote, but joined to the acceptance of 'managed migration' for his own and the Italian economy's interests (Calavita, 2005; Zincone, 2006; Geddes, 2008; Menz, 2009: 66–8; 232–49; Cento Bull, 2010).

But intolerance of the 'Other' transcended the Right/Left boundary and the red/white political cultures which were still very robust in the 1980s. Even given the uncontrolled spread of the *periferia* (suburbs and urban sprawl) since the 1950s, a series of sociological and historical studies have demonstrated the parochial nature of Italian political culture: national, North/South divide and regional forms of identities were and probably still are trumped by bedrock city, town, and indeed neighbourhood identities (for some provincial town studies, see Cento Bull, 1996; Daly 1999; Riccio, 1999). This came out very strongly in an extensive survey carried out by a team of American social scientists, published as long ago as 1994, which demonstrated that a parochial culture was not particularly open to outsiders sharing civil space with it (Sniderman et al., 2001). Thus not only did the Southern 'Other' become a template for transferring the fears and anxieties of Italians in the North onto other out groups (as the Lega Nord did when it shifted its mobilisation strategy from the South to the Islamic or Roma 'Other') but the arrival of migrants in small or medium-sized towns, or more to the point their suburbs, mobilised considerable electoral support for the Lega Nord in the 2008 and 2013 elections in the red zones of central Italy, as I have previously mentioned. Left-wing administrations in Rome or Bologna were not noted for their tolerance of or sensitivity towards migrant groups, particularly Roma from the Balkans (Diamanti, 2009: 202–13; Però, 1999; Clough Marinaro, 2003). The veteran centre-left journalist and historian Giorgio Bocca seemed to suffer from false memory syndrome when recalling Southern migration to the industrial northern cities from the 1950s to the 1970s as somehow different from the next wave of migrants in the 1990s. Thus the earlier Southerners were easier to integrate because they were 'people who had language, religion, skin colour and cultural history in common with the Milanese', even though cultural differences and even skin tone were regularly invoked as barriers by commentators when the migrations were actually occurring (Foot, 1999: 162).

Simultaneously, in the South one academic claimed that in Palermo racist sentiments were not present because Sicilians identified with the plight of the newcomers, but the later cases of Rosarno in Calabria and others elsewhere in the Mezzogiorno tell another story, although the recent positive example of Riace is closer to the original findings (Cole, 1997; Booth and Cole, 1999; Donaldio, 2010; Kington, 2013b). The violence against immigrants displayed in a series of incidents in Florence in 1990, when shopkeepers and immigrant street hawkers clashed and neo-Nazis went on the rampage against immigrants, did not happen in Sicily in the 1980s and 1990s because here immigrants did not seem to endanger the livelihoods of shopkeepers. Violence was inflicted on foreign and Italian farmworkers alike by Mafia labour contractors, but this was merely the modus operandi of the Mafia, and in any case agricultural workers and fishermen from North Africa had been a feature of Sicilian life for decades (Ben-Yehoyada, 2011). But here too, it is hard to draw hard-and-fast conclusions. Violence against immigrants flared up in Naples and Bari, for example, throughout the 1990s and the 2000s, and marginality haunted the lives of many (Dines, 2012; Lucht, 2012). Most importantly, the seasonal arrival of boat people on the island of Lampedusa focused the debate on the deepest South of Italy.

Although Italy served as a temporary reception and transport centre for Jewish, East European, and Russian refugees from the end of the Second World War, through the Cold War, until the 1990s Italy did not operate fully under the 1951 Geneva Convention and then several challenges confronted Italy simultaneously. Waves of Albanians, Kurds, Yugoslav and Kosovar Roma and mixed migrations of refugee and economic migrants from the north coast of Africa became a feature of Italian life and from the early 1990s a perennial staple of Italian journalism. Italy wanted to qualify as a Schengen member, to prove to suspicious neighbours to its north that it was not a porous entry point for illegal migrants from the Global South. Thus Italy had to develop an asylum and refugee policy which at once nodded in the direction of the humanitarian and legal requirements of the Geneva Convention but simultaneously abided by the increasingly restrictive policies of the European Union following the disintegration of Yugoslavia and the ensuing wars of succession. If the Centre-Right governments of the 2000s adopted a more restrictive policy towards migrants, with the Bossi-Fini and other 'security packages', in turn magnified by bloodcurdling pronouncements of various politicians, it was not difficult to find similar cases amongst Italy's partners (Cinalli, 2008; Finotelli, 2009; Finotelli and Sciortino, 2009). In what way was the illegal deportation of Romanian Roma from France by the none too tolerant administration of Nicolas Sarkozy any different from the Italian government's 'national emergency' in the summer of 2008 and the illegal pushbacks of boat people by joint task forces of the Italian and Libyan navies and coast guards? (Indeed one of the unintended consequences of Berlusconi's murky deals with the Libyans was a final settling of the legacy of colonial crimes inflicted on Libya by Liberal and Fascist Italy: Labanca, 2010; Paoletti, 2010.) Later, during the Arab Spring, for a brief moment the Italians and French engaged in a disgraceful game of pass the human parcel as Italian demands for stricter European help to control the Mediterranean led to channelling of boat people to the French border, which was then shut in retaliation (Richey, 2012); albeit the brief episode of Mare Nostrum was a remarkable change.

Restrictive policy in Italy, however, was accompanied in the 2000s by the two largest amnesties for illegal immigrants ever seen in Europe, which alarmed and angered her European partners. Thus, simultaneously, Italy was criticised in the European Union for being too liberal and too vocally racist. In fact Italy received more illegal immigrants from Germany through individuals (mainly from former Soviet states) with expired work visas who moved south than from Africa, and certainly more through airports than the alarming and heart-rending landings on Lampedusa, although the latter fed the populist grandstanding policies of maritime pushbacks in the Mediterranean and the shameful collaboration of the Italians in extraterritorial camps in Libya. In Germany the granting of asylum remained much more widespread than in Italy (although significantly restricted from its heyday in the early 1990s) but in practice a similar number of refugees found an ad hoc regime of protection through Italy's porous, if precarious and exploitative, labour markets. How could one measure whether in practice German or Italian approaches were more racist (Levy, 2010: 103–4)? In any case, racist discourse within the Centre-Right was at times contested by the voices of employers and certain Catholic currents whose motives ranged from the bottom line to religious ethics (Garau, 2010). Migrants, illegal or legal, were wanted but not welcome in much of Italy: the blast furnaces of 'Deep North' *leghista* Brescia would fall silent without their labour (Andall, 2007), and the Italian welfare state would have had to spend far more if migrant nannies tending to young children and carers helping the elderly were not present in the bosom of many Italian families (Andall, 2000; Colombo, 2007; van Hooren, 2010; Degiuli, 2011; Sciortino, 2013).

Conclusion: imperial memories, 'New Italians', agency and citizenship

Racism in Italy in the early twenty-first century is crafted by a series of historical legacies. The notion of the good Italian dies hard and prevents a realistic appraisal of where the nation is now. The parochial nature of much of Italian culture has not been exceptionally open to different cultures sharing space with it. Indeed it could be argued that the weakness of the Italian state, the contested legitimacy of the Left and Right in Italian politics even after the end of the Cold War, and the relatively recent emergence of a national culture, which has only partially supplanted regional or more importantly local subcultures, may have made it harder for Italians to deal with the reality of mass migration and the shifting contours of Italian identity and citizenship. Amnesia about the Italian imperial past perhaps initially made it harder to accept non-European cultures in Italian cities. Imperialism has always been a double-edged sword (see Pergher in this volume and also Labanca, 2002: 464–70; Palumbo, 2003; Triulzi, 2003; Andall and Duncan, 2005; Andall and Duncan, 2010; Baratieri, 2010). On the one hand, it fostered racism and cultural superiority but, on the other hand, the myth of a motherland for colonials to some extent forced the French and British, in their own ways, to come to terms with multicultural realities through historically determined path-dependent constitutional arrangements (from Anglican liberal-minded state Church (encased in the multi-ethnic British Isles) to the militant laicism and republicanism of the French) (Levy, 2010: 103–4). In any case, although Albanians and Romanians far exceed the populations of other newcomers, immigrants in Italy hail from nearly two hundred different ethnic and national groups, which are largely fragmented, relatively unorganised and largely without strong champions. Groups are not differentiated into such categories such as Afro-Caribbean or *beur*, although the Islamic marker may become one (for overviews, see Colombo and Sciortino, 2004; Bonifazi, 2007; Einaudi, 2007; Colombo and Sciortino, 2008). In the 1990s the Albanians (with their unique relationship to Italy), it was argued, had become the new Southerners: mirror to the nation, to be civilized, when not feared as criminal barbarians (Mai, 2003). By 2013 both the Albanians and non-Roma Romanians were being integrated into Italian society (King and Mai, 2008). The entry of Romania into the EU eased the way for hundreds of thousands of illegal Romanian migrants, and new commercial and chain migration networks seemed to assist this process (Anghel, 2008). Their scapegoat replacements, the Roma from the Balkans (Clough Marinaro, 2003; Sigona, 2003; Sigona, 2005; Clough Marinaro, 2009; Costi, 2010; Sigona, 2010; Clough Marinaro and Sigona, 2011; Tosi Cambini, 2011), did not even possess those rather dubious mitigating stereotypical features that acceptable migrants are sometimes given to ease their acceptance into the host nation (as for instance Italian-Americans in the USA) (Guglielmo, 2003; Guglielmo and Salerno, 2003), but, as we shall see, the Roma were not without their own agency.

The Catholic Church is still an important presence in Italian life and politics, even if daily religious practice languishes. Indeed the end of the 'First Republic' has witnessed the spread of noticeable political influence in the Centre-Right to the Centre-Left. The Church has become an important veto player with reference to civil unions, stem cell research and other bioethical issues (Bernini, 2010). In terms of migration and citizenship, there are voices in the hierarchy reminiscent of inter-war anti-Semitism, which warned that followers of the Islamic faith may be tolerated as guests in Italy, but they can never be accepted into the intimate fabric of national life, while some of the last Pope's statements and writings did not inspire confidence. Since the 1960s, the Church has undergone a painful reappraisal of its behaviour towards the Jews, and thus other currents within the Church, witnessing the events of the summer of 2008 and their shocking parallels to 1938 took a brave and principled stand. Indeed it could be argued that the defence of the Roma by *Famiglia Cristiana* (a mass-circulation family-oriented magazine) was far more forthright than anything the mainstream Left mounted (Famiglia Cristiana, 2008). And even if there is a disturbing anti-Islamic current in Catholic circles, it is also the case that the overlapping of Catholicism with the essence of Italian ethnicity by more sectarian elements in the hierarchy has given migrants from Catholic backgrounds (some Albanians, Filipinos or Latin Americans, and Poles) an opportunist route to the mainstream. Nevertheless, the Catholic Church's privileged relationship with the State means that the growing numbers of Muslims in Italy, who do not possess the same guarantees, are set for further battles to assert their right to practise their religion publicly (Allievi, 2002; Clough Marinaro and Walston, 2010: 12; Garau, 2010).

The labelling of Roma as nomads, the generic and disconcerting term used for Roma and Sinti in Italy, which brings to mind the ambiguity of already mentioned *extracomunitario*, was first advanced as a progressive recognition by local authorities of their cultural rights, but just as the 'concentration' of the Jews into one legally recognised category after the Lateran Pacts of 1929 was at first applauded in the Jewish community by traditionalists and Zionists as a method of guaranteeing cultural autonomy through separateness, in both cases, the effect was and could be a way to make strict segregation easier to implement when other factors came or come into play. Thus the far-right mayor of Rome Gianni Alemanno during the 2008 'crisis' redefined the Roma issue as a humanitarian problem that could be solved through the identification of 'nomads' (perhaps numbering 7,000 to 15,000), even if this was not intended to be the illegal practice of ethnic profiling. Like the Roma, the Jews of 1938 were a miniscule minority of the population but they too brought forth 'extraordinary methods': the Roma in 2008 and the Jews in 1938 were by their very presence in public society causing 'an emergency'. The Roma were rehoused 'for their own good' so that the authorities 'could look after their welfare', while the Jews were driven from civil society and transformed into non-persons, 'discriminated not persecuted', so Mussolini argued, until their segregation was followed by a more sinister denouement after 1943 (for the Jews in 1938, see Visani, 2009 and for the Roma in 2008, see Lerner, 2008a and Lerner, 2008b).

It is vital to emphasise the differences between the two. Mayor Alemanno was obliged to abide by or at least acknowledge national, European and international, liberal, democratic human rights laws (and the concerned intervention of the Italian President); he was forced to address the Roma directly, and to allow them to 'co-manage' their own segregation on the periphery of Rome, but in so doing he gave them a voice they were never afforded under the previous 'benevolent' policies of the left-wing municipality of Bologna (Clough Marinaro and Daniele, 2011; Picker, 2011; for elsewhere in Italy, see Vitale, 2011; for the use of the law to defend the rights of citizen, resident and refugee Roma and Sinti in Italy, see Loy, 2009; Bonetti *et al.*, 2011 (volumes one and two)). The paradoxes of liberal democracy and global capitalism also lessened the repressive impact of the Bossi-Fini immigration act of 2002 and other 'security packages' passed by later Berlusconi governments in the 2000s. Centre-Left policies in the 1990s shared characteristics with the 'security packages' of the 2000s. Both resulted in a series of massive regularisations of undocumented immigrants and both maintained a basic if threadbare welfare system for undocumented immigrants. Thus the need for domestic, agricultural and industrial labour, the fragility of political coalitions, the contradictory messages of human rights laws, Schengen and the war on terrorism, but also and importantly the agency of 'New Italians', migrants, and the Roma shaped realities on the ground far more significantly than lurid but static accounts in newspapers or indeed the overblown pessimistic dystopias woven by Giorgio Agamben and his prolific followers would lead one to believe (for the agency of Roma women, see Pesarini, 2013 and for political participation of Roma in Italy, see Sigona, 2009; for an example of a vast and predictable literature influenced by Agamben, see Buckel and Wissel, 2010).

The role of agency leads us to the conclusion of this chapter. The definition of second-generation 'New Italians' may have its methodological and legal challenges; nevertheless, in the public square, young people have not waited for academics and policymakers to act, shaping a new Italian reality through such social movements as Rete G2 (Thomassen, 2010; Zinn, 2010; Zinn, 2011). Direct action however is played out through Italian legal realities. The comparison with Germany is instructive. Until fairly recently, the German citizenship law of 1913 emphasised parental descent as the chief basis of citizenship; in Italy a rather similar law of 1912 has shaped the parameters of the current debate. German and Italian diasporas and the privileging of their denizens' roads to citizenship raised the issue of 'New Italians' and 'New Germans', who had far more immediate relationship with present-day Germany or Italy than those of Italian descent in Argentina or German speakers in the former Soviet Union. In Germany, the loosening of restrictions on naturalization only partly discredited the notion of *jus sanguinis* (Pastore, 2004; Tintori, 2009; Clough Marinaro and Walston, 2010). Indeed by the early twenty-first century the general consensus in Europe has settled for a modified form of *jus sanguinis* or at least a discrediting of a multicultural road to citizenship and constitutional patriotism, an unarticulated presumption that the essence of citizenship and belonging was rooted in a culture and history that transcended the mere acquisition of the legal, linguistic and educational competences of civic citizenship, that somehow ancestry made one a more authentic member of the national community, but accompanied by an equally official vigorous and public disclaimer of the rhetoric of biological racism or the notion of a Christian Europe (for the mainstream it was always Judaeo-Christian, a term not generally used before 1945 or even perhaps the 1960s). Modern mass migration was a newer phenomenon than in Germany, Sweden or Britain, so the Italians have not yet caught up in policy and rhetoric with their neighbours: there is no grand bargain as witnessed in Germany, in which asylum laws were tightened (yes in both) and citizenship laws liberalised (not yet in Italy). Nevertheless, the situations are not so different: certain critiques of multiculturalism in Italy have been a convenient rhetorical blind for the advocates of an ethnically based *Italianità* who wish to keep their rather bog-standard ethnic nationalism hidden (Grillo and Pratt, 2002; Bianchi, 2011).

Nevertheless, fieldwork studies have demonstrated how hyphenated or otherwise defined Italians have forged their selves through multiple and shifting identities. The phrase 'suspended between two worlds' (Clough Marinaro and Walston, 2010: 9) is found frequently in this literature, but the New Italians have taken action, drawing on the legacies of their parents but also shaping a hybrid Italian culture from 'translocal' and European influences, even if their use of the geographical imaginary of Europe is rather different from the ethnic exclusivist connotations of the term *extracomunitari* by which many of these Italian-born individuals are still defined by their fellow Italians (Arnone, 2011; Bello, 2011; Colombo et al., 2011; Riccio and Russo, 2011). 'We do not crave acceptance or fear rejection,' declared a self-identified 'Brown Italian'. 'We are already part of your reality' (Berrocal, 2010: 85–6). But it remains to be seen whether or not the rich resources of their multilingual and cosmopolitan competences will be utilised in Italy (Menin, 2011; Pedone, 2011), or whether future generations of 'New Italians' will find themselves trapped in a state of alienated marginality. The Italian nation state is a recent development and the widespread use of the Italian language is relatively new, really only two generations old (Coluzzi, 2009). Thus Italians have the opportunity to use an imaginary which counters the myth of ethnogenesis and transcends the parochial xenophobic provocations of the Lega Nord, as Dario Franceschini, former head of the *Partito Democratico* argued in answer to their rhetoric (see also the potential of Trieste as a model for Italian and European cosmopolitanism in Waley, 2009):

> Our own current identity, which we of course want to defend, is the result of thousands of years of encounters between different cultures and languages. Let us think of the cities of Northern Italy: I say this to the representatives of the Northern League. Let us think of Genoa, the crossroads of sailors and traders, where, over the course of centuries, our language has been enriched by Arabic, Spanish, French and many other influences. Or think of Venice, a crossroads, a miracle built by Italians but also by Byzantine mosaic artists, by Arabic carvers and Turkish decorators. Let us think of our dialects: of the Greek cadence of Barese, of the Arabic tones of Sicilian and Calabrian; of the communities which, after thousands of years still speak ancient Albanian today; of the French influences on Piemontese; of the Spanish influences in Lombardy; of Slavic ones in the North-East. To this unique heritage we must give a future.
>
> *(Berrocal, 2010: 85–6)*

Bibliography

Allievi, S. (2002). Islam in Italy. In S. T. Hunter (ed.), *Islam, Europe's Second Religion. The New Social, Cultural, and Political Landscape*. Westport, CT: Praeger.

Andall, J. (2000). *Gender, Migration and Domestic Service. The Politics of Black Women in Italy*. Aldershot: Ashgate.

Andall, J. (2007). Industrial districts and migrant labour in Italy. *British Journal of Industrial Relations*, 45(2), 285–308.

Andall, J. and Duncan, D. (eds) (2005). *Italian Colonialism: Legacy and Memory*. Oxford/Berne: Peter Lang.

Andall, J. and Duncan, D. (eds) (2010). *National Belongings: Hybridity in Italian Colonial and Postcolonial Cultures*. Oxford: Peter Lang.

Anghel, R. G. (2008). Changing statuses: freedom of movement, locality and transnationality of irregular Romanian migrants in Milan. *Journal of Ethnic and Migration Studies*, 34 (2), 787–802.

Arnone, A. (2011). Talking about identity: Milanese-Eritreans describe themselves. *Journal of Modern Italian Studies* 16 (4), 516–27.

Avanza, M. (2010). The Northern League and its 'innocuous' xenophobia. In A. Mammone and G. A. Veltri (eds), *Italy Today. The Sick Man of Europe*. London: Routledge.

Bale, T. (2003). Cinderella and her ugly sisters: the mainstream and extreme right in Europe's bipolarising party systems. *West European Politics*, 26 (3), 67–90.

Ballinger, P. (2003). *History in Exile. Memory and Identity at the Borders of the Balkans*. Princeton, NJ: Princeton University Press.

Baratieri, D. (2010). *Memories and Silences Haunted by Fascism: Italian Colonialism*. Berne: Peter Lang.

Bar-On, T. (2007). *Where Have All the Fascists Gone?* Aldershot: Ashgate.

Bar-On, T. (2013). *Rethinking the Fascist New Right: Alternatives to Modernity*. London: Routledge.

Battiston, S. and Mascitelli, B. (2008). The challenges to democracy and citizenship surrounding the vote to Italians overseas. *Modern Italy*, 13 (3), 261–80.

BBC (2013). Italian racism row: Cécile Kyenge compared to orang-utan. Available at www.bbc.co.uk/news/world-europe-23310837 (accessed 15 July 2013).

Bello, B. G. (2011). Empowerment of young migrants in Italy through nonformal education: putting equality in practice. *Journal of Modern Italian Studies*, 16 (3), 348–59.

Ben-Ghiat, R. (2004). *Fascist Modernities: Italy 1922–1945*. Berkeley: University of Calfornia Press.

Ben-Yehoyada, N. (2011). The moral perils of Mediterraneanism: second-generation immigrants practicing personhood between Sicily and Tunisia. *Journal of Modern Italian Studies*, 16 (3), 386–403.

Bernini, S. (2010). Family politics, the Catholic Church and the transformation of family life in the Second Republic. In A. Mammone and G. A Veltri (eds), *Italy Today. The Sick Man of Europe*. London: Routledge.

Berrocal, E. G. (2010). Building Italian-ness through the logic of the 'other in us' and the 'self in the other': an anti-nationalism approach to the Italian debate on a new citizenship law. *Bulletin of Italian Politics*, 2 (1), 69–90.

Bianchi, G. E. (2011). Italiani nuovi o nuova Italia? Citizenship and attitudes towards the second generation in contemporary Italy. *Journal of Modern Italian Studies*, 16 (3), 321–33.

Bidussa, D. (1994). *Il mito del bravo italiano*. Milan: Il Saggiatore.

Bigot, G. and Fella, S. (2008). The Prodi government's proposed citizenship reform, and the debate on immigration and its impact on Italy. *Modern Italy*, 13 (3), 305–15.

Bonetti, P., Simoni, A. and Vitale, T. (eds) (2011). *La condizione giuridica di Rom e Sinti in Italia*. Milan: Giuffrè Editore (2 vols).

Bonifazi, C. (2007). *L'immigrazione straniera in Italia*. Bologna: il Mulino.

Booth, S. S. and Cole, J. F. (1999). An unsettling integration: immigrant lives and work in Palermo. *Modern Italy*, 4 (2), 191–205.

Buckel, S. and Wissel, J. (2010). State project Europe: the transformation of the European border regime and the production of bare life. *International Political Sociology*, 4 (1), 33–49.

Burgio, A. (2000). Per la storia del razzismo italiano. In A. Burgio (ed.), *Nel nome della razza. Il razzismo nella storia d'Italia*. Bologna: il Mulino, 2nd edn.

Calavita, K. (2005). *Immigrants at the Margins. Law, Race and Exclusion in Southern Europe*. Cambridge; Cambridge University Press.

Cento Bull, A. (1996). Ethnicity, racism and the Northern League. In C. Levy (ed.), *Italian Regionalism. History, Identity and Politics*. Oxford and Washington, DC: Berg.

Cento Bull, A. (2000). *Social Identities and Political Cultures in Italy: Catholic, Communist and Leghist Communities between Civicness and Localism*. New York: Beghahn Books.

Cento Bull, A. (2008). The Italian transition and national (non)reconciliation. *Journal of Modern Italian Studies*, 13 (3), 405–21.

Cento Bull, A. (2010). Addressing contradictory needs: the Lega Nord and Italian immigration policy. *Patterns of Prejudice*, 44 (5), 411–31.

Chang, A. (2010). 'Birds of Passage' and 'Sojourners': A Historical and Ethnographic Analysis of Chinese Migration to Prato, Italy. BA dissertation, Duke University.

Cinalli, M. (2008). 'Weak immigrants' in Britain and Italy. Balancing demands for better support versus tougher constraints. In A. Chebel d'Appollonia and S. Reich (eds), *Immigration, Integration, and Security. America and Europe in Comparative Perspective*. Pittsburgh: University of Pittsburgh Press.

Cingolani, P. (2009). *Romeni d'Italia. Migrazioni, vita quotidiana e legami transnazionali*. Bologna: Il Mulino.

Clough Marinaro, I. (2003). Integration or marginalization? The failures of social policy for the Roma in Rome. *Modern Italy*, 8 (2): 203–18.

Clough Marinaro, I. (2009). Between surveillance and exile: biopolitics and the Roma in Italy. *Bulletin of Italian Politics*, 1 (2): 265–87.

Clough Marinaro, I. and Daniele, U. (2011). Roma and humanitarianism in the Eternal City. *Journal of Modern Italian Studies*, 16 (5), 621–36.

Clough Marinaro, I. and Sigona, N. (2011). Anti-Gypsyism and the politics of exclusion: Roma and Sinti in contemporary Italy. *Journal of Modern Italian Studies*, 16 (5), 583–89.

Clough Marinaro, I. and Thomassen, B. (eds) (2014). *Global Rome: Changing Faces of the Eternal City*. Bloomington, IN: Indiana University Press.

Clough Marinaro, I. and Walston, J. (2010). Italy's 'second generations': the sons and daughters of migrants. *Bulletin of Italian Politics*, 2 (1), 5–19.

Cole, J. (1997). *The New Racism in Europe: A Sicilian Ethnography*. Cambridge: Cambridge University Press.

Colombo, A. (2007). 'They call me a housekeeper, but I do everything.' Who are domestic workers today in Italy and what do they do? *Journal of Modern Italian Studies*, 12 (2), 207–37.

Colombo, A. and Sciortino, G. (2004). Italian immigration: the origins, nature and evolution of Italy's migratory systems. *Journal of Modern Italian Studies*, 9 (1): 49–70.

Colombo, A. and Sciortino, G. (eds) (2008). *Stranieri in Italia. Trent'anni dopo*. Bologna: il Mulino.

Colombo, E., Domaneschi, L. and Marchetti, C. (2011). Citizenship and multiple belonging. Representations of inclusion, identification and participation among children of immigrants in Italy. *Journal of Modern Italian Studies*, 16 (3), 334–47.

Coluzzi, P. (2009). Endangered minority and regional languages ('dialects') in Italy. *Modern Italy*, 14 (1), 39–54.

Cossu, A. (2010). Memory. Symbolic conflict and changes in the national calendar in the Italian Second Republic. *Modern Italy* 15 (1), 3–10.

Costi, N. (2010). The spectre that haunts Italy: the systematic criminalisation of the Roma and the fears of the Heartland. *Romani Studies*, 20 (2), 105–36.

Daly, F. (1999). Tunisian migrants and their experience of racism in Modena. *Modern Italy*, 4 (2), 173–89.

Degiuli, F. (2011). Labouring lives: the making of home eldercare assistants in Italy. *Modern Italy*, 16 (3), 345–61.

Del Boca, A. (1994a). *Una sconfitta dell'intelligenza. Italia e Somalia*. Rome-Bari: Laterza.

Del Boca, A. (1994b). *La trappola somala. Dall'operazione Restore Hope al fallimento delle Nazioni Unite*. Rome-Bari: Laterza.

De Mauro, T. (2001). Linguistic variety and linguistic minorities. In D. Forgacs and R. Lumley (eds), *Italian Cultural Studies. An Introduction*. Oxford: Oxford University Press.

Diamanti, I. (2009). *Mappe dell'Italia politica: bianco, rosso, verde, azzurro e tricolore*. Bologna: il Mulino.

Dines, N. (2012). *Tuff City. Urban Change and Contested Space in Central Naples*. New York and Oxford: Berghahn Books.

Donaldio, R. (2010). Race riots grip Italian town as Mafia is suspected. *The New York Times*, 10 January. Available online at www.nytimes.com/2010/01/11/world/europe/11italy.html?-r=0 (accessed 2 March 2014).

Duff, M. (2009). Milan train segregation idea row. *BBC News*, 5 September 2009. Available online at http://news.bbc.co.ukgo/pr.fr/-/1/hi/world/europe/8041974.stm (accessed 7 March 2014).

Einaudi, L. (2007). *Le politiche dell'immigrazione in Italia dall'Unità a oggi*. Rome-Bari: Laterza

Famiglia Cristiana (2008). Razzista e indecente l'idea sulle impronte per i bimbi rom, 30 June, 1.

Favero, P. (2010). Italians, the 'Good People': reflections on national self-representation in contemporary Italian debates on xenophobia and war. *Outlines. Critical Practice Studies*, 2, 138–53.

Finotelli, C. (2009). The north-south myth revised: a comparison of the Italian and German migration regimes. *West European Politics*, 32 (5), 886–903.

Finotelli, C. and Sciortino, G. (2009). The importance of being southern: the making of policies of immigration control in Italy. *European Journal of Migration and Law*, 11, 119–38.

Focardi, F. and Klinkhammer, L. (2004). The question of Fascist Italy's war crimes: the construction of a self-acquitting myth (1943–1948). *Journal of Modern Italian Studies*, 9 (3), 330–8.

Foot, J. (1999). Immigration and the city: Milan and mass immigration, 1958–98. *Modern Italy*, 4 (2), 159–72.

Galli della Loggia, E. (1999). *La morte della patria*. Rome-Bari: Laterza.

Garau, E. (2010). The Catholic Church, universal truth and the debate on national identity and immigration. A new model of 'selective solidarity'. In A. Mammone and G. A. Veltri (eds), *Italy Today. The Sick Man of Europe*. London: Routledge.

Geddes, A. (2008). Il rombo dei cannoni? Immigration and the centre-right in Italy. *Journal of European Public Policy*, 15 (3), 349–66.

Gentile, E. (1997). *La Grande Italia. Ascesa e declino del mito della nazione*. Milan: Mondadori.

Gilardoni, G. (2011). Segmented assimilation in Italy? The case of Latinos. *Journal of Modern Italian Studies*, 16 (4), 450–64.

Gilmour, D. (2011). *The Pursuit of Italy. A History of a Land, its Regions and their Peoples*. London: Allen Lane.

Glendinning, L. (2008). Obama is young, handsome and tanned, says Silvio Berlusconi. *The Guardian*, 6 November. Available online at http://www.theguardian.com/world/20008/nov/06/italy-barackobama (accessed 2 March 2014).

Grillo, R. and Pratt, J. (eds) (2002). *The Politics of Recognizing Difference: Multiculturalism Italian-style*. Aldershot: Ashgate.

Guglielmo, J. and Salerno, S. (eds) (2003). *Are Italians White? How Race is Made in America*. New York and London: Routledge.

Guglielmo, T. A. (2003). *White on Arrival. Italians, Race, Color and Power in Chicago, 1890–1945*. Oxford: Oxford University Press.

Hanretty, C. and Hermanin, C. (2010). Nominalisation as racialisation in the Italian press. *Bulletin of Italian Politics*, 2 (2), 75–94.

Hooper, J. (2009). Italian town where a White Christmas is a police matter. *The Guardian*, 20 December: 5.

Janoski, T. (2010). *The Ironies of Citizenship. Naturalization and Integration in Industrialized Countries*. Cambridge: Cambridge University Press.

Johanson, G, Smyth, R. and French, R. (eds) (2009). *Living Outside the Walls: The Chinese in Prato*. Newcastle: Cambridge Scholars Press.

King, R. (ed.) (1999). Special Issue: New Immigration in Italy. *Modern Italy*, 4 (2), 133–257.

King, R. and Mai, N. (2008). *Out of Albania. From Crisis Migration to Social Inclusion in Italy*. New York and Oxford: Berghahn Books.

Kington, T. (2013a). Italy's first black minister: I had bananas thrown at me but I'm here to stay. *The Observer*, 8 September: 33.

Kington, T. (2013b). The tiny Italian village that opened its doors to migrants who braved the sea. *The Observer*, 12 October. Available online at http://www.thegurardian.com/world/2013/oct/12/italian-village-migrants-see (accessed 2 March 2014).

Labanca, N. (2002). *Oltremare. Storia dell'espansione coloniale italiana*. Bologna: il Mulino.

Labanca, N. (2010). The embarrassment of Libya. History, memory, and politics in contemporary Italy. *California Italian Studies Journal*, 1 (1), 1–16.

Leonard, T. (2009). Michelle Obama keeps Silvio Berlusconi at arm's length at G20. *Daily Telegraph*, 25 September. Available online at www.telegraph.co.uk/news/worldnews/michelle-obama/6232298/Michelle-Obama-keeps-Silvio-Berlusconi-at-arms-length-at-G20.html (accessed 2 March 2014).

Lepschy, A. L., Lepschy, G. and Voghera, M. (1996). Linguistic variety in Italy. In C. Levy (ed.), *Italian Regionalism. History, Identity and Politics*. Oxford and Washington, DC: Berg.

Lerner, G. (2008a). Con la scusa del popolo. *La Repubblica*, 16 May: 1.

Lerner. G. (2008b). Quel censimento etnico di settanta anni fa. *La Repubblica*, 5 July: 1.

Levy, C. (1999). Historians and the 'First Republic': Italy fifty years after 1945. In S. Berger et al. (eds), *Writing National Histories: Western Europe since 1800*. London: Routledge.

Levy, C. (2010). Refugees, Europe, camp/state of exception: 'into the zone', the European Union and extraterritorial processing of migrants, refugees, and asylum-seekers (theories and practices). *Refugee Survey Quarterly*, 29 (1), 92–119.

Levy, C. (forthcoming). *Italy and its racisms*.

Lombardi-Diop, C. and Romeo, C. (2012). *Postcolonial Italy: Challenging National Homogeneity*. New York: Palgrave Macmillan.

Loy, G. (2011) Diritto e legislazione su Rom and Sinti 'dal nostro punto di visita', in P. Bonetti, A. Simoni and T. Vitale (eds), *La condizione giuridica di Rom e Sinti in Italia*. Milan: Giuffrè Editore (2 vols).

Lucht, H. (2012). *Darkness before Daybreak. African Migrants Living on the Margins in Southern Italy Today*. Berkeley, CA: University of California Press.

Mai, N. (2003). The cultural construction of Italy in Albania and vice versa: migration dynamics, strategies of resistance and politics of mutual self-definition across colonialism and post-colonialism. *Modern Italy*, 8 (1), 77–96.

Mammone, A. (2006). A daily revision of the past: Fascism, Anti-Fascism and memory in contemporary Italy. *Modern Italy*, 11 (2), 211–26.

Mammone, A. (forthcoming). *Transnational Neofascism in France and Italy*. Cambridge: Cambridge University Press.

Menin, L. (2011). Bodies, boundaries and desires: multiple subject-positions and micro-politics of modernity among young Muslim women in Milan. *Journal of Modern Italian Studies*, 16 (4), 504–15.

Menz, G. (2009). *The Political Economy of Managed Migration. Nonstate Actors, Europeanization, and the Politics of Designing Migration Policies*. Oxford: Oxford University Press.

Meret, S., Della Corte, E. and Sangiuliano, M. (2013). The racist attacks against Cécile Kynege and the enduring myth of the 'nice' Italian. *openDemocracy*. Available online at www.opendemocracy.net (accessed 30 August 2013).

Messina, P. (2001). *Regolazione politica dello sviluppo locale. Veneto ed Emilia Romagna a confronto*. Turin: UTET.

Moore, M. (2008). Berlusconi faces Muslim clash. *Daily Telegraph*, 4 May: 5.

Moss, H. (2000). Language and Italian national identity. In G. Bedani and B. Haddock (eds), *The Politics of National Identity. A Multidisciplinary Approach*. Cardiff: University of Wales Press.

Mudu, P. (2006). Patterns of segregation in contemporary Rome. *Urban Geography*, 27 (5), 422–40.

Palumbo, P. (ed.) (2003). *A Place in the Sun. Africa in Italian Colonial Culture from Post-Unification to the Present*. Berkeley, CA: University of California Press.

Paoletti, E. (2010). *The Migration of Power and North-South Inequalities. The Case of Italy and Libya*. Basingstoke: Palgrave Macmillan.

Pastore, F. (2004). A community out of balance: nationality law and migration politics in the history of post-unification Italy. *Journal of Modern Italian Studies*, 9 (1), 27–48.

Patriarca, S. (2001). Italian neopatriotism: debating national identity in the 1990s. *Modern Italy*, 6 (1), 21–34.

Patriarca, S. (2010). *Italian Vices. Nation and Character from the Risorgimento to the Republic*. Cambridge: Cambridge University Press.

Pedone, V. (2011). 'As a rice plant in a wheat field': identity negotiation among children of Chinese immigrants. *Journal of Modern Italian Studies*, 16 (4), 492–503.

Però, D. (1999). Next to the dog pound: institutional discourses and practices about Rom refugees in left-wing Bologna. *Modern Italy*, 4 (2), 207–24.

Pesarini, A. (2013). The reinvention of tradition: new configuration of gender identity and economic strategies within Roma communities in Italy. *Refugee Survey Quarterly*, 32 (1), 101–21.

Picker, G. (2011). Welcome 'in'. Left-wing Tuscany and Romani migrants (1987–2007). *Journal of Modern Italian Studies*, 16 (5), 607–20.

Riccio, B. (1999). Senegalese street-sellers. Racism and the discourse on 'irregular trade' in Rimini. *Modern Italy*, 4 (2), 225–39.

Riccio, B. and Russo, M. (2011). Everyday practised citizenship and the challenges of representation: second-generation associations in Bologna. *Journal of Modern Italian Studies*, 16 (3), 360–72.

Richey, M. (2012). The North African revolutions: a chance to rethink European externalization of the handling of non-EU migrant flows. *Foreign Policy Analysis*, 9 (4), 409–31.

Rusconi, G. (1993). *Se cessiamo di essere una nazione*. Bologna: il Mulino

Saitta, P. and Cole, J. E. (2011). Final remarks: Italy, dreams of a monochrome society? *Journal of Modern Italian Studies*, 16 (4), 528–30.

Schneider, J. (ed.) (1998). *Italy's Southern Question: Orientalism in One Country*. Oxford: Berg.

Sciortino, G. (2013). Immigration in Italy: Subverting the logic of welfare reform? In E. Jurado and G. Brochmann (eds), *Europe's Immigration Challenge*. London: I. B. Tauris.

Sciortino, G. and Colombo, A. (2004). The flows and the flood: the public discourse on immigration in Italy, 1969–2001. *Journal of Modern Italian Studies*, 9 (1), 94–113.

Sigona, N. (2003). How can a 'nomad' be a 'refugee'?: Kosovo Roma and labelling policy in Italy. *Sociology*, 37 (1), 69–79.

Sigona, N. (2005). Locating 'the Gypsy Problem'. The Roma in Italy: stereotyping, labelling and 'nomad camps'. *Journal of Ethnic and Migration Studies*, 31 (4), 741–56.

Sigona, N. (2009). The 'Problema Nomadi' vis-à-vis the political participation of Roma and Sinti at the local level in Italy. In N. Trehan and N. Sigona (eds), *Romani Politics in Contemporary Europe. Poverty, Ethnic Mobilization, and the Neo-Liberal Order*. Basingstoke: Palgrave Macmillan.

Sigona, N. (2010). 'Gypsies out of Italy!': social exclusion and racial discrimination of Roma and Sinti in Italy. In A. Mammone and G. A.Veltri (eds), *Italy Today. The Sick Man of Europe*. London: Routledge.

Sigona, N. (2011). The governance of Romani people in Italy: discourse, policy and practice. *Journal of Modern Italian Studies*, 16 (5), 590–606.

Sniderman, P. M., Peri, P., de Figueiredo, R. J. P. and Piazza, T. (2001). *The Outsider: Prejudice and Politics in Italy*. Princeton, NJ: Princeton University Press.

Squires, N. (2009). Italy allows vigilantes for first time since Mussolini's Blackshirts. *Daily Telegraph*, 15 May: 5.

Srivastava, N. and Bhattacharya, B. (eds) (2012). *The Postcolonial Gramsci*. London: Routledge.

Thomassen, B. (2010). 'Second generation immigrants' or 'Italians with immigrant parents'? Italian and European perspectives on immigrants and their children. *Bulletin of Italian Politics*, 2 (2), 21–44.

Tintori, G. (2009). Nuovi italiani e italiani nel mondo. Il nodo della cittadinanza. In P. Corti and M. Sanfilippo (eds), *Storia d'Italia: Annali 24: Migrazioni*. Turin: Einaudi.

Tosi Cambini, S. (2011). The social dangerousness of the defendant is 'at one with her condition of being nomadic': Rome and Sinti in Italian courts of law. *Journal of Modern Italian Studies*, 16 (5), 652–66.

Triulzi, A. (ed.) (2002). La colonia: Italiani in Eritrea. Special issue of *Quaderni Storici*, 109 (1).

Triulzi, A. (2003). Adwa: from monument to document. *Modern Italy*, 8 (1), 95–108.

van Hooren, F. (2010). When families need immigrants: the exceptional position of migrant domestic workers and care assistants in Italian immigration policy. *Bulletin of Italian Politics*, 2 (2), 21–38.

Ventresca, R. (2006). Debating the meaning of Fascism in contemporary Italy. *Modern Italy*, 11 (2), 189–209.

Visani, A. (2009). The Jewish enemy. Fascism and anti-Semitism on the seventieth anniversary of the 1938 race laws. *Journal of Modern Italian Studies*, 14 (2), 168–83.

Vitale, T. (2011). Gli stereotipti che ingombrano politiche e rappresentanze, in P. Bonetti, A. Simoni and T. Vitale (eds), *La condizione giuridica di Rom e Sinti in Italia*. Milan: Giuffrè Editore (2 vols).

Waley, P. (2009). Introducing Trieste: a cosmopolitan city? *Social & Cultural Geography*, 10 (3), 243–55.

Walston, J. (2010). Appendix: immigration statistics. *Bulletin of Italian Politics*, 2 (1), 115–20.

Zincone, G. (2006). The making of policies. Immigration and immigrants in Italy. *Journal of Ethnic and Migration Studies*, 32 (3): 347–75.

Zinn, D. L. (2010). Italy's second generations and the expression of identity through electronic media. *Bulletin of Italian Politics*, 2 (1): 91–113.

Zinn, D. L. (2011). 'Loud and clear': the G2 Second Generations network in Italy. *Journal of Modern Italian Studies*, 16 (3): 373–85.

5

ROLE AND PERCEPTIONS OF WOMEN IN CONTEMPORARY ITALY

Elisabetta Ruspini

Italian women between familism and feminism: an introduction

The aim of this chapter is to discuss some aspects of the changing role of women in Italy. These changes will be analysed taking into account the peculiarities of the Italian cultural system. Italian culture[1] may be defined as *familistic*. By *familism* we mean a set of normative beliefs that: describes a strong attachment and loyalty to one's family, emphasises the centrality of the family unit and stresses the obligations and support that family members owe to both nuclear and extended kin (see, for example, Saraceno, 2003; Rossi, 2009). The norms and traditions of the family are transmitted to the younger generation, and people usually perceive these norms to be fair and legitimate. If family is seen as the crucial foundation of society, a sense of society is not very strong, nor is a sense of the state (Ginsborg, 1989 and 1994; also Chapter 2 in this volume).

The survival of the familistic cultural system depends heavily on 'traditional' gender relations. Familism requires and encourages a specific, two-gender model, where the gender categories 'woman' and 'man' carry with them specific expectations about how to act, what to do, whom to love and so on. The familistic culture also tends to assume that all family members experience family life in the same basically positive ways. This assumption persists despite considerable evidence that women and men often experience the rhythms of family life together from quite different perspectives (See for example Rubin, 1976; Code, 1987).

Familism has its good sides: in Italy (the same is true, for example, for Spain, Greece and Mexico:[2] Gérman *et al.*, 2009) family has acted as an informal support network (a social security cushion), offering care services for children, the elderly and sick people – services provided by the welfare state in other countries. This has contributed to reinforce family solidarity between generations, as well as to create broad family networks. The negative compensation of this family economy model has affected the female collective: familism implies a prioritisation of the needs of the family over those of women (Saraceno, 1994). Familism thus influenced the visibility of women in history: in not acknowledging what women contribute to society overall, women were rendered invisible and marginalised. According to Valentini (2012), familism is one of the key elements that may explain why in Italy the question of women's rights and roles is probably the 'last thing' to be dealt with.

The familistic culture influenced the Italian feminist movement, which has some unique characteristics. Feminism and the cultural revolution of the late 1960s and 1970s played a key role in Italy in reconfiguring women's lives. The discourse of the second wave[3] of feminism put women's identity and the search for the feminist consciousness at the centre of reflection. It is also true that, just like the American feminist movement, the second wave of Italian feminism began with primarily upper- and upper-middle-class women, but expanded to include women of different educational and socio-economic levels, primarily through the organised labour movement. As Bianca Beccalli (1994) writes, this may be attributed to the social basis of Italian feminism: in most phases of its history, the movement has included women from different social backgrounds, both intellectuals and working-class activists. Through the practice of consciousness-raising (*autocoscienza*), the women's movement spread across the North and South of the country – starting in the large cities of the North and Centre, where the politics of 1968 had originated and been most influential. Small workshop collectives were organised in large and smaller cities and it is necessary to mention the diffusion of autonomous women's cultural centres and of feminist journals and magazines, most of which were self-funded and self-distributed (Longo, 2003). If the national scale of the movement was a significant achievement, we should not underestimate the persistence of regional peculiarities and differing rates of development (Adler Hellman, 1987; Beccalli, 1994). As other chapters in this Handbook show (see Chapter 2 for details), Italy has a high degree of territorial heterogeneity and territorial conflicts.

As we have said, the feminist message had to confront the familistic culture and to compromise with it. According to Paola Bono and Sandra Kemp (Bono and Kemp, 1991; on this topic, see also de Lauretis, 1989) one of the most distinctive features of Italian feminism is its non-institutional basis. This reflects the need to adapt to the coexistence of both a strong Catholic and a socialist culture, both of which give the family a central role (Guadagnini and Donà, 2007). As Dalla Zuanna (2001) writes, Catholic values are filtered by the familistic way of thinking. As the Catholic Church has emphasised some values easily compatible with familism in Italy, Catholicism has reinforced familism, and to some extent the latter has reinforced the former. Another key feature of the Italian feminist movement is the focus on sexual difference. As Dalla Torre (2010) writes, at the start of the 1970s Italian feminism went from being a feminism of equality and emancipation to a separatist politics articulated by women for women and emphasising sexual difference (see also Cavarero, 1993). According to Pravadelli (2010), both its non-institutional basis and separatist orientation may explain the late institutionalisation of women's studies (see also Bono and Kemp, 1991). Indeed, only in the late 1990s did such studies become institutionally formalised.[4] However, as Chiara Saraceno argues (2010), the weak institutionalisation of gender studies was mainly the consequence both of the Italian institutional framework and of the weak position women academics had within it. It is also true that the gender perspective is increasingly present in Italy, in sociology, economics, linguistics, psychology and literature, and within the 'hard sciences' as well (Saraceno, 2010; also Magaraggia and Leone, 2010).

Today the situation is becoming more complex. As we will see later on, male and female life courses appear to be converging: this convergence challenges the polarisation of gender roles and thus the familistic culture. Moreover, the Millennial generation is becoming more numerous. Currently including young people up to 30 years of age, the Millennials have surpassed the Baby Boomers (those born during the years 1946 and 1964, in the post-Second World War period) as the larger and more influential generation worldwide. These young women and young men are politically and socially independent, and they are spearheading a period of sweeping change around the world (Greenberg and Weber, 2008). This is primarily because of individual and family change (for example, divorced families, single-parenting, LGBT parenting, etc.), and the revolution of advanced Internet technologies.

There is thus a strong need to understand and manage the generation turnover. Starting from these premises we will look at the relationship between familism and women's roles (the next section of this chapter); in the third section, we will discuss some of the challenges posed by the postmodern turn (Lyotard, 1979; Beck, 1992; Giddens, 1990; Bauman, 1992; Beck and Grande, 2010).

The 'pleasure' of living in Italy: familism and gender discriminations

Italian women had to grow up in, adapt to, and make compromises in a very patriarchal and misogynistic culture: the familistic one. As we will shortly see, not an easy task, indeed.

As we have said, familism discourages individual autonomy and takes women's moral obligation to care for granted. In a familistic culture there is a strong belief that family members' behaviours should meet with familial expectations. Lugo Steidel and Contreras (2003) identified four components of familism, namely family honour, respect for family elders, family interdependence, and subjugation of the self to the family.

Connected to familism is a strong emphasis on the quality of intra-family care. This is seen in the 'dramatisation' of the investment of personal resources in family life, in hostility towards forms of externalisation of family care (that is, the transfer of care tasks to institutions/outside the home: Mingione, 2001) and in the difficulties of adopting strategies to redistribute care duties between men and women. Indeed, Italian men contribute very little to housework and childcare. The *Harmonised European Time Use Survey* (HETUS),[5] shows that Italian men perform the second-lowest amount of domestic work among men in the countries considered,[6] with only Spanish men doing less, while Italian women stand out as the least active in the labour market. However, a study by Bloemen *et al.* (2010) found that Italian fathers' childcare time increases significantly when there are young children in the household. Gender differences are still present in how sons and daughters are expected to help with the housework. Boys are asked and expected to do less housework, and are given greater freedom by parents than are girls (Facchini, 2002; Ruspini, 2012). The redistribution of domestic responsibilities to men is fairly limited even in young couples with a high level of education.

In order to balance the limitations of formal care services and cultural resistance to externalisation, migrant women today replace family carers and thus play a very crucial role in the maintenance of Southern European care systems (Lyberaki, 2008; Ambrosini and Beccalli, 2009; Wall and Nunes, 2010). Some authors talk about a distinctive Southern European immigration pattern (King, 2001; Bettio *et al.*, 2006), where a new 'migrant-in-the-family' care model emerges.

As Dalla Zuanna (2001) explains, familism is not only a general attitude toward the 'traditional family', based on marriage and children, with the breadwinner-father and the housewife-mother. Familism and the traditional family are certainly linked, but familism can persist even where traditional family life declines. This is what happens in contemporary Italy, where fertility is low and where 'new' marital and reproductive behaviours (divorce, cohabitation, extramarital fertility) are spreading.

Familism (and the gender differences tied to it) may indeed explain why the Italian fertility rate is falling (Livi Bacci, 2001) and also account for the low levels of women's participation in the labour market. The Italian fertility rate – 1.33 children per woman in 2004; 1.39 in 2011 – has been one of the lowest in the world for some years now. As we have said, in Italy the experience of parenthood implies a strong specialisation of gender roles, with an increase in female time spent on housework and childcare (as well as a reduction in their time for paid work and free time), and an increase in men's time dedicated to paid work (Tanturri and Mencarini, 2009). As Tanturri and Mencarini (2008) wrote, recent fertility theories have taken into consideration gender inequality as a possible explanation of lowest low levels of fertility in Southern Mediterranean countries (McDonald, 2000a and 2000b; Cooke, 2003).

Because care work still remains the responsibility of women, women's job opportunities can be seriously compromised by having children (Pacelli *et al.*, 2007; Istat, 2007). Maternity forces many women to retire from their professional life. In Italy, the employment rate among mothers with children is one of the lowest in Europe. If the employment rate for women decreases as the number of children increases in a majority of member states, in Italy the employment rate for women aged 25–54 with one child was, in 2009, 59 per cent (EU27: 71.3 per cent); with two children 54.1 per cent (EU27: 69.2 per cent) and with three children or more 41.3 per cent (EU27: 51.7 per cent) (Eurostat, 2011a; Istat, 2011a).

Not surprisingly, the situation of women and work in Italy is one of the worst in Europe in terms of employment. The target set by the European Union ('Strategy for Development and Employment') calls for 75 per cent of the population aged 20–64 to be employed by 2020. In 2010 the value of the indicator in Italy (61.1 per cent) was 14 percentage points below this target and summed up an extremely large gender imbalance (72.8 per cent for men and 49.5 per cent for women: Istat, 2010b).

The gender imbalance with regard to employment rates is accompanied by a strong regional divide. Higher employment rates characterise the Northern regions, particularly the North-East, where the employment rate for the population aged 20–64 (70.1 per cent) exceeds the average national value by 9 percentage points (Istat, 2010b). In the Southern regions, only 20.7 per cent of women between the ages of 18 and 29 are employed, compared with 45.7 per cent in the North (Italian Labour Force Survey data, second quarter of 2012). Moreover, in the Italian labour market flexible working hours and part-time work are still rare: less than 30 per cent of mothers with children under six work part-time (Reyneri, 2007). In the EU rankings, Italy, with lower-than-average values, comes eleventh for the incidence of female part-time employment and twentieth for the incidence of male part-time employment (Istat, 2010a).

Familism also means a strong reliance on the family as a provider of social protection, with minimum state intervention (see, for example, Trifiletti, 1999; Saraceno, 2003; Moreno Mínguez, 2007; see also Chapter 21 in this Handbook). Familism has led to a distinctive gender regime (with informal rules) in which females are considered caretakers in a traditional family role and a single-earner family is promoted.

Italian governments lag behind other European countries in the resources they provide for family policies (around 4 per cent of overall expenses in Italy compared with a European average of 8 per cent; Eurostat, 2005). Childcare services for children under three offer only an 11 per cent coverage at the national level, with a range of variation from 24 per cent in Emilia Romagna to less than 5 per cent in Sardinia and Basilicata (Istat, 2008). Childcare for preschool children is also expensive. Moreover, access to childcare in Italy varies a lot by region. Empirical evidence shows that Italian children are much more likely to be cared for by their parents, grandparents, relatives or friends between the ages of 0–2 years than children in the majority of other OECD countries (OECD, 2007). The work of grandmothers appears crucial to solving the problem of insufficient state childcare services in Italy, which reinforces the central role of the family as an institution that provides for social welfare (Saraceno, 2003; Oppo and Perra, 2008).

According to Dalla Zuanna (2001), thanks to family support, Italian society can bear high youth (between 15–24 years) unemployment rates: in 2013, more than 50 per cent in some Southern areas of the country (male unemployment rate: 46.7 per cent; female unemployment rate: 56.1 per cent), in the absence of public unemployment benefit and social upheaval. While, on the one hand, the role played by the family ensures greater flexibility for those entering the labour market, on the other hand, many young people are not actively encouraged to seek employment. It is often considered preferable for the young to stay at home, unemployed, rather than accept a low-status occupation. As we have said, familism discourages individual autonomy, and parents find it hard to accept a 'low-status' child.

Familism is also at the root of the very common attitude that considers young people in perpetual need of care and assistance. The tie binding parents and children is a peculiarity in the Italian model.[7] This relates to the heightened importance attributed to children and the intense support given to them – continuing even after they have married – in terms of emotional support, closeness and availability of time and money. In Italy, young adults of both sexes live with their parents until they get married and are provided for by them as long as they stay within the family – even in families with a single breadwinner – whether the young person has a separate income or not. Children, after leaving home to establish new families, still maintain strong relationships with their parents. Usually they live very near to one of the two parental families and visit them regularly (often weekly) (see Chapter 6 in this Handbook for details). In other words, there is a lengthening of the time span that people spend in their family of origin. This phenomenon has come to be known as the *famiglia lunga* (Scabini and Donati, 1988).

In sum, the Italian cultural system and welfare model are still constructed on a rigid polarisation of gender roles; on the moral duty of family subsidising (according to which the family, enlarged to include the network of relatives, is always obliged to protect its members); on women's unpaid care work; on the indefinite prolonging of financial bonds between generations. The lack of public family and care measures to reconcile work and family life in Italy is the result of a political context based on a consensual democracy characterised by a unique ideological cleavage. As we said in the introductory section, the coexistence of both a strong Catholic and a socialist culture affected the type of gender equality that emerged in Italy, which had to maintain a central role for the family (Guadagnini and Donà, 2007). The cultural and political influence of the Catholic Church as an institution, together with the low priority that family policies have had for left-wing parties and trade unions, reduced the possibility of changing not only the legal definition of the family, but the system of social protection focused on core (mostly male) workers, particularly in the face of tight budget constraints (Knijn and Saraceno, 2009).

The Italian cultural system and welfare state based on familism have proven difficult to change, also as a result of the persistence of a strong male domination of political life, with a low percentage (11 per cent) of women's representation in Parliament over the last decade, and the political culture, with a widespread idea that women's main role is in the private sphere of the family rather than in the public, political and professional arenas (Guadagnini and Donà, 2007).

Italy's inertia in achieving gender equality seems to have been enhanced by its recent political leadership. Berlusconi's actions and statements, media support for those actions and statements, and official insensitivity, if not hostility, to women, 'has made the workplace an unwelcoming if not downright hostile environment for women with even moderately serious ambitions' (Turesky *et al.*, 2011).

Today, the Italian political sphere is showing some positive signs. In November 2012, the Italian government (led by Prime Minister Mario Monti) approved a Decree-Law (Decreto Legge no. 215/2012) to promote a more balanced gender representation in the legislative and executive bodies of Italian local entities (Municipalities, Provinces and Regions). Specifically, the law introduces stricter rules for the protection of gender equality in municipal and regional representative assemblies, governing councils (i.e. *Giunte*) and selection committees. The law stipulates that during elections for representative assemblies both sexes must be represented on the electoral list. In fact, neither sex must be represented by more than two-thirds of the candidates. Furthermore, it is envisaged that voters can express a 'gender preference': electors can express up to two preferences (instead of the single-preference system previously in effect) only if they vote for two candidates of different genders; otherwise, the second preference will be considered void. The law also provides for equal access for both women and men to the media during election campaigns and for stricter rules to enforce gender equality on selection committees (one third of the seats should be reserved for women). In order to make these provisions effective, the law strengthens the role of the so-called 'equality advisors', with powers to ensure compliance with the principle of equality on the selection committees.[8]

Recently the Italian government has seen other changes, as Prime Minister Enrico Letta appointed seven women, the highest proportion to date. Italy's new government has been active on the reform front, introducing key legislation to achieve gender equality. One of the first major reforms, passed in late May 2013, was to approve the adoption of the Istanbul Convention on combating violence against women. The convention would create an international framework to provide protection for women by encouraging prevention, assistance, cultural awareness and education on the issue. The Italian government also passed a new law (Decree-Law 14 August 2013) that will make it easier to protect women against domestic violence. The new legislation includes mandatory arrest for stalking and family abuse, with the abusive spouse subject to immediate removal from the home when there is any risk of violence. In Italy, gender violence is still a widespread phenomenon. The joint research report by EURES and ANSA[9] found that between 2000 and 2012, more than 2,200 women were murdered in Italy, an average of 171 per year. Of these women, 70.8 per cent were killed by family members and 79.7 per cent of the femicides were committed at home.

However, a legislative process cannot be disconnected from the long-term planning of gender change. In other words, legislative measures should be supported, preceded and followed by gender-sensitive, comprehensive education and training programmes. Education is especially needed to rethink the traditional male identity in an anti-sexist logic, converging with feminist and women's thought.

Converging life courses and the Millennial generation

As we have just said, the situation of women in Italy is slowly changing. Women's policy agencies began to develop in the 1980s and 1990s. The main institutions set up to develop gender equality policies in Italy are the National Commission for Equal Treatment (*Comitato Nazionale di Parità*), established in 1983 as part of the Ministry of Labour to deal with employment matters; the National Committee for Equal Opportunities in the Labour Market (*Comitato Nazionale di Parità e Pari Opportunità nel Lavoro*), established in 1991; and the Ministry for Equal Opportunities (*Ministero per le Pari Opportunità*), created in 1996. These institutions, which have contributed to the promotion of gender policies in Italy, were influenced by the political leaning of the party in government, with greater progress coming from centre-left than from centre-right governments (Guadagnini and Donà, 2007).

The rate of women's employment (between 15–64 years) has recorded a gradual rise over the last ten years: from 39.6 per cent in 2001 to 46.1 per cent in 2010 (Eurostat, 2011b). Working mothers declare themselves more satisfied than housewives and mothers, although they are weighed down by an enormous amount of work when one adds the work in the house to that outside it. Women's traditional role of wife and mother is no longer appealing, and young housewives perceive their situation more as a necessity than a choice (Sabbadini, 2004).

This decline in motivation is consequent upon more extensive education and growing schooling rates. Not only do more women attend secondary school, but they are also more successful there than their male counterparts. At the university level women outnumbered men in 1990–1 (Istat, 2011b). Today young women place work and financial independence at the top of their priorities and see them at the core of their identity. Interviews and research conducted among women in their late twenties and thirties in Italy present quite a different picture from that of the past (Piazza, 2003). These women feel no sense of inferiority with regard to their male contemporaries and expect equal treatment. They tend to see family, work and education primarily in terms of self-fulfilment (Piazza, 2003). Empirical evidence also shows that Italian young women (aged between 18 and 34) appear to be more likely to achieve their goals and become autonomous if they spend a period of time outside the parental home (Ferrari *et al.*, 2013). Also the choice to remain childfree – that is, when women and men have made a personal decision not to have children – is growing (Tanturri and Mencarini, 2008). In the 2001 Eurobarometer survey 6 per cent of Italian women aged 20–34 express an 'ideal' number of children of zero (Goldstein *et al.*, 2003).

Changes in female identities increasingly have implications for male partners, workers and fathers. Younger men are beginning to claim a greater share in bringing up their children although, in the father–child relation, playing dominates the other dimensions (see for example Rosina and Sabbadini, 2005; Zajczyk and Ruspini, 2008). The number of men willing to question the stereotyped model of traditional masculinity is also growing (Ruspini *et al.*, 2011).

Men's and women's life courses seem to be converging in terms of delayed transitions to adulthood. Research evidence (Toulemon, 2010; Mencarini and Solera, 2011) shows that in Southern European countries the differences between men and women are declining. Leaving the parental home is delayed until after the first job, for men as well as for women. Similarly, the proportion of men and women having a first child before having worked full-time is declining. The proportion of women who leave the parental home before cohabiting for the first time is increasing, and the large gap present in the cohorts born in the 1940s is no longer visible for the cohorts born in the 1970s.

The convergence of life courses is strengthened by the generation turnover. In recent years, the Millennial generation has emerged as a powerful political and social force. The Millennials are a group of young people born from 1980–2 onwards. The Millennial generation has been defined as a generation that is 'competent, qualified, technological, and in search of a new form of citizenship' (Balduzzi and Rosina, 2009). This is so for various reasons. First, they are the most ethnically and racially diverse cohort of youth in history. Second, the Millennials grew up with the Internet and thrive in a multimedia, highly communicative environment. Learning online is 'natural' to them – as much as retrieving and creatively creating information on the Internet, blogging, communicating on mobile phones, downloading files to iPods and instant messaging. Third, they feel empowered, have a sense of security and are optimistic about the future. Unlike the generations that came before them (Baby Boomers and Generation Xers), these young women and men are not left to make key decisions on their own; their parents are involved in their daily lives. Their parents helped them plan their achievements, took part in their activities and were very confident about their children's abilities. A book by Greenberg and Weber (2008) that explores the values, dreams and potential of the Millennial generation shows that they are poised to change the world for the better, and lays out a powerful plan for progressive change that today's youth is ready to implement (see also Taylor and Keeter, 2010; Rainer and Rainer, 2011). The Millennials are more tolerant than adults in other generations of a wide range of 'non-traditional' behaviours relating to marriage and parenting: from mothers of young children working outside the home to unmarried adults living together. The Millenials are also distinctive in their social values; they stand out in their acceptance of homosexuality, interracial dating and expanded roles for women and migrant people.

With regard to gender equality and women's mobilisation, the emergence of Information and Communication Technologies (ICTs) has changed feminist organising, writing and networking. The feminist movement can find support and community online: today there are multiple online feminisms and feminist communities (Del Greco, 2013; Rossi, 2013). Fourth-wave feminism allowed young women (and men) to raise issues and express opinions (and to organise) in a way that print publications never afforded. In Italy, the women's and men's movement *Se Non Ora Quando?*[10] (If Not Now, When?), born in February 2011, was helped and inspired by social networking. The movement aims to protect the rights of women, including the right to work, promote a gender-sensitive culture and mobilise public opinion in favour of (gender) equality. The movement has been spreading its message via email, Facebook, Twitter and YouTube. Through the use of these tools, *Se Non Ora Quando?* has organised marches and protests against Berlusconi, his misogynistic regime and conservative politics. Besides protests, *Se Non Ora Quando?* has also organised flash mobs and forums in various Italian cities to bring to light the situation of Italian women, and plans on how to move forward.[11]

Within this evolving context, the cultural gap between second-wave feminists and today's feminism seems to be increasing (Cirant, 2005). For example, the close association between feminism and the Left and the exclusion of men are increasingly problematic matters. Contemporary feminism has been described as the ultimate acceptor of diversity: multiple truths, multiple roles and multiple realities are part of its focus. The field of women's studies – formed in the wake of the feminist movement – indeed finds itself in a precarious position in what is now called a 'postmodern', 'postfeminist' society. Are the aims and goals of feminism still relevant in the twenty-first century? How must the field adjust its goals and methods to continue to effect change in the future (Lapovsky Kennedy and Beins, 2005)? This raises challenging issues for universities, students and administrators.

Some conclusions, hard challenges

In Italy, empirical evidence also shows a trend of convergence between women and men in their behaviours, desires, and in their gender attitudes and roles, in and out of the home. These changes could effectively challenge sexism and gender stereotypes. The new women's and men's lifestyles, attitudes and roles may promote trends that encourage gender equality, a crucial element for social justice.

However, the interplay between the past and present raises the key question of how contemporary modernity relates to and interacts with the 'old' institutions, norms, rules and values, and with the familistic culture. This question is especially crucial for the Italian context. One of the biggest challenges for Italy and its culture is indeed how to support the positive convergence of gender identities, perceptions and roles, the generational turn, women's empowerment, but also men's changes. This in order to prevent generational and gender conflicts.

Gender education has a key role to play in raising public awareness of gender biases in society and promoting change. The future of gender education and gender studies seems, however, uncertain. Education on gender is still lacking in Italy, both in the process of primary socialisation and in educational programmes. On the one hand, the topics of gender and sexuality continue to be taboo subjects in Italian families. People outside the family (often friends) seem to be the main vehicles of information on these issues, which is, however, often inexact, distorted or in any case insufficient. On the other hand, in Italy there is no national legislation regulating gender and sex education in schools and the prevalent forms of learning in school and professional training systems are still constructed to highlight values and behaviours linked to traditional masculine and feminine roles (Boffo *et al.*, 2003). Moreover, gender education is undergoing severe budget cuts; this is also because most people think that gender studies has no tangible educational or job outcomes. The lack of information and education opportunities arising from this lack of funding, together with the many prejudices and stereotypes with regard to gender and sexuality, offers fertile ground for a definite increase in phenomena such as bullying, femicide and violence against women, sexual harassment, homophobia and transphobia.

The role of gender education in fighting bullying, femicide and gender violence, sexual harassment, homophobia and transphobia is indeed crucial. Gender education would also mean encouraging both young women and young men to place themselves at the centre of their lives and to acquire knowledge that releases them from traditional social identities such as those of masculinity and femininity, as well as ethnic, regional and local and national identifications (Beck and Beck-Gernsheim, 2002; Fennell and Arnot, 2009).

Notes

1 By the concept of culture we may refer to all the symbols, beliefs, meanings, behaviours, values and objects shared by member of a particular group, in contrast to other groups. Through culture, people and groups define themselves, understand meanings and social expectations, and conform to society's shared values.

2 There is an implicit assumption in the existing literature that familism is primarily applicable to Italian or Hispanic people. However, as Schwarz (2007) notes, there is some evidence that familism may apply to other cultures and ethnic groups as well. For example, Papadopoulos (1998) speaks about a 'Greek familism'. Coohey (2001) found that familism was protective against child abuse for both Hispanics and non-Hispanic Whites.

3 Second-wave feminism differentiates the women's movement that began in the late 1960s from the suffrage movement of the late nineteenth and early twentieth centuries (or 'first-wave' feminism). First-wave feminism arose in the context of the industrial society and liberal politics but was connected to both the progressive women's rights movement and early socialist feminism in the late nineteenth and early twentieth century in the United States and Europe. Third-wave Feminism began in the late 1980s as a response to the perceived failures of the second wave. It is a theoretical perspective that is both a continuation of, and a break with, second-wave feminisms. It shared many of the interests of the first two waves, i.e., the empowerment of women, but it was also attributed to the desire of women to find a voice of their own and to include various diverse groups like women of colour, lesbian, bisexual and trans women. Fourth-wave feminism (also 'first-wave equalism') is, or will be, a child of the Internet (see note 11 for details).

4 According to Magaraggia and Leone (2010), before that period women's studies was forced to adapt to existing university structures, 'hidden' inside single courses and single disciplines.

5 www.h2.scb.se/tus/tus/ (accessed 25 January 2015).

6 Belgium, Bulgaria, Germany, Estonia, Spain, France, Italy, Latvia, Lithuania, Poland, Slovenia, Finland, United Kingdom and Norway.

7 On the basis of data of the first wave (2004–6) of the SHARE-Project (Survey of Health, Ageing and Retirement in Europe) it appears that Scandinavian countries have the least traditional family structure, whereas Mediterranean countries, in particular Spain and Italy, have the most traditional one: more coresidence and late ages of leaving the parental home among adult children (Moor and Komter, 2008).

8 Palomar, Osservatorio di Diritto Costituzionale, n. 21, January 2013: www3.unisi.it/dipec/palomar/italy021_2013.html (accessed 27 January 2015).

9 Il femminicidio in Italia nell'ultimo decennio. Dimensioni, caratteristiche e profili di rischio, Indagine istituzionale, Eures, Ansa, Dicembre 2012.

10 https://strugglesinitaly.wordpress.com/equality/the-womens-movement-se-non-ora-quando/ (accessed 27 January 2015).

11 http://lachristagreco.com/lachrista-greco-1/2011/08/07/italian-feminism-and-the-power-of-social-networking (accessed 27 January 2015).

Bibliography

Adler Hellman, J. (1987). *Journeys Among Women: Feminism in Five Italian Cities*. Oxford: Polity Press.

Ambrosini, M. and Beccalli, B. (2009). Uomini in lavori da donne: il lavoro domestico maschile. In R. Catanzaro and A. Colombo (eds), *Badanti & Co, Il lavoro domestico straniero in Italia*. Bologna: Il Mulino.

Balduzzi, P. and Rosina, A. (2009). *Competent, Qualified, Technological: In Search of a New Form of Citizenship. Brain Drain in Italy*. Paper presented at the Conference *Nomad Power. Values, Illusions, Aspirations of Errant Youth*, Rimini.

Bauman, Z. (1992). *Intimations of Postmodernity*. New York and London: Routledge.

Beccalli, B. (1994). The Modern Women's Movement in Italy. *New Left Review*, I/204, March–April (available online at http://newleftreview.org/I/204/bianca-beccalli-the-modern-women-s-movement-in-italy).

Beck, U. (1992). *Risk Society: Towards a New Modernity*. London: Sage.

Beck, U. and Beck-Gernsheim, E. (2002). *Individualisation: Institutionalised Individualism and its Social and Political Consequences*. London: Sage.

Beck, U. and Grande, E. (2010). Varieties of Second Modernity: The Cosmopolitan Turn in Social and Political Theory and Research. *British Journal of Sociology*, 61 (3), 409–43.

Bettio, F., Simonazzi, A. and Villa, P. (2006). Change in Care Regimes and Female Migration: The 'Care Drain' in the Mediterranean. *Journal of European Social Policy*, 16 (3), 271–85.

Bloemen, H. G., Pasqua, S. and Stancanelli, E. G. F. (2008). *An Empirical Analysis of the Time Allocation of Italian Couples: Are Italian Men Irresponsive?* IZA Discussion Paper No. 3823, November.

Boffo S., Gagliardi F., and La Mendola, S. (2003). La luce che non c'è. Indicatori di genere in campo formativo. In F. Bimbi (ed.), *Differenze e disuguaglianze. Prospettive per gli studi di genere in Italia* (pp. 189–221). Bologna: Il Mulino.

Bono, P. and Kemp, S. (eds) (1991). *Italian Feminist Thought: A Reader*. Cambridge, MA: Basil Blackwood.

Cavarero, A. (1993). Towards a Theory of Sexual Difference. In S. Kemp and P. Bono (eds), *The Lonely Mirror: Italian Perspectives on Feminist Theory* (pp. 189–221). London: Routledge.

Cirant, E. (2005). 'Io non sono femminista ma . . .' Immagini di giovani donne nello specchio incrinato dell'identità di genere. In E. Ruspini (ed.), *Donne e uomini che cambiano* (pp. 91–120). Milan: Guerini.

Code, L. (1987). The Tyranny of Stereotypes. In K. Storrie (ed.), *Women: Isolation and Bonding* (pp. 195–209). Toronto: Methuen.

Coohey, C. (2001). The Relationship between Familism and Child Maltreatment in Latino and Anglo families. *Child Maltreatment*, 6, 130–42.

Cooke, L. P. (2003). *The South Revisited: The Division of Labor and Family Outcomes in Italy and Spain*. Iriss Working Paper Series 2003–12.

Dalla Torre, E. (2010). *French and Italian Feminist Exchanges in the 1970s: Queer Embraces in Queer Time*. Dissertation submitted in partial fulfilment of the requirements for the degree of Doctor of Philosophy in the University of Michigan.

Dalla Zuanna, G. (2001). The Banquet of Aeolus: A Familistic Interpretation of Italy's Lowest Low Fertility. *Demographic Research*, 4, article 5 (available online at http://www.demographic-research.org/volumes/vol4/5/4–5.pdf).

de Lauretis, Teresa (1989). The Essence of a Triangle or, Taking the Risk of Essentialism Seriously: Feminist Theory in Italy, the US, and Britain. *Differences*, 2, 1–37.

Del Greco, M. (2013). Voci femminili, blog, seconde generazioni. Il caso di Yalla Italia. In M. G. Turri (ed.), *Femen. La nuova rivoluzione femminista* (pp. 89–107). Milan-Udine: Mimesis.

Eurostat (2005). *European Social Statistics, Expenditure and Receipts*. Data 1994–2002. Brussels: European Union.

Eurostat (2011a). *8 March 2011: International Women's Day. Women and Men in the EU Seen through Figures*. Eurostat News Release, 36/2011, 4 March 2011 (available online at http://epp.eurostat.ec.europa.eu/cache/ITY_PUBLIC/1–04032011-AP/EN/1–04032011-AP-EN.PDF).

Eurostat (2011b). *Statistiche dell'occupazione*. European Commission (available online at http://epp.eurostat.ec.europa.eu/statistics_explained/index.php/Employment_statistics/it).

Facchini, C. (2002). La permanenza dei giovani nella famiglia di origine. In C. Buzzi, A. Cavalli and A. de Lillo (eds), *Giovani del nuovo secolo:Quinto Rapporto iard sulla condizione giovanile in Italia* (pp. 159–86). Bologna: Il Mulino.

Fennell, S. and Arnot, M. (eds) (2009). *Gender Education and Equality in a Global Context: Conceptual Frameworks and Policy Perspectives*. London: Routledge.

Ferrari G., Rosina, A. and Sironi, E. (2013). *The Decision Making Process of Leaving Home: A Longitudinal Analysis of Italian Young Adults*. Extended Abstract for the Population Association of America annual meeting, New Orleans, June 11–13 (available online at http://paa2013.princeton.edu/papers/131530).

Gérman, M., Gonzales, M. A. and Dumka, L. (2009). Familism Values as a Protective Factor for Mexican-Origin Adolescents Exposed to Deviant Peers. *Journal of Early Adolescence*, 29 (1), 16–42.

Giddens, A. (1990). *The Consequences of Modernity*. Cambridge: Polity Press.

Ginsborg, P. (1989). *Storia d'Italia dal dopoguerra a oggi. Società e politica 1943–1988*. Torino: Einaudi.

Ginsborg, P. (ed.) (1994). *Stato dell'Italia*. Milan: Il Saggiatore e Bruno Mondadori.

Goldstein, J., Lutz, W. and Testa, M. R. (2003). The Emergence of Sub-replacement Family Size Ideals in Europe. *European Demographic Research Papers* 2. Vienna: Vienna Institute of Demography.

Greenberg, E. H. and Weber, K. (2008). *Generation We: How Millennial Youth Are Taking over America and Changing Our World Forever*. Emeryville, CA: Pachatusan.

Guadagnini, M. and Donà, A. (2007). Women's Policy Machinery in Italy between European Pressure and Domestic Constraints. In J. Outshoorn and J. Kantola (eds), *Changing State Feminism* (pp. 164–81). Basingstoke: Palgrave Macmillan.

Inter-Parliamentary Unit (2010). *Women in National Parliaments*. Situation as of 1st February 2013 (available online at http://www.ipu.org/wmn-e/world.htm).

Istat (National Institute of Statistics) (2007). *Essere madri in Italia*. Rome: Istat (available online at http://www3.istat.it/salastampa/comunicati/non_calendario/20070117_00/testointegrale.pdf).

Istat (National Institute of Statistics) (2008). *Indagine censuaria sugli interventi e i servizi sociali dei comuni. Anno 2005*. Rome: Istat.

Istat (National Institute of Statistics) (2010a). *Part-time Employment*. Rome: Istat (available online at http://noi-italia2012en.istat.it/index.php?id=7&user_100ind_pi1%5Bid_pagina%5D=101&cHash=23ebf6f13f606568a4489a4e0e4681ee).

Istat (National Institute of Statistics) (2010b). *Employment Rate (20–64 years)*. Rome: Istat (available online at http://noi-italia2012en.istat.it/index.php?id=7&user_100ind_pi1%5Bid_pagina%5D=98&cHash=7410b059e61cae3bff4f10f6b61eaa6a).

Istat (National Institute of Statistics) (2011a). *La conciliazione tra lavoro e famiglia. Anno 2010*. Statistiche report, 28 dicembre 2011. Rome: Istat (available online at http://www.istat.it/it/archivio/48912).

Istat (National Institute of Statistics) (2011b). *L'Italia in 150 anni. Sommario di statistiche storiche 1861–2010*. Rome: Istat

King, R. (ed.) (2001). *The Mediterranean Passage: Migration and New Cultural Encounters in Southern Europe*. Liverpool: Liverpool University Press.

Knijn, T. and Saraceno, C. (2009). *Family Law and Family Policy Reforms in Italy and the Netherlands: Different Timings, Increasingly Different Focuses*. Paper presented at the 7th ESPAnet conference 2009, Urbino, 17–19 September 2009 (available online at http://www.espanet-italia.net/conference2009/paper/21%20-%20KnijnSaraceno.pdf).

Lapovsky Kennedy, E. and Beins, A. (eds) (2005). *Women's Studies for the Future: Foundations, Interrogations, Politics*. New Brunswick, NJ: Rutgers University Press.

Livi Bacci, M. (2001). Too Few Children and Too Much Family. *Daedalus*, 130 (3), 139–55.

Longo, P. (2003). *Italian Feminism: Past, Present*. Future Department of Politics Saint Mary's College of California. Paper prepared for delivery at the National Meeting of the American Political Science Association, Philadelphia, PA, August 28–31.

Lugo Steidel, A. G. and Contreras, J. M. (2003). A New Familism Scale for Use with Latino Populations. *Hispanic Journal of Behavioral Sciences*, 25, 312–30.

Lyberaki, A. (2008). '*Deae ex Machina*': *Migrant Women, Care Work and Women's Employment in Greece*. GreeSE Paper n. 20, Hellenic Observatory Papers on Greece and Southeast Europe (available online at http://www2.lse.ac.uk/europeanInstitute/research/hellenicObservatory/pdf/GreeSE/GreeSE20.pdf).

Lyotard, J.-F. (1979). *La condition postmoderne: rapport sur le savoir*. Paris: Minuit.

McDonald, P. (2000a). Gender Equality, Social Institutions and the Future of Fertility. *Journal of Population Research*, 17 (1), 1–16.

McDonald, P. (2000b). Gender Equity in Theories of Fertility Transition. *Population and Development Review*, 26 (3), 427–39.

Magaraggia, S. and Leone, M. (2010). Gender and Women's Studies in Italy: Looking Back to Look Forward. *European Journal of Women's Studies*, 17 (4), 425–9.

Mencarini, L. and Solera, C. (2011). *Changing Paths to Adulthood in Italy. Men and Women Entering Stable Work and Family Careers*. Carlo Alberto Notebooks, n. 219 (available online at http://www.carloalberto.org/assets/working-papers/no.219.pdf).

Mingione, E. (2001). Il lato oscuro del welfare: trasformazione delle biografie, strategie familiari e sistemi di garanzia. In *Tecnologia e società, Atti dei Convegni Lincei n. 172* (pp. 147–69). Rome: Accademia Nazionale dei Lincei.

Moor, N. and Komter, A. (2008). *Demographic Changes, Intergenerational Solidarity and Well-being in Europe: A Comparative Approach*. Multilinks Position Paper, April (available online at http://www.multilinks-project.eu/uploads/papers/0000/0035/Demographic_changes_intergenerational_solidarity_and_well-being_in_Europe_final__Moor___Komter_.pdf).

Moreno Mínguez, A. (2007). *Familia y empleo de la mujer en los estados del bienestar del sur de Europa. Incidencia de las políticas familiares y laborales*. Madrid: Centro de Investigaciones Sociológicas.

OECD (2007). *Babies and Bosses – Reconciling Work and Family Life: A Synthesis of Findings for OECD Countries* (available online at http://www.oecd.org/social/family/babiesandbosses-reconcilingworkandfamilylifeasynthesisoffindingsforoecdcountries.htm).

Oppo, A. and Perra, S. (2008). Solidarietà tra le generazioni. In C. Facchini (ed.), *Conti aperti. Denaro, asimmetrie di coppia e solidarietà tra le generazioni* (pp. 319–42). Bologna: Il Mulino.

Pacelli, L., Pasqua, S. and Villosio, C. (2007). *What does the Stork Bring to Women's Working Career?* Working Paper 58, Working Papers Series from LABORatorio R. Revelli, Centre for Employment Studies, Moncalieri, Torino.

Papadopoulos, T. N. (1998). *Greek Family Policy from a Comparative Perspective*. In E. Drew, R. Emerek and E. Mahon (eds), *Women, Work and the Family in Europe* (pp. 47–57). London: Routledge.

Piazza, M. (2003). *Le trentenni: fra maternità e lavoro alla ricerca di una nuova identità*. Milan: Arnoldo Mondadori Editore.

Pravadelli, V. (2010). Women and Gender Studies, Italian Style. *European Journal of Women's Studies*, 17 (1), 61–7 (available online at http://peer.ccsd.cnrs.fr/docs/00/61/28/25/PDF/PEER_author_10.1177%252F1350506809350863.pdf).

Rainer, T. and Rainer, J. (2011). *The Millennials: Connecting to America's Largest Generation*. Nashville, TN: B&H Publishing Group.

Reyneri, E. (2007). Lavoro e lavori nel contesto italiano. In A. Perulli (ed.), *Il futuro del lavoro* (pp. 143–66). Matelica: Halley.

Rosina, A. and Sabbadini, L. L. (eds) (2005). *Diventare padri in Italia. Fecondità e figli secondo un approccio di genere*. Rome: Istat.

Rossi, G. (2009). Development and Dynamics of the Family in Southern Europe. In O. Kapella, C. Rille-Pfeiffer, M. Rupp and N. F. Schneider (eds), *Die Vielfalt der Familie. Tagungsband zum 3. Europäischen Fachkongress Familienforschung* (pp. 365–89). Opladen: Barbara Budrich.

Rossi, M. (2013). *Donne e femminismi tra significati ed esperienze*. In M. G. Turri (ed.), *Femen. La nuova rivoluzione femminista* (pp. 109–54). Milan-Udine: Mimesis.

Rubin, L. (1976). *Worlds of Pain: Life in the Working Class Family*. New York: Basic Books.

Ruspini, E. (2012). Girls, Boys, Money. Economic Socialisation, Gender, and Generations in Italy. *International Review of Sociology – Revue Internationale de Sociologie*, 22 (3), 514–29.

Ruspini, E., Hearn, J., Pease, B. and Pringle, K. (eds) (2011). *Men and Masculinities Around the World. Transforming Men's Practices*. Basingstoke: Palgrave Macmillan.

Sabbadini, L. L. (2004). *Come cambia la vita delle donne*. Rome: Istat (available online at www3.istat.it/salastampa/comunicati/non_calendario/20040308_00/volume.pdf).

Saraceno, C. (1994). The Ambivalent Familism of the Italian Welfare State. *Social Politics*, 1 (1), 60–82.

Saraceno, C. (2003). *Mutamenti della famiglia e politiche sociali in Italia*, 2nd edition. Bologna: Il Mulino.

Saraceno, C. (2010). Women and Gender Studies in Italy: Lack of Institutionalization or a Different Kind of Institutionalization? *European Journal of Women's Studies*, 17 (3), 269–74.

Scabini, E. and Donati, P. (eds) (1988). *La famiglia 'lunga' del giovane adulto. Verso nuovi compiti educativi*. Milan: Vita & Pensiero.

Schwartz, S. J. (2007). The Applicability of Familism to Diverse Ethnic Groups: A Preliminary Study. *The Journal of Social Psychology*, 147 (2), 101–18,

Tanturri, M. L. and Mencarini, L. (2008). Childless or Childfree? An Insight into Voluntary Childlessness in Italy. *Population Development Review*, 34 (1), 51–77.

Tanturri, M. L. and Mencarini, L. (2009). *Fathers' Involvement in Daily Childcare Activities in Italy: Does a Work–Family Reconciliation Issue Exist?* ChilD n. 22/2009 (available online at http://www.childcentre.unito.it/papers/child22_2009.pdf).

Taylor, P. and Keeter, S. (eds) (2010). *Millennials: A Portrait of Generation Next. Confident, Connected, Open to Change*. Washington, DC: Pew Research Center, February (available online at http://www.pewsocialtrends.org/files/2010/10/millennials-confident-connected-open-to-change.pdf).

Toulemon, L. (2010). *Transition to Adulthood in Europe: Is There Convergence between Countries and between Men and Women?* Research Note, European Commission, Directorate-General 'Employment, Social Affairs and Equal Opportunities' Unit E1 – Social and Demographic Analysis.

Trifiletti, R. (1999). Southern European Welfare Regimes and the Worsening Position of Women. *Journal of European Social Policy*, 9 (1), 49–64.

Turesky, E. F., Cloutier, K. S. and Turesky, M. F. (2011). *Feminine Paths to Leadership in Italy: Perceptions of Female Italian Leaders in a Masculine Society* (available online at http://integralleadershipreview.com/3995-feminine-paths-to-leadership-in-italy-perceptions-of-female-italian-leaders-in-a-masculine-society).

Valentini, C. (2012). *O i figli o il lavoro*. Milan: Feltrinelli.

Wall, K. and Nunes, C. (2010). Immigration, Welfare and Care in Portugal: Mapping the New Plurality of Female Migration Trajectories. *Social Policy & Society*, 9 (3), 397–408.

Zajczyk, F. and Ruspini, E. (2008) (with B. Borlini and F. Crosta). *Nuovi padri? Mutamenti della paternità in Italia e in Europa*. Milan: Baldini Castoldi Dalai.

6

NEW GENERATION AT A CROSSROADS: DECLINE OR CHANGE?

Young people in Italy and their transformation since the nineties

Gianluca Argentin

Introduction

The aim of this chapter[1] is to investigate the state of young people in Italy and how it has changed since the 1990s. Our interpretation is based on transition from childhood to adulthood (Cavalli and Galland, 1993). In this approach, the term young people describes individuals at a particular time when they are facing major changes: concluding their studies, finding a job, and leaving their family (and, eventually, creating a new family and having children). In keeping with this theoretical framework, we reviewed not only previous research explicitly focused on young people but also research on the social institutions that play a crucial role in the transition processes (in particular, labour market, family and welfare state). Therefore, we focused on literature on the Italian family, educational system and labour market. In the sections that follow we describe the peculiar characteristics of these institutions in the Italian case and we analyse how they have changed in recent decades. In particular, we show how the policy reforms and cultural changes in these social domains have strongly affected the new generation's living conditions. We also focus on an issue which has arisen from these changes and is now emerging in youth literature, namely intergenerational equity.

The chapter is structured as follows. In the first part, in an attempt to identify the cultural climate guiding researchers and shaping their questions on young people, we review Italian research on the state of young people since the 1950s. In the second, we present the results described in previous literature and try to identify the peculiarity of Italian young people within the European perspective. The third briefly describes the major changes that have occurred in Italian social institutions in recent years and how these changes have affected the characteristics of young people. Finally, we conclude by trying to identify the key tensions of the new generation in Italy.

A long story: previous research on young people in Italy

As Cavalli and Leccardi (2013) recently observed, it is possible to identify four periods characterising research on Italian young people: the emergence of this topic during the 1950s; the second period of the unexpected youth movements of the 1960s; a long period lasting almost thirty years, which established the key findings about Italian young people and focused on the slow transition into adulthood; and finally, the new issue of youth penalisation and intergenerational inequity.

Whereas research during the 1950s focused on the apathy of young people towards politics, the unexpected youth movements of the 1960s caused researchers to examine completely new issues. Indeed, in those years, the autonomy of young people emerged in many different ways. Researchers detected elements of youth emancipation from families and investigated the role of young people as innovators in respect of collective values and attitudes.

For our purposes, the third and fourth periods of research are the most relevant. The third, the 1980s and 1990s, shaped the main characteristics of young people in the Italian context and researchers have been able to bring into focus a large set of key findings. Moreover, it was during the 1980s and 1990s that IARD (Istituto Assistenza Ragazzi Dotati), a private research institute focused on young people, developed national large-scale surveys on the younger generation (Cavalli, 1984; Cavalli and de Lillo, 1988, 1993; Buzzi *et al.*, 1997, 2002, 2007). This data collection, running for many decades on the same topic with a stable questionnaire, is quite unique in Italian social research and, thanks to these verified data scholars have obtained many crucial findings about Italian young people. It was during those years that researchers identified the crucial issues of young people's slow transition into adulthood and its dramatic lengthening over a number of years. Indeed it is interesting to observe how the definition of young people changed by comparing the different waves of IARD surveys: in 1983 the age range for being considered young was 15–24 years old; it became 15–29 in 1990 and it ended up 15–34 in 2000. During the 1980s and 1090s, it was necessary to stretch the definition to be able to describe the transition processes to adulthood. Part of this research period focused more on values, underlining the increasing relevance of family ties and the enclosure of young people in micro-networks as they abandoned the political scene. During the 1980s and 1990s, young people ceased to identify themselves as a category promoting specific needs and issues and shifted more in the direction of a consumer cluster. The young generation, during that period, enjoyed hitherto unknown opportunities: more education, but also more free time and an increasing amount of resources to spend in the leisure market. Yet, shadows characterised this period as well and the issue of youth penalisation started to emerge, predictably in the labour market, where youth unemployment rose and became a social concern, but also in leisure because of an increase in addictive behaviours. We describe the main findings of this research period in greater depth later: what is relevant here is that a wide spectrum of themes was investigated and the conceptual framework of 'youth condition' was explicitly adopted.

The fourth period of research on young people emerged at the beginning of the new century and exploded in recent years. Those of the young generation are considered a penalised category and, as we show below, this strand of research adopts the frame of intergenerational equity (Schizzerotto *et al.*, 2011; Fasano and Mignolli, 2012). Many recent studies have centred on concerns about the state of young people and show a strong orientation towards policy recommendations. A crucial topic in this research period is labour market flexibility and its consequences for young people's occupational stability. Changes in labour market regulation (adopted in the late 1990s) and the economic crisis led to a worsening of Italian young people's situation, exacerbating unresolved long-term problems. Many studies investigate how labour market precariousness affects family formation and fertility choices and also young people's attitudes and feelings about the future. An increasing social concern about the young generation is that it could be lost, trapped in a sequence of unstable jobs impoverishing its human capital and not allowed to plan for the future. Media, policymakers and social science researchers underline this risk (Dell'Aringa and Treu, 2011; Schizzerotto *et al.*, 2011; Samek Lodovici and Semenza, 2012; Buzzi, 2013; Cavalli and Leccardi, 2013). As we will see, the general picture is mixed, but the forecasts are not good. What happens to the young generation of Italians will probably happen to the entire country. Indeed, in general, but especially regarding young people, Italy is at a turning point and must choose between trying to maintain the fragile equilibrium and introducing structural changes to establish a new one.

State of young people: long-standing but unsustainable equilibrium

The aim of this section is to describe the state of young people in Italy at the beginning of the twenty-first century to provide an overall picture of the strengths and weaknesses of the pre-crisis equilibrium. This general view should support the next section, in which we focus on the changes introduced by new economic and social conditions. As we have stated above, our review considers key findings regarding young people in three crucial domains/institutions: education, labour and family. Moreover, we enrich the structural description by extending it to cover young people's values, focusing especially on the role played by the new generation in the political arena.

In terms of the educational system, young Italians have, for some time, shown lower levels of education compared with their European peers (OECD, 2012). The main gap appears at the tertiary level, primarily as a consequence of the Italian university system. Almost all university courses require four or five years for completion and lack vocational skills training. Also, at the upper secondary level, participation and completion rates are lower than in other countries. Moreover, the only academic track strongly orientated to the university, the *licei*, is not very popular and recruits its students mainly from the upper classes. On the other hand, the formal vocational upper secondary schools ('istituti tecnici' and 'istituti professionali') are not so integrated into the labour market and do not strongly hone their students' skills (Buzzi, 2013). Not surprisingly, research has detected persistent social inequalities in education (Pisati, 2002a) and, with a few exceptions, recent analyses confirm this general picture (Ballarino and Schadee, 2006; Barone *et al.*, 2010). If we look at wage returns in relation to educational credentials in the labour market, university graduates have little (if any) advantage over high school graduates (Reyneri, 2002, 2010), but the economic crises hit young people with a lower level of education harder (Reyneri and Pintaldi, 2013). What emerged during the 1990s was that participation in education in Italy was not only lower and less rewarding than elsewhere but also that Italian students developed lower skills than their colleagues in both maths and reading. More precisely, Italy showed sharply different local performances in international standardised tests: the Northern regions had good results whereas the South performed at the lowest level (Bratti *et al.*, 2007). These gaps were (and still are) huge and are largely due to the sparse economic resources available to schools in the South (Bratti *et al.*, 2007), and the consequent higher dropout rates in that region (Caretta and Mengoli, 2007). These results are not surprising considering that the economy of Southern Italy depends largely on public expenditure and the labour market relies heavily on the public sector.

These considerations introduce another crucial dimension into our analyses of the state of youth: Italy is (like Spain) a country characterised by incredibly high occupational penalisation of young people. The entry phase into the labour market is characterised by long-term unemployment and the risk of job loss is higher among the young generation than among adults (Reyneri, 2002). Moreover, passive policies to protect the earnings of people who become unemployed were not readily available to young workers and there is no minimum wage or any other form of earning protection for young people who have not had a job for a while; at the same time, active policies to support the transition into the labour market are extremely weak (Gualmini, 1998; Reyneri, 2009). This situation is clearly worse in the South, where long-term unemployment rates are extremely high, especially for young people trying to get a public sector position and, in the interim, taking irregular and underpaid jobs. The situation is possibly worse for females, considering the conciliation issue (Reyneri, 2002), which forces them to get a job in the protected labour segment and therefore defer motherhood (Mencarini and Solera, 2011; Migliavacca, 2013), despite their increasing investment in education and labour market participation (Scherer and Reyneri, 2008). To sum up, Italy is an emblematic case of the Mediterranean welfare system (Esping-Andersen, 1998; Ferrera, 1998) where labour market regulation and workfare are designed to support the male breadwinner; not surprisingly, this system disadvantages young people and females and affects birth rates and new family formation processes. Indeed, Italian young people have shown a very slow transition into adulthood, leaving their parental home very late (Buzzi *et al.*, 1997, 2002, 2007). IARD surveys have shown very clearly the sharp increase in the rate of young people living with their parents across cohorts throughout the 1980s and 1990s. All the cohorts born after the 1960s have been affected in this context (Mencarini and Solera, 2011) and the process lasted until the beginning of the new millennium, stabilising before the economic crisis (Buzzi, 2007, 2013). It must be said that this long-term residence at home was not entirely due to the longer duration of studies or to occupational difficulties: indeed it was higher in the South, but widespread also in the Northern regions among young workers who had the economic opportunity to leave home. A crucial role in regulating the transition seems to be played by social norms. Living for a long time with parents and leaving to form a new family are considered normal in the Mediterranean model (Rosina, 2013; Cicchelli and Galland, 2009). Not surprisingly, during the 1980s and 1990s, the step order in the transition to adulthood (finishing studies, getting a job, leaving home to create a new family, having children) remained mainly the same (Pisati, 2002a). Only two minor changes occurred in the transition process: more often, new generations started work before finishing university (Argentin and Triventi, 2010) and new couples more often cohabited than got married. The consequence of this secularised choice is that marriage is postponed even more than in the past (Micheli, 2006), because young partners prefer to test their relationship's stability (Cicchelli and Galland, 2009). This is coherent with young people's preference for reversible choices (Buzzi, 2007). Another reason behind the late transition to adulthood is that the family of origin is a comfortable place to stay: most parents are not demanding about housework or contributions to the family budget and allow a high degree of autonomy, especially in the case of sons (Sartori, 2007). Moreover, the family helps sons and daughters get jobs through social networks (Reyneri, 2002; Vinante, 2007) and also provides money transfers for young people, especially in the South. Evidently, the family of origin is a sort of refuge (Scabini and Donati, 1988), a place where everything can be negotiated (Buzzi *et al.*, 2007), and where young people find strong and wide support. Youth can also rely on familial alliances to face the difficulties caused by labour markets and welfare state failures. This affective protection is expanding its domain and parents are more frequently defending children from their educational failures, even coming into conflict with teachers at school (de Lillo, 2013).

Not surprisingly, the surveys of values carried out since the mid-1980s show that young people attribute increasing relevance to family, partnership and friendship and decreasing relevance to politics, social effort and political and civic participation. This general trend in youth values has been labelled the 'rise of narrow sociality' (de Lillo, 2007). It is notable that during the 1990s research also detected an increase in the rate of young people manifesting repugnance towards politics and a sharp decline in trust in political institutions (de Luca, 2007). Therefore, the public sphere was not only losing relevance in the daily life of new generations, but also being perceived more and more as dominated by forces far removed from young people and not representing their interests. Furthermore, this perception seems quite realistic, considering that policymakers decided to hit the new generation with a large number of the budget cuts and reforms required by the European Union and, afterwards, the spending reductions necessitated by the economic crisis. Later, we will come back to the relevance of those policies for young people. What seems clear is that the configuration of values and social norms, which emerged during the 1990s, seemed a perfect fit with the parallel equilibrium between the new generation, family and other social institutions. Despite its internal coherence, this equilibrium clearly showed tensions and unresolved issues, such as high youth unemployment, a decline in fertility, persistent inequality and increasing disparity in living conditions between North and South. All these well-known problems made the old equilibrium clearly unsustainable. As a consequence of the economic constraints imposed at first by the European Union and, later, by the economic crisis, the situation worsened at the beginning of the new millennium. As we will argue, it seems that Italy is facing a time of change regarding the state of its youth: the equilibrium of the 1990s seems to be collapsing under the weight of its contradictions and is not easily adaptable to the new macro-economic context.

Recent changes and their implications for Italian young people

At the end of the 1990s, two crucial reforms changed the institutional context framing young people's transition to adulthood: in 1997 the government approved a labour market reform (the so-called 'Legge Treu'), making it possible for firms to use temporary workers more easily and giving employees fewer rights than those provided in the usual standard contracts. The idea was that temporary jobs should substitute unemployment and moonlighting, especially among young people. In 2003, a second reform took place, the so-called 'Riforma Biagi', which simply reinforced the previous flexibility process. This 'partial and targeted deregulation' (Esping-Andersen and Regini, 2000) was primarily directed at young cohorts entering the labour market. In 1999, Italy joined the so-called 'Bologna process' and in 2001, universities changed to a three-tier structure. The new academic certification structure is constituted by three steps: a first-level degree ('Laurea triennale' based on a course lasting three years), a second-level degree ('Laurea magistrale', based on two additional years) and doctoral studies (three years in addition to the 'Laurea magistrale'). The reform produced a considerable increase in the number of courses and programmes offered by university colleges around the country, including those in small and peripheral cities.

The mix of these two reforms generated a significant shift in the institutional settings in which new generations transition into adulthood (Argentin and Triventi, 2010). More precisely, research detected an increase in university enrolment up to a level exceeding labour market demand for highly skilled workers (Reyneri, 2010; Barone, 2012). This judgement is strongly debated at the moment and scholars do not agree about the labour market equilibrium regarding degree holders (see *Scuola Democratica. Learning for democracy*, vol. I (2013), which collects the opinions of various authors on this topic). The parallel increase in temporary contracts concentrated mainly on people entering the labour market raised worries about its precariousness for new generations (Barbieri and Scherer, 2009). Labour market flexibility meant young workers were less frequently unemployed than in the past but generated precarious working conditions because of the absence of active labour market policies (Anastasia *et al.*, 2011; Sestito, 2011).

Educational expansion, which led to a minor decline in the effects of social origins on university enrolment, but probably also to an increase in dropping out, must also be taken into account (Argentin and Triventi, 2010; Ballarino and Schizzerotto, 2011; Barone, 2012). University growth led to more educational inflation than equalisation: indeed, enrolment on post-tertiary courses increased at the beginning of the new millennium and research has shown persistent inequality at the top of educational distribution (Argentin, 2011; Argentin *et al.*, 2012). At the same time, a new factor increased inequality at the bottom of the educational system: young immigrants or children born in Italy of foreign parents show lower educational achievement (Azzolini and Barone, 2012) and higher risks of dropping out (Checchi, 2011). The traditional gender gap switched from female to male disadvantage during the 1990s and the first decade of the twenty-first century (Del Boca and Giraldo, 2011). Moreover many tertiary degrees do not meet firms' occupational demands (Cappellari and Leonardi, 2011), which leads to declining returns for education. This is particularly true of an economic phase characterised by saturation of skilled occupational positions. This structural contingency is even affecting social mobility opportunities for middle-class children (Marzadro and Schizzerotto, 2011). This situation undermines the perception of benefits associated with education (Giorgi *et al.*, 2011) and, not surprisingly, university expansion has stopped in recent years. The risk of a return to a decline in educational investment is especially relevant in an Italian context, in which young people do not consider skills to be the crucial factor determining labour market success (Vinante, 2007) and in which family networks play a crucial role in employment allocation (Reyneri, 2002). It should be understood that the reduction in public expenditure affected education directly, for example, by increasing university tuition fees or reducing teacher turnover (through restrictions on retirement and increased school/class sizes). This meant that within 20 years Italy had the oldest teaching labour force among the industrialised countries (Argentin, 2013): this is a factor which probably affects innovation in schools (i.e., information and communication technologies use and the development of digital skills) and plausibly underlies the widespread student feeling that school is a meaningless experience (Argentin, 2007; Fondazione Gianni Agnelli, 2011).

The economic constraints due to EU agreements and economic crisis affected labour market opportunities for young people in many ways (Sestito, 2011). In the last decade the new generation has been facing a reduction in recruitment by the public sector, increasing unemployment (non-renewable temporary contracts) and small firms' closure on a massive scale. The worsening labour market conditions have led to a situation where unemployment is accompanied by permanent employment in unstable jobs (Buzzi, 2013; Migliavacca, 2013) and lower wages for young cohorts entering the labour market (http://www.lavoce.info/chi-paga-la-crisi-30–40-anni/). This problem has affected young people in particular because of the existence of many fake self-employed workers (the so-called *parasubordinati*; Reyneri, 2009) and because many temporary contracts do not guarantee workers protection (Anastasia, 2011; Cappellari and Leonardi, 2011). This occupational instability translates into high levels of perceived uncertainty for young people and their parents (Simonazzi and Villa, 2007), generating worries for the future at the individual level (Fellini, 2006; Bertolini, 2012) and probably threatening pre-existing solidarity networks among temporary workers (Fullin, 2004).

Moreover, the financial crisis restricted bank rules on mortgages, another factor reactivating delay mechanisms in the transition to adulthood (Buzzi, 2013). A powerful reinforcement of social concerns about uncertain youth employment lies in the fact that this problem is affecting highly skilled young workers, a group not traditionally targeted by labour market policies but now facing serious difficulties (Samek Lodovici and Semenza, 2012). Furthermore, it must be recognised that labour market disadvantages are greater for young females, because of their persistent segregation in less rewarding fields of study (Barone, 2011) but probably also because of labour market discrimination (Argentin and Triventi, 2010). Moreover, childcare is an activity managed mainly by the family, namely grandmothers and grandfathers (Saraceno, 2011). Occupational and welfare state politics do not properly support young women's labour market participation (Del Boca and Giraldo, 2011) and, not surprisingly, conciliation is one of the problems raised most frequently by young workers (Migliavacca, 2013).

This is the general picture, but the situation is very much worse in the Southern regions, which are economically weaker than the North and strongly reliant on the public sector. The concentration of NEETs (Not in Education, Employment or Training) in Southern Italy is extraordinary from a comparative perspective (Delzio, 2011). A clear sign of this divide is the re-emergence of South–North migration, a phenomenon that characterised Italian society of the 1960s (Pannichella, 2009; Moccetti and Porello, 2011) and the parallel appearance of long-distance commuters (Delzio, 2011). Migration is particularly worrying nowadays, because the young people who move are highly skilled. Indeed, low-skilled jobs are assigned to foreign immigrants in the Northern regions and this labour market sector does not attract young workers from the South. Conversely, sons and daughters from high social classes have the opportunity to improve the returns on their investment in education by migrating from the South to the North (Moccetti and Porello, 2011). This process has a clear side effect: a brain drain and impoverishment of human capital in Southern Italy. The problem is even more severe: indeed it affects the entire country; the available data show that there is an increase in the number of skilled young Italians living abroad and that Italy is not able to attract skilled foreign researchers (Balduzzi and Rosina, 2012; Moccetti and Porello, 2011).

Consequently, because of longer study duration, labour market difficulties and home market rigidities, the new generations are delaying family formation once again. The positive signals which emerged at the beginning of the new millennium have faded (Buzzi, 2013) and research findings have detected a decrease in the number of young people living with parents through choice and an increase in the number who say that it is a consequence of external constraints (Facchini, 2013). The crucial difference, compared with the 1990s, is that the Mediterranean family is not as strong as it was in the past (Micheli, 2006). Currently, the bad economic situation is affecting parents as well, and they are older than the previous cohort of mothers and fathers (Migliavacca, 2012). Moreover, the investment required by new generations is higher than in the past: longer studies in more distant regions, more expensive lifestyles, and daughters more frequently active in the labour market and requiring childcare. Sociologists and demographists suggest that, within families, intergenerational exchanges are facing increasing pressure (Saraceno, 2012; Facchini, 2013). Mothers and fathers are now taking charge of their children's uncertainty and, at the same time, facing their own. This shift is clearly a powerful lever of change in the Italian welfare equilibrium, based mainly on traditional roles within families. The increasing (and hitherto non-researched) relevance of grandparents in their families' life (Saraceno, 2011) is one of the more visible restructurings of family boundaries and ties (Donati and Naldini, 2012). The risk is twofold: on the one hand, Italian welfare, strongly based on family and intergenerational exchanges, would collapse if the households' solidarity networks weaken; on the other hand, the new Italian generations could experience different citizenship on the basis of their family background and economic resources, living with social inequalities that are greater than in the past (Saraceno, 2012; Brandolini and D'Alessio, 2011).

A slow decline or an (un)expected sea change?

The general picture drawn in previous pages shows that, in Italy, young generations have been facing increasing difficulties since the 1990s. More precisely, the structural constraints on their transition to adulthood have become stronger in recent years because of the economic crisis and cuts in public expenditure. The Italian government has not been investing in young people for a long time (Livi Bacci, 2011), instead, relying on the key role played by families to support their well-being. This lack of investment is odd, considering that Italian young people are a group numerically smaller across cohorts. Moreover the condition of Italian young people is becoming highly problematic. Indeed, as we have seen in the previous paragraph, there are many signs of deterioration in the state of Italian young people and concerns about their future are increasing. Especially in the Southern regions, young people's economic and social situation seem unsustainable in the long run: we are losing entire new generations unable to build their pathway to adulthood. It must be remembered that the new Italian generations are experiencing better living conditions than their parents did (i.e., more education); at the same time, there is converging evidence that the last cohorts (born after the 1960s) are losing ground and that the constant intergenerational improvement of the past is no longer so obvious (Schizzerotto *et al.*, 2011). Income distribution is typical of the general trend of many other living conditions: it has been growing for people born in the first half of the twentieth century, but declining for recent cohorts (Brandolini and D'Alessio, 2011). A crucial role in this worsening of inter-generational equity has been played by the policies introduced since the 1990s (Pertile *et al.*, 2011). Are younger Italian generations destined to experience declining opportunities and worse living conditions?

Until now, in contrast to many other Mediterranean countries, Italian young people have not started collective movements or at least demonstrations against the status quo; resignation has prevailed (Delzio, 2011; Meloni, 2011), although new parties and political actors are emerging. The new generations, unlike those of the past, are not fighting to impose their rights. This absence of collective action is probably due to an orientation towards narrow sociality; however, the anaesthetic of family resources (Livi Bacci, 2011) and intergenerational economic transfers (Brandolini and D'Alessio, 2011) have played a crucial role. But, as we have seen, the familiar welfare state is facing increasing tensions and seems less and less able to maintain the previous equilibrium. Moreover, it is possible to identify at least three other engines of change, which could potentially lead to policy interventions and significant changes in the state of Italian young people.

The first engine of change is that the intellectual and political system is (finally!) focusing on the intergenerational inequality of policy interventions (Schizzerotto *et al.*, 2011; Dell'Aringa and Treu, 2011). The inter-temporal balance in policymaking is a perspective gaining relevance (Fasano and Mignolli, 2012) and the idea that young people are a penalised category is widespread in Italy. The idea of considering the effects on young people of each policy intervention is emerging (Livi Bacci, 2011), such as the proposal to design an extraordinary plan to support young people, especially in the Southern regions (Rosina and Voltolini, 2011; Delzio, 2011) and with regard to labour market policies (Sestito, 2011).

A second engine of change is a (so far) underestimated transformation of the young population living in Italy. The decline in the Italian birth rate is mainly due to the increase in the number of children born to foreign families; these are not Italian citizens, despite their permanent residence in Italy and their participation in the Italian educational system. These young people are living a double life (Ricucci, 2012), belonging at the same time to their culture of origin and to Italian culture and actively helping to reshape it. It should be noted that Italian young people are ambivalent towards immigrants, showing openness but also the persistence of stereotypes (Peri, 2007). The young 'foreign Italians' are the group mainly affected by the general crises of the Italian model, because they have fewer family resources on which to rely (Livi Bacci, 2011; Saraceno, 2012) and, at the same time, they are not fully recognised by the State. Hence, a new (large) generation of young people is growing up in our country: it would not be surprising if, in the future, they asked for the recognition of their rights, expecting full citizenship.

The third engine of change lies in the political system. Older people govern the entire Italian representation system (parties, firms, trade unions, professions) and the system was not open to youth participation and innovation (Cavalli and Leccardi, 2013). This lack of representation is probably one of the reasons for the poor attention to young people in the policies implemented in the last 20 years. Nonetheless, something is quickly changing at this level: in the last elections, a striking result was the consensus gained by 'Cinque stelle', a political movement born on the Web with a conspicuous number of young members and supported by young voters (Biorcio and Natale, 2013). More recently something even remarkable occurred: the current prime minister is the youngest in Italian history. He is a 40-year-old who started his political career as mayor of Florence and gained electoral consensus promoting the idea of renewing the political class through a decisive change in people in leading positions. Hence, it seems that, finally, the political system is invested in the need for change, driven by young people's worries about the country's decline. The political answers to these requests for transformation will decide not only the future of Italy but also the story of Italian young people and their movements.

Note

1 Antonio de Lillo asked me to help him with this chapter, because his illness was causing him sight problems and did not allow him to write properly. Despite his situation, he was willing to reflect upon Italian research on young people, one of his favourite topics. We were supposed to work together on this text, but we did not in the event have enough time. I want to dedicate this chapter to his memory and to his passion for social research. I thank Mauro Migliavacca for his useful bibliographical suggestions.

Bibliography

Anastasia, B. (2011). Sulla 'trappola della precarietà': quali indicazioni dalle ricerche empiriche e dalle statistiche disponibili? In Dell'Aringa, C. and Treu, T. (eds.). *Giovani senza futuro? Proposte per una nuova politica*. Bologna: Il Mulino.

Anastasia, B., Paggiaro, A. and Trivellato, U. (2011). Gli effetti sulle disuguaglianze generazionali delle riforme nella regolazione del welfare e del lavoro. In Schizzerotto, A., Trivellato, U. and Sartor, N. (eds.). *Generazioni disuguali. Le condizioni do vita dei giovani di ieri e oggi: un confronto*. Bologna: Il Mulino.

Argentin, G. (2007). Come funziona la scuola oggi: le esperienze e opinioni dei giovani italiani. In Buzzi, C., Cavalli, A. and de Lillo, A. (eds.). *Rapporto giovani. Sesta indagine dell'Istituto IARD sulla condizione giovanile in Italia*. Bologna: Il Mulino.

Argentin, G. (2011). Studying after the degree: new pathways shaped by old inequalities. Evidence from Italy, 1995–2007. *AlmaLaurea working papers/RePEC*, 45.

Argentin, G. (2013). Come cambia la forza lavoro nel sistema scolastico. Le tendenze demografiche degli insegnanti italiani, 1990–2010. *Sociologia del lavoro*, 131, 74–88.

Argentin, G., and Triventi, M. (2010). Social Inequality in Higher Education and Labour Market in a Period of Institutional Reforms. Italy, 1992–2007. *Higher Education*, 61(3), 309–23.

Argentin, G., Ballarino, G. and Colombo, S. (2012). Accesso ed esiti occupazionali a breve del dottorato di ricerca in Italia. Un'analisi dei dati ISTAT e Stella. *Sociologia del lavoro*, 126, 165–81.

Azzolini, D. and Barone, C. (2012). Tra vecchie e nuove disuguaglianze: la partecipazione scolastica degli studenti immigrati nelle scuole secondarie superiori in Italia. *Rassegna Italiana di Sociologia*, 4, 687–718.

Balduzzi, P. and Rosina, A. (2012). Ridare peso alle giovani generazioni per tornare a crescere. In Cordella, G. and Masi, S. E. (eds.). *Condizione giovanile e nuovi rischi sociali. Quali politiche?* Rome: Carocci.

Ballarino, G. and Schadee, H. M. A. (2006). Espansione dell'istruzione e disuguaglianza delle opportunità educative nell'Italia contemporanea. *Polis*, 20(2), 207–32.

Ballarino, G., and Schizzerotto, A. (2011). Le disuguaglianze intergenerazionali di istruzione. In Schizzerotto, A., Trivellato, U. and Sartor, N. (eds.). *Generazioni disuguali. Le condizioni di vita dei giovani di ieri e oggi: un confronto.* Bologna: Il Mulino.

Barbieri, P. and Scherer, S. (2009). Labour market flexibilization and its consequences in Italy. *European Sociological Review*, 25(6), 677–92

Barone, C. (2011). Some Things Never Change: Gender Segregation in Higher Education across Eight Nations and Three Decades. *Sociology of Education*, 84(2), 157–76.

Barone, C. (2012). Contro l'espansione dell'istruzione (e per la sua ridistribuzione). Il caso della riforma universitaria del 3+2. *Scuola Democratica*, 4.

Barone, C. and Fort, M. (2011). Disparità intergenerazionali di istruzione e riforme scolastiche: i casi della scuola media. In Schizzerotto, A., Trivellato, U. and Sartor, N. (eds.). *Generazioni disuguali. Le condizioni di vita dei giovani di ieri e oggi: un confronto.* Bologna: Il Mulino.

Barone, C., Lijux R. and Schizzerotto, A. (2010). Elogio dei grandi numeri: il lento declino delle disuguaglianze nelle opportunità di istruzione in Italia. *Polis*, 24(1), 5–34.

Bertolini, S. (2012). *Flessibilmente giovani. Percorsi lavorativi e transizione alla vita adulta nel nuovo mercato del lavoro.* Bologna: Il Mulino.

Biorcio, R. and Natale, P. (2013). *Politica a 5 stelle. Idee, storia e strategie del movimento di Grillo.* Milano: Feltrinelli.

Brandolini, A. and D'Alessio, G. (2011). Disparità intergenerazionali nei redditi familiari. In Schizzerotto, A., Trivellato, U. and Sartor, N. (eds.). *Generazioni disuguali. Le condizioni di vita dei giovani di ieri e oggi: un confronto.* Bologna: Il Mulino.

Bratti, M., Checchi, D. and Filippin, A. (2007). *Da dove vengono le competenze degli studenti? I divari territoriali nell'Indagine OECD-PISA 2003.* Bologna: Il Mulino.

Buzzi, C. (2007). La transizione all'età adulta. In Buzzi, C., Cavalli, A. and de Lillo, A. (eds.). *Rapporto giovani. Sesta indagine dell'Istituto IARD sulla condizione giovanile in Italia.* Bologna: Il Mulino.

Buzzi, C. (2013). La transizione in crisi: difficoltà occupazionali e precarietà esistenziale. *Quaderni di sociologia*, 57(62), 149–56.

Buzzi, C., Cavalli, A. and de Lillo, A. (eds.) (1997). *Giovani verso il duemila.* Bologna: Il Mulino.

Buzzi, C., Cavalli, A. and de Lillo, A. (eds.) (2002). *Giovani del nuovo secolo. V Indagine sulla condizione giovanile in Italia.* Bologna: Il Mulino.

Buzzi, C., Cavalli, A. and de Lillo, A. (eds.) (2007). *Rapporto giovani. Sesta indagine dell'Istituto IARD sulla condizione giovanile in Italia.* Bologna: Il Mulino.

Cappellari, L. and Leonardi, M. (2011). A favore di un sistema di 'vocational tertiary education' Italia. In Dell'Aringa, C. and Treu, T. (eds.). *Giovani senza futuro? Proposte per una nuova politica.* Bologna: Il Mulino.

Caretta, A. and Mengoli, P. (2007). Le politiche di contrasto dell'abbandono precoce dell'istruzione e della formazione. In Villa, P. (ed.). *Generazioni flessibili. Nuove e vecchie forme di esclusione sociale.* Rome: Carocci.

Cavalli, A. (ed.) (1984). *Giovani oggi. Indagine IARD sulla condizione giovanile in Italia.* Bologna: Il Mulino.

Cavalli, A. and de Lillo, A. (eds.) (1988). *Giovani anni 80.* Bologna: Il Mulino.

Cavalli, A. and de Lillo, A. (eds.) (1993). *Giovani anni 90. Terzo rapporto IARD sulla condizione giovanile in Italia.* Bologna: Il Mulino.

Cavalli, A. and Galland, O. (eds.) (1993). *L'Allongement de la jeunesse.* Arles: Actes Sud.

Cavalli, A. and Leccardi, C. (2013). Le quattro stagioni della ricerca sociologica sui giovani in Italia. *Quaderni di sociologia*, 57(62), 157–69.

Checchi, D. (2011). È possibile combattere il fenomeno del 'drop out' scolastico? In Dell'Aringa, C. and Treu, T. (eds.). *Giovani senza futuro? Proposte per una nuova politica.* Bologna: Il Mulino.

Cicchelli, V. and Galland, O. (2009). Le trasformazioni della gioventù e dei rapporti tra le generazioni. In Sciolla, L. (ed.). *Processi e trasformazioni sociali. La società europea dagli anni 60 ad oggi.* Rome-Bari: Laterza.

Cordella, G. and Masi, S. E. (eds.) (2012). *Condizione giovanile e nuovi rischi sociali. Quali politiche?* Rome: Carocci.

Cutuli, G. (2008). Lavoro atipico e salari: una discriminazione nascosta nel mercato del lavoro italiano. *Polis*, 22(3), 403–22.

Del Boca, D. and Giraldo, A. (2011). Politiche di conciliazione e occupazione femminile: disparità tra generazioni negli ultimi quarant'anni. In Schizzerotto, A., Trivellato, U. and Sartor, N. (eds.). *Generazioni disuguali. Le condizioni di vita dei giovani di ieri e oggi: un confronto*. Bologna: Il Mulino.

Dell'Aringa, C. and Treu, T. (eds.) (2011). *Giovani senza futuro? Proposte per una nuova politica*. Bologna: Il Mulino.

de Lillo, A. (2007). I valori e l'atteggiamento verso la vita. In Buzzi, C., Cavalli, A. and de Lillo, A. (eds.). *Rapporto giovani. Sesta indagine dell'Istituto IARD sulla condizione giovanile in Italia*. Bologna: Il Mulino.

de Lillo, A. (2013). Preadolescenza: un'età problematica. *Quaderni di sociologia*, 57(62), 7–21.

de Luca, D. (2007). Giovani divisi fuori e dentro la politica. In Buzzi, C., Cavalli, A. and de Lillo, A. (eds.). *Rapporto giovani. Sesta indagine dell'Istituto IARD sulla condizione giovanile in Italia*. Bologna: Il Mulino.

Delzio, F. (2011). I 'senza futuro'. Dalla rassegnazione alla reazione: la traversata dei giovani laureati del Sud nel deserto delle opportunità. In Dell'Aringa, C. and Treu, T. (eds.). *Giovani senza futuro? Proposte per una nuova politica*. Bologna: Il Mulino.

Donati, E. and Naldini, M. (2012). Generazioni e scambi di cura. In Naldini, M., Solera, C. and Torrioni, P. M. (eds.). *Corsi di vita e generazioni*. Bologna: Il Mulino.

Esping-Andersen, G. (1998). *The Social Foundations of Welfare Regimes*. Oxford: Oxford University Press.

Esping-Andersen, G. and Regini, M. (2000). *Why Deregulate Labour Markets?* Oxford: Oxford University Press.

Facchini, C. (2013). Le giovani coppie tra continuità e mutamenti. *Quaderni di sociologia*, 57(62), 171–84.

Fasano, A. and Mignolli, N. (2012). L'impatto intergenerazionale nella valutazione delle politiche: metodologie ed esperienze a confronto. In Cordella, G. and Masi, S. E. (eds.). *Condizione giovanile e nuovi rischi sociali. Quali politiche?* Rome: Carocci.

Fellini, I. (2006). La flessibilità a lungo termine dei giovani adulti. In Micheli, G. A. (ed.). *Strategie di family formation. Cosa sta cambiando nella famiglia forte mediterranea*. Milano: Franco Angeli.

Ferrera, M. (1998). *Le trappole del welfare*. Bologna: Il Mulino

Fondazione Gianni Agnelli (2011). *Rapporto sulla Scuola in Italia 2011*. Rome-Bari: Laterza.

Fullin, G. (2004). *Vivere l'instabilità del lavoro*. Bologna: Il Mulino

Giorgi, F., Rosolia, A., Torrini, R. and Trivellato, U. (2011). Mutamenti tra generazioni nelle condizioni lavorative giovanili. In Schizzerotto, A., Trivellato, U. and Sartor, N. (eds.). *Generazioni disuguali. Le condizioni di vita dei giovani di ieri e oggi: un confronto*. Bologna: Il Mulino.

Golini, A. and Rosina, A. (eds.) (2011). *Il secolo degli anziani. Come cambierà l'Italia*. Bologna: Il Mulino.

Gualmini, E. (1998). *Le politiche del lavoro in Italia*. Bologna: Il Mulino.

Livi Bacci, M. (2011). La sindrome del ritardo. In Dell'Aringa, C. and Treu, T. (eds.). *Giovani senza futuro? Proposte per una nuova politica*. Bologna: Il Mulino.

Marzadro, S. and Schizzerotto, A. (2011). Le prospettive di mobilità sociale dei giovani italiani nel corso del XX secolo. In Schizzerotto, A., Trivellato, U. and Sartor, N. (eds.). *Generazioni disuguali. Le condizioni di vita dei giovani di ieri e oggi: un confronto*. Bologna: Il Mulino.

Meloni, M. (2011). La fuga dei cervelli: un ritratto dell'Italia. In Dell'Aringa, C. and Treu, T. (eds.). *Giovani senza futuro? Proposte per una nuova politica*. Bologna: Il Mulino.

Mencarini, L. and Solera, C. (2011). Percorsi verso la vita adulta tra lavoro e famiglia: differenze per genere, istruzione e coorte. In Schizzerotto, A., Trivellato, U. and Sartor, N. (eds.). *Generazioni disuguali. Le condizioni di vita dei giovani di ieri e oggi: un confronto*. Bologna: Il Mulino.

Micheli, G. A. (ed.) (2006). *Strategie di family formation. Cosa sta cambiando nella famiglia forte mediterranea*. Milano: Franco Angeli.

Migliavacca, M. (2012). Giovani tra passato e futuro. Risorsa o vincolo? In Cordella, G. and Masi, S. E. (eds.). *Condizione giovanile e nuovi rischi sociali. Quali politiche?* Rome: Carocci.

Migliavacca, M. (2013). Un futuro instabile. Come cambia la condizione lavorativa dei giovani. In Rosina, A. (ed.). *Rapporto Giovani 2013*. Bologna: Il Mulino.

Moccetti, S. and Porello, C. (2011). Mutamenti dei processi migratori giovanili dalla seconda metà del XX secolo ad oggi. In Schizzerotto, A., Trivellato, U., and Sartor, N. (eds.). *Generazioni disuguali. Le condizioni di vita dei giovani di ieri e oggi: un confronto*. Bologna: Il Mulino.

Naldini, M., Solera, C. and Torrioni, P. M. (eds.) (2012). *Corsi di vita e generazioni*. Bologna: Il Mulino.

OECD (2012). *Education at a Glance: OECD Indicators 2012*. Paris: OECD Publishing.

Panichella, N. (2009). La mobilità territoriale dei laureati meridionali: vincoli, strategie e opportunità. *Polis*, 23(2), 221–46.

Peri, P. (2007). L'atteggiamento dei giovani verso gli immigrati. In Buzzi, C., Cavalli, A. and de Lillo, A. (eds.). *Rapporto giovani. Sesta indagine dell'Istituto IARD sulla condizione giovanile in Italia*. Bologna: Il Mulino.

Pertile, P., Polin, V., Rizza, P. and Romanelli, M. (2011). L'equità intergenerazionale delle politiche di bilancio. In Schizzerotto, A., Trivellato, U. and Sartor, N. (eds.). *Generazioni disuguali. Le condizioni di vita dei giovani di ieri e oggi: un confronto*. Bologna: Il Mulino.

Pisati, M. (2002a). La transizione alla vita adulta. In Schizzerotto, A. (ed.). *Vite ineguali. Disuguaglianze e corsi di vita nell'Italia contemporanea*. Bologna: Il Mulino.

Pisati, M. (2002b). La partecipazione al sistema scolastico. In Schizzerotto, A. (ed.). *Vite ineguali. Disuguaglianze e corsi di vita nell'Italia contemporanea*. Bologna: Il Mulino.

Reyneri, E. (2002). *Sociologia del mercato del lavoro*. Bologna: Il Mulino.

Reyneri, E. (2009). Occupazione, lavoro e disuguaglianze sociali nella società dei servizi. In Sciolla, L. (ed.). *Processi e trasformazioni sociali. La società europea dagli anni 60 ad oggi*. Rome-Bari: Laterza.

Reyneri, E. (2010). I giovani istruiti e la difficile ricerca di un lavoro qualificato. *Italianieuropei*, 4, 74–81.

Reyneri, E. and Pintaldi, F. (2013). *Dieci domande su un mercato del lavoro in crisi*. Bologna. Il Mulino.

Ricucci, R. (2012). Figli dell'immgrazione. In Naldini, M., Solera, C. and Torrioni, P. M. (eds.). *Corsi di vita e generazioni*. Bologna: Il Mulino.

Rosina, A. (ed.) (2013). *Rapporto Giovani 2013*. Bologna: Il Mulino.

Rosina, A. and Sironi, E. (2013). Diventare adulti in tempo di crisi. In Rosina, A. (ed.). *Rapporto Giovani 2013*. Bologna: Il Mulino.

Rosina, A. and Voltolina, E. (2011). Politiche a favore dell'indipendenza intraprendente delle nuove generazioni. In Dell'Aringa, C. and Treu, T. (eds.). *Giovani senza futuro? Proposte per una nuova politica*. Bologna: Il Mulino.

Samek Lodovici, M. and Semenza, R. (eds.) (2012). *Precarious Work and High-skilled Youth in Europe*. Milan: Franco Angeli.

Saraceno, C. (2011). Nonni e nipoti. In Golini, A. and Rosina, A. (eds.). *Il secolo degli anziani. Come cambierà l'Italia*. Bologna: Il Mulino.

Saraceno, C. (2012). Solidarietà e obbligazioni intergenerazionali. In Naldini, M., Solera, C. and Torrioni, P. M. (eds.). *Corsi di vita e generazioni*. Bologna: Il Mulino.

Sartori, F. (2007). La vita con la famiglia di origine. In Buzzi, C., Cavalli, A. and de Lillo, A. (eds.) (2007). *Rapporto giovani. Sesta indagine dell'Istituto IARD sulla condizione giovanile in Italia*. Bologna: Il Mulino.

Scabini, E. and Donati, P. (1988). *La 'famiglia lunga' del giovane adulto*. Milan: Vita e Pensiero.

Scherer, S. and Reyneri, E. (2008). Com'è cresciuta l'occupazione femminile in Italia: fattori strutturali e culturali a confronto. *Stato e Mercato*, 84(2), 507–18.

Schizzerotto, A. (ed.) (2002). *Vite ineguali. Disuguaglianze e corsi di vita nell'Italia contemporanea*. Bologna: Il Mulino.

Schizzerotto, A., Trivellato, U. and Sartor, N. (eds.) (2011). *Generazioni disuguali. Le condizioni di vita dei giovani di ieri e oggi: un confronto*. Bologna: Il Mulino.

Sciolla, L. (ed.) (2009). *Processi e trasformazioni sociali. La società europea dagli anni 60 ad oggi*. Rome-Bari: Laterza.

Sestito, P. (2011). Il disagio giovanile: sono le politiche giovanili la risposta? In Dell'Aringa, C. and Treu, T. (eds.). *Giovani senza futuro? Proposte per una nuova politica*. Bologna: Il Mulino.

Simonazzi, A. and Villa, P. (2007). Le stagioni della vita lavorativa e la fine del 'sogno americano' delle famiglie italiane. In Villa, P. (ed.). *Generazioni flessibili. Nuove e vecchie forme di esclusione sociale*. Rome: Carocci.

Villa, P. (ed.) (2007). *Generazioni flessibili. Nuove e vecchie forme di esclusione sociale*. Rome: Carocci.

Vinante, M. (2007). I giovani e le rappresentazioni del mercato del lavoro e delle professioni. In Buzzi, C., Cavalli, A. and de Lillo, A. (eds.) (2007). *Rapporto giovani. Sesta indagine dell'Istituto IARD sulla condizione giovanile in Italia*. Bologna: Il Mulino.

7

MAFIAS, ITALY AND BEYOND

Ercole Giap Parini

Preliminary remarks

The word mafia is very well known far from Italy's borders. However, instead of designating precisely a specific organized crime phenomenon, it appears to be a kind of cultural sign of Italy, a typical symbol of the country just like pizza, spaghetti and the mandolin. If you type into *Google*'s search box the words "mafia café," you receive back more than 18,000 links, testifying to an image of the mafia in which the "criminal" evaporates into the "folkloristic" and which may be useful for commercial reasons. And the impressive number of T-shirts with the face of Marlon Brando playing the title role in *The Godfather* is another sign of this misrepresentation.

The problem with the word mafia is that internationally it evokes a large number of stereotypes, that is, it brings to mind fake or quasi-fake conceptual images. In daily life people use this term in a confused way together with words like boss, honorable men, feud, all of them flavored with a certain Italian taste. Among scholars, too, the presence of stereotypes, particularly of a cultural/ethnic type, together with the lack of a common framework for defining the mafia phenomenon, very often leads to models that emphasize some aspects more than others to the detriment of a general understanding.

For a long time mafias had been considered nothing more than a diffuse behavior, a set of practices based on violence embedded in a particular culture; therefore the existence of specific organizations had been explicitly ignored (Blok, 1974). Henner Hess emphasizes the "mafia spirit" from which at most little, scarcely organized groups stem (Hess, 1970: 18). Pino Arlacchi, in his book *La mafia imprenditrice* (*The Entrepreneurial Mafia*), which is a valuable representation of the entrepreneurial characters of the mafia groups, wrote: "The mafia is a behavior and a form of power, it is not a formal organization. Behaving as mafiosi means behaving in an honorable way" (Arlacchi, 1983: 22).[1]

This perspective has strengthened the prejudice about the existence of a "diversity" in Southern Italian culture and receives the blame for neglecting the relational aspects of the mafias: by considering them nothing more than a kind of regional heritage, many have underestimated the fact that the emergence and the strengthening of the Italian mafias is to be read together with the main phases of Italian politics since the times of the national unification process.

One of the most convincing attempts to define the mafias is that proposed by Umberto Santino in the mid-nineties and based on the so called "paradigm of complexity":

> The mafia is a set of criminal organizations, of which the most important—but not the only one—is Cosa nostra, which operates inside a vast and articulated context of relations and produces a system based on violence and illegality and directed towards the accumulation of capitals, the achievement and the managing of power, which makes use of a cultural code and enjoys a certain social consensus.
>
> *(Santino, 1995: 129–130)*

This perspective describes a dynamic phenomenon well embedded in a relational system which is of an instrumental nature for the mafiosi.

The main problem with the definition of the mafia is the possibility of distinguishing it from the other phenomena of organized crime (OC). In accordance with Finckenauer (2005), it is not only incorrect to assimilate mafia to OC, but it is also dangerous in terms of planning the policies and practices to counter it. His proposal is to focus on the mafia's main character, that is, the ability to set up a system of government through violence where there is a power vacuum (Finckenauer, 2005: 74). Finckenauer hits the nail on the head by identifying the specific character of the mafia in relation to its territories, in particular by filling the space the legitimate state has left free. Moreover, the proposal bypasses the tendencies to describe the mafia in an ethnic way or by assuming cultural traits as fundamental to its definition.

Nevertheless, if this view works for the understanding of the functioning of the mafias in their specific territories, in accordance with present-day evidence, we need to articulate it with their movement strategies (Minuti and Nicaso, 1994; Nicaso and Lamothe, 1995; Parini, 2011), as well as with their ability to have a role in the network of worldwide illicit business activities (both, at an international level and of a transnational type).

That is, I try to take as an important fact the idea that the mafias have, for a long time, expanded their activities outside their traditional territories.[2] And this represents critical aspects for any perspectives studying the mafias as phenomena typical of institutionally weak or intrinsically vulnerable territories. This is the case with large areas in the Northern regions of Italy, for instance, whose economy and institutional performances are considered the most advanced among Western countries (e.g. Putnam *et al.*, 1993) and where the mafias are strongly present.

Moreover, it is a widespread opinion that the Italian mafias proliferate mostly in the traditional sectors. For instance, when the *'ndrine* (the single cells of the 'Ndrangheta) started to settle in Lombardy, their main activities were the construction sector and in particular earth-moving; through these, the mafiosi used to provide the Northern Italian economic fabric with easy services and control over the workforce from Southern Italy (see Ciconte, 1996: 167). Therefore, the importance of the traditional sectors has to be considered as a kind of "spearhead" strategy aimed at infiltrating new territories' economies with their activities. Nevertheless, things change when the mafias set up complex money-laundering systems in which they are able to deal with high-level sectors of economic institutions. For instance, in Germany the *cosche* of the 'Ndrangheta, which have transplanted their activities there, invest their illicit profits in the stock exchange by setting up huge and complex money-laundering systems. In Africa different mafia groups are involved in the trafficking of coltan, a mineral of fundamental importance for the manufacture of electronic goods, such as cell phones, tablets, and so on.

Because of their rootedness in Southern Italy, together with their importance in worldwide trafficking, this chapter is focused on Cosa Nostra and the 'Ndrangheta. They are paradigmatic cases of the control mafiosi can exert over territories of original settlement as well as of the permeation of legal markets, and of the ability to constitute a relatively organized system between original settlement territories and those of new expansion.

The organization and the origins

It is reductive to consider Cosa Nostra and the 'Ndrangheta as mere parts of the large family of OC. In fact, they are not just criminal systems, since they have a political agenda aimed at accumulating power. This target is pursued through organizational resources:

> Cosa Nostra and the 'Ndrangheta possess the distinguishing trait of organisations: independent government bodies that regulate the internal life of each associated family and that are clearly different from the authority structure of their members' biological families. Starting from the 1950s, moreover, superordinate bodies of co-ordination were set up—first in the Cosa Nostra, then in the 'Ndrangheta as well.
>
> *(Paoli, 2004: 20)*[3]

The confusion and misunderstanding about the definition of the Italian mafias are emphasized by the existence of foundation myths introduced *ex post* in order to consolidate the inner organization through initiation rites of an exoteric type (Paoli, 2003) as well as to exert fascination outside the organization (Parini, 2003). Take, for instance, the legend of the three Spanish knights Osso, Mastrosso and Carcagnosso who founded, respectively, the Neapolitan Camorra, the Calabrian 'Ndrangheta, and the Sicilian Mafia, as is usually reported in the affiliation codes of the mafiosi.[4] The following example has been drawn from the initiation rite of Serafino Castagna, a young man who was a member of the 'Ndrangheta and then became a kind of early *pentito* or police informer.

> In the name of the organized and sacred society, I consecrate this place in the same way our ancestors Osso, Mastrosso and Carcagnosso consecrated it, through irons and chains. I consecrate it through my faith and through my long words. If until now I used to know this place as an obscure one, from now on I know it as a sacred, holy and inviolable place, where it is possible to set and to dismantle this honoured society. "Thanks!," the others said together.
>
> *(Castagna, 1967: 33)*

In accordance with mainstream studies about the Sicilian mafia, the original scenery was semi-feudal Sicily and in particular the *latifundium*, and the first mafiosi are described as intermediary people between the landowners and the poor peasants who were able to subjugate the latter to the former. The historian Salvatore Lupo gives us a more detailed history, in which the Sicilian mafiosi carried on their activities in and around Palermo more than in the *latifundia* of Trapani or of Agrigento. The Palermo area is for the mafiosi a place of articulation of different activities: "a system of control of the territory which begins with the dense network of the agricultural guards and extends to control over licit as well illicit business activities, such as cattle stealing, smuggling and the first intermediation of the citrus fruit trade and of other products of a rich agriculture" (Lupo, 1996: 18). It is consequently possible to place the role of the Sicilian mafia in the complex and paradoxical processes of modernization rather than considering it as a mere heritage of the past.

According to the social historian Sharo Gambino, "the prehistory of the Calabrian mafia is to be investigated in the events that have interested the land owners since the XVII century to the unification process of Italy, in those fights in which baronies, together with gentlemen and bourgeoisie, were opposed [. . .] to the peasants [. . .] in order to affirm their position and consolidate it through the so-called legality" (Gambino, 1975: 69). In this struggle, though nourished by the people's discontent, the 'Ndrangheta has easily become an instrument of powerful people for social control.

Gratteri and Nicaso (2006: 25–6) stress this fact, since in those years violence was the sole flourishing industry in Calabria and consequently the *picciotteria* (the first step of affiliation) was an occasion for outcast people to become richer, more powerful, and, above all, respected.

As in the case of the Sicilian mafia, the 'Ndrangheta very soon based its power on what is called social capital (see Levi, 1996):

> Now as in the past, the strength [of the Calabrian mafia] as well as the adaptive ability, rootedness and diffusion of the mafiosi are based on the external relations: a kind of social capital without which the 'Ndrangheta would not be the 'Ndrangheta.
>
> *(Gratteri and Nicaso, 2006: 33)*

During the first phases of consolidation of their power the mafiosi built up, in their original territories, what scholars have called *Signoria territoriale* (territorial seigniory), which is a key concept describing the particular way the mafia exerts its control over the traditional territories. In these areas, in Calabria, Campania and Sicily, mafiosi are widely considered benefactors willing to help people in the daily minute necessities. As a counterpart, the bosses assume power over those persons living in "their" territory, for instance by claiming (and ensuring) that any decisions have to pass through them. That is what we call territorial *signoria*, a concept defining a type of power which is totalitarian and based on pervasiveness: the "seigneur" is a person who makes a kind of personal property of the territory.

According to Renate Siebert, territorial *signoria* is:

> A kind of domination focused on the persons and diffused: the organization, the bosses—the little ones as well as the biggest—expect to know and to decide, roughly, on anything that is related to life, the activities, the relations among persons living in the subjugated territory.
>
> *(Siebert, 1996: 18)*

Territorial *signoria* is based on a mix of violence (actual or threatened) and the ability to stay at the center of a system of acquaintanceships based on small or large advantages.

Nowadays, these original traits, far from being abandoned, have been strengthened.

Building a system of economic protection

The entrepreneurial dimension of the mafias has been systematically revealed and studied since the early eighties (Arlacchi, 1983), when researchers and scholars realized that, in order to understand and prosecute them, it was crucial to understand the economic behavior, which has some traditional elements though it is continuously adapted to present-day needs.

On 13 December 1982 in Italy, Law n. 646 was enacted, which introduced the crime of association (Article 416 bis) and defines the mafia organization not only as a violent phenomenon, but also as an articulation of social and economic strategies aimed at the accumulation of power through the permeation of the mechanisms of legal markets.

The diffusion and the distribution of the so-called "warning-light" crimes may help in understanding the continuous pressure of the mafias on the economic fabric, particularly in the Southern Italian regions. Researchers label as "warning crimes" damage and setting fire to businesses as well as reported extortions.[5] It is worth mentioning that, because of the unwillingness of those persons living in the territories under pressure by the mafias to report these activities, the data represent just the tip of the iceberg; nevertheless, by taking into consideration the distribution of these crimes among the Italian regions, two elements appear clearly: first, the continuous pressure that the mafias exert on their traditional territories and, second, the diffusion of these crimes in non-traditional regions (Dia, 2011, II).

These two elements confirm that the mafias in their evolutions tend to expand their activities well beyond their traditional borders while continuing to stay rooted in their traditional territories.

The use of violence represents only the first phase of the mafias' strategy aimed at achieving control over the territories but it remains the "last" resource when some entrepreneurs are reluctant to accept the system the mafiosi impose.

In Sicily, Calabria and Campania, the mafias tend, through a heterogeneous strategy of violence and their ability to share small or large advantages with the victims, to constitute a dense network of accomplices through which it becomes possible to build up a huge system of economic protection. By the expression "economic protection" I mean a strategy aimed at controlling a part of the economic fabric in an area to increase consensus (by sharing very small advantages with people) and to make things easier for the most profitable businesses (from illicit activities) by providing them with efficacious money-laundering systems. The diffusion of the influence they exert, and in general of the pressure on the economic fabric in the areas of origin as well as those of new settlement, has a twofold effect. There are, in fact, many businesses that the owners have to hand over to the mafiosi because of the oppression they have to put up with from them. Moreover, many business people decide to become their accomplices and consequently are drawn into a huge network of money laundering. In fact, as has been suggested by Antonio Nicaso in the case of the 'Ndrangheta,[6] the true problem for the mafias today is not making money but justifying it.

In the Southern regions of Italy, this pressure reaches such high levels that the economic system is, particularly in specific areas, strongly compromised. The expansion of these activities in new territories in Italy could represent a serious danger for the national economy.

The political bond

"The relation with politics has to be read in that complex dimension. They (the mafiosi, nda) address a politician when no other way to obtain what is necessary remains" (Antimafia Parliamentary Commission, 1993: 27). Acquaintanceships with politicians are to be inscribed in a complex relation of mutual advantages in which parts of the ruling class cooperate in order to maintain their power. From the mafiosi's point of view, it is an important way of consolidating consensus and providing themselves with "high-level" protection.

In the early nineties, the information given by a number of *pentiti* (police informers) (ex-bosses of the caliber of Tommaso Buscetta, Antonino Calderone, Gaspare Mutolo and many others) has made clear the importance for the mafiosi of becoming acquainted with politicians at different levels, from the local to the national. Tommaso Buscetta declared in 1993 in front of the Antimafia Parliamentary Commission that the "Mafioso has always been looking for political support [. . .]. I myself, in 1962 when I used to import butter in Milan, had my politicians to address to have the import licence" (Antimafia Parliamentary Commission, 1993: 206). And Gaspare Mutolo stated: "for instance, if a person was looking for a job [. . .] he addressed the Mafioso, instead of the employment agency, and the Mafioso would have talked to the employment officer" (Antimafia Parliamentary Commission, 1993: 406).

In the 1993 report of the Antimafia Parliamentary Commission it is emphasized that "[t]he relations between Cosa Nostra and institutional and professional sectors are of extraordinary importance in the strategies of the mafia-type organization" (Antimafia Parliamentary Commission, 1993).

In order to have a raw account of the phenomenon, it is useful to consider the data of the municipal councils that were dismantled because of suspected mafia infiltration.[7] From the early nineties to the end of December 2012 this decree was applied 205 times to municipal councils. Most of the dismantled councils are in the Southern regions of Italy (85 in Campania; 56 in Sicily; 53 in Calabria; 7 in Apulia). Nevertheless, it is worrying that in recent years councils in Lazio, Piedmont and Liguria have been dismantled since that testifies to the continuing geographical advance of the mafia and its ability to infiltrate the political fabric.

It is worth mentioning that four Local Health Agencies were dismantled for the same reasons. This testifies that another sector whose control is crucial for the mafiosi is the public health services because of the important economic resources connected to their management (more than 60 percent of regional public budget—in Calabria and in Sicily—is represented by it). Moreover, by controlling these services they have the possibility of consolidating social consensus through control of a primary right such as health.[8]

It is possible to suggest some hypotheses about the importance for the mafiosi of the relationship with and the control of politics. First of all, the possibility of controlling a number of local administrations is of a crucial importance in terms of the consensus the mafia boss can get from the daily managing of local public resources, whether economic or not (see, for instance, Mete, 2009).

Then the importance of the control mafiosi can exert on a local level on politics has to be referred to the control of economic resources provided by the control of public contracts, some of them of conspicuous economic importance.[9] But overall, through these alliances the *cosche* seek full social legitimacy and a stronger integration in the local economy and local politics (for the case of the 'Ndrangheta, see Forgione, 2008: 25).[10]

The local level of relationships with politicians is somehow functional to the national one, since from the control of the specific territories it is possible to build up networks of reciprocal help between mafiosi and high-level politics. Mafiosi are willing to ally themselves to members of any government parties, since their pragmatism does not allow of any ideological view. In order to focus on this strategy, aimed at receiving a kind of political protection, let me report what the Corte d'Appello wrote in its sentence against Giulio Andreotti, one of the most important and powerful Italian politicians during the so-called First Republic: "Senator Giulio Andreotti had full knowledge that his party companions in Sicily had maintained friendly relations with the mafia bosses [. . .]; he showed to these [the bosses] a not fictitious willingness"[11] (Sentence of the Palermo Corte d'Appello, 2 May 2003, quoted in Pepino, 2008: 419).

In search for legitimation

As we have seen, in order to provide protection for themselves, the mafiosi entered a multilevel system of relationships with members of the Italian ruling class. Far from the mafiosi being external actors endangering the order of the State, inside this articulation of relations they have been trusty allies of Italian governments in crucial moments of Italian history, and this has provided them with a kind of "hidden" legitimation.

In his discussion of Luigi Barzini's and Anton Blok's findings about the mafiosi, Mark Findlay states that

> They are an outgrowth of the particular process of state formation in Italy, presumably from the expansion of national systems of power which failed to subsume and obliterate local quasi-feudal systems of power. For long periods of time, various central governments in Italy were forced to work with the rural landlords and the mafiosi whom they helped to create and patronise. The central government was continually compromised by the forces of traditional corruption and partisanship.
>
> *(Findlay, 2004: 152)*

This is a long history, which started immediately after the national unification process, when the so-called "briganti" were considered a danger to the affluent classes, as well to the Italian authorities, much more than the mafiosi. That is when the mafiosi started to be the instruments of the so-called "manutengoli," that is, members of the ruling classes who were accomplices and protectors of the mafiosi in a relationship of reciprocal advantage. According to the historian Salvatore Lupo, Raffaele Palizzolo, "charged as 'manutengolo,' could be remembered after years as being a 'champion of morality,' the leader of the owners' league in the resistance against the brigantaggio" (Lupo, 1996: 84). Raffaele Palizzolo was a Palermo municipal councilor and then member of the Italian Parliament who was accused of being the instigator of the murder of the Marquis Emanuele Notarbartolo on 1 February 1893. This fact is considered to be the first mafia murder of a prominent figure and it is worth mentioning that the assassins were two mafiosi, Matteo Filippello and Giuseppe Fontana.

Some decades later, the mafiosi played a controversial role during the landing in Sicily of the Allied forces. Lucky Luciano, a Mafioso who had emigrated to the United States, after complex and unclear events in which mafiosi like Vito Genovese and masonic powers took part, would seem to have been put in charge of facilitating the landing in Sicily of the Allied forces at the end of World War II. This operation—whose real significance and the mafia's role in it are still not clear (see Lupo, 1996)—was, nevertheless, crucial to legitimate the Sicilian mafiosi in the post-war Italian political fabric. With regard to Luciano, the *pentito* Tommaso Buscetta said:

> He [Luciano] told me about his role during the Allied landing. He placed his influence on Cosa Nostra at the disposal of the success of the operation without bloodshed. And in fact the Americans took a good walk in Sicily.
>
> *(Arlacchi, 1994: 51)*

Moreover, in Sicily and in Calabria at that time the peasants' leagues were demanding a new system of agricultural ownership in which resources (in particular land) were to be given directly to the peasants. This attempt was opposed by the owners of the land, who often utilized the violence of the mafiosi against the peasants demanding land (see Lupo, 1996; Santino, 2009). The Portella della Ginestra attack on unarmed peasants on 1 May 1947—for which the bandit Salvatore Giuliano was charged—is a blatant example of this strategy of defending traditional interests and order. In those years a number of labor union members were killed by the mafia in Sicily, among them, Accursio Miraglia (January 4 1947), Placido Rizzotto (March 10 1948), Calogero Cangelosi (April 2 1948) and many others in the years that followed.

Another obscure period of Italian history in which interests of some hidden powers inside the state encountered some mafia strategies was during the attempted *coup d'état* planned by the general Junio Valerio Borghese at the end of 1970. Important mafia bosses such as Tommaso Buscetta, Salvatore Greco and Luciano Liggio took part in the planning of the conspiracy to give support to the subversive armies in Sicily; the same happened in Calabria, where the

De Stefano family was involved in the conspiracy by means of the subversive political right as well as members of the secret services (cf. Ciconte, 2008: 92–3). This fact testifies to the interests of the mafiosi in taking part in the political conflict even in extreme cases, such as an attempted coup, in order to exert continuous pressure on politics.

In the middle of seventies, the Calabrian *cosche* decided to deal more effectively with their relationships with masonic lodges and other hidden powers of the Italian State in order to consolidate their legitimation inside the articulation of the power system in Italy. That is the reason why a number of *doti*, that is levels endowed with high prestige and, consequently, decisional power, were introduced, starting with the *Santa* (see Gratteri and Nicaso, 2006: 75; Ciconte, 2008: 97). The persons belonging to those levels of the organization have the exclusive power of staying in contact with the so-called "gray area" of Italian power in order to consolidate their hidden legitimation. They are a kind of *diplomatic corps* of the mafiosi.

Transnational business activities and the search for a second legitimation

> One shipment which arrived at Montreal in October 1974, most likely choreographed by the transnational Cuntrera-Caruana-Rizzuto factions of the Cotroni decina, consisted of 5.5 kilos of pharmaceutical cocaine that had been shipped in London, England, and disappeared from a bonded warehouse at Dorval Airport.
>
> *(Schneider, 2009: 506)*

From the mid-seventies, the Cuntrera-Caruana and Rizzuto families of Cosa Nostra achieved a leading position in international drug trafficking especially because of their ability to work in Montreal (a very important crossroad in the drug traffic for the North American continent and where cocaine processing laboratories had been set up) in close relation with South American importers. It is worth mentioning that those families have been established in Venezuela since the seventies in order to consolidate their strategic position and rule in drug trafficking. Some years later, in the Pizza Connection Trial evidence was given of a huge heroin trafficking operation, the organizer of which was the Sicilian boss Gaetano Badalamenti: in the seventies, the mafiosi, in a "franchise agreement with American organized crime groups" (Roth, 2010: 73) set up a multimillion business using a nationwide network of pizzerias for distribution.

Partly because of the Italian State's reaction against Cosa Nostra after the murders of judges Falcone and Borsellino, from the mid-nineties Calabrian mafia groups became very important actors in the worldwide cocaine market and reached their peak in the 2000s.

> By 2005 the area around Locri on Calabria's east coast was deemed the narco-capital of Italy. Links were discovered between the eastern 'Ndrangheta and Colombian, Turkish, German, Dutch, Belgium, and French criminal organizations. Two investigations—"Borsalino" and "Super Gordo"—yielded players in several countries, including Canada. Arrests in Calabria were made in Platì, Marina di Gioiosa, and San Luca, all key towns in the growth of the *'ndrangheta.*
>
> *(Nicaso and Lamothe, 2005: 29)*

Particularly relevant is the evidence that has emerged from the so-called "Decollo" inquiry which testifies to the high favor and the reputation of Italian mafias among other criminal groups. Actually the inquiry has revealed cocaine trafficking groups of the Calabrian mafia planned with the right-wing paramilitary army called the AUC (Autodefensas Unidas de Colombia).[12]

Italian mafias operate within a huge network of illicit markets thanks to alliances in many parts of the world and to their subsequent control of crucial functions for the carrying out of this trafficking. On the global stage, the mafias are becoming

> a true power system developed at the border between what is licit and what is illicit, by mixing together typical elements of the socio-political behavior with those typical of the economic ones. [Their] success derives from the capability to take together local and global better than the backward model of the national state can do.
>
> (*Armao, 2000: 298*)

On the basis of this suggestion, it is possible to forecast a slow move towards the managing of the illicit aspects of the licit economy. This pertains essentially to illicit waste disposal, since it represents an important part of its budget that the industrial system is interested in cutting.[13] Moreover, it is worth mentioning too that in times of global crisis, the mafias, through the revenues from their illicit business activities, are introducing significant monetary resources into a thirsty economy. The "Metropolis" inquiry, carried out in the first months of 2013 by the District Antimafia Agency of Reggio Calabria, shows an impressive money-laundering system through the selling of tourist products in very upmarket villages in Calabria, allegedly made with money from drug trafficking in Great Britain and in Ireland.

"The ability to make money through money, to finance other activities through accumulated illegal capital has multiplied the power of the 'Ndrangheta members enormously" (Pellegrini, 1997: 74). It has multiplied, too, the chances of becoming a crucial—and somehow tolerated—actor in the licit economic system.

Notes

1 Pino Arlacchi in one his subsequent books (1994) has honorably recognized his under-evaluation of the mafias' organizational aspects.

2 It is worth mentioning the proposal by Francesca Longo (2010) for a general definition of Organized Crime to keep together the local and the transnational level: "Organized crime is, at the same time, a contextualized phenomenon which is strongly connected with local dynamics, and a transnational reality in that different organized groups create reciprocal links, structures of interdependency and forms of cooperation which affect the global system. Secondly, it permits us to govern in a more coherent way the activities of prevention, tackling and combating organized crime and TOC both at national and/or international levels" (Longo, 2010: 27).

3 I want to mention here that the 'Ndrangheta is based on family groups, called *'ndrine*, which can be anyone exerting independent power in their specific territories. The only superior organism, the *crimine*, has coordinating and representative functions. In contrast, Cosa Nostra has a structure based on a territorial division and has a vertical structure: each group is subordinated to the ones above.

4 This is an ancestral myth widely considered as constitutive of all the mafia organizations: the three knights, belonging to the Garduna, a secret sect, were imprisoned for thirty long years because they had avenged the honor of their sister. After their imprisonment, they decided to remain in Italy and took different paths. Osso went to Sicily, where he founded the mafia; Mastrosso went to Calabria and founded the 'Ndrangheta, while Carcagnosso, once he had arrived in Campania, founded the Camorra. As we can see, the myth of the three knights is aimed at describing the mafia's organizations as stemming from a culture characterized by a strong attachment to traditional values of honor.

5 In 2011 (data from Dia, 2011, II), cases of damage, mainly to shops, numbered 388,207; there were a little more than ten thousand (10,075) cases of damage followed by fires. Extortions number more than five thousand (5,293). With regard to damage followed by fires, in the second half of 2011 the majority is concentrated in the Southern regions (1,186 in Sicily; 606 in Calabria; 317 in Campania; and 753 in Apulia); nevertheless, in Northern regions, where the presence of the mafias is relatively recent, such as Lombardy, the same data is significant (418) as it is in Lazio (331). The data on the

number of extortions is particularly significant since Lombardy is the second region in Italy (395) for the diffusion of this type of crime.

6 http://rotocalcoafricano.wordpress.com/2012/09/20/ndrangheta-e-coltan/

7 In 1991 in the Italian system the legislative decree N. 164 allowing the dissolution of municipal councils and other local policy's agencies in case of suspected mafia infiltration was adopted.

8 Moreover, the influence over the health system may be a good occasion for the bosses in jail to illegally lighten their conditions of imprisonment. In Calabria, in 2012 judicial inquiries pointed out the role of complaisant physicians working in two private clinics where the bosses used to be admitted on the basis of false medicals by their testifying to a state of mental illness (Badolati and Sabato, 2012).

9 In the recent past the Calabrian *cosche* managed to control the public contracts for the modernization of the A3 highway, the principal highway in Southern Italy, by imposing on contractors a fee of 3 percent (as "Tamburo" and "Arca" judicial inquiries made clear). In general the *cosche*, particularly in the traditional territories, but also in some regions of expansion, control the building sector from concrete to asphalting, and manage to distort the assignments of public contracts to the firms with which they are in collusion (Antimafia Parliamentary Commission, 2012: 111–13).

10 The 'Ndrangheta, for instance, has from the seventies come into contact with the Masonic lodges, by setting up a kind of "cupola," the so called "Santa" whose function is to keep in touch with politicians, professionals and masonic lodges. Cosa Nostra has a long history of connections with politicians.

11 In the sentence, Andreotti's role in covering the bosses' responsibilities in the murder of the former President of the Sicilian Region Piersanti Mattarella is criticized.

12 The "Crimine 3" inquiry carried on by the Dda (District Antimafia Agency) has confirmed the great ability of the 'Ndrangheta to work together with other criminal groups in huge criminal networks—in the specific case the Mexican cartel "Las Zetas," and this confirms the attitude of the mafias to working in criminal consortia (Nicaso and Lamothe, 1995).

13 According to the 2012 Legambiente Report on the so-called *Ecomafie*, since 2006 there have been 1,229 inquiries into organized illicit waste traffic and more than 3,500 people who have been reported. These activities involve Italy as well as some 23 different countries around the world. Through these activities, a huge amount of waste is taken from the legal disposal firms' system, whose processing costs are significantly higher.

References

Antimafia Parliamentary Commission (1993). *Relazione sui rapporti tra mafia e politica.* In O. Barrese (ed.), *Mafia, politica, pentiti.* Soveria Mannelli: Rubbettino.

Antimafia Parliamentary Commission (2012). *Relazione.* Rome.

Arlacchi, P. (1983). *La mafia imprenditrice.* Bologna: Il Mulino.

Arlacchi, P. (1994). *Addio a Cosa Nostra. La vita di Tommaso Buscetta.* Milano: Rizzoli.

Armao, F. (2000). *Il sistema mafia.* Turin: Bollati-Boringhieri.

Badolati, A. and Sabato, A. (2012). *Codice rosso. Sanità tra sperperi, politica e 'Ndrangheta.* Cosenza: Pellegrini.

Blok, A. (1974). *The Mafia of a Sicilian Village, 1860–1960: A Study of Violent Peasant Entrepreneurs.* New York: Harper and Row.

Castagna, S. (1967). *Tu devi uccidere.* Milan: il Momento.

Ciconte, E. (1996). *Processo alla 'Ndrangheta.* Rome-Bari: Laterza.

Ciconte, E. (2008). *'Nrandgheta.* Soveria Mannelli: Rubbettino.

Dia (Direzione Investigativa Antimafia) (2011). *Semestrial report II.* Rome.

Finckenauer, J. O. (2005). Problems of Definition: What is Organized Crime? *Trends in Organized Crime* 8(4), 63–83.

Findlay, M. (2004). *The Gobalization of Crime.* Cambridge: Cambridge University Press.

Forgione, F. (2008). *'Ndrangheta. Boss, luoghi e affari della mafia più potente del mondo.* Rome: Baldini Castoldi Dalai.

Gambino, S. (1975). *La mafia in Calabria.* Reggio Calabria: Parallelo 38.

Gratteri, N. and Nicaso, A. (2006). *Fratelli di sangue. La 'ndrangheta tra arretratezza e modernità.* Cosenza: Pellegrini.

Hess, H. (1970). *Mafia.* Rome-Bari: Laterza 1991.

Legambiente (2012). *Ecomafie. Rapporto 2012.* Rome.

Levi, M. (1996). Social and Unsocial Capital: A Review Essay of Robert Putnam's *Making Democracy Work. Politics and Society* 24(1), 45–55.

Longo, F. (2010). *Discoursing Organized Crime.* In F. Longo, F. Allum, D. Irrera and P. A. Kostakos (eds.), *Defining and Defying Organized Crime. Discourse, Perceptions and Reality.* London and New York: Routledge.

Lupo, S. (1996). *Storia della mafia. Dalle origini ai nostri giorni.* Rome: Donzelli.

Mete, V. (2009). *Fuori dal comune. Lo scioglimento delle amministrazioni locali per infiltrazioni mafiose.* Acireale-Rome: Bonanno.

Minuti, D. and Nicaso, A. (1994). *'Ndranghete: le filiali della mafia calabrese.* Vibo Valentia: Monteleone.

Nicaso, A. and Lamothe, L. (1995). *Global Mafia: The New World Order of Organized Crime.* Toronto: Macmillan.

Nicaso, A. and Lamothe, L. (2005). *Angels, Mobsters & Narco-Terrorists. The Rising Menace of Global Criminal Empires.* Mississauga: Wiley.

Paoli, L. (2003). *Mafia Brotherhood: Organized Crime, Italian Style.* Oxford: Oxford University Press.

Paoli, L. (2004). Italian Organised Crime: Mafia Associations and Criminal Enterprises. *Global Crime* 6(1), 19–31.

Parini, E. G. (2003). Miti e ritualità dell'affiliazione alla mafia. Note per una definizione del fenomeno mafioso a partire dalla sua segretezza. *Ou* XIV(1), 125–31.

Parini, E. G. (2011). *'Ndrangheta. Un prisma di potere.* In A. Mammone, N. Tranfaglia and G. A. Veltri (eds.), *Un paese normale? Saggi sull'Italia contemporanea.* Milan: Dalai.

Pellegrini, A. (1997). The 'Ndrangheta: an Account of the Situation. Direzione Investigativa Antimafia, Centro Operativo Reggio Calabria. Summary Translation in *Trends in Organize Crime* Winter 1997, 70–5.

Pepino, L. (2008). *Politica e mafia.* In L. Pepino and M. Mareso (eds.), *Nuovo dizionario di mafia e antimafia.* Turin: EGA.

Putnam, R., Leonardi, R. and Nanetti, R. Y. (1993). *Making Democracy Work: Civic Tradition in Modern Italy.* Princeton, NJ: Princeton University Press.

Roth, M. P. (2010). *Globalized Crime. A Reference Handbook.* Santa Barbara, CA: ABC-CLIO.

Santino, U. (1995). *La mafia interpretata.* Soveria Mannelli: Rubbettino.

Santino, U. (2009). *Storia del movimento antimafia.* Rome: Editori Riuniti.

Schneider, S. (2009). *ICED. The Story of Organized Crime in Canada.* Mississauga: Wiley.

Siebert, R. (1996). *Mafia e quotidianità.* Milan: il Saggiatore.

PART II

Democratic life and institutions

8

INSTITUTIONS AND THE POLITICAL SYSTEM IN ITALY

A story of failure

Martin J. Bull

Introduction

Italy is exceptional amongst advanced western democracies for the extraordinary focus it has placed in the past thirty years on reforming its political system through institutional reform – and largely failing to do so. In the first thirty years of the Republic, Italian democracy was perceived to have been unstable and functioning poorly, but little focus was placed on institutions as being at the heart of the problem. From the early 1980s, however, the political class saw a solution in changing the institutional framework of the Republic, a position which was reinforced by the implosion of the party system in the early 1990s, and the beginning of what most observers viewed as a transition to a more stable and effective democracy. A change in the electoral system in 1993 away from proportionality towards plurality – forced on an unwilling political class by popular referendum – and the subsequent bipolarizing effect on the party system led to an assumption that reforming institutions would be a natural and fundamental outcome of this process. Yet, despite significant efforts, the political class visibly failed to achieve this goal. Important reforms that were achieved (e.g. regional reform and further change to the electoral system) were regarded as largely partisan in origin and technically deficient.

This chapter first outlines the institutional framework and the functioning of the Italian political system until the early 1990s; then, second, documents the rise of institutional reform from the early 1980s and especially its trajectory since the early 1990s, highlighting the long-term failure of the political parties to achieve comprehensive reform; and third, analyses the Italian political system today and how, despite the absence of root-and-branch institutional reform, it differs in its operation from the so-called 'First Republic' as a result of the impact of a mixture of institutional and non-institutional changes.

Institutions and the functioning of Italian democracy until the 1990s

The Italian post-war settlement produced a conventional parliamentary system, albeit with some distinctive traits. It was commonly accepted that the system did not work well; yet the cause was identified not so much in the core institutions as such but in the role of the political parties and how their behaviour distorted, or at least exploited, the system's distinctive features to the detriment of the Italian democratic model (Bull, 2004).

Cabinet government never worked effectively because of the dominance of the political parties which sapped authority from the prime minister and the Cabinet. A pure PR electoral system produced a large number of political parties in parliament, with 'anti-system' parties to the left (Italian Communist Party, PCI) and right (Italian Social Movement, MSI), and with two parties (the PCI and Christian Democracy, DC) significantly bigger (in votes and seats) than the rest. The 1948 elections, conducted in a climate of Cold War hostility, established a party system that would effectively prevail until the early 1990s, based on the permanence in office of the centrist DC in alliances with parties to its immediate right and left, the alliances designed primarily to keep out the 'anti-system' PCI. This situation persisted despite the electoral strength of the PCI in several communes, provinces and 'red regions', which saw the party playing a positive role in the governance of the country. The closest the PCI came to national office was during the Historic Compromise (1976–9) when – in a situation of economic and political crisis – the party allowed DC minority governments to stay in office through the former's policy of 'not no-confidence'. This party system had an important conditioning effect on institutions and their performance.

Governments were formed on the basis of post-election negotiations focused primarily on the allocation of ministerial posts amongst the different parties, rather than on policies, which also for that reason did not figure prominently in election campaigns. The prime minister had little control over his ministers since they perceived themselves as accountable to their parties, which had secured their appointment. Ministries were often treated as fiefdoms by ministers, safe in the knowledge that, for a prime minister, sacking a minister could result in the collapse of his government. Prime ministers were, therefore, 'mediators' rather than 'authoritative leaders'.

Governments, moreover, were weak and unstable in parliament since their legislation and their own fate depended less on their policies than on internal factional struggles in the parties, often taking place outside the parliamentary arena. A government rarely fell as a result of a vote of no confidence or parliamentary defeat, and it invariably produced 'peripheral turnover' (in place of alternation) through a reshuffling of ministries amongst the parties.

Parliament also found its powers circumscribed by the self-same factors. The power to dissolve a government through a vote of no confidence was rarely exercised, it was not an arena for the proper discussion of policy differences, and it failed to exercise properly its watchdog function. Four structural features of parliament reinforced these weaknesses, and in particular made the formation and processing of substantive policy difficult: genuine bicameralism (both chambers with identical powers); extraordinary powers of the committees system (which could pass some bills into law without going through the parliament in plenary); no limits on private members' legislation; and the use of the secret ballot on legislation voted on in parliament (allowing members of the government to vote secretly against a bill).

The result for policymaking was inefficiency and an absence of coherence. Because of the way they were formed, governments rarely had a clear programme of legislation they wished to achieve. As a result of their coalitional nature, they struggled both to design substantive legislation and then to get it passed either in a timely manner or without substantial amendment.

To circumvent this problem, governments frequently resorted to repeated use of decree legislation (where a decree would be issued which had to be ratified by parliament within sixty days, but the decree was simply reiterated when parliament failed to act). At the same, time a large amount of legislation of a particularistic nature was produced by parliament, often originating in private members' bills and passed through the committee system.

If we use Lijphart's (1999) widely accepted typology, Italy in the post-war period until the 1990s can be described as a 'consensual' rather than 'majoritarian' democracy (Morlino, 2013). Yet, it was a curious, or at least malfunctioning, form of consensualism, characterized by several features which tended to work against each other. On the one hand, the nature of the party system produced a system of predominant party rule and an absence of alternation in government. On the other hand, the design and operation of the institutions entrenched the power of 'minorities' (within both the governing coalition and the opposition), which made governments highly unstable and policymaking ineffective. This paradox of 'stable instability' (Bull and Newell, 1993) was supported by a party system which proved adept at adapting to absorb the increasing pressures on the system and thereby retaining its anomaly (absence of alternation in government): from centrism in the 1950s to the centre-left in the 1960s to the Historic Compromise in the 1970s and the *pentapartito* in the 1980s. This situation led to the development of a 'spoils system' in which state positions could be used clientelistically to reinforce electoral support, a system which provided a foundation for more insidious forms of corruption in the 1980s.

Institutional reform: goals, debate, achievements, effects

While it was widely recognized that the political system did not perform well, there was little focus, before the early 1980s, on institutional reform as a means of overcoming the deficiencies.[1] In the 1980s, the system's distortions became more acute, the parties became trapped in their own clientelistic logic, the party system (after the *pentapartito*) had no further coalition options and the system unknowingly approached its dénouement (Bull and Newell, 2005: ch. 1). In this situation the political class turned to root-and-branch institutional reform as the solution to the system's problems.

This had been originally launched in 1976 as the 'great reform' by the leader of the Italian Socialist Party (PSI) Bettino Craxi, but was only first attempted when Craxi became Prime Minister in 1983, thus starting a 'long quest in vain' on the part of the political class (Bull and Pasquino, 2009). The goals and procedures adopted were nothing short of ambitious. The notion of a 'great reform' meant not just root-and-branch in substance but, as it were, a 'Constituent Assembly' in style, although on a smaller scale. Large unwieldy Constitutional Commissions were the preferred mode, with representatives of all the parties present. The first attempt – the Bozzi Commission (1983–5) – set the trend. It worked for two years but it failed to meet its goals through division and partisanship. The second attempt – the De Mita/Iotti Commission (1992–4) – was set up in the throes of the dramatic upheaval in the party system (which entailed the wholesale destruction or transformation of the existing parties and the birth of new parties), and the Commission died with the end of the legislature. There were high hopes for the third attempt – the Bicameral Commission (*Bicamerale*) of 1997–8 – because this had been established on the back of the transformation of the party system – which had, by then, gained some stability – and two changes to the electoral system extracted from the political class by popular referendum: the removal of preferences in 1991 and a shift from proportionality to majoritarianism in 1993 (for one Chamber, followed in 1994 by similar legislation for the other).

The bipolarizing impact of the electoral reform on the new and transformed parties became visible in 1994 as two broad coalitions – centre-left and centre-right – took shape, with the centre of the spectrum no long acting as the fulcrum of governing coalitions but increasingly squeezed itself, and the 1994 and 1996 elections witnessed the achievement of alternation in office. It seemed natural, therefore, that the new 'majoritarian' drives in the system should be facilitated – if not a transition to a new model of democracy completed – by significant changes to the Constitution. Yet, the proposals produced after eighteen months' work by the Bicameral Commission (chaired by Massimo D'Alema) were sunk in parliament by Berlusconi's withdrawal of his party's support for the project. Berlusconi's action was commonly viewed as a reaction to the commission's failure to circumscribe the role of the judiciary. However, the institutional reforms proposed by the commission were widely perceived to be poorly conceived compromises and unlikely to produce the intended effects (Pasquino, 2000).

If this action confirmed the partisan stamp of the institutional reform debate (originally placed on it by Craxi, whose proposals seemed designed to break the PCI–DC hegemony and increase the powers of his own prime ministerial office), the centre-left subsequently destroyed an apparent 'sacred cow' designed to offset the dangers of such partisanship: that institutional reform should be a product of wide-ranging consultation and consensus across party lines. In 1999–2001, the centre-left governments drove through a significant reform of the Constitution on the back of its majority. Following the so-called Bassanini reforms in 1997, which empowered central government to transfer administrative responsibilities to the regions in their area of competence and placed limits on central controls, a constitutional law was passed in 1999 which strengthened the role of regional presidents mainly through making them directly elected, and Title V of the Constitution was revised, which provided greater legislative autonomy to the regions and reduced further the scope for centralized control over their acts. This reform, which was widely regarded as prompted by a partisan agenda (Massetti and Toubeau, 2013: 367–8), was opposed by the centre-right, which petitioned a 'confirmative' referendum (made possible since the reform had not been passed with a two-thirds majority), which took place on 7 October 2001, the Italian people approving the changes, albeit on a very low turnout of 34 per cent.

In the short term, this reform was perhaps less significant for its substance than the fact that it had been passed *a colpi di maggioranza* (on the strength of its parliamentary majority), which thus treated the Constitution like any other law and undermined its sacrosanct nature. This set a precedent which the centre-right, on the back of a decisive electoral victory, did not hesitate to mimic, but on a much larger scale. Indeed, the centre-right's constitutional reform proposals of 2005 promised to rewrite about a third of the Constitution (most of Part II). The principal two aspects of the proposed reform concerned wide-ranging 'devolution' to the regions and an increase in the powers of the prime minister, alongside important changes to parliament. The reform was highly controversial not only because of its scale and the manner in which it was passed (using Article 138 of the Constitution to bundle the different proposals together to be voted en bloc and then mustering its majority to see it passed) but also because it was seen to be the product of an unwieldy compromise between the different parties of the governing coalition and therefore technically deficient, if not dangerous (Sartori, 2006: 54–5).

Part of that compromise involved, as a separate matter, reintroducing proportionality into the electoral law. In December 2005, shortly after definitive parliamentary approval of the constitutional reform package, the centre-right changed the electoral law which had served for the previous three national elections (1994, 1996, 2001). The 1993 reform, admittedly, had not delivered everything expected of it. Indeed, some argued that, as a mixed system, it delivered the worst aspects of both the proportional and plurality models. The need to construct all-encompassing coalitions to secure the single-member constituencies increased the bargaining power of small parties and led to conflict-ridden coalitions. At the same time, the proportional component of the electoral law exacerbated the fragmentation of the party system, with parties retaining their identities and undermining the consolidation of the coalitions. However, the efforts of those who favoured shifting the system further in a 'majoritarian' direction had been thwarted by a large number of 'proportionalists' who campaigned against and successively defeated (through the participation rate not reaching quorum) two referenda in 1999 and 2000 which would have introduced a majoritarian system. Then in December 2005, with the centre-right having been defeated in the 2005 regional elections and opinion polls predicting a centre-left victory in the 2006 national elections, the centrist Union of the Democratic Centre (UDC) extracted from an all too willing Berlusconi a return to proportionality, partly because it ensured the UDC's support for the constitutional reform and partly because the new law (through a 25 per cent bonus to the winning coalition) was designed to place a cap on the size of the likely centre-left victory. The reform was 'elite-imposed' and unashamedly partisan in its origin and design, Roberto Calderoli (the minister responsible) himself describing it as a *porcata* (pig's dinner) (Baldini, 2011: 654–5).[2]

The passage of the electoral reform poured further fuel on the fire of the institutional reform debate, and the centre-left managed to sink the constitutional proposals through a popular referendum. This resulted in an unequivocal entanglement of constitutional reform in partisan debate, since the referendum took place in June 2006 only two months after the national elections, the parties lining up for or against the referendum according to coalition lines. In short, a referendum on one of the most significant reforms since the birth of the Republic became little more than a political instrument of the two coalitions. The referendum's decisive defeat of the proposals (61.7 per cent against 38.3 per cent on a turnout of 53.7 per cent) led to a pause in attempts to achieve root-and-branch institutional reform (as well as attempts to reform the Constitution by majority), but it did not end the institutional reform debate itself. On the contrary, nothing could quash the political parties' putative aspiration for a 'modernization' of Italian democracy and their conviction that it could not be achieved without institutional reform (Bull, 2007).

Following the centre-left election victory in 2006, the Constitutional Affairs Commission was tasked with identifying specific reforms which might improve the functioning of the Constitution, rather than producing a comprehensive blueprint for constitutional reform: 'constitutional gardening' as it was dubbed at the time. This was an all-party affair and it presented its proposals (known as *Il Projetto Violante*, after its main spokesman, Luciano Violante) to the Chamber of Deputies in 2007, but its work effectively died with the collapse of the government in 2008 and fresh elections. The Berlusconi government elected in 2008 committed itself to constitutional reform, including a reform of the electoral system before the next election. But both these projects died with the collapse of the Berlusconi government in the midst of the economic crisis in November 2011. The Berlusconi government, however, did pass a reform introducing 'fiscal federalism', although the full implementation of the reform depended on enacting legislation which never saw the light of day.

The Monti 'technical' government which followed the Berlusconi government in 2011 had primarily economic aims, but the parties supporting him also committed themselves to reforming the electoral law before the next elections. This they failed to do and the February 2013 elections took place with the old electoral law. The outcome of those elections produced a 'perfect storm' in Italian politics: no party or coalition secured an absolute majority in both houses and was therefore able to form a government; the President of the Republic, Giorgio Napolitano, no longer had the power to dissolve parliament and call fresh elections because he was in the so-called 'white semester' (the last forty days of his office); and the outgoing technocratic prime minister was no longer credible as the focus for a continuing technocratic solution since he had entered the election as a politician at the head of a party list.

In this situation, President Napolitano, in effectively his last substantial act of his term of office, set up a working group of 'ten wise men' who were entrusted with the task of identifying a set of proposed reforms which might provide the basis for the development of a government programme which Napolitano could hand on to his successor. The 'ten wise men' divided themselves into two working groups, one producing a report on socio-economic reforms and the other on institutional reforms (Mauro *et al.*, 2013). The fact that, in the midst of what was Italy's worst political crisis since 1992, a working group was established to identify a set of institutional reforms for the country was testimony to the importance with which such reforms were viewed, nearly forty years after Craxi's first initiative.

When the parties proved unable to agree on and vote in a new presidential candidate, they turned to Napolitano, who agreed to stand for a second term of office. When Napolitano was sworn in to office in April 2013, he delivered (in his acceptance speech) a devastating indictment of the politicians and political parties for their failure to deliver urgently needed institutional reforms. He said that what had prevailed over many years was 'contradictions, delays, hesitations . . . calculations of expediency, tactical manoeuvres and instrumental moves'. He described as 'unforgivable' the failure to reform the 2005 electoral law, especially when the Constitutional Court had called on Parliament to review specifically the clause providing a premium to the majority party irrespective of any threshold of seats or votes. He argued that this had helped create fierce competition between parties to secure the premium, difficulties in forming a government after the election and further citizen disenchantment because of being unable to choose their representatives directly. It was also equally unforgivable, he said, to have done nothing about Part II of the Constitution, where even reforms of a limited nature, laboriously agreed, had then been sunk, and where there seemed to be an obsession with protecting, at all costs, 'symmetric bicameralism'. Napolitano went on to argue that the working group's recommendations would provide the basis for the next government and he warned the parties to live up to their responsibilities (*La Stampa*, 22 April 2013).

In short, the 'perfect storm' of the early months of 2013 brought to a head in the most dramatic manner possible the long-standing failure of the political class to achieve institutional reform. It symbolized how fanciful it had been – even in the context of the partial renewal of the Italian political class in the 1990s – to have imagined that there existed a consensus on reinforcing the system's new majoritarian tendencies by carrying through appropriate institutional reforms.

Yet, Napolitano's attempt to overcome this deadlock was not without problems. While the government of Enrico Letta that was cobbled together was not a 'technical' government as such, it resembled closely its predecessor (Monti's) in so far as it was effectively presidentially 'owned' and 'transitional' in nature, with a limited (eighteen-month) tenure and a programme shaped from above. In this way, the report of the 'ten wise men' and Napolitano's savage indictment of the political parties made electoral and institutional reform a central tenet of the Letta government. In June 2013 Letta set up a 'Commission for the Reform of the Constitution' consisting of 35 people, mostly from universities, tasked with mapping out possible reforms, based on the same objectives that inspired the work of Napolitano's 'wise men': 'to revitalize democratic participation, assure efficiency and stability to the political system and reinforce public ethics' (Commissione per le riforme costituzionali, 2013: 6). The commission submitted its report to the prime minister in September 2013. It was highly generic in nature and reflected divisions inside the commission, especially over the broad direction that institutional reform should take (offering three possible options) but nevertheless managed to propose certain common reforms, including: reduction in the number of members of parliament; the overcoming of 'symmetric bicameralism; a strengthening of the government in parliament; and an overhaul of sub-national government' (ibid.).

In parallel with the work on the Report, a ddl (*disegno di legge* or draft law – no. 813) was formulated and presented to parliament in June 2013. This draft law was less controversial for the 'Committee of 40' it proposed to establish specifically to draft a package of constitutional reforms (i.e. based on the Commission's ideas) than for the procedures it outlined to achieve the reform, which would have set aside one of the provisions contained in Article 138 of the Constitution. This article requires constitutional amendments to be passed by each chamber after two successive debates at intervals of three months. The draft law reduced this to just over a month, and at the same time contained other provisions to ensure that the reform would be achieved within eighteen months of the draft law being passed.

In view of the wide scope of the committee's brief – the examination of Titles I, II, III and V of the Constitution pertaining to the form of state, government and bicameralism, as well as considering (under ordinary legislation) proposals for reform of the electoral system – the provisions in the draft law 813 were highly controversial, not only amongst the opposition (and especially the populist Five Star Movement (of Beppe Grillo), which filibustered the bill), but amongst elements of those parties supporting the government. The bill was approved twice by the Senate and once by the Chamber of Deputies, to which it was returned for a required second reading. However, by then, the procedural provisions had lost the bill all credibility, and the prime minister eventually, in December 2013, formally withdrew it, thus ending this attempt at constitutional reform.

In the same month, a Constitutional Court ruling on the existing electoral system compounded the failure of the draft law. The Letta government had not overlooked electoral reform. The Senate had set up a commission to consider options for electoral reform, which would then be considered by the Committee of 40, but progress had been interminably slow. The withdrawal of the draft law 813 coincided with a ruling by the Constitutional Court – in response to a case brought to it by a lawyer – that the existing electoral law (the so-called Porcellum) was unconstitutional. The Court's reasoning (published in mid-January 2014) focused on both the premium awarded to the winning party and the lack of preferences given to voters. The effect of its ruling was that the provisions invalidating the electoral law had to be removed, which meant – unless parliament carried through electoral reform before the subsequent election – a return to a proportional electoral system.

The combination of this latest failure to achieve both electoral and institutional reform threw the issues back into the political arena and caused an apparent 'mad dash' for reform of both institutions and electoral system in early 2014, initiated and primarily shaped by the newly elected leader of the Democratic Party, Matteo Renzi, who started work on trying to forge agreement with the other parties on a package of proposals. In early 2014, however, it remained uncertain what chances of success this latest attempt would have.

In short, the severity of the crisis of early 2013 led many into false expectations: that what had proved impossible to achieve through consensus over forty years could then be secured on the back of Napolitano's admonishment of political parties for their 'irresponsible' behaviour. Today there is little evidence that the constraining factors have disappeared, and notably the extent to which partisan considerations on the part of parties override any concerns about national interest and coherence in the design of reform proposals (Pasquino, 1998). Italy is almost unique in so far as 'a lack of agreement on the fundamental rules, mechanisms and institutions shaping Italian democracy has pervaded the system for so long it seems to have become a predominant element in the country's political culture' (Bull and Pasquino, 2009: 34).

The Italian political system today

The long-term failings of the political class, however, do not mean that the Italian political system remains unchanged. On the contrary, several reforms have changed the way in which institutions and the system function today compared with the period until the early 1990s. It is clear that, if the political system until the early 1990s was a 'consensual' democracy, then the changes of the 1990s and 2000s have introduced a stronger element of majoritarianism in the way in which that democracy operates, although this trajectory (as an expressed aspiration on the part of so many) remains incomplete. The principal motivator of that change, however, has not been institutional reform as such but a combination of changes in the electoral and party systems.

The principal development (which itself has been the cause of other changes) has been the bipolarization of the party system (under the impact of its implosion and the 1993 electoral reform) into two broad blocs (centre-left and centre-right), with the accompanying disappearance of anti-system parties and the decline of the centre as the pivot around which coalitions are made (Millefiorini, 2007), and a significant turnover in the political class (see Verzichelli in this volume). Bipolarization has consequently led to alternation in government and a greater stability in the duration of governments, relative to those before the early 1990s (when the average life of a government was almost half of that today). This has led to an increased focus on the design of policy manifestos at elections and use of them in election campaigns, with a stronger sense of a government being elected to carry through a programme, as opposed to a programme being a by-product of a post-election set of compromises over the formation of government and allocation of ministries.

These changes have, with other factors, had spillover effects on the relationship between the legislature and the executive, with a 'shift . . . from a parliament-centred system to a government-centred system' (Fabbrini, 2012: 15). Successive governments from the 1990s onwards – partly drawing on reforms already introduced in the 1980s, such as a significant restriction on the use of the secret ballot – have drawn on the implications, obligations and expectations of bipolarization to increase their muscle in the policymaking process through various changes and developments, including: control over the parliamentary agenda; a transformation in the role of Speaker, who has become responsible for oversight of the viability of government bills (and as a consequence of which Speakers of the two Houses are now regularly elected from the majority coalition); greater use of decree laws and ability to transform those decree laws into legislative acts within the required sixty days, especially following the Constitutional Court's ruling in 1996 that constant reiteration was illegitimate; a marked increase in the use of legislative decrees, promulgated by government on the basis of prior authorization of parliament (according to 'directive principles and criteria') and having the immediate force of proper laws; more extensive use of 'regulations', which are legislative provisions issued directly by the government but without having the status of laws as such; greater use of the vote of confidence both to accelerate the tabling of government legislation (which is prioritized when it is subject to a vote of confidence) and to increase its likelihood of approval (since voting is by roll call, which makes it more difficult for individual MPs to vote against); and greater use of the so-called 'maxi-amendment', whereby a government amendment completely replaces a bill at the same time as integrating it with other provisions which have nothing to do with the original bill, with the possibility also of calling a vote of confidence on the amendment (Vassallo, 2007: 696–703).

This is evidenced in an improvement in public policymaking performance, with an increase in the successful passage of government legislation (including legislation linked to its manifesto programme), as part of a more general shift from 'government by transaction' – where policies are secondary to government formation – towards 'government by achievement' – entailing greater responsiveness to the wishes of the electorate, as expressed in its vote for a programme (Conti, 2012; CIRCaP, 2011). The 'centrality of parliament' of pre-1990s Italy has, therefore, been considerably undermined.

At the same time, there has been a notable shift inside the executive itself, with the rise of the prime minister as the key focal point, and therefore a shift from prime minister as 'mediator' towards prime minister as 'authoritative leader'. This is partly because of the collapse of the old parties, based on traditional organizations and ideologies, and their replacement with parties which, in many cases, resemble personal machines at the service of their leaders (of which Berlusconi's Forza Italia is the example par excellence). However, it is also because the old system of checks and balances as well as bargaining between different positions has largely unravelled and been replaced by centripetal forces converging around the prime ministership. External pressures – and notably those emanating from the European Union in a situation of economic crisis – have reinforced the strength of these centripetal forces because of the need for swift and effective responses which only a powerful Executive can provide (Calise, 2010; Fabbrini, 2012).

The rise of the Executive and within that, the prime minister's office, has been reflected in changes of an organizational nature, most of which were carried through in the 1990s: a reduction in the number of ministries and a streamlining of the ministerial apparatus; decentralization of certain public administration functions; privatization of key public and semi-public enterprises; an increase in the number of political appointees to the Civil Service (to drive through the government's programme); and reforms to rationalize the bureaucracy and improve coordination between different departments (Vassallo, 2007: 703–8). Finally, the territorial reforms carried out between 1996 and 2001 brought into effect a significant decentralization of the Italian political system, which could develop further if the necessary legislative decrees were to be passed on the back of the May 2009 'framework law' on fiscal federalism (Massetti and Toubeau, 2013: 373–6).[3]

Yet, in looking at the core institutions, many of the changes in operation are largely conjunctural rather than structural in nature, and therefore unstable. Indeed, some of them (use of decree legislation, votes of confidence, maxi-amendments) resemble precisely the sort of practices derided in the 'First Republic'. They represent adjustments to primarily non-institutional factors (parties, party system, electoral system – although this last has institutional aspects) which themselves are unstable and changing. The parties remain polarized, and until the 2008 elections high in number. They are effectively constrained into a bipolarized logic by an electoral law which offers a 'premium' to the winning coalition and which, because of party lists, has the effect of alienating citizens from directly choosing their representatives in parliament. While it is true that governments since the 1990s have expressed a stronger will to lead the legislative process in a stronger adversarial context, at the same time, 'parliament continues to be shaped by a structure and procedures that favour fragmentation and induce individual MPs into exploiting legislative decrees, and forcing parliament's hand, and sometimes that of its own majority, with last-minute maxi-amendments and votes of confidence' (Vassallo, 2007: 703). Analyses of policy performance over time confirm the rather ephemeral and unstable nature of the trend towards more effective majoritarian government, with marked differences not only between different governments but within the same government during its term of office, when 'centrifugal forces in the system cause government instability' (Conti, 2012: 14).[4]

Admittedly, this is not a unique situation, since the exact manner in which the institutional arrangements in any democracy will function is dependent upon various non-institutional factors. Yet the Italian case stands out for the degree of change it has undergone (from consensualism towards majoritarianism) on this basis, combined with the failure of these conjunctural changes to be reinforced or consolidated through reforms of a more lasting, structural nature.

Conclusion: whither the Italian political system?

How best can the Italian political system and the functioning of its core institutions be captured today? Under the impact of the dramatic changes of the early 1990s and the political will of (putatively 'majoritarian') reformers, the functioning of the political system has undergone change, largely through the development of adversarial politics and the adoption of some of the practices of the 'Westminster' model, something which has allowed the system to overcome the chief failure of the 'First Republic': to achieve alternation in government. At the same time, these changes, if analysed according to the different dimensions of the two Lijphartian models of democracy (consensus v. majoritarian), remain partial and incomplete, leaving Italy in a kind of hybrid state of 'adjustment and stalemate' (Morlino, 2013: 338). What Italy has experienced thus far has been a complex 'process of institutional (re-)stabilisation and negotiated change in which the "new" (or at least substantial parts of it) looks remarkably similar to the "old"' (Bull and Rhodes, 2009: 6). Moreover, even though it is difficult to envisage a complete return to the consensual model of the 'First Republic', the direction of future change is anything but predictable (Bull, 2012).

The reason for this state of affairs is that the conjunctural features of change have not been accompanied by structural reforms necessary to consolidate the majoritarian tendencies. This is not to say that there has been inactivity on the structural front. On the contrary, in some areas (e.g. territorial reform and – if one counts it as institutional – electoral reform), the opposite could be argued. Regarding the latter, it is worth nothing that 'today Italy is the only democracy in the world that finds itself discussing its third important electoral reform in less than 15 years' (Baldini, 2008: 105); yet, this is due to little more than 'electoral reform cycles' in which publicly inspired reforms are then subject to 'a backlash from the political elite who try to get more of what they want out of the system by reforming it', provoking a further backlash from the public (Baldini, 2011: 660). And regarding the former, while it is true that there have been four substantial territorial reforms since 1996, this is largely because the Northern League managed to force the two coalitions (centre-left and centre-right) to adopt an electoral logic which 'gave territorial reforms a strongly partisan flavor and heightened the salience of the territorial dimension in mainstream political competition' (Massetti and Toubeau, 2013: 376). Finally, those attempts at producing a root-and-branch overhaul of the core institutions – Bozzi (1983–5), De Mita/Iotti (1992–4), *Bicamerale* (1996–7), the centre-right's constitutional package (2005–6), the Napolitano–Letta attempt (2013) – have been subject to intense partisanship once under way, which has coloured the outcome and ensured failure.

What makes the scale of this failure all the greater is that a consensus exists and has long existed not just on the inadequacy of the existing institutional framework but also on the general trajectory that institutional reform should take ('majoritarian') *and* on the types of reforms perceived as necessary to stabilize Italian democracy around a new institutional equilibrium. If one looks at the 'high points' of the institutional reform debate over the past twenty years, from Bozzi through to the 'ten wise men' and the '35 wise men' of 2013 (and even to the proposals of Matteo Renzi in 2014), one finds a common and repeated thread of proposed reforms, including: ending symmetric bicameralism; streamlining the legislative process; reducing the size of parliament; modifying the relations between the executive and legislature; consolidating the power of the prime minister; modifying the role of the president; introducing fiscal federalism; and reforming the electoral system to stabilize the bipolar logic and the reduced number of parties.

The problem is that once the reform process is commenced and the detail of such reforms negotiated, the parties tend to adopt approaches which place their partisan interests over any national interest, which leads to conflict, procrastination, partial and poorly designed reforms and, ultimately, failure. In this way, the very process of institutional reform has, paradoxically, had the effect of delegitimizing further the existing institutional framework by simultaneously highlighting its inadequacies at the same time as the incapacity of the political elites to achieve its reform.

Notes

1 Save for the introduction of regional governments in the 1970s (supported mainly by the PCI and PSI), which did not begin to operate properly until the late 1970s, and were, in the 1980s, regarded as having failed to meet expectations.

2 Sartori, therefore, dubbed it the *Porcellum* since the 1993 reform had been called the *Mattarellum* after its chief proponent.

3 The prospects of this receded with the onset of the economic crisis, when the reform was effectively used for cutting public spending and raising taxes (Massetti, 2012) although the report of the 'Ten Wise Men' in April 2013 recommended it as 'an essential component of the policies to relaunch the country' (Mauro *et al.*, 2013: 18).

4 The 2008–11 Berlusconi government is a good example: it started out cohesive and able to legislate but then endured, from within its supporting coalition, a complete collapse in its authority and capacity to legislate (CIRCaP, 2011).

References

Baldini, G. (2008). The Campaign for an Electoral Law Referendum and the Prospects for Reform. In M. Donovan and P. Onofri (eds.) *Italian Politics: Frustrated Aspirations for Change* (pp. 104–22). Oxford: Berghahn.

Baldini, G. (2011). The Different Trajectories of Italian Electoral Reforms. *West European Politics*, 34 (3), 644–63.

Bull, M. J. (2004). Parliamentary Democracy in Italy. *Parliamentary Affairs*, 57 (3), 550–67.

Bull, M. J. (2007). The Constitutional Referendum of June 2006: End of the 'Great Reform' but Not of Reform Itself. In J.-L. Briquet and A. Mastropaolo (eds.) *Italian Politics. The Center-Left's Poisoned Victory* (pp. 99–118). Oxford: Berghahn.

Bull, M. J. (2012). The Italian Transition that Never Was. *Modern Italy*, 17 (1), 103–18.

Bull, M. J. and Newell, J. L. (1993). Italian Politics and the 1992 Elections: From 'Stable Instability' to Instability and Change. *Parliamentary Affairs*, 46 (2), 203–27.

Bull, M. J. and Newell, J. L. (2005). *Italian Politics: Adjustment under Duress*. Cambridge: Polity.

Bull, M. J. and Pasquino, G. (2009). A Long Quest in Vain: Institutional Reforms in Italy. In M. Bull and M. Rhodes (eds.) *Italy – A Contested Polity* (pp. 14–35). Abingdon: Routledge.

Bull, M. J. and Rhodes, M. (2009). Introduction – Italy: A Contested Polity. In M. J. Bull and M. Rhodes (eds.) *Italy – A Contested Polity* (pp. 1–13). Abingdon: Routledge.

Calise, M. (2010). *Il Partito Personale*. Bari: Laterza.

CIRCaP (2011). Centre for the Study of Political Change, *VI Rapporto sul Governo Italiano*, 16, 1–22.

Commissione per le riforme costituzionali (2013). Relazione della Commissione per le riforme costituzionali al Presidente del Consiglio dei Ministri (Rome). Available online at http://riformecostituzionali.gov.it/documenti-della-commissione/relazione-finale.html (accessed 26 February 2014).

Conti, N. (2012). Dalle parole ai fatti: l'attuazione del programma di governo. Paper presented to the annual meetings of the Società Italiana di Scienza Politica (SISP), 13–15 September, 1–22.

Fabbrini, S. (2012). The institutional odyssey of the Italian Parliamentary Republic. *Journal of Modern Italian Studies*, 17 (1), 10–24.

Lijphart, A. (1999). *Patterns of Democracy*. New Haven, CT: Yale University Press.

Massetti, E. (2012). La riforma federale: la fine dell'inizio o l'inizio dell fine?. In A. Bosco and D. McDonnell (eds.) *Politica in Italia: i fatti dell'anno e le interpretazioni*. Bologna: Il Mulino, Kindle edition.

Massetti, E. and Toubeau, S. (2013). Sailing with Northern Winds: Party Politics and Federal Reforms in Italy. *West European Politics*, 36 (2), 359–81.

Mauro, M., Onida, V., Quagliarello, G. and Violante, L. (2013). Relazione Finale del Gruppo di Lavoro sulle riforme istituzionale. Istituto il 30 marzo 2013 dal Presidente della Repubblica. Available online at: www.quirinale.it: 1–29 (accessed 18 April 2013).

Millefiorini, A. (2007). Bipolarismo, leadership e governabilità. La resistibile modernizzazione del sistema politico italiano. In R. Segatori and G. Barbieri (eds.) *Mutamenti della politica nell'Italia contemporanea* (pp. 13–32). Soveria Mannelli: Rubettino.

Morlino, L. (2013). The impossible transition and the unstable new mix: Italy 1992–2012. *Comparative European Politics*, 11 (3), 337–59.

Pasquino, G. (1998). Reforming the Italian Constitution. *Journal of Modern Italian Studies*, 3 (1), 42–54.

Pasquino. G. (2000). A Postmortem of the Bicamerale. In D. Hine and S. Vassallo (eds.) *Italian Politics: the Return of Politics* (pp. 101–120). London: Berghahn.

Sartori, G. (2006). *Mala costituzione e altri malanni*. Rome-Bari: Laterza.

Vassallo, S. (2007). Government under Berlusconi: the functioning of the core institutions in Italy. *West European Politics*, 30 (4), 692–710.

9

THE MISSING RENEWAL OF THE RULING CLASS

Luca Verzichelli

Introduction

As reported by all the international observers, the Italian general elections of February 2013 have brought about a situation of extreme political uncertainty. However, one can unquestionably argue that the political composition of the parliament in the XVIIth republican legislature exactly mirrors the different attitudes of the Italian public towards politics and political elites: the pyrrhic victory of the Democratic Party (PD) – actually a poor performance in comparison with the 2008 results – and, more generally, the centre-left coalition represent those Italians who desired a turning point from the era of Berlusconi, but still believed in a 'party-democracy' based on mass-party organizations ruled by established elites: the leaders of the PD and of its smaller allies had hoped that the effect of an important innovation such as the direct consultation of the voters in a primary election for the choice of the chief of the coalition could be a sufficient instrument to overcome the decline of trust in the traditional political actors. However, this message did not reach more than 30 per cent of valid votes (roughly one-fourth of potential voters) supporting the centre-left.

On the other hand, the share of centre-right voters – more or less the same size – who confirmed their support for the coalition led by the inexhaustible TV tycoon, represents the part of Italy that simply does not believe in the previous message. They do not believe in the centre-left parties and they still prefer their antagonistic hero: a populist leader who was able to keep the 'leftists' out of government for years, and to be the most long-lasting occupant of the Palazzo Chigi – the base of the Italian Chief Executive – in the Republic's history: indeed, in his eighteen years of political engagement (with about 100 months spent as *Presidente del Consiglio dei Ministri*), Berlusconi put a very varied body of politicians together, from some truly complete beginners, selected from the managers of his own firms, to some members of traditional governing parties, as well as some former neo-Fascists and former representatives of the radical left. Berlusconi has always been personally involved in the selection of the most important candidates of a very weak de-institutionalized party organization: *Forza Italia* and, since 2008, the larger PDL – the *Popolo della Libertà*.

A lot has still to be written about the incredible recovery of Silvio Berlusconi in the 2013 campaign, but at the beginning of 2015 he is still the leader of a major party, and only history will show whether this was just the swansong of a leader with no more chances to have any impact on Italian politics. However, it is a fact that the success of the centre-right is, to a large extent, due to Berlusconi's personal appeal: all his competitors within the centre-right coalition disappeared after trying to challenge him, and even the recent attempts of some centre-right second-rank leaders to distance themselves from his very disputable political performance were basically unsuccessful. For instance, notwithstanding its opposition to the technocratic government in charge after November 2011, the Northern League has been dramatically reduced in its electoral performance, while the other lists allied to the PDL in 2013 had very poor results.[1]

A third (and relatively new) force now represented in Parliament thanks to the astonishing result of the Five Star Movement (*Movimento Cinque Stelle*, or M5S) corresponds to those Italians who reject the antagonistic logic between the two previous visions. They are simply fed up with all the narratives of the past, and they ascribe the entire responsibility for the Italian crisis to the whole political establishment, refusing any kind of distinction within it and promoting – a unique case of a widely supported purely populist movement in Europe – a 'democracy of citizens' which should replace the parliamentary chain of delegation with some kind of direct representation managed through the Internet. To some extent, the rejection of the bipolar logic centred on the distinction between old party elites is shared by a share of about 10 per cent of centrist voters supporting the list *Scelta Civica* led by Mario Monti. When the technocratic prime minister decided to take the leadership of a coalition including the small parties at the political centre, he tried several times to approach those voters tempted by M5S, putting forward a simple argument: 'I share your protest against the ineffective, incompetent and unfair party elites who have devastated the Italian social structure and the economy'.

Mutual mistrust among the supporters of these three visions is evident in the development of Italian politics, and this is actually the main reason for the impasse following the 2013 election. More than different policy preferences, what divides the political actors lies in their different estimations of the relationship between the public and the elites in Italy today. In the present chapter I will focus on the explanations for this impasse, which makes the process of *elite settlement*[2] weak, if not impossible. Starting from very simple data on the difficult process of elite renewal, I will argue that the responsibilities for this difficult situation have to be shared between national and mid-level party leaders, who alternated themselves on the political ladder during the last twenty years. These politicians (but the same should be probably said of the Italian social and economic elites) did not realize the persistent and increasing distance between the elite and the ordinary people. Then, I will put forward the argument that there is a serious disease affecting political parties, which is surely not an Italian peculiarity but it has, in this country, particularly heavy implications.[3] In this general context of lack of foresight shown by party elites in Italy, I will highlight two dimensions: the high degree of intergenerational conflict and the persistence of a familistic view of politics. Finally, I will summarize the state of the Italian political elite, trying to understand possible scenarios for the near future.

The difficult emergence of a new ruling class: some pieces of evidence

An uninterrupted discussion about the necessity to renew the ruling class has accompanied the changes within the Italian political system after 1994. The March general elections, that year, marked the evaporation of the old parties and the striking victory of Berlusconi's personal party, which brought about an astonishing rate of turnover in the parliamentary elite.

However, since then, all the attempts to establish a new core of politicians on the two sides of the new bipolar party system have failed. The permanence of two leaders like Berlusconi and Prodi was not the effect of the consolidation of a whole dominant party elite, but quite the opposite: a lack of alternatives was basically the reason for their duration, and those who challenged them have been defeated one after the other, sometimes provoking splits and dramatic changes within the coalitions. As a result, a very unpredictable scenario has characterized the Italian democracy since 1994: the illusion of a simplified party system with more durable and authoritative cabinets lasted for a while, especially when Berlusconi was in power (2001–6 and 2008–11), with quite large majorities, a certain capability of control over his own coalition and an evident effect of cohesion within the opposite camp. However, during these two decades the Italian political system experienced a lot of unprecedented phenomena connected to the crisis of the parties: continual splits, repeated cases of individual defectors among MPs, a rather high degree of 'legislative rebellion' by political representatives, manifest conflicts among members of the executive bodies, other opportunistic behaviour by individual politicians such as inappropriate dual mandates and other unfair practices sometimes contrary to the statutes of their own parties.

The literature on the delays and missed promises of the Italian politicians after 1994 is huge, and reflects the problems of credibility of the whole ruling class. Here we can simply recall that sociological research has extensively illustrated the inadequacy of the Italian ruling class and an increasingly deteriorating link to public opinion (see Carboni, 2010). On this line of reasoning, political scientists have often underlined the uncertainties in the processes of elite settlement and elite institutionalization, which are the crucial processes at the core of a stable democratic accountability. These persistent rates of uncertainty and instability are evident when we consider long term survey data about the degree of democratic satisfaction (Morlino and Tarchi, 1996) but the evidence of positional studies of the elites is also useful for seeing the magnitude of the problem.

The amount of turnover and the rate of seniority are usually considered good indicators for describing the solidity of a given parliamentary elite. Here we can briefly show the data for these indicators in a long term perspective (for reasons of simplicity we are using only the data for the lower chamber) as in Figure 9.1.

The data clearly illustrate the difficulties in the consolidation of a new parliamentary elite in Italy: after the exceptional elections of 1994, the rate of emergence of new politicians remained high. This is to be connected to the alternation of victories of the two opposing coalitions, but also to the continual rearrangement within the political parties and within the same coalitions. Interestingly enough, the rate of *senior deputies* (here defined as MPs with at least two legislatures' experience) never reached the very stable threshold of 40 per cent which had characterized the age of the First Republic. This is a clear sign of deinstitutionalization of the party elites. Especially after 2005, when the introduction of a blocked list system allowed a centralized procedure of parliamentary selection, party selectors were not able to ensure the consolidation of parliamentary elites. The experience of the XVIth legislature, which started in 2008, is particularly significant: both the new PDL (which, as expected, had won the elections with a clear majority) and the PD (created the year before from the merger of two parties, heirs of the traditional Christian Democrats and Communist Party) reinforced their positions thanks to a strong concentration of seats[4] and to their new organizations. The PD in particular had experienced a highly participative process of foundation, with the elections of a general party assembly and with the primary elections of its first leader, Walter Veltroni. The success of both parties and the consequent simplification of the parliamentary scenario towards a quasi-two-party system were seen by all observers as the starting point for a new phase of consolidation of the Italian political elite, but these premises were soon contradicted in both parties: in the case of PDL, the personalized leadership of Berlusconi was contested by a number of internal challengers,[5] while the PD was endangered by internal fragmentation, which led to a new leadership change (from Veltroni to

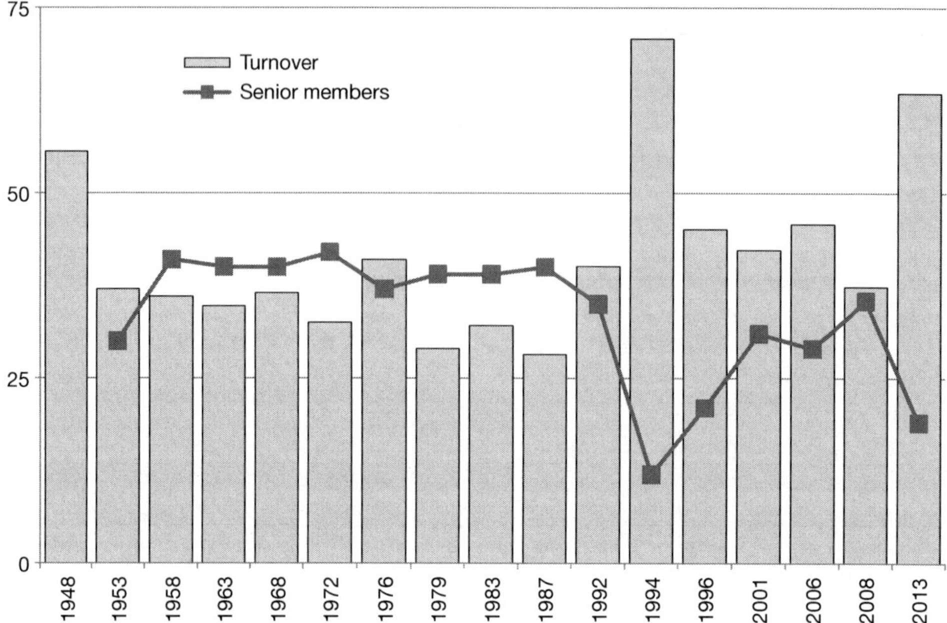

Figure 9.1 New MPs and senior MPs in the Lower Chamber, 1948–2013

Note: New MPs are those MPs elected for the first time to one of the two parliamentary chambers. The figures for senior MPs are defined as the percentage of MPs who had experience of at least two legislatures (no matter in which of the two chambers) before being elected.

Source: CIRCaP Parliamentary Elite Archive

Bersani, with the interlude of Dario Franceschini as interim secretary) and to splits with some moderate figures (including one of the founder leaders, Francesco Rutelli) who left the party during the legislature.

The problems of consolidation of a new ruling class are even better illustrated by the data on the profiles of top national leaders, i.e. the selected group of people who hold responsibilities within the national executive. Using a short summary of data extracted by larger surveys (Verzichelli, 2009; Verzichelli and Cotta, forthcoming), we can show in Table 9.1 the profile of the people included in the ministerial inner circle in comparison with some analogous data for the First Republic.

The first piece of evidence to be stressed is the discrepancy between the increasing stability of the governments of the Second Republic and the relative ministerial instability in recent years: although cabinet duration is now approaching two years, the mean duration of ministerial careers does not exceed the limit of 2.6 years, since most of the ministers have had just one appointment. Once again, political alternation is a strong explanatory factor for this high rate of turnover, but not a sufficient one: while the top executive positions have been reoccupied by indestructible leaders (in particular, Berlusconi and Prodi, who served as prime minister for about 75 per cent of the time between the 1994 and the 2013 elections) second-rank ministers have followed one after another with a very high rate of turnover, as a consequence of the uncertain equilibrium in both the political coalitions.

Table 9.1 provides additional information about the profile of ministers from the Second Republic: they are no younger (actually they are a bit older!) than the average age of their predecessors. This has to do with the relatively old age of ministerial aspirants. Throughout the Second Republic, the mean age of MPs new to parliament rose from legislature to legislature (Figure 9.2). This means that the renewal of the new political forces was done selecting rather old personnel to replace the defeated politicians. This trend of progressive ageing of the political class continued without interruption until the 2008 elections, characterized by the predominance

Table 9.1 Profile of Italian ministers. First and Second Republic compared

	Ministers: First Republic (1948–94)	*Ministers: Second Republic (1994–2012)*
Mean duration of government (days)	320	591
Mean duration of ministerial career (years)	3.5	2.6
Mean number of ministerial offices	4.3	1.8
Ratio of appointments/different jobs	1.9	1.3
Mean age of entry into government	54.3	54.8
% Ministers with previous parliamentary experience	85.3	62.5
% Ministers with previous junior ministerial experience	42.8	15.6
% Ministers with just one ministerial experience	24.9	64.2
% Ministers directly recruited to 'core executive'	11.2	20.1
Total number of individuals appointed as ministers	294	179

Note: The core executive includes the offices of Prime Minister and Vice Prime Minister, and the office of Minister of Economy and Finance (as well as the corresponding offices existing until the nineties: Budget, Treasury, Finance), Justice, Foreign Affairs, Interior, and Defence.

Source: CIRCaP Parliamentary Elite Archive

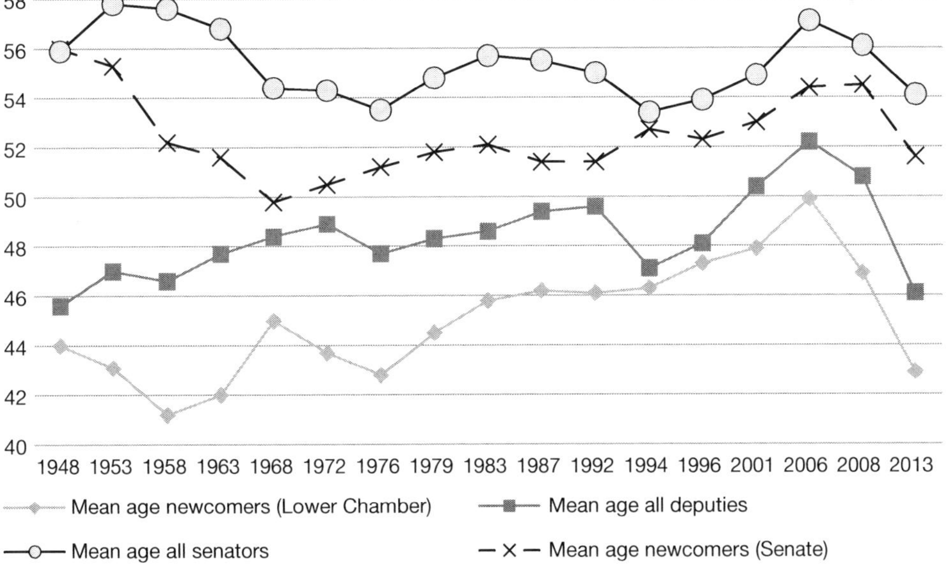

Figure 9.2 Mean age of Italian MPs (Lower Chamber and Senate, all MPs and new MPs), 1948–2013

Source: CIRCaP Parliamentary Elite Archive

of two 'majoritarian' parties (see above) and, above all, in 2013, by the significant rejuvenation of the ranks of the PD and the impressively young mean age of the M5S representatives.

With regard to the important features of the profile of the ministerial elite, another innovation from the Second Republic is the presence of different 'surrogates' of career politicians, such as techno-political policy experts, part-time professional politicians or figures with a less defined political profile. The data confirm that, in recent times, ministers tended to be more connected to specific 'policy roles'. On the other hand, ministers from the Second Republic show a higher probability of having been recruited directly within the inner circle,[6] without a period of training in the second ranks of government. The traditional feature of a relatively long parliamentary experience as a precondition for entering the ministerial elite has decreased by about twenty points, and the requirement of having experience as a junior minister has almost completely disappeared. Overall, a sort of hybridization between different types of careers has emerged: some ministers are recruited for their evident expertise, being suitable only for specific policy-related offices; other ministers are generalist politicians who take not more than a couple of important offices; and others still are purely technocrats (sometimes recruited also by 'political' cabinets) dealing with delicate issues such as the economy, environment, infrastructure or health.

However, ministers with more clearly technocratic profiles seem, in general, to have shorter expectations for their ministerial life and they are much more exposed to reshuffles decided by the prime minister. Interesting cases of sacking can be identified in the deselection of technical ministers of the Second Republic: the ministers Ruggero, Tremonti and Siniscalco lost their posts under the Berlusconi governments after policy disagreements with the chief executive. Personalization and concentration of power because of the increasing legitimacy of the government leader have thus been important phenomena in recent years, impacting on the relationship between leadership and ministerial elite.

I do not need to summarize here detailed evidence about the difficult reconstruction of a credible political class in Italy after 1994. What seems more useful for the purposes of this chapter is providing a comprehensive analysis of some peculiar aspects such as the 'lost opportunities' and the 'lack of continuity' within the elite formation and circulation. This will lead me to a more robust interpretation of the unproductive renewal of the Italian political elite. My proposal is therefore to move to a qualitative picture, first, capturing the important moments of stalemate in the selection of the political class and, second, analysing the most critical aspects of the relationships between political leaders and their immediate followers.

Lost opportunities: critical elections and the missed consolidation of the political class

The image of a lost opportunity for the formation of a new and prominent ruling class in Italy has been repeatedly used in different contexts. Michele Salvati (2000) has connected the *lost opportunities* for a renewal of the Italian elites with the delay in modernizing the economic system. From a different perspective, Lorenzo Ornaghi and Vittorio Parsi have argued (2001) that the elites who survived the crisis of the mid-nineties lost the opportunity to recreate a strong link with the very fragmented sectors of Italian society.[7] According to these authors, Italian leaders have shown a lack of vision, abdicating their duty to drive change and trying to survive by employing purely *technical adaptations*. As a consequence, the political change would have proved incomprehensible and disappointing to a large part of the Italian public. More recently, a book edited by eminent economists has shown the lost opportunities for a radical renewal of the *labour market of politicians* (Boeri *et al.*, 2010), and even the recent empirical studies of political careers in Italy illustrate a number of promises that have been not kept (Verzichelli, 2010).

The list of references could be much longer: many observers have in fact stressed the problem of lost opportunities for a fruitful elite change. In order to add more qualitative evidence on the missed renewal of the political class, at least four important points in time can be identified. A first critical period was that following the 1994 elections: Italians immediately understood that the transition would be neither easy nor decisive. This not just because of the sudden failure of the first Berlusconi government and the birth of the first full technocratic experience (the Dini government), but because of the diffuse awareness that the new leadership was not going to bring a real renewal of the political elite. With the passing of time, the *liberal revolution* claimed by Berlusconi in the spring of 1994 became a vague memory and *Forza Italia*, which would have lost many of its founder members, transformed itself in a sort of personalized *party*, with no solid internal organizations and no chance to grow new and autonomous leaders. Until the foundation of a larger but still personalized party such as the PDL, in 2008, *Forza Italia* kept being an incomplete construction: grounded on a mix of territorial second-rank politicians from the parties of the First Republic and a group of managers directly co-opted from Berlusconi's environment, the party was always ready to support the leader, showing a remarkable reactivity during the electoral campaigns, but it also proved to be extremely weak and divided in day-to-day politics.

On the centre-left, the difficult life of the *Olive tree* (*L'Ulivo*) coalition and the breakdown of the Prodi government (1998) marked a second lost opportunity: the attempt to overcome the immobility of the pre-existing elites, moving to a federation of progressive forces, failed because of the resistance of the party apparatus to such a radical change of direction. According to Alfio Mastropaolo (1997), the *Cashmere Revolution* represented by the new entrants of 1994 was followed by a *Cashmere Restoration*, dominated by the party establishments.

A third phase of disillusion occurred after the defeat of the centre-right coalition at the regional elections of 2005. The doubts raised by some of the allies of Mr Berlusconi were solved with a minor reshuffle of the ministerial team and with the enlargement of the larger coalition, now opened to some small personalized parties. The new political equilibrium sought by the leader of the Catholic centre (Marco Follini, who would soon leave the centre-right coalition) was not achieved and Berlusconi went back to his populist approach, changing the electoral system a few months before the end of the legislature and standing again as a candidate for the premiership in the next legislative elections (2006).

Finally, one should remember the above-mentioned lost opportunity of the XVIth legislature, the most impressive in terms of measurable negative consequences such as mistrust of politicians and rejection of the classic idea of 'political party'. If the failure of the PDL can be directly linked to the personal conduct of Berlusconi (both his very questionable private life while he was serving as prime minister, and his style as party leader), the problems within the PD were connected to the strong conflicts between its internal factions and, particularly, between 'old' and 'new' leaders. To some extent, this is still the problem to be faced by the PD and the centre-left camp, which has not yet succeeded in 'turning the page'.

Missing changes in party leadership: the fate of 'second fiddles'

No doubt, the amount of political change produced after 1992 has not created stable stratifications and clear hierarchies within the political elites. On the contrary, the political confrontation has taken the shape of a *bellum omnium contra omnes*: the notion of party discipline has almost disappeared in a country where, for about half a century, a factionalized party like the DC had always found the necessary equilibrium to remain in power and the largest communist party in the Western hemisphere used to be the main opposition.

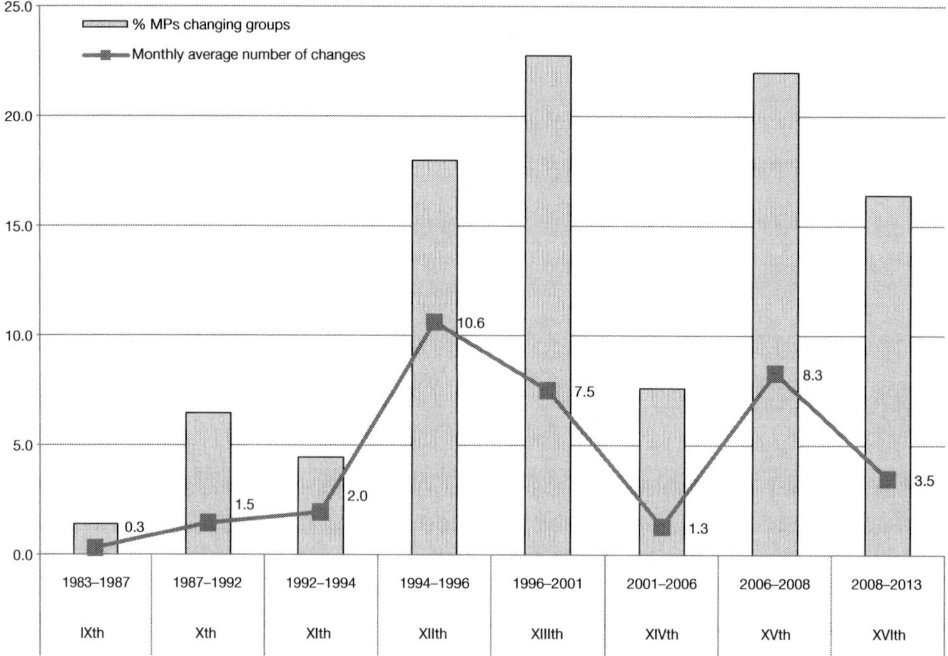

Figure 9.3 MPs changing parliamentary groups and monthly average number of changes, 1987–2013
Source: CIRCaP Parliamentary Elite Archive

The extreme consequence of party indiscipline – the disappearance of party establishments – is actually a recurrent situation in the Italian Second Republic. If one counts the number of defections from parliamentary groups (an almost unprecedented phenomenon in the First Republic), it can easily be seen that the four previously mentioned points of stalemate were followed by dramatic increases in parliamentary fluidity (Figure 9.3). This is actually a complex phenomenon which includes the effects of real splits and/or phases of merging between forces, but even a number of individual moves, because of opportunistic decisions by single MPs (those defecting to other parties). However, the combined effects of all these factors are the weak consolidation of parliamentary parties and the disarray among the elite ranks.

Moreover, the patterns of internal party competition developed during these two decades denote some paradoxical situations that can be described as a lack of rapport between leaders and followers. The common denominator in all the important cases is the disappearance of the traditional system of selection delegated to party congresses: not a single party was able to organize regular conferences during the past two decades, and in any case the leadership selection was generally made before the pre-congress debate or proposed to the general acclaim of the whole party conference.

In terms of leader effectiveness, a different fate has characterized the two sides of the system: on the right, leaders such as Berlusconi (Forza Italia, PDL), Bossi (Northern League), Casini (Democratic Centre) or even Fini (leader of the right wing *National Alliance*, who subsequently joined PDL and then founded the FLI) remained the undisputable heads of their organizations for about twenty years, although with very different degrees of charisma and autonomy. Berlusconi has surely shown some of the characteristics of other Western populist leaders as a prime minister (Campus, 2006), but his relationship with the top party leaders has always been rather peculiar, given the personal nature of his leadership (McDonnell, 2013). As a consequence, interactions within the party elite have been characterized by an absence of any open confrontation and by bilateral relationships between the leader and individual followers.[8] Even the events following the electoral decline of the party, which readopted its old title of Forza Italia at the end of 2013, confirm the peculiarities of such a personal party: the faction opposing the decision of Berlusconi to leave the *grand coalition government* was forced to split (founding the *New Centre-Right* party) while the weak internal opposition led by the former minister Raffaele Fitto was soon neutralized by Berlusconi. Bossi has been a strong charismatic leader, able to build a relatively structured party (probably the most effective party machine in the Second Republic) but, at the same time, to personalize the central structure of the party.[9] The destiny of the 'colonels' in all these parties (as well as within the other centre-right parties) has been really sad: working hard in a context of competition for power with no chance of a promotion.

A dissimilar situation, with a not very different outcome, has characterized the left of the political system, which has always suffered a systematic lack of leadership, to be filled by external figures (first of all the coalition leader Romano Prodi, and to some extent other figures such as Giuliano Amato and Carlo Azelio Ciampi). The competition for the leadership of the main parties of this camp has always been uncertain and unclear.[10] This has led to some forms of shared leadership (both in the PDS and in the post-Christian Democratic forces leading the centre-left coalition) and, above all, to a very litigious establishment, which has been inherited by the PD. The introduction of the primary election, strongly demanded by Veltroni at the beginning of the adventure of this innovative form of party, did not pacify this fragmented elite, which is still experiencing a very difficult phase of harsh confrontation (see below).

Still waiting for the 'good Italy': perspectives for a new ruling class

So far, two phenomena have been discussed: the inability of Italian leaders to take the various chances they had to change the political system, and the lack of communication between political leaders and their immediate followers, which has undermined continuity within each party organization. These are two sides of the same coin, that, in short, can be defined as a persistent empty space characterizing at least twenty years: throughout this time, the Italian ruling class has in fact been characterized by an incessant lack of political responsibility and by the 'abdication' of its duty to keep cultivating the reputation of all the political institutions. A full comprehension of the nature of this phenomenon is surely beyond the goals of this short analysis, but we can try at least to better focus the factors which have probably contributed to such a situation.

A first element to be stressed is the *intergenerational gap*. Italian politicians have been, and to a large extent they remain, an expression of the 'older' generation, and the renewal at the top elite level has not been made possible. With the passing of time, this distance increased, and all the strategies provided by the parties of the Second Republic do not seem to be working in reducing the gap. Indeed, the striking success of M5S in the Lower Chamber elections in 2013[11] proves that, for the very first time, the youngest cohorts of voters had a remarkably different reaction. Other signs of this generational problem are evident in the PDL, with the shy attempts to create some degree of autonomy from Berlusconi and, above all, in the duel between two PD candidates at the centre-left primary elections of 2012: a large part of the party establishment supported the secretary, Pierluigi Bersani, against the mayor of Florence, Matteo Renzi, who is the main figure in a generational movement within the left party, openly demanding the *scrapping* of the old elite.

The second element concerns the egocentricity and the high self-esteem of Italian politicians. A lot of facts should be adduced here to show the widespread arrogance of Italian career politicians, especially in respect of the repeated episodes of bribery and corruption. The most transparent evidence, however, lies in the continued attempts made in the past two decades to maximize the direct and indirect benefits guaranteed by different pieces of legislation, for instance allowances to representatives, electoral reimbursements and fiscal facilitation for parties and political think tanks. All these benefits were basically increased until the shocking crisis that led to a technical government in the autumn of 2011. In any event, parties represented in parliament have so far prevented the adoption of a law implementing the constitutional provisions concerning the transparency of political parties and a structural limit on the use of public resources devoted to the political organizations.

Not least, the persistence of familistic and clientelistic attitudes within the political class is another aspect to be stressed in explaining the stalemate of the Italian political class. Although it is impossible to calculate the extent of *familism* in Italian politics, all sociological surveys and, in particular, journalistic reports[12] speak about an increase in the 'private' transmission of political benefits. The lesson of *tangentopoli* has been not learned, as is shown by the large-scale use of political patronage and an illogical (and sometimes illegal) use of public resources by elected politicians. If it was the centre-right coalition at the heart of the repeated scandals before 2013 (with a high perception of political corruption especially in the two symbolic regions of Lombardy and Lazio, where the centre-right governments were forced to resign), the scandal of the political management of a bank considered very close to the centre-left camp, the *Monte dei Paschi di Siena*, had very similar effects of producing mistrust, showing long-term connivances and the precise responsibilities of the political leaders.

Is this elite decay irreversible? The film *Girlfriend in a Coma* – a critical analysis by the *Economist* editor Bill Emmott on the decline of the Italian political system over the past twenty years – proposes a sort of double conclusion: the sign 'the end' evolves into 'this is not the end', while a number of excerpts from the interviews collected for the film, including that with the prime minister Mario Monti, describe the problems of *mala Italia* and some relatively optimistic perspectives for a *good Italy* in the years to come.

From the perspective of an elite-centred analysis, one cannot be particularly optimistic. The Italian ruling class has demonstrated an inability to change, and to a large extent it did not want to change, its mind. Political elites, in particular, proved to be egocentric, ungenerous and not forward-looking at all. This applies particularly to the top leaders who have not ensured continuity in their ideas and in their parties, but their defects have been mirrored by the incompetence and the disreputable behaviour of many local politicians and administrators.

The results of the 2013 elections highlight the consequences of these mistakes. The conflicting 'faces' of Italian public opinion, perfectly mirrored in the XVIIth legislature, are, respectively, instinctive trust in the leader (and only in him) still shown by Berlusconi's followers; the open but self-destructive self-analysis of a party elite which cannot recognize the real world (especially embodied by the PD elite, but somehow scattered in other sectors of the political elite); and finally the total rejection of the existing order, which is well represented by the instances of M5S.

This is clearly the most difficult point of departure for anybody who wants to rebuild a viable political perspective in this amazing political system. The main difficulty lies, in the short run, in the very narrow path leading to a new political equilibrium: how to keep the present elites sufficiently unified to give the country a new government, to start a few 'emergency' policy plans to give a chance to the Italian economy to start again, and to implement the basic institutional (and perhaps constitutional) reforms which can allow the political system to regain some of the large amounts of time wasted.

What seems to be particularly hard to reach is a sufficient degree of *elite settlement*, a necessary condition in the attempt to reconstruct a positive relationship between elites and public. In comparison with twenty years ago this goal seems even more ambitious, since the factors at work then, the bipolar simplification of the political space and the high rate of trust in EU institutions seem to be much less incisive now. A new set of endogenous and, if possible, exogenous factors are therefore needed to bring the Italian political elite back to an acceptable level of legitimacy.

Notes

1 Of an overall result of 29.1 per cent of the popular vote (Chamber of Deputies) for the centre-right coalition, PDL achieved 21.6 per cent, while the Northern League had 4.1 per cent of the votes (nationwide) and the total of the other centre-right lists was not more than 3.5 per cent. This is an interesting piece of evidence in terms of the personal success of Berlusconi, with crucial implications for the selection of the political elite: Berlusconi has now a much greater control over the MPs of PDL, and most of his former and current competitors have been excluded from parliament.

2 The notion of elite settlement as a necessary condition for the consolidation of the democratic order is suggested by the extensive research of John Higley on the relationships between elites and regime stability. See, in particular, Higley and Burton (2006).

3 Recent reflections by some well-known Italian opinion makers insist on the ineffectiveness of political parties. Two books in particular, by Piero Ignazi (2012) and Marco Revelli (2013), stress, with quite different tones and implications, the peculiarities of the crisis of the Italian parties.

4 The overall figures for the *index of bipartitism* were in 2008 higher than 70 per cent (votes) and higher than 75 per cent (parliamentary seats). These figures mark the highest peak of bipartitism in the whole republican experience.

5 Among the traditional allies of Berlusconi, the leader of the democratic centre Casini had refused to enter the new party since 2008, leaving the coalition before the elections, while Fini joined the new party and obtained the office of Speaker of the Lower Chamber. From this position, Fini criticized Berlusconi several times, until his decision to quit supporting the government (December 2010) and the consequent split of his little party (*Futuro e Libertà*). Among the other important leaders who left Berlusconi's party most recently one should mention the former ministers Frattini (close to the position of Mr Monti), Tremonti (elected in 2013 with the Northern League), La Russa and Meloni (elected in a satellite list allied to the PDL in 2013).

6 Besides governmental leaders recruited from other elite pyramids (Ciampi, Dini, Monti) or immediately called to the top of the government after their emergence on the political ladder (Berlusconi, Prodi), other important ministers such as Tremonti, D'Alema, Padoa Schioppa, Mancino, Napolitano and Fini have been directly appointed to a top governmenta office during the Second Republic.

7 Their criticism is, correctly, addressed to the whole ruling class, which means not just the top political class but the whole group of policymakers who were in charge of the most important policy processes in the years of the transition.

8 Needless to say, the use of his personal resources to finance party initiatives and even the (supposed) exchanges to 'buy' the consensus of some MPs elected in other parties. In particular, Berlusconi has been accused of fraud for having obtained the support of a few deputies from the opposition parties on 14 December 2010, when his government survived a confidence vote in the Lower Chamber by just three votes.

9 With the passing of time, the leading group of the League was indeed overlapping the restricted circle of Bossi's friends and relatives. After the scandals of 2012 and the involvement of several of the League's top leaders in various episodes of illegal party financing and corruption, the divide between Bossi's circle and the reformists (led by the new secretary Roberto Maroni) emerged, endangering the present and the future assets of the party.

10 A paradigmatic example was the decision of the *Democratic Left Party* national council, in 1994, to appoint Massimo D'Alema as the successor of Achille Occhetto (the last leader of the Communist party, who had founded the new PDS in 1991) despite the fact that a large consultation of the membership had indicated the name of Walter Veltroni.

11 In the contest for the Senate, where the minimum age for the active electorate is 25 years, M5S achieved 23.79 per cent, that is to say almost 2 points less than the result of the same list in the Lower Chamber.

12 Investigative reports by some famous journalists on maladministration and clientelism have had an amazing success over the past two decades, particularly the book by two journalists from *Corriere della Sera* (Rizzo and Stella, 2007), who reintroduced the term *casta* ('caste') to describe the attitudes of many Italian politicians to practising political clientelism and patronage.

References

Boeri, T. A. Merlo and Prat, A. (eds.) (2010). *The Ruling Class: Management and Politics in Modern Italy*. Oxford: Oxford University Press.

Campus D. (2006). *L'antipolitica al governo. De Gaulle, Reagan, Berlusconi*. Bologna: Il Mulino.

Carboni, C. (2010). Elites and the democratic disease. In A. Mammone and G. A. Veltri (eds.), *Italy Today. The Sick Man of Europe* (pp. 19–33). London: Routledge.

Higley, J. and Burton, M. (eds.) (2006). *Elite Foundations of Liberal Democracy*. Lahnam, MD: Rowman & Littlefield.

Ignazi, P. (2012). *Forza senza legittimità. Il vicolo cieco dei partiti*. Rome-Bari: Laterza.

McDonnell, D. (2013). Silvio Berlusconi's Personal Parties: From Forza Italia to the Popolo Della Libertà. *Political Studies*, 61, 217–33.

Mastropaolo, A. (1997). La «nuova» classe politica. Innovazione o trasformismo? In I. Diamanti and M. Lazar (eds.), *Stanchi di miracoli. Il sistema politico italiano in cerca di normalità* (pp. 89–108). Milan: Guerini & associati.

Morlino, L. and Tarchi, M. (1996). The Dissatisfied Society: The Roots of Political Change in Italy. *European Journal of Political Research*, 30, 1, 41–63.

Ornaghi L. and Parsi, V. E. (2001). *Lo sguardo corto. Critica della classe dirigente italiana*. Rome-Bari: Laterza.

Revelli, M. (2013). *Finale di partito*. Turin: Einaudi.

Rizzo, S. and Stella, G. (2007). *La casta. Così i politici italiani sono diventati intoccabili*. Milan: Rizzoli.

Salvati, M. (2000). *Occasioni mancate. Economia e Politica in Italia dagli anni sessanta ad oggi*. Rome-Bari: Laterza.

Verzichelli, L. (2009). Italy. The Difficult Road Towards a More Effective Process of Ministerial Selection. In K. Dowding and P. Dumont (eds.), *The Selection of Ministers in Europe. Hiring and Firing* (pp. 79–100). London: Routledge.

Verzichelli, L. (2010). *Vivere di Politica. Come (non) cambiano le carriere politiche in Italia*. Bologna: Il Mulino.

Verzichelli L. and Cotta, M. (forthcoming). Shades of Technocracy. The Variable Use of Non-partisan Ministers in Italy. In A. Costa Pinto, M. Cotta and P. Tavares De Almeida (eds.), *Non-partisan Ministers in European Democracies*. Oxford: Oxford University Press.

10

MEDIA AND DEMOCRACY

Cinzia Padovani

Introduction

The interrelationship between media and democracy in Italy has historically been characterized by *lottizzazione*, a practice through which managerial, as well as editorial, positions in the public service broadcaster (RAI, *Radiotelevisione Italiana*) were assigned on the basis of an elaborate party-quota system. Whereas this system, in place from the late 1970s to the early 1990s, was often criticized as a sign of corruption and undue influence, it also had the lofty intention of improving political pluralism, after decades of the Christian Democrats' cultural hegemony in Italy's main cultural industry (Mancini, 2009).

Since the first appointment of Silvio Berlusconi as prime minister (1994), the relationship between the political system and the media sphere has changed. In RAI, there was a shift from *lottizzazione* to a "spoils" system, as key positions inside the public broadcaster were occupied by managers and journalists close to the media mogul. Indeed, during the 2000s, the public broadcaster came to represent the very core of Berlusconi's conflict of interest: owner of Mediaset, RAI's competitor in the commercial broadcasting sector, and head of government.

Media concentration

The level of media concentration, and the size of Berlusconi's conflict of interest, reached levels that had no equals in other liberal democracies. Concentration in the television sector was of great concern: since the mid-1980s, the broadcasting market had become structured in a duopoly, with RAI and Mediaset controlling more than 90 percent of the audience share. High levels of market concentration continued to characterize the television sector throughout the 2000s. By 2007 the concentration ratio for the two broadcasters was still an alarming 4,639 points in the Herfindahl-Hirschman index (Colapinto, 2010: 62).[1] In 2008, Mediaset alone controlled 55 percent of national advertising revenues for television (AGCOM, 2009: 80).

For these reasons, the Italian case has received wide attention. A considerable body of work has been published in English that has investigated the challenges facing public broadcasting in the country (Richeri, 1990), analyzed the practice of *lottizzazione* inside RAI (Mancini, 2009), studied the evolution of the Fininvest/Mediaset conglomerate (Balbi and Prario, 2010), analyzed media policies and pluralism (Padovani, 2009; Casarosa and Bolgi, 2011), and contextualized those policies within broader trends in the cultural industries (D'Arma, 2009). In this chapter, after briefly reviewing some of this history, I focus attention on media policies for the print media, and discuss the difficulties of properly regulating conflicts of interest in Italy. Finally, I examine changes that have occurred in the media sector since the early 2000s, with a focus on developments in television and online media, and the significance of these changes for Italian democracy.

Media policies

The history of media regulation in Italy has brought to full visibility the tension between a pro-market media sector, where antitrust limits have been lax, and the normative ideal of a pluralistic public sphere, where citizens should be informed and entertained by a variety of sources.[2] We notice this tension in the ways in which governments have developed their media policies: whereas public interventions through direct and indirect support of some media sectors, such as public service broadcasting and the print media, have been put in place to increase diversity of viewpoints in the public sphere, the legislator has been reluctant to set limits on concentration in the television sector.

Media policies that have favored market concentration in the TV sector have been amply discussed elsewhere (Padovani, 2009; 2015). For the purposes of this chapter, I call attention to Law No. 223 of 6 August 1990 (the so-called Mammì law), which originally legitimated the duopoly in television broadcasting. Although subsequent laws[3] had tried to set stricter antitrust measures, various loopholes *de facto* allowed the status quo to continue and Mediaset to maintain its dominant position as the main commercial broadcaster in the country.

Print media

Whereas media policies for the TV sector had failed to set limits to concentration, rules for the print media had been stricter. Even the Constitutional Court (Sent. 420, 1994) had pointed out the "incoherence" and "irrationality" between the two different legislative approaches, and underlined that antitrust limits for the print media sector (according to which no group could control more than 20 percent of national circulation) should have informed the legislation in the broadcasting sector in order to protect "pluralism of voices" (Art. 14, Par. 5).

Indeed, the legislation for the print media sector had traditionally been more in tune with the need to secure transparency and encourage plurality of opinions in the public sphere. Historically, the most important reform law in this sector was Law No. 416 of 5 August 1981, which detailed the conditions for the ownership structure of print media and established that such ownership should be made public and transparent (Art. 1, Par. 5.a). Most importantly, the law set up a system of direct as well as indirect public intervention in favor of the printing press (Art. 4).[4] Publications run by cooperatives, political parties, publications for expatriates, or those published in any of the languages spoken in the autonomous regions of the Northern borders (French, Ladin, Slovene, and German), have been among those benefiting from this law.

Although inefficiencies in the system, and even abuses of public funds, have pointed to the need to fundamentally revise some of the ways in which those fundings have been appropriated (Polo, 2010: 140–1), the legislation of the publishing sector has contributed to expanding pluralism of expression, as well as political and linguistic pluralism. The sheer availability of tens of national dailies (155 in 2013, according to the Italian Federation of Newspapers Publishers) on the newsstands gives visibility to the vibrant diversity of opinions and political positions that exist in the country. This presence is important. Indeed, although the print media sector is not as concentrated as television,[5] powerful capitalists with interests in a multiplicity of sectors have traditionally owned the most established publications.

A brief review of the ownership of newspapers and magazines illustrates the web of interests behind Italy's popular press. For example, in 2011, the two most powerful publishing groups in the country, *Gruppo Editoriale L'Espresso* and *RCS Corriere della Sera*, shared approximately 36.8 percent of the market (AGCOM, 2012: 139). In the same year, Mondadori (of which Silvio Berlusconi's Fininvest owned approximately 53 percent)[6] commanded 14 percent of magazines sales (AGCOM, 2012: 149).

Who was behind some of these groups? At the time of writing (Winter, 2014), Giuseppe Rotoli, who controlled the business of private health care in the wealthy northern region of Lombardy, remained the single most prominent stockholder of the newspaper *Corriere della Sera* (the Italian newspaper of record). Another prominent figure in the newspaper sector was Andrea Riffser, who owns the dailies *La Nazione* and *Il Resto del Carlino*, and the news agency Polypress. Riffser is the heir of a family business with interests in the gasoline sector.

Compagnia Industriale Riunita (CIR), controlled by the De Benedetti family, was behind the *Gruppo Editoriale L'Espresso*, publisher of the weekly magazine *L'Espresso* (among others) and of *La Repubblica*, the second newspaper in Italy in terms of circulation. The group's core business, however, was not the news media, but energy production and distribution (CIR owns Sorgenia, active in the sector of gas and electricity), as well as elder care, the private health care business, venture capital, and private equity.

These examples raise the legitimate question of whether—and, if so, to what extent—news content might have been slanted in favor of these powerful stakeholders. The public financing system, originally established in 1981, created an important counterbalance to private interests. The subsidies have sustained smaller publications, those that do not have large amounts of capital behind them, as well those that express points of view that are not in the mainstream. This has represented a crucial support for promoting pluralism in the public sphere.

From *lottizzazione* to the spoils system

The public service broadcaster has provided, at least in principle, another important contribution to the public sphere. However, this ideal function has often been challenged by a political party system always ready to intervene in RAI's affairs.

The kind of power exercised inside RAI through the *lottizzazione* system of the 1970s and 1980s, with its party logics of assigning administrative and editorial positions based on quotas, had begun to change during the 1990s. Various elements seemed to delegitimize the logic of strict party control over the broadcaster: the emphasis on formal training and professional values of objective reporting, the debacle of the post-war party system during *tangentopoli* (the *bribesville* scandals of 1992–3), and the growing competition of online news, which required more frequent and direct interactions with audiences (through blogs and, later, social media). Market and industrial imperatives seemed to have replaced the strict control of the political establishment. An emphasis on objectivity in reporting, especially coveted by the new generations of journalists (Padovani, 2005), together with a focus on "lifestyle" politics and "soft" news, seemed to break away from the tradition of advocacy journalism. This, however, was only partly true.

Indeed, the right-wing coalition in power for most of the 2000s exercised ample control over the broadcaster. As has been discussed elsewhere (Padovani, 2010; Curran, 2011: 20–1), this was the time when people from the entourage of the prime minister, from Mediaset, or from Berlusconi's own political party, or his coalition, occupied top managerial posts and editorial positions. This created great concerns for those advocating for media independence in the country and was evidence of Berlusconi's far-reaching conflicts of interest.

Conflicts of interest

Indeed, a key area of concern for the relationship between media and democracy in Italy, has been the issue of regulating conflicts of interest. Even though Berlusconi himself had promised that he would relinquish control over his media empire after being appointed prime minister, that never happened. Quite the contrary: Fininvest, the holding company that controls Mediaset TV channels, remained firmly in his hands. Moreover, his family tightened its grip over Mediaset and expanded its presence in various other fields, including newspapers and film production, soccer, finance, banking, and insurance.

Pier Silvio Berlusconi (Silvio's son) became chief executive officer of *Reti Televisive Italiane* (RTI), the corporation in charge of television activities for Mediaset, and later chairman of Mediaset's board of directors. Marina Berlusconi (Silvio's oldest daughter) was president of Fininvest and, in 2003, became chairman of the board of the publisher group Arnaldo Mondadori. She also continued to be a member of Mediaset's board of directors. Both Marina and Pier Silvio held executive positions in various other firms, including the insurance group Mediolanum, the film production house Medusafilm, and the investment bank Mediobanca.

Another daughter, Barbara, sat on the board of directors of Fininvest and, since 2011, on the directors' board of the premier league soccer team AC Milan, of which Fininvest was 100 percent owner. Paolo, Silvio's brother, became majority stockholder of the daily *Il Giornale* (previously owned by Silvio), after Silvio had relinquished his shares in compliance with the 1990 Mammì law prohibiting cross-media ownership. In 2011, Paolo acquired the national daily *Il Foglio*, previously owned by Veronica Lario, Silvio's second ex-wife.

A law regulating conflicts of interest?

Law No. 215 of July 2004, passed during the second Berlusconi government, defined conflict of interest and established that those who hold government responsibilities should "dedicate themselves exclusively to the care of public interests and abstain from putting into action and participating in deliberations . . . in situations of conflicts of interest" (Art. 1, Par. 1). Whereas the law forbade those with government responsibilities from holding other titles or other positions while in office (Art. 2), it never challenged the issue of media ownership. In fact, it defined conflict of interest as a situation in which an elected government official "participates in or omits an act" that might have a direct repercussion on his patrimony, or the patrimony of his immediate family (Art. 3).

Conflict of interest was therefore defined as a subjective, potential problem, rather than an objective one. This meant that it was sufficient for Silvio Berlusconi to leave the room while lawmakers voted or discussed any regulations that might have personally benefited him, for Berlusconi not to be in breach of the law. The irony was evident: according to this formulation, conflict of interest was only a *potential* problem, rather than an a priori condition that had to be prevented. As such, conflict of interest could be sanctioned only after lengthy procedures would have provided evidence of any "specific" and "preferential" impact of a government act or a law on somebody's patrimony. Certainly, not a very efficacious rule!

Whereas it would have been naïve to expect that any Berlusconi government could have imposed stricter regulations on conflicts of interest, a more vigorous position would have been expected from the center-left coalitions, in power on various occasions since the 1990s (1996–2000; 2006–8). During the XVth legislature (2006–8), for instance, a bill was proposed establishing that those with a patrimony of more than 15 million euros would have to put their corporations under a blind trust if they occupied top government positions, at the national as well as at the local level. The bill declared that those with such patrimony were *incompatible* with public office, but failed to establish that they would be *ineligible* for public office. For obvious reasons, ineligibility would have been vehemently opposed by the right-wing coalition, intent on protecting Berlusconi's interests and political ambitions. At the same time, the bill was considered "too weak" by those on the left who wanted stricter rules (Fusani, 2007). Eventually, the proposal failed to gather enough support even within the left-wing government coalition.[7]

In interviews with lawmakers and media professionals, the importance of regulating conflicts of interest was unequivocally stated. A prominent Democratic Party official, the former Minister of Communications for the Prodi government (2006–8) stated that "regulating conflicts of interest will be high on the agenda of any future government" (Gentiloni, personal interview). For the head of the Italian Press Federation (*Federazione Italiana della Stampa*), conflict of interest was the "cancer" of the country's democracy (Natale, personal interview). Still, at the time of writing (Winter, 2014) there had been no new regulations in this field and discussions about it have remained taboo in public discourse (d'Arcais, 2013). In part, this was due to the composition of the governing coalition that resulted from the 2013 national elections (the center-left, center-right-wing government led by Enrico Letta, April 2013–February 2014) and the continuing prominence of Silvio Berlusconi on the political scene. Still, addressing the question of conflict of interests remains one of crucial importance for the future of Italian democracy and should be a priority on the agenda of any government.

The duopoly

After having examined the regulations in support of the publishing industry and the unresolved issue of conflicts of interest, we need to analyze the conditions of the television industry, as television remains a crucial factor in the relationship between media and democracy in Italy. Is this sector still dominated by the duopoly? Have new delivery technologies, including digital terrestrial television and satellite television, changed its conditions?

In the sector of free-to-air television during the 2000s and early 2010s, the broadcasting channel LA7[8] was particularly successful. Although the channel had initially struggled to make a profit, given its relatively low audience share compared with RAI and Mediaset, its focus on high-end audiences and on news and public affairs programs has been a winning strategy.[9]

Still, RAI and Mediaset maintained their prominence in the very important sector of news and public affairs programs, a sector that has traditionally represented the core of the electronic public sphere, as news bulletins remain the main source of information for the majority of Italians.[10]

For instance, in 2011, RAI's main news bulletins, TG1, generated an audience share of 23.7 per cent, while TG5, Mediaset's flagship news program, commanded a 20.1 percent share. However, it is important to notice that the performance of LA7 was also particularly impressive in this sector, as the audience share for its prime-time news bulletin, TGLA7, grew from 5 percent in 2010 to 10 percent in 2011 (AGCOM, 2012: 118). These data reveal that, overall, news programs on generalist, free-to-air television, have continued to occupy a central position in the electronic public sphere. In comparison, the audience share of SKY TG24's prime-time edition (TG24 is the news bulletin on SKY Italia satellite television), for instance, has been minuscule (0.32 percent in 2011, according to AGCOM, 2012: 118).

Throughout the 2000s, the "historical" channels (RAI and Mediaset) also maintained a prominent position in the digital terrestrial television sector, even as audience share for generalist television slowly decreased during the decade. In 2001, the six generalist channels of RAI and Mediaset combined had an audience share of 90.4 percent (RAI, 2002: 27); by 2012, that share had dropped to 62.0 percent (RAI, 2012: 30). During the same period, new national channels were growing: from a share of only 2.9 percent in 2009, they had reached 11.9 percent of audience share in 2011 (E-media, 2012: 3). Among those new channels, there was *Cielo*, News Corporation's channel on the digital terrestrial platform. During the 2000s and early 2010s, the consumption of mobile television was also increasing. In 2007, viewership of mobile TV was only 1 percent; in 2013 it had reached 6.8 percent (CENSIS, 2013: 2). The sector of mobile television had opened up to global competition, with operators such as the Chinese H3G and Vodafone Omnitel alongside Telecom Italia.

In the sector of pay TV, Sky Italia, the satellite television platform owned by Rupert Murdoch's News Corporation and in operation since 2003, has remained the dominant player. By 2011, it had almost five million subscribing households and controlled 77.4 percent of the pay TV market (AGCOM, 2012: 124). Mediaset Premium (Mediaset's pay-per-view offer on the digital terrestrial television platform) was a distant second, with 17.4 percent of the market.

From this overview, it is clear that the duopoly has been losing ground as new operators have entered the market and new technologies have been developed. However, RAI and Mediaset still represent key players, especially in the sector of news and public affairs programs, a sector that is vital for the relationship between media and democracy.

Emerging media

A chapter on media and democracy must also include references to emerging communication technologies and how these might have contributed to the creation of a more diverse media environment in the country. In line with developments elsewhere, social media have greatly contributed to changing the ways in which Italians receive and share information and news. Increasingly, users have interacted on popular mainstream sites such as Facebook and Twitter to gather information, and in 2013, the number of downloads of informative apps for smartphones and tablets had doubled compared with the previous year (CENSIS, 2013: 3).

The use of social media might have a positive impact for the promotion of a more pluralistic public sphere as sources multiply exponentially and users become more active. Politicians and journalists have certainly taken notice. Even Silvio Berlusconi attempted to engage different publics and modalities of communication when he set up a Facebook page and Twitter account in 2000 and 2013, respectively. Yet his "friends" and "followers" had been consistently less numerous than, for instance, those of Matteo Renzi, then mayor of Florence (since 22 February 2014, Italy's prime minister). When Berlusconi announced his decision to run for the 2013 national elections, the hashtag #nonlovoto immediately became a trending topic on Twitter. Still, his surprisingly positive showing at those elections reminds us that online behaviors are not valid predictors of offline voting preferences!

Conclusions

The history of the relationship between media and politics in Italy has illustrated the importance of supporting public media in the face of commercialization and consolidation of the cultural industries. In particular, the presence of a lively print media sector and an established public service broadcaster, might have contributed to improving pluralism in the public sphere.

Indeed, neither a free market nor technological innovations can guarantee diversity of viewpoints. For pluralism to be supported, public sector need to be strengthened. Moreover, regulation of conflicts of interest, aimed at preventing the consolidation and centralization of political and media power in the hands of a few, is also necessary for promoting a healthy relationship between media and democracy.

Notes

1 The Herfindahl-Hirschman index is a measurement (0–10,000 points) of market concentration. As a point of comparison, notice that the United States government defines firms with indexes in excess of 2,500 points as "highly concentrated" (Department of Justice and the Federal Trade Commission, 2010).

2 The notion of the public sphere received wide attention after the publication in English of Jürgen Habermas's *The Structural Transformation of the Public Sphere* (Habermas, 1989). According to that initial formulation, the public sphere was to be conceived as a sphere protected from both government pressures and market imperatives, where citizens could freely share information and deliberate on issues of public interest. The notion of the public sphere gained influence in the field of media studies thanks primarily to the work of Nicholas Garnham (1992) and his analysis of public service broadcasting as the embodiment of the ideals of the public sphere. Although various scholars (Benhabib, 1992 and Fraser, 1992, among others) have mounted important critiques of what they considered to be a male-dominated and ethnocentric concept, the notion of the public sphere, as a "community of authors, readers and writers" (Benhabib, 2008), continues to be a central category for the study of the role of the media in democracy. For an analysis of the relevance of the notion of the public sphere in contemporary media studies, see Lunt and Livingstone (2013).

3 Other milestones in the history of media legislation are: Law No. 249 of 31 July 1997, Law No. 112 of 3 May 2004, and Legislative Decree No. 177 of 31 July 2005.

4 For an in-depth analysis of this law, see Murialdi (1998).

5 In 2011, the Herfindahl-Hirschman index for newspapers in Italy was 886 (AGCOM, 2012: 139).

6 See www.fininvest.it/en/group/company_structure (accessed 20 December 2014).

7 The proposal is available at: www.lucianoviolante.it/images/pdf/pdl_leggi/1318_conflitto%20interessi.pdf?phpMyAdmin=VF18taLp7KbGqqxaWwkw2Zr8753&phpMyAdmin=840bf80888bf75b93091498f492547c0 (accessed 20 December 2014).

8 Owned by Cairo Communications.

9 The prime-time audience share of LA7 grew from 2.6 percent in 2008 to 4.0 percent in 2012. For a detailed analysis of LA7's performance despite a declining market share for generalist television channels in Italy, see Siliato (2012).

10 In 2011, 86.4 percent of Italians used news bulletins as their main source of information (CENSIS, 2013: 2).

Bibliography

AGCOM (2009). *Annual Report*. Available online at www.agcom.it/documents/10179/15859/1_Sistema_2009.pdf/1e9cc48c-8661–4bc1–83c8-dd094c1762fc (accessed 24 January 2015).

AGCOM (2012). *Annual Report on the Activity Carried Out and on the Work Programmes*. Available online at www.agcom.it/documents/10179/16144/RELAZIONE+ANNUALE+2012.pdf/e4ab0ad8-fb88–44ec-96be-26888af508e3 (accessed 23 January 2015).

Balbi, G. and Prario, B. (2010). The history of Fininvest/Mediaset's media strategy: 30 years of politics, the market, technology and Italian society. *Media, Culture & Society*, 32 (3), 391–409.

Benhabib, S. (1992). Models of Public Space: Hannah Arendt, The Liberal Tradition and Jürgen Habermas. In C. Calhoun (ed.) *Habermas and the Public Sphere* (pp. 73–98). Cambridge, MA: MIT Press.

Benhabib, S. (2008). On the Public Sphere, Deliberation, Journalism and Dignity. (Interview by Karin Wahl-Jorgensen), *Reset: Dialogues On Civilizations*, 4 August. Available online at www.resetdoc.org/story/00000000965 (accessed 15 January 2015).

Casarosa, F. and Bolgi, E. (2011). *Case Study Report. Does Media Policy Promote Media Freedom and Independence? The Case of Italy*. Report prepared for the European Commission Seventh Framework Programme. Available online at www.mediadem.eliamep.gr/wp-content/uploads/2012/01/Italy.pdf (accessed 5 January 2015).

CENSIS [Centro Studi Investimenti Sociali] (2013). *Rapporto sulla situazione sociale del paese. Comunicazione e Media. [Annual Report on the Country's Social Conditions. Communications and Media]*. Available online at www.censis.it/7?shadow_comunicato_stampa=120944 (accessed 23 January 2015).

Colapinto, C. (2010). Moving to a multichannel and multiplatform company in the emerging and digital media ecosystem: The case of Mediaset Group. *The International Journal of Media Management*, 12, 59–75.

Constitutional Court. *Sentence N. 420/1994*. Available online at http://www.ilfattoquotidiano.it/2013/05/01/conflitto-dinteressi-vietato-parlarne/580226/ (accessed 15 December 2014).

Curran, J. (2011). *Media and Democracy*. London: Routledge.

d'Arcais, P. F. (2013). Conflitto d'interessi, vietato parlarne. *Il Fatto Quotidiano*, 1 May. Available online at www.ilfattoquotidiano.it/2013/05/01/conflitto-dinteressi-vietato-parlarne/580226/ (accessed 23 January 2015).

D'Arma, A. (2009). Broadcasting policy in Italy's "Second Republic": National politics and European influences. *Media, Culture & Society*, 31 (5), 769–86.

Department of Justice and the Federal Trade Commission [U.S.A.] (2010). *Horizontal Merger Guidelines (5.3, Market Concentration)*. Available online at www.justice.gov/atr/public/guidelines/hmg-2010.html#5c (accessed 15 December 2014).

E-media (2012). Analisi. Gli Ascolti TV in Europa nel Passaggio al Digitale. No. 35, May. Available online at www.dgtvi.it/news.php (accessed 15 January 2014).

Fraser, N. (1992). Rethinking the Public Sphere: A Contribution to the Critique of Actually Existing Democracy. In C. Calhoun (ed.) *Habermas and the Public Sphere* (pp. 109–42). Cambridge, MA: MIT Press.

Fusani, C. (2007). Conflitto di interessi, l'Udeur si astiene. Berlusconi: "La legge non passerà". *La Repubblica*, 16 May. Available online at www.repubblica.it/2007/05/sezioni/politica/conflitto-interessi/udeur-si-astiene/udeur-si-astiene.html (accessed 23 January 2015).

Garnham, N. (1992). The Media and the Public Sphere. In C. Calhoun (ed.) *Habermas and the Public Sphere* (pp. 359–76). Cambridge, MA: MIT Press.

Habermas, J. (1989). *The Structural Transformation of the Public Sphere*. Cambridge, MA: MIT Press.

Law no. 416 (5 August 1981). *Disciplina delle imprese editrici e provvidenze per l'editoria*. Available online at www.medialaw.it/editoria/1981416.htm#TitoloII (accessed 15 December 2014).

Law no. 223 (6 August 1990). *Disciplina del sistema radiotelevisivo pubblico e privato*. Available online at www.camera.it/_bicamerali/rai/norme/l223–90.htm (accessed 23 January 2015).

Law no. 249 (31 July 1997). *Istituzione dell'Autorità per le garanzie nelle comunicazioni e norme sui sistemi delle telecomunicazioni e radiotelevisivo*. Available online at www.parlamento.it/parlam/leggi/97249l.htm (accessed 23 January 2015).

Law no. 112 (3 May 2004). *Norme di principio in materia di assetto del sistema radiotelevisivo e della RAI-Radiotelevisione italiana S.p.A., nonché delega al Governo per l'emanazione del testo unico della radiotelevisione [Norms for the Radio and Television System and RAI]*. Available online at www.camera.it/parlam/leggi/04112l.htm (accessed 23 January 2015).

Law no. 215 (20 July 2004). *Norme in materia di risoluzione dei conflitti di interessi [Norms for the Resolution of Conflicts of Interest]*. Available online at www.camera.it/parlam/leggi/04215l.htm (accessed 23 January 2015).

Legislative Decree n. 177 (31 July 2005). *Testo unico dei servizi di media audiovisivi e radiofonici [Consolidated Law]*. Available online at www.camera.it/parlam/leggi/deleghe/05177dl.htm (accessed 15 December 2014).

Lunt, P. and Livingstone, S. (2013). Media studies' fascination with the concept of the public sphere: critical reflections and emerging debates. *Media Culture & Society*, 35 (1), 87–96.

Mancini, P. (2009). *Elogio della lottizzazione. La via italiana al pluralismo*. Rome-Bari: Laterza.

Murialdi, P. (1998). *La stampa italiana dalla Liberazione alla crisi di fine secolo*. Rome-Bari: Laterza.

Padovani, C. (2005). *A Fatal Attraction: Public Television and Politics in Italy*. Boulder, CO: Rowman & Littlefield.

Padovani, C. (2009). Pluralism of Information in the Television Sector in Italy: History and Contemporary Conditions. In A. Czepek, M. Hellwig and E. Nowak (eds.) *Press Freedom and Pluralism in Europe: Concepts and Conditions* (pp. 289–304). Bristol: Intellect, ECREA book series.

Padovani, C. (2010). Public Service Communication in Italy: Challenges and Opportunities. In P. Iosifidis (ed.) *Reinventing Public Service Communication: European Broadcasters and Beyond* (pp. 183–96). Basingstoke: Palgrave Macmillan.

Padovani, C. (2015). Berlusconi's Italy: the media between structure and agency. *Modern Italy*, 20 (1), 41–57.

Polo, M. (2010). *Notizie S.p.A.* Rome-Bari: Laterza.

RAI (Radiotelevisione Italiana) (2002). *RAI Annual Report 2002.* Available online at www.bilancio 2002.rai.it/uk/dwl/pdf/eciv.pdf (accessed 15 December 2014).

RAI (2012). *RAI GROUP Reports and Financial Statements 2012.* Available online at www.rai.it/dl/bilancio2012/eng/bilancio/civ05.htm (accessed 15 December 2014).

Richeri, G. (1990). Hard Times for Public Service Broadcasting: The RAI in the Age of Commercial Competition. In Z. Baranski and R. Lumley (eds.) *Culture and Conflict in Postwar Italy* (pp. 256–69). London: Macmillan Press.

Siliato, F. (2012). *Dall'oligopolio alla coda lunga: la televisione è digitale.* Milan: FrancoAngeli.

11

NO LONGER PRO-EUROPEAN?

Politicisation and contestation of Europe in Italy

Nicolò Conti

Politicising Europe in Italy: long-term trends

Although one of the founding members of the EU, for a long time (1940s–1970s) Italy was characterised by a polarisation of the Italian party system that also affected politicisation of the issue of European integration. The country was divided between fervent Europhilia on the side of government parties and hard Euroscepticism on the side of the Italian Communist Party (PCI), the second-largest Italian party and main opposition force (it was never in government). In this context, the pro-European governments represented membership of the EEC not just as a matter of economic interest: it was a choice for the Western camp, one that found its other main pillar in membership of NATO. This conception of two nested supranational communities (one strategic and one mainly economic) developed among Italian government parties (particularly the Christian Democrats, DC) in a context of bilateralism and Cold War, when the country was under the double pressure resulting from physical proximity to the Warsaw Pact bloc and significant popular support for the PCI (the largest communist party in Western democracies) domestically. Thus, the choice of the Italian government to join the Common Market was part of a broader strategy primarily inspired by Atlanticism, so the EEC was not considered as a potential third force, but rather as a means of stabilising capitalism, consolidating democracy and developing interdependences within the framework of the Western strategic alliance. Conversely, for the same reasons, the Italian left (including the socialists until the 1950s; then only the communists) rejected the Common Market, which they considered an engine of capitalism and a tool of American influence in Europe.

However, from the 1970s, as a consequence of international developments in Soviet imperialism (such as the repression of the Prague Spring), ideological revision by some prominent left-wing thinkers and widespread benevolent attitudes towards the West and the EEC among leftist voters (Isernia and Ammendola, 2005), the PCI started a process of realignment on the issue of European integration that finally took the party closer to the continental mainstream. Consequently, the positions on the European issue gradually became linear, moving from polarised positions on the EEC (centrist principled support vs. leftist rejection) to a simplified version of widespread support. Radicalism on the EEC was gradually banned from the political discourse of the main political actors and their reciprocal distance became drastically reduced. Indeed, once the PCI changed its position and supported Italian participation in the European Community, particularly after it was renamed Party of Left Democrats (PDS, later simply DS) in 1991, no party of any significance could be found that would question Italian participation in the integration process.

Thus, consensus on European integration developed in Italy after a process of realignment taking over three decades that, in the end, transformed the country into one of the most pro-European member states (Conti and Verzichelli, 2012). Party consensus on the EEC/EU was shared by Italian citizens as well, who, in the same period, proved amongst the most Europhile in the whole continent (Bellucci and Serricchio, 2012). In the Italian case the permissive consensus on European integration was not the result of a choice of the elites that citizens would tolerate but not share; on the contrary it was a phenomenon rooted in widespread consensus between elites and masses. Such popular support was determined by several factors: identification with the Western camp and the Atlantic community (Isernia and Ammendola, 2005), greater trust in the European level of government than in the domestic government, which was considered inefficient and corrupt (Battistelli and Bellucci, 2002), and perceived economic benefits of membership (Italy was a net recipient in the EEC/EU budget).

Finally, consensus involved most Italian socio-economic and technocratic elites as well. On the one hand, the majority of employers saw the advantage in being allowed access to a broader market and a consequent higher demand for Italian goods abroad. Indeed, the Common Market was a driving factor in the export-driven economic boom of the 1960s in Italy, since exports have always been crucial for the Italian economy whose internal demand has maintained comparatively low rates (whereas savings have instead been high). On the other hand, unions saw the free movement of labour as an opportunity for the economic migrants of the *Mezzogiorno* and hoped that membership of the EEC/EU would push the country to develop a welfare state as modern as in other member states such as France and Germany (until the 1970s the Italian welfare was still based on a corporatist non-universalistic model). Finally, experts and top-level technocrats (particularly those operating in crucial ministries in the economic field and foreign affairs, or in the Bank of Italy) have always supported putting the country at the heart of the integration process and complying with the main EU challenges. Even more, they have contributed to binding the country to the most ambitious European commitments when the domestic political scene was more unstable (as in the early 1990s because of the transition from the First to the Second Republic), thus promoting domestic stabilisation by securing the government agenda within a European frame (Dyson and Featherstone, 1996). Actually, these elites considered the European external constraint necessary in order to stop the distributive laxity and abuse of public spending of the Italian government and to rescue the country from drifts caused by political clientelism and corruption (Cotta and Isernia, 1996; Ferrera and Gualmini, 1999).

In the end, at least since the 1980s, for different and often asymmetric reasons, the most important Italian political actors converged in supporting European integration. However, the end of the so-called First Republic in 1993 – that was mainly due to corruption scandals involving the main political parties, and to the end of the communist/anti-communist confrontation – marked the disappearance of the traditional parties (DC, PCI and other smaller parties governing in coalition with the Christian Democrats for several decades, including the socialist PSI), a depolarisation of the party system, and the creation of a new party system based on bipolarity and alternation in government. At the same time, negotiations for European Monetary Union were taking place. As we have seen, in the past, few voices were heard outside the two positions of principled support (definitely prevailing in the long term) and principled rejection of the

Common Market (declining over time), since any pragmatic approach to the issue of European integration was scantly represented in the Italian party system. But since 1994, for the first time all positions – from hard Euroscepticism, to pragmatic attitudes, to principled pro-Europeanism – have been represented, which has thus made Europe a divisive issue and one of renewed politicisation and increased salience.

A first discontinuity to note concerns the new centre-right parties, which have shown clear signs of Euroscepticism from the very beginning. Their political discourse has been described as moving back and forth from soft Euroscepticism to vagueness to broad unspecific pro-Europeanism. On the other side of the political spectrum, the literature documents that the Italian centre-left has Europe at the centre of its programme more than the right does and that the former has firmly developed the traditional commitment of the Italian governments of the First Republic to the idea of a united Europe (Conti and Memoli, 2010). It is worth noting that several authors maintain that across Europe, parties have swapped their positions on the EU and from the 1990s the left has become more pro-European than the right (Gabel and Hix, 2002; Ladrech, 2000). Although other authors (Conti, 2014) contend that left and right exert an influence on attitudes towards the EU that is not linear, it is a matter of fact that Italy is in line with the above pattern, as in this country the centre-left really has become more pro-European than the centre-right.

Second, at the extremes of the political spectrum, hard Euroscepticism has become a remarkable feature, though not a stable one. The small Communist party *Rifondazione Comunista* showed signs of strong opposition to European integration, for example, by voting in parliament against the ratification of the Maastricht Treaty, the Treaty of Nice and the Treaty establishing a Constitution for Europe.[1] At the other extreme of the political spectrum, the Northern League (LN) has also criticised the achievements of European integration and voted against the ratification of the Treaty establishing a Constitution for Europe (but in favour of the Lisbon Treaty). However, the fact that these parties have been in government several times made their stance rather ambivalent and their anti-European rhetoric has rarely been followed by coherent institutional behaviour but rather by alignment with the mainstream parties (Conti and De Giorgi, 2011). *Rifondazione Comunista* and the Northern League have become electorally weak in recent times, particularly the former, which has become unimportant and since 2008 has not been represented in the Italian parliament. However, a new Internet party (the Five Star Movement, M5S) made its appearance on the political scene in 2012 with an unprecedented success in the general elections of 2013, when, in a context of a fragmented party system, it became the largest party with over 25 per cent of the vote. The M5S failed to reach a majority in parliament only because the Italian electoral law benefits substantially those parties that make pre-electoral alliances. For this reason this party gained 40 per cent of seats less than the Democratic Party (PD, a merger of PDS-DS and other centrist parties such as *Margherita*), which came second in the elections but gained a generous seat bonus thanks to its pre-electoral alliance with other smaller parties. Despite the asymmetrical allocation of seats in parliament, for the first time since the deradicalisation of the PCI, the Italian party system finds in a radical force such as M5S one of its main internal units and a tendency toward polarisation again. The ideological character of the M5S is indeed protest-based, with a charismatic leader and a populist rhetoric, a mix of extreme left/right preferences and a hard Eurosceptic stance. Being an anti-establishment party, the M5S has refused cooperation with any other party in parliament. This has made the legislative process more disputed and polarised but has also made its capacity to influence the conduct of the Italian government on European issues directly very limited.

It is likely, however, that the electoral success of a fiercely Eurosceptic party like the M5S marks the end of the honeymoon between the Italians and Europe. Indeed, in recent times an increase in Euroscepticism has concerned public opinion as well as socio-economic elites. As to the former, the fall in public support for the EU has been impressive over the past twenty years, to the point that in the last decade the attitudes of the Italians have become more pessimistic than the European average, mainly because of perceived threats to their personal economic security and to their identity and values. Italians consider the most recent steps in European integration (monetary union, measures to manage financial instability such as the Fiscal Compact, enlargements) as the main determinants of the worsening of their economic condition and social security, as well as a threat to their culture and way of life (trust in other Europeans has reached a negative peak: see Bellucci and Serricchio, 2012). Considering that the centre-right had a majority and was in government for most of the recent past (in 2001–6 and 2008–11, then again in a grand coalition in 2012–13), one could argue that both Italian citizens and the government have shared a broad Eurosceptic stance. It is also possible that these two actors have exerted a mutual influence on each other, as parties represent citizens and the latter are indeed influenced by party discourse and ideology. Additionally, the fact that a party such as the M5S became so popular confirms that in the country there is a large electoral market available for a Euroseptical platform.

The Italian socio-economic elites have also become more cautious about the EU. Their support for the integration process has become more contingent on costs and benefits as long as they have started to perceive the impact of the EU on their interests less favourably in consequence of increased competitive pressures from the Common Market and the Eurozone. Their approach to the issue of European integration has become more pragmatic; for example they now express mixed views on EU institutions and policies and they support inter-governmentalism as a decision-making mode more than supranationalism, because in their view national interests can be better defended through the influence and veto power of national governments (De Giorgi and Verzichelli, 2012).

Certainly, the increased resistance to the EU and to European integration by a substantial part of public opinion, socio-economic elites and by so many major parties marks a shift in the widespread attitudes of Italians and, in the future, could give birth to an enduring social bloc that may change the overall relationship between Italy and Europe.

Different views on EU integration

Among the parties of the Second Republic, the major forces of the centre-right, *Forza Italia* and the National Alliance (AN) that merged into the People of Freedom Party (PDL) in 2008, but then split again into *Forza Italia* and several small parties in 2013, showed from their origins clear hints of Euroscepticism. Their political discourse has moved back and forth from soft Euro-scepticism to vagueness to broad unspecific pro-Europeanism, where the latter is mainly comprised of a supportive rhetoric largely used to gain domestic and international legitimacy for those parties whose leadership (respectively, the media tycoon Berlusconi and the post-fascist Fini) was distrusted by many, both domestically and internationally. Indeed, their support for European integration was rarely issue-specific. Throughout their life *Forza Italia* and National Alliance alternated hints of support for the general idea of integration with issue-specific Eurosceptical stances. In particular, the record of *Forza Italia* – until 2007 the largest Italian party and the main component of every centre-right coalition government – and of the PDL (the largest party in government in 2008–11) is striking. Forza Italia started in 1994 with a rather pro-European stance, but over time became more reticent with the lowest level of programmatic commitment to EU issues in the entire party system, while AN's rhetoric referred more intensely to the EU, but alternated pro-European and Eurosceptical stances.

Forza Italia and National Alliance agreed on the broad principle of the defence of national interests and on a preference for intergovernmentalism within the EU. Otherwise, on other issues the distance between the positions of these two parties was remarkable. For instance, AN was very interested in the EU playing an autonomous (even from NATO) international role, something that in the end would indirectly enhance the international role of Italy (otherwise a middle-ranking power with limited international influence). AN also showed an interest in the capacity of the EU to protect European economies from the challenges of globalisation. The focus was on the protection of goods produced in the EU from the low-cost products of non-EU countries. Ultimately the party saw in the European arena an environment in which a defensive strategy of economic protectionism could more successfully be achieved. On the other hand, the priority of *Forza Italia* was to create an ever-larger free-market area, more than a federal and politically integrated entity (several times the party proposed Russian and Israeli membership of the EU). The issue of the international role of the EU was instead little developed by *Forza Italia*, but its preference was openly for a predominant role for NATO. The stance of the PDL on the EU was hesitant and confused, probably as a result of different orientations of its internal factions linked either to Christian Democrat ideology, conservative neo-liberal thinking or political nationalism.

As a result of the economic crisis and the related austerity measures, the EU has become a more contentious issue in recent times, also because of greater politicisation by the PDL, as was shown for example in the general elections of 2013. Some of the patterns already at work in the party system were reinforced on this occasion and the PDL developed its critical stance into bitter antagonism against EU institutions. In particular, the Commissioner for Economic and Monetary Affairs, Olli Rehn, was represented by the party as an enemy of the Italian state and, together with the German Chancellor Angela Merkel, a conspirator against Italians' national interests. The electoral campaign conducted by the PDL built on stories of socio-economic panic and conspiracy against Italy. For example, Berlusconi accused the EU technocracy of forcing his government (in office in 2008–11) to resign, under the threat of economic sanctions against the country. According to Berlusconi's accusations, the EU exerted pressure to replace his government with one led by the former European Commissioner Mario Monti, in order to make the Italian executive more acquiescent to German and EU interests and demands. This is clear evidence of how the PDL has made efforts to demarcate itself from the mainstream and politicise the EU issue in order to give representation to an emerging split that divides advocates and opponents of the EU within Italian society.

At the other end of the political spectrum, from the early 1990s the Italian centre-left has placed Europe at the heart of its programme. The Italian People's Party/*Margherita* – a party which then merged with the Democratic Party[2] – developed the traditional commitment of the Christian Democrats to the idea of a united Europe, while the social democrats (PDS-DS)[3] reflected the positive international commitment of this family of parties. These two parties put forward within the country the principle of an ever-closer union. When in government, they appointed Romano Prodi (President of the European Commission from 1999 to 2004) prime minister twice. Both parties supported indeed the idea of a federal Europe and, therefore, of intense political integration. For this reason they were also in favour of supranational decision-making and critical of intergovernmentalism. Specifically, they supported the reinforcement of the EP and the Commission to the detriment of the Council and the overall improvement of popular legitimacy and powers of EU institutions through the direct election of the President of the Commission. They proposed EU (either exclusive or shared) involvement in the management of many policies as yet not so Europeanised, such as foreign and defence, justice, immigration and social policies. They were also in favour of a strong role for the EU in the international arena and the creation of an independent European military force, while in their view NATO should be transformed into an instrument of the United Nations. Finally, they proposed a permanent seat for the EU on the Security Council. Since 2007, the Democratic Party has proved coherent with the pro-European line of its founders. During the electoral campaign of 2013, there was indeed an attempt by the PD to put on the agenda the issues of economic growth and the relaxation of EU austerity measures, still within a framework of general loyalty and commitment to the EU process. It was not until 2014 that a newly formed coalition cabinet led by the new PD secretary Matteo Renzi announced a project of renegotiation of the Eurozone criteria and, in particular of the maximum allowed ratio of the annual general government deficit relative to gross domestic product. The idea is to allow Eurozone countries to exceed this ratio (3 per cent) for investments in infrastructure and measures to combat the crisis. Although at the time of writing the exact nature of these proposed measures is not clear, nor the terms of the supposed negotiation with the EU, it is interesting to note that under the pressure of a growing Eurosceptical front, a government led by the PD has for the first time introduced a critical note in its representation of the EU, arguing that its external influence is not entirely positive, but that it creates obstacles to growth and to overcoming the economic crisis in the country. It might be an exaggeration to interpret this as a shift in the attitudes of the centre-left towards the EU. Still, it is a sign of growing competition on the EU in a context of growing Euroscepticism on the part of citizens. Increasingly, parties including the PD respond to citizens' fears and perceived threats by promising the defence of national interests from the EU.

The 2013 general elections saw the creation of a new party (Civic Choice) led by the incumbent prime minister Mario Monti. This party and its leader made loyalty to the EU a firm priority. Needless to say, Monti's government gained an international reputation for its capacity to respond positively to EU recommendations and create a climate of international trust in the Italian government. Many austerity measures have been introduced under this government to meet EU demands and to comply with the competitive pressures imposed on Eurozone countries. The fact that during the same elections, the commissioner Rehn made a public endorsement of the Italian pro-European parties, in particular Monti's Civic Choice, contributed to the bitterness of the campaign and to increasing domestic polarisation with regard to the EU whose institutions became an easy target for political rivalry. After a disappointing result in the 2013 elections, the Europhile Civic Choice party split into many different factions of limited importance and, although represented in government with a limited presence and role, it has almost disappeared from the political scene and the electoral market.

As we have already mentioned, at the extremes of the political spectrum, throughout the past two decades Euroscepticism has been a solid feature. The small Communist party *Rifondazione Comunista* showed strong signs of opposition to European integration and the radical right-wing party, the Northern League, also held positions of fierce opposition to the EU. After the decline of the Northern League and the Communists, the M5S developed those parties' stances, which have taken it to unprecedented electoral success. In the past, the anti-capitalist *Rifondazione Comunista* defined the EU as an instrument of Americanisation and as an enemy, like other international technocratic powers such as the IMF and the WTO. The party voted against the ratification of the Maastricht Treaty and fiercely opposed monetary union and the creation of a European Central Bank. The reconstructed communists opposed the involvement of the EU in most policy fields, with the exception of social policy, where, in their view, the role of the EU in promoting best welfare practices could be beneficial in overcoming asymmetries across the member states. It is interesting to note that, contrary to the centre-left, in its discourse *Rifondazione* mainly presented the negative outcomes of the integration process and its external constraints on Italy. It defined European politics as a cause of the diminishing quality of life of lower classes and disadvantaged social groups and of stagnation in consumer demand. *Rifondazione* started a process of realignment from the mid-2000s that eventually led to the party becoming part of a government led by Europhile Prime Minister Romano Prodi in 2006–7. However, after this period the party became largely irrelevant with minimal electoral support and little coalition potential; hence its shift was not really conducive to any major change on the left of the political spectrum, beyond a simple decline of this area.

At the other end of the political spectrum, the regionalist Northern League (LN) strongly criticised the results that European integration had achieved as well. While defending intergovermentalism within the EU, it accused the European institutions of aiming at a process of state-building whose final goal is to replace nation states with a new undemocratic superstate. It expressed a pessimistic evaluation of the EU's impact on the main goal promoted by the party – the self-determination of the Northern regions of Italy – as well as on its targeted social groups – such as farmers, milk producers and small firms. LN rejected EU policy competence in most fields and framed stories of moral panic when describing the integration process, anticipating immigrant flows from the new member states and candidate countries, job losses and mounting unemployment of Italian citizens. Interestingly, the Northern League presents the preservation of the European meta-culture – rooted in Christianity and set apart from the other cultures – as a main political goal. Actually, the discourse on a shared identity among Europeans has become a central point in the rhetoric of this party. However, it is one used to justify another theme on which the party exerts a sort of issue-ownership within the system: the rejection of non-EU citizens (particularly Muslims), considered aliens and enemies of European civilisation. Indeed, this discourse does not include any reference to the shared identity of Europeans based on the common experience of the EU process and is not conducive to building a European identity, but rather to marking distance from non-Europeans, sometimes with overtly xenophobic tones.

Finally, the M5S is a new party with no past record before 2013, when it contested national elections for the first time. On this occasion the party leader, Beppe Grillo, made the EU central to its campaign. Interestingly, the Eurosceptical discourse of Grillo is similar to – but much more radical than – the recent discourse of the centre-right. Furthermore it develops many old Eurosceptic arguments made by the radical left and right. This phenomenon shows that competition has developed at the Eurosceptic end of the political spectrum and that a growing number of parties now give salience to a pessimistic representation of Europe. During the campaign, the M5S insisted in particular on stories of conspiracy on the part of the EU and other European countries against Italy. Grillo contended that the European Central Bank lent money to Italian banks to make them buy Italian government bonds that before were held by German and French banks. This would serve as a means to free France and Germany from toxic assets, while shifting to Italy the whole burden of financial uncertainty and indebtedness. Additionally, many times Grillo proposed a referendum on Italy leaving the Eurozone. Rejection of the EU by this party is therefore important in all aspects of the integration process, including policy, institutional representation and identity. At the time of writing, the future of this party is very uncertain, and it remains to be seen whether it will survive the institutionalisation and political responsibility that are normally associated with parties with such a large share of the vote. The 5SM is a personality-based party lacking a central office and subject to the discretionary decisions of the party leader. It delegates its main political choices and policy stances to a single leader who decides every time, often following public opinion and without necessarily formalising it in a programmatic platform. Thus, we have limited systematic information on the overall stance of this party and it is difficult to assess whether the party rank and file all share the same Europhobic attitude. Ultimately, it is interesting to note that a party with such a hard Eurosceptical stance could be so successful in Italy. It is a clear sign of a shift in the attitudes of citizens towards Europe and of its impact on the party system.

On the whole, the picture of party politicisation and preference formation on Europe could be seen in the light of two points of view proposed by the comparative literature. The first concerns the European vocation of social democrats in several countries (Hix *et al.*, 2007; Ladrech, 2000) that has clearly emerged in Italy as well. The second concerns the Eurosceptical attitudes of parties on the edges of the political spectrum (Szczerbiak and Taggart, 2008) that have also found fertile ground in Italy. The two oldest radical parties (*Rifondazione Comunista* and the Northern League) have been in government several times in coalition with the mainstream parties, and this contributed to their reducing their anti-EU rhetoric and aligning their institutional behaviour with regard to the EU with that of mainstream parties.[4] However, this is not the case with the M5S, which has taken a confrontational and anti-system stance within the Parliament and whose Euroscepticism seems firmly principled. The Left (Europhile) and the Right (Eurosceptical) used the EU issue to demarcate themselves from each other. However, of late the EU has become so unpopular with public opinion that the most recent signs are in the direction of an adoption of a critical stance by the centre-left as well.

Ultimately, over a long period of time, Italy evolved from having a polarised party system with polarised attitudes to the EU, to a segmented party system with Euroscepticism confined to its edges, to a segmented party system with a tendency to become polarised again (witness the role of the M5S). Competition over the EU issue has overlapped with – and even strengthened – the dominant pattern of competition in the party system. Indeed, conflict over the European issue produced a *divergence* when polarisation of the party system was higher and a *convergence* when polarisation was lower. In this respect, Conti and Verzichelli (2012) proposed the argument of the *internalisation* of the European issue along the established lines of party division: a process largely characterised by a *fit* between the conflict over EEC/EU and the domestic patterns of party competition. The European issue has neither disrupted the Italian party system, nor has it created a new cleavage. Typically, Europe becomes more politicised as long as the system becomes more polarised and citizens become more divided. In the end, competition over the EU has been internalised by the patterns of competition characterising the party system, and it might also have contributed to their reinforcement.

Final remarks

Italy was a country of extraordinary Europhilia until the mid-1990s. The symbiosis between integration, modernisation and economic stability was very effective in the eyes of domestic politicians and decisionmakers and enjoyed a widespread permissive consensus on the part of citizens. However, this pattern completely changed after the signing of the Maastricht Treaty and the new parties born after the end of the First Republic have channelled the growing unhappiness of citizens with the EU within the party system. Since the economic crisis, Euroscepticism and protest voting have become more significant in the country, so even mainstream parties have made their anti-EU rhetoric central in their discourse (PDL) or have at least encompassed some aspects of criticism (PD). However, the fact that in Italy the discourse on the EU has become largely Eurosceptical does not mean that the institutional behaviour of parties and of institutions follows the same tendency. On EU matters, after the Europhile Monti government, Italy had a more divided government based on a grand coalition, which, however, has not changed its behaviour towards the EU. Indeed, changing the roots of loyalty (or even acquiescence) of the Italian government to the EU might prove very difficult for the

Eurosceptical forces even when they are in government, especially in the context of the economic vulnerability of the country. For example, despite a broad debate within the government on the necessity of renegotiating the EU criteria for Eurozone countries, in recent years the loyalty of the Ministry of the Economy to the EU proved very solid. Certainly, the lack of consensus on the EU trajectory and the mounting Euroscepticism on the political scene are emergent phenomena of great interest. However, the Italian government looks very much embedded in a role of a government that rules but does not represent. In particular, it rules under the external constraint of the EU – particularly severe during the economic crisis – but it does not represent those demands of change in the trajectory of the EU that have become so prominent in Italy, once a Europhile country.

Notes

1 As of 2008, the party is not represented in the Italian parliament any more. Therefore it has not participated in the process of ratification of the Lisbon Treaty.
2 The Democratic Party was created in 2007 when the Left Democrats (DS) merged with *Margherita*. Today, it is the main party on the centre-left.
3 This party became the largest heir of the Italian Communist Party (PCI), which was dissolved in the early 1990s. It has moved from a post-communist legacy to a more moderate social democrat platform. Dissident members of the old PCI created a separate and more extreme party, *Rifondazione Comunista*, and other fringe parties.
4 For example, it has been shown that, when in government, these parties voted in favour of the ratification of EU legislation as much as the mainstream incumbent parties (Conti and De Giorgi, 2011).

References

Battistelli, F. and Bellucci, P. (2002). L'identità degli italiani tra euroscetticismo e europportunismo. *Il Mulino*, 1(52), 77–85.

Bellucci, P. and Serricchio, F. (2012). Cosa pensano i cittadini dell'Europa? In P. Bellucci and N. Conti (eds.) *Gli Italiani e l'Europa*. Rome: Carocci.

Conti, N. (2014). Introduction. In N. Conti (ed.) *Party Attitudes Towards the EU in the Member States* (pp. 1–19). London: Routledge.

Conti, N. and De Giorgi, E. (2011). L'Euroscetticismo a parole: Lega Nord e Rifondazione Comunista, tra Retorica e comportamento istituzionale. *Rivista Italiana di Scienza Politica*, 41(2), 265–89.

Conti, N. and Memoli, V. (2010). Italian parties and Europe: problems of identity, representation and scope of governance in the Euromanifestos (1989–2004). *Perspectives on European Politics and Society*, 11(2), 167–82.

Conti, N. and Verzichelli, L. (2012). Italy? In E. Kulahci (ed.) *Europeanisation and Party Politics*. Colchester: ECPR Press.

Cotta, M. and Isernia, P. (1996). *Il Gigante dai Piedi d'Argilla*. Bologna: Il Mulino.

De Giorgi, E. and Verzichelli, L. (2012). Classe politica e integrazione europea: segnali di crisi? In P. Bellucci and N. Conti (eds.) *Gli Italiani e l'Europa*, Rome: Carocci.

Dyson, K. and Featherstone, K. (1996). Italy and EMU as a 'Vincolo Esterno': empowering the technocrats, transforming the state. *South European Society and Politics*, 1(2), 272–99.

Ferrera, M. and Gualmini, E. (1999). *Salvati dall'Europa*. Bologna: Il Mulino.

Gabel. M. and Hix, S. (2002). Defining the EU political space. *Comparative Political Studies*, 35(8), 934–64.

Hix, S., Noury, A. and Roland, G. (2007). *Democratic Politics in the European Parliament*. New York: Cambridge University Press.

Isernia, I. and Ammendola, T. (2005). L'Europa vista dagli Italiani: I Primi Vent'Anni. In M. Cotta, P. Isernia and L. Verzichelli (eds.) *L'Europa in Italia. Elites, Opinione pubblica e decisioni*. Bologna: Il Mulino.

Ladrech, R. (2000). *Social Democracy and the Challenge of European Union*. London: Lynne Rienner Publishers.

Szczerbiak, A. and Taggart, P. (2008). *Opposing Europe: The Comparative Party Politics of Euro-scepticism*, vols. 1–2. Oxford: Oxford University Press.

12

RELIGION AND THE STATE

Donatella Loprieno

A brief introduction

To examine the issue of the relations between religion and the Italian state it is necessary to consider the very close relations that the latter has maintained with the Catholic, Roman and Apostolic Church throughout history. Rome has always had a primacy of honor compared with the other core cities of Christian Europe (e.g. the role of the Church of Constantinople), universally recognized as the see of the Apostle Peter (Cardia, 2010: 22) and the center of world Catholicism. The almost millenary existence of a State of the Church (Papal State), which covered most of the (modern) regions of central Italy, before the unification of the country and the question of the role of Rome, see of the temporal power of the pope, but also capital of Italy (the so-called Roman Question), raised after 1861, have inevitably marked the issue of the creation and consolidation of the Italian state, thereby delaying the birth and progressive consolidation of lay ethics. Even if many other denominations exist and are embraced in Italy today, and, at least formally, atheism, agnosticism and indifferentism cannot be the direct cause of discriminations, there can be no doubt that the Catholic Church and its hierarchies are deeply rooted and play a key role at all levels of political and social life. Financial, fiscal and educational resources, in all their different aspects, which the Catholic Church benefits from, are incomparably more considerable than those enjoyed by other religious confessions (see www.icostidellachiesa.it). In ethically sensitive issues (end of life, medically assisted reproduction, scientific research, etc.) or in those concerning aspects to which the magisterium is particularly attentive (family, sexuality, legal recognition of homosexual relationships), a prominent role is still played in Italy by Catholic hierarchies and the unilateral ethics promoted by them. Instead, public decisions (whether taken or not) on the rights of the freedom of people, as in the case of homosexuals or sterile couples, or of those who want to die with dignity, in a democratic constitutional state should stand above any single and partial ethics of each religious confession and protect believers, non-believers and "individuals with different beliefs" in their earthly existence.

The presence of the state of the Vatican City, which is an absolute monarchy with the pope as its undisputed head, has therefore hindered, and still hinders, the full emancipation of politics and law from the religious dogmas and the social doctrine of the Catholic Church. The orientation of the ecclesiastical authorities to directly address the people and the political class in Italy has been maintained intact, going well beyond the rules governing the relations between the two states (the Italian state and the Vatican state), thereby invading spaces that are undoubtedly "temporal." On the other hand, those who hold the political power in Italy are, in many cases, not only willing to satisfy the Church's desiderata, but even tend to anticipate them. Perhaps, the historical events of Italy have made its religious belonging so static and viscous that the Italian population, although strongly secularized, still finds it difficult to perceive itself as a lay, multiethnic and multicultural society.

That having been stated in general, this chapter has been structured as follows:

An initial and very short section will account for the "original" fracture between the newly born unified Italian state and the Catholic Church, as well as the attempts to set such a fracture by a compositional approach during the Fascist regime. In this section, we will place emphasis on the words of Carlo Arturo Jemolo, one of the most outstanding experts on religious matters in Italy, who, in his reconstruction of the relations between the state and the church in Italy, highlighted the need not to interpret the past through the present (Jemolo, 1974: 52).

A second section will analyze the constitutional provisions on the Catholic religion, other religious beliefs and, more generally, on the protection of religious freedom. In particular, the focus will be on how the Catholic Church has kept its traditional dominant position for about two decades after the entry into force of the Italian Republican Constitution of 1948. It was not until the late eighties that the Italian Constitutional Court formulated the supreme principle of the *laicità* (principle of secularism) of the state, which, however, has never implied indifference of the state to religions "but the State guarantee for the protection of freedom of religion, under the religious and cultural pluralism" (Decision No. 203/89). The actual implementation of the principle of *laicità* in Italy still faces great difficulties, since it is continually challenged and its content is too often even debased.

In this respect, the last section of the chapter will consider some aspects, already settled in a large number of European countries, which are in Italy still held hostage by a political *élite* that is too indulgent to the requests of the clerical authorities.

Unification and the Roman question

The unification of the Italian state, which had been divided into several small states, did not occur until the second half of the nineteenth century, more specifically in 1861. The annexation of Rome to the Kingdom of Italy and, therefore, the end of the Papal State and the temporal power of the popes took place on 20 September 1870 with the famous "Breach of Porta Pia."

In previous centuries, religion-based law had a key role in Europe. The alliance between the throne and the altar found its logical justification insofar as each of the two orders could have recourse to the powers of the other to better control the subjects of the former, who were at the same time also the believers of the latter. In the historical process, which led to the birth of the modern separatist state and started in the late eighteenth century, the political and legal framework progressively separated "from Christian religion and from any specific religion as the foundation and haven" (Böckenförde, 2007: 34). It has rightly been pointed out that separatism identifies with modernity in that it "expresses the need of the community to free from any authoritarian clerical tie" (Cardia, 2010: 73), thereby introducing the issue of laicity in continental Europe in a modern sense. In this process of the foundation of the state and of public institutions, the religious profile of individuals has little importance insofar as they are taken into consideration by laws exclusively for their status as citizens. Summarizing the concept, we could affirm that the European states in the nineteenth century developed an exclusively "profane" profile, becoming emancipated from the sacred and confining the religious aspirations and feelings of individuals to the private sphere. The universality of the new organization of political power is no longer based on the dogmatic heritage of one of the various religions, but it is anchored to a system whose objectives are things and values of this world. If in the liberal state model, politics and law must be desacralized as a matter of principle and need, it is not surprising that the Catholic Church has refused the ideology of liberalism as a whole, perceiving the separatist change as a clear departure from the natural order of things. The conflict was more political than religious and the state was in need of defending itself from an alternative project promoted by the Church. In brief, the historical assertion of secularism "as a positive political value, took place *against* the Church, not *with* the Church and, even less, *by* the Church" (Zagrebelsky, 2010: 11).

As we have already anticipated, one of the thorniest issues of the newborn Kingdom of Italy was the so-called Roman Question, originating from the historical events which led to the liberation of the city of Rome on 20 September 1870 and its annexation to the Kingdom of Italy. The solutions devised by the Law of Guarantees of 13 May 1871 for regulating relations between the Kingdom of Italy and the Holy See, although internationally appreciated for their balance, left the Holy See dissatisfied, and it maintained its opposition on principle against the Italian state until 1929.

For their part, the first governments of the unified Italy tended to award the state the functions that are typical of a legal system[1] that had above all to become emancipated from the interference of the Catholic Church, which, instead, asserted its will to deal with sacred issues but also and especially with earthly ones. The anti-unitary vocation of the Papacy should be attributed to the lack of participatory "'patriotic' grounds which prevented the development of an 'Italian National Church' over time. Nothing comparable to what would be the homeland churches of the great European nations, indeed incorporated in the universal Church, but national first of all" (Bellini, 2011: 14).

Some documents issued by the Church can be mentioned in confirmation of the Holy See's attitude of refusal and hostility towards the Italian liberal state and modernity, in general. The encyclical[2] *Quanta cura* (1864) and its annex *Syllabus* listed, for example, pantheism, naturalism, rationalism, indifferentism (i.e. freedom of religion), socialism and communism among the main *errores*. The so-called *Non expedit*,[3] a policy of the Holy See pronounced for the first time in 1868 and reasserted several times in subsequent years, prohibited any possibility of Italian Catholics cooperating with the institutions of the state and participating in political elections and, therefore, in the political life in Italy. Inevitably, such a policy, which was not revoked until 1919, caused a delay in the creation of a Catholic party able to adjust to the mechanisms of a liberal democracy. It should be pointed out, however, that in liberal Italy religious pluralism has never been a feature of the nation and that Catholicism has never had real competitors. Catholicism, for better or worse, whether accepted or refused, was the reference religion of the Italian people. In other words, historically, there has always been poor familiarity with religious pluralism and the consequences it has for the legal system.

Part of the earthly power lost by the Catholic Church at the time of separatism[4] would be recovered with the agreements of the 1920s–30s, at the price, however, of a strategic and political alliance with the totalitarian states of Fascist inspiration based on surrenders, silences and complicities. When the Lateran Pacts were signed on 11 February 1929, the Fascist Italian state and the Catholic Church settled the Roman Question and finally made "peace." The Lateran Accords of 1929 were peculiar in that they were made up of two separate acts which were different both formally and substantially. The treaty provided a new solution to the Roman Question, by creating the state of the Vatican City, setting out the relations between the latter and the Italian state, and recognizing the independence and sovereignty of the Holy See and the pontiff. Annexed to this act was a Financial Convention whereby Italy, "in consequence of the events of 1870" agreed to a number of financial commitments as an indemnity "through the loss of the patrimony of S. Peter constituted by the ancient Pontifical States." The other document of the Lateran Pacts was concluded to "regulate the position of religion and the church in Italy." The Concordat reactivated – also from a formal point of view – the religious confessionality of the State, thereby making the Catholic religion "the only state religion." Article 1 of the Lateran Treaty specifies that "Italy recognizes and reaffirms the principle established in the first Article of the Statute of the Kingdom, according to which the Catholic Apostolic Roman religion is the only State religion." This provision, although not having immediate legal application, has become, over time, the prism through which many other provisions of the Concordat could be read and construed in favor of the requirements of the Catholic confession on the one hand, and on the other hand it left a distinct confessional hallmark on the Italian legal system, to the detriment of the freedom of other faiths existing in the Italian state. Suffice it to mention, among the other things, the crime of defamation of the Catholic religion, which, envisaged for the first time in the Sardinian Code of 1859 and dropped from the new criminal code of 1889, was reintroduced in the Rocco Code of 1930. The secular punishment for defamatory behavior – even if eroded by the constitutional doctrine – has crossed the threshold of the twenty-first century. In the micro-system of Articles 402–6 of the Rocco Code of 1930, within a general authoritarian framework, the provisions laying down penalties for the crime of defamation of the Catholic religion and to a lesser extent of other "admitted beliefs" was derived not from the consideration of religion as an individual interest, but from its consideration for the purposes of the preservation of the political–institutional context, or of the social peace, or of the defense of the community's religious identification, or of a greater ideological control. All these matters would inevitably be in conflict with the new system of rights of freedom, under the sign of pluralism, outlined by the new Constitutional Charter of 1948.

The protection of the freedom of religion in the Republican Constitution of 1948 and the supreme principle of the *laicità* of the state

On 2 June 1946, after two decades of Fascist dictatorship and the atrocities of World War II, Italian male and female citizens were called to the polls to chose between the Republic and the Monarchy and elect the members of the Constituent Assembly whose task was to draft the new Constitution. The Constituent Assembly was characterized by different political orientations: left-wing, liberal and Catholic. It was inevitable that these different orientations emerged, encountering and clashing with each other, in the elaboration of the constitutional provisions which, directly and indirectly, affected aspects of religious issues. If on the one hand, the overall result cannot be considered as the exclusive outcome of any of the political powers participating in the Constituent Assembly, on the other hand it turned out to be thornier and more complex than was expected by the protagonists themselves. It was not by chance that Art. 7 of the Constitution,[5] on the subject of relations between the Italian state and the Catholic Church, was the provision most hotly debated by the Assembly and it is still today open to diverging (if not opposite) interpretations, to such an extent as to be considered a "complete constitutional monstrosity" (Viano, 2008: 15). The central issue to be solved was the status to be attributed to the Lateran Pacts in the future context of democracy and pluralism. Relatively more straightforward was the approval of Article 8[6] on the position to be given to non-Catholic religious confessions. Many members of the Constituent Assembly, and especially the lay wing, perceived the disparity between the Catholic Church, protected by the Constitution's explicit reference to the Lateran Pacts of 1929, and the other religious confessions, which were not sufficiently protected by safeguards on individual religious freedom. The first paragraph of Article 8 ("All religious confessions are equally free before the law.") grants the same amount of freedom and absolute equality of treatment in the enjoyment of the freedoms guaranteed by the Constitution to all religious confessions. However, whereas the Catholic Church is "independent and sovereign" from the state, other religious confessions "have the right to organize themselves in accordance with their own statutes, provided that these statutes are not in conflict with Italian law"; whereas relations with the Catholic Church are regulated by the Lateran Pacts (whose amendments, where agreed upon between the Italian state and the Catholic Church, do not require any constitutional review), those with non-Catholic confessions are "regulated by law on the basis of accords between the state and the respective representatives." As can be easily inferred, the constitutional text contains an undeniable inconsistency in the treatment of non-Catholic religious confessions (same freedom, but different treatment).

On the whole, the right of religious freedom has become a key element within the framework of the whole set of rights and freedoms protected by the Constitution. It is guaranteed in its individual and collective expression by Article 19 ("All persons have the right to profess freely their own religious faith in any form, individually or in association, to disseminate it and to worship in private or public, provided that the religious rites are not contrary to public morality."); it is closely linked with the principle of equality formulated in Article 3, which guarantees equality and equal social dignity without discrimination of religion, with the "personalist principle" laid down by Article 2, according to which "The Republic recognizes and guarantees the inviolable rights of the person, as an individual and in the social groups where human personality is expressed. The Republic expects that the fundamental duties of political, economic and social solidarity be fulfilled." This core constitutional provision outlines a polyhedric idea of the human person, whose protection is not limited to primary needs, which are indeed fundamental, but it extends to a more intimate sphere: the need for moral freedom, self-determination, self-actualization, as well as active and conscious participation in democratic institutions. Freedom of religion is also referred to in a variety of other constitutional provisions regulating issues connected to it: the right to freedom of thought, the rights to freedom of association and assembly, the freedom of art and science (and their teaching); the moral and legal equality of spouses on which marriage is based.

The different collocation and content of the formulations chosen by the Constituent Assembly to regulate relations with the Catholic Church and the other religious confessions have contributed to maintaining the undisputed supremacy of the Catholic confession vis-à-vis all other religions, especially in the first years of the Republic's life, and the predominance of the religious culture of the majority. In religious matters (as well as in other sectors) the laws adopted during the Fascist period remained in force and public bodies continued to act as if the Constitution did not exist. It was legislation very favorable to the Catholic religion and discriminatory against other minority confessional groups and non-religious and irreligious ideologies. Throughout the sixties and the seventies, Italian society underwent an important process of secularization with the emergence of a new lay conscience. In the sectors in which, in previous years, legislative policy had been more subject to the Catholic Church (sexual morals, the concept of family, the role of women and abortion) new issues were introduced: divorce, law on abortion and the new family law, to mention but a few.

The new idea of civil ethics and the separation of them from religious morality paved the way – in the early eighties – to the end of the long process of the revision of the Concordat of 1929. On 18 February 1984, the so-called "new concordat," which is still in force,[7] was concluded in Villa Madama. From a formal point of view, the new concordat is a bilateral and consensual amendment of the Concordat of 1929, even if from the point of view of substance, several amendments and innovations were introduced. It was certainly necessary to "update" the anachronistic old concordat in line with the constitutional, social and cultural evolution of Italy but also with the renewal of the Catholic Church after the Second Vatican Council. In the Additional Protocol to the new concordat, the contracting parties in relation to Art. 1 ("The Italian Republic and the Holy See reaffirm that the State and the Catholic Church are each in their own way independent and sovereign and committed to this principle in all their mutual relations and to reciprocal collaboration for the promotion of man and the good of the Country.") mutually stated that the principle of the Catholic religion as the sole religion of the Italian state, originally referred to by the Lateran Pacts, should no longer be in force.

The 1984 Agreement, despite several contradictions, triggered a number of transformations consolidating the pluralism embodied in the Constitution and fostering actual secularism. Many agreements have been progressively concluded with different religious confessions on the basis of the provision of Art. 8 of the Constitution[8] and, above all the Constitutional Court[9] has rendered secularism the supreme principle of the Italian legal system. With decision No. 203 of 1989, the Italian Constitutional Court started the important and difficult process of the definition and development of the supreme principle, that is the principle of *laicità*, which is not expressly mentioned in the Constitution, although it permeates it. Such a principle stemmed from Articles 2, 3, 7, 8, 19 and 20 of the Constitution and outlines one of the profiles of the form of State envisaged by the Charter of the Republic. It "does not imply indifference to religion, but the State guarantee for the protection of freedom of religion, under the religious and cultural pluralism" (Decision 203/89). Starting from this decision, the Italian Constitutional Court has progressively set out the principle of *laicità* and its corollaries, expunging the provisions which – in an anachronistic way and in contrast to the Constitution – awarded extra protection to the Catholic religion. In more recent decisions, the principle was set out as the "neutrality of the State in religious matters" (Decision 235/97), "equidistance and impartiality of legislation with respect to all different religious denominations" (Decision 329/97) and "distinction between civil matters and religious matters" (Decision 334/96).

What has become of the principle of *laicità* and its corollaries?

The years following Decision No. 203 of 1989 have been characterized not only by "the persistent failure to implement the constitutional principle of *laicità*, but also by a subtle neutralization of the principle itself, pursued through the introduction of provisions which . . . have led to the depletion of the innovative profiles of the constitutional model of laicity" (Fiorita, 2011). In recent years, moreover, the intervention of the Constitutional Court has become less frequent, while ordinary and administrative courts have provided a minimal and, in too many cases, even an elusive interpretation of this principle.[10] The substantiality of the political interest and of the millenary attitude of the Church to the *potestas indirecta in temporalibus* has continued to prevail over the abstract purity of the principle. The issue is very subtle: laicity is never denied, but provisions favoring the Catholic Church are justified and legitimated through interpretations redefining the concept of laicity itself, emptying it of its emphatic and libertarian content.

It seems that, especially over the last two decades, the decrease in the political unity of Catholics[11] and the loss of appeal of Catholic morality have been flanked by the temptation of a part of the Catholic hierarchy to compensate for a lack of authority and authoritativeness (e.g. the scandal of pedophilia) by increasing pressure on politics "to support with the authority of the political power and the judiciary the moral rules which the Church is no longer able to impose on consciences" (Prodi, 2005: 266–7). How else could we explain the several *non possumus* with which the Holy See opposes any possible form of recognition of unions between people of the same sex? Or abortion? Or medically assisted reproduction? Or euthanasia?

The *non possumus* of the Catholic Church and the fullness of rights of Italian citizens

Very often, in public discussions and in parliament in Italy, references to encyclicals eclipse or completely nullify references to the articles of the Constitution. On an almost daily basis, the Italian Episcopal Conference or the pope himself lavishes *non possumus* on matters or problems they consider "ethically sensitive" and, thus, of their competence in that they are the sole guardians "of morals supported by truth and reason" (Zagrebelsky, 2010: 101). But, is it possible to recognize a certain ethical/moral superiority in the believers of any religious denomination and in its highest representatives, which leads the public powers to favor any, and only, one instance? Contraception, abortion, scientific research, conception and death, recognition of loving unions between homosexuals, discrimination, and physical and verbal violence against homosexuals are only some of the issues with which Italian citizens are confronted every day. No doubt that, if desacralisation of law and politics is seriously taken into account, these are issues of public ethics which need law provisions with general scope and validity for everyone (believers, non-believers, and individuals with different beliefs) and, therefore, for those who pursue a discordant *ethos* vis-à-vis the values that are considered as the only right, moral and natural ones for the Catholics. The question for non-religious Italian citizens is not the *tout court* exclusion of the Catholic religion and its institutionalized agencies from the public sphere, but simply the refusal to attribute a special status to their *non possumus* or to their non-negotiable values.

Well aware that it cannot lead any battle against divorce or abortion (which has actually become complicated by the possibility for medical and paramedical staff to exercise conscientious objection) or against other institutions that are now part of the cultural and ethical background of Italian society, the Catholic Church is concentrating a large part of its efforts against the legal recognition of loving and sexual relationships between people of the same sex. Such efforts have clearly been evidently well invested, since no legislation on unions between homosexuals has been passed in Italy so far. In 2000, the Pontifical Council for the Family issued an interesting document titled *Family, marriage and "de facto unions,"* stating that "with the pretext of regulating one context of social and juridical cohabitation, attempts are made to justify the institutional recognition of de facto unions. In this way, de facto unions would turn into an institution, and their rights and duties would be sanctioned by law to the detriment of the family based on marriage. In today's open and democratic societies, the State and the public authorities must not institutionalize de facto unions, thereby giving them a status similar to marriage and the family, nor much less make them equivalent to the family based on marriage." According to Vatican hierarchies, lawmakers in all European countries (except for Greece), in having recognized rights and duties to members of gay couples, have used their power arbitrarily "because the original nature of marriage and the family proceeds and exceeds, in an absolute and radical way, the sovereign power of the State." The (unexplained and unexplainable) option is that the orientation "of discriminating against marriage by attributing an institutional status to de facto unions that is similar, or even equivalent to marriage and the family, is a serious sign of the contemporary breakdown in the social moral conscience, of 'weak thought' with regard to the common good, when it is not a real and proper ideological imposition exerted by influential pressure groups."

Stances of this kind, which are legitimate if addressed to the faithful and not so legitimate when addressed to the state and the public powers that belong to everyone (believers and non-believers) and whose mission is completely earthly, are at the basis of the criticism energetically promoted by Vatican hierarchies and especially the current pope against relativism. The condemnation of the cultural predominance of relativism (an all-encompassing formula including a large range of things that are often very different from one another), is in conclusion a "condemnation of the pluralism of the ethical views of life and the establishment of a sole assertion that is legitimate in that it is 'true,' as compared to all other assertions that are illegitimate, in that they are 'false'" (Zagrebelsky, 2010: 95). The fear of relativism could be interpreted as the request not to confine religion exclusively to the private sphere of the individual. Anyone who is up to date on Italian current events through the media well knows how intensely and loudly the voice of the Catholic Church is raised in the public sphere. No day passes without the Italian media covering the opinions of the pope or the Italian Episcopal Conference on all the main items on the political agenda. What is disquieting for non-religious Italian people is, rather, the consequences that would follow from the unquestionable meddling of the Catholic Church in the public sphere: "the recognition of a new 'temporalism,' with the attribution of a power of social government to the Church" (Rodotà, 2009: 133), which could stray from the principle of the separation of orders, embodied in Article 7 of the Constitution and establishing the supreme principle of the *laicità* of the state.

If the principle of the *laicità* of the state and its corollaries were taken into account seriously, as in other Western democracies, then the Church's magisterium should not affect the development and the content of public decisions. On the other hand, Italian lawmakers should show greater autonomy and, finally, assume the responsibility of lay choices in ethically sensitive issues. However, Italian lawmakers, even the most progressive ones, were totally unable to pass provisions (even very "soft" ones) on issues such as unions between people of the same sex or end-of-life treatment (euthanasia) and, in contrast, they approved a very severe, or even liberticidal law on medically assisted reproduction.

A kind of short-sighted cultural backwardness seems to pervade large sectors of Italian society, which is manifestly not yet mature enough for laicity. In 2013, journalists asked the political leaders who were candidates for the government of Italy what family meant for them, what they intended to do for homosexual couples and whether they considered it acceptable for homosexual couples to be able to adopt children. They did not dwell too much on other much more ethically relevant issues such as the fight against organized crime or environmental crimes or corruption. Is it because they scrape together more votes by fighting against gay people rather than mafia?

Notes

1 By way of illustration, mention is made here of the so-called *leggi eversive* of 1866–7, the introduction of the institution of government authorization for clerical entities to purchase assets, the Casati law on education, depriving the Church of a role in the education of children and the young to the advantage of public schools; the introduction of civil marriage (Civil Code of 1865) and finally the Crispi Law of 1890 calling for the nationalization of all charitable institutions belonging to the Catholic Church.

2 Encyclicals are pastoral letters written by the pope and addressed to the bishops of the Catholic Church and through them to all the faithful on matters of doctrine, morals or social issues.

3 "It is not expedient," in English.

4 It should not be forgotten that the theoretical scheme of the liberal, separatist State was rarely fully implemented even in legal systems which more coherently adopted such a system (see Cardia, 1980: 40ff.).

5 Art. 7 of the Italian Constitution states: "The State and the Catholic Church are independent and sovereign, each within its own sphere. Their relations are governed by the Lateran Pacts. Changes to the Pacts that are accepted by both parties do not require the procedure for constitutional amendment."

6 Art. 8: "All religious confessions are equally free before the law. Religious confessions other than the Catholic one have the right to organize themselves in accordance with their own statutes, provided that these statutes are not in conflict with Italian law. Their relations with the State are regulated by law on the basis of accords between the State and the respective representatives."

7 Adopted with Law No. 121 of 25 March 1985 (Ratification and implementation of the agreement with additional Protocol, signed on 18 February in Rome, bearing amendments to the Lateran Concordat of 11 February 1929, between the Italian Republic and the Holy See).
8 There are currently eleven approved agreements.
9 The Constitutional Court is the body entrusted by the Italian Constitution with the task of deciding (inter alia) on the conformity of laws with the Constitution itself.
10 The regional administrative court of Veneto, in a judgment of 17 March 2005, No. 1110, argued that the display of the crucifix in State schools is at the basis of the principle of laicity itself, in that it is a symbol of a system of values of freedom, equality, human dignity and religious tolerance. The issue of the display of the crucifix in Italian state schools was brought before the European Court of Human Rights, which, in its ruling on the case *Lautsi and Others v. Italy*, of March 2011, declared that such display was in conformity with the principles of the European Convention on Human Rights.
11 There is no large political party such as *Democrazia Cristiana*, which represented the Catholic world in a unitary manner from 1946 until the early 1990s.

References

Bellini, P. (2011). La Chiesa e la politica. In G. Leziroli (ed.), *Atti del Convegno sul tema "La Chiesa in Italia: oggi* (pp. 11–37). Cosenza: Pellegrini.

Böckenförde, E. W. (2007). *Diritto e secolarizzazione. Dallo Stato moderno all'Europa unita* (G. Preterossi, ed.). Rome-Bari: Laterza.

Cardia, C. (1980). *La riforma del Concordato. Dal confessionismo alla laicità dello Stato.* Turin: Einaudi.

Cardia, C. (2010). *Principi di diritto ecclesiastico. Tradizione europea legislazione italiana.* Turin: Giappichelli.

Fiorita, N. (2011). *L'insostenibile leggerezza della laicità italiana.* Available online at www.statoechiese.it (accessed 23 May 2011).

Jemolo, C. A. (1974). *Chiesa e Stato. Dalla unificazione a Giovanni XIII.* Turin: Einaudi.

Prodi, P. (2005). *La Chiesa nella società italiana.* Rome: Carocci Editore.

Rodotà, S. (2009). *Perché laico.* Rome-Bari: Laterza.

Viano, A. C. (2008). *Laici in ginocchio.* Rome-Bari: Laterza.

Zagrebelsky, G. (2010). *Scambiarsi la veste. Stato e Chiesa al governo dell'uomo.* Rome-Bari: Laterza.

PART III

Politics

13

GENIUS LOCI

The geography of Italian politics

John Agnew

Thinking about Italian politics in terms of "place" is to emphasize how the geographies of everyday life figure in how political movements arise in some places but not others, parties put down roots better in some places than elsewhere, and local attachments arise that animate political behavior to the extent that liberating those places from the rest of the country becomes the object of political action. The two dominant genres of writing about Italian politics are those that focus on the "making" of Italy as a nation and those that see it as divided/united essentially by national social classes and a powerful left/right political division that pervades the country whatever the current political regime or system of parties happens to be. Most commentators also acknowledge that the country has had longstanding geographical differences economically, socially, and politically. But both dominant genres implicitly view these as residual: destined to fade in significance as national unity overcomes regional and local identities or as nationwide class divisions trump local and regional affiliations and interests.

This chapter refuses to partake of these particular narratives. This does not mean that I would deny the existence of an Italian national project or the reality of social classes organizing nationally. It is that these only take on meaning for people and thus affect who they are and how they act in terms of the practical routines and pathways of everyday life. It is important to emphasize, however, that this does not entail a vision of Italy in which geographical differences informing present-day politics are simply inheritances from the dim and distant past. I prefer to provide an account of Italian politics that takes geographical divisions seriously as the result not of primordial identities or fixed interests residing in different places, as most approaches to the geography of Italian politics have tended to do, but as emergent features of the sociality of life as lived by people across Italy, representing the blending together in different places of workplace, religious, residential, and demographic differences that inform people's life experiences and condition their political attitudes and behavior.

The chapter begins with a brief overview of why place matters to politics irrespective of country but with particular attention to Italy. This challenges both the nationalist and the individualist premises upon which much political analysis tends to rely: that the sole context in which individuals operate is that of their respective nation states. I then provide a selective survey of how geographical differences in social and political behavior across Italy have been considered by students of Italian politics. A third section provides an empirical analysis of Italian electoral politics covering both the so-called First Republic or party system from 1948 to 1992 and then, in somewhat more detail, the recent period from 1994 to 2008. I then turn to one of the most interesting phenomena of recent Italian politics: the rise of the Northern League as a political party invested in representing a particular region of Italy. This is a politics *of* place more than just a politics arising in places. Finally, I address the issue of whether centralized command over national communications networks and the spread of new technologies (such as the so-called social media) portend the declining significance of place, particularly as the parties that have lain at the center of Italian politics lose their role as transmission belts for popular demands and citizens become consumers of messages to which they supposedly respond in lockstep rather than as active social participants in political life.

Place and politics

A commonplace of social psychology is that people's attitudes are shaped by where they are. Situational factors enter into interpersonal interactions, the attribution of trust and knowledge, judgments about ethics, and consumption decisions. From this viewpoint, there is no such thing as discrete individuals. The boundaries of the "me" are fluid. As a result, decisions, choices, and actions are all inspired by links with others. Terms such as "social networks" and "the social logic of action" have been coined to describe these interdependencies. "Network effects" are well established: people can and often do change preferences simply on the basis of what others say and do. Face-to-face relationships are absolutely central to the development of selves. From parental and household influences to friendship and acquaintanceship circles, people are social beings whose lives and behavior circulate around well-worn paths and routines. These are anchored to the sites in which social situations are located. Numerous studies have shown that the social contexts in which people develop their attitudes are spatially defined (e.g. Zuckerman, 2005). The heuristics or rules of thumb that we come to rely on to make decisions are the result of social interaction conditioned by where we work, play, worship, and learn. This does not mean that everyone in a given place agrees on everything. Far from it: rather, it is from the experience of anchored social networks that emanate whatever attitudes people exhibit. But different people have different experiences that reflect their command over resources, their relative social power, and restrictions on the range of their sites of social interaction. Hence, though some common orientations can be expected, there is absolutely no expectation of complete uniformity in attitudes.

It is the social spaces arising in different places, therefore, that are most at stake in defining how political attitudes and behavior arise and change. But the relative presence of different types of sites or locales for interaction ultimately conditions how interpersonal and communal influences really operate. The "background geography" of places underpins the social spaces of interaction (e.g. Newburger *et al.*, 2011; Sampson, 2012). Some places have big factories, others do not; some places have many peasants, others do not; some places are dominated by agribusiness, others are not; some places have longstanding cultural and recreation activities tied to churches, others do not; some places are heavily urbanized, others are not; some places are well tied into transportation and communication networks, others are not; some places have been affected by natural calamities, others have not; some places have very specialized economies (and equally narrow elites), others do not; some places are magnets for immigrants, others are not; and so on. There are systematic correlations between these different types of place and the sorts of political attitudes and behavior that they encourage (Agnew, 1987).

Places, the settings for sites of social interaction, structure the ways in which political attitudes and organization develop. In Italy, a number of obvious historic geographical features lie behind the more dynamic churning of the economy and society to produce the basic template of geographical differences. These would include, for example, the long-established political division of the peninsula before final unification in one state only in 1870, the settlement system with its lack of a single dominant city and its orientation fundamentally affected by the long coastline and long mountainous spine of the Apennines, the more successful history of large-scale industrialization in the country's northwest, the diffuse urbanization that has characterized large parts of central and northeastern Italy since the 1970s, notwithstanding major efforts at redistributing industry and supplementing incomes, the lag of most southern regions behind the North in terms of economic growth, and the peculiar geography of Catholic Italy, with practice reflecting the prior political divisions of the peninsula and attendant views of the Church as much as the relative pace of secularization (e.g. Coppola, 1997; Cartocci, 2011; Cozzo, 2011). Other countries have their own, if very distinctive, repertoires of such differences. In that regard, Italy is by no means unique.

This way of thinking about politics is by no means new, if the ideas of social psychology that inform it could sound unfamiliar to many current students of politics. Indeed, until the 1950s in the United States and elsewhere, the social logic and social geography of politics was everywhere predominant. Political sociology retained an emphasis on "territorial" or geographical cleavages and the impact of "neighborhood effects" on voting behavior for even longer. Italian Fascism, for example, was widely understood as a movement that had its roots in the towns of the Po Valley and among the middle classes of areas with a powerful socialist presence. The US South was the dominion of the Democratic Party until the 1960s, when the passage of the federal Civil Rights Act of 1964 led many southern whites to turn against the party whose President, Lyndon Johnson, introduced the legislation. Two trends in social science since the 1960s have obscured this heritage of geographical thinking about politics and made writing about "place and politics" appear more novel or exotic than is actually the case. The first was the borrowing from microeconomics, arguably the most "scientific" of the social sciences in terms of its reliance on a nineteenth-century model of physics, of an ontology of action focused on autonomous individual actors engaged in rational calculation about political goals (often called "methodological individualism"). From this viewpoint, social environments are solely sources of informational and material constraints, not the identities, interests, and preferences associated with the individuals themselves. Recently, however, the more sociological view has undergone something of a revival, suggesting, for example, that prejudices as much as reasons underpin motivations and that social influences cannot be reduced to the effects of separate individuals simply bumping up against one another (Massey, 2012).

The second was the presumed victory of the nation state as the sole locus of political activity. This has had two implications. One is the focus on national electoral politics as a sort of sporting event or horse race in which national-level majorities are all that is of much interest. The actual "making" of such majorities might involve political operatives with detailed local knowledge but academic students of politics need to know only how to predict the overall outcome, not how to explain how it comes about. The other is to collect national-level survey data that gives you the traits and opinions of individual voters divorced from any concern about social context other than the national. The presumption is that as long as you sample sufficiently across demographic characteristics (age, sex, race, ethnicity, class, etc.), you can know enough to predict results. Yet, increasingly not only local and regional differences but also influences emanating from beyond national borders make the presumption of national containment of political determinants open to doubt (Veltri, 2010). But the combination of methodological individualism and "methodological nationalism" has undoubtedly become the "common sense" of political studies in Italy as elsewhere.

Whether it represents "good sense" is another question entirely. The increased complexity of political offerings, rising electoral abstentionism, and the emergence of place-specific political movements have made it less and less useful in its own terms. The paradigm is in trouble. In the words of Ilvo Diamanti (2012a: 103), after offering a similar diagnosis to mine:

> It is therefore difficult to understand what is happening in politics without taking account of the everyday life, of the common sense of the territory; without profoundly exploring the places where the parties, the institutions, and democracy find the roots to their legitimation and their consensus.

Fixing regions

"Geography" has figured more centrally in a number of approaches to Italian politics. But in each, geography is subordinated to some other imperative, be it economic, cultural, or political. Three distinctive conceptions can be distinguished. The first, predominant among scholars of elections in the 1960s and still important in reporting election results, is that of voting regions and the association between some of these and so-called regional subcultures. The classic division of Italy is into four regions, the industrial Northwest, the "traditionally" white or Catholic Northeast, the "traditionally" red or socialist Center, and the economically underdeveloped South. These electoral regions came into existence after World War II and are seen as reflecting structural differences, sometimes entirely economic and sometimes pre-eminently cultural, between discrete areas. If the Northwest and the South are seen as based on the relative success of mass politics because of the relative presence of the organized working class in the former and its absence in the latter, the Northeast and the Center represent deep-seated cultural traditions based on a complex of historical differences such as differences in rural land tenure, family types, attitudes towards the Church hierarchy, and the differential colonization of the regions by political movements such as Christian Democracy and Socialism before Fascism.

The second approach has a much more long-term understanding of regional difference. In this case the emphasis is on how in the distant past, when Italy was divided politically into a variety of states, very different political cultures developed and ever since have conditioned the practice of politics in the places that, though now parts of a unified Italy, still betray their older characteristics. Associated most closely with the research project of Robert Putnam (1993), this approach does have much deeper roots in the cultural sociology that identifies southern Italy, in particular, with such ideas as "amoral familism," a cultural syndrome in which immediate family ties trump any sort of wider civic culture or collective action, and an instrumental as opposed to consummatory attitude towards national citizenship. From this perspective, contemporary political differences such as extent of identification with parties as vehicles for distinctive ideologies, rates of political participation, and relative volatility in votes for all parties across elections are put down to longstanding geographical differences in the degree of civic culture and/or cultural capital present in a particular place.

A final approach focuses much more on the regional pattern of returns to political incentives as these have evolved over time. Thus, voting in the South has come to reflect the dependence of the region on policy initiatives coming from Rome, redistributive politics, and the relatively high level of government employment in the region. This, along with the historical incidence in some parts of the South of alliances between some parties and criminal organizations, has encouraged high levels of so-called exchange or quid pro quo voting. Voting in the main metropolitan areas and the Northwest, however, fits more closely with the model of so-called opinion voting in which people respond to party programs as rational individual voters. Finally, in some regions so-called identity voting tends to prevail. This is the result both of well-entrenched parties providing locally desired services (that the central government fails to provide) and of the attachment to parties on the part of sizable local majorities remembering crucial historical events (rescue from the Austrian Empire or the end of Fascism, for example). "Types" of voting, therefore, correlate highly with different places. But these places are, as with the two other perspectives on geography, presumably homogeneous regions that have not changed much down the years.

Mapping place and politics

The word "geography" does often convey a sense of permanence, so it is not surprising that fixed regional divisions have tended to be the major way in which geographical analysis has entered into understandings of Italian politics. Persisting regional differences, particularly that between the North and the South, have been elemental in Italian political discourse down the years. Thinking of geography as "dynamic" or based on the complexities of micro-geography described earlier, however, leads in a different direction.

Examining the long period of Italian national elections from 1948 until 1987 reveals a number of realigning elections when national vote changes were greater than usual and involved flows of votes beyond the typical left, right, and center "families" of parties within which votes were usually exchanged. The main shifts occurred in 1948 and 1953, when the Communist Party (PCI) emerged as the major party of the left and the Christian Democratic Party (DC) as the major party of the center; 1963, when the DC lost votes to the right and began its collaboration with the Italian Socialist Party (PSI) and the PCI began moving towards a center-left ideological position; and 1976, when the PCI increased its national vote from both new voters and voters from the center, and the DC received votes from the right. These substantial changes can be linked to shifts in the political geography of electoral choice (Agnew, 2002: 92–110). A breakdown of the variance of votes for the DC and PCI across all elections to the Chamber of Deputies from 1953 to 1987 at the provincial level shows that the provincial standard deviations from the national means go up from 1953 to 1968 but then drop precipitously from 1968 to 1976 with a significant increase from 1979 to 1987. I take these to signify the following: that before 1963 most of the variance was at the regional scale (the fourfold regionalization of Italy made by Galli and Prandi in 1970), which suggests that geographical difference was concentrated regionally; between 1963 and 1976 the votes for the two parties nationalized, which suggests a decline in regional clustering but without an increase in variance from within-region means; and between 1976 and 1987 a dramatic increase in within-region variances, which suggests an overall localization of trends in voting for the two parties. There was thus a dynamic flow to the political geography of Italian national elections – three regimes (regionalizing, nationalizing, and localizing) – that a static regional account or one focused entirely on national trends would have missed.

Different "logics" in different places seem to have determined how the votes were formed over time. No single national "cause" can account for these shifts in electoral variance. There certainly were some important forces at work throughout Italy: the arrival of administrative regions across the entire country in 1970, the movement of significant numbers of people from the interior of the south of the peninsula and from the islands to the industrial Northwest in the 1950s and 1960s, the "economic miracle" of the late 1950s and early 1960s increasing incomes and consumption across the board, the emergence of a dynamic sector of small firms geared towards artisanal production particularly in the Center and Northeast in the 1960s and 1970s, the differential secularization of the country with the Northeast standing out the longest against the overall trend, the increased role of organized crime in politics in parts of the South in the 1970s and 1980s, and the deradicalization of the Communist Party and the emergence of widespread political violence associated with the extreme right and the extreme left in the 1970s. But these changes were all refracted through local lenses depending on the historical constellation of different parties and movements in different places and the mix of local and regional conditions and issues that one would expect would lead to different responses to external pressures. Such factors as prevalence of churchgoing, type of workplace and employment conditions, rural versus urban, loss of population, degree of local organized criminality, the prevalence of exchange voting, and so on are by most accounts crucial to the emergence of distinctive "logics" to aggregate vote shifts over time (Brusa, 1984; Cartocci, 1990; Agnew, 2002).

Between 1992 and 1994 the party system that had dominated Italy since 1948 disintegrated. This had its roots in both the collapse of the Cold War geopolitical division of the world that had given both of the major Italian parties a core part of their identities and the corruption scandals relating to the funding of the Socialist and Christian Democratic parties of the same epoch. In 1993, an electoral system based on 75 percent of seats from single-member majority vote districts and 25 percent from multi-member proportional representation (PR) contests replaced the previous proportional/party list system. The idea was to encourage parties to enter into pre-election compacts rather than post-election coalitions that had not had popular endorsement. In some quarters the hope was that the new system might also stimulate a more bipolar party system with alternation in office between left- and right-leaning parties. This system lasted until 2005, when it was replaced by a "top-up" PR system that rewarded the winning coalition with extra seats. This system was introduced by the then-center-right government to improve its electoral chances and lasted through the 2013 election. Its topping-up of seats at the regional level in Senate elections and nationally for the Chamber of Deputies was to prove particularly destabilizing in February 2013, when the center-left won (if narrowly in votes) in the Chamber, and the Senate was left divided because of the surprising success of the M5S Movement critical of the "party system" in the Senate election in crucial regions (see pp. 165–6).

After 1992 three political formations came to dominate Italian national politics until 2013: a center-right grouping under the leadership of the media tycoon Silvio Berlusconi, a center-left grouping that has become the Democratic Party, and a regionalist party, the Northern League. Berlusconi made himself the indispensable figure in putting together for substantial periods of time cross-regional and locality coalitions between his own party, initially called Forza Italia, Alleanza Nazionale (a party that developed from the neo-Fascist MSI), with most of its core support in Rome and scattered places in the South, and the Northern League (Diamanti, 2003; Shin and Agnew, 2008). Over the long haul, Berlusconi's grouping was particularly successful in the North, especially in and around the largest cities such as Milan, and in the South around Naples and in Sicily. The center-left, meanwhile, retained a strong hold in central Italy and gained a hold in Basilicata in the South. The Northern League, for its part, tended to have its greatest success in the more rural parts of Lombardy and the Veneto in the North but with some expansion into similar settings in the Piedmont region (in the Northwest) and in Emilio Romagna (a "traditional" stronghold of the left) between 2006 and 2008.

In national terms, two coalitions organized along a basic left–right continuum increasingly accounted for most votes everywhere. This was so even if the left was increasingly neoliberal and decreasingly social democratic, and the center-right increasingly clerical and statist and decreasingly liberal in ideological orientation. The polarizing capacity of Berlusconi was undoubtedly important in this regard as he recruited other right-wing factions into his camp and institutionalized his alliance with the Northern League after 2001. Yet, there was a definite geography to this bipolarity. If in the North Berlusconi had to share votes and seats with the Northern League, elsewhere he was faced with serious competition in the South but a dearth of opportunities in Central Italy, where the center-left party still exercised a considerable draw. Down the years, Berlusconi's personality and activities, both business and personal, became increasingly central to his political appeal and to the arguments of his adversaries. No Italian political leader since Mussolini had attracted the attention and criticism that Berlusconi did inside and outside of the country (Agnew, 2011).

This attention was largely because his rise to political prominence had much to do with shepherding his business interests, and his wealth allowed him to behave according to norms that were exceptional by the public standards of other Italian politicians. As a political leader he was particularly attractive to those with instrumental views of government, fear of increased state regulation of their activities, and an attraction to the model of wild consumer capitalism with which Berlusconi strongly associated himself through the programming and advertising on his private television channels. Such people are to be found all over Italy. Italy has the largest number of self-employed people of any major industrialized country, symptomatic of the small average size of most businesses. But as maps of tax evasion (overwhelmingly in the South and areas of small firm concentration in the North: Corriere della Sera, 2011) and intensive television watching (urban peripheries everywhere and the rural South) tend to attest, there are also geographic pools of such people in places with histories of off-the-books employment, narrow profit margins in small businesses, and credit-based consumption. Berlusconi's promises to reduce tax pressures, condone illegal building, and limit entry into professions all speak to this side of his appeal. At the same time, and ironically in light of charges about his personal behavior, he allied himself with the Church on questions relating to euthanasia, gay rights, and women's rights. Such positions made him attractive to the most conservative Catholic constituencies concentrated in parts of the Veneto and the South (see Veltri, in this volume).

It was the unraveling of the Italian public economy because of increased spreads in bond yields between Italian and German bonds in late 2011 that put paid to Berlusconi's last government. Berlusconi had been prime minister for all but five of the seventeen years from 1994 to 2011. He could not finally evade responsibility for the weakness of Italy within the Eurozone (e.g. Pianta, 2012). Even though his credentials as a successful businessman had helped bring him repeatedly to office, his failure to seriously address or arrest the declining state of the Italian economy must be the final epitaph on his role as a political leader. Perhaps the very secret of his political success, appealing to entrenched conservative business interests and religious identities, created the barrier to moving Italy as a whole in a new direction.

Though he made a remarkable comeback in the February 2013 national election after his seeming "disgrace" in 2011, partly through making promises for the repeal and restitution of previous payments for the property tax introduced by the "technocratic" Monti government in 2012, Berlusconi was not able to reconstitute the coalition of political forces located in different regions that had been the secret of his previous national electoral success (Repubblica, 2013).

The politics of place: the Northern League

Since the 1990s one of the most important political novelties of Italy has been the prominence of an avowedly regionalist party, the Northern League, within Italian national politics. This began life as a series of "leagues" across the different northern regions. If Berlusconi provided a substitute for the DC and PSI (particularly in the Northwest and South) and the Democratic Party was the result of a split in the PCI and the attraction of some of the more progressive elements in the DC, the Northern League, which debuted in the 1992 election, was the outcome of colonizing the perimeter and then achieving a high degree of electoral consensus in the core areas traditionally associated with strong support for the Christian Democrats in Lombardy and the Veneto (Shin and Agnew, 2008: 49–64; Passarelli and Tuorto, 2012: 21–42). This party appealed to a new territorial formulation of the problems facing "the North" or, as in a later formulation, "Padania," particularly those of small businesses now without their old DC allies in Rome or local government. The onset of globalization had produced an ever-greater competitiveness in the economic sectors in which many places in northern Italy specialized and the League arose to answer the anxieties of those for whom the national government was an increasing irrelevance in this context. The overall approach emphasized the relative deprivation of the affluent North in relation to redistributive (and patronage) politics in Rome, which favored the "unproductive" South. Defense of local cultural differences from the Italian "norm," hostility to immigrants, notwithstanding their role in the economy, and resentment directed at globalization and the powers of the European Union were all added to the repertoire of complaints at the center of the League's electoral success.

Though claiming a regional basis to its complaints, the League has mainly appealed to localized identities and interests that are entrenched in only some sorts of places. Its activists are particularly localistic in their attachments (Passarelli and Tuorto, 2012:180–1). They and many of the party's voters are united on such themes as the lack of local return on revenues sent to central government and the need to have greater local control over local resources. But this does not extend to massive support across the North from voters as a whole for the proposed secession of "Padania" from Italy, a major theme of the party in the late 1990s while out of government, or even to supporting the proposed devolution of powers to the administrative regions as proposed in a referendum of 2006. Indeed, that referendum revealed major differences within the North with only the most rural and peripheral areas in Lombardy and the Veneto giving a majority of votes in favor. Elsewhere in the North the "no vote" also tended to prevail. The Northern League's roots, therefore, tend to be strong in only some types of place across northern Italy. So, even as its leaders have made claims about a larger region, these only resonate in certain places, not in others (Shin and Agnew, 2008: 128–31; Panebianco, 2010).

The League started out as a protest movement that few commentators expected to last as a significant presence in national politics. Obviously the movement found a niche for itself within the center-right constellation that Berlusconi put together in the early 1990s. Though the League was initially uncomfortable in the role of junior partner, after 1999 its leaders turned the party into a party of government, at local, regional, and national levels (Diamanti, 2011). Since then the party's historical leader, Umberto Bossi, has also drifted away from the secessionist logic and neo-pagan rhetoric about northern cultural roots that had characterized the party in the late 1990s and that continued to inspire a certain element among the party's active supporters (e.g. Passarelli and Tuorto, 2012; Guolo, 2011). By early 2012 Bossi's diminished health, reliance on a dysfunctional family, and lack of ideological coherence had taken a toll. In a poll taken in early February 2012 most League supporters said they wanted him to leave his role as party secretary (Nasi, 2012a). In the 2013 national election, the League faded across the North, particularly in Piedmont and the Veneto, although at least partly as a result of re-entering into alliance with Berlusconi's PDL. The only bright spot was the success of Roberto Maroni in being elected as governor of Lombardy in February 2013 in the same election that saw the party in retreat in national politics (Diamanti, 2013).

The dependence of the party on Bossi's rhetorical excess or what the journalist Marco Belpolito (2012) calls his "oratory of gestures" had kept the party in the news at a time when the culture of celebrity was in the ascendancy in Italy as elsewhere. But in the end this diminished the party in two ways that came to a head in 2012. The first was the failure of the party to deliver much to its electorate by way of federalism or a shift in Italy's public economy in favor of the North from its long period in office alongside Berlusconi (Ricolfi, 2012a, 2012b). The other was that the centrality of Bossi's family and circle of friends to the enterprise and the lack of internal democracy within the party left it open to the scandal over the use of public funds that led to Bossi's forced resignation as secretary of the party (Maltese, 2012; Repubblica, 2012). The League was the sole oppositional voice in the Italian parliament to the technocratic government of Mario Monti that had replaced Berlusconi in late 2011, so its future was hostage to whether it could ever find a new niche for itself in the absence of both Bossi and Berlusconi, the two men who had brought the League into a governing position but whose maneuverings had in the end not achieved much of anything for the mythic North or Padania that Bossi had singlehandedly invented.

Placeless politics?

It is not just the politics of place as exemplified by the Northern League that is now open to question. Recent trends can be read as signifying a crisis for thinking in terms of politics in place as well. This takes two forms, although both relate to issues of communication over distance.

The first, illustrated by the phenomenon that is Berlusconi, is the signal importance of control over the mass media, particularly television, for political outcomes. In this light, the conventional wisdom about the rise of Berlusconi has been almost entirely that his control over the main private television channels (gifted to him by his mentor Bettino Craxi when he was prime minister), plus his influence over the public ones (RAI) when in office, has given him a stranglehold over political messages and viewing a diet of shows devoted to consumption and the promise of celebrity habituated the population at large to his interests. Daniele Zolo (1999: 739) puts this as follows:

> Not only is political communication almost totally absorbed by television, but so is the whole process of the legitimization of politicians, of the production of consensus and of the definition and negotiation of the issues that have no other location and, so to speak, no other symbolic places except television studios and popular entertainment programmes – to which the stars of the political firmament are invited.

Berlusconi undoubtedly has benefited from the agenda-setting potential of his television interests. Italians in general watch more television and receive more of their news from television than people in many other countries. That said, however, television tends to reinforce and mobilize voters who already share the perspectives they are absorbing (Diamanti, 2012a: 93–101). These they tend to acquire by other means, including from face-to-face social interaction. Television messages also must be interpreted in familiar terms. This is so much the case that, as Giovanni Sartori (1989: 189) says, television can encourage localism more than national homogenization because it takes attention off parties and puts it on politicians and their service to constituencies. Sartori worries that any sort of national "good" is lost between the extremes of "no place" and "my place." Berlusconi's success, therefore, must be put down more to his capacity to weld together a center-right coalition more successfully than his adversaries than simply to his control over television (Shin and Agnew, 2008).

A second trend involves the increased significance of so-called social media organized in relation to the Web and the technologies such as smartphones, laptop computers, and Skype associated with it. Politics need no longer have much if any grounding in place but people can be mobilized for various political goals over differing time spans by social media such as Twitter and Facebook and by means of Internet listservs and billboards. Exhibit A for this phenomenon in Italy has been the recent success of the *Movimento Cinque Stelle* (M5S movement) organized by the comedian Beppe Grillo (Corbetta and Gualmini, 2013; Bartlett *et al.*, 2013). In the 2012 local elections, the M5S movement polled about 10 percent of the vote nationally and won several mayoral contests, including Parma's (e.g. Severgnini, 2012; Urbinati, 2012). In the 2013 national elections it polled the largest number of votes of any single "party" (excluding Italian residents abroad), although was outnumbered overall by each of the two main electoral alliances. Its success led to its holding the balance of power in the Senate. The movement is organized almost entirely on the Web, which Grillo has used to effect mainly through a funny blog about the sins and vices of all existing parties and politicians, above all those in and supporting Italy's previous technocratic government. The appeal, as with many current politicians, is to an "anti-politics" that casts political parties in a particularly dim light as instruments of corruption and destitution. It finds resonance with those most tuned in to new technologies (although Grillo himself is in his sixties) and facing a terrible job market in an Italian economy that has seen better days (e.g. Dinmore, 2011). But it also reflects the increasing disassociation between politics, in terms of popular demands and issues, on the one hand, and the realities of representative democracy, with politicians increasingly out of touch with ordinary people, on the other (Diamanti, 2012b). It is not simply an anti-politics movement. The "Grillo" phenomenon signifies a new way of articulating interests and identities but as yet without the capacity to aggregate these satisfactorily into a legislative agenda in the presence of existing parties with which the "movement" must negotiate. Mainstream political parties everywhere are in deep trouble because they no longer seem to either articulate or aggregate interests and identities adequately (Economist, 2012a). To outlast its current basis as a protest movement, the M5S will have to do both.

As with television but more interactively, the Web does portend a different range of information sources and cross-place mobilizing opportunities than existing mass media such as newspapers and magazines. But much of the newness associated with the technologies is simply a matter of fingertip delivery and timeliness more than a qualitative break with past modes of information and mobilization. Even as new technologies have expanded the total amount of communication, data from the United States suggest that some other modes of communication such as print and inter-personal of all types have maintained their popularity while radio and television have declined (Economist, 2012b). More interestingly in terms of the presumed effects of new technologies, numerous studies of social networking show that geographic constraints still exercise a strong influence over all social media. The probability of having social ties still decreases as a function of distance, which suggests strongly that the new social media tend to facilitate flows among existing social networks rather than serving to create them (e.g. Onnela *et al.*, 2011). Polling data suggest that, irrespective of how they have been mobilized, the supporters of M5S differ little in fact from other voters in terms of their expectations of how future Italian governments should be formed (Nasi, 2012b) and that they can be found in some places much more than in others (lower-religiosity and higher-income areas, in particular) (Nasi, 2012c). Beppe Grillo himself has taken to traveling around Italy by bus to give his movement the "ground game" that retail politics still requires (Diamanti, 2012c). The "party" was the primary party in votes cast in 50 provinces out of 108 in 2013 but achieved its greatest successes in Sicily (where the Internet is not that widely used) and in Lazio and Lombardy, where a better case for the Internet's role can be made but which are also the seats of Italy's largest metropolitan areas and plausibly the largest concentrations of those most disillusioned with the existing party system. A placeless politics does not yet seem on the immediate horizon.

Conclusion

Italian politics has long been about a variety of projects – national, class, regional, and anti-politics – but all of these and the parties and movements that have been their instruments have been mediated geographically through the exigencies of everyday life as grounded in places. The "geography" of Italian politics has hitherto been thought of mainly in terms of fixed regions having continuous effects. But even this approach has been eclipsed in the face of trends to think of politics in terms of autonomous individuals operating entirely in relation to national-level influences. The burden of this chapter has been to lay out the case for a social psychology of politics that grounds political behavior in the settings of everyday life and that rather than seeing these as in decline sees them as of persisting, if dynamically charged, significance as the places they define change their configurations over time.

References

Agnew, J. A. (1987). *Place and Politics: The Geographical Mediation of State and Society*. London: Allen and Unwin.

Agnew, J. A. (2002). *Place and Politics in Modern Italy*. Chicago: University of Chicago Press.

Agnew, J. A. (2011). The big seducer: Berlusconi's image at home and abroad and the future of Italian politics. *California Italian Studies*, 2. Available online at http://escholarship.org/uc/item/2bt6w92c (accessed 3 July 2013).

Bartlett, J., Littler, M., McDonnell, D., and Froio, C. (2013). *New Political Actors in Europe: Beppe Grillo and the M5S*. London: Demos.

Belpolito, M. (2012). *La canottiera di Bossi*. Parma: Guanda.

Brusa, C. (1984). *Geografia elettorale nell'Italia del dopoguerra. Edizione aggiornata ai risultati delle elezioni politiche 1983*. Milan: Unicopli.

Cartocci, R. (1990). *Elettori in Italia. Riflessioni sulle vicende elettorali degli anni ottanta*. Bologna: Il Mulino.

Cartocci, R. (2011). *Geografia dell'Italia cattolica*. Bologna: Il Mulino.

Coppola, P. (ed.) (1997). *Geografia politica delle regioni italiane*. Turin: Einaudi.

Corbetta, P. and Gualmini, E. (eds.) (2013). *Il partito di Grillo*. Bologna: Il Mulino.

Corriere della Sera (2011). Dalla banca dati del Fisco: la radiografia dell'evasione in Italia. *Il Corriere della Sera*, 3 April: 1.

Cozzo, P. (2011). Un paese all'ombra del campanile. Immagini del parocco nell'Italia unita. In S. Soldani (ed.) *L'Italia alla prova dell'Unita* (pp. 65–85). Milan: Franco Angeli.

Diamanti, I. (2003). *Bianco, rosso, verde . . . e azzurro. Mappe e colori dell'Italia politica*. Bologna: Il Mulino.

Diamanti, I. (2011). L'anima romana della Lega. *La Repubblica*, 7 February: 1.

Diamanti, I. (2012a). *Gramsci, Manzoni e mia suocera. Quando gli esperti sbagliano le previsioni politiche*. Bologna: Il Mulino.

Diamanti, I. (2012b). La dissociazione tra politica e democrazia rappresentiva. *La Repubblica*, 20 August.

Diamanti, I. (2012c). L'autobus di Grillo nel paese della politica-che-non-c'è. *La Repubblica*, 13 July: 3.

Diamanti, I. (2013). Paradosso Lega: mai così debole. Eppure adesso comanda al Nord. *La Repubblica*, 27 February: 3.

Dinmore, G. (2011). Italy's lost generation sceptical of new order. *Financial Times*, 18 November: 5.

Economist (2012a). Lonely at the top. Is the mass political party on its way out? And does it matter? *The Economist*, 4 August: 15.

Economist (2012b). Wordy goods. Americans are exchanging ever more words. *The Economist*, 22 August: 18.

Guolo, R. (2011). *Chi impugno la Croce. Lega e chiesa*. Rome-Bari: Laterza.

Maltese, C. (2012). *La crisi della Lega*. Rome: La Repubblica e-book.

Massey, D. S. (2012). Location matters. *Science*, 336, 35–6.

Nasi, A. F. (2012a). Sette leghisti su dieci sono stufi di Umberto. *Libero*, 5 February: 1.

Nasi, A. F. (2012b). Il 90% degli italiani boccio l'inciucio: alleanze chiare prima delle elezioni. *Libero*, 5 August: 2.

Nasi, A. F. (2012c). Padani, liberisti e non giustizialisti. I grillini non sono l'antipolitica. *Libero*, 3 May.

Newburger, H. B., Birch, E. L. and Wachter, S. M. (eds.) (2011). *Neighborhood and Life Chances: How Place Matters in Modern America*. Philadelphia, PA: University of Pennsylvania Press.

Onnela J.-P., Arbesman S., González M. C., Barabási A.-L., and Christakis N. A. (2011). Geographic Constraints on Social Network Groups. *PLoS ONE* 6(4), e16939. doi:10.1371/journal.pone.0016939.

Panebianco, A. (2010). La questione non è Padana. *Il Corriere della Sera*, 24 June: 1.

Passarelli, G. and Tuorto, D. (2012). *Lega e Padania. Storie e luoghi delle camicie verdi*. Bologna: Il Mulino.

Pianta, M. (2012). *Nove su dieci. Perché stiamo (quasi) tutti peggio di 10 anni fa*. Rome-Bari: Laterza.

Putnam, R. D. (1993). *Making Democracy Work: Civic Traditions in Modern Italy*. Princeton, NJ: Princeton University Press.

Repubblica (2012). I soldi in nero e le auto per I figli Bossi era a conoscenza di tutto. Cronaca Milano. *La Repubblica*, 7 April: 14.

Repubblica (2013). L'Istituto Cattaneo fotografa il voto: Pd e Pdl crollano rispetto al 2008. *La Repubblica*, 26 February: 1.

Ricolfi, L. (2012a). Il sogno svanito del federalismo. *La Stampa*, 13 April: 1.

Ricolfi, L. (2012b). Chi difende le ragioni del Nord. *La Stampa*, 7 April: 1.

Sampson, R. J. (2012). *Great American City: Chicago and the Enduring Neighborhood Effect*. Chicago: University of Chicago Press.

Sartori, G. (1989). Videopolitica. *Rivista Italiana di Scienza Politica*, 19, 185–98.

Severgnini, B. (2012). The allure of Italy's Jiminy Cricket. *Financial Times*, 4 June: 9.

Shin, M. E. and Agnew, J. A. (2008). *Berlusconi's Italy: Mapping Contemporary Italian Politics*. Philadelphia, PA: Temple University Press.

Urbinati, N. (2012). La politica degli antipolitica. *MicroMega*, 10 May: 1–4.

Veltri, G. A. (2010). Sulle spalle di nessuno. Il ruolo delle scienze sociali nel dibattito culturale e politico in Italia. In A. Mammone, N. Tranfaglia, and G. A. Veltri (eds.) *Un paese normale? Saggi sull'Italia contemporanea* (pp. 47–65). Milan: Dalai.

Zolo, D. (1999). From "historic compromise" to "telecratic compromise": notes for a history of political communication between the First and Second Republic. *Media, Culture & Society*, 21 (6), 727–41.

Zuckerman, A. S. (2005). *The Social Logic of Politics: Personal Networks as Contexts for Political Behavior*. Philadelphia, PA: Temple University Press.

14
THE POLITICAL RIGHT

Francesco Raniolo and Marco Tarchi

General context

Since the unification of Italy, several models of party systems have followed each other on the national political stage (Cotta and Verzichelli, 2008; Salvadori, 2013). However, since the foundation of the Italian Republic, the party system has been largely stable. This was a defining feature of the political system until the early 1990s, when Italian democracy entered a phase of endless transition (Ignazi, 1997; Pasquino, 2002; Morlino, 1998). More generally, the dismantlement of the old party system could be seen as the *result* of some deeply rooted conditions (Morlino and Tarchi, 1996; Morlino, 1998): a crisis of ideology, the secularization of political subcultures, Europeanization, globalization, the mediatization of politics. Furthermore, other elements contributed to this change: the *Manipulite* ('Clean Hands') judicial investigation, the crisis of distribution policies, and the April 1993 referendum results. Endogenous and exogenous factors, operating in the short and medium term, can help explain the reasons for the crisis of the Italian political system in the 1990s and its consequent transition (1994). A decade later, it is now necessary to account for the failure to reach political stability in Italy and for the outbreak of the new crisis in 2010–11, with the 2013 election providing a truly uncertain political outcome (Morlino et al., 2013) Furthermore, it will give rise to some considerations with regard to three more specific aspects relevant for the purpose of this chapter. The first aspect relates to the transformation of the post-Fascist right and, therefore, the emergence of conservative, not confessional and 'majority vocation' parties. The second aspect concerns the role played by Berlusconi's party (FI and then PDL) in the 1993–2013 political cycle. In fact, the 2011 political crisis could be considered as the failure to institutionalize a personal party. The third aspect is connected to the nature of this institutionalization, which appeared not only weak but also inconsistent and ineffective (Levitsky, 1998). FI and PDL are personal parties – depending on Berlusconi – whose partial consolidation affects both political competition (which tends to radicalize) and party system (which remains fluid). The 2013 general election confirmed this scenario but showed, for the first time, the risk of marginalization for the PDL, which no longer represented the party of change.

From *Forza Italia* to *Popolo della Libertà* and back

The rise of Berlusconi's party can be better understood by looking at the Italian political situation in the early 1990s. In those years, the restructuring of the party system laid the basis for a new subject, requiring a political entrepreneur. Although a movement for institutional and political renewal was organized around Mario Segni, it was Silvio Berlusconi who succeeded in this enterprise of transforming Italian politics. *Forza Italia*, however, was not just 'another party', but a totally new party, as Berlusconi himself said (2003). It was a personality-driven party; organizationally lightweight and flexible, based on political marketing and extensive use of media; an anti-political movement able to address the crisis of the parties.

That said, considering both institutional constraints and the main right-wing party evolution, the 1994–2013 period can be easily divided into three main stages: the *transitional phase*, or *imperfect bipolarism* (1993–2001), *asymmetrical alternance and fragmented and polarized bipolarism* (2001–11), with Berlusconi governments replacing the two-year Prodi government, and finally *depoliticized competition* (2011–12), which characterized the crisis of Berlusconism and the 'technical' government led by Mario Monti. The 2013 general election opens the door to a new political stage which witnessed the survival of the considerably weakened PDL.

The foundation and 'the crossing of the desert' (1993–2001)

On 26 January 1994, in a message broadcast on his Channel 5, Berlusconi announced his 'entry into the political arena' and presented his own political movement, *Forza Italia*. A few months later, more than 8 million Italian citizens supported him at the general election. His *Forza Italia* party topped the polls with 21 per cent of votes and obtained an overall 15.7 per cent of the seats (99 seats in the Chamber of Deputies and 32 in the Senate). In a short time and starting from scratch, he set up a formidable machinery to gain popular consensus and an exceptional and asymmetrical electoral coalition, which included in the North of Italy a regional party, *Lega Nord*, and in South and Central Italy, the post-Fascist party *Alleanza Nationale* (AN) led by Gianfranco Fini. The success of the centre-right opened the door to an anti-establishment coalition government. FI, AN and LN reflected a mixture of anti-state, anti-party feelings and an aversion to the political regime of the First Republic set up by the 1948 Constitution with the allied Christian Democratic Centre (CCD), the political group originating from the old Christian Democracy, which played the difficult role of balancing the different needs.

Berlusconi's party was characterized by a negative identity stemming from anti-party statements and by the 'primary, fundamental, original and irreplaceable factor' of anti-communism (Are, 1997: 186). By contrast, in a positive way, the identity of FI (and then of the PDL) tried to reconcile, albeit with some contradictions, different values coming from 'strongly rooted Italian political traditions' (Berlusconi, 2003: 13) such as populism, reformist socialism and liberalism. Berlusconi's style, inclined to radicalization and divisions, favoured the polarization of political competition which characterized the last two decades. Such politics, moderate in political discourses but radical in strategies, cannot be understood without considering at least one other factor: Silvio Berlusconi's personality and biography (Frattini, 2003: 76).

The characterizing feature of the original model of FI, and later PDL, is that of 'personal party' (Calise, 2000; Raniolo, 2013). This label can be seen in a twofold way. First, FI's 'electoral appeal is not based on any program or ideology, but rather on the personal charisma of the leader or candidate, who is portrayed as indispensable to the resolution of the country's problems or crises' (Günther and Diamond, 2001: 28). Second, its formation called for considerable use of human and logistical resources, which, almost without exception, came from companies belonging to the financial group founded and chaired by Berlusconi (Poli, 2001: 30). However, on the whole, FI is an organization in which the dividing line between public and private, as well as between business and party, is blurred – which resulted in a corrosive effect on the rule of law in the decade following. FI tends to rely on Berlusconi's personal

Table 14.1 Main centre-right parties in Italian general elections, 1994–2013: percentage of vote

	1994	*1996*	*2001*	*2006*	*2008*	*2013*
FI	21,01	20.57	29.43	23.72	37.39	21.56**
AN	13.47	15.66	12.02	12.34	–	–
LN	8.36	10.07*	3.94	4.58	8.30	4.1
UDC	–	5.84	3.22	6.76	5.62*	1.78
FLI						0.46
FDI						1.95

Source: McDonnell (2013) and Italian Ministry of the Interior. (*) Indicates when parties did not run as part of the centre-right coalition. (**) Since 2008 FI and AN ran together as the PDL.

charisma, which is largely an impure charisma – or, better, a manufactured charisma (Ginsborg, 2003; Ceri, 2011) – with strongly patrimonial connotations.

Silvio Berlusconi's centre-right coalition included his own FI and other six parties, among which was the League, which defected from the coalition, unwilling to cooperate with the 'post-Fascist' National Alliance. The inclusion in the government of ministers from AN for the first time caused concerns and misgivings at the international level (Ignazi and Katz, 1995). Thus, owing to all those factors of weakness the first Berlusconi government was obliged to resign after only seven months (December 1994).

A period of institutional tensions followed, characterized by a conflict with the head of state and political uncertainty. Under the technical government led by Dini – a former minister in Berlusconi's cabinet – the foundation stage of FI could be considered over. The 1996 elections were won by the centre-left coalition formed by the *Ulivo* (the Olive Tree) backed by the *Partito di Rifondazione Comunista*, PRC (Party of Communist Refoundation) under Romano Prodi's leadership. FI, without *Lega Nord*, LN (Northern League), won 20.6 per cent of the vote (7,715,342 votes) and obtained 123 seats in the Chamber of Deputies (only 47 in the Senate) with 420,000 fewer voters than in the 1994 elections (see Table 14.1). Thus, FI's 'crossing of the desert' started, as was emphatically depicted by its leader.

While FI was in opposition, Berlusconi addressed some issues aimed at strengthening the internal party organization and spreading it throughout the country, which culminated in the first National Party Congress held on 16–18 April 1998. During this period, several attempts to institutionalize FI were undertaken by adopting different organizational models: Previti's original project (1994), based on the American party model, a more sophisticated plan drafted by Giuliano Urbani, but immediately discarded, and finally Claudio Scajola's proposal which laid the basis of the new Statute of FI (18 January 1997). From an organizational point of view, it can be said that a few years after its creation and after having lost its symbiotic relationship with Fininvest, FI was no longer an 'instant party'. Yet, party institutionalization remained weak, with strong centrifugal forces in the periphery, especially during negative electoral stages.

From hegemony to crisis (2001–11)

The elections of 13 May 2001 provided Berlusconi and his allies with the chance to win and rule the country. They represented a historic turning point: 'the first legitimate, peaceful changeover in the Italian political system, decided by the electorate and accepted by the losers' (Pasquino, 2002: 19). But the elections were especially crucial for FI, which obtained 10,923,146 votes, 29.4 per cent, equivalent to more than 50 per cent of the votes gathered by the *Casa delle libertà* (House of Freedoms), the new name of the centre-right coalition. FI won 187 seats in the Chamber of Deputies and 83 in the Senate. In contrast to 1994, there was also a considerable gap between *Forza Italia* and the second national party, the *Democratici di Sinistra*, DS (Democrats of the Left), which got only 16.6 per cent of the vote. As a result, FI became the largest party in Italy, 'capable of establishing itself anywhere and everywhere' (Diamanti, 2003: 90) (see Table 14.1).

Over the years, the party showed an unstable trend, registering an increase in its membership from 139,546 to 312,863 from 1997 to 2000, and a drop to 190,000 members in 2006 (Raniolo, 2006; Paolucci, 2007). The party carried out the important function of rooting itself throughout the country thanks to FI local representatives at regional, provincial and municipal levels, according to the model of a franchising party (Carty, 2004). Consequently, FI local representatives preserved a high degree of autonomy from the centre without any strong organizational structure able to connect the periphery with the centre.

Forza Italia's success was also due to Berlusconi's politics of alliance. In 2001, the first bipolar election in Italian history took place under the slogan 'united we can win': the fracture between the *Lega Nord* (LN) and the centre-right coalition was therefore repaired (Di Virgilio, 2001). The League, once again allied with FI and AN within the *Casa delle Libertà* (House of Freedoms) with a clear, shared programme to which all subscribed, governed throughout the 2001–6 legislature, as was expected. The other coalition partners were *Biancofiore* (Whiteflower), the Centre Christian Democrats (CCD), and the Christian Democratic Union (CDU), the New Italian Socialist Party and the Italian Republican Party. In total, the cabinet consisted of 84 people, with 14 ministers, nine of them without portfolio, and five technical ministers. In order to guarantee stability in government coalition, key posts were assigned to the leaders of majority parties.

The second Berlusconi goverment will be remembered as the longest in the history of the Italian Republic, exceeded only by his fourth government (16th legislature). However, severe tensions emerged between the prime minister and the parties in the coalition (Cotta, 2002; Campus, 2002). Government policymaking was affected by external factors as well as by 'sudden and unexpected events' (Cotta, 2002: 180), such as the economic crisis and, after September 11, a new international scenario. In addition, in recent years, this led to the radicalization of relationships with trade unions, especially the CGIL. It also triggered a twofold coordination problem for Berlusconi, the first within the party, concerning the relationship with the peripheral structures, the second within the coalition and the government.

Signs of crisis became more evident after the results of the European and the regional and local elections held in 2004 and 2005 respectively. The outcome of this negative trend was the resignation of the Berlusconi government and the formation of a new one: the so-called Third Berlusconi government (23 April 2005). The 2006 general election marked a slim victory for the centre-left led by Romano Prodi. Berlusconi's centre-right performed better than expected and came closer to returning to power. This outcome was arguably due to the new electoral law, which entailed a proportional system with a majority bonus (known as the *Porcellum Bill*). Berlusconi questioned the legitimacy of the election, stressing its irregularities and making a strong challenge to Prodi's victory by mobilizing his supporters (Donovan, 2008).

Only two years after the rise to power of the centre-left under the Prodi government, the centre-right took its revenge. The announcement and creation of a united centre-right party, *Partito del Popolo della Libertà* (the People of Freedom Party, later renamed simply as *Popolo della Libertà* (PDL)), enabled Berlusconi to reassert his role as an innovative leader. The idea of a single party within the right was not new, it was raised without success within the CDL, but it was only in 2009 that it was realized, favoured by a more competitive political framework.

Berlusconi was, therefore, able to respond to the creation of the single centre-left party *Partito Democratico* (PD, Democratic Party), under Walter Veltroni's leadership. Whereas DS and *Margherita* merged following a so-called 'cold fusion', Berlusconi looked for direct popular involvement in this process. In the end, UDC refused to join PDL and only AN and other small centre-right parties did.

This strategy was rather successful in attracting media attention and in paving the way for Berlusconi's triumph. Table 14.1 shows that the PDL won a fairly impressive 37.4 per cent (1.3 per cent more than the combined votes gained by FI and AN in 2006), compared with 34 per cent for the PD; the nine-point gap between the two coalitions (PDL + AN + LN vs PD + IDV) was unprecedented compared with the rounds of voting in the history of the Italian Second Republic (Corbetta, 2009: 81). The 2008 election highlighted a bipolarism characterized by the reduction of fragmentation and by the enduring dominance of the right over the left (ibid.: 91). Nevertheless, political competition was still radicalized, both between the parties and within the ruling coalition and the PDL. Likewise, the conflictual relationship between the judiciary and other state institutions caused an institutional stalemate.

Berlusconi is dead. Long live Berlusconi (2011–13)

Some of the events that occurred after the 2008 election were largely unexpected. Although the fourth Berlusconi government enjoyed high levels of support and solid majorities in both parliamentary chambers, after three years the strength of the majority coalition was threatened by internal conflicts (between PDL and LN) and disagreements within the ministerial team (between Berlusconi and Tremonti). Gianfranco Fini subsequently withdrew from the PDL to form a rival centre-right party, *Futuro e Libertà* (Future and Freedom). Moreover, by the end of 2011, the international credibility of Berlusconi and his government was damaged by a long series of scandals and the increasing anti-European attitude adopted by the prime minister. This, in turn, alienated the PDL from its electorate, the business world and traditionally conservative Catholic voters. Over the years the relationship with the opposition, with Italy's largest trade union federation, the left-wing CGIL, as well as with the President, the Constitutional Court and the judges had become highly antagonistic. Against this background, the political crisis under the pressure of the global financial speculations reached its peak.

The inability to find a suitable successor to Berlusconi negatively affected the stability of Italian politics and even of the PDL itself. The leaders of coalition government parties were unable to deal with the events whilst the opposition showed a low degree of coordination (Diamanti *et al.*, 2012). The only solution to managing the political, fiscal and, once again, moral crisis of the country was the formation of a fully non-partisan and technical government, led by Mario Monti (16 November 2011), supported by the president of the Republic, with the approval of European institutions (e.g. the European Commission and the European Central Bank) and international bodies (e.g. the IMF). Monti's government introduced emergency austerity measures backed by a large parliamentary majority, except for *Lega Nord* and *Italia dei Valori* (Italy of Values) following a model of party cartelization (Katz and Mair, 1995).

The consequences of these changes within the *Popolo della Libertà* were rather ambiguous. The choices made by Angelino Alfano, appointed secretary of the party, were not independent and were often undermined by Berlusconi himself, as in the case of holding primaries in the PDL, often announced on television, but in practice denied by Berlusconi even prior to the official declaration that he would be running for prime minister again. In addition, whereas the PDL took a strong stance against corruption scandals involving its staff in the regions of

Lombardy and Lazio, within parliament the party delayed the approval of an anti-corruption bill. The summer of 2012 was characterized by internal conflicts, with Berlusconi expressing his willingness to change the name and identity of the party, his decision to return to the electoral race, growing scandals around him, as well as the threats of defections from former AN members.

This period was well described by a PDL member: 'We are all on the run, but no one knows where to go' (*Corriere della Sera*, 3 October 2012, p. 13). In this political landscape, Berlusconi's return was more about the implosion of, and the dramatic loss of support for, the PDL. This was also an answer to the centre-right electorate, strongly affected by the Monti government's austerity policies. However, Berlusconi's return was not entirely unexpected and many observers in Italy suspected that it had been orchestrated from the beginning. Tensions with the judges – with verdicts of uncertain outcome expected in the early months of 2013 – influenced the electoral campaign, where the search for a prospective rather than retrospective vote prevailed.

Against this background, the 2013 elections produced a significant change in the Italian political system. The *Movimento Cinque Stelle* (M5S, the Five-Star Movement), led by the popular comic actor Beppe Grillo performed far better than the major parties, PD and PDL, standing as Italy's single largest party. The PDL obtained 21.6 per cent of votes, about 14 percentage points down on 2008 and reached only 29.2 per cent with its coalition partners. On the other hand, the centre-right alliance lost 18 percentage points compared with the previous elections, registering its worst historical result of 22 per cent in the last twenty years. In absolute values, the PDL lost over six million votes compared with 2008, as well as its control over its traditional strongholds, Lombardy in the North and Sicily in the South. Certainly, Berlusconi prevented the collapse of the PDL and the centre-right coalition, but this was mainly due to declining support for its rival party, the PD, rather than its own growth (Diamanti, 2013).

That makes it hard to read the PDL result as an unquestionable victory. The PDL is no longer the party of change, as this role is taken by M5S, nor is its future clear, while the leader appears weakened by new scandals (he was accused of having bribed Senator Di Gregorio to bring down Prodi's government in 2008) and the verdicts of the trials. After the 2013 elections, Italy is a special case of floating party systems (Rose and Munro, 2010), similar to Eastern Europe. In November 2013, after the split with Alfano and the other PDL ministers (who have subsequently formed the New Centre-Right), Berlusconi then created a new *Forza Italia*, orienting it towards anti-European positions and a radical opposition to the government led by Letta. There is a paradox here: Berlusconi has been one of the main actors in the birth of the bipolar system, albeit polarized and imperfect, but he seems no longer able to guarantee it. Twenty years after the 'Clean Hands' investigation, the crisis of the parties and the party system is contributing once again to making the Italian political situation highly unstable.

The parable of neo-Fascism: from 'custom clearance' to extinction

The earthquake caused by the *Tangentopoli* scandal brought a decisive change in the country's political system. The neo-Fascist MSI, which since 1971 had been excluded from any local or national government because of its distinctive illegitimate identity (Chiarini, 1991), emerged as the front-runner against the left dominated by former Communists. Silvio Berlusconi subscribed to this view by endorsing the candidacy of the MSI leader, Gianfranco Fini, as mayor of Rome.

After its unexpected success at 1993 municipal elections, the party started moderating its approach by enforcing the process of integration into the democratic system, which it had started long before but never completed. The moment had come to modify its name, symbol and strategy in order to set up a larger coalition of the right. As a result of these changes, a new label, *Alleanza Nazionale*, was adopted, even if this change was not well accepted by all its middle-level elite and supporters (Tarchi, 1995b and 1997).

Allies and competitors (1994–99)

Forced to look for cooperation, the party, unused to this practice, had early difficulties in relations with its new allies. Because of the veto by the Northern League, the National Alliance was unable to join the Pole of Freedom in Northern Italy and had to run its own list at the 1994 general elections. By contrast, in other regions it joined FI along with the CCD, under the Good Governance Pole. Despite this difficulty, the success of the MSI-AN was clear: 13.5 per cent of the votes, 109 deputies and 48 senators (see Table 14.1).

The AN's first foray into government with five ministers and twelve secretaries and the question, raised especially abroad, over the so-called 'rebirth of Fascism' pushed Fini to actively try to transform the party's neo-Fascist image by dropping its original ideology. The Congress held on 25–29 January 1995 sanctioned the end of MSI and the birth of *Alleanza Nazionale*.

In fact, at the very beginning there was an identifiable continuity between the MSI and the AN (Ignazi, 1994a). Having changed its status as a pariah party (Tarchi, 1995a) and following their leader's decision, almost all members accepted the new situation. Only one of the historical leaders, Pino Rauti, opposed this decision and founded the *Movimento Sociale–Fiamma tricolore*, which gained only very modest support. Fini tried to emphasize the originality of this transformation. The manifesto launched by the Fiuggi Congress claimed to 'embrace the democratic values that Fascism had denied', but it was not enough to achieve AN's political legitimization at large. The new positions of the party still showed consistent traces of MSI illiberal imprinting (Griffin, 1996; Ignazi, 1998; Baldini and Vignati, 1996) and intended solely to 'create the illusion of a core change in ideology and programs' (Ignazi, 1994b: 856). According to the data from a survey conducted among party delegates (Bertolino and Chiapponi, 1999), they displayed contradictory political attitudes towards the past which had inspired the creation of the MSI.

The political parties that formed the first Berlusconi government returned to opposition in early 1995. Overshadowed by the personality of Berlusconi, AN gave new priority to concerns about differentiating the *Alleanza* from its allies. Assuming that *Forza Italia* could quickly fall apart, AN progressively moved to more moderate positions, showing that the policy of the Italian right was oriented toward the centre (Ruzza and Fella, 2009), although an inner faction, *Destra sociale*, continued the traditional political culture of the MSI. Despite its allies' attempts at mediation, AN called for early elections, thus obtaining a good result (15.7 per cent), but as a result of its competition with MS-FT, the centre-right was defeated.

From that moment onwards, AN openly competed with FI. Rifts arose mainly over the reform of the judiciary and other institutions. The new party ideology, presented at the 1998 Programmatic Conference held in Verona, advocated liberalism in the economy and assumed conservative positions on ethical issues, a strategy aimed at attracting moderates. According to Fini, the era of anti-communism and ideological conflicts that had plagued the nineteenth century was over, whereas Berlusconi stressed his strong aversion to communism (Chiarini and Maraffi, 2001). At the same time, AN established a cooperation with some former Christian Democrats and members of the Radical Party to promote a referendum on the electoral law which culminated in the formation of a joint list at the 1999 European elections. The poor outcome of both initiatives confirmed the failure of an isolation strategy and reinforced confrontational stances within the party.

Governmental right (2000–5)

The crisis of the centre-left governments relaunched the necessity of unifying the opposition. Despite the harsh confrontation in previous years, AN did not refuse an alliance with the LN and it led to the centre-right coalition's victory in the main regions in April 2000. Its hopes of drawing voters away from *Forza Italia* waned (25.6 per cent vs 13.1 per cent, as Table 14.1 shows), but AN acquired a higher number of regional councillors and assessors, and gained the presidency of Lazio and Abruzzo. The increase in the number of party representatives in local government and the progressive professionalization of its cadres favoured a transition from a party of true 'believers' to one of 'careerists' (Panebianco, 1988). Notwithstanding the dramatic increase in the official number of members to 467,539 in 1995, the party was characterized by an emphasis on its presence 'in public office' rather than 'on the ground', through a large number of promotions to positions of power in the public sector. It was even clearer that the positions expressed in the AN programme documents presented at the Naples conference of February 2001 with the leitmotif of the 'Destra di governo' aimed at shifting towards moderate tendencies (Tarchi, 2003).

After the 2001 elections (AN 12 per cent, FI 29.4 per cent), the AN acquired ministerial positions in Berlusconi's government and the nomination of its leader as deputy prime minister. Fini tried to affirm himself as a serious and responsible conservative politician, now distancing himself from his old dream of reviving a 'Fascism of 2000' (Negri, 2010). He was appointed as the official representative of the Italian government at the European Convention, endorsed the military attack against Iraq and, while taking a hard line on law and order (repression of the anti-G8 protesters in Genoa, use of 'very severe' punishments for drug dealers), assumed more 'progressive' positions. In 2003 the party leader launched a proposal to provide legal immigrants with the right to vote at local elections, revised previous positions on ethical issues, opening up to some libertarian options, retracted his statement on Mussolini, whom he called in 1994 'the greatest Italian statesman of the twentieth century', and, during his visit to Jerusalem, he defined Fascism as an 'absolute evil' because of its racial laws. Fini's image as leader of a modern and moderate right-wing force was highlighted after his appointment as foreign minister in November 2004. However, the fact that, together with the Lega Nord's leader Umberto Bossi, he had signed a bill on stricter immigration regulations gave the members of the European People's Party cause for reservations about the prospect of the inclusion of AN's MPs in its parliamentary group in the Strasburg Assembly.

The break with the past was carried out mainly by the party leader but among its members the picture was less clear, since in some cases they displayed political attitudes close to the traditional MSI both in terms of authoritarian values and in their evaluation of the Fascist regime. Despite increasing its external attractiveness by emphasizing the new course of its programme, the political positions adopted by the party reflected only the choices of a restricted inner circle of party leaders. AN was governed according to the principle of 'plebiscitary centralism', in which the party leader had almost absolute power over the internal decision-making bodies, appointed half of its members in the National Assembly and exerted full control over financial resources. The president also violated the party statute which stipulated the need to organize a conference every three years, whereas only three conferences took place from 1995 to 2009. This, however, did not prevent the flourishing of internal factions that competed for hegemony within the party, though Fini's leadership was never questioned, and sought to influence ideologically the AN's official position. This explains why the programme presented at the 2002 National Party Congress was drafted by a committee made up of representatives of the three internal factions of the party.

Fini adopted the strategy of 'divide and rule', but such divisions raised notable friction within the party. His clear statement on the 'absolute evil of Fascism' provoked uproar amongst the members and resulted in the departure of Alessandra Mussolini, who founded *Alternativa Sociale* (an umbrella coalition of extreme-right parties, including *Forza Nuova* and *Fronte nazionale*), and some public expressions of dissent among senior party leaders. The poor performance of the centre-right in the 2005 regional elections, at which the House of Freedoms won only in Lombardy and the Veneto – thanks to the Northern League – increased these difficulties.

The risks of 'cold fusion' and the diaspora (2006–13)

The disagreements within the coalition suggested that the centre-right should present itself at the 2006 elections with a better articulated formula, emphasizing the specific programmes tabled by FI, AN and CCD. The defeat left room for Fini to make efforts to move towards the centre, with the purpose of obtaining membership of the EPP, even at the cost of causing the exit of the populist wing of Alleanza Nazionale, loyal to the MSI heritage, led by Francesco Storace, who founded a new party *La Destra* (which got 2.4 per cent of votes at the 2008 general election, as Table 14.1 shows). Fini's strategy was overshadowed by Berlusconi's invitation to merge all the forces of the centre-right into a single party, *il Popolo della Libertà*. Whereas at first Fini had strongly opposed it, then, under the pressure of elections just around the corner and the fear of loss of votes, he agreed to run on a joint list. After the success of the new strategy promoted by Berlusconi, Fini organized a purely formal third congress of the party and announced both the dissolution of the AN and its merger with the PDL.

The 'cold fusion', despite the entry into government with four ministers, the election of Gianni Alemanno as mayor of Rome and Fini's appointment as president of the Chamber of Deputies, worsened previous rifts and created new ones. Within the PDL, a party without its own political identity and centred on Berlusconi's personal leadership, Fini was, for the first time in twenty years, no longer the only party leader. His reiterated anti-Fascist statements contributed to distancing him from most former leading members of the AN, who never accepted his ideological repositioning. Incorporating party officials and members into the new party proved hard to implement because of their failure to share a common organizational structure. Furthermore, the decision that 70 per cent of political positions and electoral candidatures would be granted to FI members, whilst only 30 per cent would be reserved to former AN members, highlighted the inequality of treatment of both founding parties by increasing conflicts within the party.

Between 2008 and 2010, relations deteriorated between Berlusconi and Fini, who, by taking advantage of his institutional role, complained about the PDL's political choices and Berlusconi's personal behaviour. In the end, Fini broke away from Berlusconi, who had become more intolerant of his ally's criticism, and quit the PDL at the April 2011 National Committee of the PDL; but only 44 MPs and a limited number of local councillors followed him. Yet, Fini's attempt to reunite all his former followers and thus force Berlusconi to resign as head of the government failed. Fini's *Futuro e Libertà* (FLI) appeared as a betrayal not only of Berlusconi but also of many members originally from the MSI. The new party experienced internal troubles because of its poor performance in the run-up to local elections and was weakened by defections. A willingness to build a central pole in a hypothetical 'Party of the Nation', including the UDC and another moderate party, *Alleanza per l'Italia*, combined with a strong support for the Monti government, did not prevent the rapid decline of Fini's party. At the general election of February 2013, FLI got a disastrous 0.4 per cent of votes, which meant it was no longer represented in Parliament and was condemned to becoming an irrelevant political actor.

The FLI was not the only victim of the neo-Fascist *diaspora*. Fini's controversial behaviour brought internal divisions among his fellow members. Within the PDL most of the AN leaders loyal to Berlusconi were marginalized and their presence reduced in the electoral lists. Others, led by former ministers La Russa and Meloni, formed a new, more nationalist and right-wing party, *Fratelli d'Italia*, with the unavowed purpose of recreating the former National Alliance, which with 1.9 per cent got only nine MPs. *La Destra* did even more poorly, scoring only 0.6 per cent. The lists of the Radical Right – *Forza Nuova, CasaPound, MS-Fiamma tricolore* – together took only 0.4 per cent of votes (see Table 14.1). Research suggests that many former MSI followers shifted their vote to the populist movement headed by Beppe Grillo. Twenty years after *Tangentopoli*, the tide that had brought the 'National Right' from the margin of politics to the centre of power has now reached a very low ebb, leaving behind the remnants of a long and controversial history. The inability to preserve its own distinct identity amongst its allies, as well as in the eyes of its opponents, has destroyed the ambitions raised by the collapse of the old party system in 1993.

Conclusions

After a long period of isolation caused by its identification with Fascism, the Italian Right emerged from the ashes of the First Republic in 1993, beset by the scandals of *Tangentopoli*. Since there was no longer a Communist threat, a large part of the electorate expressed conservative views, albeit in rather different ways. Disappointed with the corrupt ruling class, citizens were in search of new political forces. *Forza Italia* was seen as appealing by anti-state 'liberal revolution' supporters. The MSI and AN were popular with those citizens who wanted to reaffirm law-and-order policies, to call for an increased sense of the state and respond to threats to national identity (migration, secessionist claims). The CCD and CDU were viewed favourably by Catholic traditionalists.

The success of the centre-right coalition, despite this heterogeneity of expectations and perspectives, can be explained by two factors: the persistent hostility of a large sector of Italian society against the left and the presence of a unifying leader, a successful entrepreneur, a man from civil society (systematically praised by the media for its virtues and opposed to 'uncivil' political society), who presented himself as a newcomer. In these conditions, enjoying the advantage of owning the most important Italian private television company, Berlusconi managed for almost twenty years to maintain control over the fragile coalition he had founded. This coalition had been repeatedly challenged by the conflicting interests and ideological aspirations of each member group: after the break-up with the Lega Nord, which was responsible for the electoral defeat of 1996, the frictions between FI, AN and CCD-CDU-UDC were frequent (Poli and Tarchi, 1999), eased only by the prospect of returning to government, and re-emerged still in the years that followed in relation to important issues such as economic policy, relations with the European Union and institutional reforms. After 2006, with the defection of the UDC and the criticism of populism launched by AN against the LN and *Forza Italia*, the instability of the coalition increased, but it was counterbalanced by the failure of the incoherent coalition supporting the Prodi government, torn by serious internal conflicts. The success of the centre-right at the 2008 election only temporarily mitigated internal tensions, triggered by Gianfranco Fini, sceptical about the opportunity to succeed Berlusconi as leader of PDL, but convinced, in the face of the economic crisis, of the possibility of being appointed to head a transitional government with the support of the centre-left party. Between 2010 and 2011, Fini's expectation was unfulfilled: the creation of the FLI was not enough to defeat the Berlusconi government in parliament, and when the weakness of the executive in dealing with the financial crisis forced the *Cavaliere* to resign as prime minister, Mario Monti succeeded him at the head of a technocratic government. Support for Monti's government was far from unanimous within the PDL: the party was close to division and its parliamentary majority was gradually being eroded, but also for the FLI the alliance with the centrists did not succeed as expected.

At the February 2013 general election, the PDL lost considerable support to the *Scelta civica di Monti* (Monti's Civic List), but most significantly to the Five-Star Movement, which had already at the 2012 local elections attracted right-wing voters keen to oppose the rise of the centre-left parties. The centre-right lost the election by an unexpectedly tiny margin, but the decline of bipolarism diminished its capacity to undertake initiatives, condemning it to depend on others' actions and decisions. The proposal to form a broad coalition government with the Democratic Party, in spite of their sharp differences in ideology and in programmatic platform, was an evident confirmation of that situation. Without a new ruling class, with a leader severely damaged by legal difficulties likely to lead to convictions on a number of charges and with the ex-AN component fragmented and weakened, the destiny of the Italian Right will be influenced by factors that are difficult to control. Given that, as is shown by the polls, its potential electorate is wide, although eroded by temporary defections and abstentions, a deep process of renewal in the organizational structure and in the programmatic platform is expected to take place sooner or later. In what direction and by whom, it is rather hard to predict in the current circumstances. Against this background, it seems that the Italian political system will find it hard to emerge from the tunnel of political transition.

Bibliography

Are, G. (1997). I riferimenti culturali. In D. Mennitti (ed.), *Forza Italia. Radiografia di un evento* (pp. 183–95). Rome: Ideazione Editrice.

Baldini, G. and Vignati, R. (1996). Dal Msi ad An: una nuova cultura politica? *Polis*, 1 (10), 81–101.

Berlusconi, S. (2003). *La nuova strada*. Rome: Fondazione Liberal.

Bertolino, S. and Chiapponi F. (1999). I militanti di Alleanza Nazionale: ancora 'Esuli in Patria'? *Quaderni di Scienza Politica*, 2 (8), 211–49.

Calise, M. (2000). *Il partito personale*. Rome-Bari: Laterza.

Campus, D. (2002). La formazione del governo. In G. Pasquino (ed.), *Dall'Ulivo al governo Berlusconi* (pp. 275–94). Bologna: Il Mulino.

Carty, K. R. (2004). Parties as franchise systems. The stratarchical organizational imperative. *Party Politics*, 10 (1), 5–24.

Ceri, P. (2011). *Gli italiani spiegati da Berlusconi*. Rome-Bari: Laterza.

Chiarini, R. (1991). La Destra italiana. Il paradosso di un'identità illegittima. *Italia contemporanea*, 185, 582–600.

Chiarini, R. and Maraffi, M. (eds.) (2001). *La destra allo specchio. La cultura politica di Alleanza nazionale*. Venice: Marsilio.

Corbetta, P. (2009). *Cronaca di una vittoria annunciata, Le elezioni politiche del 13–14 aprile*. In G. Baldini and A. Cento Bull (eds.), *Politica in Italia. Edizione 2009* (pp. 73–96). Bologna: Il Mulino.

Cotta, M. (2002). Berlusconi alla seconda prova. In P. Bellucci and B. Martin (eds.), *Politica in Italia. Edizione 2002* (pp. 163–84). Bologna: Il Mulino.

Cotta, M. and Verzichelli, L. (2008). *Il sistema politico italiano*. Bologna: Il Mulino.

Diamanti, I. (2003). *Bianco, rosso, verde. . . e azzurro. Mappe e colori dell'Italia politica*. Bologna: Il Mulino.

Diamanti, I. (2005). Il Cavaliere senza partito. *Repubblica*, 17 April: p. 20.

Diamanti, I. (2013). L'illusione del Cavalieri e la 'rimonta' del Pd. *Repubblica*, 4 March: p. 11.

Diamanti, I., Ceccarini, L. and Lazar, M. (2012). *Fine di un ciclo: la destrutturazione del sistema partitico italiano*. In A. Bosco and D. McDonnell (eds.), *Politica in Italia. Edizione 2012* (pp. 63–82). Bologna: Il Mulino.

Di Virgilio, A. (2001). Uniti si vince? Voto e politica delle alleanze. *Il Mulino*, 4, 635–44.

Donovan, M. (2008). *Il centro-destra: conflitti, unità e mobilitazione.* In M. Donovan and P. Onofri (eds.), *Politica in Italia. Edizione 2008* (pp. 87–108). Bologna: Il Mulino.
Frattini, F. (2003). Una grande svolta. *Liberal*, 15, 76–8.
Ginsborg, P. (2003). *Berlusconi.* Turin: Einaudi.
Griffin, R. (1996). The 'post-Fascism' of the Alleanza Nazionale: a case study in ideological morphology. *Journal of Political Ideologies*, 2 (1), 123–45.
Günther, R. and Diamond, L. (2001). Types and functions of parties. In L. Diamond and R. Günther (eds.), *Political Parties and Democracy* (pp. 3–39). Baltimore, MD and London: Johns Hopkins University Press.
Ignazi, P. (1994a). *Postfascisti?* Bologna: Il Mulino.
Ignazi, P. (1994b). La resurrezione postfascista. *il Mulino*, 6 (43), 853–62.
Ignazi, P. (1997). *I partiti politici in Italia.* Bologna: Il Mulino.
Ignazi, P. (1998). Gianfranco Fini è in fuga ma il suo plotone arranca. *Il Mulino*, 3 (47), 233–40.
Ignazi, P. and Katz, R. S. (1995). Introduzione. Ascesa e caduta del governo Berlusconi. In P. Ignazi and R. Katz (eds.), *Politica in Italia. Edizione 1995* (pp. 27–48). Bologna: Il Mulino.
Katz, R. S. and Mair, P. (1995). Changing models of party organization and party democracy: the emergence of the cartel party. *Party Politics*, 1 (5), 5–28.
Levitsky, S. (1998). Institutionalizaton and Peronism. *Party Politics*, 4 (1), 77–92.
McDonnell, D. (2013). Silvio Berlusconi's personal parties: from Forza Italia to the Popolo Della Libertà. *Political Studies*, 61 (1), 217–33.
Mennitti, D. (ed.) (1997). *Forza Italia. Radiografia di un evento.* Rome: Ideazione Editrice.
Morlino, L. (1998). *Democracy between Consolidation and Crisis.* Oxford and New York: Oxford University Press.
Morlino, L. and Tarchi, M. (1996). The dissatisfied society. Protest and support in Italy. *European Journal of Political Research*, 30, 41–63.
Morlino, L., Piana, D. and Raniolo, F. (eds.) (2013). *La qualità della democrazia in Italia 1992–2012.* Bologna: Il Mulino.
Negri, L. (2010). *DoppiFini.* Florence: Vallecchi.
Panebianco, A. (1988). *Political Parties.* New York: Cambridge University Press.
Paolucci, C. (2007). *Forza Italia.* In L. Bardi, O. Massari and P. Ignazi (eds.), *I partiti italiani* (pp. 97–149). Milan: Università Bocconi Editore.
Pasquino, G. (2002). *Il sistema politico italiano.* Bologna: Bononia University Press.
Poli, E. (2001). *Forza Italia.* Bologna: Il Mulino.
Poli, E. and Tarchi, M. (1999). I partiti del Polo: uniti per cosa? In D. Hine and S. Vassallo (eds.), *Politica in Italia. Edizione 99* (pp. 79–100). Bologna: Il Mulino.
Raniolo, F. (2006). Forza Italia. A leader with a party. *South European Society and Politics*, 3–4, 439–55.
Raniolo, F. (2013). *I partiti politici.* Rome-Bari: Laterza.
Rose, R. and Munro, N. (2010). *Parties and Elections in New European Democracies.* Colchester: ECPR Press.
Ruzza, C. and Fella, S. (2009). *Re-inventing the Italian Right. Territorial Politics, Populism and 'Post-Fascism'.* London and New York: Routledge.
Salvadori, M. (2013). *Storia d'Italia e crisi di regime.* Bologna: Il Mulino.
Tarchi, M. (1995a). *Esuli in patria. I fascisti nell'Italia repubblicana.* Milan: Guanda.
Tarchi, M. (1995b). *Cinquant'anni di nostalgia. La destra italiana dopo il fascismo*, intervista di Antonio Carioti. Milan: Rizzoli.
Tarchi, M. (1997). *Dal Msi ad An. Organizzazione e strategie.* Bologna: Il Mulino.
Tarchi, M. (2003). The political culture of the Alleanza Nazionale: an analysis of the party's programmatic documents (1995–2002). *Journal of Modern Italian Studies*, 2 (8), 135–81.

15

FROM COMMUNISM TO CENTRE-LEFT*

Analysis of an unprecedented political trajectory

Marc Lazar and Lilia Giugni

Any study of the Italian left must be anchored in the general framework of the significant change the boot-shaped peninsula has gone through—a change with very specific features, when compared with the transformations that affected many other European countries (Meyer and Hinchman, 2002; Poguntke and Webb, 2005). Almost everywhere, indeed, national politics have undergone a quadruple process of presidentialization, personalization, mediatization and intensification of marketing strategies. Such transformations, which contribute to the rise of what Bernard Manin calls 'audience democracy', took place in Italy with extraordinary intensity and rapidity (Manin, 1997). Moreover, they have been accompanied by a systemic and institutional upheaval and strengthened by the prodigious social changes that also altered Italians' attitudes towards politics.

We are going to illustrate the unprecedented trajectory followed by the Italian Communist Party (PCI). Why should we concern ourselves with this organization? On the one hand, because the PCI has long embodied the Italian left, by dint of a merciless competition with the Italian Socialist Party (as during the 1970s–1980s, when the latter was led by Bettino Craxi) and with some far-left groups (which, especially during the 1960s–1970s, vehemently contested its politics and even embraced terrorist violence). On the other hand, because this party enjoyed the worthwhile reputation of an open, intelligent and creative political force, autonomous, if not totally independent, from Moscow. After the opening of the Soviet archives, historians put such originality back in its true perspective, albeit without denying it completely. Nonetheless, notably from the 1960s to the 1970s, the PCI wielded a real influence not only over the whole European left (in the West as in the East, where it attracted dissidents keen on democratic socialism), but also in American leftist intellectual coteries. Explicitly situated on the left of the political spectrum, the PCI painfully renounced both its name and its communist identity, in order to call itself the *Partito Democratico della Sinistra* (PDS), then the *Democratici di Sinistra* (DS), before finally adopting the title of the Democratic Party (*Partito Democratico*, or PD). Since then, Italy has been one of the few European countries where the main antagonist of the right-wing forces not only refuses the name 'socialist' or 'social-democrat', but has also rejected the word 'left', preferring to replace it with the expression 'centre-left'.

We will restrict our investigation to two essential aspects of the transition experienced by the former Italian communists, and then carefully consider the situation of the Democratic Party.

First of all, by scrutinizing the strategies adopted by the subsequent party elites, we will explore how the evolution of the political system, of potential allies and rivals, of public opinion and of the electoral mechanism shaped the party in question. Then, inversely, we will investigate how the latter tried to influence the external environment and to turn it to its own advantage. Second, the organization, the political culture and the identity, three essential and deeply interconnected dimensions within the old PCI, will be investigated. The party, indeed, was characterized by a solid organizational structure and clearly recognizable identity and political culture. Therefore, studying what has become of the organizational components will allow us to evaluate the reality of the changes claimed by the party leadership.

By analysing these two topics, we aim to understand how a party evolves in a context of democratic transition in which the phases of consolidation and legitimization of the new institutions and party system still seem rather remote. The purpose is thus to identify the real ruptures which took place within the Italian Left and to uncover eventual elements of continuity hidden behind the claims of a complete renewal.

A strategy of interaction with the environment

PCI, PDS and DS: the main steps between 1991 and 2007

After its spectacular success in the 1970s,[1] by the early 1980s the PCI had started to be obsessed by fear of the decline which was affecting the communist parties all over Western Europe, as is shown by its poor electoral performance in 1987 (26.6 per cent). The fall of the Berlin Wall and the Soviet collapse heightened the internal debate and, in 1989, precipitated the decision of the leader Achille Occhetto to change the party's name and identity.

After two years of lively controversies, the majority of the PCI decided to scuttle itself and to create the PDS, against the opinion of a minority, which adopted the name of *Rifondazione Comunista* (PRC). This 'Party of the Democratic Left' was neither a 'socialist' nor a 'social democratic' party, not only in order to differentiate itself from the PSI, which was sinking into a corruption scandal, but also because the former communists kept their old aversion towards social democracy.

The PDS soon had to prove itself in elections characterized by a new voting system. It ran in the 1994 political elections within a coalition called *Alleanza dei Progressisti* (Alliance of the Progressives), led by Occhetto and rather left-oriented, despite the presence of some moderate groups which joined the left-wing forces and the Green Party. The PDS believed in its chances of victory: the Christian Democrats and the Socialists had disappeared; the voters shared a commitment to change, as demonstrated by the success of many leftist or left-friendly candidates at the 1993 local elections; the manifesto of the Progressives was moderate.

The defeat was shocking. Silvio Berlusconi triumphed for different reasons. He managed to present his candidacy as a real break with the previous system, revolutionizing political communication by relying on his own TV channels and on the sales techniques he had perfected after several decades as a businessman, and imposed a new type of leadership. Last but not least, he built up a large and heterogeneous coalition, very suitable to the new electoral system (75 per cent of the seats assigned by uninominal plurality method and the remaining 25 per cent by proportional representation) and able to attract most of the conservative and moderate voters, who were anti-leftists but also willing to enter a new political era.[2]

The PDS drew some lessons from such humiliating failure, whose price was paid by Occhetto, who was immediately obliged to resign. As the new leader Massimo D'Alema (symbol of a new generation of party cadres, as well as his younger rival Walter Veltroni) suggested, the PDS considered the left unable to win the elections. Because of many contingent factors, such as the voting system or the unwieldy communist past, Berlusconi had successfully revitalized the anti-communist feelings which were deeply entrenched in Italian society.[3]

At the same time, there were some structural reasons related to the country's history, its social stratigraphy and its cultural features, particularly the role played by the Catholic Church.

The purpose was thus to deepen the decommunization of the party (through a complete reconversion to reformism and thanks to concepts such as modernization, Europeanization or welfare reform) and to try to attract some of the centrists. Divided during the 1994 elections, these latter collected above 15 per cent of the votes and were experiencing a troublesome crisis. Hence, the idea of forming a centre-left coalition rather than a mere leftist alliance, guided by a leader free from a communist past but weak and easily controllable according to the communist tradition. The choice fell on Romano Prodi, a Catholic economist who had served as a minister without being too closely linked to the Christian Democrats, and had proven managerial skills without being a party man.

This ingenious operation transformed the Italian political system, which organized itself around two main poles, the centre-left and the centre-right. Admittedly, in the endless confrontation between the two fields, the centre-right often defined its rivals as 'leftists', in its view synonymous with 'communists', whereas the centre-left referred to its adversaries as 'rightists', which was clearly intended to mean 'fascists'. Nevertheless, the two blocs shared a common interest in building two main polar coalitions in order to reduce competition. Moreover, on the one hand they attempted not to leave any space on their respective flanks, and on the other hand competed to win over moderate voters and snatch them away from the centrists. Such strategy backed up the PRC's criticisms, while a leftist tendency arose within the PDS itself, as a consequence of the leadership's moderate policies. However, the PDS proved itself able to adapt to the current electoral system: it turned the tables and put Berlusconi on the defensive, especially after the defection of the Northern League at the end of 1994. The Olive Tree, the name of the centre-left coalition, won by a few votes in 1996, when Prodi successfully played the card of professional expertise, rather than challenging Berlusconi's showman skills.

Two years later, in February 1998, the PDS changed its name again. By transforming itself into the DS (*Democratici di Sinistra*), it aimed to emphasize its break with the past. Apart from the PDS, the new party collected various left-wing forces—socialist, republican, secular and Catholic. It aspired to cover the space of the reformist left, in contrast to the extreme-leftists, and to strengthen its alliance with the centre. A few months later, after the PRC had caused the collapse of the Prodi administration, the DS got rid of such an unreliable ally: Massimo D'Alema became the first Italian prime minister from the communist experience (despite his attempt to remove his heavy past). His premiership was brief and in 2000 he resigned, after a humiliating debacle in the regional elections. The following year, the centre-left, led by Francesco Rutelli (a former Radical and Green who focused on mediatization and personalization but did not manage to hide the coalition's internal divisions), was heavily defeated by Berlusconi.

Traumatized by this new failure, vehemently criticized by some civil society members for their incapacity to oppose Berlusconi (the so-called *girotondi* movement), the DS were split between a tiny minority supporting further centrist realignment and a more powerful social democratic tendency wanting to anchor the party to the left. With their new secretary, Piero Fassino, the DS opened itself up to the creation of a new large centre-left coalition, which performed satisfactorily in local and regional elections. In October 2005, primary elections were organized to choose the leader of the *Unione*, the new centre-left coalition. Back from his experience as president of the European Commission, Romano Prodi won a ballot which involved more than 4,300,000 voters. In the spring of 2006, he won a knife-edge political election characterized by a new voting mechanism (proportional method with a majority premium for the winning party or coalition). However, his majority was too fragile and heterogeneous to resist the attacks of the centre-right. In 2008 he resigned and new elections were then called.

The Democratic Party, 2007–13

In the meantime, the tables were turned again. Piero Fassino promoted a rapprochement with the Daisy (*Margherita*), an aggregation of several centrist and Catholic forces. The purpose, already clarified by Prodi and his followers, but also by Veltroni, was to put an end to the heterogeneity of electoral alliances and to assure governability thanks to a dominant party able to appeal to moderate voters. With this in mind, despite the opposition of tiny minorities in both organizations, in the spring of 2007 the DS merged with the Daisy to form a new party, the PD. The latter considered the left/right distinction as outdated in Italian politics.[4] Therefore, it repudiated the left *tout court* in order to present itself as a majoritarian centre-left party, supposed to compete against a centre-right organization. Also, it wanted to open itself up to civil society and in the autumn of 2007 organized primary elections to select its National Assembly and leader, in the person of Walter Veltroni (former communist and eternal rival of D'Alema, vice prime minister in the first Prodi administration and secretary of the DS between 1998 and 2001, more recently mayor of Rome). For his part, Berlusconi did the same, by announcing out of the blue in November 2007 the creation of the People of Liberty (PDL), born from the fusion of *Forza Italia* and *Alleanza Nazionale* and formalized in 2009.

The 2008 elections were marked by the struggle between the two main organizations, the PD and the PDL (at that moment a mere electoral coalition). Veltroni ran an 'Americanized' electoral campaign and tried to forge a majoritarian centre-left party, free from any electoral deal. Nonetheless, Silvio Berlusconi achieved his third victory. Moreover, although the ballot had initially led to a certain simplification of the parliamentary representation by erasing the communists and the extreme right from the two Chambers, the two-party system defended by Veltroni appeared stillborn. An imperfect bipolar quadrille was established, where the two main parties, the PD and the PDL, were partnered by two allies, respectively the Italy of Values (IDV) and the Northern League, whereas the centrists of the UDC attempted to survive the siege. The PD strategic paradox thus became evident. On the one hand, its birth contributed to modifying the electoral competition and obliged the centre-right to go in the same direction, as Veltroni had hoped by claiming for an 'appeased democracy'. However, on the other hand, the PD did not manage to impose itself as the majoritarian party (as this was almost impossible because of the voting mechanism) and suffered from a troublesome institutional fragility shown by the succession of three leaders in less than three years.

The electoral defeat saw the beginning of a period of destabilization. In February 2009, Veltroni, who had been strongly criticized, resigned and soon worsened by the debacles in the following local and European consultations. After a temporary mandate of the deputy leader Dario Franceschini, Pierluigi Bersani won the October 2009 primaries, which were characterized by a real confrontation between the former, the latter and their challenger Ignazio Marino and by a significant participation (more than 3,100,000 voters, compared with 3,500,000 in 2007). The new secretary, who intended to incarnate a new type of leadership, adopted a 'D'Alemian' rather than 'Veltronian' programme: to set up a reformist party, close to European social democracy but respectful of other sensibilities. In spite of his tactfulness, he could not prevent the defection of the moderates, starting with Rutelli and his followers in November 2009 and the Catholic Paola Binetti in 2010.

Despite its success in the 2011 and 2012 local elections, the PD struggled to organize its opposition against Berlusconi and to take full advantage of his decline, provoked by sexual scandals, his loss of international credibility and by the deterioration of the economic and social context. Above all, it hesitated in matters of alliances, to be stipulated with the centrists of the UDC or with the left embodied by the IDV of Antonio Di Pietro and by *Sinistra, Ecologia e Libertà* of Nichi Vendola: the centre-left strategic dilemma was anything but solved.

In November 2011, the PD accepted the suggestion of President Napolitano to appoint Mario Monti as prime minister rather than dissolving the chambers and calling early elections. During the following months, the party backed the new government, but insisted on differentiating itself and protecting its core voters from policies such as the labour market flexibilization.[5] What is more, it appeared profoundly divided over the austerity measures adopted by the executive as well as over the party management and leadership. Bersani was criticized not only by Veltroni but also by some young party officers, such as Giuseppe Civati and above all by Matteo Renzi, mayor of Florence.

In autumn 2012, Renzi officially presented his candidacy in the primaries supposed to select the centre-left candidate for the 2013 general election by spectacularly placing the battle for generational renewal at the centre of the party debate. A part of the old dominant coalition closed ranks behind Bersani, considered as the most trustworthy guarantor of internal unity, despite his attempt to exploit Renzi's challenge in order to get rid of the older elite guardianship. As for the young generations, they were rather divided over Renzi's liberal democratic vision and Bersani's social democratic programme. Political economy remained, indeed, a very controversial matter, besides generational change. After trying to reconcile different histories and sensibilities, the party witnessed a struggle for the definition of its own political culture.

Nevertheless, Bersani's clear victory and Renzi's fairly honourable performance, as well as the openness of the internal debate, seemed to temporarily strengthen the leadership and reassure the party over its state of health. Therefore, the bitter surprise of the 2013 general election (see Table 15.1), which saw the triumph of the movement led by the comedian Beppe Grillo and the partial recovery of Berlusconi, proved even more painful. The centre-left, unable to win a majority in the two chambers, struggled to form a new government. The Democrats appeared divided over the strategies to adopt, the government to form and the candidate to present for the Presidency of the Republic, which led to the resignation of Bersani and of the whole executive.

In a nutshell, the PCI, the PDS and then the DS and the PD made some strategic breaks, most spectacularly when they renounced a leftist name in favour of the term centre-left, seen as more suitable to the political circumstances, the electoral system and the voters' expectations. The former communists have often trailed behind other political actors, particularly in understanding the voting mechanism and in adapting to the processes of presidentialization, personalization, mediatization and adoption of political marketing techniques. At the same time, they have been able to take the initiative by forming unprecedented coalitions in order to attract moderate voters, or by committing themselves to the cause of a short-lived bipolar polity. The other important innovation, which inspired the centre-right as well as other European organizations, has been the usage of primaries.

Lastly, although Enrico Letta assumed the leadership of a national unity government, after the 2013 elections the PD seems to be at a crossroads and about to implode. Shaken by the electoral result and by several corruption scandals, lacking a clear identity, without an attractive project, it is more than ever on the defensive. It is suffering as a result of the so-called anti-political protest and of the context of general deconstruction of the whole political system, which sees all Italian parties equally under deconstruction.

Its only (relative) reason for satisfaction is the awareness that the PDL and the centre-right are experiencing an even more troublesome crisis.

Organizations, cultures and identities

From the PCI to the PDS

The organizational doctrine of the PCI relied on democratic centralism. This was achieved through the considerable power of the leading bodies and more specifically of the party secretary, the social entrenchment of the membership, the imposition of an iron discipline and, above all, the numerous bureaucrats forming the apparatus. The same centralizing logic ruled the relations between the party and the collateral organizations (trade unions, diverse associations, youth and women's movements, etc.). The sacralization of the party was an essential feature of the communist culture.

Nevertheless, by the 1960s and most evidently at the end of the following decade, this system became more flexible. The new 1979 statute defined democratic centralism as a 'method' rather than a doctrinal principle. Several political and ideological sensibilities were then able to express themselves within the party and the right to dissent (but not to give rise to organized tendencies) was formalized in 1986. In the meanwhile, various collateral 'mass organizations' obtained an increasing autonomy. The last two years of the PCI, shaped by the debate over its future, meant the end of democratic centralism and the creation of organized factions (Accornero and Ilardi, 1979; Accornero *et al.*, 1983; Ignazi, 1992; Lazar, 1992; Bosco, 2000).

The PDS had to break from the communist organizational model, and consequently to develop its own institutional culture and invent a way to penetrate society. However, the communist legacy, evident in terms of the vertical distance between leadership and base, size and importance of the membership (see Table 15.2), values and references, could not disappear overnight and jeopardized the new party's first initiatives (Baccetti, 1997; Bellucci *et al.*, 2000; Morlino and Tarchi, 2006).

The 1991 statute was characterized by ambiguity. On the one hand, this document erased any leftovers of democratic centralism and set up a democratic and pluralist organization, ensuring the proportional representation of all factions within the party conference, respectful of civil society autonomy and aware of its own limits. On the other hand, the structure remained rather centralized, thanks to the primacy of the central and regional bodies over the local ones. Once the Central Committee had disappeared and the Direction had been so massively enlarged as to become ineffective, the role of the party leader was strengthened and some new executive organs were created (the Political Coordination Office, the only real executive committee, with 27 members, and the Operational Coordination Office, with three members representing the different internal positions).

The apparatus and the membership also experienced significant renewal. For example, new professional experts, often more emancipated than the traditional apparatchiks, rose to join the bureaucrats, especially in the communication, surveys and political marketing field. As for the members, the new organizational philosophy appeared less demanding than the communist one: the new party considered itself a centre of expression and participation rather than indoctrination, and encouraged individual contributions and critique.[6] Nonetheless, the persistent importance of apparatus and membership, despite their resizing, represented an element of continuity between

Table 15.1 Election results for the Chamber of Deputies (data expressed as percentages)[1]

1987	*1992*	*1994*[2]	*1996*	*2001*	*2006*	*2008*	*2013*
PCI: 26.6	PDS: 16.1	PDS: 20.4	PDS: 21.1	DS: 16.6	Union: 31.3	PD: 33.2	PD: 25.4

1 Data reported in European Elections Database. Available online at www.nsd.uib.no/european_election_database/country/italy/parliamentary_elections.html (accessed 26 October 2014).
2 For the elections of 1994, 1996 and 2001, the results refer to the proportional part of the voting process.

Table 15.2 PCI, PDS and DS membership

PCI[1]	*PDS*[2]	*DS*[3]	*PD*[4]
1987: 1,508,140	1991: 989,708	1999: 655,146	2009: 831,042
1988: 1,462,281	1992: 769,944	2000: 555,171	2010: 620,000 (estimate)
1989: 1,424,035	1993: 690,414	2001: 598,085	
1990: 1,319,905	1994: 698,287	2002: 531,358	
	1995: 682,290	2003: 549,372	
	1996: 686,713	2004: 560,141	
	1997: 640,838	2005: 561,193	
	1998: 613,412		

1 Data reported in C. Baccetti (1997). *Il PDS: verso un nuovo modello di partito?* Bologna: Il Mulino.
2 Data reported in R. De Rosa (2007). Partito Democratico della Sinistra e Democratici di Sinistra. In L. Bardi, P. Ignazi, and O. Massari (eds.), *I partiti italiani. Iscritti, dirigenti, eletti* (pp. 76–92). Milan: Università Bocconi Editore.
3 Ibid.
4 Partito Democratico: data available online at www.partitodemocratico.it (accessed 26 October 2014). No further data available after 2010.

the PCI and PDS. What is more, youth movements, trade unions and leftist cultural associations (such as ARCI) became almost completely independent. Similarly, the party's parliamentary component was also selected and organized according to softer criteria.[7]

The DS

During its nine-year life, the DS constituted an additional step in the organizational transition, although it also reflected the former communists' hesitation about renewal.

The DS intended to complete the transformation of the old, formidable communist organization into a 'weak institution' and to enlarge the leading elite, albeit (as we are going to see) without renewing it at all (Mulé, 2007). The 1998 statute officially formalized the party factions and created the post of president (specifically conceived for Massimo D'Alema, forced to resign as party secretary after having been appointed Prime Minister).

In 2000 and 2005, two further constitutional amendments deepened the decommunization. The first achieved a certain degree of decentralization, by strengthening local bodies at the expense of central ones and by introducing some autonomous organs, the so-called Thematic Autonomies, Councils and Forums.[8] The second enacted a new deliberative committee (the National Council), with the purpose of ensuring a permanent linkage between the Direction and the Congress (convened every three years).[9] Relative structural flexibility was provided, even if at the expense of a certain organizational power dispersion.

In a nutshell, the DS contributed to removing any organizational leftovers of the pre-existing communist system. The new force shared common features with most of the European parties ('light' structure, opening up to non-members, shrinkage in the proselytizing activities traditionally pursued by the militants), though it kept a hybrid nature. The debate nourished by the incertitude affecting both the party and civil society played an important role in the future foundation of the Democratic Party.

The PD

Organizational renewal

The PD, as the last product of the long transition process accomplished by the former communists, rose from the '*in vitro* fusion' of these with the Daisy. This explains the contradictions in its organizational system, born from the marriage of totally different cultures, both aspiring to adapt to the external environment.

Nevertheless, the 2008 statute reveals a conception of the party, of Italian society and of the democratic system which is very different from those defended by the PCI, the PDS and the DS. Thus, the whole organizational philosophy of the PD relies on the principles of internal and participative democracy.[10] It hopes to stress the break with the communist tradition and, at the same time, to 'heat up a cold fusion' (according to Michele Salvati, to get civil society involved in the shaping of the party).

The constitution defines the party as 'federal' and recognizes the political, programmatic and financial independence of regional and local bodies. It also regulates the party's local branches (the clubs), constituted online or on a territorial basis, and creates some 'instruments of political participation, elaboration and training', such as the Thematic Forums, the internal referendums or the Annual Programmatic Conference. Even though these guidelines aim to decentralize and diversify the decision-making process, their implementation is still ambiguous and incomplete, whereas the party organization as a whole appears rather complex and confused.

Officially, the national secretary represents the party and expresses its political positions. Moreover, he or she will be presented by the party as candidate for the premiership, as a proof of the majoritarian and pro-presidentialism commitment of the PD. The role is supported by some vice secretaries, whose enactments facilitate the power-sharing between the two original founding organizations, which essentially share between them all the existing leading positions. The executive bodies are the Secretariat and the National Coordination Office (120 members). In addition, there is a supreme deliberative organ, the National Assembly.

The 2008 statute includes only very general and vague references to official relations with possible collateral organizations.[11] Rather than stipulating institutional links with trade unions and associations, the PD prefers to invent a new relationship with civil society, above all thanks to the organization of primary elections. These constitute its main innovation and an essential feature of its identity.

The primaries

The primaries were adopted by the PD, as we have said, in order to stimulate public participation in its project and to attract those in civil society who had become more and more sceptical towards parties and politicians. They enabled the personalization process and inaugurated a direct relationship between leaders and voters. Thus, at least initially, they were conceived by the leadership as an instrument of legitimization for its authority thanks to a form of plebiscitary approbation. Consequentially, the continuous claims for a participative democracy are paradoxically accompanied by a rather elitist conception of democracy itself.

The primaries are open to PD members as well as to non-members, either Italian or EU citizens over 16 years of age, who share party values and accept being registered on a voters' list. Those who are mere voters enjoy essentially the same rights as members (with the exception of the chance to present their candidacy for party executive positions), which greatly modifies the concept of militancy and of the party itself, by affecting one of its traditional functions, the selection of future candidates. This choice focuses public attention on the electoral procedure, but weakens the link between the party and the electorate.

Two types of primaries need to be distinguished. The first aims to elect the national secretary and adopts a top-down mechanism. The 2007 ballot took place during the foundational phase of the party and set out to select the Constituent Assembly and the leader. Walter Veltroni easily won against his main adversaries, Rosi Bindi and Enrico Letta (Lazar, 2009b). The 2009 primaries, whose rules were slightly modified, were preceded by a preliminary consultation open to club members only (theoretically in order to choose candidates able to get over the threshold of 15 per cent) and designated the leader and the National Assembly. They were more open and significant and led to the victory of Pierluigi Bersani against his main challengers, Dario Franceschini and Ignazio Marino (Hanretty and Wilson, 2010). In both cases, as we have noticed, the turnout was considerable.

The primaries held to appoint candidates for upcoming local elections enact a totally different process. Even though the party constitution imposes organizing them for the post of mayor, president of province and region, in practice they have been used 'à la carte'. Such elections can involve only the PD or rather turn into coalition primaries and become even more competitive. These witnessed the success of the front runners Piero Fassino in Turin and Virgilio Merola in Bologna in 2011, but also promoted outsiders such as Matteo Renzi in Florence in 2009, Nichi Vendola in Puglia in 2010, Giuliano Pisapia in Milan in 2010 and Marco Doria in Genoa in 2012, who all challenged the party elite and demonstrated a robust commitment towards leadership renewal (Massari, 2004; Pasquino, 2009; Seddoni and Valbruzzi, 2009; Pasquino and Venturino, 2010; Pasquino and Venturino, 2011; Bobba *et al.*, 2012).

The autumn 2012 primaries, organized to select the centre-left candidate for the 2013 general elections, constitute a very specific case. Constitutionally, the party secretary was not obliged to call for a ballot, but the formidable challenge embodied by Renzi's candidacy did not leave him any choice. The rules were soon clarified, although not universally endorsed. Candidates other than the party leader were admitted only if supported by ten per cent of the National Assembly or by three per cent of party members. The voting modalities seemed even more restrictive: exclusion of young voters between 16 and 18 years of age; a second ballot if no candidate reached the majority of 50 per cent; registration on a voters' list and necessity for preregistration (also possible online, thanks to Renzi's insistence). Nevertheless, several candidates ran in the leadership race. After a bitter campaign, the secretary was confirmed at the second ballot. Once again, public attention for the pre-election debate and voter turnout were significant. In December 2012, the PD organized its first primaries to choose parliamentary candidates.

However, it is worth noticing that the massive participation which marked the primaries of 2007 and 2012 in neither of the two cases ensured victory at the following general election, which certainly gives food for thought to the party leadership. Overall, we can conclude that such consultations, perceived as a key element of the PD organizational identity, helped to reinforce the party's cohesion and image, but also turned into an unsettling indicator of its unsolved problems and into a multiplier of its internal conflicts. It is no wonder that in 2013 several elite members suggested another constitutional amendment in order to prevent Renzi from conquering power. The proposal, still under discussion, consists in differentiating the primaries which designate the leader (limited to members) from those electing the party candidate for the general election (open to all supporters of the centre-left).

Leadership, membership and values

The contrast embodied by the physiognomy of the PD is striking. On the one hand, the party membership had greatly changed, notably in terms of generational belonging. On the other hand, its apparatus and leading group, despite some undeniable transformations, form an oligarchy which prevents the circulation of the elites. These essentially rose, indeed, from the fusion of the former DS and Daisy leadership, with an evident imbalance in favour of the former communists. This nourishes the malaise of the Catholics, of the new members who joined the PD directly, and of the young cadres who are clamouring for further responsibilities. And this also backs the critics of the adversaries who accuse the PD of reframing itself in the old political system.

Thus, the percentage of the DS members who already belonged to the PCI was 78 per cent in 2006, against 94.7 per cent in 1991, and 93.04 per cent in 1993 within the PDS.[12] One could argue that the proportion of former PCI members (as well as former PDS and DS) within the PD is decreasing, although there are no specific data available. In the party apparatus, the changes are contradictory. In 2000, 54.4 per cent of DS Congress delegates were former communists.[13] In 2007, of PD Constituent Assembly delegates, 45.8 per cent came from the PCI-PDS-DS, 27 per cent from the Daisy and 27 per cent did not previously belong to any of the founding parties, whereas in the 2009 Congress the percentages were respectively 44.8, 33.4 and 21.8.[14] In addition, in 2009, 11 out of 16 in the PD Secretariat were former PCI-PDS-DS members (although, in 2006, 16 out of 18 members of the DS Secretariat were from the PCI-PDS).[15]

As for values and identity, confusion is extreme. A sort of hybridization, carefully planned in theory but resulting in a fragile compromise in practice, has been set in motion. Reformism, democracy, and commitment to ecology, feminism and pacifism are widely shared values within both the founding parties.[16] The Catholic tradition has imposed references such as attention to the individual, freedom, Europe and the West, while the old communist left has suggested equality, social policies, labour and solidarity with the trade unions. Since the very beginning, two different souls, a social democratic and a liberal democratic one, have (not always pacifically) coexisted. However, at the 2007 PD Assembly, 57 per cent of the delegates called themselves Catholic and 54 per cent of them considered religion an important matter (Fasano, 2008).

The Catholic sensibility of the Daisy is thus clearly evident. This explains the embarrassment of the PD over issues such as the rights of homosexual couples, bioethics questions, and more generally secularism, the role of the State, the functions of the party or the concepts of left and centre-left. The controversies about the way to address fellow members of the PD (the terms *compagni* and *compagne*, seen as a communist legacy, being rejected by a minority and by the youngest members) are certainly very telling.

Similarly, the problem of the European collocation of the party shows that the Italian centre-left is divided not only over its political culture but also over its essential aims, strategies and policies. The PD is a member of the Progressive Alliance of Socialists and Democrats in the European Parliament, created in 2009 to integrate the Italian organization into a group able to merge socialists with other progressives and to avoid the previous ambiguity (in 2004–9 the DS was a part of the European Socialist Party and the Olive Tree deputies of the Alliance of the

Liberals and Democrats for Europe). Nonetheless, nowadays the PD does not belong to the ESP. This low (and confused) profile exacerbates the controversies and weakens the PD political project.

The transition process accomplished by the former communists has been long and troublesome and the physiognomy of the PD is nowadays very different from that of the old PCI. However, the renewed party is not a new party yet. It has got rid of most of the organizational, ideological and identity leftovers inherited by its communist ancestor, but it is still unable to adopt a strategy, forge a political culture and design an innovative organizational structure. Likewise, it struggles to secure a strong leadership (considering the election of Guglielmo Epifani as temporary secretary in May 2013, for different leaders guided the PD between 2007 and 2013). Its genetic phase, to quote Angelo Panebianco, has been particularly weak and its institutionalization process is still fragile: such uncertainties play without a doubt a central role in the difficulties the party is currently facing (Panebianco, 1988).

Furthermore, the elements of continuity have not completely disappeared. Thus, the territorial entrenchment of the PD is almost a mirror of that of the old PCI: the core voters are mainly located in central Italy, despite a slight resizing and the adoption of different membership recruitment modalities (Agnew, 2002; Ramella, 2005; Almagisti, 2006; Diamanti, 2007 and 2009; Schin and Agnew, 2008; Lazar, 2009a; De Sio, 2011). As for the leading group, it is dominated by former members of the PCI-PDS-DS, although these do not completely dominate the party and have profoundly changed their references.

Despite its attempts at renewal and dialogue through the invention of the primaries, the PD is nowadays affected, as are other parties, by the extreme distrust of Italian voters towards theirs institutions, party system and politicians, and it struggles to understand the transformations in society. It is weakened by the traditional disagreements among the former communists, divided over strategic guidelines and personal rivalries, and by the malaise of the moderates, the Catholics and the young cadres. It calls itself reformist and so it is, but it is not able to develop a mobilizing project. It has not yet cut the Gordian knot of the alliances and, despite its awareness of the current importance of leadership, its six secretaries in eleven years demonstrate its chronic inability to find a strong, uncontested and charismatic leader. Needless to say, such incapacity has been dramatically underlined by the low-profile campaign run by Bersani during the 2013 elections.

The PD experiences, thus, a strong strategic tension: by moving to the left of the political spectrum it is scared to condemn itself to a minority position, but to develop a common centre-left culture and identity seems an exhausting and complex enterprise—an enterprise still very peculiar, if not unique, in the whole of Western Europe, which brings us to formulate an urgent question: is the PD a mere exception or does it represent a preview of future transformations the European left will undergo? That is the point.

Notes

* This chapter was written in February 2013.

1 The second Italian party after the Christian Democrats, the PCI performed particularly well in 1976 (34.37%) and 1979 (30.38%). At the 1984 European elections, shortly after the death of their charismatic leader Berlinguer and just before entering a very unfortunate phase, the communists even managed to surpass the Christian Democrats.

2 See the chapters by Bull and by Verzichelli in this volume for a more detailed analysis of the electoral systems and of the political context.

3 For the impact of anticommunism, see, for example, Corbetta (2002).

4 See, for example, Fassino (2007) and Ricolfi (2002).

5 The disagreements within the PD over the government's political economy tend to complicate its choices in matters of foreign policy. On the one hand, indeed, support for Mario Monti represents the heart of the centrists' political project. On the other hand, the extreme left has continually criticized the new administration's policies (Vendola and Di Pietro have also promoted a referendum in order to abolish certain measures on the right to sack employees, approved instead by the PD).
6 It is worth noting that, apart from the rights and duties of the membership, the 1991 statute also sets the obligations of the party towards its members, particularly in terms of participation and internal democracy.
7 The nominations to the main elective functions had to respect a specific procedure adopted by the Direction, which could consist in any of the following modalities: regulated selection, 'open' or 'closed' primary elections.
8 The Thematic Autonomies include members and simple sympathizers, at both local and national level, in order to contribute to programme development by reflecting upon specific issues. The Councils and the Forums are platforms for debate, the former commissioned to discuss urgent questions, the latter to 'unify the competences of institutions, trade unions and associations'.
9 According to the 1998 statute, the National Council's task is to 'define the party's political orientations and programme on the basis of the guidelines established by the Congress' and to summon the National Congress and elect the Direction.
10 The 2008 statute, structured rather differently from the constitutions of the old PCI, PDS and DS, begins with the party's commitment to promote pluralism, gender equality and cooperational elaboration of programmes. Moreover, it creates an additional warranty body: the Committee for the Actuation of the Ethics Code.
11 The text simply states the willingness of the PD to establish cooperation with foundations and political or cultural associations, whose independence it commits itself to respect
12 Data reported in Baccetti (1997) and Mulé (2007).
13 Data reported in Bellucci *et al.* (2000).
14 Data reported in Fasano (2011).
15 Data reported in Pasquino and Venturino (2009). For the DS, data are available online at www.dsonline.it (accessed 26 October 2014).
16 See, for example, the study on Tuscany by Recchi *et al.* (2011).

Bibliography

Accornero, A. and Ilardi, M. (eds.) (1979). *Il Partito comunista italiano: struttura e storia dell'organizzazione 1921–1979.* Milan: Feltrinelli.

Accornero, A., Mannheimer, R. and Sebastiani, C. (eds.) (1983). *L'identità comunista: i militanti, la struttura, la cultura del PCI.* Rome: Editori Riuniti.

Agnew, J. A. (2002). *Place and Politics in Modern Italy.* Chicago: Chicago University Press.

Almagisti, M. (2006). *Qualità della democrazia. Capitale sociale, partiti e culture politiche in Italia.* Rome: Carocci.

Baccetti, C. (1997). *Il PDS.* Bologna: Il Mulino.

Bellucci, P., Maraffi, M. and Segatti, P. (2000). *PCI-PDS-DS. La trasformazione dell'identitá politica della sinistra di governo.* Rome: Donzelli.

Bobba, G., Sozzi, F., Venturino, F. and Viotti, F. (2012). *Le primarie del centro sinistra a Genova.* Working Paper 2/2012, *Candidate & Leader Selection.* Available online at www.candidateandleaderselection.eu (accessed 16 January 2015).

Bosco, A. (2000). *I comunisti.* Bologna: Il Mulino.

Cacciari, M., De Giovanni, B., Galasso, G., Salvati, M., Scoppola, P. and Racinaro, R. (2003). *Sul Partito Democratico.* Naples: Guida.

Corbetta, P. (2002). Forza Italia: il 'nuovo' che non c'è. *il Mulino*, 3, 479–89.

De Rosa, R. (2007). Partito Democratico della Sinistra. Democratici di Sinistra. In L. Bardi, P. Ignazi and O. Massari (eds.), *I partiti italiani Iscritti, dirigenti, eletti* (pp. 55–96). Milan: Università Bocconi Editore.

De Sio, L. (ed.) (2011). *La politica cambia, i valori restano? Una ricerca sulla cultura politica dei cittadini toscani.* Florence: Florence University Press.

Diamanti, I. (2007). The Italian Centre-Right and Centre-Left: Between Parties and the 'Party'. *West European Politics*, 30(4), 733–62.

Diamanti, I. (2009). *Mappa dell'Italia politica. Bianco, rosso, verde, azzuro e . . . tricolore.* Bologna: Il Mulino.

Fasano, L. (2008). *L'Assemblea costituente nazionale del PD. Fisionomia di un ceto politico fra vecchie appartenenze e nuove lealtà*. Paper for the XXII Congress of the Società Italiana di Scienza Politica.
Fasano, L. (2011). L'Assemblea nazionale del PD. In G. Pasquino and F. Venturino (eds.), *Il Partito Democratico di Bersani. Persone, profilo e prospettive* (pp. 35–66). Bologna: Bononia University Press.
Fassino, P. (2007, May 23). Le vieux schéma tripolaire droite, centre, gauche, ne fonctionne plus. *Le Monde*.
Hanretty, C. and Wilson, A. (2010). The Partito Democratico: A Troubled Beginning. In M. Giuliani and E. Jones (eds.), *Managing Uncertainty. Italian Politics* (pp. 76–92). Oxford–New York: Berghahn Books.
Ignazi, P. (1992). *Dal PCI al PDS*. Bologna: Il Mulino.
Lazar, M. (1992). *Maisons rouges. Les Partis communistes français et italien de 1945 à nos jours*. Paris: Aubier.
Lazar, M. (2009a). *L'Italia sul filo del rasoio. La democrazia nel paese di Berlusconi*. Milan: Rizzoli.
Lazar, M. (2009b). The Birth of the Democratic Party. In M. Donovan and P. Onofri (eds.), *Frustrated Aspirations for Change. Italian Politics* (pp. 51–67). Oxford–New York: Berghahn Books.
Manin, B. (1997). *The Principles of Representative Government*. Cambridge: Cambridge University Press.
Maffei, M. and Gennaccari, F. (2008). *Al voto, al voto! L'Italia delle elezioni 1946–2008*. Rome: Armando Curcio Editore.
Massari, O. (2004). *I partiti politici nelle democrazie contemporanee*. Rome-Bari: Laterza.
Meyer, T. and Hinchman, L. (2002). *Media Democracy: How the Media Colonize Politics*. Cambridge: Polity.
Morlino, L. and Tarchi, M. (2006) *Partiti e caso italiano*. Bologna: Il Mulino.
Mulé, R. (2007). *Dentro i DS*. Bologna: Il Mulino.
Panebianco, A. (1988). *Political Parties: Organization and Power*. Cambridge: Cambridge University Press.
Pasquino, G. (ed.) (2009). *Il Partito Democratico. Elezione del Segretario. Organizzazione e potere*. Bologna: Bononia University Press.
Pasquino, G. and Venturino, F. (eds.) (2010). *Il Partito Democratico di Bersani. Persone, profilo e prospettive*. Bologna: Bononia University Press.
Pasquino, G. and Venturino, F. (eds.) (2009). *Le primarie comunali in Italia*. Bologna: Il Mulino.
Poguntke, T. and Webb, P. (eds.) (2005). *The Presidentialization of Politics*. Oxford: Oxford University Press.
Ramella, F. (2005). *Cuore rosso? Viaggio politico nell'Italia di mezzo*. Rome: Donzelli.
Recchi, E., Grifone Baglioni, L. and Colloca, C. (2011). Veterani e neofiti in un partito nuovo: chi sono e in che cosa credono gli attivisti del Partito Democratico in Toscana. In A. Montanari (ed.), *In libera uscita. La partecipazione politica nell'Italia di inizio millennio* (pp. 163–205). Rome: Carocci.
Ricolfi, L. (2002). *La frattura etica. La ragionevole sconfitta del centro sinistra*. Naples: L'Ancora del Mediterraneo.
Salvati, M. (2003). *Il Partito Democratico*. Bologna: Il Mulino.
Schin, M. E. and Agnew, J. A. (2008). *Berlusconi's Italy. Mapping Contemporary Italian Politics*. Philadelphia, PA: Temple University Press.
Seddoni, S. and Valbruzzi, M. (2009). *Le primarie comunali di Firenze*, Working Paper 1/2009, *Candidate & Leader Selection*. Available online at www.candidateandleaderselection.eu (accessed 16 January 2015).

16

FROM THE *DEMOCRAZIA CRISTIANA* TO THE ARCHIPELAGO OF CATHOLIC AND CENTRIST PARTIES

Mark Donovan

The changed role of party political Catholicism and centrist parties in the so-called First and Second Republics could scarcely be greater: central, even dominant in the former (Tarrow, 1990); marginal, tending to absence, in the latter. This is far from meaning the marginalization of Catholicism's political influence. This has remained considerable thanks to the Church's entrenched position in society and conservative and Catholic politicians supporting it or seeking its favour (Pollard, 2011). The difference is in the party system. The Christian Democratic Party (*Partito della Democrazia Cristiana*, DC) dominated government throughout the First Republic. From 1945 to 1981, every prime minister (president of the council) was a Christian Democrat and, up to 1994, half of all ministers (including the prime ministers, 1987–92) were still Christian Democrats. In the Second Republic, with its fundamentally bipolar party system no longer dominated by a centrist governmental bloc, Christian Democrats were everywhere and nowhere. Mostly they were scattered among other parties.

From 1995, and especially from 2001–7, it looked as though two small post-DC parties, one on the left and one on the right, would contest elections. In 2001–2, the Italian Popular Party (*Partito popolare italiano*, PPI), the principal DC successor party, had fused with some other minor centrist, more or less Catholic parties to found the Margherita-Democracy is Freedom (*Margherita-Democrazia è Libertà*). In 2007–9, however, this party fused with the post-communist Democrats of the Left (*Democratici di sinistra*, DS) co-founding the Democratic Party (*Partito democratico*, PD), abandoning its distinct Catholic identity. On the centre-right, the Union of Christian and Centre Democrats (*Unione dei Democratici Cristiani e di Centro*, UDC), whose forerunners had been allied to Silvio Berlusconi since 1994, asserted their independence in 2007, refusing to dissolve themselves into Berlusconi's new 'fusion party' (Arter, 2012), the People of Freedom (*Popolo della Libertà*, PDL). Allied with other, largely Catholic fragments as the Union of the Centre, the UDC (the acronym remained the same) was the only political formation allied to neither the PD nor the PDL to gain parliamentary representation in 2008. It won a precarious 5.6 per cent of the vote. From 2011, the UDC sought to boost its vote by championing the technocratic government of Mario Monti. Ideally, indeed, it sought to realign the centre-right electorate which it regarded Berlusconi as having hijacked. Whilst a formidable array of Catholic interest group leaders, some prominent business and financial leaders, and two or three ministers showed interest in the UDC's attempt to re-establish a new, improved Catholic party, the Roman Catholic hierarchy gave only limited and ambiguous support. At the end of 2012, Monti's decision to seek electoral legitimation as a political leader then led to his Civic Choice list allying with the UDC, now a firmly centrist party. The alliance proved fatal to the UDC. In the Senate, a single list was presented in order to overcome the 8 per cent threshold – under Monti's name. Only two of the 19 senators elected were from the UDC, one being Pierferdinando Casini, the de facto leader of the Catholic centre-right since 1994. In the Chamber of Deputies a distinct UDC list was presented, but was squeezed to just 1.8 per cent of the vote, electing eight deputies. A distinct Catholic parliamentary presence ceased to exist, since the numbers were too small to form an officially recognised group in either Chamber (ten are required in the Senate, 20 in the Chamber of Deputies).

The proposition of this chapter is that whilst the post-DC archipelago, like the DC itself, must be understood as being a self-constituted product of political Catholicism, it is also the product of its systemic context. And in the end, that system's structuration process 'organized out' the autonomous representation of Catholic political forces (Mair, 1997). That is to say, in the logic of bipolar confrontation that developed, a specifically Catholic identity became irrelevant. Contrariwise, the DC, which had been the core government party of the Cold War era, *c.*1947–91, whilst partly successful because of its own undoubted merits (and despite its demerits), was as successful as it was because of the nature of the then party system – 'polarized pluralism'. In such a system the destiny of centre parties is 'to govern indefinitely' (Sartori, 1976: 138). Government alternation was not possible in a NATO country in which the leading opposition party was the Communist Party (*Partito comunista italiano*, PCI). Crucially, moreover, at the critical juncture at which the party system was formed, the DC had hegemonized the centre, becoming *the* anti-communist bulwark. By contrast, at the critical juncture that led to the bipolarization of the party system in the early 1990s, the post-DC parties were marginalized. Their survival was jeopardized by a *ventennio* (20-year period) in which the principal line of conflict was defined in terms of support for, or opposition to, Silvio Berlusconi. And that conflict was mobilized around *Forza Italia* (and later the PDL) and its allies on the one hand, whilst, on the other, the primarily post-communist opposition was dominated by debates over its social democratic identity, or otherwise; alternatives being, simply: 'democratic', or perhaps reformist or progressive – but not 'Christian', or even 'Popular', given the debacle of the East European, communist people's parties.

The international context was also important. The Berlusconi era coincided with the heyday of the neo-liberal paradigm of boundless, market-led growth – boundless, because markets were presumed self-correcting, and because, with Deng Xiaoping's 'capitalist turn' in China (from *c.*1978) and the collapse of the USSR, capitalism was triumphant. In Italy, as elsewhere, electoral programmes became very similar (Conti, 2008). Consequently, differentiation in terms of Berlusconism could more easily dominate. But whilst states and political economy were on the back foot for most of the Berlusconi era, this changed from 2008 (Bordoni, 2012). Thereafter, the global financial and economic crisis led institutional investors and key political actors to recognize that 'actually existing capitalism' was undergoing a major crisis that required effective polity management at the state–national level. In this respect, Italy was found wanting. Thus party government was supplanted in November 2011 by the technocratic administration of Mario Monti. Over the winter of 2012–13, however, Monti's electoral initiative, backed by the UDC, was marginalized by the partial recovery of the PDL. The 2013 parliament was thus split three ways, between the PD and PDL, each with some 30 per cent of the vote, and Beppe Grillo's anti-establishment Five Star Movement with its 25 per cent (see Chapter 19). Let us look, then, at party political Catholicism in the Second Republic, and its role in creating this failure of party government.

The crisis of Christian Democracy, 1990–4

The fall of the Berlin Wall in November 1989 was followed by the ending of Soviet suzerainty over central and eastern Europe and, in 1991, by the collapse of the USSR itself. The DC's initial reaction was triumphalism. Its historic enemy had been defeated. The PCI, whose vote had peaked at 34 per cent in 1976, abandoned its name, which provoked a split. In the 1992 election the party's principal successor party, the Democratic Party of the Left (*Partito democratico della sinistra*, PDS) gained only 16.1 per cent of the vote. Communist Refoundation obtained 5.6 per cent. The DC was also weakened, however, its vote falling to fractionally under 30 per cent, mainly because of the Northern League (*Lega Nord*, LN), whose success evidenced a major failure of representation by the DC. Until the early 1980s, the DC had hegemonized the north-east thanks not to its own organizational strength but to the pervasiveness of Catholicism in the area's rich, deeply historically rooted associational life (see Chapter 13). For itself, the DC was increasingly seen as failing to represent the region's small and medium-sized businesses. Once the communist threat was removed, voters turned to the League (Gangemi, 1997).

No longer bound to 'hang together, or hang separately' in the face of the communist threat, splits began to take place in the DC too. In 1990, the left-oriented Network was formed, in large part by former Sicilian Christian Democrats led by the mayor of Palermo (1985–90), Leoluca Orlando. As the so-called *Tangentopoli* phenomenon got under way, that is, the uncovering of systemic party corruption, the splits grew. In 1993, the tiny Christian Socials joined the PDS. More significant was the formation of the *Popolari*. This movement was led by Mario Segni, a backbencher who had championed the two waves of referendums on electoral reform which, in the period 1990–3, unintentionally mobilized the country against the partyocracy. Segni's ill-defined project of state and party reform, which at a key moment flirted with the PDS as a possible ally, earned the displeasure of the Vatican and ended when the 1994 elections ushered in the so-called Second Republic. Segni obtained just 4.7 per cent of the vote and a mere 13 seats – 2.1 per cent of the total, insufficient to form a parliamentary group. The main reasons for this outcome were the new electoral system and the bipolarization of the electorate between Berlusconi's conservative alliance and the Progressives, as the left, including the Christian Socials, was known. The PPI and Segni were left to claim a 'centre' ground which was no longer the anti-socialist bastion that it had been in the days of the DC. It had become a no-man's-land. This development had not been properly anticipated.

By late 1993, the DC's elites had expected to survive the turmoil as a major anti-socialist force winning seats predominantly in the centre-south. The League was expected to dominate the north, and the left the 'Red Belt' (which runs across central-northern Italy, south of the river Po). In January 1994, the PPI and Segni's Pact sought an alliance with the League, affirming the primacy of the left–right conflict, with them central to it. The League, however, renounced that alliance, opting instead to back Berlusconi. Berlusconi's entry into politics confirmed the domination of left–right conflict but did so in terms of a battle against communism which marginalised the predominantly Catholic centrists. Allying with the League and other parties, Berlusconi usurped the DC/PPI's role as the principal anti-socialist force. Part of the DC foresaw that their party's neo-centrist strategy was doomed and broke away to ally with Berlusconi as the Centre Christian Democrats (*Centro cristiano democratico*, CCD). Later, in 2001, this party would form the core of the UDC. The CCD/UDC remained loyal to Berlusconi, at least in formal alliance terms, until 2008.

The 1994 election was disastrous for the PPI and especially Segni. The latter's movement was reduced to a rump and wasted away; the former was forced to recognize the reality of bipolarization. There was no room for a centre party. In 1995, the PPI split. The fate of party political Catholicism was not entirely sealed, but survival could now only be as minor components of the *new* left and right. Had Segni accepted Berlusconi's backing to become the core of a new anti-socialist centre-right in late 1993, then the course of the Second Republic would have been very different, but Segni regarded himself as already one of Berlusconi's foes (Segni, 1994: 7–18).

Bipolarization: the crisis of party political Catholicism, 1995–9

The split in the PPI had a profound impact on the Catholic world. For half a century the myth of Catholic 'political unity' had dominated Catholic political thinking. Now, looming regional elections (in 1995) imposed the strategic imperative to opt left or right, for the electoral system would severely punish parties that failed to do this. More than this, opting for the right, as the party's leader, Rocco Buttiglione planned, would guarantee Berlusconi's victory, establishing the ascendance of a bloc of parties whose success in 1994 had shocked world opinion. The ability of a reunified Catholic party (PPI plus CCD) to 'pull' the right-wing bloc's policies and style of government to the centre, as Buttiglione intended, can only be a matter of conjecture. The PPI-Left would not accept alliance with Berlusconi's new right. The party split. Catholics were forced to acknowledge that they were politically divided to the point of rival Catholic forces competing against each other for office. The end of Catholic 'political unity' thus became a key theme of Italy's political transition (Pace, 1995: 9).

In an overwhelmingly Catholic country, Catholics had, in fact, always been electorally divided. From 1946 onwards, millions had voted for the PCI or the markedly anticlerical Socialists (PSI) despite two-thirds of Catholics – though 'only' two-thirds, not all – believing it impossible to be a good Catholic and a Marxist, or to vote PCI (Wertman, 1982: 99). This material division had been suppressed ideationally by the myth of Catholic political unity, according to which the country's principal electoral cleavage juxtaposed democratic Catholics (the DC) and their 'lay' allies against atheist Marxists. By 1985, however, barely a quarter of Italians thought Catholicism and Marxism incompatible (Segatti *et al.*, 1999). Secularization had brought immense change. In 1974 the divorce referendum had established that ethical norms were contested within the Catholic world, and that they could be overturned by a secular state. Even more shockingly, the 1981 abortion referendum introduced a liberal regulatory regime considered genocidal by conservative Catholics. By the 1990s, nevertheless, the fear of terminal secularization had proven mistaken. The number of regularly practising Catholics stabilized at around 30 per cent (Garelli, 1991: 58–9; ITANES, 2008: 124). The abortion battle had also encouraged the diverse world of organized Italian Catholicism to recompact and, although sharp internal divisions were not overcome, the idea, at least, of Catholic unity had been reasserted. DC links with the Catholic world had been reinforced too, in an attempt to reform the party (Formigoni, 1998: 181–5). In fact, the DC's electorate was, to the end, overwhelmingly close to the 'Catholic world', with some 90 per cent substantially identifying with the model of religious behaviour proposed by the Church, and high rates of regular Church attendance (Garelli, 1996a: 126). The DC, which had never been a clerical party, having itself done much to secularize Italian Catholicism, had become 'a party of Catholics', even though it was no longer 'the Catholics' party' (Pace,

1995: 145). Catholic 'investment' in the DC was profound. Renewed in the party's last years, it underlay the Church's hostility to Segni's reform initiatives and would help explain alleged papal support for the attempt to prevent the PPI/CCD split in January 1994 (Verucci, 1999: 110) as well as episcopal opposition to the 1995 split (Franco, 2000: 193–4). The 1995 split, in fact, much more than that of 1994, made visible the existence of rival Catholic parties. In these circumstances, Catholic unity was reformulated in terms of 'overarching' cultural values, ethically 'above politics', as well as in more sophisticated terms regarding Italian democracy and national unity. The explicit presence of Catholics on both left and right, it was argued, could reinforce national identity at a time when it was challenged by the Northern League. Equally, loyal competition, acknowledging the legitimacy of the opposition, would confirm that competitive democracy promoted a common good. This was a vitally important idea, and one that failed to establish itself as 'common sense' in the Second Republic.

In 1995, then, Buttiglione's proposed alliance with Berlusconi was challenged by the party's National Council. A long legal dispute followed, becoming entangled with others, and was resolved, if then, only by a Supreme Court ruling in 2010 (Maestri, 2012). Meanwhile, the politically brokered outcome of the 1995 split was that Buttiglione *et al.* kept the DC's historic symbol, a white shield with a red cross inscribed with the word *Libertas*, becoming the United Christian Democrats (*Cristiani Democratici Uniti*, CDU), whilst the remainder kept the name PPI. It is perhaps not too much to argue that the PPI's alliance with the left shaped much of the subsequent history of the Second Republic – alongside Silvio Berlusconi, of course. To anticipate, then: in 1995, Buttiglione's opponents proposed Romano Prodi, an industry technocrat associated with the DC, as the left's prime ministerial candidate for the 1996 election. On this basis they formed the Olive Tree alliance with the post-communist PDS, the main centre-left party. Prodi won the election, as he did again in 2006. In 2007–8 the PPI's successor party, the Margherita-DL, fused with the DS (*Democratici di sinistra*, Left Democrats) as the PDS had become in 1998, becoming the Democratic Party, the would-be catch-all, centre-left party intended to reduce party system fragmentation and consolidate the bipolar format. These aims were not achieved, the party system substantially losing its structure following the collapse of Berlusconi's fourth government in 2011 (Ceccarini *et al.*, 2012), which facilitated Grillo's success in 2013. The PD, nevertheless, remained one of Italy's major parties, and the predominant party on the left.

Meantime, the bifurcation of Catholic politics was confirmed in the 1996 elections, the CCD-CDU allying with Berlusconi confronting the PPI (in the Olive Tree). The electorates of both formations were markedly more Catholic, in terms of those regularly practising their faith, than those of other parties: perhaps as much as 77 per cent of the CCD-CDU, and 69 per cent of the PPI. The next closest was the short-lived Dini list, at 51 per cent (which became part of the Margherita-DL in 2001–2), followed by *Forza Italia* at 46 per cent (Diamanti, 1997: 348). Jointly, the PPI and CCD-CDU gained 12–13 per cent of the total vote, yet some 23 per cent of weekly practising Catholics. Even more, however (*c.* 29 per cent), did not vote (Garelli, 1996b: 891). The other half divided between left and right. In fact, whereas regular Church attendance had correlated with high participation rates in the First Republic, now it was an incentive to abstention. Catholic voters were disorientated by the turmoil and division in the political 'supply' made available to them. Not surprisingly, then, the idea of – the hope for – Catholic political unity did not die easily.

In February 1998 no less a figure than former President of the Republic (1985–92) Francesco Cossiga sought Catholic party reunification, allegedly to build a 'normal' European party system. By this he meant one based on the juxtaposition of liberal-conservatives, perhaps including most Catholics, and social democrats, free of the determining influence of the extremes: the Northern

League on the right (and perhaps the National Alliance too), and Communist Refoundation on the left. At this point, the League had been only briefly in government and was widely seen as an anti-system party, proposing the secession of northern Italy ('Padania'), whilst its electoral support in local elections was shortly to plummet. For its part, Communist Refoundation was relatively small (8.6 per cent in 1996) and it suffered a split that autumn when it brought down the Prodi government ('proving' Cossiga's concerns). To this extent, Cossiga's project was understandable. The post-Fascist National Alliance (AN), however, had obtained nearly 16 per cent of the vote and was too big for Berlusconi to abandon if he wished to return to government. Crucially, however, Cossiga, like many people, expected Berlusconi *not* to continue his political adventure.

Cossiga's project was primarily based on the construction, at the parliamentary level, of a new party, the Democratic Union for the Republic (*Unione democratica per la repubblica*, UDR). Inevitably this was based on MPs abandoning the parties they had been elected in or, as in the case of the CDU, abandoning the alliance it had been elected with. Thus the CDU switched almost in its entirety, providing nearly 20 of the new party's 50-odd MPs. Since the party was born in the (correct) expectation that it would support a centre-left government if and when Communist Refoundation brought the Prodi government down, this meant the UDR facilitated a major act of 'transformism', that is, opposition MPs being 'transformed' into government supporters. Whilst historically the practice has found some intellectual justification, given its strategic objectives, it is more routinely seen as typifying MPs' unscrupulous office-seeking behaviour (Donovan and Newell, 2008). This mix of judgements fits this case. The fall of the Prodi government in October 1998 led to the formation of a centre-left government including the UDR. At the same time, Cossiga achieved one of his objectives, a centre-left independent of the Communist left.

The second objective, the construction of a centre-right rooted in liberal values was far more challenging (not that success with regard to the centre-left endured). A liberal centre-right required the marginalization of the League and possibly some reunification of conservative Catholics via the dissolution of *Forza Italia*, the latter being expected by many, in late 1997 (Repubblica, 1998; Franco, 2000: 98). None of this happened. The CCD remained loyal to Berlusconi, who, furthermore, was invited to join the European People's Party in June 1998 despite Cossiga's furious opposition. Berlusconi did not abandon Fini's National Alliance and he worked hard, and successfully, to resuscitate the alliance with the League. In sum, Cossiga's impact on the right was negligible. On the left, meanwhile, the possibility that the PPI might join the UDR resulted in Prodi forming a party – the Democrats – specifically opposing Catholic reunification lest it promote the collapse of the nascent bipolar system. This was, perhaps, a danger, given that many in the PPI, and in the Church hierarchy, felt that the PPI was far too subordinate to the DS. By early 1999 Prodi was also no longer prime minister, so the project bolstered his position as still a potential leader of a pan-left 'pole', whilst Berlusconi remained leader of the right. The UDR collapsed. In the 1999 European election, the Democrats' vote (7.68 per cent to the PPI's 4.25 per cent) ensured the PPI maintained its alliance with the DS, confirming the binary development of party political Catholicism – and of the party system.

Weak consolidation: the 'bipolar' party system, 2000–8

The 2001 election appeared to signal the consolidation of a bipolar party system with Catholic parties on left and right. On the right, the League had re-allied with Berlusconi in the 2000 regional elections, creating the Home of Freedom (*Casa della Libertà*, CDL) with *Forza Italia*, the National Alliance and the CCD-CDU. On the left, the four small, more or less Catholic parties had formed an electoral alliance: the Margherita, which competed independently for the PR seat allocation whilst confirming the Olive Tree alliance with the DS to compete for the majoritarian seats. The Margherita comprised the PPI, the Democrats, the Dini list and the Udeur (a remnant of Cossiga's UDR). A new Catholic party, European Democracy, was formed shortly before the election by Sergio D'Antoni, the leader, 1991–2000 of the Catholic trade union confederation, the CISL. It ran as a centre party and obtained about a million votes, electing two senators. Its failure to elect any deputies confirmed the impact of the electoral system on unaligned parties and in 2002 the party merged with the CCD-CDU to form the Union of Christian and Centre Democrats – the UDC. The non-viability of Catholic centrism was confirmed. Meanwhile the unification of the Margherita allies into a party (the Margherita-DL) in 2002 left the tiny Udeur as a lone centrist fragment. By 2003, then, three Catholic parties could be identified as 'relevant' according to Sartori's 'counting' rules (Sartori, 1976): the Margherita-DL, the UDC and the Udeur with, respectively and approximately, 14 per cent, 5 per cent and perhaps 1–2 per cent of the vote each, i.e. about 20 per cent in total. The relevance of the Udeur was entirely contingent on the closeness of the election results. In 2006, Prodi's pan-left Union won the election with the narrowest of majorities. The Udeur could bring the government down if it withdrew its support. In fact, this became true of any two or three senators who switched to the opposition hoping to gain reward if their action led to early elections and alternation, as happened in 2008.

The apparent consolidation of a bipolar party system and the Catholic parties' place in it was deceptive. On the right, the UDC's relationship with Berlusconi was one of rather hostile dependency. In 2005, the UDC brought the government down to demonstrate, as its leader put it, the sovereignty of parliament versus that of a plebiscitary leader, whilst Berlusconi's attempts to reform the law on media coverage of elections in favour of the larger parties were repeatedly vetoed. More than this, the government's constitutional reform, largely driven by the *Lega Nord*, was sabotaged by procrastination: eventually passed in 2005, it was overturned by referendum in 2006 following a change of government which, according to Berlusconi among others, the UDC expected and intended. Berlusconi managed to avoid taking the blame for the defeat, however, and the much-anticipated 'post-Berlusconi' restructuring of the right, supposedly to the advantage of the UDC and of Christian Democrats in *Forza Italia*, notably Roberto Formigoni, the President of Lombardy, was again postponed. The situation on the left was also uncertain. Many in the Margherita wished to reinforce the alliance with the DS at the expense of the more radical Greens and communists whilst so-called 'theo-dems', for whom conservative Catholic ethics loomed large, regarded the relationship with the DS as too close. When the Left won the 2006 election, it was as a pan-left alliance that put nine parties in the government with the tiniest of majorities in the Senate. Exploiting this weakness and his media strengths, Berlusconi continued his electoral mobilization, first claiming that the result was fraudulent, then claiming the government's policies were outrageous, and then that it was illegitimate because it no longer had the backing of the people. In 2008, the government fell and early elections were held. By then, however, the party panorama had changed yet again.

Fusion, and autonomy in vain, 2008–13

In the period 2007–9 the two main centre-left parties, the DS and the Margherita-DL, underwent a process of fusion. There were two main reasons for this: first, to overcome the fragmentation and instability of the left by creating a party able to assert its leadership over potential allies; second, by so doing, to offer voters stable, effective government. Such an offer would, it was believed, mobilize voters who appeared to want stronger government. Thus the

Democratic Party was born. Its new leader, Walter Veltroni, sought to win the 2008 election by emphasising the prospect of a quasi-two-party system were Berlusconi to take up the challenge and similarly fuse the parties of the right. This Berlusconi partly did, presenting his allies with an ultimatum: dissolution in his new party, the People of Freedom (PDL), or compete against him. Initially, all three main allies, the League, the UDC and the National Alliance (AN), rejected the ultimatum. When an early election was called almost immediately, however, the AN switched its position, offering to 'co-create' the new party. The UDC, like the LN, maintained its autonomy, though losing defectors whilst gaining others, as *Forza Italia* and the AN reorganized. The UDC thus became the core of the Union of the Centre. The new formation's Catholic identity was no longer explicit, but the party continued to be seen as an essentially Catholic, neo-centrist party. The UDC survived the election, the only force not allied with either the PD or PDL to do so, becoming part of the disparate opposition to the fourth Berlusconi government (2008–11).

Initially the Berlusconi government looked strong, whilst the oppositions (*sic*) were so divided that some feared a predominant party system might be established. A year later, however, internal disagreements were again raising concerns about government paralysis. In 2010 the PDL split. The government lost its parliamentary majority, but managed to survive as the oppositions remained divided. The UDC now joined other centrist fragments, most notably Future and Freedom for Italy (FLI), the split from the PDL, to form the Pole of the Nation, still hoping that disillusion with Berlusconi would enable reaggregation around the – 'post-Catholic'? – 'centre', implicitly an alternative centre-right. A year later the centrist pole was renamed as the New Pole for Italy but local elections showed there was little interest in these superficial name changes and micro-party shufflings. Attempts to reaggregate Catholic social forces at a much-heralded summit in the Umbrian town of Todi in October 2011 foundered, moreover, over the issue of party political unity. It simply wasn't possible. For all that the socio-economic cleavage was programmatically minimal, enduring left–right perceptions prevailed among both elites and voters. What the Todi meeting did do was consolidate the sense of disillusion with the Berlusconi government and, indeed, the entire Berlusconi era. A month later, Berlusconi resigned. The continuing division of opposition forces still meant no alternative parliamentary majority could be found. Thus Monti's technocratic government was formed, backed by the PD, PDL and the centrists. The government included some prominent Catholics, perhaps most notably Corrado Passera, Andrea Riccardi, Lorenzo Ornaghi and Renato Balduzzi, ministers respectively for the Economy, International Cooperation, Culture, and Health. These men were leaders in the worlds of banking, international peace activism and academia. As such, they confirmed the availability of an elite able to administer Italy, yet also the absence of an elite able to mobilize consensus for an economically hard-pressed nation. Nor was Mario Monti the person to galvanize such a force.

In the spring 2012 local elections the Five Star Movement of Beppe Grillo became a significant political force, taking 12–13 per cent of the vote in the Red Belt and northern Italy, if only 3 per cent in the south. By the summer, the movement had overtaken the PDL in the polls to become the second party, at some 15 per cent, only some 10 per cent behind the PD, the largest party. By December, the PD was polling at *c.*30 per cent. It was against this background that Monti entered the electoral fray. However, in November Berlusconi had reasserted his leadership of the PDL/the centre-right. In the following three months he remobilized some 10 per cent (in absolute terms) of the PDL vote. Between the PDL's partial recovery and the emergence of Monti's Civic Choice, the UDC was marginalized. The Vatican and Catholic Church, which appeared to back Monti in early January, rapidly reasserted their more traditional, neutral stance. In the election, the UDC, only a junior partner in Monti's alliance, all but disappeared. Together with the FLI it took 1.8 per cent of the vote. And whilst it perhaps took nearly double its share of the regularly practising Catholic vote (3.3 per cent), abstention probably remained above the national average (25 per cent). Of those who voted, 20 per cent swung behind the Five Star movement, below the national average (also 25 per cent), but confirming Grillo's ability to mobilize voters across the spectrum and nationwide. About a half divided roughly equally between the PD and PDL (Guarasci, 2013).

Conclusion

In the aftermath of the Second World War, the two main mobilizing forces in Italy were Catholicism and socialism. By mobilizing Catholics, including even some social Christians on the myth of Catholic unity, the DC was able to align a large bloc of the electorate against the 'Socio-Communists', as the Socialists and communists were known. The DC was, thus, the anti-socialist party as much as it was a Catholic party. Yet it was that too; or at least it was a party for Catholics, and it remained thus into the 1980s. When the parties of the First Republic disintegrated in 1992–3, the Catholics began to split, fragmenting in all directions, though those who split leftwards were initially only a tiny minority. In 1994, the DC split sharply, between the centre (the PPI) and the centre-right (the CCD). Both forces saw themselves as alternative to the left, but the centrists saw themselves as opposed also to Berlusconi's right (rather as the DC had also opposed the neo-Fascist right). These events largely sealed the fate of Catholic party representation, since the nature of the electoral system effectively precluded the survival of a centrist pivot party.

The disappearance of the DC and the lack of a single successor party or one with a similar role and status also meant that abstention became a prominent trait among practising Catholics. Given the limited visibility of the CCD-PPI split, the much more high-profile split of the PPI in 1995 encouraged relatively high abstention rates among regularly practising Catholics. At the same time, the majority of such Catholics who did vote were split more or less equally between the centre-left which, led by Romano Prodi, a Roman Catholic technocrat, won the election, and the centre-right. Subsequently, victory for the right in 2001 saw a preponderance of such Catholics voting for the centre-right and this was confirmed subsequently, including in 2006, despite Prodi winning again for the centre-left. Despite this imbalance, most analysts agree that these 'Catholic' voters are voting largely for the same reasons as others, whatever they may be. Nevertheless, in the period to 2008, such voters could still vote for a party with a significant Catholic identity, whether on the left or on the right. That particular bipolar format, with Catholic 'twins' either side of the principal cleavage, did not survive. The reasons for this were probably more contingent than structural. The immediate cause of the disappearance of the Margherita-DL was the attempt to reduce political fragmentation and instability by an act of political volition, the construction of the would-be, catch-all Democratic Party, perhaps because appropriate institutional reforms were negated by mutual vetoes. Initially, the UDC avoided subsumption within Berlusconi's PDL, but in 2013 it was overwhelmed by the rise of Grillo, the continuing bipolar confrontation between Berlusconi and the left, and Mario Monti's capture of the 'centre' ground. Party political Catholicism had been 'organized out' of the party system.

Bibliography

Arter, D. (2012). Analysing 'successor parties': the case of the true Finns. *West European Politics*, 35(4), 803–25.

Bordoni, G. S. (2012). Autobiografia di un sistema politico. *il Mulino*, 3, 555–62.

Ceccarini, L., Diamanti, I. and Lazar, M. (2012). Fine di un ciclo: la destrutturazione del sistema partitico italiano. In A. Bosco and D. McDonnell (eds.), *Politica in Italia. I fatti e le interpretazioni* (pp. 63–82). Bologna: Il Mulino.

Conti, N. (2008). The Italian parties and their programmatic platforms: How alternative? *Modern Italy*, 13(4), 451–64.

Diamanti, I. (1997). L'identità cattolica e il comportamento di voto: l'unità e la fedeltà non sono più virtù. In P. Corbetta and A. M. L. Schadee (eds.), *A domande risponde* (pp. 317–60). Bologna: Il Mulino.

Donovan, M. and Newell, J. (2008). Centrism in Italian politics. *Modern Italy*, 13(4), 381–97.

Formigoni, G. (1998) *L'Italia dei cattolici. Dal Risorgimento a oggi*. Bologna: Il Mulino.

Franco, M. (2000). *I voti del cielo. La caccia all'elettorato cattolico*. Milan: Baldini and Castoldi.

Gangemi, G. (1997). C'è qualcosa di nuovo, anzi antico. In G. Gangemi and G. Riccamboni (eds.), *Le elezioni della transizione* (pp. 3–18). Turin: UTET.

Garelli, F. (1991). *Religione e chiesa in Italia*. Bologna: Il Mulino.

Garelli, F. (1996a). *Forza della religione e debolezza della fede*. Bologna: Il Mulino.

Garelli, F. (1996b). 'Cattolici senza partito'. *il Mulino*, 45, 888–98.

Guarasci, A. (2013). Quei cattolici cha stanno con Grillo, *Famiglia cristiana*. 5 March. Available online at www.famigliacristiana.it/articolo/quei-cattolici-che-stanno-con-grillo.aspx (accessed 13 Jan 2015).

ITANES (2008). La fine della questione cattolica? In *Il ritorno di Berlusconi. Vincitori e vinti nelle elezione del 2008* (pp. 123–35). Bologna: Il Mulino.

Maestri, G. (2012). Appena 'tornata' e già diffidata: la Democrazia cristiana senza pace (e i partiti senza regole). *Forum di Quaderni costituzionali*. Available online at www.forumcostituzionale.it/wordpress/images/stories/pdf/documenti_forum/paper/0334_maestri.pdf (accessed 13 Jan 2015).

Mair, P. (1997). On the freezing of party systems. In P. Mair (ed.), *Party System Change. Approaches and Interpretations* (pp. 3–16). Oxford: Clarendon Press.

Pace, E. (1995). *L'unità dei cattolici in Italia. Origini e decadenza di un mito collettivo*. Milan: Guerini.

Pollard, J. (2011). A state within a state: the role of the church in two Italian political transitions. *Modern Italy*, 16(4), 449–59.

Repubblica (1998). Centro, la ricetta di Cossiga 'sciogliere Forza Italia'. *La Repubblica*, 26 September: 6.

Sartori, G. (1976). *Parties and Party Systems. A Framework for Analysis*. Cambridge: Cambridge University Press.

Segatti, P., Bellucci, P. and Maraffi, M. (1999) Stable Voters in an Unstable Party Environment: Continuity and Change in Italian Electoral Behaviour, Working Paper 1999/139, Madrid: Instituto Juan March de Estudios e Investigaciones.

Segni, M. (1994). *La rivoluzione interrotta*. Milan: Rizzoli.

Tarrow, S. (1990). Maintaining hegemony in Italy: the softer they rise, the slower they fall. In T. J. Pempel (ed.), *Uncommon Democracies: The One-Party Dominant Regimes* (pp. 306–32). Ithaca, NY: Cornell University Press.

Verucci, G. (1999). *La Chiesa cattolica in Italia dall'Unità a oggi*. Rome-Bari: Laterza.

Wertman, D. (1982). The Catholic Church and Italian politics: the impact of secularization. *West European Politics*, 5(2), 87–107.

17

THE FLUCTUATING FORTUNES OF THE *LEGA NORD*

Anna Cento Bull

Introduction

In February 2013 the *Lega Nord* lost half of its electorate compared with the 2008 elections, gaining 1,390,156 votes or 4.1 per cent of the total of votes cast, as against 3,026,844 or 8.3 per cent in 2008. Already in 2011–12 the party had witnessed a series of setbacks at the polls and was rocked by a major financial scandal involving links to the Calabrian Mafia, which struck at the heart of Umberto Bossi's leadership, forcing him to resign as general secretary. These crucial two years also marked the fall of the fourth Berlusconi government and its replacement by a technocratic government headed by former EU commissioner Mario Monti, in what is widely considered as the dissolution of the political and party system – generally known as the Second Republic – that in the early 1990s had succeeded the First Republic, itself marred by a major financial scandal. Twenty years later, history appears to have repeated itself, this time engulfing, in an ironic twist of events, the very party that in 1992 had been at the forefront of the protest against systematic corrupt deals between business and politics, often involving criminal organizations.

The events of 2011–13, therefore, provide a good vantage point for attempting to achieve an overall assessment of the politics and policies of the *Lega Nord* since its inception. On the one hand, its political influence kept increasing, especially after the party struck a deal with Berlusconi and later joined his centre-right governments in 2001–6 and again in 2008–11. Similarly, its media exposure was constantly on the rise, not least thanks to its many publicity stunts, controversial statements and aggressive style of leadership. Conversely, its growing influence and public notoriety have been accompanied by fluctuating electoral fortunes over the years, as well as significant shifts in political strategies and policies, which has led to its veering towards an extreme-right ideology and platform. These shifts gave rise to some scholarly controversy concerning the definition and interpretation of the *Lega Nord* as a specific type of party. Furthermore, the party has often appeared to prioritize media-grabbing statements and stunts over concrete and effective policymaking, which has led some scholars to refer to its politics as 'symbolic' or 'simulative'.

This chapter will examine and assess the trajectory of the *Lega Nord* from the early 1990s to the present in the light of the above issues and taking into account scholarly debates and interpretations. In particular, it will analyse this party's role in attacking and bringing down the First Republic, its preferential relationship with a specific electoral and territorial constituency, its ideology and rhetoric, its alliance with Berlusconi and resulting policy impact within the centre-right governments and finally its current predicament and likely future scenarios.

The early years: reasons for success

The *Lega Nord* was formed in December 1989 as a merger of previously distinct regional leagues, including the *Lega Lombarda*, formed in 1985 by Umberto Bossi, a long-time student-worker who had become an enthusiastic believer in regionalist and autonomist movements. The new party's breakthrough came at the 1992 general election, when it unexpectedly gained 8.7 per cent of the votes nationally and 17.3 per cent in the North, becoming the fourth party after Christian Democracy, the Democratic Party of the Left and the Socialist Party. At the 1993 administrative elections, in which voters directly elected the local mayors, the *Lega* triumphed in the North, especially in the provincial capitals and smaller communes. Its biggest success was in Milan, where Marco Formentini was elected mayor, with the party list securing 41 per cent. In light of such a positive performance, heralding dramatic future events, what factors allowed this newly formed party to emerge as a significant player in Italian politics?

Most commentators agree that the electoral success of the *Lega Nord* in the early 1990s must be explained on the basis of both structural and agency factors. At the structural level, the crisis of the Italian state, following the fall of the Berlin Wall in 1989 and the *Tangentopoli* scandal of 1992, opened the door for new political actors to enter the electoral market, as witnessed two years later even more spectacularly with the emergence of Berlusconi's *Forza Italia*. In addition, the burgeoning state deficit, together with the increasing fiscal pressure experienced by both ordinary citizens and business people, created the preconditions for an anti-tax protest movement, especially in those northern regions whose model of economic development rested on a myriad of small and medium-sized firms which, after two decades of export-oriented growth, towards the end of the 1980s had started to experience increasing competition from abroad. According to Biorcio (1997: 123), in 1991 half of northern voters supported requests for tax reductions, while a third were in favour of greater regional autonomy, which thereby indicated the potential for the success of a new party ready to intercept these sentiments.

However, structural factors do not in themselves explain the success of a political actor. Bossi's entrepreneurship cannot in any way be underestimated, especially in constructing a 'Northern Question' in opposition to the classic 'Southern Question'. Specifically, he combined a strong fiscal protest and a headlong attack upon the political class, seen as guilty of leading the country towards bankruptcy, with an ethno-regionalist ideology and a populist stance. In 1991, at the first Congress of the party, Bossi made it clear that ethno-federalism, while justified by the existence within Italy of different 'ethnic nations', with the productive North exploited by the parasitic South, represented primarily 'an instrument for attacking the centralist state' as well as for controlling the public purse.

The *Lega* was aware however, that there was a consensus among both voters and parties in favour of public spending and that the only way it could gain substantial electoral support would be through mobilizing those voters who could regard themselves as net givers as opposed to receivers. Thus the party pitted business people and entrepreneurs based in the North in areas of small-scale industrialization against all those voters who could be portrayed as 'parasites' living off the state: public sector employees, people on the dole or receiving benefits, and more generally southerners. As for the remedies advocated, these ranged from full-scale privatizations to radical reforms of the pension, health and labour systems, to draconian measures against tax evasion and organized crime, all of which, the *Lega* argued, would only be possible through a federalist reform of the state accompanied by fiscal responsibility. Its proposal was to divide Italy into three macro-regions, each of which would have responsibility for most policy areas, leaving the 'federal' level responsible only for a handful of matters.

The remedies put forward to the diagnosed 'Italian malaise' were thus in many respects Thatcherite (Agnew, 1995: 168; Gilbert, 1995: 61). They were innovatively associated by Gianfranco Miglio, the *Lega*'s most influential thinker during this early phase, with the ideas of libertarian federalism and radical liberalism promoted by the Austrian classical school of Ludwig von Mises. Yet the party also adopted a crude populist language and style which bordered on racism in its negative portrayal of lazy and Mafiosi southerners as opposed to hard-working and law-abiding northerners. Xenophobia was also already in evidence, albeit to a much lesser extent than it was to become in later years. Nevertheless, the *Lega* made it clear that immigration had to be curbed and that immigrants had to be fully assimilated into the host society, while simultaneously excluding some groups a priori as non-assimilable.

In terms of the party's electorate, the early years saw a preponderance of young, male, less-educated voters from the lower-middle, the independent-middle and the working classes, who had previously voted for Christian Democracy (Mannheimer, 1991, 1993; Diamanti, 1991). The majority resided in areas of small-scale industrialization, especially in Lombardy and the North-East and held inward-looking attitudes towards foreigners and immigrants, as well as deep-seated feelings of distrust towards state and political institutions (Mannheimer, 1991, 1993; Diamanti, 1993; Cento Bull, 1992, 1993; Cento Bull and Gilbert, 2001). Hence the *Lega* clearly succeeded in tapping into these voters' material grievances and cultural values, offering an innovative response to both in the guise of ethno-federalism.

Membership rose rapidly, from 18,000 in 1989 to 40,000 in 1990 and 140,000 in 1994 (Gold, 2003: 88), consisting mainly of people who were new to political participation and prepared to dedicate time and resources to the party. As for organizational structure, at the 1991 Congress Bossi made it clear that he would not take over the post of party secretary unless he were in a position of pre-eminence vis-à-vis the secretaries of the various regional leagues. Bossi got his way, since the party's 1991 statute established that its secretary had the power to request the Federal Congress to dissolve, by simple majority, any 'national' councils 'operating in contrast with the political, moral and administrative line established by the Federal Congress' (Art. 12) and had 'coordination and supervisory functions towards all the organs of the movement'. Furthermore, Bossi made systematic use of expulsions to eliminate possible rivals and impose his strategy upon the party. As Dematteo (2011: 62) remarked, 'In the *Lega Nord* expulsion has always been the means by which internal conflicts are managed, thus confirming the absence of a democratic culture at the level of the party leadership.'

An important question related to this early period concerns the role played by the *Lega Nord* in bringing down the First Republic. The general consensus among scholars and commentators is that the rise of the party contributed to, but did not in itself cause, the demise of the old political system. However, there is no doubt that Bossi's entrepreneurship and his party's electoral success, mainly at the expense of Christian Democracy, accelerated the dismantling of the political system that had sustained the First Republic, opening the way for other political actors to enter the fray.

The *Lega Nord* between 1994 and 2001

After 1994 the party underwent a significant shift in its ideological and political position, with a dual move away from neo-liberal values towards a radical right-wing stance and away from federalism towards secessionism. This shift must be explained at least in part by Berlusconi's decision to form his own party, *Forza Italia*, and to stand at the 1994 elections, proposing similar themes to those advocated by the *Lega* and competing for the same electorate.

The year 1994 turned out to be a crucial one. In January, Berlusconi took the decision to form a new party and Bossi accepted his offer of an electoral pact, being afraid that direct competition with *Forza Italia* would consign the *Lega Nord* to a marginal position, particularly in view of the largely majoritarian electoral system introduced in 1993. Berlusconi devised a three-way pact that saw *Forza Italia* in coalition with the *Lega* in the North and with *Alleanza Nazionale* (AN), the heir to the neo-fascist party *Movimento Sociale Italiano* (MSI) in the South. This convoluted pact reflected the deep differences that existed at the time between a northern-based, pro-free market party like the *Lega* and a southern-based, statist party like AN. The new elections saw the triumph of *Forza Italia* and the MSI-AN with 21.0 per cent and 20.3 per cent of the votes respectively. The *Lega Nord*, with 8.4 per cent, managed to remain at the level of the 1992 elections but could no longer aspire to become the main party in the North. Bossi went on to form a government with Berlusconi which proved short-lived, as in December of the same year he decided to withdraw from the coalition, losing more than fifty MPs, who opposed this decision, in the process. In retrospect, it is easy to understand how irksome the cohabitation between these three parties turned out to be, as well as the embarrassment of the *Lega* in finding that the new government was more interested in occupying the state than cutting it down to size (Cento Bull and Gilbert, 2001: 36).

The following years were to prove especially difficult for the *Lega*. In electoral terms, a remarkable success at the 1996 general election, when the party obtained its best result to date, with 10.1 per cent of the votes, was not sufficient to allow Bossi to play a pivotal role in the new legislature. It was followed by a steep decline at the 1999 European elections and a debacle at the 2001 elections, when the party had to settle for a meagre 3.9 per cent, losing votes heavily in its northern heartlands. In terms of its political strategy and ideology, the *Lega* embarked on a secessionist campaign, engaging in highly choreographed nationalist rites which culminated in the proclamation of the independence of Padania in September 1996. This campaign was aimed primarily at galvanizing its activists and supporters, as well as relaunching the *Lega* as the true interpreter of the identity and interests of the North (Giordano, 2000). Furthermore, secessionism reinforced the *Lega*'s ability to make people think of politics in terms of territorial, as opposed to social, issues (Agnew and Brusa, 1999; Dickie, 1996; see also Chapter 13 in this volume).

This phase also marked a process of radicalization of the party. Internal expulsions became more frequent and a strident nationalist discourse was adopted. Globalization, once portrayed in apolitical terms, was redubbed 'mondialism', following the terminology of the French New Right. Immigration and multiculturalism became the spectre of the future, to be resisted at all costs. European integration, viewed favourably prior to Italy's entry into the Eurozone, not least in the belief that it would promote greater regional autonomy, was now viewed with suspicion, as leading to the creation of a centralist superstate. Instead of hailing the cohesiveness, inventiveness and success of the Northern community of producers and entrepreneurs, the *Lega* now lamented its fragility and vowed to protect it from both internal and external threats. Thus the twin themes of fear and security rose to the top of the party's agenda, where they were to remain dominant for more than a decade.

The *Lega*'s ideological steer towards the extreme right was accompanied by a change in the composition of its voters, losing support among business people but gaining the votes of 'workers and artisans living in small towns and working in or for the myriad of small and medium-sized factories located throughout Lombardy and the northeast' (Beirich and Woods, 2000: 132).

According to the authors, in 1996 the *Lega* had become 'Italy's largest working-class party', as a result of a fear of globalization and its impact.

It is in light of this political and ideological shift that we ought to examine Bossi's decision to ally himself once again with Berlusconi' s coalition for the 2001 general election. At one level, in fact, the decision marked the end of the secessionist phase and signalled the return of the party to its early dual goal of reining in the public deficit and implementing federalism (now renamed 'devolution' to distinguish it from the federalist reform introduced by the centre-left government in 2000). An electoral pact, signed on 5 April 2001, put devolution at the top of the agenda, together with new legislation aimed at curbing immigration, which seemingly indicated that the *Lega* was prioritizing reforms of a substantive nature over any identity politics. At another level, however, the politics of identity was retained and even emphasized, which constantly interfered with the party's reforming drive. This raises the issue of whether the party in government subordinated its populist rhetoric to mainstream and pragmatic policy initiatives or, conversely, whether its rhetoric and ideology took precedence over any functional policymaking. In order to address these questions, we need first to examine the role and impact of the *Lega* in government.

Participation in government

The *Lega Nord* took part in the second and third Berlusconi governments (2001–6) and, after a brief period when the centre-left was back in power, participated in the fourth Berlusconi government (2008–11). On both occasions, the party prioritized two specific policy areas, immigration and federalism, in exchange for a series of legislative measures that were of interest to Berlusconi. At the same time, the *Lega* strove to differentiate itself from its coalition allies and to preserve its distinctive identity, both by behaving as an 'opposition within government' and by retaining its image as a party of the periphery, alien to Rome's corrupt ways (Albertazzi and McDonnell, 2005).

In 2001–6 the *Lega* shared power with *Forza Italia*, AN and the *Unione dei Democratici Cristiani e di Centro* (UDC), a centrist Catholic party. This made for an uneasy alliance, as the UDC was adverse to the populist radical-right posturing of the *Lega*, while AN's leader Gianfranco Fini was opposed to any reform that would weaken the central state. The party controlled key ministerial posts, with Roberto Castelli as Minister of Justice, Roberto Maroni responsible for Welfare and Bossi Minister for Devolution, the last determined to devolve exclusive powers in health, education and local policing to Italy's regional governments. However, negotiations within the coalition turned out to be complex and protracted, and Bossi had to give in to the requests of his allies. Hence, 'Everyone obtained something, and in the end this reform was an absolute dog's dinner of contradictions' (Donovan, 2010: 494). In 2006, the reform was put to the test of a national referendum, as required by the Italian Constitution, but failed to achieve the support of voters, except in Lombardy and the Veneto, the *Lega*'s own strongholds.

The party was more successful with its anti-immigration policy, as it gained approval for a new law, known as the Bossi-Fini from the names of its proponents. Introduced in 2002, the law envisaged tough sanctions for illegal immigrants and paved the way for their expulsion from the country. However, it was widely considered ineffective, especially in view of a substantial increase in immigration in the following years, as well as the government's subsequent decision to regularize the situation of almost 700,000 immigrants.

While the party's performance in terms of policymaking was not a clear-cut success, the *Lega* was, nevertheless, able to place the blame for any failure upon its allies and, thus, to preserve its distinctive and 'pure' political image. As a result, the party fared much better than its coalition partners at the 2005 local and regional elections, which signalled an overall loss of support for the government.

In 2008, following a strong performance at the general election of that year, when it secured 8.3 per cent of the votes, the *Lega* was back in power, in alliance with the *Popolo della Libertà* (PDL), the party formed by a merger between *Forza Italia* and the AN. The pact between Bossi and Berlusconi continued to revolve around the former's support for federalism and anti-immigration measures in exchange for policies aimed at solving Berlusconi's personal and judicial problems. This time the *Lega* announced that it would focus on 'fiscal federalism'. In May 2009, a framework law established the guidelines for financing local and regional governments, based upon the calculation of 'standard costs', applicable to all communes and regions, with a view to cutting spending. Given the complex nature of this reform, the government set up a Bicameral Commission with the task of producing detailed proposals within two years. As in the case of the devolution bill, the *Lega* was at risk of reaching the end of the legislature without a tangible result in this priority area.

The party also focused on new anti-immigration measures, known as the 'security package', introduced in August 2009. In an even more draconian manner than the Bossi-Fini legislation, the new law aimed at curbing the entry of new immigrants and facilitating the expulsion of illegal immigrants. As had happened with its predecessor, it gave rise to strong criticisms and protests, and incurred the same accusations of being largely ineffective, constituting primarily a form of 'symbolic politics'. We will come back to these issues in a later section.

After a period of popularity, the government started to lose internal cohesion and electoral support. On 15 November 2010, the leader of the AN, Gianfranco Fini, and some MPs left the government in protest, because of irreconcilable personal and political differences with Berlusconi. At the local elections of May 2011, both the PDL and the *Lega* lost votes, the latter even in its traditional strongholds. In the course of the same year, the government was seemingly caught unawares by the gravity of the financial crisis and it was increasingly seen as unreliable by its European allies. Amid repeated calls for Berlusconi to stand aside, the governing coalition barely survived a vote of confidence on 14 October. Finally, on 12 November Berlusconi handed in his resignation and was replaced by Mario Monti at the head of a technocratic government. While the PDL decided to support the new government, the *Lega* went into opposition, a decision adopted at least in part to regain credibility among its voters through resuming its autonomist stance.

Quite apart from these dramatic events, the *Lega*'s participation in the fourth Berlusconi government was less beneficial to the party than its previous collaboration. The reason is twofold. First, the party found it more difficult to behave as an 'opposition within government', blaming various allies for any policy failure, given that the UDC was no longer part of the coalition and Fini had left the government. Second, the long delays in introducing fiscal federalism and the inability to cut back the public deficit did not sit well with the *Lega*'s northern constituency. Hence the voters punished the *Lega* as much as the PDL at the polls in 2011, unlike in 2005. However, much worse was to come.

The *Lega* in crisis

An issue which had been brewing for some time within the party exploded in January 2012. This concerned the excessive influence exercised by the so-called 'magic' circle surrounding Umberto Bossi, made up of his wife and children as well as his closest friends, which had been set up ever since a stroke, suffered in March 2004, had left him severely impaired. The fact that Bossi managed to continue to lead the *Lega* after this episode is nothing short of miraculous and owes much both to his charismatic image and to his wife, who ensured that only the most trusted allies (and her own children) would exercise power alongside her husband.

Opposition to the magic circle revolved around former Interior Minister Roberto Maroni, who seized his chance early in 2012, when a financial scandal involving payments from party funds to Bossi's children and even corrupt deals with the Calabrian Mafia rocked the party. Maroni publicly declared that he would clean up the *Lega* and restore it to its original mission and 'purity'. He then proceeded to dismantle the magic circle and put himself forward as candidate for the party secretaryship. However, this did not prevent the *Lega* from losing votes heavily at the April 2012 local elections, with its candidates failing to be elected mayors even in its heartlands, with the exception of Flavio Tosi, a close ally of Maroni, in Verona. How much this was due to the scandal that had engulfed the party is unclear, but the *Lega* clearly failed to profit from its intransigent opposition to the Monti government.

After becoming party secretary in July 2012 and relegating Bossi to the newly created role of honorary President,[1] Maroni claimed that his new *Lega* would focus on becoming the main party of the North and resume its original mission of representing the interests of northern society and citizens, with particular attention paid to the needs of small and medium-sized entrepreneurs. He then decided to stand as candidate for the presidency of the Lombardy Region, declaring that his party wanted to create a strong and autonomous Euroregion of the North. After the fall of the Monti government in November 2012 and with new elections scheduled for February 2013, Maroni opted to resume an alliance with Berlusconi, despite strong opposition from the grass roots. As it turned out, this alliance secured Maroni election as regional president and consoled the party for its heavy loss of votes elsewhere in the North.

Having analysed the party both in opposition and in government, we must now examine the nature of the *Lega Nord* in both these roles and assess how it can best be defined and categorized. We will then explore where the party currently stands and its likely future trajectory.

Categorizing the *Lega* in opposition and in government

In light of the above analysis, it is now possible to address the moot question of whether the *Lega Nord* can be located within one of the established party families and, if so, to which it actually belongs. Initially the *Lega* was included in the category of ethno-regionalist (De Winter and Türsan, 1998) or subcultural parties (Natale, 1991; Cento Bull, 1992, 1993; Messina, 1998). However, the most influential interpretation categorized it as a populist or regional-populist party (Biorcio, 1997; Leonardi and Kovacs, 1993; Diani, 1996). One strand of scholarship viewed it more specifically as a radical-right populist party, in view of its xenophobic and quasi-racist stance (Betz, 1994; Kitschelt, 1995; Taggart, 1995). Recently, there was renewed controversy over whether the *Lega* should be categorized as a regionalist-populist party (McDonnell, 2006; Albertazzi and McDonnell, 2011) or an extreme-right one (Zaslove, 2004, 2007).

What at times risks appearing as sterile polemics masks in fact an interesting dilemma: is the *Lega* to be considered as belonging to the European New Right or has it made use of populism in an opportunistic manner? If the former, did the party embrace an extreme-right ideology from its inception or following its 'turn to Padania'? These questions have wider implications as regards the Italian political system, not least because they are closely linked to the issue of the future direction and even survival of this party in light of its internal turmoil in 2012.

It is the view of this author that the *Lega Nord* can indeed be classified as a party of the radical-right variety (see Chapter 4 in this volume). A recent study by Passarelli and Tuorto (2012) in fact revealed that nowadays its voters and supporters, as well as its elected representatives, place themselves and the party well on the right of the political spectrum. Indeed Woods (2009: 176) argued that the *Lega*'s antiglobalization and xenophobic stances were in evidence from its inception, even though they took centre stage only from the mid-1990s. However, it seems important to distinguish between two phases of development in the party's history. In the early 1990s the *Lega Nord* was the first and only party to have squarely identified in the huge public deficit the primary source of Italy's socio-economic problems, innovatively proposing (ethno)-federalism as the remedy. While these were to remain key themes for the *Lega*, the events of the following years, above all Berlusconi's decision to enter the field of politics, growing immigration, increasing economic competition and an uncertain outlook for the areas of small-scale industrialization that formed the backbone of the party's electoral support, all combined to convince Bossi to veer to the right, prioritizing a politics of identity. Padania was no longer the means through which the party was to attack and dismantle the centralist state, but a nation under threat from internal and external 'Others'.

We can therefore agree with Albertazzi and McDonnell that the *Lega* has proved opportunistic in its approach to politics. Yet the above-mentioned study by Passarelli and Tuorto also indicates that a change of strategy and ideology would not be an easy task to accomplish, unlike in the 1990s, because the *Lega* is now much less a movement than a structured party. Furthermore, the unexpectedly strong performance of the *Movimento 5 Stelle* at the 2012 local elections and above all at the 2013 general election, due in great part to its ability to attract votes from the whole of the political spectrum, shows that the political space has already been occupied by a new populist player in direct competition with the *Lega*. Thus a repositioning of the latter along the left–right axis is severely constrained both by the current nature of the party and its supporters and by the electoral and political context in which it operates.

Another important issue concerns the overall assessment of this party's role in government. Did the party pursue a radical-right agenda in government or did it carry out fairly mainstream policies? This question has been addressed by scholars largely with reference to immigration policy, because of the *Lega*'s intransigent stance on this issue. While Zaslove (2004: 114) argued that the *Lega*'s extreme-right ideology had indeed influenced public policy, Ruzza and Fella (2009: 231) distinguished between 'symbolic' politics and policymaking, stating that the *Lega* had in fact implemented 'mainstream conservative policies' (2009: 190). Other commentators (Albertazzi and McDonnell, 2005; Geddes, 2008; Woods, 2009) argued that the policies implemented by the government responded to functional socio-economic needs and/or to the logic of intra-coalitional bargaining rather than being inspired by an extreme-right ideology.

This author (Cento Bull, 2010: 429) put forward a somewhat different interpretation, acknowledging the largely 'simulative' character of the *Lega*'s policymaking in the field of immigration, yet also arguing that it has had a real and concrete impact, establishing a differentiated system of rights and 'creating an entire category of workers who are easily hired and fired'. Furthermore, the *Lega*'s intransigence has prevented any changes to the country's citizenship laws, which are among the most hostile in Europe to immigrants and their children. Therefore, at least in the short run, the party's radical stance addressed 'both the material and economic needs of the *Lega*'s electorate, as well as their anxieties and fears concerning culture and identity' (430).

Conclusion: whither the *Lega Nord*?

While the outcome of the 2013 elections showed a substantial decrease in electoral support compared with 2008, the party was still at a higher level than in 2001, from which it managed to recover. It is therefore too early to assess the long-term consequences of the important events of 2012, not least as regards the possibility that they marked the beginning of the end for a party that had dominated Italian politics for over twenty years, consistently grabbing the headlines and punching above its weight.

Maroni's strategy to relaunch the party represented a balancing act between strengthening the *Lega*'s northern identity and federalist mission, though stopping short of secessionism, on the one hand, and regaining consensus among its traditional supporters by focusing on concrete socio-economic policies on the other. Hence his slogan 'The North First' and the idea of a macro-federation of the North. Maroni's victory in Lombardy seemingly vindicated this strategy, as the *Lega* ended up controlling the three main northern regions. However, while the party retained considerable support in Lombardy, it lost heavily in Piedmont and above all in the Veneto, where Beppe Grillo, leader of the 5 Star Movement, successfully campaigned on a platform of lower taxes and anti-politics, thus stealing the *Lega*'s thunder. Hence even in its strongholds the party was no longer perceived as a radical alternative and it was challenged by new populist actors untainted by corruption charges.

In the course of 2013, amid worsening living standards and rising levels of social protest, the *Lega Nord* steered further to the right and attempted to relaunch its radical vocation. The new strategy was strengthened by the election of Matteo Salvini as general secretary on 7 December, when he won 82 per cent of the vote and relegated the historic leader, Umberto Bossi, to a marginal position with only 18 per cent of the vote. Salvini's triumph marked yet another U-turn in policy, as he openly denounced the years spent in government, stating that the *Lega* 'tried to change things from Rome but failed, what with devolution and the referendum they took us for a ride for the last 14 years' (Madron, 2013). He then asserted that the way forward consisted in pursuing the independence of Padania. Salvini linked independence to a battle against the euro, which he dubbed 'a crime against humanity'. By joining a new pan-European alliance between radical right parties spearheaded by the French *Front National* and the Dutch Freedom Party, the *Lega Nord* headed by Salvini was obviously trying to capitalize on a wave of anti-EU sentiment ahead of the 2014 elections to the European Parliament (on this alliance, see Mammone, 2013; Muller, 2013).

We can envisage two main scenarios. The first is that Salvini's strategy proves successful and the party starts to recover consensus in the North, riding on a popular wave of anti-politics, yet also managing to re-establish links with its traditional socio-economic electorate. Alternatively, the *Lega* may continue to lose ground and ultimately become a spent force, with voters deserting it either in favour of other populist players, especially Beppe Grillo's movement, or indeed in favour of more mainstream conservative parties, including Berlusconi's re-formed *Forza Italia* and the new party created by Angelino Alfano, the *Nuovo Centro Destra* (New Centre Right, NCD).

Whether or not it survives or even manages once more to thrive in electoral terms, the party which started out to change the nature and functioning of the Italian state and aggressively redress the public debt cannot attract a positive overall assessment in terms of its substantive performance. It proved innovative in terms of political style and discourse and contributed to accelerating the end of the First Republic, but it was unable to tackle the deficit, lower the fiscal pressure or indeed renew the political system along federalist lines. While it succeeded in putting the 'Northern Question' centre stage, taking on the representation of the interests and anxieties of much of the northern electorate, it ultimately failed to address the root causes of its malaise.

Note

1 For the new role of 'honorary President' and other changes to the party's structure approved on 1 July 2012, see the 2012 Statute of the *Lega Nord* accessible on its website: http://www.leganord.org/index.php/il-movimento/lo-statuto-della-lega-nord (accessed 7 March 2013). For a comparison with the 2002 Statute, see http://www.ilsole24ore.com/pdf2010/SoleOnLine5/_Oggetti_Correlati/Documenti/Notizie/2012/04/lega_nord_statuto.pdf?uuid=14f2bc08-7e2d-11e1-a3cb-d6fcc09c039f (accessed 7 March 2013).

Bibliography

Agnew, J. (1995). The rhetoric of regionalism: the Northern League in Italian politics 1983–94. *Transactions of the Institute of British Geographers*, 20 (2), 156–72.

Agnew, J. and Brusa, C. (1999). New rules for national identity? The Northern League and political identity in contemporary Northern Italy. *National Identities*, 1 (2), 117–33

Albertazzi, D. and McDonnell, D. (2005). The Lega Nord in the second Berlusconi government: in a league of its own. *West European Politics*, 28 (5): 952–72.

Albertazzi, D. and McDonnell, D. (eds.) (2011). *Twenty-First Century Populism: The Spectre of Western European Democracy*. Basingstoke: Palgrave Macmillan.

Beirich, H. and Woods, D. (2000). Globalisation, workers and the Northern League. *West European Politics*, 23 (1), 130–43.

Betz, H.-G. (1994). *Radical Right-Wing Populism in Western Europe*. Basingstoke: Macmillan.

Biorcio, R. (1997). *La Padania promessa. La storia, le idee e la logica della Lega Nord*. Milan: il Saggiatore.

Cento Bull, A. (1992). The Lega Lombarda. A new political subculture for Lombardy's industrial districts. *The Italianist*, 12, 179–83.

Cento Bull, A. (1993). The politics of industrial districts in Lombardy. Replacing Christian Democracy with the Northern League. *The Italianist*, 13, 209–29.

Cento Bull, A. (2010). Addressing contradictory needs: the Lega Nord and Italian immigration policy. *Patterns of Prejudice*, 44 (5), 411–31.

Cento Bull, A. and Gilbert, M. (2001). *The Lega Nord and the Northern Question in Italian Politics*. Basingstoke: Palgrave.

Dematteo, L. (2011). *L'idiota in politica. Antropologia della Lega Nord*. Milan: Feltrinelli.

De Winter, L. and Türsan, H. (eds.) (1998). *Regionalist Parties in Western Europe*. London: Routledge.

Diamanti, I. (1991). Una tipologia dei simpatizzanti della Lega. In R. Mannheimer (ed.), *La Lega Lombarda* (pp. 159–90). Milan: Feltrinelli.

Diamanti, I. (1993). *La Lega. Geografia, storia e sociologia di un nuovo soggetto politico*. Rome: Donzelli.

Diani, M. (1996). Linking mobilization frames and political opportunities: insights from regional populism in Italy. *American Sociological Review*, 61 (6), 1053–69.

Dickie, J. (1996). Imagined Italies. In D. Forgacs and R. Lumley (eds.), *Italian Cultural Studies: An Introduction* (pp. 19–33). Oxford: Oxford University Press.

Donovan, M. (2010). Berlusconi: truly, Craxi's heir? *Modern Italy*, 15 (4), 485–99.

Geddes, A. (2008). *Il rombo dei cannoni*? Immigration and the centre-right in Italy. *Journal of European Public Policy*, 15 (3), 349–66.

Gilbert, M. (1995). *The Italian Revolution: The End of Politics, Italian Style?* Boulder, CO and Oxford: Westview Press.

Giordano, B. (2000). Italian regionalism or 'Padanian' nationalism – the political project of the Lega Nord in Italian politics. *Political Geography*, 19 (4), 445–71.

Gold, T. W. (2003). *The Lega Nord and Contemporary Politics in Italy*. New York: Palgrave Macmillan.

Kitschelt, H. (with A. J. McGann) (1995). *The Radical Right in Western Europe. A Comparative Analysis*. Ann Arbor, MI: University of Michigan Press.

Leonardi, R. and Kovacs, M. (1993). The Lega Nord: the rise of a new Italian catch-all party. In S. Hellman and G. Pasquino (eds.), *Italian Politics: A Review* (pp. 123–41). London: Pinter.

McDonnell, D. (2006). A weekend in Padania: regionalist populism and the Lega Nord. *Politics*, 26 (2), 126–32.

McDonnell, D. (2007). Beyond the radical right straitjacket: a reply to Andrej Zaslove's critique of 'Regionalist Populism and the Lega Nord'. *Politics*, 27 (2), 123–6.

Madron, L. (2013). Lega, il salto di Salvini. Dai comunisti padani all'amicizia con l'estrema destra. *Il fatto quotidiano*. 15 December. Available online at www.ilfattoquotidiano.it/2013/12/15/lega-il-voltafaccia-di-salvini-dai-comunisti-padani-allamicizia-con-lestrema-destra-ue/813511/ (accessed 20 December 2013).

Mammone, A. (2013). The rise of the far right is overplayed – but austerity increases the threat. *The Guardian*. 16 November. Available online at www.theguardian.com/commentisfree/2013/nov/16/europe-fascist-takeover-austerity-wilders-le-pen (accessed 20 December 2013).

Mannheimer, R. (ed.) (1991). *La Lega Lombarda*. Milan: Feltrinelli.

Mannheimer, R. (1993). The electorate of the Lega Nord. In G. Pasquino and P. McCarthy (eds.), *The End of Post-War Politics in Italy* (pp. 85–107). Boulder, CO and Oxford: Westview Press.

Messina, P. (1998). Opposition in Italy in the 1990s: local political cultures and the Northern League. *Government and Opposition*, 33 (4), 462–78.

Muller, J. W. (2013). How Europe could face its own shutdown. *The Guardian*. 21 October. Available online at www.theguardian.com/commentisfree/2013/oct/21/europe-own-shutdown-anti-eu-parties (accessed 20 December 2013).

Natale, P. (1991). Lega Lombarda e insediamento territoriale: un'analisi ecologica. In R. Mannheimer (ed.), *La Lega Lombarda* (pp. 83–121). Milan: Feltrinelli.

Passarelli, G. and Tuorto, D. (2012). *Lega & Padania: Storie e luoghi delle camicie verdi*. Bologna: Il Mulino.

Ruzza, C. and Fella, S. (2009). *Re-inventing the Italian Right: Territorial Politics, Populism and 'Post-Fascism'*. Abingdon and New York: Routledge.

Taggart, P. (1995) New populist parties in Western Europe. *West European Politics*, 18 (1), 34–51.

Woods, D. (2009). Pockets of resistance to globalization: the case of the Lega Nord. *Patterns of Prejudice*, 43 (2), 161–77.

Zaslove, A. (2004). Closing the door? The ideology and impact of radical right populism on immigration policy in Austria and Italy. *Journal of Political Ideologies*, 9 (1), 99–118.

Zaslove, A. (2007). Alpine populism, Padania and beyond: a response to Duncan McDonnell. *Politics*, 27 (1), 64–8.

18

MAGISTRATES GOING INTO POLITICS

Antonio Di Pietro and Italy of Values

James L. Newell

Introduction

With the outcome of the Italian general election of 2013, Antonio Di Pietro's *Italia dei Valori* (Italy of Values, IdV) found itself excluded from Parliament for the first time in ten years. It had fielded candidates as part of the left-wing coalition, *Rivoluzione Civile* (Civil Revolution, RC) headed by another public prosecutor, Antonio Ingroia. But in the Chamber election RC managed only 2.3 per cent of the vote and therefore failed to cross the 4 per cent exclusion threshold, while in the Senate election it did even worse failing everywhere to come close to the 8 per cent exclusion threshold applied regionally. In some respects this was surprising; for the most spectacular result was the explosion of support for Beppe Grillo's *Movimento Cinque Stelle* (Five-star Movement, M5S), with which IdV had much in common. Both were political independents, 'non-coalitionable' for some or all of their history (McDonnell and Newell, 2011: 444); both sought to challenge the stranglehold on political life of the mainstream parties, perceived as corrupt, remote from ordinary citizens and incapable of the reform of the political system they had promised twenty years earlier at the time of the great *Tangentopoli/Mani pulite* ('Bribe City'/'Clean Hands') scandal; neither formation could be easily located on the left–right spectrum and drew members and supporters from all parts of it. They even had overlapping styles of political communication, both giving a privileged place to the Internet and the piazza. Grillo's movement had not been present at the general election held less than five years before: now it took 25.6 per cent of the vote.

Of course, to a large extent it was the overlap in the nature of their appeals that explained the sharp contrast in the two forces' performance. Ecological analyses carried out by the Istituto Cattaneo (Colloca *et al*., 2013) confirmed that significant proportions of IdV's 2008 electorate had shifted to the M5S. But this left open the question why, despite the similarities, Di Pietro's followers (whose best performance was the 8 per cent achieved in the 2009 European elections) had never managed to achieve the striking success that Grillo's now achieved. Of course, the M5S explosion will have had to do with conjunctural factors not present when IdV was the only player in town; but on the other hand, popular discontent with 'politics as usual' from which both drew so much of their sustenance was long-standing, not new. And why was it that, aware of the risk of being cannibalised by Grillo in 2013, Di Pietro had not reached an accommodation with him that might at least have kept the size of the feast to a minimum?

The remainder of this chapter is designed to shed light on these and other questions by exploring the factors underlying the emergence of IdV and the political debut of its leader; the nature of IdV as a party; and its strategy and electoral performance. IdV has often been criticised for the patrimonial style of leadership of its founder, from whose identity it has hardly been possible to separate its own. At the same time, it initially seems odd that Di Pietro, having won such enormous standing for his role in *Mani pulite* should then have decided to join a political class so negatively viewed by citizens, a class whose malfeasance he had done so much to expose. We therefore begin by examining the career of Antonio Di Pietro himself, seeking to uncover what drove his choices from the early 1990s on.

Emergence

A feeling for the degree to which Di Pietro was revered by the Italian public in the early 1990s can be obtained from the telegram sent to him by Anna Maria Florio on 18 May 1992:

> It is sad when in a nation a member of the judiciary as intelligent, honest, capable and courageous as you are is considered a hero. I hope no one, whether one of your superiors or a minister, perhaps from the Justice Department, stops you. Lined up behind you, you have almost the whole of Italy, which is saying to you: 'Thank you Di Pietro!'
>
> *(Carlucci and Di Pietro, 1995: 48, my translation)*

The scandal that turned Di Pietro into a popular hero had few to rival it. 'It might even qualify, in some meaningful sense, as the twentieth century's "greatest scandal"' (Newell, 2005). It began on 17 February 1992, when Mario Chiesa, the head of a Milanese old people's home, was arrested in the act of taking a 7 million lire bribe from the owner of a cleaning company. A member of the Italian Socialist Party (*Partito Socialista Italiano*, PSI), Chiesa owed his position to the system of the governing parties' control, for patronage purposes, of large parts of the state apparatus, and assumed that the party would now erect a protective wall around him. In the past it had got representatives accused of accepting bribes elected to Parliament – whose members had then obligingly voted against the judicial authorities' requests that their parliamentary immunity be lifted. But Chiesa had been caught 'with his hands in the till' and a general election was due on 5 April. Frequently the object of media satire for its shaky grasp of probity, the party abandoned him to his fate. He was, in party secretary Bettino Craxi's words, 'a little rascal' who had thrown 'a shadow over the entire image of a party which in fifty years in Milan . . . [had] never had an administrator convicted for grave crimes against the public administration'. Faced with this evidence that his political career was in ruins, Chiesa decided to confess all.

What came to light was a massive network of 'mutually beneficial linkages' (Waters, 1994: 170) between the political parties and powerful economic groups in the City: a network whose illegality required there to be, among those involved, a trust that would necessarily have been very difficult to establish – but very easy to break in the event of the slightest suspicion that the wall of silence surrounding the network had been breached. One confession therefore led to another and by November 1993, over half the members of Parliament found themselves under investigation for corruption, as did four former prime ministers and all those who had been members of the government at the time the scandal broke.

The effect of the exposure of corruption on this scale was to bring about a complete disintegration of the traditional parties of government and a complete restructuring of the party system through impacts that were financial, organisational, electoral and institutional. Financially, the parties had become increasingly dependent on corrupt forms of funding while facing mounting accumulated debts. They were therefore pushed fairly quickly towards bankruptcy. This led to their organisational disintegration as they were deserted by venal members – aware that the parties could no longer serve as vehicles for upward mobility – and by ideologically committed members who had been kept in ignorance of the corrupt networks within them. The electoral impact was a haemorrhage of support as voters who had once supported the governing parties out of fear of the opposition communists no longer felt, now that the Berlin Wall was down, any particular compulsion to do so. The tidal wave of indignation the scandal provoked provided the popular backing required by a range of cross-party groups that now attempted – successfully – to bring about a change in the electoral law – through a referendum held in 1993 – and with it a change in the party system, which they hoped would produce more honest government.

Di Pietro's role in this was as a public prosecutor who since the early 1980s had stood out for an ability to use information technology to increase the efficiency and effectiveness of judicial investigations. It was Di Pietro who had brought about Chiesa's arrest by persuading Luca Magni, the aforementioned cleaning-company owner who had complained about being asked for a bribe, to present himself at Chiesa's office with a briefcase containing marked banknotes and several listening devices while four *carabinieri* waited outside.

What caused his involvement to give him the status of popular hero was the high profile he had as a leading member of a group of investigators whose enquiries captured the public imagination. The downfall and humiliation of so many powerful figures delighted Italians, who had voted for them less because of any positive commitment than because of the feeling that they had little choice: they supported them either for reasons of clientelism – which, by turning citizens' *rights* into *favours*, itself bred cynicism and resentment – or because they were frightened by the prospect of the communists taking power, or both. They knew that the world of politics was dark and labyrinthine and that its practitioners were powerful people with the ability to 'fix things' in such a way that they were immune from the impositions of a hostile state that ordinary citizens had to endure. Consequently, the sight of once untouchable figures at last getting their comeuppance was intoxicating (Newell, 2005).

The proceedings were framed in the media less as threats to the reputations of the individuals involved than as the trial of an entire political class, with Di Pietro cast in the role of moraliser of public life. Judicial reforms from the late 1950s had considerably increased the extent of prosecutors' de facto discretion in deciding what to investigate. Combined with generational turnover this had led increasing numbers of judges and prosecutors, since the 1970s, to see their role less as a passive '*bouche de la loi*' (Guarnieri, 1997: 158), than as one demanding – through penal initiatives in the areas of workplace safety, environmental pollution, tax evasion, fraud and so forth – that they use their powers to act as problem-solvers, attempting to tackle the great social issues of the day (Di Federico, 1989: 33). Not surprisingly then Enrico Pozzi (1997) recounts that, having endured three years of grinding routine at the Milan public prosecutor's office, Di Pietro's first 'big break' came with a 1987 investigation into corruption in the issuance of driving licences – where, according to biographers, what was at stake for Di Pietro was less the identification of offenders than the prevention of a potential massacre, his mission being 'to rid Milan of "this cancer", "to clean up the region of Lombardy", "to enact a process of social disinfestation", to reclaim the State' (Pozzi, 1997: 335, my translation). Consequently, the later 'Clean Hands' investigations would tend to be framed as a re-edition of David and Goliath, a morality play in which Di Pietro was depicted as doing battle, single-handedly, with the forces of evil.

Why, under these circumstances, would Di Pietro have decided – as he did in 1996 when he became Minister of Public Works in the first Prodi Government and then in 1997 as the centre-left's successful candidate for a place in the Senate – to take to the field of politics? Hitherto he had been the leader, not of a group or a movement, but the impartial leader, above party politics, of an entire nation; in politics he would inevitably divide opinion around him, not unite it. Moreover, individual politicians had long used informal relations of connivance with members of the judiciary to trade political favours (e.g. help in getting a seat in Parliament) for judicial favours (such as damaging a political opponent), while often accusing the judiciary of political interference: The appearance, if not the substance, of an imperfect separation of the roles of judge and politician would hardly be lessened by a political debut.

Di Pietro's own account of his decision was given in the preface to a lengthy interview published in 2008:

> Public life is like a football match: there are those who play and those who are good at giving advice and making angry criticisms from the sidelines. The basic choice, however, is between being a player or a spectator and I chose to be a player, with all the risks and uncertainties of the job, but also all of the satisfactions to be had from the pride that comes with being on the pitch ready to play the game of one's life ... as a magistrate I had revealed the illnesses of Italy's political and business systems, so I thought that as a politician I would be able to contribute to the search for a cure, which for me consisted and still consists in a generational change in the composition of the political class
>
> *(Di Pietro, 2008: 7–8, my translation)*

Di Pietro's charisma would have provided the required confidence of success. He spoke a language that was colourful and informal, free of technicalities, flavoured with proverbial sayings and idioms, a language that was quickly dubbed in the media '*dipietrese*'. Such qualities made it possible to stake a claim to be the authentic voice of the people and thus to compete on the same terms as politicians such as Berlusconi and Umberto Bossi, who had met with considerable success precisely by adopting such strategies.

Italia dei Valori

Di Pietro originally set up his party in March 1998, some four months after he had been elected to the Senate. In fact, he set it up twice. Less than a year after its original founding the party was merged with the *Democratici* (Democrats) – conceived as the first of a series of steps[1] designed to lead to the unification of all of the parties of the centre-left, one of the two main coalitions in the new, bipolar, party system that had emerged in the aftermath of *Tangentopoli*. Little more than a year after that, in 2000, Di Pietro left the Democrats and re-established IdV in protest at the decision of the former to support the formation of a government headed by the socialist, Giuliano Amato, who had been a close collaborator of former Prime Minister Bettino Craxi, one of the most high-profile defendants in the *Mani pulite* trials.

Cross-nationally, new parties tend not to last very long (Lucardie, 2000: 175). However, much depends on the political opportunity structure, and in the Italy of the late 1990s circumstances were rather propitious. Promoters of the 1993 referendum had assumed that the single-member simple plurality (SMSP) system they had achieved for the assignment of most parliamentary seats would result in party-system bipolarity by obliging parties close on the left–right spectrum to form electoral coalitions in order to avoid ideologically more distant parties taking seats at their joint expense with less than 50 per cent of the vote. It *did* produce this – but the bipolar system was highly *fragmented*: the disintegration (or in some cases transformation) of the traditional post-war Italian parties left large numbers of voters orphaned; and though disinclined to switch between coalitions, voters were rather weakly attached to the new parties *within* each coalition. Under these circumstances SMSP, which in other circumstances might have acted as a disincentive to potential newcomers, gave them a unique opportunity: as elections approached they could tell potential allies that they would run independently if their demands for safe seats were not met, aware that if non-aligned candidacies had few prospects of victory, 'what was much more certain was that they could make their larger rivals lose' (Newell, 2010).

Of course to be able to exercise such blackmail power potential newcomers have to have a credible *project*, that is, some problem – specific or general, of policy or ideology – on which they may reasonably expect to mobilise some minimum number of voters. IdV had such a project: the moralisation of public life, which citizens' reactions to *Mani pulite* had already revealed to be one with considerable resonance.

It is interesting, under these circumstances, to ask why IdV emerged as a party forming part of the coalition of the centre-left. After all, there was nothing particularly left-wing about justice and legality, which might, indeed, be perceived as having more in common with law-and-order themes typical of the conservative right. Moreover, besides – or perhaps because of – this, the party's location on the left–right spectrum was unclear, as its founder was clearly aware:

> I am a pragmatist . . . This does not mean that the right and the left are both good or amount to the same thing. I grew up, yes, with a negative perception of the right: my parents had no nostalgia for Fascism and always spoke negatively of the period of *il duce*. They associated the right with arrogance, and I have always hated arrogance. As far as . . . the left is concerned . . . mine was a Catholic family . . . so for my parents [communism] represented sin. Only with time did I understand that . . . among communists too – as among anti-communists – there were many who could be taken as models of social and civic engagement . . . My experience has led me, over time, to develop a political outlook that has certain basic principles: on the one hand, the concept of a liberal economy, the free market, respect for private property and economic freedom; on the other hand, the recognition of individual rights and of solidarity towards the weak and unfortunate . . . It's not right that the weakest are always the ones to lose, don't you think?
>
> *(Di Pietro and Barbacetto, 2008: 63–5, my translation)*

IdV found itself joining forces with the parties of the centre-left because of Silvio Berlusconi, the media magnate. Like Di Pietro, Berlusconi went into politics with a new political party which, like IdV, was its leader's own creation, as were its rules and values, identity and organisation. But while Di Pietro had gone into politics seemingly with the ambition of leading a crusade to clean up public life, Berlusconi had done so to protect his business interests. His party, *Forza Italia* (FI), had emerged in 1994 as the fulcrum around which the coalition of the centre-right was built, and from then on, thanks to his high profile in the post-Cold War world of 'personalised politics', he *himself* had become the main political cleavage in Italian politics.

This had two significant consequences for Di Pietro and IdV. First, it created a political competitor whose conflict of interests as prime minister and owner of Italy's three largest private television stations, and whose willingness to pass legislation to solve the legal problems to which he was subject as a private citizen, rendered him immensely controversial. It therefore provided IdV with the perfect target: the personification of the immorality whose expunging from public life went to the heart of its *raison d'être*. Second, it naturally drew the party to the centre-left: for both Di Pietro and the centre-left, Berlusconi's position and the type of control he exercised over the centre-right rendered his coalition inherently illegitimate as a potential governing actor.

Like FI, IdV was a 'personal party': a party created to further the political ambitions of its founder and whose internal organisation therefore reflects the founder's more or less complete control (Calise, 2000). It also had characteristics of the 'franchise party' (Carty, 2004): a party the use of whose 'brand' is granted to autonomous local branches but whose political and communications strategies are the prerogative of the centre (Floridia, 2013). Formally, the distribution of power within the party was federal in nature: its regional structures had administrative, financial and statutory autonomy; they were to make decisions about whom to admit to the party. On the other hand, membership of the party was not to give membership of the 'Association', a legally separate entity whose control of the party's assets and its symbol would ensure that these resources were protected from the potential claims of breakaway groups. Moreover, the fledgling IdV's statute assigned the presidency of the Association, until such time as he decided to relinquish it, to Di Pietro while also stipulating that the role of president of the party was to be filled by the president of the Association. The president was given wide powers, including ownership of the party symbol, newspaper and website, and powers to amend the party statute, select candidates, appoint personnel, choose the party treasurer and so on (Pisicchio, 2008: 43).

These features of the party's organisation help to explain two of its most distinctive characteristics. First, later complaints that Di Pietro ran the party as if it were a private fiefdom: as Calise (2000: 5–6) points out, in the personal party, the relationship between leaders and followers is governed by patrimony and charisma rather than rational-legal authority. Second, as a franchise party, IdV's central organisations were 'responsible for providing the basic product line (policy and leadership) . . . and for establishing standard organizational management', while the local units were 'charged with delivering the product', i.e. 'mobilizing campaigns to deliver the vote on the ground' (Carty, 2004: 11). This being the case, there seemed to be a rather strong correlation between vote share and the presence of local leaders able to interact with voters directly, adding to their own appeal the 'brand value' of the party (Pisicchio, 2008: 9). This is hardly surprising, but it might explain IdV's tendency, initially at least, to do better in the smaller than in the larger towns and cities (Emanuele, 2011); and as was suggested by the outcome of the 2001 general election, when the party failed by some 18,000 votes to cross the exclusion threshold, the matter was important for a small party like IdV insofar as it could make the difference between achieving some parliamentary representation or none at all.

Later, in 2008, the relationship between population density and the party's support went into reverse, as then it did much better in the large urban centres than elsewhere, this in no small part thanks to the large influx of votes that came to it from the radical left (see below). This influx revealed a third characteristic of the party, namely, its tendency to draw volatile support[2] from across the political spectrum – this thanks to its ambiguous left–right placement and to the anti-Berlusconi emphasis on legality (understood as public probity and due process), which made it attractive both to the 'right-thinking', moderate petit bourgeois, and to the anti-system protester on the radical left (Pisicchio, 2008: 78–9). Not surprisingly, then, unlike with other parties with significant regional strongholds, support for IdV was distributed more or less evenly across the national territory (Emanuele, 2011: Table 2).

A final distinctive feature of IdV that deserves highlighting is the considerable investment the party made in Internet technology. This enabled it to connect more effectively with radical left protesters, given that those with their social characteristics – youth, high levels of education and political efficacy – were disproportionately represented among assiduous Internet users. And by making it possible for the party to act as the focal point for relatively innocuous forms of protest, this enabled it to deal more effectively with the dilemmas posed by its need to speak simultaneously to those who wanted it to be a *partito di lotta* ('party of struggle') and the centrists among its supporters who wanted it to be a *partito di governo* ('party of government'). Finally, by facilitating dialogue and interaction with activists and potential activists, it held out the prospect of overcoming the late twentieth-century conflict faced by parties everywhere between the electoral imperatives to centralise power in the hands of a charismatic leader, and the equally strong pressures (deriving from declining memberships, post-materialism and so forth) to increase the powers of activists.

Electoral strategy and performance

Thanks to factors such as these, IdV was always a minor party: by the time it came onto the scene, Berlusconi had already consolidated his hold on the centre-right (the centre-left was dominated by the DS) and the popular passion aroused by the great scandal had long cooled. The popular distrust of governing institutions that the passion expressed had since been channelled by Berlusconi into hostility towards the judiciary with his repeated complaints that his legal difficulties were the product of a witch-hunt by judicial officials with communist sympathies out to exploit their positions to damage him politically.

But though it remained a minor party, IdV was always – at least until the general election of 2013 – a 'relevant' party (Sartori, 1976). Early confirmation came with the outcome of the 2001 general election at which IdV refused to coalesce with the rest of the centre-left. This was largely because of the latter's unwillingness or inability to act decisively on the matter of Berlusconi's conflict of interests and because, going into his first general election as leader of IdV, Di Pietro wanted to establish a clear identity for his party and make a bid for the leadership of a potentially new coalition of anti-Berlusconi forces (Giostra, 2009: 219). In the end, the votes his party received in the SMSP arena (1,487,287), though insufficient to enable it to surmount the exclusion threshold, were of consequence for the outcome overall: if we make the counterfactual assumption that Di Pietro's supporters would have voted for the centre-left in the absence of their preferred candidate, then the number of seats lost to the coalition as a result of its failure to reach an agreement with Di Pietro can be set at fifty-seven – fifty-seven being the number of colleges where the sum of the votes received by the centre-left *Ulivo* ('Olive Tree') candidate and the candidate representing Di Pietro's party was larger than the vote received by the winning candidate of the centre-right. And had the *Ulivo* won all these seats, then what was a centre-right majority of 107 in the Chamber, might have been a centre-left majority of four.[3]

By the time the next general election was held in 2006, the electoral law had been changed, and had been changed in such a way that Di Pietro no longer needed to fear that running in harness would result in his party's distinctive identity being submerged. The centre-right felt disadvantaged by the existing law because, as the outcomes of the 1996 and 2001 elections revealed, many of those who chose a centre-right party in the proportional arena were unwilling also to support the centre-right's candidate in the plurality arena,[4] whereas the opposite was true for supporters of the centre-left. Late in 2005, therefore, the centre-right used its parliamentary majority to force onto the statute book a law providing that seats would henceforth be distributed proportionally and that there would be a majority premium for the party or coalition of parties with the most votes overall. This disadvantaged the centre-left as the more fragmented of the two coalitions; for, given some uncertainty about the election's likely outcome, the coveted majority premium encouraged the largest aggregations of lists possible – making it likely, by the same token, that any centre-left governing coalition would be too large and unwieldy to provide stability. This is what in fact transpired: IdV along with the other minor parties were encouraged to emphasise their distinctiveness and raise their profiles, knowing that the majority premium ensured that no votes would be wasted. Then, after the centre-left took office with a wafer-thin majority, the veto power of its many components and its consequent ineffectiveness ensured that the necessity for each party to distance itself from unpopular policies and thus from its allies 'became ever more dominant with the passage of time' (Floridia, 2008: 319).

This circumstance was decisive for the way in which IdV would be obliged to position itself at the 2008 election following the government's early demise. By then, the DS and the *Margherita* had merged to form the PD which, notwithstanding the electoral law, now declared that it would run alone, without allies – a decision driven by the belief that the former coalition was now 'unelectable', that victory for the centre-right was a near certainty and that by damaging its former minor-party allies, such a strategy would free it of their constraints in the future. IdV was an exception to this policy and thus found itself running in harness with the PD – this largely because it added a radical hue to the alliance, so assisting PD leader Walter Veltroni's appeal to supporters of the now excluded radical left parties, to cast a '*voto utile*' in favour of the only coalition (his own) with a realistic prospect of stopping Berlusconi (Bull and Newell, 2009: 340).

In the aftermath of the election, as the fourth largest party in a now much less fragmented Italian parliament, IdV became a considerable thorn in the side of its larger PD ally. Strengthened by a considerable inflow of votes from former *Ulivo* supporters and supporters of the radical left, and by a system of public funding which tied the amounts available to the votes a party had won, IdV's representatives could now expect, in the much simplified party system that emerged from the election, to get a level of media attention they might once have only dreamt of. There thus followed a series of initiatives designed to outflank the PD, initiatives that would consolidate the images of Di Pietro and IdV as much more consistent and resolute opponents of the incumbent government and prime minister than Veltroni and the PD (Newell, 2009: 90–1).

In the short term, these initiatives were highly successful, enabling, as revealed by local and European elections, the party to grow at the expense of its larger ally (Newell, 2009). In the longer term, Di Pietro found that he had painted himself into a corner: attacks on the PD could only sustain an image of litigiousness on the centre-left, which kept it weak and therefore unattractive as an alternative to a Berlusconi government whose solidity, as the legislature progressed, was undermined by personal rivalries, by scandals and by divisions over how to confront the growing international financial crisis. Twenty years after *Tangentopoli*, promises of cleaner, more effective government seemed to vast swathes to have gone unfulfilled and the mainstream parties to be useless as vehicles for bringing about reform. Thus it was that demands for political overhaul were now expressed in growing support for Grillo's M5S, which, by the local elections of May 2012, was in some areas achieving as much as 20 per cent of the vote, with the established parties in full retreat. This created seemingly impossible dilemmas for Di Pietro thinking of the general election of 2013: already in 2008, when in a famous incident Di Pietro had shared a platform with Grillo, the alliance had led to a number of high-profile resignations from the party (Newell, 2009: 95). The May elections confirmed that a re-edition of the 2008 alliance with the PD would almost certainly be a losing proposition; on the other hand, so might alliance with Grillo, a strategy that also exposed IdV to the risk of losing its distinctive profile. This left the alternative of alliance with the radical left – the one which Di Pietro in the end chose – but this too involved a loss of identity: it was clear under the circumstances that none of the parties alone would clear the 4 per cent exclusion threshold; therefore all were obliged to merge their identities with that of RC, under whose symbol all of their candidates were fielded. The threshold was not cleared in any event. By the end of March 2013, Di Pietro had announced that IdV would be dissolved, eventually to be replaced by a constituent assembly that would give birth to a new party of a liberal democratic and reformist persuasion.

Conclusion

Italian politics is always full of surprises, and predictions, unless heavily qualified, are for the unwary. A few months before this was written few would have been willing to bet that Silvio Berlusconi had much of a political future, but he has made something of a comeback and his 'opposite number', Antonio Di Pietro, may yet do so too. On the other hand, the political adventure of the former prosecutor and his political party does seem to have come to something of a conclusion, permanent or temporary as it might be. In many respects, politician and party were the creation of their arch enemy, Silvio Berlusconi, someone with whom Di Pietro has more than a little in common – like Berlusconi, he is a self-made man; he shares the entrepreneur's unshakeable self-confidence; for him, as for Berlusconi, politics is the means to an extra-political goal – and whose politics were necessary to his own success. In fact it might be said that the two men needed each other: for Berlusconi, Di Pietro was living proof of the desire for political interference of members of the judiciary; for Di Pietro, Berlusconi was the embodiment of immorality in public life. With the outcome of the 2013 election, many argued that the Second Republic which had come into being in the early 1990s had now been eclipsed; few doubted that Italian politics faced a highly uncertain future. What, on the other hand, was certain was that for better or worse Antonio Di Pietro had been one of the key actors, if not the key actor, both in bringing the Second Republic about and, now, in bringing it to an end. He had earned his place in history.

Notes

1 Continued in 2002 with the merger of the Democrats and others to form the *Margherita* (the 'Daisy') and in 2007 with the merger of the *Margherita* and the *Democratici di Sinistra* (Left Democrats, DS) to form the *Partito Democratico* (Democratic Party, PD).
2 Its vote share declined from 3.9 per cent in the 2001 general election to 2.3 in 2006 before almost doubling to 4.4 per cent at the election of 2008.
3 Actually, the matter is slightly more complicated than this, for technical reasons explained in Newell and Bull (2001), but the basic point holds.
4 In Chamber elections voters had two votes: one for the 75 per cent of deputies to be elected in the SMSP arena, another for the 25 per cent to be elected proportionally.

Bibliography

Bull, M. J. and Newell, J. L. (2009). The General Election in Italy, April 2008. *Electoral Studies*, 28 (2), 337–42.

Calise, M. (2000). *Il Partito Personale*. Rome-Bari: Laterza.

Carlucci, A. and Di Pietro, A. (1995). *Grazie Tonino: Le lettere degli italiani al giudice di Mani Pulite*. Milan: Baldini & Castoldi.

Carty, K. R. (2004). Parties as Franchise Systems: The Stratarchical Organizational Imperative. *Party Politics*, 10 (1), 5–24.

Colloca, P., Corbetta, P., Galli, E., Marangoni, F., Passarelli, G., Pedrazzani, A., Pinto, L., Tronconi, F. and Vignati, R (2013). Elezioni politiche del 2013. I flussi elettorali in 9 città: Torino, Brescia, Padova, Bologna, Firenze, Ancona, Napoli, Reggio Calabria, Catania. Available online at www.reset.it/wp-content/uploads/2013/02/Analisi-Istituto-Cattaneo-Elezioni-politiche-2013-Flussi-elettorali.pdf (accessed 7 April 2013).

Di Federico, G. (1989). The Crisis of the Justice System and the Referendum on the Judiciary. In R. Leonardi and P. Corbetta (eds.). *Italian Politics: A Review*, 3 (pp. 25–49). London: Pinter.

Di Pietro, A. (2008). Premessa. In A. Di Pietro and G. Barbacetto. *Il guastafeste: La storia, le idee, le battaglie di un ex magistrato entrato in politica senza chiedere il permesso* (pp. 7–8). Milan: Adriano Salani Editore.

Di Pietro, A. and Barbacetto, G. (2008). *Il guastafeste: La storia, le idee, le battaglie di un ex magistrato entrato in politica senza chiedere il permesso*. Milan: Adriano Salani Editore.

Emanuele, V. (2011). Riscoprire il territorio: dimensione demografica dei comuni e comportamento elettorale in Italia. Paper presented to the annual conference of the Società Italiana di Scienza Politica, Palermo, 8–10 September.

Floridia, A. (2008). Gulliver Unbound. Possible Electoral Reforms and the 2008 Italian Election: Towards an End to 'Fragmented Bipolarity'? *Modern Italy*,16 (3), 317–32.

Floridia, A. (2013). M5S, il partito in franchising alla prova del Parlamento L'intervento. *l'Unità*. 7 March. Available online at http://cerca.unita.it/ARCHIVE/xml/2525000/2522034.xml?key=n.l.&first=181 &orderby=0&f=fir&dbt=arc (accessed 10 April 2013).

Giostra, A. (2009). *Il tribuno: storia politica di Antonio Di Pietro*, Roma: Castelvecchi.

Guarnieri, C. (1997). The Judiciary in the Italian Political Crisis. In M. Bull and M. Rhodes (eds.). *Crisis and Transition in Italian Politics* (pp. 157–75). London: Frank Cass.

Lucardie, P. (2000). Prophets, Purifiers and Prolocutors: Towards a Theory on the Emergence of New Parties. *Party Politics*, 6 (2), 175–85.

McDonnell, D. and Newell, J. L. (2011). Outsider Parties in Government in Western Europe. *Party Politics*, 17 (4), 443–52.

Newell, J. L. (2005). Introduction. In J. A. Garrard and J. L. Newell (eds.). *Scandal in Past and Contemporary Politics* (pp. 1–9). Manchester: Manchester University Press.

Newell, J. L. (2009). Center Left, Radical Left, Anti-Politics and Center: Four Oppositions in Search of a Comeback. In G. Baldini and A. Cento Bull (eds.). *Italian Politics*, 24 (pp. 81–98). New York: Berghahn.

Newell, J. L. (2010). *The Politics of Italy: Governance in a Normal Country*. Cambridge: Cambridge University Press.

Newell, J. L. and Bull, M. J. (2001). The Italian General Election of May 2001. *Keele European Parties Research Unit (KEPRU)*, Working Paper 4, University of Keele.

Pisicchio, P. (2008). *Italia dei valori: Il post partito*. Soveria Mannelli: Rubbettino.

Pozzi, E. (1997). Antonio Di Pietro: invenzione di un Italiano. In S. Berilli (ed.). *La chioma della vittoria: Scritti sull'identità degli italiani dall'Unità alla seconda Repubblica* (pp. 316–53). Florence: Ponte alle Grazie.

Sartori, G. (1976). *Parties and Party Systems: A Framework for Analysis*. Cambridge: Cambridge University Press.

Waters, S. (1994). 'Tangentopoli' and the Emergence of a New Political Order in Italy. *West European Politics*, 17 (1), 169–82.

19

SOCIAL MOVEMENT CAMPAIGNS FROM GLOBAL JUSTICE ACTIVISM TO MOVIMENTO CINQUE STELLE

Maria Fabbri and Mario Diani

On 24–25 February 2013, the Movimento Cinque Stelle (Five Stars Movement, M5S), a political organization officially founded by comedian Beppe Grillo only in 2009, obtains 8,700,000 votes in the elections for the lower chamber (Camera dei Deputati), where it secures 109 MPs, as well as 54 in the Senate. Corresponding to 25 per cent of the vote, this figure makes M5S very close to the Partito Democratico (PD) as the party in the country with most votes.[1] Although M5S cannot be regarded as an offspring of the global justice movement (GJM) that had mobilized in Genoa in 2001 or against the Iraq war in 2003, nor of the subsequent struggles for public morality and in defense of the commons, it cannot be dismissed as a mere expression of anti-politics sentiments either. This is actually the first time in the country that many elements of progressive social movements' agendas co-exist with strong disdain for the established political class within an organization with such a strong parliamentary representation. In this chapter we are going to identify the main lines of contention in the country in the 2000s, paying special attention to the following: the global justice and peace campaigns of 2001–3; the opposition to major public works (*grandi progetti*); the initiatives in support of legality and against (political) corruption; the new wave of contention in 2011 and the emergence of M5S as a major national political actor. We do not claim to provide a thorough account of all the important campaigns that have taken place over the decade. Rather, we look at some processes that are in our view illustrative of the changes that have occurred in the repertoires and organizational forms of contention, and in patterns of social movement representation. Space limitations prevent us from considering the role as promoters of collective action played by right wing organizations like CasaPound, an association connecting grassroots groups that define themselves as "Fascists of the third millennium," follow a model quite close to left-wing social centers, address many themes of the GJM, and attempt to reformulate classic issues of the right-wing agenda such as migration (Toscano and Di Nunzio, 2012).

Global and local justice activism

Since the 1990s, many have tried to combine environmental, women's, peace, human rights, and development issues, central to the "new social movements" agenda (Melucci, 1996), with issues of social exclusion and workers' rights. The crisis of the traditional political cleavages facilitates alliances between organizations from the leftist and the Catholic tradition, promoting both activist campaigns and voluntary work on issues such as cooperation for development, environmental crises both in the North and in the South of the world, labor exploitation, in particular child labor, human rights, and peace issues. Catholic peace and development organizations like Beati costruttori di pace, Pax Christi, and Mani Tese join with environmental groups like Legambiente, grassroots unions like COBAS and cultural associations of the left like ARCI in promoting a counter-summit against the G7 summit in Naples in July 1994 (Reiter, 2007: 54). Italian support for NATO intervention in Kosovo in 1999, approved by the center-left government in 1999, renders the relationship between civil society actors and the institutional left more problematic, but the climax of global justice initiatives is reached in 2001. In July, more than 800 groups join the Genoa Social Forum to challenge the G8 summit, hosted by the newly appointed right-wing government led by Mr. Berlusconi. The meeting will be mostly remembered for the death of a local protestor, Carlo Giuliani, during clashes between the military police and activists from *centri sociali* (social centres), the serious damages to property by small sections of demonstrators, mostly linked to the black bloc, and the unprecedented levels of police violence inflicted on peaceful demonstrators (della Porta *et al.*, 2006). The meeting also vividly illustrates the heterogeneity of the actors mobilized on global justice issues. Some are closest to eco-pacifism, promoting voluntary and solidarity action, fair trade, critical consumption, alongside anti-war and large scale environmental campaigning. Apart from the Catholic organizations or Legambiente, which we have already mentioned, environmental groups like WWF also play a role alongside innumerable local initiatives, coordinated by Rete Lilliput.[2] Others focus primarily on the critique of neo-liberal policies. These include Attac Italy and organizations from the institutional left, such as ARCI, or FIOM, the metalworkers' union of the major left-wing union CGIL.[3] More critical sectors of the movement, such as the *centri sociali* and *tute bianche* (literally "white overalls," from their chosen outfit) and the Network for Global Rights, voice a broader anti-capitalist critique. They have a complex relation to more radical sectors like the anarchists or the black bloc, whose boundaries are admittedly vague (Reiter, 2007: 56–60). Despite the violent repression in Genoa and the difficult political climate following the Twin Towers attack in NYC in September 2001, global justice mobilization continues in the Fall of that year with the organization of the European Social Forum, which mobilizes – this time without incident – hundreds of thousands of demonstrators in Florence in November.

Initiatives on global justice issues continue in the years that follow, through the formation of local social forums, with about 170 being recorded as active in the spring of 2003 (Reiter, 2007: 60). With the intensification of US and allied forces' intervention in Afghanistan and later Iraq, global justice activism increasingly overlaps with peace activism. On 15 February 2003, a vast demonstration takes place in Rome against the imminent attack on Iraq, with over 80 per cent of the participants expressing some level of identification with the GJM (della Porta and Diani, 2004). The demonstration is promoted by the Italian branch of the international coalition Stop the War, with the support of about 400 associations, 350 local councils and 136 MPs. It is preceded and followed by innumerable and diverse local initiatives: occupations of buildings, parades, sit-ins, hunger strikes, prayer vigils. Hugely attended marches occur in various cities on the days following the start of the war (20 March), and again in Rome on 12 April, with about 250,000 demonstrators. On 12 October 2003 the annual peace march from Perugia to Assisi, promoted by Tavola della pace,[4] attracts more than 300,000 people.

After the end of 2003, peace mobilization fragments, and most of the organizations involved in the 2003 campaigns go back to their main areas of intervention, such as defense of the commons, housing, migrant rights, infrastructure, environment, land conservation. Global justice initiatives experience a variable degree of success in the following years. In July 2009, the G8 summit in L'Aquila is challenged by only a few thousand protestors. While this is in line with diminishing attendance at counter-summits and European social forums over the decade (Andretta and Chelotti, 2010), a new phase of intense activism develops in 2011, although it fails to reach the heights and diffusion of the Indignados and Occupy campaigns across the globe (Zamponi, 2012). The most important event of the period will be the demonstration that takes place in Rome on 15 October 2011, as part of the international day of mobilization against economic inequality and the influence of the European Commission, the European Central Bank, and the International Monetary Fund on politics. Endorsed by several political groups on the left of the PD as well as by critical unions, and voicing strong opposition to the neo-liberal policies adopted by the government led by the economist Mario Monti, the protest turns violent, as hundreds of hooded demonstrators attack property and clash violently with the police, with over 100 people injured and 13 arrested.

Throughout the 2000s there are recurrent attempts to bring labor issues back to the core of social movements' agendas. Alongside actions promoted by established "official" (CGIL, CISL, UIL) and "critical" unions (such as COBAS, particularly strong in the public sector), a number of networks mobilize on behalf of workers without basic rights and protection in both the highly qualified and unqualified tertiary sectors. Broadly identified under the label "movimento di San Precario," combining a reference to job precariousness with one to the Christian tradition, these initiatives expand the agenda from job-related issues, on which traditional unionism focuses, to the pursuit of broader rights for the individual citizen. They somehow manage to transform the traditional May Day celebrations, previously dominated by established unions, into occasions for representing broader issues associated with unemployment, precarious jobs, and citizenship rights (Mattoni, 2012; Murgia and Selmi, 2012). Concerns about unemployment and welfare cuts are also voiced at recurring protests by high school and university students against neo-liberal reforms of the education system, for example on the occasion of the Onda Anomala (Anomalous Wave) campaign against cuts to the educational budget and the reform of the education system promoted by the Berlusconi government in the fall of 2008, and of similar initiatives in the spring of 2009, in the fall of 2010 as well as (this time against the Monti government) in the fall of 2012 (Sciolla, 2009).

Fighting for the land: local initiatives against *grandi opere*

In a phase in which large-scale mobilizations are few, because of the weakening of the GJM following 9/11 and the end of the peace campaigns of 2003, and because of the lack of strong mobilizing structures capable of mobilizing huge numbers of people, local struggles take on a new role. Actions against existing plants, damage to local communities, and plans to build new large infrastructure projects with a strong environmental impact (such as those against high-speed trains, or the bridge over the Strait of Messina, or the US military base in Vicenza) attract much broader attention than the areas directly affected and turn in some cases into major national confrontations (della Porta and Piazza, 2008).

The "No Dal Molin" campaign opposes the conversion into a US air force base of the Dal Molin airport, located on the outskirts of the artistic and monumental city of Vicenza, in the north-east region of the Veneto. Originally agreed between the US government and Silvio Berlusconi's government, the plans are confirmed by the center-left administration led by Romano Prodi between 2006 and 2008. The protest campaign starts in 2006 and peaks in February 2007, when about 200,000 people from all over the country demonstrate outside the airport; a few weeks earlier, a protest camp has been set up. From that moment the conflict becomes a major issue for peace and nonviolent campaigners across the country, to whom the local campaign is strongly indebted in terms of repertoires of action, networking practices, and narratives.

At the other extreme of Northern Italy in Piedmont, the "No TAV" protest campaign against the construction of a 57 km tunnel in Val di Susa as a part of a new high-speed railroad (*TAV – Treno Alta Velocità*) between Turin and Lyons is a long-lasting mobilization. It starts back in 1991, promoted by the environmental associations and the mayors of the valley, worried about the environmental and health impact of the excavation works on the local community. In its early phase it consists primarily of information campaigns, promoted by local residents, environmental groups and concerned technical experts from the University of Turin, in dialogue with local institutions. Mobilization in the valley grows after 2000, supported by local "No TAV" citizens' committees, left-wing parties of a communist or environmental persuasion, rank-and-file unions, farmers' associations, social forums, etc. Local activists also start playing a role in broader campaigns and initiatives, such as the 2001 Genoa and Florence Social Forums, and the French campaigns against high-speed railroads. In November 2005, the violence of the police, intervening to evict the occupants of a protest gives the campaign a national dimension, with a large media coverage of the event, followed by a series of rail and road blockades in the valley and by marches held in solidarity throughout Italy (40,000 people). While the Prodi center-left government (2006–8) slows down work on the building sites, though without abandoning the project, works restart in 2009 following Berlusconi's return to power the previous year. On 22 May 2011 activists establish a permanent protest camp in Chiomonte, where excavation work on the preliminary tunnel is supposed to begin. The site will become a major ground of confrontation between protestors and police. At times violence will break out, e.g. on 3 July 2011, when, following a peaceful demonstration with about 60,000 in attendance, some demonstrators lay siege to the building site, which is heavily guarded by the police: in the resulting confrontation about 200 people get injured, 90 per cent of them police officers, and five demonstrators are arrested. The conflict continues up to the present day with periodic traffic blockades and other initiatives, also boosted by the electoral success of M5S, which has an explicit "No-TAV" stance. Throughout the conflict, local administrators play a major role in the opposition to the project, often in explicit contrast to their parties (even at the regional level, the PD is also in favor of the project). Operating through a mix of institutional procedures and public events, the "No-TAV" mayors fail, nonetheless, to gain any attention not only from the government but also from the President of the Republic, Giorgio Napolitano, who refuses to meet them on the occasion of his visit to Turin in March 2012,[5] while protests continue.

Fighting for public morality

Apart from their environmental impact, critics blame big infrastructural projects for the opportunity they open up for large-scale bribes. For example, protestors against the location of waste-disposal areas in Southern Italy insist that they are being largely managed by criminal organizations. Accordingly, mobilizations on *grandi opere* partially overlap with actions on moral and legal issues, the defense of the *stato di diritto*, the equality of citizens before the law, the fight against organized crime as well as corporate crime and its depenalization by the Berlusconi government. While protests have addressed political corruption across the political spectrum, the personal position of Berlusconi as a defendant in innumerable court cases, and as a womanizer driven by a macho culture, has attracted most attention. It is possible to identify a few major waves of mobilization on these themes.

First to emerge is the so-called "movimento dei girotondi" (literally, "circles movement"/ "round dances movement"), which between 2002 and 2003 promotes in many Italian cities actions in support of basic principles of legality and democracy. The newly elected Berlusconi government is not the only one to come under attack, as criticism extends to the leadership of the major center-left Democratici di Sinistra.[6] The name of the campaign comes from its original, distinctive form of action, creating human circles around the buildings of public institutions that need protection from their enemies: law tribunals, public broadcasting stations, etc. While *girotondi* are usually seen as originating from leftist milieus, they have appealed to people of different political persuasions on issues like democracy, defense of the constitution and of freedom of information, and independence of the judiciary. The campaign originates from an appeal that the then chief justice of Milan, Francesco Saverio Borrelli, makes in January 2002 to the citizenry in defense of the judiciary and the basic principles of law. After a first, small demonstration in front of the Ministry of Justice in Rome, a number of public actions occur, including major demonstrations in Florence, with about 15,000 people (January), the first *girotondo* with 4,000 people in Milan two days later, and in Rome on 2 February 2002. This last event, organized by center-left parties, turns into an explicit critique of the traditional left leadership, as popular film director Nanni Moretti vehemently accuses them of political ineptitude and lack of vision. On 23 February in Milan, 40,000 people commemorate with Nobel laureate Dario Fo and other prominent intellectuals the tenth anniversary of the start of the Milan investigation that undermined the political system that emerged from WWII. The event, promoted by the magazine *MicroMega*, is followed by a march in Naples that attracts about 20,000 people. After March the focus moves to the Italian public broadcaster RAI, and Berlsuconi's supposed attempt to reduce its pluralism. For a few months, the network "Girotondi per la democrazia" promotes in several cities an agenda that combines the above-mentioned issues with broader criticisms of Berlusconi's government, targeting for example the reform of the school system promoted by secretary for education Letizia Moratti. However the movement loses momentum and by September is virtually finished. Its trajectory is illustrative of a pattern of a quick rise and a similarly quick disbanding that is quite recurrent in the decade.

A new wave of mobilization corresponds to the start of the second Berlusconi government of the decade in 2008. Regarded as one of the earliest examples of a digital movement in Italy, the Popolo Viola[7] is established originally to oppose attempts by the new Berlusconi government to pass legislation intended to rescue its leader from his legal problems. Under particular attack comes the so-called lodo Alfano, a piece of legislation passed in 2008 that grants immunity to the four highest roles of the state, including the prime minister, from any legal procedures during the period of their incumbency. The opposition against this act, which will be erased by the Constitutional Court the following year, is coordinated through a number of Facebook pages that enable forms of self-organization. The first public event in the "offline" sphere takes place in Rome in December 2009, the "No Berlusconi Day," demanding the resignation of Berlusconi as prime minister and denouncing the crisis of consensus that affects the Italian political class as a whole. Mobilizations continue in 2010. In September splinter groups from the Popolo Viola form the Rete Viola ("Violet Network"), which advocates an organizational model based on local meetings of activists, promoting real-life rather than virtual participation, and coordinated through a national body elected on the basis of principles of direct democracy. Rete Viola promotes several militant initiatives. The first, a protest in front of Berlusconi's villa near Milan, which attracts huge media coverage, degenerates into clashes with the police in which activists from social centers also participate. The agenda of Rete Viola goes beyond legal issues, however, to include unemployment and labor issues, environment, health, and the commons.

The Popolo Viola represents one of the first instances of collective action that largely emerged from the connections existing on the Web between sites associated with several localities and events: it consists of local groups scattered across the country, and communication between groups relies heavily on social networks and the Web (Facebook pages, activists' blogs, dedicated Web TV channels for the streaming of events, an official website, online discussion groups, etc.). This organizational form aids in facilitating communication between dispersed actors but also, and most important, in ensuring multipolar and non-hierarchical forms of coordination (Mosca and Vaccari, 2011). These allow for a multiplicity of perspectives and for different degrees of involvement by specific organizations in any specific campaign or cause; they also contribute to the growth of critical communities that are not associated with a specific location and can neither easily rely on previous organizational forms, nor on the workplace or the local community as foci for mobilization. Several campaigns are mainly located in the virtual sphere, with a few key events conducted offline. One example is the "*Se non ora quando?*" campaign (If not now, when?). On 13 February 2011 almost a million people (not only women) take to the streets in different Italian cities to express outrage at Berlusconi's machismo and his indictment for underage sex and prostitution, but also to address broad issues linked to women's condition in the country (Saraceno, 2012). In a reversal of the most usual pattern, the huge public initiative of February 2011 is not so much an outcome as an inspiration for the establishment of the network, which promotes both offline and (primarily) online activities in the following years (Pavan, 2012). ICT is also particularly helpful in the case of initiatives on issues of broad relevance but unlikely to attract huge constituencies, and therefore mostly promoted by small epistemic communities of like-minded people, such as those on communication rights, or for open software (Padovani and Pavan, 2009).

A distinctive role is played by anti-mafia mobilizations, particularly in Sicily, where they have gained momentum after the killing in 1992 of senior prosecutors Giovanni Falcone and Paolo Borsellino. In 2009, the brother of Paolo Borsellino, Salvatore, is among the promoters of the "red diaries movement," after the color of his sibling's diary, which has mysteriously disappeared from the scene of the killing. The campaign calls for truth to be revealed and justice to be obtained for the mafia killings of the early 1990s. It also aims at protecting, once again, magistrates from the attacks brought against them by politicians and journalists close to Berlusconi. The latest episode in this ongoing confrontation takes place in Milan in March 2013, when Berlusconi's MPs literally invade the tribunal to voice their support for their leader, the victim of a "persecution" by Milan judges, and a counter-demonstration occurs the following day with Mr. Borsellino among the participants. The anti-mafia initiatives are also interesting in that they suggest the spread of "critical consumption" to new terrains. Between 2004 and 2006 groups are founded in Palermo and Catania with the goal of supporting those storekeepers who report extortion from criminal gangs, and inviting consumers to patronize stores whose owners refuse to pay *pizzo*, the slang term for criminal protection – hence the name "Comitati Addiopizzo" ("Farewell Pizzo Committees") (Forno, 2013). Of course, support for businesses that resist organized crime is just one form of critical consumption. A large part of sustainable consumption and fair-trade activities is coordinated through *Gruppi di Acquisto Solidale* (literally, "Solidarity Purchasing Groups"), local networks of citizens coordinating their purchasing practices with a view to supporting greater social and environmental sustainability. While members of these groups cannot be equated with standard social movement activists, they represent a specific community of people sharing similar worldviews and lifestyles, culturally close to many themes of the GJM, as well as of the most critical and socially engaged sectors of the Catholic church (Graziano and Forno, 2012).

The rise of Movimento Cinque Stelle

The "five stars" in the name of M5S represent its five core themes: the safeguarding of public water and the environment, the growth of public transport and Internet connectivity, and sustainable development.[8] It originates from the civic engagement of Beppe Grillo, a well-known comedian, who after reaching popular fame in the 1980s, was denied further access to the national media for his explicitly anti-establishment stances. In the years that follow he performed in highly successful live shows, in which he voiced his opinions on public issues such as political corruption, sustainable development, the criticism of global corporate and financial dominance, or the alternative potential of technology. The creation of his own blog (beppegrillo.it) in 2005 quickly turned Grillo into an influential opinion maker, acknowledged by international media like *Time*, while disconnected from, and indeed in explicit confrontation with the established Italian media scene. The growing influence of the blog led in 2005 to the creation of a number of local groups of sympathizers, coordinated through the meetup.com web platform.[9]

Meetups are the main channel for promoting a series of initiatives aiming primarily at the moralization of Italian politics and in defense of the commons. On 8 September 2007, the first "V-Day"[10] promoted by Grillo attracts 50,000 people at a meeting in Bologna and more in other Italian cities, where 350,000 signatures are collected in support of proposals for new laws preventing people with criminal convictions from serving in the Italian parliament, limiting MPs to two terms, and restoring the old voting system with personal preferences for candidates in national elections. A similar event occurs on 25 April the following year, this time with public subsidy to the media system, regarded as dependent on political parties, as the main target. In 2008 there are also the first instances of participation in local elections with "citizens' lists" (*liste civiche*). The failure of Grillo's attempt to run for the post of secretary of the Democratic Party (PD) prompts his decision to enter the electoral arena directly. On 2 August 2009 Grillo announces the foundation of Movimento 5 Stelle.[11] After good results in the regional elections in Piedmont in 2010 and in Molise in 2011, the local elections of May 2012 see 150 "*grillini*" elected as city councilors and four as mayors, including in an important city like Parma. In October 2012, M5S becomes the largest party at the regional elections in Sicily, with 15 per cent of the vote. Its elected members collaborate with the center-left regional government despite not joining it formally.[12]

The great success of the 2013 elections is probably due to the capacity of M5S to combine the many elements of a GJM agenda (environmentalism, opposition to *grandi opere*, minimum wage for all citizens) with a very strong and aggressive – in many ways, populist – critique of the political class, labeled as a "*casta*" (caste) in its entirety, that resonates with disenchanted sectors of the right-wing electorate. Survey data on voters suggest that they have grown to match almost perfectly the profile of the Italian population in both territorial location and social profile, with a very strong presence (around 50 per cent) among the under twenty-fives (Bordignon and Ceccarini, 2013).

The overall structure of the M5S combines multiple modes of coordination (Diani, 2013). At one level it is still close to the original model of an online community which connects different local groups and individual sympathizers. Local "organizers" promote meetings and other local activities, enabling the shift from the virtual to the offline sphere. The *Movimento* can thus be regarded as a web-like structure consisting of micro-organizations conducting a heterogeneous range of activities. These groups have considerable independence and are only loosely coordinated, at the central level, by the blog, and therefore by Grillo and his team. Control is strict, however, when it comes to constituting an electoral list associated to M5S, in order to compete in elections. On that issue, one needs to receive approval from Grillo himself. Candidates must meet some requirements, such as not to be members of any political party or political organization, have no criminal convictions (even subject to appeal), and not have served on any local council or in any national assembly for more than one term. Another element of centralization has to do with the management of the website, which plays a central role in the life of the organization. This is entrusted to a company specializing in web marketing, Casaleggio Associati. Gianroberto Casaleggio,[13] despite his preference for acting "behind the scenes," is actually a co-founder of M5S with Grillo. His company is responsible not only for the management of the blog but for the Meetup network, the organization's communication strategies, publishing books and pamphlets, and organizing Grillo's tours. The organizational model adopted by M5S seems close to franchising in business, with the brand Cinque Stelle legally owned by Mr. Grillo.

Finally, despite its rhetorical insistence that there be no leaders and that "*uno vale uno*" ("any member is worth one"), the success of the M5S has not changed – if anything, it has reinforced – the process of personalization that has been going on for a long time in the Italian political system. Although activists refer to Grillo as a mere spokesman ("megaphone") for the movement, on crucial issues of national relevance such as possible support for a center-left government, or the vote for the president of the Republic, other prominent members of the organization have always aligned with the "leader." Moreover, the centralization and lack of internal discussion have been pointed out not only by unsympathetic media, but also by some activists of the organization, frustrated, for example, at the ban on appearing on talk shows and the limitations to the contacts that movement representatives in the elected assemblies may have with the media. This has led to expulsions, particularly in Bologna in the fall 2012. However, this particular structure has probably so far spared M5S from the factionalism that has marred the innumerable left-wing groups that since the 1970s have tried to act as political representatives of anti-establishment stances. It has also made the organization more visible – for better or worse – to public opinion. It is of, course, questionable how long this model will survive now that the organization has a significant presence in Parliament and has faced difficult decisions following the elections. In the negotiations for the new government in the spring of 2013 the M5S representatives in Parliament displayed a substantive lack of autonomy vis-à-vis their "leader," Grillo. Dissenting voices (or those who did not abide by the rule of not participating in TV talk shows) found little room within the party, with at least six MPs expelled or leaving the parliamentary group in dissent with the official line between the spring and the summer of 2013.

Conclusions: changing patterns of representation?

While the 2000s have been rich in protest actions, it is more disputable whether coordination between them has been enough to secure the passage from "protest" to "social movements" proper (Diani, 1999). To this end, it is useful to look at the cultural schemata (or frames) with which actions are interpreted. Frames are essential for giving some level of commonality to phenomena of protest that might as well develop in total independence and disconnection from each other. One can indeed speak of social movement processes – as opposed to mere single-issue campaigns – to the extent that there are shared representations of the world that provide some meaningful connection between themes and issues, and some criteria for defining the collectivities involved in them (Diani, 1992 and 2013). Narratives need not be fully comprehensive nor have fully coherent agendas, but actors need some common ground to be able to recognize what connects them to each other and differentiates them from their opponents. In the absence of such characteristics it is difficult to think of collective actors able to change the balance of power within a polity. In Italy up to the 1980s, such a role has been played by some version of anti-capitalism, even allowing for the libertarian nature of some of the great campaigns of the 1970s such as those on abortion and divorce. Since the emergence of environmentalism in the 1980s, however, such ideological glue has lost its power, without really being replaced by any comparably broad narrative. In the 2000s, opposition to capitalism and neo-liberalism as such does not represent even in the case of the GJM the most diffuse narrative, trying to assign meaning to the different actions undertaken in those years. The most common theme is the need for a democratization of the political process from below, coupled with attention to social justice, eco-pacifism, and themes of public morality (Reiter, 2007: 67–71).

Now, several of the themes listed above are certainly present – with variable emphasis –in M5S's program too. But are they enough to provide the basis for a new major political actor, or at least to enable M5S to play a coordinating role for movement sectors? In order to address the question properly we need to reconsider – if very briefly – the relation between civil society, alternative social movements, and the political system. In the 1970s, for all their differences and conflicts, the traditional left and the social movements of the time shared a similar cultural model, critical of capitalist society, and their activists often coexisted in organizations (e.g. the unions, or the cultural associations of the left such as ARCI) that acted as a bridge between movements and parties. Since the 1980s the link between social movements and traditional leftist ideology has become weaker, with the spread of ideas close to the "new social movements" model of personal transformation (Melucci, 1996). Coupled with the growing professionalization of political parties, the relation between social movements of the 1980s or 1990s (most conspicuously, the environmental movement) and the party system has taken the form of ad hoc collaborations on specific issues in a political field characterized by the fragmentation of previous ideological references. There has been, however, an element of continuity in two respects at least. On the one hand, the established parties of the left (the Communist but also the Socialist party in the 1970s, the Democratici di Sinistra in the 1990s, following the disbanding of PCI in 1991) have secured a strong share of the support of people active in the social movement sector, and incorporated several of their issues into their own agenda. On the other hand, attempts to give social movements a direct political representation have kept following a bottom-up approach, with (some) local groups of a movement creating local party branches, linking into regional and ultimately national structures, while keeping strong ties to civil society groups. Parties as diverse as Democrazia Proletaria, Verdi (the Greens), Rifondazione Comunista, and more recently SEL (Sinistra, Ecologia e Libertà) have all followed similar paths, combining critical views of established parties with a will to collaborate on specific issues.[14]

The same pattern of complex webs of alliances between multiple, heterogeneous actors with a variable relation to the established political parties of the center-left can be can be found in most of the mobilizations of the 2000s. For example, the networks mobilizing on behalf of migrants' rights include organizations created by migrants themselves, as well as organizations close to political parties, unions, and the Catholic church, alongside other radical movement organizations (Pilati, 2010). This is also evident in the composition of the committees that support the call for four referendums aiming at abolishing laws enabling the privatization of water resources, reintroducing nuclear power, banished in the late 1980s in the aftermath of the Chernobyl accident, and allowing Berlusconi not to give evidence in court on the ground of his public commitments. For example, the committee mobilizing in particular on public water includes many of the major Italian cultural associations such as ARCI or voluntary groups such as Mani Tese alongside grassroots unions, established unions, Church-related organizations, or local branches of the PD, SEL, or the Greens, and indeed of M5S.[15] The referendum, held in June 2011, results in a resounding success for the proponents, with a 95 per cent rate of approval for all proposals, and more than 50 per cent of electors actually taking part in the vote.

What appears problematic in Italy in the 2000s is, however, translating these single-issue alliances into a broader political project, and eventually into parliamentary politics. First, it is disputable whether the PD would be able to offer social movement activists the same space that the PCI offered social movements of the 1970s and 1980s. While local chapters of the PD have been involved in virtually all the campaigns of the 2000s, the leadership's attitude toward those campaigns has swung between cautious (as in the case of the referenda on public water and nuclear energy) and vehemently hostile (as in the campaigns against high-speed trains). To judge by the electoral results of 2013, PD has only marginally profited from the wave of mobilization that led to success in the June 2011 referenda (one should remember that the absolute majority of the electorate voted not only against the privatization of water but also against laws protecting Berlusconi's interests in courts). It is actually M5S that seems to have gained most of the benefits in electoral terms.

At the same time, it is far from clear whether M5S should be seen as an expression of the social movements of the 2000s. The answer to this is ambiguous. It is certainly the case, and it is reflected in the biographies of the M5S MPs, that many M5S activists and groups have been involved in local initiatives, close to the GJM or to other campaigns such as the one on public water. But the conversion of a group of local and/or single-issue campaigners into a national political actor is not automatic. Likewise, it is certainly true that the decision that M5S took, following the vote of its registered members, to propose Stefano Rodotà, a highly respected law professor, as president of the Republic was shared by many movement activists who were not particularly close to M5S, but recognized the role that Rodotà has played in defense of the commons, particularly as a promoter of the referendum on public water. This candidacy, which was rejected by the PD in favor of a new alliance with Berlusconi to re-elect the outgoing president, Giorgio Napolitano, may have been the first ground on which to test a new alliance between M5S, the SEL party, which also voted for Rodotà in opposition to Napolitano's re-election, the growing number of dissenters within the PD, and many movement activists.

At the same time, some distinctive traits of M5S may prove a major obstacle to the consolidation of such alliance. First, the rigid exclusion of any strategic, and not purely contingent, collaboration with any group somehow linked to existing political parties may cast doubt on the opportunity for social movements to form close links with a party with such a limited coalitional capacity (the formation of a new government supported by both the PD and Berlusconi may be at least partially blamed on M5S's refusal to support a vote of confidence in a government led by the PD leader Pierluigi Bersani). The heavy dependence of M5S on a non-elected leadership when it comes to decisions of national importance may also be a serious problem, especially in light of the fact that a withdrawal by Grillo and/or Casaleggio may deprive activists of the Web infrastructure that enables them to act as a national rather than a mere local political actor. Finally, one should not ignore M5S's outright rejection of the left–right distinction. Not focusing one's approach on anti-capitalism is one thing; claiming that left and right are meaningless, empty categories is quite another, at least for activists of social movements. Rather than the emergence of a unified political actor, the immediate future may well see the consolidation of M5S into an anti-political, populist force, and the emergence of a new political group, including SEL, movement activists, and PD dissenters, with relatively little in common.

Notes

1 Only 148,116 votes separate the two: see http://elezioni.interno.it/ (accessed 24 April 2013).
2 The Lilliput Network is a network of various associations, groups and individuals that since the late 1990s have coordinated various grassroots associations involved in protest campaigns on global justice and solidarity.
3 The CGIL as a confederation decides not to take part in the Genoa mobilization, although they will become fully involved in the aftermath of it (Reiter, 2007).
4 The Peace Table is an original permanent network involving civil society entities (NGOs and social movements) and local government institutions that every two years organizes the march for peace between Perugia and Assisi and the Assembly of Peoples of the United Nations Organization.
5 See e.g. http://torino.repubblica.it/cronaca/2012/03/06/news/napolitano_in_visita_a_torino_non_incontra_i_sindaci_no_tav-31022341 Interestingly, in March 2013 the president will have no problems meeting the representatives of Berlusconi's MPs after they storm the law courts in Milan in protest against their leaders' judicial "persecution" (http://ricerca.repubblica.it/repubblica/archivio/repubblica/2013/03/12/pdl-corteo-assedio-al-tribunale-basta-perseguitare.html?ref=search) (both accessed 27 April 2013).
6 The party disbands in 2007 to found, with former Christian Democrats from the Margherita, the Democratic Party (PD).
7 The name "Violet People" comes from the desire to adopt a color that is not associated with any of the existing political parties.
8 Empirical information for this section comes primarily from Biorcio and Natale (2013), Corbetta and Gualmini (2013), and Bordignon and Ceccarini (2013).
9 Meetup (or meetup.com) is a social network, founded in 2001 in the US and later imported to Italy, that enables people to set up meetings on any subject of interest to them throughout the world. On 21 April 2013 the website beppegrillo.meetup.com reports 1,173 local groups (including very few located abroad) and over 140,000 registered members.
10 Here "V" stands for "*vaffanculo*," a quite crude invitation to politicians to "bugger off."
11 In order to join the organization it suffices to embrace its ideas, commit to respecingt the basic principles outlined in the "non-statute," and contribute to the diffusion of the program, downloadable from the site.
12 By April, 2013, the collaboration is under strain, as even in Sicily M5S regards the PD as too close to Berlusconi's party.
13 Gianroberto Casaleggio has developed a senior career in telecommunications, first at Olivetti, later at Telecom Italia before starting his own business in 2004. He has also authored books and multimedia products that summarize his vision for a future society centered on the Web.
14 Democrazia Proletaria (Proletarian Democracy) starts as an electoral coalition of several left-wing political groups in 1975 and operates until 1991, when it joins hard-liners from the disbanded Communist Party in the new Partito della Rifondazione Comunista (Party of Communist Refoundation, PRC). The Federazione dei Verdi (Federation of the Greens) is created in 1990 out of the merging of two Green political networks that have run in elections in the late 1980s. Both PRC and the Greens have gone through a number of splits and new alliances, with declining electoral success (in the national elections of 2008 and 2013, the coalitions of which they are both part fail to elect any MPs). Sinistra, Ecologia e Libertà (Left, Ecology and Freedom) is founded in 2009 by a group of left-wing and environmental groups. Thanks to its electoral alliance with the Democratic Party it gets 37 MPs in the lower house and 7 in the senate at the February 2013 elections. Later, relations between the two parties dramatically worsen following the re-election of Giorgio Napolitano as president and the formation of a government including both the PD and the PDL.
15 http://www.acquabenecomune.org/raccoltafirme/index.php?option=com_content&view=article&id=47:comitato-referendario-2-si-per-lacqua-bene-comune&catid=34:quesiti&Itemid=139 (accessed 27 April 2013).

Bibliography

Andretta, M. and Chelotti, N. (2010). Il G8 in Italia tra politica e protesta: un caso di successo? In M. Giuliani and E. Jones (eds.), *Politica in Italia 2010*. Bologna: Il Mulino.

Biorcio, R. and Natale, P. (2013). *Politica a 5 stelle. Idee, storia e strategie del movimento di Grillo*. Milan: Feltrinelli.

Bordignon, F. and Ceccarini, L. (2013). Five Stars and a Cricket. Beppe Grillo Shakes Italian Politics. *South European Politics & Society* (in press; published online February 2013, DOI: 10.1080/13608746.2013.775720).

Corbetta, P. and Gualmini, E. (2013). *Il partito di Grillo*. Bologna: Il Mulino.

Della Porta, D. and Diani, M. (2004). "Against the war with no ifs or buts": The Protests Against the Iraq War. In S. Fabbrini and V. della Sala (eds.), *Italy Between Europeanization and Domestic Politics*. Oxford: Berghahn Books.

Della Porta, D. and Piazza, G. (2008). *Le ragioni del no. Le campagne contro la Tav in Val di Susa e il Ponte sullo Stretto*. Milan: Feltrinelli.

Della Porta, D., Andretta, M., Mosca, L. and Reiter, H. (2006). *Globalization From Below: Transnational Activists and Protest Networks*. Minneapolis, MN: University of Minnesota Press.

Diani, M. (1992). The Concept of Social Movement. *Sociological Review*, 40, 1–25.

Diani, M. (1999). Protesta senza movimenti? *Quaderni di Sociologia*, 21, 3–13.

Diani, M. (2013). Organizational Fields and Social Movement Dynamics. In J. van Stekelenburg, C. Roggeband and B. Klandermans (eds.), *The Future of Social Movement Research: Dynamics, Mechanisms, and Processes*. Minneapolis, MN: University of Minnesota Press.

Forno, F. (2013). L'economia solidale forma di autorganizzazione sociale contro la mafia. *Il Ponte*, 69, 85–92.

Graziano, P. and Forno, F. (2012). Political Consumerism and New Forms of Political Participation: The "Gruppi di Acquisto Solidale" in Italy. *Annals of the American Academy of Political and Social Science*, 644, 121–33.

Mattoni, A. (2012). *Media Practices and Protest Politics. How Precarious Workers Mobilise*. London: Ashgate.

Melucci, A. (1996). *Challenging Codes*. Cambridge and New York: Cambridge University Press.

Mosca, L. and Vaccari, C. (eds.) (2011). *Nuovi media, nuova politica? Partecipazione e mobilitazione online da MoveOn al Movimento 5 Stelle*. Milan: FrancoAngeli.

Murgia, A. and Selmi, G. (2012). "Inspire and conspire": Italian precarious workers between self-organization and self-advocacy. *Interface*, 4, 181–96.

Padovani, C. and Pavan, E. (2009). Fra reti tematiche e reti sociali. Un ritratto delle mobilitazioni sui diritti di comunicazione in Italia. *Quaderni di Sociologia*, 53, 11–41.

Pavan, E. (2012). Collective Action within Socio-Technical Systems. Unpublished paper, University of Trento.

Pilati, K. (2010). *La partecipazione politica degli immigrati. Il caso di Milano*. Roma: Armando.

Reiter, H. (2007). The Global Justice Movement in Italy. In D. della Porta (ed.), *The Global Justice Movement*. Boulder, CO: Paradigm.

Saraceno, C. (2012). La protesta delle donne: un successo con molte ombre. In A. Bosco and D. McDonnell (eds.), *Politica in Italia 2012*. Bologna: Il Mulino.

Sciolla, L. (2009). Generazioni nell'Onda. *Il Mulino*, 1, 48–57.

Toscano, E. and Di Nunzio, D. (2012). Il movimento CasaPound: l'affermazione dell'individuo e i limiti per la democrazia. *Rassegna Italiana di Sociologia*, 53, 631–60.

Zamponi, L. (2012). "Why don't Italians Occupy?" Hypotheses on a Failed Mobilisation. *Social Movement Studies*, 11, 416–26.

PART IV

Italian welfare and economy

20

WELFARE, ITALIAN STYLE

From Bismarckian beginnings to crisis and reform[1]

Julia Lynch and Peter Ceretti

At one time, the Italian welfare state was the envy of social reformers in the advanced industrialized nations. International observers lauded Italy's leadership in introducing pension and unemployment insurance programs for agricultural workers as early as 1919; and admired the generous system of family allowances set up in the 1950s and the 1960s (Fargion, 2013: 176; Lynch, 2006: 93). Yet by the late 1980s Italy seemed to offer an object lesson in how not to run a welfare state—and an expensive one, at that. The first section of this chapter describes the development of the main structural features of the Italian welfare state through the end of the First Republic. The second section analyzes reforms and continuities in the Second Republic. Finally, in the third section we assess prospects for significant reform of the Italian welfare state going forward.

A very brief history of the Italian welfare state

The Italian welfare state combines occupationally based social insurance for old age and unemployment; citizenship-based national health insurance; and regionally based provision of social services and safety net programs. The system began in classic Bismarckian style, with benefits conditional on participation in the labor market and gradated according to earnings. The Fascist government expanded the corporatist system of social insurance, further fragmenting it into separate schemes for different groups of workers in order to reward supporters and punish potential opponents of the regime. At the same time, both Liberal (anti-state) and Catholic elements left important traces on the system in the form of weak state participation, inadequate funding, and minimal state intrusion into the spheres of charity and early childhood education (Fargion, 1997; Quine, 2002; Lynch, 2009).

After World War II, the occupational foundations of the Italian welfare state persisted, even as many other countries in Europe began shifting toward social entitlements based on citizenship rather than labor market participation. In 1948, the D'Aragona Commission, convened by the De Gasperi IV government, recommended that Italy consider moving toward a citizenship-based model of social provision similar to Britain's, but opined that in the short to medium term, the country's fiscal infrastructure was better suited to a system in which benefits could be financed by employment-based contributions. Subsequent efforts to broaden and deepen social protection took place primarily through the social insurance system, which expanded to include new groups (e.g. agricultural workers and housewives [Zoli government 1957]; the self-employed [Segni government 1959, Moro III government 1966]); more generous pension benefits (e.g. Fanfani II government 1958, Moro II government 1965); and new programs intended to provide relief for those who were not eligible for full coverage—e.g. minimum pensions (De Gasperi VII government 1952) and social pensions (Rumor I government 1969). By the end of the 1970s, entitlement to income support in old age or in case of disability was nearly universal, with the amount of support largely dependent on the recipient's (or spouse's) employment history.

Despite its strengths and even at the height of its generosity, however, the social insurance system contained blind spots. For example, compared with other Bismarckian welfare states, Italy's regular unemployment insurance benefits were minimal (less than 20 percent of average wages), and first-time job seekers had no protection. Certain groups of laid-off workers could receive *Cassa integrazione guadagni* (CIG and CIGS; regular and extraordinary short-term earnings supplements) and, later, "mobility allowances." However, these forms of income support were subject to discretionary action by the state, not entitlements. Moreover, family allowances languished after 1964 (Moro I and II governments), so that a once generous system designed to provide a substantial benefit to families with children became a minor wage supplement.

A major departure from the occupational model in Italy came in 1978 (under the Andreotti IV government) with the introduction of the Servizio Sanitario Nazionale (SSN), modeled on the British National Health Service. A victory for the Italian left, which was at the peak of its power when the SSN was adopted, the SSN promised healthcare free at the point of service to all Italians. Despite lack of clarity in the financial arrangements governing the system and significant out-of-pocket payments introduced by Liberal health ministers responsible for the SSN's implementation, the Italian healthcare system has been generally well regarded outside of Italy for its universalism, low costs, and good health outputs. However, as will be discussed in the next section, regionalized administration of healthcare services has raised questions about the equity and fiscal sustainability of healthcare in Italy.

Aside from healthcare, other typical elements of a citizenship-based welfare state, such as robust social services and a national minimum income, remain conspicuous by their absence in Italy. As we have seen, elements of income protection—minimum pensions, social pensions, and disability pensions—were integrated into the occupational social insurance system. However, Italy did not develop a statutory minimum income guarantee, and poverty alleviation and other social services remained almost entirely in the hands of local and regional authorities. Regional variation in entitlements, actual availability of services, and quality of services resulted in a highly variable "geography of citizenship" (Fargion, 1997).

By the 1980s, Italian policymakers recognized systemic problems with their welfare state. Incomplete protection against social risks combined with structural unemployment and underdevelopment in Italy's Mezzogiorno to produce heavy demands on those social insurance and other programs such as disability pensions or minimum pensions that could be used, often illicitly, to buffer incomes. Italy's already expensive contribution-financed occupational pension system was thus additionally burdened with social assistance functions. Some of the costs of this system were covered by the government via deficit spending, which was sustainable only as long as Italy maintained control over its own currency exchange rates. Some restrictions were placed on the improper use of social insurance benefits from the mid-1980s (e.g. introduction of a means test for receipt of minimum pensions in 1983 and reform of eligibility for disability pensions in 1984, both under the Craxi I government). But at the same time, the social insurance system continued to grow, with more generous indexation of high-end pensions introduced in 1983 (Craxi I government), and a rise in the ceiling on earnings allowed to count toward setting the level of pensions in 1988 (Goria government). In 1990 (Andreotti VI government), self-employed persons were permitted to opt into the system at a contribution rate far lower than that paid by employees and their employers (12 percent vs. 25.9 percent of wages). To combat growing debts in the social insurance system, contributions were raised five times between 1980 and 1990, which created a "fiscal wedge" that made it expensive for employers to hire additional workers. This contributed to higher unemployment and to the development of two classes of workers in Italy: overprotected, often older, labor market "insiders" who enjoyed generous pensions and supplemental unemployment protection; and underprotected, often younger "outsiders" who spent long spells without work or in the informal labor market with no benefits.

By the dawn of the Second Republic, then, the Italian welfare state faced several structural problems: stark regional divergence in social protection; incomplete protection against both "old" social risks such as unemployment or earnings insufficient to support a large family, and "new" social risks such as youth unemployment or child care needs due to female employment; systematic misuse of benefits such as disability pensions to make up for poor employment prospects; fiscally

Table 20.1 Italian social spending, poverty and inequality in comparative perspective

	Public social spending % of GDP (2012)	*Relative poverty rate: total population (2004–5)*	*Relative poverty rate: children (2004–5)*	*Gini, household disposable income (2007)*
US	19.5	17.189	20.945	0.37
Spain	25.3	14.092	17.256	0.313
Ireland	19.8	13.209	15.857	0.289
Canada	19.3	12.977	16.872	0.328
Australia	16.1	12.187	13.96	0.324
Italy	**26.4**	**12.038**	**18.256**	**0.334**
Greece	23.1	11.867	12.429	0.307
UK	22.9	11.221	12.983	0.345
Luxembourg	23.6	8.882	13.494	0.292
Germany	25.8	8.518	10.9	0.3
France	29.9	8.489	10.174	0.292
Switzerland	18.5	8.001	9.308	0.29
Norway	22.4	7.073	5.264	0.256
Austria	28.1	7.07	6.82	0.261
Finland	28.0	6.617	4.008	0.258
Netherlands	21.5	6.338	9.15	0.297
Sweden	26.5	5.596	4.72	0.259
Denmark	29.5	5.586	3.872	0.243

Total public social expenditure from OECD (2013), OECD Social Expenditure Database.

Poverty rates calculated as share of population with size-adjusted household incomes below 50% of national median income. Data from Luxembourg Income Study (2013), Key Figures.

Gini coefficient from OECD (2011). *Divided We Stand: Why Inequality Keeps Rising* (available online at www.oecd.org/els/social/inequality).

unsustainable social insurance programs; an insider/outsider cleavage in the labor market and the occupational benefits linked to labor market participation; and intergenerational imbalances in both access to social protection and responsibility for financing the system. The absence of a nationwide safety net exacerbated pre-existing divergences in living standards resulting from varying levels of economic development between Italy's North and South, so that despite social welfare spending near the West European average (23.7 percent of GDP in 1990, versus the EU15 average of 24.4 percent [Eurostat]), levels of poverty and inequality in Italy have approached those in the United States (see Table 20.1).

The incomplete transformation of the Italian welfare state during the Second Republic

As the First Republic began to crumble, the speculative crisis that forced Italy's exit from the European Monetary System in 1992 made it clear that comprehensive welfare state reform could wait no longer. Stabilizing the public finances and structural reforms to the economy suddenly became urgent priorities, and the next twenty years saw an incremental series of reforms to pensions, unemployment benefits, healthcare, and social assistance. These efforts have been more successful in some areas (e.g. pensions) than others (e.g. social assistance).

Pensions

Pension spending had reached 12.8 percent of GDP in 1992, and was projected to balloon to 23.4 percent of GDP by 2040 if left unchecked (Ferrera and Jessoula, 2007: 431). Measures adopted since 1992 have gradually harmonized pension eligibility requirements between genders and across sectors, increased the retirement age, and curbed seniority pensions (available to those below the statutory retirement age who have made a certain number of years of contributions). As a result, the sustainability of the social insurance system has greatly increased, but the pace of adjustment has begun to raise new concerns about generational fairness, pension adequacy, and poverty in old age.

The pension reform process began with the Amato reform in 1992, which lengthened the reference period for calculating benefits, adjusted indexation, increased the retirement age for private sector workers, and gradually raised contributory requirements for seniority pensions. The Dini government passed another significant reform in 1995, introducing a flexible retirement age and shifting from a defined-benefit to a "notional defined contribution" system, in which workers' accumulated contributions are linked more directly to eventual benefits. However, the price of union support for both the Amato and the Dini reforms was a slow phase-in period to protect older workers (Schludi, 2005: 116; Ferrera and Jessoula, 2007: 433–7; Schludi, 2005: 56).

Subsequent reforms in 1996 and 2004 further tightened requirements for seniority pensions, introduced incentives to forgo early retirement, and gradually increased the retirement age. In 2009–10, in response to the financial and sovereign debt crises, retirement ages for men and women in the public sector were made identical, the statutory retirement age was linked to life expectancy, and retirement flexibility was limited (Jessoula, 2012: 14–15). Finally, under pressure from the European Central Bank, the 2011 Fornero reform sped up the phase-in of the Dini reform and post-crisis measures. All benefits accrued since 2012 are now calculated according to the new formula. Indexation of benefits to aggregate life expectancy and harmonization of pension plans have been accelerated, and retirement flexibility has been restored. Seniority pensions have been replaced with an early retirement scheme that penalizes retirement before 62. By 2018, the retirement age is projected to be a uniform 66 years and 7 months for all, increasing to at least 67 by 2021.

Steps have also been taken since 1993 to develop funded, supplementary pensions on both an individual and a collective basis. Nevertheless, supplementary pensions remain fragmented across occupational and geographic lines, and coverage is limited. At the end of 2011, supplementary schemes covered about 5.5 million workers, or 24 percent of those employed (Finocchiaro, 2012: 11). While still modest, the coverage rate is a substantial increase over 2005, when only 13 percent of workers were enrolled (Coletto, 2007). In other regards, however, the changes to the pension system have been significant, and signal a breakthrough of the policy stalemate of the First Republic that had protected pension spending at the expense of more thorough protection for non-elderly Italians, particularly labor market outsiders.

Unemployment benefits

In contrast to pensions, since the early 1990s unemployment benefits have become more generous, but starting from a very low level. By 1993, the ordinary unemployment benefit (OUB) was still substantially less generous than in most other European countries, but had been raised to a 25 percent replacement rate (with duration capped at 6 months, and substantial insurance and contribution requirements: 2 years of insurance coverage, and 52 weeks of contributions in the year before unemployment) (Madama and Coletto, 2009). Between 2001 and 2008, both duration and generosity gradually rose, but benefits were differentiated according to age, with longer and more generous benefits for older workers (Leombruni *et al.*, 2012: 11–12). Unemployment benefits were also limited mainly to cases of involuntary job loss and tied more tightly to availability to work than in the past (Sacchi and Vesan, 2011: 8).

The Monti government's 2012 labor reform then made broader changes to unemployment insurance, bringing the replacement rate closer to the 80 percent offered by the CIG/CIGS schemes and phasing out mobility allowances as of 2017 (CGIL Rimini, 2012). The reform replaced the standard OUB with a new "social insurance for employment" benefit (Aspi) from January 2013. Contribution and insurance requirements remain the same, but the duration and age differentiation of benefits have been adjusted, and coverage expanded. When fully phased in, the Aspi will last a maximum of 12 months for workers up to 55 years of age, and 18 months for those 55 and over. The replacement rate is 75 percent for monthly incomes up to €1,180 in 2012, bringing the benefit in line with that offered in other European countries. The benefit falls to 60 percent for months 6–12, and to 45 percent thereafter. Eligibility has been extended to all categories of dependent employees, and coverage is expected to increase from about 4 million workers in 2013 to 12 million in 2017 (Consiglio Nazionale Economie e Lavoro [CNEL], 2012: 247–8, 262).

Given the high contributory and insurance requirements for the OUB and Aspi, younger and temporary workers are more likely to qualify for the less generous "reduced requirement unemployment benefit" (RUB), which by 2012 had a 35 percent replacement rate for the first 4 months of eligibility, and 40 percent thereafter, for up to 6 months (CGIL Rimini, 2012). Until the Monti government's reform, the RUB had a lengthy insurance requirement (2 years of insurance coverage), but lower contributory requisites than the OUB (78 days in the year before unemployment). However, the benefit was paid out in a lump sum in the year after job loss (Madama and Coletto, 2009). The 2012 Monti reform set the replacement rate of the RUB, renamed the "mini-Aspi," equal to that of the full-fledged Aspi. The insurance requirement has been eliminated, but the contributory requirement has been increased (13 weeks in the year before job loss). Workers will now be able to collect the benefit for half as many weeks as they contributed in the previous year. Not only has coverage been expanded as in the case of the Aspi, but the benefit is also paid out at the time of job loss, which eliminates the peculiar *ex post* nature of the RUB (CGIL Rimini, 2012).

Expanding and strengthening the Aspi and mini-Aspi required additional contribution-based financing, which aggravated the already substantial tax wedge on employment. To finance the new unemployment benefits, employers now pay a further 1.61 percent for apprentices and regular employees on top of the prior total social contribution of 33 percent of wages (shared by employers and employees). The contribution addition is 3.01 percent for fixed-term contracts, both to increase the attractiveness of apprenticeships and to cover the higher likelihood of recourse to the Aspi or mini-Aspi by less-protected temporary workers.

Despite significant improvements in social protection for the unemployed in Italy since the start of the Second Republic, labor market "outsiders" remain vulnerable. For example, most workers on short-term contracts are eligible only for mini-Aspi benefits, with a maximum duration of 26 weeks. Similarly, formally self-employed workers under contract to single firms must bear the costs of their own insurance. In short, the social insurance logic of the Italian welfare system is poorly adapted to an economic reality in which 60 percent of new jobs are "atypical" (part-time, fixed-term, or contracted-out) (Fargion, 2013: 189).

Healthcare

Like unemployment and social insurance, Italy's healthcare system has also undergone profound changes over the last twenty years. Reforms have professionalized management, increased the role of the private sector in care provision, and devolved policy-setting competencies to regional governments (Jessoula and Pavolini, 2012: 16). Despite these changes, serious quantitative and qualitative disparities between the North and South persist; and while Italian healthcare spending is lower than in many other rich democracies, cost containment remains a challenge in some regions.

The healthcare reform process began with the 1992 "reform of the [1978] reform," which began the decentralization of the healthcare system and introduced greater competition in care provision (Ferrera and Gualmini, 2004: 114; Frisina Doetter and Götze, 2011: 4). Health agencies and larger hospitals previously run by elected committees and political appointees were given over to professional executives, and were required to run balanced budgets to keep their independence. Deficits were to be covered by regional tax additions or higher co-pays. The central government retained its planning role, providing the regions with funding to deliver a standard package of mandatory or "essential" services (LEAs).

A third healthcare reform in 1999 and other legislation passed between 1998 and 2000 accelerated regional devolution and created new funding sources. The 1999 reform reorganized the national government's and the regions' financing responsibilities, restricted the private activities of full-time SSN doctors, and altered regulations on supplementary health insurance funds (Ferrera and Gualmini, 2004: 117). During this period, a regional business tax (the IRAP) was introduced to finance healthcare spending; revenue sharing and the scope for regional tax additions were expanded; and a redistributive fund was created to complement the regions' independent resources (Frisina Doetter and Götze, 2011: 6). Finally, in 2001, the reform of Title V of the Italian Constitution confirmed the regions' responsibility for organizing and delivering healthcare.

In 2009, the third Berlusconi government's framework law on fiscal federalism attempted to link funding allotted to the regions to cover essential services to "standard cost" benchmarks, determined by the cost of provision in several regions with "virtuous," efficient healthcare systems. However, the Monti government left the standard cost provisions unimplemented: federalization was not a priority for Monti's technocratic administration, which was appointed with a mandate to stabilize the public finances and enact structural reforms. In fact, in an effort to control spending, Monti instead sought to reassert central government's primacy over local administrations. As a result, the financing of regional health budgets remains in limbo until cost benchmarks can be worked out.

Social assistance

As with healthcare, progress in the field of social assistance got off to a bright start in the Second Republic, but in contrast to other welfare policy areas, eventually flagged. The overall picture is one of an attempted transition to a universal system that was halted by the process of federalization and devolution. As a result, social assistance remains regionally variegated and largely transfer-based, with services in kind insufficient to meet demand, particularly in many Southern regions.

The path to reforming social assistance began with the Onofri Commission, which was tasked with reviewing the performance of the welfare state in 1997. The Onofri Commission's final report recommended a citizenship-based assistance architecture and more effective selection criteria for determining eligibility. It also called for further decentralization of service provision, a greater emphasis on services in kind rather than cash transfers, and better offerings in the areas of long-term care and child care, among other reforms (Bosi *et al.*, 2003: 2–3).

Although the Commission prescribed incisive reforms to pensions, healthcare, and unemployment insurance, as well, social assistance was one of the few areas where its recommendations were taken up in earnest (Ferrera and Gualmini, 2004: 114–20). In response to the Onofri Commision's recommendations, and satisfying a long-term desideratum of both unions and large employers that social assistance functions be separated from the contribution-based social insurance system, the Prodi government passed clearer, more transparent rules on social assistance financing. Then, in the 1998 budget law, provisions were laid out for an experimental "minimum insertion income" (RMI), a means-tested minimum wage with an activation component. A new scale for measuring eligibility, the "indicator of the economic social equivalent" (ISEE), was also introduced. The ISEE would be applied to all new means-tested benefits (Ferrera and Gualmini, 2004: 117; Sacchi and Bastagli, 2005: 68).

The most important innovation was a framework law on social assistance, adopted in 2000. The planning architecture was modeled on the healthcare system, which allowed the government to set national standards for decentralized provision of child care, elder care, rehabilitation, and other social services. The law fit into the federalization process by defining national, regional, provincial, and municipal responsibilities for social assistance. However, it also gave the state firm powers to set guidelines for various aspects of assistance policy through national plans (Sacchi and Bastagli, 2005: 69). Nevertheless, the new policy framework was only used briefly, however, as the 2001 constitutional reform devolved greater control over social assistance to regional and local governments, much as in the area of healthcare policy. Central government planning powers were watered down, and although the state still retains the power to set essential levels of provision for social assistance transfers and services, crafting territorially coherent policies is now much more difficult (Sacchi and Bastagli, 2005: 70), and very substantial regional variation in provision remains (Fargion, 2013).

Poverty and family policy

Poverty has long been a challenge for Italy, particularly among children, a group for whom Italy still has by far the highest poverty rate in Western Europe (see Table 20.1). Absolute measures of deprivation confirm the vulnerability of families with three or more children (Coromaldi and Zoli, 2012; Devicienti *et al.*, 2012; Sacchi and Bastagli, 2005). These same studies also reveal a marked North–South divergence in relative and absolute poverty; in 2002, poverty rates in the South and Islands were more than three times higher than in the Center, and four and a half times higher than those in the North (Sacchi and Bastagli, 2005: 73). However, after its experimental period ended in 2002, the RMI was discontinued. Thus, Italy still lacks a national minimum income that could effectively combat poverty.

A number of categorical benefits have anti-poverty effects. "Civil disability" pensions have no contribution requirement, and are intended for those who are almost totally disabled. The "social allowance," introduced by the Dini reform of 1995 to replace social pensions, can be collected by those over 65 who are ineligible for a pension, or whose contributions would yield a monthly pension less than the social allowance itself.[2] Within the social insurance system, means-tested family allowances, pension supplements (available until the Dini reform), disability pensions, and inability pensions for those totally disabled all play some poverty-alleviation role (Sacchi and Bastagli, 2005: 80). Since 1999, a means-tested benefit for all families with three or more children (*assegno per il nucleo familiare*) has been available to Italian and other EU-member families resident in Italy. Arcanjo *et al.* (2013: 16) estimate, however, that family cash benefits reduce child poverty in Italy by only 8 percent.

The same legislation also provided for a new, five-month maternity benefit for legal resident households ineligible for an insurance-based maternity benefit. Means-testing is performed according to the ISEE (Sacchi and Bastagli, 2005: 80). Despite these new additions, the Italian family policy arsenal remains antiquated. For example, child care spaces are inadequate to meet demand in many regions, and private solutions have not been adequate to fill the gap (Da Roit and Sabatinelli, 2013). Italian family policy has lagged behind other European countries in other respects as well: very low replacement rates (30 percent of wages) result in low take-up of parental leave by fathers, and many primary schools in southern Italy lack cafeterias, which stunts female labor force participation (Naldini and Jurado, 2013: 52–5).

Reforms in political context

Many of the changes in the Italian welfare state since the 1990s are due to the transformation of Italy's domestic politics and international position since *Tangentopoli*, and the commitment to join the EU's Economic and Monetary Union (EMU). The politics of decentralization have also strongly affected the evolution of the welfare state in the areas of healthcare and social assistance. While pressure from the Northern League triggered the start of federalization of the Italian state, this policy "solution" was adopted by the center-left and center-right alike as something of a panacea with respect to healthcare and welfare (Fargion, 2005: 139; Frisina Doetter and Götze, 2011: 6). Federalization has not always led to positive outcomes, as persistent healthcare disparities (especially between northern and southern regions) and the stunted process of social assistance reform demonstrate.

The external constraints posed by financial markets and deepening European integration have also played an instrumental role in encouraging reform (Ferrera and Gualmini, 2004; Jessoula, 2012). In the 1990s, the goal of EMU accession pushed the social partners and technocratic (or left-leaning, partly technocratic) governments into a process of institutional learning.

The search for policy solutions in an adverse fiscal climate led unions, employers, and governments to collaborate on measures such as the Dini reform and a series of social pacts. In addition, EU initiatives such as the European Employment Strategy helped to clarify policy priorities and increase institutional capacity (Ferrera and Gualmini, 2004: 104).

In recent years, welfare state reform has been less collaborative, though the external constraints are as real as ever and continue to tighten in step with European fiscal integration. This point is underscored by the experience of the Monti government, which was appointed largely in response to pressure from financial markets and EU institutions, and relied on these external factors to facilitate the passage of strict austerity measures and pension and labor reforms (Jessoula, 2012: 25–7).

In light of the results of the 2013 parliamentary elections, in which the center-left "Italy, Common Good" coalition and Mario Monti's centrists were penalized by the public for supporting austere fiscal policy and structural reforms, the outlook for future changes to the welfare state is uncertain. The scope for collaboration with the social partners also appears to have diminished in recent years, thanks in part to the heavy-handed approach to negotiations espoused by the center-right under Berlusconi and the severity of the reforms imposed by the Monti government. With a public suffering from the beginnings of reform fatigue and significant developments in the party system underway, it looks increasingly unlikely that the changes in the welfare state to come will be well-planned, far-sighted ones. Despite significant progress in recent years, welfare state reform is now in a "holding pattern," awaiting the emergence of a government with a political mandate strong enough to continue the work left unfinished in the Second Republic.

Sources of policy stability in welfare *all'italiana*

Why has the Italian welfare state, with its recognized territorial, generational, gender and insider/outsider inequities, proved resistant to fundamental change? The nature of political competition in Italy—marked as it is by longstanding patterns of clientelism and conflict over territorial economic divergence—constitutes a serious impediment to reform. This impediment has persisted throughout the First and into the Second Republic, and continues to bedevil serious welfare reform efforts.

Clientelist political competition during the First Republic, aided and abetted by a pattern of polarized pluralism in the party system (Ferrera *et al.*, 2012), was directly responsible for many of the Italian welfare state's pathologies, including the insider/outsider cleavage and the strong elderly and male-breadwinner orientation (see Lynch, 2006 for more detail). A tradition of exchanging tailored policies and even individual benefits for votes in Italy helped maintain occupationalist welfare programs even in the face of calls by high-level commissions (the CNEL in 1963, the Onofri Commission in 1992) for a system of universal benefits. Extreme fragmentation of pensions, in particular, benefited clientelist politicians, but made it difficult for citizens and even policy specialists to project the long-term budgetary consequences—which were grave indeed when combined with population aging, declining labor force participation, and a weakening contribution base. The use of selective welfare benefits for clientelist purposes, predominantly by the DC and later the PSI, altered the preferences of those political actors who had an ideological affinity for more equitable universalist solutions: the PCI and labor unions came to fear that expansion of the state's role in the areas of unemployment insurance and poverty relief would provide even more fodder for DC and PSI clientelist activities, and so eventually opposed universalizing reforms despite having shown some enthusiasm for them in the early post-war period. Additionally, since the PCI was excluded from power under the system of polarized pluralism, it was tempted to make promises in the realm of welfare policy that it would never have to keep, which led to a pattern of leap-frogging promises that resulted in the extraordinarily generous and expensive pension system put in place from 1969 (Ferrera *et al.*, 2012).

Clientelism, then, was a major determinant of the configuration of the welfare regime up to the end of the First Republic. And because welfare state policies are complex institutions that tend to "stick" once enacted, the Italian welfare state still bears strong traces of this aspect of political competition that so dominated the political context of the First Republic. Does clientelism pose a continued obstacle to reform in the Second Republic? Persistent scandals in regional healthcare administrations—Lazio and Lombardy are two prominent examples—suggest that despite the disappearance of the two parties most implicated in clientelism during the First Republic, the longstanding link between the Italian welfare state and clientelist politics has yet to be dissolved. Under Berlusconi, the familiar pattern of clientelist exchange appears to have been grafted onto a neo-liberal agenda. The protection of key center-right clienteles—for instance, business owners and professionals for the PdL, northern pensioners for the Northern League—has led to ambiguous stances on tax evasion and hesitance to overhaul certain welfare policy instruments, such as seniority pensions. All of these factors have tended to slow the process of recalibration initiated in the early years of the Second Republic.

The second key feature of Italian politics that has rendered the welfare state so resistant to thoroughgoing reform is the perennial political salience of the North–South economic divide. Throughout its history, many aspects of the Italian welfare state were invented or survived because they provided a political buffer against the economic mal-integration of the South. For example, minimum, seniority, and disability pensions have all found political support in part because of the way they have been (mis)used as subsidies for underemployment and low household incomes in the South. Until the regional economic divide lessens, there will be political pressure to retain those aspects of the welfare state that provide resources for Southern families—even if rebuilding the entire edifice of the welfare state might itself contribute to lessening the economic divide, and could in any case lead to more effective and efficient policies.

Of course, the welfare state itself has also served as a cause of interregional tensions. The Lega Nord's cries of "*Roma ladrona*" refer not only to politicians on the take, but also to government social spending that the party claims benefits the South at the expense of the North. The federalizing reforms pushed by the Lega Nord have resulted in substantial regional autonomy in the health and social assistance sectors, while tensions over newly visible fiscal transfers between regions necessitated by federalization have hindered both national-level oversight and the eventual completion of these decentralization processes. Further, while devolution has led to some fruitful experiments in alternative welfare and healthcare models at the sub-national level, continuing regional disparities in the benefits and services available to citizens have also occasioned invidious political comparisons, and make it difficult to rationalize the state's investment in major infrastructure such as hospitals and medical centers to reduce costs and create greater geographic equity in access to healthcare.

Prospects for further reform

Italy's social insurance model is highly resilient. Transformation to a universal, citizenship-based model with flat-rate benefits is exceedingly unlikely. At best, Italy will probably come to more closely resemble the continental social insurance systems of Germany, the Netherlands, or France. Furthermore, while pressure from international financial actors to increase productivity and decrease unit labor costs could provoke some convergence, the structural economic differences between Italy's North and South also seem unlikely to recede. Should we then expect the Italian welfare state's occupational, insider-protecting, and regionally variegated welfare state to persist indefinitely?

Perhaps not. Once reform of the electoral law is accomplished, there may be opportunities for subsequent governments to undertake further reform. We see three reasons for cautious optimism in this regard. First, the financial crisis has brought pressure from the ECB and international financial actors that introduces a fundamentally new kind of *vincolo esterno*. Instead of demanding adherence to general fiscal targets, generating fixes that may unravel once targets have been met, international actors are now pressing for (and receiving) very specific reforms. For example, the ECB outlined a series of specific pension reforms that needed to be undertaken after 2011 in return for Frankfurt's support in secondary bond markets (Jessoula, 2012: 25). This significant reduction in domestic policy autonomy may generate political ill will toward both European and domestic political elites, and it is almost certain to result in a decrease in the total resources available for social protection. On the other hand, it may also give reformers the political cover needed to undertake very unpopular reforms, freeing up resources to devote to new protections for labor market outsiders and younger Italians.

A second cause for cautious optimism is that the details of fiscal federalism cannot remain in limbo indefinitely. Unless the federalist project is abandoned altogether, which seems unlikely at this point, standard costs will have to be defined. Once this occurs, the central government will have increased control over health and social assistance spending, and may also be able to press for greater uniformity of social provision across regions.

Third, and most speculatively, there are indications that the Italian welfare state's harsh intergenerational inequities—which despite the quicker phase-in of pension reforms may have actually gotten worse since the crisis—have finally generated a meaningful political backlash. After decades of gerontocracy, the recent elections have returned a younger parliament than in France, Germany, Spain, Great Britain, or the United States. There is also a larger share of female parliamentarians than in the past (Coldiretti, 2013), which may be a result of the primaries held by the PD and M5S. This parliament is unlikely to last long, or to undertake any substantial welfare policy changes. But if parties continue to hold primary contests, it seems likely that the increase in younger and female parliamentarians may also persist and lead to a reorientation of welfare policy away from highly protected insiders, and toward the needs of families and younger workers.

Notes

1 This chapter was drafted in March 2013, shortly after Italy's general elections and at a moment of considerable political volatility. Since then, the political outlook has changed significantly, and some welfare policy changes—most notably with respect to the unemployment insurance system—are currently under way or have already been enacted.

2 Thanks to the third Berlusconi government's pension measures and the Fornero reform, the eligibility age for the social allowance is now indexed to life expectancy, much like the retirement age. This means that the elderly poor will effectively be forced to wait longer for relief as the eligibility requirement is revised upwards over time (Jessoula and Pavolini, 2012: 140).

Bibliography

Arcanjo, M., Bastos, A., Nunes, F. and Passos (2013). Child poverty and the reform of family cash benefits. *Journal of Socio-Economics*, 43, 11–23.

Bosi, P., Dirindin, N. and Turati, G. (2003). Reform paths in Italian health and social assistance expenditure. *The Consolidation of the General Budget in Italy: Tools, Costs, and Benefits*. Available online at http://www.esri.go.jp/jp/prj-rc/macro/macro15/10-4-R.pdf (accessed 9 March 2013).

CGIL Rimini (2012). Mini A.S.P.I. (Come cambia la disoccupazione stagionale). Available online at http://www.cgilrimini.it/ARCHIVIO/Volantini/volantinoDSstagionale2013.pdf (accessed 16 March 2013).

Coldiretti (2013). Elezioni: Coldiretti, parlamento più giovane storia. 48 anni in media. Available online at http://www2.coldiretti.it/News/Pagine/141-26-Febbraio-2013.aspx (accessed 18 March 2013).

Coletto, D. (2007). Agreement reached on end-of-service allowance. Available online at http://www.eurofound.europa.eu/eiro/2006/11/articles/it0611039i.htm (accessed 21 October 2012).

Consiglio Nazionale Economie e Lavoro (CNEL) (2012). Rapporto sul mercato di lavoro 2011–2012. Rome.

Coromaldi, M. and Zoli M. (2012). Deriving multidimensional poverty indicators: methodological issues and an empirical analysis for Italy. *Social Indicators Research*, 107 (1), 1–18.

Da Roit, B. and Sabatinelli, S. (2013). Nothing on the move or just going private? Understanding the freeze on child- and eldercare policies and the development of care markets in Italy. *Social Politics*, 20 (3): 430–53.

Devicienti, F., Gualtieri, V. and Rossi, M. (2012). The persistence of income poverty and lifestyle deprivation: evidence from Italy. *Bulletin of Economic Research*, 66 (3), 246–78.

Eurostat (2013). Main tables. Social protection. Expenditure on social protection (tps_00098). Available online at http://epp.eurostat.ec.europa.eu/tgm/table.do?tab=table&init=1&language=en&pcode=tps00098&plugin=1 (accessed 26 August 2013).

Fargion, V. (1997). *Geografia della cittadinanza sociale in Italia: regioni e politiche assistenziali dagli anni settanta agli anni novanta*. Bologna: Il Mulino.

Fargion, V. (2005). From the Southern to the Northern Question: territorial and social politics in Italy. In N. McEwen and L. Moreno (eds.), *The Territorial Politics of Welfare* (pp. 127–47). London: Routledge.

Fargion, V. (2013). Italy: a territorial and generational divide in social citizenship. In A. Evers and A. M. Guillemard (eds.), *Social Policy and Citizenship: The Changing Landscape*. Oxford and New York: Oxford University Press.

Ferrera, M., Fargion, V. and Jessoula, M. (2012). *Alle radici del welfare all'italiana: origini e futuro di un modello sociale squilibrato*. Venice: Marsilio.

Ferrera, M. and Gualmini E. (2004). *Rescued by Europe? Social and Labour Market Reforms in Italy from Maastricht to Berlusconi*. Amsterdam: Amsterdam University Press.

Ferrera, M. and Jessoula M. (2007). Italy: a narrow gate for path-shift. In K. Anderson, E. Immergut and I. Schulz (eds.), *Handbook of West European Pension Politics* (pp. 396–453). Oxford and New York: Oxford University Press.

Finocchiaro, A. (2012). COVIP: Commissione Di Vigilanza Sui Fondi Pensione: Relazione per L'Anno 2011: Considerazioni Del Presidente. Available online at http://www.covip.it/wp-content/files_mf/1337766508RelazionePresidente2011.pdf (accessed 20 October 2012).

Frisina Doetter, L. and Götze, R. (2011). The changing role of the state in the Italian healthcare system. *TransState Working Papers*, 150. University of Bremen.

Jessoula, M. (2012). Like in a Skinner box: external constraints and the reform of retirement eligibility rules in Italy. *Laboratorio di politica comparata e filosofia pubblica*, 4. Centro Einaudi.

Jessoula, M. and Pavolini, E. (2012). *Pensions, Health Care and Long-term Care in Italy. Asisp Annual National Report*. European Commission DG Employment, Social Affairs and Inclusion.

Leombruni, R., Paggiaro, A. and Trivellato, U. (2012). Per un pugno di euro. Storie di ordinaria disoccupazione. *LABORatorio R. Revelli Working Papers Series*, 120. LABORatorio R. Revelli, Centre for Employment Studies.

Lynch, J. (2006). *Age in the Welfare State: The Origins of Social Spending on Pensioners, Workers, and Children*. Cambridge and New York: Cambridge University Press.

Lynch, J. (2009). Italy: A Christian Democratic or clientelist welfare state? In K. V. Kersbergen and P. Manow (eds.), *Religion, Class Coalitions, and Welfare States* (pp. 91–118). Cambridge and New York: Cambridge University Press.

Madama, I. and Coletto D. (2009). Italy: flexicurity and industrial relations. Available online at http://www.eurofound.europa.eu/eiro/studies/tn0803038s/it0803039q.htm (accessed 16 March 2013).

Naldini, M. and Jurado, T. (2013). Family and welfare state reorientation in Spain and inertia in Italy from a European perspective. *Population Review*, 52 (1), 43–61.

Quine, M. S. (2002). *Italy's Social Revolution: Charity and Welfare from Liberalism to Fascism*. Houndmills and New York: Palgrave.

Sacchi, S. and Bastagli, F. (2005). Italy – striving uphill but stopping halfway: the troubled journal of the experimental minimum insertion income. In M. Ferrera (ed.), *Welfare State Reform in Southern Europe: Fighting Poverty and Social Exclusion in Italy, Spain, Portugal and Greece* (pp. 65–109). London and New York: Routledge.

Sacchi, S. and Vesan P. (2011). Interpreting employment policy change in Italy since the 1990s: nature and dynamics. *Carlo Alberto Notebooks*, 228. Collegio Carlo Alberto.

Schludi, M. (2005). *The Reform of Bismarckian Pension Systems: A Comparison of Pension Politics in Austria, France, Germany, Italy and Sweden*. Amsterdam: Amsterdam University Press.

21
CLIENTELISM

Jean-Louis Briquet

Clientelism has been a central issue throughout the history of modern Italy and a prominent factor in analyses of its political system. Since the country's unification in 1860, numerous historians, intellectuals, politicians and, more recently, social and political scientists have documented the persistence and ubiquity of individualized and localized political ties in which votes and political support are obtained in exchange for favours and services provided by political representatives to their voters.[1] Political and social modernization, the democratization of suffrage and the weakening of traditional notables' patronage did not do away with clientelism; it has in fact persisted up to the present in new and different forms within mass parties and state institutions (see Chapter 8 in this volume).

This hallmark of the history of Italy is often presented as one of the manifestations of the country's political 'anomaly'. It has been associated with obstacles and difficulties in building the unitary state and forming national identity in the second half of the nineteenth century and the beginning of the twentieth, as it was later with the shortcomings of the country's civic culture, the imperfections of the republican regime after the Second World War, or the spread of corruption that led to the fall of the 'First Republic' at the beginning of the 1990s. But clientelism may appear as something other than the symptom of a flawed democracy: not only has it taken on 'virtuous' forms by supporting the economic development of certain regions, but it has also constituted a 'consensus mechanism' involving in public life part of the electorate (interest groups, local social networks) because of their clientelistic bonds with part of the state bureaucracy, politicians or local party machines. However, this mechanism, based on principles far removed from democratic legitimacy, involves the risk of undermining citizens' trust in the political system and accentuating tendencies to delegitimize the state.

From notables' clientelism to party clientelism

As in many other Mediterranean societies, clientelism was commonly the form that social and political ties took in late nineteenth- and early twentieth-century Italy (Davis, 1977). Exchange of goods and services between notables (*notabili*) and the populations by and large structured political dependencies and loyalties, particularly in rural communities. For these, clientelism was a means of gaining access to scarce resources (land, employment, charity or protection) as a trade-off for their recognition of the prestige and statutory authority of the property owners and the members of the commercial bourgeoisie, the administration and the liberal professions, who constituted the majority of the political class of unified Italy. The gradual extension of suffrage between the 1882 reform (which gave the right to vote to almost a quarter of men aged 21 and over) and the establishment of universal suffrage for men in 1912 consolidated the power of notables. In a predominantly rural society marked by local particularisms, clientelism-based relations were one of the main means of mobilizing voters (Banti, 1996). They were also an instrument for territorial penetration of central government. The state was in fact able to intervene in peripheral regions through the mediation of notables, who relayed public action (administrative regulations, land-development and planning policies, social policies, etc.) and adapted it locally. The mediation of notables helped to familiarize people with modern political institutions while consolidating their own power through a clientelistic distribution of state resources (Silverman, 1965).

In the decades following the Second World War, economic development and urbanization, increased social and geographic mobility, the rise of mass parties and the expansion of state bureaucracies eroded the power of traditional notables considerably. This did not, however, do away with clientelism. Italy's socio-economic and political modernization ushered in 'party clientelism', based on control over the distribution channels of public resources by a new political elite made up of 'professional party politicians' (Caciagli and Belloni, 1981). Particularly in the southern regions (the Mezzogiorno), first the agrarian reform and then regional development policies (for example, through the Cassa per il Mezzogiorno, a government agency set up in 1950 to support agricultural and infrastructure modernization) offered the new politicians significant resources to capture and keep their clienteles. These facilities chiefly benefited the members of the government parties, and most of all the Christian Democracy (Democrazia Cristiana, or DC) party. Under the leadership of its Secretary General, Amintore Fanfani, the DC adopted as of the second half of the 1950s a strategy of penetration of state institutions (national and local government, banks and public industries) thanks to which, by distributing public goods to voters through its elected officials and the agencies attached to them (organizations, unions, etc.), it was able to establish its hegemony for three successive decades (Ignazi, 1999). Clientelism, in this case, not only characterizes personal relationships in which political loyalty and support is given in return for jobs and services (as it appears in the traditional communities studied by anthropologists), but also a system of government in which patronage networks are incorporated into the State apparatus and participate in the running of modern political parties and bureaucracies

'Political machines' and Christian Democratic power

This system of clientelistic distribution of resources through an organized mass party helped to reconcile traditional political practices with the economic and social modernization promoted by the DC and the Italian state. As has been demonstrated by Sidney Tarrow (1967), the transformation of the clientelism of the notables into the 'clientelism of the bureaucracy' was how the expanding of urban services, the new welfare policies (see Chapter 20 in this volume), programmes of support for the Mezzogiorno, etc. were concretely established. Client networks were deeply changed as a consequence, both in the nature and volume of resources circulating within them and in their forms of organization. This is perfectly illustrated by the case of Naples, which was studied by Percy Allum (1973). The growth in public resources (jobs, housing, assistance, funding of enterprises and organizations, public contracts, etc.) went hand in hand with the strengthening of the channels of their allocation by the local DC machinery. The latter thus became a top-down organization, linking groups of voters (neighbourhood committees, professional associations, territorial sociability networks, as well as trade-union sections or economic interest groups) to mid-level leaders (local elected representatives, DC section secretaries, business leaders and public administration managers), themselves connected with the highest party leaders. These party leaders, backed by the electoral power they gained through clientelist exchanges within these networks, could then trade on this power with the national DC structures and obtain positions for themselves and their collaborators in the government and in the 'parallel government-related institutions' (*sottogoverno*). This in turn increased their ability to meet their voters' demands and thereby to broaden and consolidate their electoral support.

This same system, in which influence on government institutions was combined with maintaining a substantial electoral base by means of the clientelism of political machines, was observed in several other southern cities. In Catania, for example, 'new notables' from the professionalized party machinery took over the DC in the early 1950s. This led to the establishment of an 'extended chain of interest and fidelity' around a 'mass client party' that could meet the demands of a wide variety of interest groups joined together in a 'bloc of interests' for which the party was the guarantor (Caciagli and Belloni, 1981: 45–6). Very similar power mechanics were highlighted in the case of Palermo, where control by the main local DC power centres allowed the party to set up differentiated clientelistic ties with the 'white-collar middle class' (the main beneficiary of public employment), the 'local entrepreneurial class' (which prospered thanks to public aid and contracts in a context of strong urban growth) and the 'urban poor' categories (integrated into personalized networks of dependency and loyalty to 'neighbourhood bosses' who provided protection and the aid resources indispensable to their livelihood) (Chubb, 1982). The mafia played an important role in these mechanisms, because of its influence on part of the electorate and its participation in corrupt networks involving entrepreneurs, politicians and criminal bosses (see Chapter 7 in this volume).

These urban political machines played a decisive role in maintaining the DC in power in the 1970s and 1980s. As has been noted by Carlo Trigilia (1992), the DC offset the decline in its vote in the northern and central regions by preserving its electoral strength in the Mezzogiorno.[2] As a consequence, the national party organization was more dependent on local demands from the southern political class. This led to the deterioration of public action for development, which was more subject to the electoral and parochial interests of political actors than to the effectiveness and neutrality imperatives expected to guide the activity of modern bureaucracies and encourage an 'autonomous' development of productive forces released from political pressure (Trigilia, 1992: 82–3). This does not, however, mean that party clientelism was an exclusively southern phenomenon. In the 'white' areas, the DC's political strength was drawn from its ability to embody and defend the values and lifestyles of Catholic circles.[3] Nonetheless, it was also explained by 'the importance of material assistance to the local populations by Catholic organizations' and by an ideological mobilization associated, in this case, with the offer of individualized resources (jobs, financial and technical support, participation in leisure activities, etc.) by numerous organizations (parishes, trade unions, banks, rural associations, etc.) attached to the DC (Allum, 1995: 33).

Clientelism and *partitocrazia*

The importance of clientelistic links in maintaining the DC electorate explains their influence, not only on the operations of local political machines but also on national political institutions and the state itself. Indeed, grounding electoral consensus in the clientelistic distribution of public resources affected the activity of public bureaucracies. Having little autonomy with respect to the dominant political parties, public bureaucracies tended to respond primarily to requests from the pressure groups most directly related to these parties through ideological proximity and social collusion (*parentela*) or best integrated into the DC leaders' client networks (*clientela*) (La Palombara, 1964). As a result of the state's strong presence in the industrial sectors (through the Ministry of State Participation and public banks), the agricultural sectors (through the Cassa per il Mezzogiorno and the many public agencies under the *Federconsorzi* umbrella) and the social sectors (pension funds, insurance, etc.), many public policies responded to a specific and fragmented logic in which decision-making processes were largely influenced by the electoral interests of political leaders and the corporatist ties they had established with certain interest groups (Paci, 1989).

The importance of clientelistic mechanisms in Italian political life also affected the legislative process, emphasizing inter-party negotiations on laws relating to corporatist or local 'micro-interests' at the expense of Parliament's capacity for taking initiatives, providing guidance and controlling public action (Di Palma, 1977). Furthermore, it encouraged the DC's splitting into competing factions, which contributed to undermining government alliances and to subjecting the decisions of the executive branch and of public administrations to the interests of heterogeneous groups and of internal currents in the majority party competing for the allocation of resources and positions in public and para-public institutions (*lotizzazione*). The DC was thus described as a coalition of 'groups of power' led by the leaders of currents (*capi correnti*) and made up of 'political clienteles depend[ing] for their survival on the control of governmental positions' and on the 'patronage opportunities' offered by these positions (Zuckerman, 1979: 136).

This extension of the logic of the local political machine across the national political system emerged as one of the characteristics of Italian *partitocrazia* (party control of the state), in which clientelistic exchanges involved organized groups at the national level: on the one hand, political parties, the parties' internal factions, central government agencies, local administrations, and/or parastatal institutions; on the other, pressure and interest groups, professional associations, trade unions, and/or local power alliances. Not only did *partitocrazia* change local clientelism into 'state clientelism', given the 'massive use of public resources' and the 'colonization' of public institutions by government parties (Pasquino, 1995: 347–8); it also translated into the generalization of client-based 'consensus mechanisms'. As demonstrated by Alessandro Pizzorno (1974), the 'individualistic voter-mobilization strategy' that prevailed in Italy since the end of the Second World War, mainly the DC's, favoured the distribution of material 'benefits' to the middle classes, who constituted the regime's main supporters, at the expense of the 'institutionalization of their collective claims'. As a result, clientelism was generalized as the 'power-formation channel' to meet the social demands of large sections of the electorate and thus to ensure the stability of the political system.

Perverse effects of clientelism

The majority of analyses of clientelism have stressed its perverse effects or, at the very least, the 'anomaly' of its massive presence in the context of a modern democracy (Briquet, 2009). This perspective was first formulated at the end of the 1950s and beginning of the 1960s by a number of political scientists such as Edward Banfield (1958) or Gabriel Almond and Sidney Verba (1963). In his monograph on a rural community in the Basilicata region, Banfield suggested for the Mezzogiorno the image of a 'backward' society marked by 'amoral familism', in which interest in public affairs was exclusively determined by the hope of maximizing the 'material, short-run advantage of the nuclear family' (Banfield, 1958: 85). Comparative research on attitudes to democracy in five European countries conducted a few years later by Almond and Verba confirmed this image. In their study, Italy was shown as a country with 'premodern' social structures and a 'parochial', weakly participatory political culture, which resulted in a chiefly 'pragmatic' and 'instrumental' relationship to public institutions amongst the major part of the population. According to the authors, this type of culture encouraged clientelism and could not support a 'stable and effective democratic system' (Almond and Verba, 1963: 308–10). Clientelism then appeared as a manifestation of the anomalies of the Italian political system, of the distance that separated it from developed democracies, which are characterized by the active participation of citizens in public affairs and the force of 'civic culture'.[4] Sidney Tarrow (1967) also pointed to clientelism as one of the signs of the gap between political systems in the south of Italy and those of a 'modern system of representation'; he related this, however, more to the 'atypical' modernization trajectory of the Mezzogiorno than to the peculiarities of its culture.[5]

Marked by a dominant paradigm consisting in identifying and explaining the deficiencies of the Italian political system and its 'deficit in modernity' (Mastropaolo, 2000), subsequent analyses of clientelism reformulated the 'anomaly' theory and extended it. According to Mario Caciagli and Frank Belloni (1981), for example, although clientelism was instrumentalized to politicize the southern populations (integrated into national politics through mass clientelistic parties) and to help the economic development of the Mezzogiorno (through redistribution of the financial flows that they were allocated), it also heightened the deviant aspects of these processes. It acted as an obstacle to citizens' 'political maturity' by preventing the autonomous expression of civil society and the collective defence of social interests. It condemned the southern regions to precarious economic development because they were almost exclusively dependent on intervention from the state, itself subjected to the electioneering aims of political leaders, whose legitimacy was weakened by the fact that voter loyalty depended only on material and short-term benefits.

Clientelism therefore affected the political system in two ways: first, it reduced the efficiency of institutions by privatizing state power and limiting the autonomy of public bureaucracies as well as their coordination and programming capacities; second, it undermined the legitimacy of those institutions by making their relationship to citizens exclusively instrumental. It thus appeared as an 'obstacle to the institutionalization of authority' and to a sustainable legitimization of the political system. It prevented the formation of diffuse political support based on collective and ideological values and on the principles of impartiality, universalism, and the separation of public roles and the private roles that constituted political leaders' 'reserves of social credit' (Graziano, 1980: 53–4). Ultimately, it made the political stability of the regime dependent on the capacity of its leaders to meet voters' material interests at the risk of seeing the legitimacy of the regime challenged if the ruling classes were no longer able to meet the material expectations of its electoral base as a result of a lack of sustained economic growth or an inflation in the social demands that were addressed to them.

The 'virtuous circles' of clientelism

Some authors have qualified the binary conception described above, which considers clientelism in an exclusively antagonistic relationship with democratic accomplishment and thereby presents it as a dysfunctional political 'anomaly'. Simona Piattoni (1998), in her comparative research on the evolution of politics in the Abruzzo and Apulia regions in the second half of the twentieth century, proposed in this regard the notion of 'virtuous clientelism'. On the basis of a strategic conception of clientelism, considered as a means chosen by politicians to maximize their power resources, she argues that clientelism may, in some cases, promote economic development and contribute to the establishment of political practices more in line with democratic standards. While in Apulia, a weak opposition, coupled with strong divisions within the government parties led to the formation of fragmented clientelism networks lavishing 'selective goods' only on their members, the political elites in Abruzzo combined the offer of private goods and public goods to strengthen their position against a powerful and unified opposition.

This resulted, in the first case, in uncoordinated and inefficient public action by the local political 'bosses', seeking primarily to manipulate administrative and political action to protect the interests of their own clienteles alone. Conversely, in the second case, the regional DC leaders consolidated their position as 'brokers' by extending provision of goods and services beyond just their supporters. To safeguard their control over the public-resource allocation channels on which their power relied, they entered into a variety of collaboration and exchange relations with all the local actors (entrepreneurs, interest groups, organizations, etc.), whose claims they conveyed and whose interests they defended to central government. They supported the industrial sector by providing the financial aid and logistical support needed for its development, and promoted collective citizenship in the form of 'constituency services' intended for the whole community.

By channelling government resources to their constituency and using the expertise of public bureaucracies, a number of political leaders therefore actively participated in the modernization of their territory while preserving their electoral influence by controlling and manipulating these resources. Clientelism practices in this case were combined with the development of modern infrastructure (transport, hospitals, housing, etc.); they contributed to the improvement of the populations' living conditions by creating jobs and improving education and social-welfare policies (Zuckerman, 1997). As has been shown in particular by Gabriella Gribaudi (1990), clientelism was the means by which modern political institutions actually took root in certain regions. In the Mezzogiorno in particular,

> the very important social and economic transformation processes found in the local societies the channels through which they were expressed. The relationship with the state and the public institutions may be thus considered as a relationship of selective and adaptive use . . . [The state] adopts the forms imposed by the local society, by controlling its resources, channelling them through non-institutional networks and chains of personal relationships governed by motivations that are different from those proclaimed by the institutions.
>
> *(Gribaudi, 1990: 284)*

The former clientelistic practices were thus reconstructed to adapt to new forms of public action, the official logic of which they altered, however, by subjecting them to the local actors' social standards and practical interests.

Recent political transformations and changes in clientelism

Clientelism thus turned out to be a channel for political and socio-economic modernization, but it was also one of the factors in the development of deviant behaviour in political spheres, in particular, corruption. Although for analytical purposes the two phenomena need to be distinguished, in practice they were frequently combined.[6] Many of the testimonies collected in the late 1980s and early 1990s by anti-corruption magistrates indicate that the services requested from 'protected' entrepreneurs by corrupt politicians were not only monetary; they could also be to provide jobs or a variety of services to the politicians' supporters. More generally, resources obtained through corruption were frequently used to consolidate the corrupt politicians' electoral base (Della Porta, 1992). The complementarity of clientelism and corruption is explained by the features they have in common. In both cases, there are benefits based on the privatization of public institutions tending to promote an instrumental conception of politics, to erode the public-commitment ideal, and to promote, within the parties, 'business politicians' who are part of exchange-and-favour networks in which electoral constituencies and circles of political and business collusion are interwoven. On the other hand, the two phenomena reinforce each other through a 'vicious circle' dynamics revealed by Donatella Della Porta and Alberto Vannucci (1994): 'business politicians' sustain their clientele by controlling significant material resources and by increasing the 'corruption offer' to entrepreneurs; corrupt politicians gain access to positions of power in the party apparatus and increase their power to influence public administrations; they thus have control over new resources, which they use to get votes and political support; this in turn fuels clientelism.[7]

The spread of corruption in political circles was one of the causes of the fall of the 'First Republic' between 1992 and 1994. By revealing the extent of illegal practices within the governing classes, anti-corruption and anti-mafia judges accelerated the moral discrediting of the regime and sparked demand for change amongst broad sectors of the electorate. This also offered new political actors powerful arguments and legitimating repertoires to assert themselves in the political arena against the old established elites in the name of the necessary revitalization of public life (Briquet, 2007). Judicial investigations, however, simply sped up a process that had originated upstream of the crisis and can be related to 'government party' dysfunctions and the clientelist political consensus-building mechanisms associated with them. Indeed, although these mechanisms had long guaranteed support to the regime by a majority of voters and ensured its stability, they had at the same time eroded its overall legitimacy. 'Macro-political' competition (relating to major social choices and ideological issues) was gradually supplanted by 'micro-political' competition (dealing with the management and defence of vested interests). As a consequence, in addition to the extension of deviant behaviour amongst the ruling elites, the government's programmatic-proposal capacities were weakened and the political system became more vulnerable as it faced an increase in particularistic voter requests and a scarcity of state resources as a result of the worsening of its financial difficulties and budgetary constraints that was related to European integration (Cotta, 1994). The crisis in the Christian Democratic regime thus appears as the ultimate manifestation of the contradictions of '*partitocrazia* clientelism', laid bare by political scandals and causing a brutal collapse of the legitimacy of the ruling class in the eyes of the citizens.

It remains to be seen whether the aspirations for change and moralization of democracy expressed during the 'First Republic' crisis has led to a lessening of the weight of clientelism in public life. Only assumptions and lines of thought can be advanced by way of conclusion. On the one hand, privatizations and the state's disengagement from productive sectors in which it had previously been massively involved, the greater autonomy of administrations with regard to political authorities, and budgetary constraints leading to fewer public-sector jobs have certainly restricted opportunities for politicians to satisfy voters' particularistic demands. In addition, local government reforms since 1993 appear to have triggered dynamics that are not conducive to the development of clientelism. Associated with local-government modernization measures, the change to a majority-based voting system for the designation of local leaders has improved the latter's decision-making capacities, weakened party tutelage over their activities, and led to the establishment of more transparent forms of consultation with representatives of local interests (Trigilia, 2002).

On the other hand, however, national and local political authorities have maintained a decisive position in the distribution of many resources that could be used for clientelistic purposes; they have them available either directly (national and local government jobs, public aid) or indirectly (through organizations, businesses, and public and para-public institutions active in the new public-management cooperation networks). Moreover, the persistence of territory-based political affiliations and personal solidarity networks and the exchanges on which they are based (Diamanti, 2012) can contribute to the formation of new local political notables inclined to secure voter loyalty through selective incentives similar to those of the former political clientelism. More generally, as has been argued by Jonathan Hopkin and Alfio Mastropaolo (2001: 171),

> the postmodern age, characterized by the absence of ideological mobilization, the decline of the great social cleavages and collective identities of class and religion, a growing social differentiation, and an exaggerated emphasis in particularistic interests, would appear to provide fertile ground for the resurgence of clientelism.

This clientelism is now one of the main instruments of social and political integration in modern societies. The revelations during the corruption scandals that punctuated Italy's recent political history, the judicial authorities' regular whistleblowing on widespread illegality in administrative action, which favours clientelist uses of public funds, and the recurrent controversies stirred by the denunciation of the privileges and abuses of the political class all tend to confirm this diagnosis. They call for social and political sciences to revive empirical research on clientelism phenomena and their reshaping today in Italy's new political landscape.

(Translated from French by Marina Urquidi)

Notes

1 For a detailed overall discussion of the concept of clientelism, see for instance Eisenstadt and Roniger (1984) or, with special attention to the case of Italy, Piattoni (2005).

2 Between 1972 and 1992, the DC's parliamentary election scores declined from 38 per cent to 25 per cent in the northern and central regions while remaining stable (42 per cent to 40 per cent) in the southern regions. The Mezzogiorno share in the DC vote thus increased during this period from 32 per cent to 42 per cent (Trigilia, 1992: 66).

3 The 'white' areas (*zone bianche*) are the northern regions of Italy in which the DC, closely associated with the Church and Catholic associations, has long been dominant.

4 Robert Putnam (1993) later proposed a revised version of this theory, in which the greater or lesser capacity of Italian regional administrations to respond effectively to the needs of the populations was attributed to the degree of civicness of a local society. In contrast to the northern regions, the long historical trajectory of which led to the formation of a culture of participation in collective life and cooperation and trust between individuals, institutional action was inefficient in those of the south, which was characterized by mistrust, the weakness of collective collaborative networks and clientelism.

5 More specifically, Tarrow attributed this 'atypical' modernization to the process of integration of the southern regions in the Italian state on the basis of the 'traditional' characteristics of their social structure (see in particular Tarrow, 1967: 71–95).

6 Corruption is an illegal exchange between public-office holders and economic actors based on mutual and specific benefits: secret funding for the former and secure access to government contracts for the latter. Clientelism is also an exchange of services involving public actors, but in which they trade favours and private services with voters in return for their electoral support in a less clearly commodified relationship than in the case of corruption, and it is not necessarily illegal (Della Porta, 1993).

7 As has been observed by Luigi Musella (2000: 141–2), their integration into corruption networks helped 'new leaders' to be given leading positions in the government parties from the late 1970s onwards. This was due in particular to the parties' increased funding needs and the crucial role taken by corruption practices to meet these needs.

Bibliography

Allum, P. A. (1973). *Politics and Society in Post-War Naples*. Cambridge: Cambridge University Press.

Allum, P. A. (1995). Le double visage de la Démocratie chrétienne. *Politix*, 30, 24–44.

Almond, G. A. and Verba, S. (1963). *The Civic Culture: Political Attitudes and Democracy in Five Nations*. Princeton, NJ: Princeton University Press.

Banfield, E. C. (1958). *The Moral Basis of a Backward Society*. New York: The Free Press.

Banti, A. M. (1996). *Storia della borghesia italiana: L'età liberale*. Rome: Donzelli.

Briquet, J.-L. (2007). *Mafia, justice et politique en Italie. L'affaire Andreotti dans la crise de la République (1992–2004)*. Paris: Karthala.

Briquet, J.-L. (2009). Scholarly formulations of a political category: Clientelism and the sociohistorical interpretation of the 'Italian Case'. *Modern Italy*, (14) 3, 339–56.

Caciagli, M. and Belloni, F. P. (1981). The 'New' Clientelism in Southern Italy: The Christian Democratic Party in Catania. In S. Eisenstadt and R. Lemarchand (eds.), *Political Clientelism, Patronage and Development* (pp. 35–55). London: Sage Publications.

Chubb, J. (1982). *Patronage, Power, and Poverty in Southern Italy: A Tale of Two Cities*. Cambridge: Cambridge University Press.

Cotta, M. (1994). Il governo dei partiti in Italia. Crisi e trasformazione dell'assetto tradizionale. In M. Caciagli, F. Cazzola, L. Morlino and S. Passigli (eds.), *L'Italia fra crisi e transizione* (pp. 119–39). Rome-Bari: Laterza.

Davis, J. (1977). *People of the Mediterranean: An Essay in Comparative Social Anthropology*. London: Routledge.

Della Porta, D. (1992). *Lo scambio occulto. Casi di corruzione politica in Italia*. Bologna: Il Mulino.

Della Porta, D. (1993). Corruzione, clientelismo e cattiva amministrazione. Note sulle dinamiche degli scambi corrotti in Italia. *Quaderni di sociologia*, 38 (5), 31–50.

Della Porta, D. and Vannucci, R. (1994). *Corruzione politica e amministrazione pubblica*. Bologna: Il Mulino.

Diamanti, I. (2012). *Gramsci, Manzoni e mia suocera. Quando gli esperti sbagliano le previsioni politiche*. Bologna: Il Mulino.

Di Palma, G. (1977). *Surviving Without Governing: The Italian Parties in Parliament*. Berkeley, CA: California University Press.

Eisenstadt, S. and Roniger, L. (1984). *Patrons, Clients and Friends: Interpersonal Relations and the Structure of Trust in Society*. Cambridge: Cambridge University Press.

Graziano, L. (1980). *Clientelismo e sistema politico. Il caso dell'Italia*. Milan: Franco Angeli.

Gribaudi, G. (1990). *A Eboli: Il mondo meridionale in cent'anni di trasformazione*. Venice: Marsilio.

Hopkin, J. and Mastropaolo, A. (2001). From Patronage to Clientelism: Comparing the Italian and Spanish Experiences. In S. Piattoni (ed.), *Clientelism, Interests, and Democratic Representation* (pp. 152–71). Cambridge: Cambridge University Press.

Ignazi, P. (1999). I partiti e la politica dal 1963 al 1992. In G. Sabbatucci and V. Vidotto (eds.), *Storia d'Italia. 6. L'Italia contemporanea dal 1963 a oggi* (pp. 101–232). Rome-Bari: Laterza.

La Palombara, J. (1964). *Interest Groups in Italian Politics*. Princeton, N.J.: Princeton University Press.

Mastropaolo, A. (2000). *Antipolitica: all'origine della crisi italiana*. Naples: L'Ancora.

Musella, L. (2000). *Clientelismo. Tradizione e trasformazione della politica italiana 1975–1992*. Naples: Guida.

Paci, M. (1989). *Pubblico e privato nei moderni sistemi di welfare*. Naples: Liguori.

Pasquino, G. (1995). La partitocrazia. In G. Pasquino (ed.), *La politica italiana. Dizionario critico 1945–95* (pp. 341–53). Rome-Bari: Laterza.

Piattoni, S. (1998). Clientelismo virtuoso: una via di sviluppo per il Mezzogiorno? *Rivista italiana di scienza politica*, 28 (3), 483–513.

Piattoni, S. (2005). *Il clientelismo. L'Italia in prospettiva comparata*. Rome: Carocci.

Pizzorno, A. (1974). I ceti medi nel meccanismo del consenso. In F. L. Cavazza and S. R. Graubard (eds.), *Il caso italiano* (pp. 315–38). Milan: Garzanti.

Putnam, R. (1993). *Making Democracy Work: Civic Traditions in Modern Italy*. Princeton, NJ: Princeton University Press.

Silverman, S. F. (1965). Patronage and community–nation relationships in central Italy. *Ethnology*, 4 (2), 172–89.

Tarrow, S. G. (1967). *Peasant Communism in Southern Italy*. New Haven, CT: Yale University Press.

Trigilia, C. (1992). *Sviluppo senza autonomia. Effetti perversi delle politiche nel Mezzogiorno*. Bologna: Il Mulino.

Trigilia, C. (2002). Dalla politica alle politiche. Comuni e interessi locali, In R. Catanzaro, F. Piselli, F. Ramella and C. Trigilia (eds.), *Comuni nuovi. Il cambiamento dei governi locali* (pp. 579–602). Bologna: Il Mulino.

Zuckerman, A. S. (1979). *The Politics of Faction: Christian Democratic Rule in Italy*. New Haven, CT: Yale University Press.

Zuckerman, A. S. (1997). Transforming a peripheral region: the consolidation and collapse of Christian Democratic dominance in Basilicata. *Regional and Federal Studies*, 7 (2), 1–24.

22

THE IMPACT OF POLITICAL CALCULUS ON THE REFORM OF INSTITUTIONS AND GROWTH

Old and new examples

Leone Leonida, Dario Maimone Ansaldo Patti and Pietro Navarra

Introduction

Italy is experiencing a dramatic economic and social crisis. It is known that the economy has lost one fourth of industrial production over the period from 2008 to 2013. In addition, and differently from other economies in the European Union, at the time of writing the economy does not seem to be in the recovery phase. However, even before the economic crisis, the economy was not performing well. In fact, Italian economic growth has been slowed down by numerous structural issues for a long time. The country is indeed known to be an example of a so-called dualistic economy, where regions in the South of Italy are known to be lacking in industrialization, in the sense that they are substantially based on the agricultural and service sectors, while regions in the North are known to be among the richest regions in Europe. There also exists a divergence pattern between the North and the South of the country. The 2012 report by SVIMEZ shows that Southern Italy has been growing at a lower rate than Central and Northern Italy over the last ten years.[1] According to the report, the southern economy shows signs of greater difficulty during the crisis period that began in 2007, which is easy to show in the trend of employment and production.

Why do regions converge to different long-term equilibria? Are multiple equilibria the result of different institutions? What is the impact of political institutions on the convergence and growth processes? Despite the (recognized) importance of the industrialization process in catching-up dynamics, its theoretical and empirical role has been largely neglected in studies of growth (De la Fuente, 1997, 2000; Durlauf and Quah, 1999; Islam, 2003) and in particular in 'growth accounting approach' studies (Temple, 1999). These theories, in addition, originally tended to put aside the role of political competition in economic development, assuming that the State plays the role of the so-called social planner and therefore acts in any case in the interest of citizens and in favour of economic growth and development.

Acemoglu and Robinson (2006) highlight instead the crucial role played by the political calculus of incumbent governments in the decision to undertake market-oriented economic reforms. The authors emphasize the role played by incumbent governments, whose political power is eventually put under threat by the implementation of institutional reforms that are in turn critical to production. They argue that the implementation of growth-enhancing reforms clearly increase societal welfare, but, at the same time, may destabilize the existing political system and reduce the possibility of incumbent governments remaining in power and resisting the political challenges posed by new competitors. They discuss the history of industrialization to support their theory.

The two main questions that we want to answer in this chapter are the following. First, we suggest using the theory put forward by Acemoglu and Robinson (2006) in order to understand the different levels of development between Northern and Southern Italy and the reasons why the economy is experiencing a lack of growth. We make use of this theory to interpret the history of industrialization in general and in the Italian case in particular, and some of the current problems associated with economic growth in Italy. In light of this theory Italy is a particularly interesting case study. The country is a developed economy as its production level is classed among the top ten in world economies. Moreover, in Italy some regions are fully industrialized; others, however, represent a case of missed industrialization, where the less industrialized regions are geographically located in the south of Italy. These experienced a slowdown of the industrialization process during the late 1960s and, since then, their ability to create growth and employment has been poor.

The second main research question, which we want to address in this chapter, refers to the explanation of why the Italian parliament is facing several difficulties in reforming the TV broadcasting sector, although such a reform is called for by several parties. As we will note, mass media development and, more generally, investment in information and communication technologies (ICT) are critical to production and growth both directly and indirectly (Daveri, 2002; Haacker and Morsink, 2002; Bandyopadhyay, 2009). Also in this case, we believe that the theory of Acemoglu and Robinson (2006) could be useful in investigating the lack of reform of the broadcasting sector.

The remainder of the chapter proceeds as follows. We summarize the theory that links economic growth to political competition, according to Acemoglu and Robinson (2006). Next we describe the convergence process across Italian regions and the extent of dualism between the two main areas of the country, and discuss how the theory we have presented can be used to interpret the absence of industrialization in the southern part of the economy. Then we discuss the case of the (lack of) reform of the Italian TV broadcasting sector, by explaining the link between mass media development, investment in ICT and economic growth. We discuss the main features of the discipline of the Italian broadcasting service and then we explain why it has not been reformed. Finally, we provide some concluding remarks.

The political replacement effect

The relationship between political competition and economic growth is more controversial than one might expect. On the one hand, some authors argue that democratic systems are needed for implementing institutional reforms that are in turn likely to deliver economic development and growth. For example, de Haan and Sturm (2003), Giavazzi and Tabellini (2005) and Amin and Djankov (2009a, 2009b) suggest that democratic institutions strongly influence economic reforms. Besley *et al.* (2010) believe that economic growth is associated with higher degree of democracy and political competition. The authors discuss the case where competition among political parties is likely to boost economic development by inducing incumbent governments to support policies leading to economic development. They support their theory by using evidence from US states. A similar approach has been applied by Padovano and Ricciuti (2008) in Italian regions and their results support the existence of a positive impact of political competition on economic performance. On the other hand, some scholars argue that authoritarian regimes are more likely to lead to economic reforms that boost economic growth. They argue that the distributional conflict that characterizes democratic systems is likely to lead to delays, and eventually failures, in the adoption of economic reforms that are critical to economic development (Fernandez and Rodrik, 1991; Rodrik, 1996). Edwards (1991) also notes that countries such as Chile, South Korea and Taiwan introduced democracy only after undergoing economic reforms. China is an obvious and recent example of this idea.

Acemoglu and Robinson (2006) offer a theoretical framework that unifies these opposing views. They highlight the crucial role played by the political calculus of incumbent governments in the decision to undertake market-oriented economic reforms. Unlike the mainstream literature that focuses on the role of distributional conflicts in discouraging changes in economic policy, the authors emphasize the role played by incumbent governments, whose political power is eventually put under threat by the implementation of institutional reforms that are in turn critical to production. The authors discuss the existence of the *political replacement effect*, and define it as the decision of incumbent governments to block economic reforms if they believe that the reforms themselves are likely to reduce their chances of staying in power. Their key argument is that the introduction of growth-enhancing reforms may change the political, economic and social characteristics of a country. While such reforms increase societal welfare, they may lead to a change of the current leadership in power, as more political competitors may emerge.

When are reforms more likely to be blocked? The authors suggest that the answer is strongly correlated to the level of political competition the economic system is experiencing. Indeed, if political competition in the country is low, then the governments' incumbent advantage with respect to other parties is high and, therefore, replacement is unlikely. In this context, the government's political power is secure and market reforms are more likely, even though they might generate political turbulence. The opposite situation is characterized by a high degree of political competition. In this case, the governing body has little incumbent advantage and prefers to carry out economic reforms because, given their potential beneficial effects on the well-being of society, they might increase the probability of their staying in power.

A particular situation occurs when the degree of political competition is neither high nor low. Since the political situation is not well-defined, the risk associated with the implementation of growth-enhancing reforms is an increase in the probability that the incumbent government may be replaced by new political competitors. Under those circumstances, the existing leadership does not have the incentives to introduce economic reforms, as the cost associated with them is greater than the benefits that it could receive.

Missing convergence and the political replacement effect

Acemoglu and Robinson (2006) present a number of historical examples to support their theory, and consider industrialization as a concrete example of the mechanism they describe and, finally, analyse cross-country differences in industrialization during the nineteenth century. Their theory appears to be able to explain why Great Britain, Germany, and the United States enacted institutional reforms that encouraged entrepreneurs to adopt new technologies leading to industrialization and economic development, while Russia and Austria-Hungary blocked those reforms, causing economic stagnation.

The theory the two authors propose is in our opinion helpful in interpreting the history of industrialization in Italy. Despite being a developed economy, as its production level is classed among the top ten in the world economies, part of Italy is known to be a case of missing industrialization. Iona *et al.* (2008), among many others, present some stylized facts about industrialization, the quality of political institutions and growth in Italy. The authors present evidence from 1960 to 2010 regarding the per capita gross domestic product as a measure of welfare in the country. They show southern regions have a per capita gross domestic product considerably smaller than the richer ones. Moreover, while regions experienced a strong convergence process until 1971, this process tended to slow down thereafter, and the difference between the per capita GDP of the South and the North is increasing. The crucial importance of industrialization to the growth process is highlighted by the evidence that, over the period 1960–5, the South had greater added value in the agriculture sector and lower production in the manufacturing sector than the North, and that investment in the industrial sector in the southern regions has been always lower than across northern regions. In summary, northern regions have experienced a faster growth process mainly because of a stronger industrialization process than that of southern regions.

Williamson (1965) looks optimistically at such a geographical imbalance. He suggests looking at these imbalances as growth-boosting devices as, because of them, southern regions would catch up in a second stage of the Italian development process. He explicitly links the level of national development with the process of absolute convergence across regional economies, introducing the hypothesis that the lower the degree of development of a nation, the faster some of its regions will grow and diverge from each other. The laggards would catch up in a second stage, by taking advantage of the progress of the fast-growing regions: 'the evidence on Italian regional dualism suggest optimistic projections regarding the future size of the north–south problem as Italy passes into mature stages of growth and rapidly ascends into high-income classes' (Williamson, 1965: 28).

In Williamson's analysis, therefore, sector imbalance causes convergence. However, this has not been the case. Southern regions have not caught up with northern ones, and it seems unrealistic to suppose that a convergence process is going to take place in the future. Why a different level of development persists between the two areas of Italy is thought to be related to the behaviour of economic elites – entrepreneurs in the North and land owners in the South – that have pushed the decision of the incumbent government towards blocking industrialization in southern economies, what is known to be part of the Southern Question (*La Questione Meridionale*; see Chapter 1 in this volume). During these years, incumbent governments did fear the consequences of a different economic policy, and the sectorial imbalance between the North and the South of Italy, which has caused economic stagnation in these regions, can be seen as a consequence the political replacement effect.

Reform of the media, economic growth and the political replacement effect

Acemoglu and Robinson (2006) make use of a notion of institutions critical to reforms that accounts for a broad range of factors which boost economic performance. According to Orr (1987) the media should be treated as an economic institution. Among other things, it should be acknowledged that the media convey information. In particular, they represent a tool for gathering and circulating information. In this view, their role is largely critical in offering individuals the correct amount of information in order to play a more active role in social life.

The media are an important part of the more general concept of ICT. The relationship between them and economic growth has been investigated from several points of view. The link between them can be both direct and indirect. For instance, Bandyopadhyay (2009) shows that a larger media development is associated with a lower level of corruption, inequality and poverty. In turn, this generates a better environment in which economic growth and production may take place. In addition, the effectiveness and completeness of the information that the media may offer is largely determined by the way in which governments treat them. As Besley *et al.* (2002) acknowledge, countries which are rated as democratic experience a larger media penetration.

In this section, we study the media law introduced by Italian government in 2004, and, in particular, we try to explain in light of Acemoglu and Robinson (2006) the reason why such an Act has not been modified, although a change is called for by several different parties and organizations.

Media penetration and economic growth

Our first concern is to explain the link between media penetration and economic growth. As we mentioned above, such a relationship may be both indirect and direct.

As far as the direct impact is concerned, there exists a large literature that acknowledges the role of investment in ICT and economic growth. Although the initial studies did not find any positive relationship, but, on the contrary, a negative one (Pohjola, 1998), there is now a general consensus on the positive impact. For instance, Haacker and Morsink (2002) show that investment in ICT leads to a large increase in total factor productivity. Clearly, there exist differences in such an impact among developed and developing countries. However, it is commonly held that the positive effect is consistent across a large cross-country sample. Indeed, Daveri (2002) shows that investment in ICT boosts significantly economic productivity in several developed countries, although in some cases, such as Germany, France, Italy and Spain, the impact of such investment is negligible.

On the other hand, the indirect impact of media penetration on economic growth is considerable. Bandyopadhyay (2009) shows that media development reduces corruption, inequality and poverty. Brunetti and Weder (2003) and Ahrend (2001) find that greater press freedom is associated with low corruption. Even more interestingly, Djankov *et al.* (2003) show that state ownership of media is negatively associated with the quality of political governance. A similar negative correlation is witnessed in Shi and Svensson (2006), where the authors show that a limited media penetration (identified in the distributions of radios among the population) finds a counterpart in larger political budget cycles. It should be acknowledged that such a relationship is not undisputed in the literature. Besley *et al.* (2002) argue that the presence of larger media groups generates sufficient conditions for the emergence of a free press. In fact, such large groups prevent any attempts at bribery by politicians.

Another indirect effect of media penetration on economic development comes from the relationship between investment in ICT and social inequality. While at a macro-level we may notice the tendency of clustering in the media industry as with any other kind of production, Quah (1996) shows that such a clustering is more pronounced in Europe than in US. In a similar fashion the lack of access to ICT may worsen the existing inequality among individuals, because of the lack of information that individuals may have access to in their lives.

As with the corruption issue, we cannot neglect that the development of mass media allows voters to exercise more effectively their control of governments' actions. If individuals are aware of politicians' choices, they can decide freely which candidate they will support in upcoming elections. This is particularly true for less developed countries. However, political accountability goes hand in hand with the issue of media ownership. Privately owned media possibly do not guarantee the necessary independence of the editors that is required to punish government's inappropriate actions and to reward the choices that are in fact beneficial for individuals' well-being.

The Italian Act on TV broadcasting

The Italian TV broadcasting industry has been subject to some legislative interventions in the last 20 years. The most important interventions were an Act introduced in 1990 on regulations for the public and private broadcasting industry (the so-called *Legge Mammì*) and another Act introduced in 2004 on regulations for the broadcasting industry and the publicly owned body, *RAI*. The last Act also authorized the Italian government to promulgate a general act on the entire broadcasting service in Italy (the so-called *Legge Gasparri*).

The 1990 Act recognized the right of private bodies to broadcast over the entire country, which broke the monopoly of public television. It came after the partial rejection of earlier regulations issued in 1985, which were declared against Italian Fundamental Law by the Constitutional Court. It recognized the role of private broadcasting bodies and introduced both *internal* and an *external* pluralism in the service. The internal pluralism was meant to guarantee adequate space in the broadcasting service for different opinions and political, social and religious ideas. The external pluralism allowed entry into the market by players different from the publicly owned broadcasting body.

The *Legge Mammì* introduced a duopoly in the Italian broadcasting industry formed by the publicly owned body and the privately owned *Fininvest* (now *Mediaset*). Each of them consisted of three channels and controlled almost the entire national broadcasting service. Admittedly other private bodies were operating in the broadcasting industry. Nonetheless, their market share was significantly smaller than the two main competitors.

The broadcasting service was severely reformed in 2004. The objective of such a reform was to offer a solution to the conflict of interest produced when the owner of *Mediaset*, Silvio Berlusconi, was appointed prime minister. The approval of that Act was unusually long and controversial. According to Italian Fundamental Law, acts are promulgated by the Head of State. However it is his right to refuse approval if he considers some elements in the bill to be in conflict with the Constitution. In the case of the *Legge Gasparri*, the president of the Republic exercised his constitutional right because of two elements. On one hand, there was the necessity of fixing a shorter term to regulate access to terrestrial digital television, while the original version of the *Legge Gasparri* aimed at postponing a deadline fixed by the Constitutional Court. On the other, the president of the Republic recognized the risk that the regulations regarding the calculation of advertising revenues could generate a detrimental situation for pluralism in the broadcasting sector.

Eventually, the *Legge Gasparri* was approved with the following characteristics:

a) definition of an integrated system, which covers among other things newspapers and TV advertising;
b) a limit of 20 per cent on the total amount of advertising obtained in a year according to the integrated system for a single body;
c) a progressive move from analogue to digital terrestrial television by the end of 2006.

It should be noted that the change to the digital terrestrial television occurred 6 years later than the date fixed in the *Legge Gasparri*.

The above Act has been criticized in several respects. The most critical was the limit on the amount of advertising revenues that each body could obtain from the integrated system. Although the percentage was reduced from the 30 per cent fixed by the previous legislation, to 20 per cent, in absolute terms this resulted in an increase from 12 to 26 billion euros. Moreover, the new Act would incentivize advertising on TV rather in newspapers. Finally, the Act did not tackle the problem of the assignment of TV frequencies. A further important point is that the European Commission required some amendments, since it recognized the presence of elements at odds with European Law.

As can be noted, the introduction of such a reform of the broadcasting sector was quite controversial. Moreover, nowadays there are continual requests for changes, which have been systematically neglected. More importantly, it was difficult to amend the *Legge Gasparri*, even when the government was supported by left-wing parties.

The crucial questions we would like to answer are consequently the following: Provided that the necessity of amending the *Legge Gasparri* was recognized by several parties, organizations and even single persons, why was it so difficult to change it and why is it still in operation after 10 years? What prevented left-wing parties changing an Act which they have always recognized as unfair and detrimental to pluralism?

Political calculus and the *Legge Gasparri*

It should be noted that the necessity of solving the so-called conflict of interest emerged when Berlusconi was appointed prime minister. This happened in 1994. After his replacement in 1995, another four governments were in office and all of them were mainly supported by left-wing parties. Although Berlusconi had already changed his status from TV tycoon to politician, nobody solved the conflict of interest. In addition, the broadcasting sector was reformed by a government run by Berlusconi himself and, as has been recognized, the *Legge Gasparri* appeared to favour the owner of the largest private broadcasting body, who was, of course, Berlusconi himself. His second government ended in 2006 and was replaced by two left-leaning governments. Eventually, Berlusconi came to power again in 2008 for another three years before resigning because of the international financial crisis.

Our objective in this subsection is to answer a simple but important question. Why did no government of the last ten years have the necessary power to change an Act which was recognized as detrimental to the effective development of the media sector? Answering the above question is not straightforward, Moreover it requires a critical interpretation of different features of the Italian broadcasting sector and political system.

The first important point concerns the relationship between political power and the publicly owned broadcasting body. As we mentioned above, Italian public television consists of three channels. The key corporate positions are determined by the political powers. Therefore, people appointed to positions are usually close to a particular party. For instance, the first channel is usually assigned to the main party, which supports the government in office, while the third channel has usually been run by people who are close to left-wing parties. It appears that the quality of the information provided may be heavily affected by political power.

The second key factor, which occurred in the same period, when the broadcasting sector was reformed, is the approval of a new Act regulating electoral competition, which was introduced in 2005. There are two features of the new Act that are interesting for our purposes. First, it allows for multiple nominations. In other words, the same person may run for a position in different constituencies. This practice has been widely used by parties which prefers to indicate as the first candidate in the list the most representative politician, in order to maximize the number of votes that they can obtain. The second characteristic is that voters cannot choose their most preferred candidate, but they can only vote for a party or a coalition. The list of candidates is chosen by the same political parties and, depending on the position of a candidate on the list, his probability of being appointed to a position is high or low. Given the characteristics of the Italian electoral rules, it is certainly true that elections are free and everyone may express his or her own preferences, but at the same time voters cannot choose their most preferred candidate, but they need to accept the choice made by parties. In this view, it could be acknowledged that Italian elections lack full freedom of choice. Therefore, competition in the political arena occurs among parties and/or coalitions but not among candidates. In this view, we may argue that political competition in Italy is not fully developed, since voters can choose their most preferred political platform, but they cannot choose the candidate that they feel could best represent their interests.

Why may the above issues explain the reasons for the absence of a change in the regulations for the broadcasting sector?

Let us consider again the theory put forward by Acemoglu and Robinson (2006). The two authors argue that the implementation of policies which are growth-enhancing is more likely to occur in those countries in which the degree of political competition is either high or low. On the other hand, when the degree of competition is neither high nor low, the government in office prefers not to introduce reforms which could generate a dramatic change in the economic, political and social structure of the country. In turn, this could lead to a change in the political leadership.

As we argued above, the elections Act introduced in 2005 removed the possibility of selecting the most preferred candidate. Therefore, broadly speaking, voters are limited in their freedom to choose. Although Italian elections are in general democratic and the degree of political competition is high, the election Act eliminates one of the most important aspects of an election.

If we couple together the above observations, we can develop the following argument. In Italy, the broadcasting service is polarized between two main bodies: one is publicly owned, while the second is privately owned (the main shareholder being the former Italian prime minister). The key figures in public television are appointed by the political powers following a procedure which gives each party some 'control' over one of the three channels. If this is the case, the broadcasting services do not play the role of conveying neutral information but it is filtered by the political powers.

Changing the regulations of the Italian broadcasting service by introducing more competition and more efficiency could have two consequences. On the one hand political parties will lose some TV channels through which they may spread information; on the other, an efficient and highly competitive sector may generate the conditions for the emergence of new political competitors. With respect to the first point, according to Acemoglu and Robinson (2006), we can explain why even left-wing governments do not manage to change the existing regulations of the broadcasting service. Although a new Act would limit the power of one of the political competitors (the main shareholders of the private broadcasting body), on the other, a government which acts in this way would lose control of public television.

The second consequence highlighted above is crucial. A more effective broadcasting sector or, more generally, investment in ICT would create an ideal environment for the emergence of political competitors which may threaten the leadership in office. This explains why ten years on, the broadcasting service has still not been reformed. An example of what may happen was given at the last general election in 2013. In a few months a new movement called the Five

Stars Movement obtained a significant result by collecting around 25 per cent of votes for the Chamber of Deputies. The main characteristic of such a movement is that it uses the Internet heavily as the main vehicle of communication among its members and with its voters (see Chapter 19 in this volume).

The provocative questions we want to pose at the end of this section are the following. What would be the result of the general elections in ten years, if each government in office from now on provided more effective regulation of the broadcasting sector and invested massively in ICT? More importantly, would we have the same political parties in Parliament? Is it convenient for a government in office to reform the broadcasting sector in light of its own political calculus?

Conclusions: political reforms as a condition for a long-term growth strategy

In the economic analysis of convergence one of the reasons why economies do not tend, in the long run, to the same equilibrium level of wealth per capita is that the markets do not transmit appropriate incentives to economic agents (Solow, 1956). If this is the case, the intervention of the government should be directed to remove such obstacles through adequate policies which would allow the market to transmit incentives properly.

The question therefore is: is such a policy possible? Italy needs a development strategy. However, the effects of such a strategy are likely to take place in a period of time that is longer than the urgent need to present voters with results. In other words, the political cycle is shorter than the time this policy requires in order to produce its effects. This reduces the likelihood of sticking to such a policy.

Moreover, the political calculus as outlined by Acemoglu and Robinson (2006) leads us to explain the behaviour of politicians who may or may not implement some growth-enhancing reforms. While in Italy there is the need for a development strategy, it should account for media development and investment in ICT. However, in the last ten years there has been no government which was able to implement such a reform. We explained this inconsistency with the argument that a more efficient television broadcasting service is not in the interests of Italian political parties. Under an electoral rule which limited the voters' freedom of choice, as they cannot vote for their most preferred politician but only for a party or coalition, the possibility of 'controlling' some public television channels is fundamental for conveying and spreading non-neutral information. In addition, the development of the television broadcasting industry may give rise to the emergence of political competitors which may challenge the leadership in power. As we have noted, this could be a big risk, as the experience of the new Five Stars Movement shows.

Note

1 In this chapter we group Italian regions according to the following classification. Northern Italy: Piedmont, Valle D'Aosta, Lombardy, Liguria, Trentino-Alto Adige, Veneto, Friuli-Venezia Giulia, Emilia Romagna. Central Italy: Tuscany, Umbria, Marche, Lazio, Abruzzo. Southern Italy: Molise, Puglia, Campania, Basilicata, Calabria, Sicily, Sardinia.

Bibliography

Acemoglu, D. and Robinson, J. (2006). Economic backwardness in political perspective. *American Political Science Review*, 100, 115–31.

Ahrend, R. (2001). Press freedom, human capital and corruption. *DELTA Working Paper*, 2002 (11).

Amin, M. and Djankov, S. (2009a). Democracy and reforms. *The World Bank Policy Research Working Paper*, 4835.

Amin, M. and Djankov, S. (2009b). Natural resources and reforms. *The World Bank Policy Research Working Paper*, 4882.

Bairam, E. I. and McRae, S. D. (1999). Testing the convergence hypothesis: a new approach. *Economic Letters*, 64, 351–5.

Bandyopadhyay, S. (2009). Knowledge-based economic development: mass media and the weightless Economy. *STICERD Discussion Paper*, London School of Economics.

Barro, R. J. and Sala-i-Martin, X. (1991). Convergence across states and regions. *Brookings Papers on Economics Activity*, 1, 1107–82.

Ben-David, D. (1994). Converging clubs and diverging economies. *CEPR Discussion Papers*, 922.

Bernard, A. and Durlauf, S. N. (1995). Convergence in international output. *Journal of Applied Econometrics*, 10, 97–108.

Besley, T., Burgess, R. and Prat, A. (2002). Mass media and political accountability. *Mimeo*, London School of Economics.

Besley, T., Persson, T. and Sturm, D. M. (2010). Political competition, policy and growth: theory and evidence from the US. *Review of Economic Studies*, 77, 1329–52.

Brunetti, A. and Weder, B. (2003). A free press is bad news for corruption. *Journal of Public Economics*, 87, 1801–24.

Buonanno, P. and Leonida, L. (2009). Non market returns of education on crime. Evidence from Italian regions. *Education of Economics Review*, 28, 11–17.

Daveri, F. (2002). The new economy in Europe: 1992–2001. *WIDER Discussion Paper*, 2002/70.

De Cecco, M. (2007). Italy's dysfunctional political economy. *West European Politics*, 30 (4), 763–83.

de Haan, J. and Sturm, J.-E. (2003). Does more democracy lead to greater economic freedom? New evidence for developing countries. *European Journal of Political Economy*, 19, 547–63.

De la Fuente, A. (1997). The empirics of growth and convergence: a selective review. *Journal of Economic Dynamics and Control*, 21, 23–73.

De la Fuente, A. (2000). Convergence across countries and regions: theory and empirics. *EIB Papers*, 2, 25–43.

Del Monte, A. and Giannola, A. (1997). *Istituzioni Economiche e Mezzogiorno*. Bologna: NIS.

Djankov, S., McLiesh, C., Nenova, T. and Shleifer, A. (2003). Who owns the media? *Journal of Law and Economics*, 46, 341–81.

Dowrick, S. and Gemmell, N. (1991). Industrialisation, catching up and economic growth: a comparative study across the world's capitalist economies. *The Economic Journal*, 101, 263–75.

Durlauf, S. N. and Quah, D. T. (1999). The new empirics of economic growth. In J. Taylor and M. Woodford (eds.), *Handbook of Macroeconomics*, Vol. 1A (pp. 235–306). Amsterdam: North-Holland.

Easterly, W. (2007). Was development assistance a mistake? *American Economic Review*, 97, 328–32.

Edwards, S. (1991). Stabilization and liberalization policies in Central and Eastern Europe: lessons from Latin America. *NBER Working Paper*, 3816.

Fernandez, R. and Rodrik, D. (1991). Resistance to reform: status quo bias in the presence of individual-specific uncertainty. *American Economic Review*, 81, 1146–55.

Ferri, G. and Mattesini, F. (1997). Finance, human capital and infrastructure. An empirical investigation on post-war Italian growth. *Banca d'Italia Working Paper Series*, 321.

Giavazzi, F. and Tabellini, G. (2005). Economic and political liberalization. *Journal of Monetary Economics*, 52, 1297–1330.

Graziani, A. (1979). Il Mezzogiorno nel quadro dell'economia Italiana. In A. Graziani and E. Pugliese (eds.), *Investimenti e Disoccupazione nel Mezzogiorno* (pp. 25–38). Bologna: Il Mulino.

Haacker, M. and Morsink, J. (2002). You say you want a revolution: information technology and growth. *IMF Working Paper*, No. 02/70.

Iona, A., Leonida, L. and Sobbrio, G. (2008). O convergence, where art thou? Regional growth and Industrialization in Italy. *Journal of Modern Italian Studies*, 13, 366–87.

Islam, N. (2003). What have we learnt from the convergence debate. *Journal of Economic Survey*, 17, 309–62.

Milio, S. (2008). How political stability shapes administrative performance: the Italian case. *West European Politics*, 31, 915–28.

Murphy, K., Shleifer, A. and Vishny, R. (1989). Industrialization and the Big Push. *Journal of Political Economy*, 97, 1003–26.

North, D. C. (1991). *Institutions, Institutional Change and Economic Performance*. Cambridge: Cambridge University Press.

Orr, D. (1987). Notes on the mass media as an economic institution. *Public Choice*, 53, 79–95.

Paci, R. and Saba, A. (1998). The empirics of regional economic growth in Italy, 1951– 1993. *Rivista Internazionale di Scienze Economiche e Commerciali*, 5, 513–42.

Padovano, F. and Ricciuti, R. (2008). Political competition and economic performance: evidence from Italian regions. *Public Choice*, 138: 263–77.

Peters, B. G. (2004). Managing horizontal government. The politics of coordination. *Research Paper 21*, Canadian Centre for Management Development.

Pohjola, M. (1998). Information technology and economic development: an introduction to the research issues. *UNU WIDER Working Paper 153*.

Putnam, R. D. (1993). *Making Democracy Work: Civic Traditions in Modern Italy*. Princeton, NJ: Princeton University Press.

Quah, D. (1996). Regional convergence clusters across Europe. *European Economic Review*, 40, 951–8.

Quah, D. (1997). Empirics for growth and distribution: stratification, polarization and convergence clubs. *Journal of Economic Growth*, 2, 27–59.

Rajan, R. G. and Subramanian, A. (2007). Does aid affect governance? *American Economic Review, Papers and Proceedings*, 2, 322–7.

Rodrik, D. (1996). Understanding economic policy reform. *Journal of Economic Literature*, 34, 9–41.

Shi, M. and Svensson, J. (2006). Political budget cycles: do they differ across countries and why? *Journal of Public Economics*, 90, 1367–89.

Solow, R. M. (1956). A contribution to the theory of economic growth. *Quarterly Journal of Economics*, 70, 65–94.

SVIMEZ (2008). *Rapporto SVIMEZ 2008 sull'Economia del Mezzogiorno*. Rome.

Temple, J. (1999). The new growth evidence. *Journal of Economic Literature*, 37, 112–56.

Terrasi, M. (1999). Convergence and divergence across Italian regions. *The Annals of Regional Science*, 33, 491–510.

Williamson, J. G. (1965). Regional inequality and the process of national development: a description of the patterns. *Economic Development and Cultural Change*, 13, 3–84.

23
ITALIAN FIRMS

Alessandro Giovannini and Raoul Minetti

Introduction

Italy is one of the major economies of Europe. In 2012 its GDP equalled 1,565 billion euros, the fourth in Europe after Germany, France and the United Kingdom. In Europe, its industrial sector (mining, manufacturing, construction and energy) is second only to that of Germany for value added (as is shown in Figure 23.1) and for employment. Italy is the fifth industrial country in the world, producing around 6 per cent of the OECD industrial output in 2011 (as is shown in Figure 23.2). Although the gap between it and the fourth, Germany, has widened in recent years, Italy has slightly increased its advantage in relation to France and the United Kingdom.

According to ISTAT data (2012a), in 2010, 33 per cent of all employees worked in the industrial sector (1,050,000 firms), and 20 per cent in services (more than 3,000,000 firms), as is shown in Figure 23.3. Within the industrial sector, a significant role is played by firms operating in the production of metal products (about 689,000 workers), textiles (about 512,000 employees) and machinery (about 462,000 workers).

The Italian economic system comprises a very large number of small and medium-sized firms and few big industrial groups or enterprises. In the 2012 ranking of the top 500 companies in the world published by the magazine *Fortune* (2012), only nine Italian firms (two manufacturers, three financial firms and two energy-related companies) were listed, while, for instance, Germany and France accounted for 32 firms each. Moreover, in 2010 the average number of employees of Italian firms was around 4, which is the lowest in Europe and well below that of other European economies such as Germany (12), the United Kingdom (10.8) and the average of EU countries (6.1). More precisely, the Italian system is based on a hard core of two elements: i) a very large number of enterprises with fewer than 50 employees (more than 4,000,000 in 2010 according to ISTAT data); ii) a relatively small number of firms with more than 50 employees (25,000) able to connect the multitude of small enterprises with global markets.

In 2010, in Italy there were about 64 firms per 1,000 inhabitants, a figure among the highest in Europe. This figure, however, hides pronounced differences across Italian regions: if the regions in the North and the Centre exhibit an even greater ratio (almost 70 firms per 1,000 inhabitants), those in the South of the country barely exceed 50 firms per 1,000 inhabitants. This North–South gap can also be grasped by looking at other indicators of industrial activity. For example, with regard to the distribution of employees, 34 per cent of employees work in the North-West, while firms in the South employ under 15 per cent. Finally, firms located in the North contributed

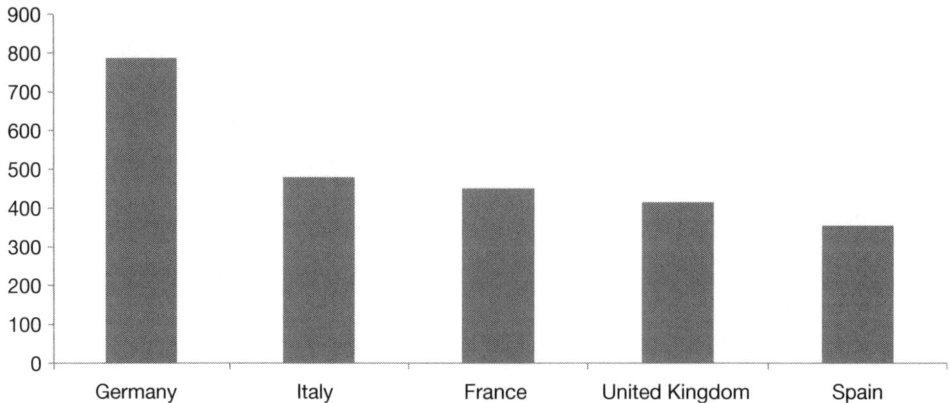

Figure 23.1 Industry, value added (current US$)

Source: World Bank, 2013

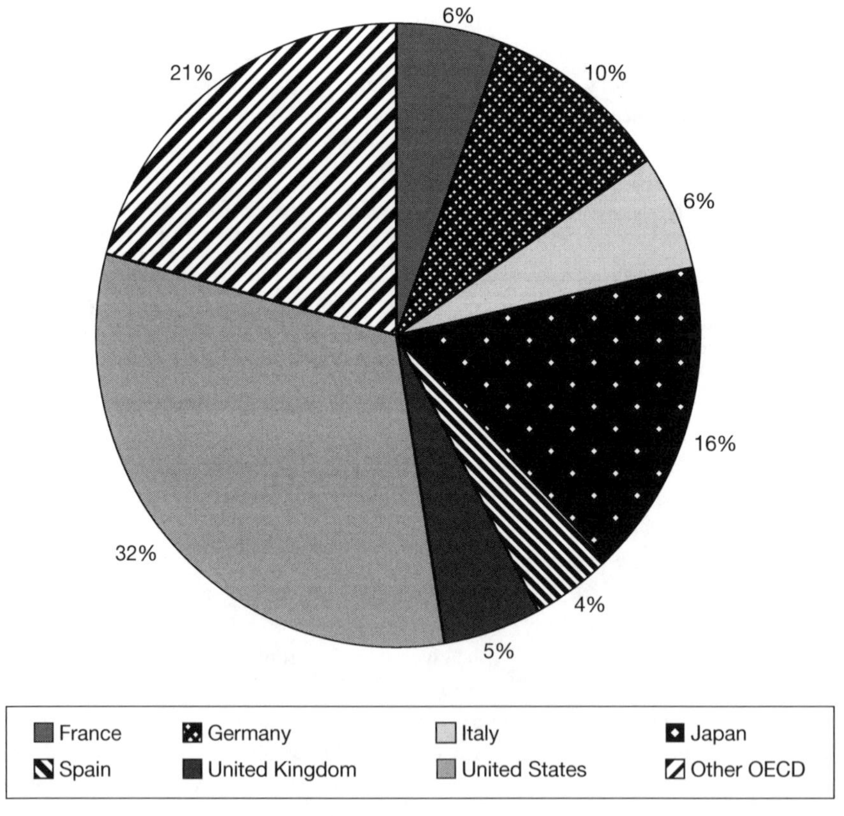

Figure 23.2 Share of OECD industrial production

Source: World Bank, 2013

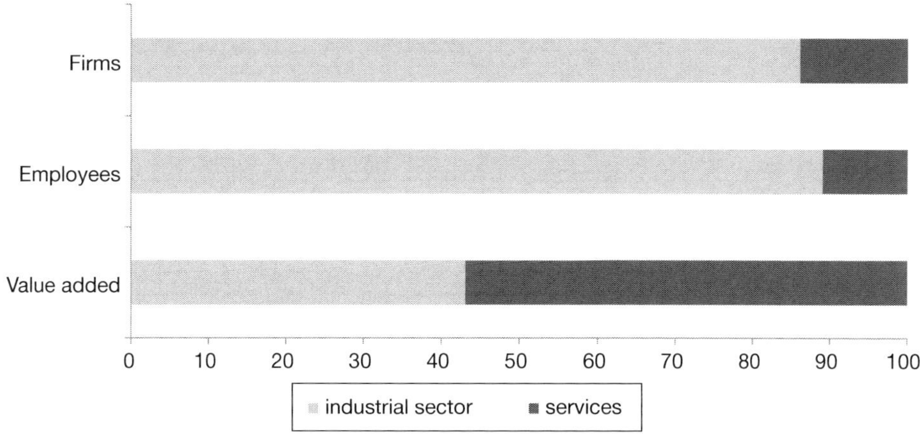

Figure 23.3 A snapshot of the Italian productive system

Source: ISTAT, 2012a

61.9 per cent to the creation of added value in the country, while those in the South only 18 per cent.

This chapter intends to examine the main features of Italian firms. The first section of the chapter analyses the main factors behind the small size of many Italian firms and the pros and cons of this feature. The next section investigates the ownership structure and governance of Italian businesses. The last two sections examine the ability of Italian firms to engage in innovation at all levels of production; and their ability to export products and internationalize their activities.

A fragmented production system

In 2010, out of 4.5 million Italian firms, those with no employees accounted for 65.44 per cent of the total; around 95 per cent of the firms had no more than 10 employees (employing 47 per cent of the total workforce). To turn to bigger firms, Table 23.1 shows that 4.5 per cent of Italian enterprises employed 10 to 49 employees, giving employment to 21 per cent of the workforce, while firms with 50 to 249 employees provided employment to 12.4 per cent of the total workforce. Only 3,718 firms had more than 250 employees, absorbing, however, 20 per cent of overall employment. The importance of small firms is a feature of several European countries: small enterprises (with no more than 10 employees) represent the vast majority of businesses in Germany (95 per cent), the United Kingdom (94 per cent) and France (93 per cent). The key difference with Italy, however, is not only the average small size of firms, but also the fact that in other countries the proportion of total employment accounted for by small firms is much lower: 34 per cent in France, 28 per cent in Germany and the United Kingdom.

Alongside an extraordinary constellation of small and medium-sized enterprises with fewer than 250 employees (mainly specialized in consumer goods), the Italian system comprises a few large firms, partly state-owned (or previously state-owned) and partly controlled by a few families. These large firms often specialize in the production of capital goods and consumer durables and have a turnover of more than 20 billion euros.

Table 23.2 shows the list of Italian groups with more than 10,000 employees and their evolution in the last twenty years (the list is based on Coltorti, 2012). It appears that the size

Table 23.1 Size structure of Italian firms

	Number of firms	*Employees*	*Turnover (000,000 Euros)*	*Value added (000,000 Euros)*	*Value added per employee (000 Euros)*	*Investments per employee (000 Euros)*
0–9	4,151,104	7,986,251	780,351	220,276	27.6	5.8
10–19	141,434	1,850,581	325,317	71,540	38.7	5.2
20–49	54,801	1,628,475	346,714	76,403	46.9	6.3
50–249	21,309	2,057,944	572,517	113,972	55.4	15.4
250	3,495	3,171,207	882,396	225,639	71.2	12.7
Total	4,372,143	16,694,458	2,907,295	707,830	42.4	8.3

Source: ISTAT, 2012a

and the role of large manufacturing firms have declined strongly during this period. Fiat is one of the groups that have maintained an adequate size in international comparisons, with, however, in 2009 a workforce 27 per cent lower than 20 years ago. A similar pattern has characterized another leading manufacturing company, Pirelli, as well as other groups producing appliances, such as Zanussi/Electrolux (which reduced its workforce by more than 50 per cent) and Montedison, Olivetti and SNIA, which went bankrupt over the last ten years. In total, between 1993 and 2009, the number of employees of the large Italian groups declined by 49 per cent. In contrast with this process, some new groups have emerged especially in the service sector and in industrial sectors characterized by lower intensity of capital. The Benetton group, for instance, is increasingly becoming a conglomerate. Alongside its core production of clothes, it has increased its participation in financial and public services (e.g. roads) and commercial activities (restaurants), mostly through the privatization programmes of state-owned enterprises that have occurred in the last twenty years. Following a different pattern, Luxottica has instead expanded its core business (albeit with investments in commercial distribution) and it has been able to increase its number of employees by 59,000.

If we look at the second pillar of the Italian economy, it appears that small businesses are specializing in sectors with lower technological content than large firms. For a long time, their small size was considered a strategic choice, because of several advantages connected with: i) the possibility of creating synergies by putting in place collaboration agreements; ii) the possibility of achieving greater diversification through the establishment of groups of several small firms able to address the growing fragmentation of demand and the spread of niche markets; and iii) the greater flexibility of small firms in reacting to exogenous market shocks. Recently, however, this peculiarity of the Italian system has increasingly been considered the result of internal and external constraints limiting firm growth. Internal constraints include cultural aspects and business practices rooted in the majority of Italian firms which may make them reluctant to expand their scale. The tight relationship between firms' management and family ownership (see also the discussion in the next section) and the tendency of families to retain management functions may also pose obstacles to the growth of firms.

In addition to internal constraints, external constraints can also hinder the growth of firms. Arrighetti and Serravalle (1997) and Micossi and Parascandolo (2010) argue that the dimensional duality seems to have been nourished by an equally pronounced institutional dualism, in turn due to three different factors. First, small businesses have been systematically supported by a system of monetary incentives, such as favourable accounting rules and tax reporting duties, as well as privileged financing channels from both private and public sources. Second, small businesses

Table 23.2 Italian groups with at least 10,000 employees (in 000 units)

Groups	*1993*	*2003*	*2009*	*Groups*	*1993*	*2003*	*2009*
Fiat	261	162	190	Merloni Indesit	7	19	16
Pirelli	42	36	30	Barilla	8	25	15
Snia	12	5	—	Parmalat	13	32	14
Zanussi/Electrolux	17	12	7	Gruppo Cir (De Benedetti)	71	10	13
Michelin Italiana	8	7	5	Menarini	5	10	13
Face/Alcatel	13	3	2	Perfetti Van Melle	—	9	13
Setemer/Ericsson	7	2	4	Unicem/Buzzi	3	12	12
Piaggio	8	5	7	Miroglio	7	8	11
Edizione (Benetton)	9	44	72	Marzotto	11	11	3
Luxottica (Del Vecchio)	3	38	61	TIBB/Asea BB/ABB	12	9	8
Riva	6	25	23	Smi (Orlando)/KME Group	10	8	7
Italcementi (Pesenti)	20	17	23	Lucchini	10	9	6
Ferrero	16	16	22				

Source: Coltorti, 2012

are exempted from the application of the rules of the Workers' Statute (*Statuto dei Lavoratori*) and other social constraints. Although there is no established empirical evidence of sharp discontinuities in the size of firms because of such regulations, it is likely that the combination of these factors can deter firm growth (Barca, 1997). Third, tax evasion and undeclared work appear to be particularly common among micro-enterprises, as is confirmed indirectly by the significant weight of the shadow economy (estimated at 20 per cent of GDP), which has showed a rapid increase since 1970, after the introduction of the Workers' Statute (Schneider, 2005).

Klapper *et al.* (2006) offer an alternative explanation for the small size of Italian firms based on external constraints on the entry of new firms. According to their analysis, the significant regulatory and bureaucratic barriers that still hinder the foundation of firms in Italy tend to depress the rate of creation of new firms. Furthermore, such barriers induce an arbitrary selection of new firms, not one based on their productivity and potential efficiency, but purely on their ability to sustain entry costs. These aspects reduce the competition faced by older incumbents, making them more 'lazy' and less interested in enhancing their productivity and expanding their scale.

Overall, we can then conclude that a distinguishing feature of the Italian economy is the inability of many small firms to grow and reach a medium scale of operations. Indeed, several medium-sized Italian companies are not the result of an expansion of small firms but rather stem from the shrinkage of large firms, as has been documented above. In the past, the small size of small firms was less of a concern as such firms led the economic growth of the country, thanks to their flexibility in production. Today, on the other hand, small firms face significant challenges, as will be discussed in the next sections. Small businesses, especially those run by families, appear to be less prone to developing a management system based on strong competences. They also engage less in research and development and innovation projects. Finally, they appear to be unable to sustain the high fixed costs associated with export activities and production abroad.

Ownership structure and governance

Family firms were the key players in the industrialization of Italy and today they still play a fundamental role in the economy. In fact, they can be considered a 'structural element' of the Italian economy. Indeed, in the evolution that has marked Italian capitalism over the past three decades, they have been an unvarying factor that assured continuity in the context of an increasingly globalized market. Despite significant changes in the regulatory framework and in institutional incentives (now more similar to those of other major developed countries), ownership and control of the Italian productive system have changed little, especially for unlisted companies (Franco, 2012).

According to the data of the Bank of Italy shown in Table 23.3, 86 per cent of Italian companies are owned by a family, a figure slightly higher than that of France (80 per cent), Spain (83 per cent) and the United Kingdom (81 per cent), but lower than that of Germany (90 per cent). Indeed, what emerges from the table is not a completely peculiar pattern of ownership structure, but rather the low propensity of Italian family businesses to rely on external management resources.

As is shown in Table 23.4, another element typical of Italian firms is the high percentage of businesses run in a 'centralized' way and the low proportion of enterprises using individual remuneration incentives.

These elements are particularly relevant to explaining the performance of Italian companies, as a management structure predominantly based on families could generate biases, such as privileging the long-term maintenance of family control rather than firm profitability and growth.

To be sure, family ownership in itself can present both advantages and disadvantages. On the minus side, some studies have underlined that family businesses tend to have a higher degree of risk aversion, because of a substantial coincidence between family assets and business assets, with possible negative effects on growth and investment. For instance, Cucculelli (2007) suggests that family businesses may be more oriented to maintaining control in the long term rather than enhancing profitability and growth. This would induce them to be less responsive to sudden changes in market demand, which would entail a reduced ability to exploit new market opportunities. More recently, Bianco *et al.* (2012) have found evidence that Italian family firms' investments are more sensitive to uncertainty than those of non-family firms. On the plus side, an advantage of family firms is that they could have a longer-term horizon, because they better internalize the utility of future generations of family owners. Minetti *et al.* (2012b) find that family-owned firms tend to export more than other types of companies, even after controlling for firm heterogeneity in productivity, size, technology and access to credit. They

Table 23.3 Family-owned firms in Europe

Country	*Family-owned firms (% of the total)*	*Only family-owned firms*	
		CEO is a member of the family (in %)	*Management is composed of family (in %)*
Italy	85.6	83.9	66.3
Germany	89.8	84.5	28.0
France	80.0	62.2	25.8
Spain	83.0	79.6	35.5
United Kingdom	80.5	70.8	10.4

Source: Bank of Italy, 2009

Table 23.4 Managerial structure in Italian firms

Country	*Centralized management structure (as % of total firms)*			*Individual remuneration incentives structure (as % of total firms)*		
	All firms	*Only family-owned firms*	*Only with family members in the management*	*All firms*	*Only family-owned firms*	*Only with family members in the management*
Italy	84.9	87.0	91.3	16.4	15.2	10.7
Germany	70.5	74.4	90.2	48.9	46.9	31.5
France	77.5	79.7	83.4	45.0	43.1	33.4
Spain	61.4	67.0	79.8	24.8	23.3	13.5
United Kingdom	62.7	66.4	78.4	47.3	44.9	39.8

Source: Bank of Italy, 2009

also find evidence that this result is especially driven by the long-termism of family owners. Minetti *et al.* (2012b) find that this longer horizon of family firms also implies a higher propensity to invest in innovation projects, but that the benefits of institutional owners increase with their equity shares.

To conclude the analysis of the ownership structure of Italian firms, it is useful to briefly discuss the limited role of financial institutions. In Italy the main source of financing for business projects consists of funds provided by the banking sector, as the use of capital market financing remains relatively underdeveloped (see Chapter 24 in this volume). So far, however, the great importance of banks has not resulted in the development of financial intermediaries that intervene directly in the ownership of firms, but mostly in a high credit exposure of the banking system to the industrial system. Table 23.5 shows that in listed companies, institutional owners (both domestic and foreign) have a smaller role in Italy than in other European economies (roughly 5 per cent compared with an average participation of 9 per cent). The presence of institutional investors in the ownership of Italian firms has changed very little in recent years (for possible theoretical explanations, see, for example, Araujo and Minetti, 2007, and references therein).

Table 23.5 Shareholder structure of listed companies (in %)

Country	*Significant shareholders (more than 3% of capital)*	*Controlling shareholders*	*Institutional investors*	*of which: domestic*	*of which: foreign*	*Others*
Italy	52.2	45.2	4.9	1.1	3.8	2.1
Germany	22.4	14.0	6.6	0.8	5.7	1.8
France	19.7	11.1	6.7	3.8	2.9	2.0
Spain	47.8	28.3	9.9	7.0	2.9	9.5
United Kingdom	18.4	6.8	11.6	8.7	2.9	0.0

Source: Bank of Italy, 2009

Innovation processes in Italian firms

Among OECD countries, Italy is characterized by the lowest level of expenditure for research and development (R&D). In 2010, compared with an OECD average expenditure of 2.4 per cent and an EU average of 1.9 per cent of national GDP, Italy allocated only 1.3 per cent of its GDP to R&D. This figure appears to be even smaller if we consider that in 2010 Italy accounted for only 8 per cent of the total R&D expenditure of the European Union. In comparison, Germany, France and the United Kingdom contributed respectively 28 per cent, 18 per cent and 13 per cent.

The low propensity of Italian firms to innovate is often mentioned as one of the primary causes of their difficulties in fostering the productivity of the country. And yet the potential of the innovations could be quite significant: in 2010 the share of turnover that resulted from sales related to innovative products equalled 25 per cent.

To continue the comparison with the main European competitors, approximately 38 per cent of Italian firms have engaged in innovation projects in the 2008–10 period. This percentage is above the EU average (35 per cent), but far below that of Germany (50 per cent). Italy's lag in relation to other major EU countries hides substantial differences among Italian regions: only 16 per cent of firms in the South have carried out innovative projects in the 2008–10 period compared with 27 per cent of firms in the North. Further analysis of the data shows that the majority of firms undertook combined innovations in products and processes (about 50 per cent), while 27 per cent innovated only in products and 24 per cent only in processes. The industrial sector has shown the highest propensity to innovate, with an expenditure for innovation of about 9,400 euros per employee, followed by the services sector (5,800 euros) and the construction sector (4,300 euros).

The propensity to innovate of Italians firms appears to be correlated not only with their geographical location and their sector, but also with their size: considering the same period, Figure 23.4 shows that more than 60 per cent of the firms with more than 250 employees have introduced innovations, compared with 47 per cent for firms with between 50 and 250 employees, and 29 per cent for those with 10–50 employees.

In terms of firms' expenditures for R&D, the situation is again not reassuring when compared with that of Italy's main competitors. In comparison with an average expenditure by EU firms of around 1.2 per cent of GDP, expenditure by Italian firms shows a substantial backwardness, equalling 0.7 per cent of GDP. Breaking down these expenses by type, we find that in 2010 applied research absorbed most of the resources spent in industrial R&D, followed by expenditure for experimental development projects, and by investment in basic research processes. More than 75 per cent of Italian industrial research is concentrated in the North, while the total expenditure of firms in Sicily, Calabria, Campania and Puglia did not even amount to 3.5 per cent of Italian industrial spending on R&D in 2010. This situation is also reflected in the distribution of employment: of the 112,200 employees in R&D activities in Italian firms, approximately 45 per cent work in the North-West, 30 per cent in the North-East, 15 per cent in the Centre and only 8 per cent in the South.

To turn to other measures of innovation, Italian firms do not appear to perform much better. If one looks at the number of patent applications filed at the European Patent Office (EPO), Italy went from 45,863 requests in 2004 to 44,442 in 2010. This reduction of 3 per cent is far worse than the decline in Europe during the same period (-0.9 per cent) and puts Italy (with 73.3 patents per million inhabitants) very far from the EU average of 109.2 patents per million inhabitants and the figures for other major European economies, such as Germany (267.4), France (135.2) and the United Kingdom (77.3). Lotti and Schivardi (2005) find empirically that the

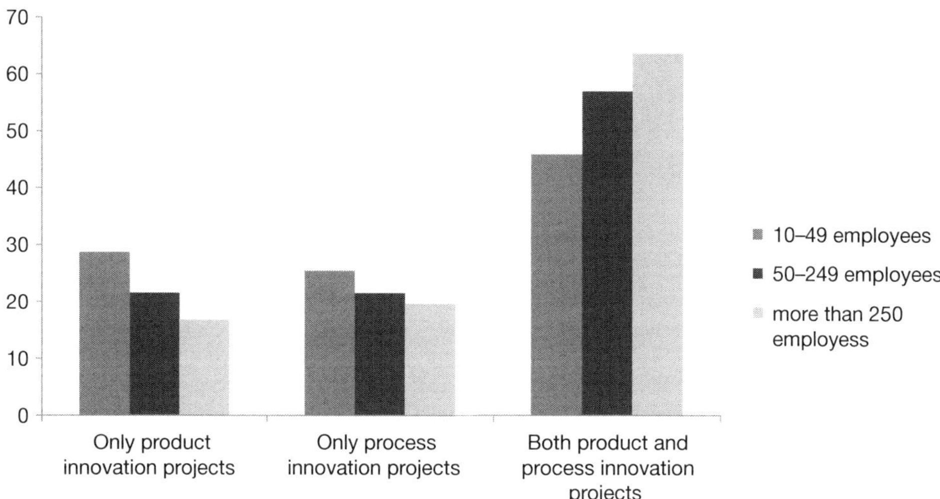

Figure 23.4 Innovation projects by size of firm

Source: ISTAT, 2013

probability of Italian firms registering new patents is significantly and positively correlated with company size, while Marini and Menon (2011) show that patent activity is highly concentrated in a few large companies. Of all the patents registered with the EPO between 1990 and 2007 by Italian applicants, approximately one quarter are owned by the 20 largest applicants, and 40 per cent by companies with a turnover of more than 10 million euros.

The reader might be concerned that the above indicators (expenditure on R&D, number of patents, and number of employees involved in R&D activity) underestimate the innovative effort of the small and medium-sized firms that undertake innovative activities without officially registering them. It is then important to analyse specifically the activity of the firms that claim to have carried out a product or process innovation without formal expenditure on R&D and compare them with those that instead report expenditure on R&D. Performing such an exercise, Bugamelli *et al.* (2012) show that innovators without research 'have a significantly lower ability to realize patents, register industrial designs, trademarks or copyrights, and the share of sales from innovative products is in their case lower'.

If we analyse innovation activity by sector, it emerges that Italy's lag in this area is partly due to a sectorial specialization biased towards traditional industries with low technological content. As we have discussed, the importance of sectors such as textiles and clothing (characterized by little propensity to innovate) is greater in Italy than in other European countries, while the sectors most likely to promote innovation activity (e.g. chemical, communications, computing hardware) account for a smaller share of GDP. This explanation, however, is not fully convincing. Bugamelli *et al.* (2012) show that the lower level of innovative activity in Italy is common in many industries and, in terms of expenditure on R&D, Italy has the lowest figure both in technologically advanced sectors and in more traditional ones. Therefore, other causes are probably crucial in explaining the low propensity to innovate of Italian firms. Such factors may include the limited size of Italian businesses (as we have discussed above) and inefficiencies in their management. Recent studies also point to a mixed role of the Italian financial system. On the one hand, Benfratello *et al.* (2008) and Herrera and Minetti (2007) find evidence that the credit relationships between banks and firms foster the innovation activity by Italian firms.

On the other hand, Minetti (2011) uncovers evidence that Italian banks tend to finance especially incremental innovations but are less willing to support radical innovations.

Exports and internationalization of Italian firms

In 2011, Italian exports of goods amounted to 24 per cent of GDP, a value lower than that of Germany, but higher than that of France, the United Kingdom and Spain. However, in the last decade the international competitiveness of Italian firms has shown signs of deterioration: their market share in world exports decreased from 3.6 per cent in 2002 to 2.7 per cent in 2011. This has mainly been the result of two factors. On the one hand, Italian exports are characterized by a technological content lower than that of goods produced by competitors (such as Germany), a peculiarity that reflects a sectorial distribution of Italian firms biased towards traditional goods and exposes them to the competition of emerging economies. On the other hand, the loss of competitiveness reflects the inferior ability of Italian firms to export to the most dynamic emerging economies such as India and China. Sales by Italian firms to China accounted for 2.7 per cent of total exports, while in Germany this figure is more than double.

In 2011, about 205,382 Italian firms carried out at least one business transaction in a foreign country, according to ISTAT (2013). Their strategies of internationalization are mainly based on traditional approaches, such as exports or sub-supply agreements based on commercial and production relationships with foreign firms. The largest proportion of firms carry out both import and export activities, followed by only exporting firms, while the number of firms that adopt forms of internationalization of their production is much lower (5 per cent and 3 per cent respectively for foreign-controlled firms and for multinational enterprises). However, in the latter categories, the average firm size is much larger: around 210 employees per firm compared with an average 13 employees for firms that only export. Moreover, Italian multinational enterprises differ also in the larger number of products exported and the higher number of foreign destination markets.

If we analyse the relationship between the presence in foreign markets and firms' performance, it emerges that the firms that have a greater level of internationalization also have higher productivity, and this relationship holds too after controlling for firm size. Nevertheless, firms with higher profitability mostly have a pattern of internationalization based on 'basic' export strategies.

The distribution of firms among categories shows that in the traditional areas of the so-called "Made in Italy" goods, the practice of exporting and importing is largely predominant: for instance, the production of textiles, clothing, and paper and related products is mainly based on bidirectional commerce. A similar pattern can be found in the remaining manufacturing sectors, such as the chemical industry, the metallurgical industry, the production of plastic, electronic, electrical and optical products, as well as the production of motor vehicles and other means of transportation. By contrast, in the production of machinery, Italian exporting firms act as global enterprises (i.e. sell at least in five non-European areas) and in no manufacturing sector is there a predominant presence of firms with direct investments abroad. ISTAT (2013) also shows that on average Italian multinationals and global firms exhibit better production results, measured as greater changes in the value added of production, than Italian firms that follow other strategies of internationalization. Finally, businesses mainly based on exporting alone are those in the fields of drinks, printing and reproduction of recorded media, manufacturing of metal products, furniture, repair and maintenance of machinery. On average, these export-only firms show a worse performance in terms of employment change and increase in value added compared with firms that follow bidirectional or more structured activities of internalization.

If we look at firms' size, exports are highly concentrated in the largest firms (ICE, 2012). In 2010, almost 45 per cent of exports were attributable to firms with more than 250 employees, while firms with fewer than 10 employees accounted for less than 10 per cent of total exports. This situation, however, does not reflect the number of export firms: more than 60 per cent of export firms had fewer than ten employees, while 7 per cent had more than 50 employees and only 1 per cent more than 250.

Therefore, despite the large presence of small exporters, the increase in the size of firms appears to have remarkable relevance for export volumes. Firms' size matters, especially because of the fixed, sunk costs that are associated with strategies of internalization and are more easily sustainable by large firms. Moreover, the small size of many Italian firms also affects their ability to reach distant markets, as is shown by the analysis conducted by ISTAT (2013): over 62 per cent of small and medium-sized firms export only to neighbour areas such as the European Union and Central/Eastern Europe and only 38 per cent of them reach markets outside Europe.

As we have mentioned, the Italian industrial system also contains a number of multinational enterprises (ISTAT, 2012b); in 2008 these generated around 190 billion euros in revenue and employed nearly 854,000 individuals. These numbers also reflect the average size of Italian subsidiaries abroad, which have around 71 employees on average, well above that of firms resident in Italy. Italian affiliates abroad mostly operate in non-financial services, followed by industrial activities. The sector with the most pronounced propensity to engage in direct foreign activity is manufacturing: the incidence of its activities abroad, over those carried out in Italy, is around 16 per cent in terms of employment. The presence of manufacturing activities abroad is particularly significant in the production of machinery and equipment, textiles and clothing, and manufacturing of means of transport. In terms of localization, in 2008 the main targeted countries for industrial activities were Romania, Brazil, China, and France, while Italian foreign subsidiaries operating in services were primarily present in the United States, Germany, Spain, and France.

Conclusion

The Great Recession has severely affected the Italian economy, and the recovery that has followed has so far been slow. The problem of the modest growth of the Italian economy is, however, structural in nature, as for over a decade before the crisis the country's productive system was unable to adapt to the radical changes that had occurred in the world economy since the 1990s. Faced with a process of international integration of production processes in advanced economies, Italian firms have reacted in different ways. On the one hand, the majority of firms, mostly those of small size, have remained oriented towards the domestic market and have engaged in innovation to only a small extent. On the other hand, a smaller group of companies, on average larger, more productive and innovative, have projected themselves onto international markets.

The internationalization of Italian firms in the next years will become even more crucial for the growth of the country, not only to reinvigorate its economic performance but most of all as a channel for increasing firms' productivity, innovation, and competitiveness. A key step in this process will be to overcome the widespread concept that 'small is necessarily beautiful'. The ability of Italian firms to expand their activity to international markets and to advance their technological frontiers will also depend on the strategies they will put in place to grow in size and to open their participation to new investors.

Bibliography

Araujo, L. and Minetti, R. (2007). Financial Intermediaries as Markets for Firm Assets. *Economic Journal*, 117 (523), 1380–402.

Arrighetti, A. and Serravalle, G. (1997). *Istituzioni e dualismo dimensionale dell'industria italiana.* In F. Barca (ed.), *Storia del capitalismo italiano dal dopoguerra ad oggi* (pp. 335–83). Rome: Donzelli Editore.

Banca d'Italia [Bank of Italy] (2009). *Rapporto sulle tendenze nel sistema produttivo italiano*, a cura di A. Brandolini e M. Bugamelli. *Questioni di Economia e Finanza*, 45.

Barca, F. (1997). *Compromesso senza riforme nel capitalismo italiano.* In F. Barca (ed.), *Storia del capitalismo italiano dal dopoguerra a oggi* (pp. 4–107). Rome: Donzelli Editore.

Benfratello, L., Schiantarelli, F. and Sembenelli, A. (2008). Banks and Innovation: Microeconometric Evidence on Italian Firms. *Journal of Financial Economics*, 90, 197–217.

Bianco, M., Bontempi, M. E., Golinelli, R. and Parigi, G. (2012). Family Firms' Investments, Uncertainty and Opacity. *Small Business Economics*, 14, 1–24.

Bugamelli, M., Cannari, L., Lotti, F. and Magri, S. (2012). *Il gap innovativo del sistema produttivo italiano: radici e possibili rimedi.* Bank of Italy Occasional Papers, 121.

Coltorti, F. (2012). Decline or Transformation? Assessing the Health of Italian Industry. *QA Rivista dell'Associazione Rossi-Doria*, 2. Milan: FrancoAngeli.

Cucculelli, M. (2007). *Owner Identity and Firm Performance in European Companies. Implications for Competitiveness.* Mimeo.

Fortune (2012). *Global 500 Annual Ranking of the World's Largest Corporation.* Available online at http://fortune.com/global500/2012/ (accessed 14 January 2015).

Franco, D. (2012). *Indagine conoscitiva sulle caratteristiche e sullo sviluppo del sistema industriale, delle imprese pubbliche e del settore energetico.* Testimonianza del Direttore Centrale per la Ricerca economica e le Relazioni internazionali della Banca d'Italia, X Commissione, Camera dei Deputati (Attività Produttive, Commercio e Turismo), Rom2 26 September 2012. Available online at www.bancaditalia.it/pubblicazioni/interventi-vari/int-var-2012/Franco_26092012.pdf (accessed 14 January 2015).

Herrera, A. M. and Minetti, R. (2007). Informed Finance and Technological Change: Evidence from Credit Relationships. *Journal of Financial Economics*, 83 (1), 223–69.

ICE (2012). *Italy in the World Economy.* Rapporto Annuale dell'Istituto per il Commercio con l'Estero.

ISTAT (2012a). *Struttura e competitività delle imprese.* Istituto Nazionale di Statistica Italiano.

ISTAT (2012b). *Struttura, performance e nuovi investimenti delle multinazionali italiane all'estero.* Istituto Nazionale di Statistica Italiano.

ISTAT (2013). *Primo studio sulla competitività dei settori produttivi.* Istituto Nazionale di Statistica Italiano.

Klapper, L., Laeven, L. and Rajan, R. (2006). Entry Regulation as a Barrier to Entrepreneurship. *Journal of Financial Economics*, 82 (3), 591–629.

Lotti, F. and Schivardi, F. (2005). Cross Country Differences in Patent Propensity: A Firm-Level Investigation. *Giornale degli Economisti e Annali di Economia*, 64 (4), 469–502.

Marini, F. and Menon, C. (2011). *L'attività brevettuale in Italia.* Banca d'Italia. Mimeo.

Micossi, S. and Parascandolo, P. (2010). Impresa privata. In C. Pinelli and T. Treu (eds.), *La costituzione economica: Italia, Europa* (pp. 173–218). Bologna: Il Mulino.

Minetti, R. (2011). Informed Finance and Technological Conservatism, *Review of Finance*, 15 (3), 633–92.

Minetti, R., Murro, P. and Paiella, M. (2012). Ownership Structure, Governance, and Innovation: Evidence from Italy. *Working Papers 10.* Department of the Treasury, Ministry of the Economy and of Finance.

Minetti, R., Murro, P. and Zhu, S. (2012b). Family Firms, Corporate Governance, and Export. *Working Paper.* Michigan State University.

Schneider, F. (2005). Shadow Economies around the World: What Do We Really Know? *European Journal of Political Economy*, 21 (4), 598–642.

World Bank (2013). *Databank.* Available online at http://data.worldbank.org/ (accessed 14 January 2015).

24

THE BANKING SYSTEM AND SAVINGS ALLOCATION IN ITALY

Alfonsina Iona, Leone Leonida and Damiano Bruno Silipo

Introduction

It is well known that banks play an important role in the economic growth of bank-oriented economic systems such as the Italian one. The Italian banking industry is in fact the main financial sector in Italy, as it represents 82 per cent of total financial activities (and 24.3 per cent of GDP). Although, by the end of 2009 the total loans of institutional investors, such as insurance companies, investment funds, pension funds and investment management companies, were about 11.8 per cent of GDP, the Italian capital market was still playing a minor role in boosting Italian economic growth. Despite the merger between Borsa Italiana SPA and the London Stock Exchange and the efforts made to create a segment of the market for small and medium-sized companies, by the end of 2009 Borsa Italiana registered just 291 listed companies, with a capitalization rate of 29 per cent of GDP. This evidence shows that savings allocation and growth perspective in Italy depend heavily on the banking system.

Aware that competition increases quality and reduces prices, throughout the nineties European governments implemented a number of reforms in the banking system in order to create a common credit market. An important step in this legislative process was the implementation of the Second Directive for Banking Coordination in 1992 (*Seconda Direttiva di coordinamento bancario*, 1992), which allowed European Union banks to open branches in other EU countries. As a consequence of this and other European directives, the Italian banking system was also involved in a period of restructuring that deeply changed its nature. From 1993 an intense mergers and acquisitions process started along with the privatization of the biggest public banks. Italy became second in Europe after Germany in terms of banking mergers. As a result, over the period 1990–2009, the number of banks fell from 1,176 to 788. Mergers have led to the integration of local credit markets via the start-up of banking groups, and the reduction in the number of independent banks. This, in turn, has changed the ownership structure of the banking system (Messori, 2002; Guiso *et al.*, 2006).

This chapter investigates the effect of the change in the ownership structure on savings allocation and on the efficiency of the Italian banking system. The main conclusion of this investigation is that competition and efficiency in the Italian banking sector are lower than those of similar financially developed countries, despite the strong process of reform in the Italian banking sector. Italian banks have the highest cost of banking services in Europe. This result is mainly due to cross-ownerships among the major Italian banking groups. In addition, our chapter studies another anomaly of the Italian financial system: the existence of massive controls on investment management companies (SGR) by Italian banks, which cause further distortions to savings allocation. Finally, we argue that poor functional efficiency in the Italian banking system prevents the banking sector from boosting Italian economic growth.

The chapter is structured in three parts. First, we compare the level of cost of banking services and the degree of efficiency of the Italian banking system with those of other European countries. Second, we analyse the determinants of banking inefficiency, such as ownership structure of Italian banks. Third, we study the characteristics of the savings allocation in investment management companies. Finally, we make some concluding remarks.

Costs and efficiency of Italian banks

The mergers and acquisitions (M&A) process in the Italian banking system since the nineties has led to the setting-up of few large banking groups able to exploit economies of scale and scope in the sector. This is the reason why the current structure of the Italian banking system is characterized by the coexistence of few large banking groups, operating both in Italy and abroad, and many small banks, segmented by market area or customers' needs and operating mainly in local credit markets.

A first helpful criterion for evaluating the effect of this M&A process is to compare the costs of banking services in Italy and other similar developed countries. In 2003, the annual worldwide survey of current account fees by Cap Gemini and the European Financial Management and Marketing Association (Efma) showed the average price (206 euros) of some *core banking services* (cheque and cash payments, account management, down payments and bank overdrafts) charged by the six biggest Italian banks was higher than that (109 euros) of the other countries analysed in the survey: Belgium, Canada, France, Germany, Netherlands, Norway, Sweden, the United Kingdom and the United States.

In 2007 consumer protection organizations received complaints from citizens about the rule on the symmetry of rates not being applied properly: banks did not adjust active and passive interest rates to the new official reference rate (*tasso ufficiale di sconto*).

The unadjusted rates badly affected families, especially low-income ones. In fact, the European Central Bank (ECB), according to consumer protection organizations, increased the cost of money five times in one year and consequently Italian banks raised fees on mortgages, loans and bank credits without raising rates on deposits, such as current accounts and savings accounts. Furthermore, banks would have charged customers a higher fee to pay off a mortgage than the fee agreed by the ABI (Associazione bancaria Italiana).

In April 2010, at the Senate Finance Committee, Antonio Catricalà, president of the Antitrust Committee (*Il Sole24 ore*, 17 April) claimed that fees and tariffs of different banking services were higher than those applied in a competitive market and similar to those applied in an oligopolistic market. He also said that new fees replacing overdraft commissions increased costs especially for account holders. Therefore, in order to reach a good level of competition, he claimed it was necessary to increase the mobility of clients and to reinforce consumers' and small and medium-sized firms' bargaining power. At the end of 2010, the Bank of Italy's representative at a Senate hearing showed that the average cost of a current account had remained stable in recent years, with a small decrease in the fees for cash withdrawals and payments, but with an increase in other variable expenses, including fees for the use of overdraft services.

Moreover, Michael Barnier, the European Union commissioner responsible for the Internal Market, recently announced the implementation of an investigation into disparity sources for costs of banking services, pointing the finger at Italy, where the average cost per customer is 246 euros per year against 43 euros in Netherlands. The vigilance commissioner for prices (*Garante per la sorveglianza dei prezzi*) expressed worries about complaints about the lack of transparency and clarity in the increase in the management costs of current accounts. He announced an investigation on costs paid by customers in the banking industry, in order to verify the single cost charged to clients and the correct application of rules on overdrafts.

Thus, by comparing levels of costs and services provided to customers across countries, we can conclude that Italian banks must still work hard to reach the same efficiency level as that of other developed European countries, even if legal and structural reforms have taken place only in recent years in the Italian banking sector.

In principle, the high cost of banking services might be compensated by a lower differential between active and passive interest rates. However, as we have mentioned, in the Cap Gemini research in 2003, Italy has a positive relationship between *spreads* and costs of banking services, whereas in the other countries in the sample (Belgium, Canada, France, Germany, Netherlands, Norway, Spain, Sweden, the United Kingdom and the United States) this is not the case. The same research shows that, after Germany, in 2003 Italy showed the highest *spread* of all those countries. Moreover, EUROSTAT data show that from 1996 to 2004 the cost of banking services rose in Italy by 78 per cent compared with the 28 per cent of the fifteen EU countries.

Competition and ownership structure in the Italian banking industry

The deregulation process in the nineties, started as a consequence of EU directives, aimed at increasing competition in the banking industry. In fact, it led to an increase in both the number of banking counters and ownership concentration in the Italian banking system, through an intense mergers and acquisitions process. Therefore, it is important to understand whether and how this increasing concentration has affected competitive mechanisms in the Italian banking system.

The theoretical relationship between competition and concentration is ambiguous. On the one hand, it is argued that the degree of competition in a market is inversely correlated to the degree of ownership concentration.[1] On the other hand, it is stated that high ownership concentration does not necessarily lead to a lower degree of competition, but it may lead to an increase in the industry's efficiency. The idea underlying this strand of research is that a more efficient firm can increase its share price through mergers more than an inefficient one. This explains why the higher the concentration, the lower the price in the sector. In Italy over the period 1995–2006, 476 banks were involved in mergers and acquisitions, which accounted for 70 per cent of total activities in the system.

However, while mergers are made to allow banks to exploit economies of scale and scope (Berger *et al.*, 2001; Berger, 2000), a more efficient firm does not necessarily impose a reduction in the level of price for customers. Therefore, evaluating the effect of mergers on prices means taking into account these two potential outcomes, along with the ability of potential competitors to enter the market and the kind of market (local, national, international), which may affect that relationship.

The first way to estimate the effect of mergers on banking competition is to evaluate the trend of interest rates on deposits after the merger. If the merger improves efficiency, we might expect that banks involved in the merger process will increase interest rates on deposits after the merger. Conversely, if the merger increases banking competition, we might expect a decrease in the interest rates on deposits. This latter can be taken as a signal that the merger is a mechanism that distorts perfect competition.

Focarelli and Panetta (2003) show that mergers in the Italian banking system led to an increase in interest rates on deposits immediately after the merger but to a decrease in the period thereafter. The authors conclude that mergers in the Italian banking sector increase market power only in the short term; in the long term, they instead cause a higher level of competition.

Angelini and Cetorelli (2003) also find that, two years after a merger, interest rates on deposits increased and they conclude that the ownership concentration in the Italian banking system in the 1990s increased competition. This conclusion is supported by Coccorese (2002), Sapienza (2002) and Cerasi *et al.* (2009). In particular, the research by the last mentioned shows that the increase in the level of competition is due to the fact that a merger creates a bank able to compete with other banks operating in the local markets.

The second way to estimate the effect of mergers is to consider the persistence of extra profits after the merger. This is because the persistence of non-competitive profits implies high market power where entry barriers prevent profits from converging to the zero long-term equilibrium level (Mueller, 1977).

In line with this strand of research, Messori shows that over the period 1990–7 the consolidation and reallocation of ownership structure, which has seen the setting-up of five big banking groups (IMI, BNL, Mediocredito, Mediobanca, San Paolo di Torino), produced an increase in efficiency and competition in the banking sector. However, since 1998 there has been an increase in revenue for the big banking groups, i.e. non-competitive profits (Messori, 2004). This result supports the hypothesis that the concentration of ownership structure has not been efficient from a competitive point of view even in the long term. Accordingly, Agostino *et al.* (2005) show the existence of a significant correlation between the persistence of profits and ownership concentration, for a sample of Italian banks over the period 1997–2000.

By investigating the potential sources of the positive relation between concentration and market power, Messori (2001 and 2004) shows that mergers and acquisitions led not to the setting-up of a few independent banking groups, but to a situation in which a small number of shareholders hold an important share in almost all the big banking groups: so-called *cross-ownership* (see also Inzerillo and Messori, 2000). These cross-ownerships have involved the biggest banking groups (Banca Intesa Unicredito, San Paolo IMI-Banco di Napoli, Banca di Roma-MCC, Banca MPS, Banca Nazionale del Lavoro, Banca Cardine, BIPOP-CARIRE, Banca Lombarda e Piemontese, CdR Firenze, Carinord, Credem) with shares held in many other banks too. In line with this, Trivieri (2007) shows that, over the period 1997–2000, small Italian banks involved in the cross-ownership process exhibited non-competitive behaviour.

Results on the effect of mergers on competition are ambiguous. On the one hand, trends in deposit rates show an increase in banking competition. On the other hand, the persistence of extra profits shows a decrease in banking competition. As far as the *spread* between active and passive rates applied by Italian banks from 1992 to 2004 is concerned, a fall in that spread from 9.4 per cent to 4.9 per cent was observed. This reflects to some extent the increase in the level of competition that has characterized the Italian banking sector since 1992. Further, the Italian spread is higher than the average spread in Europe, which shows Italian banks' greater market power with respect to other European countries (Silipo, 2009).

In light of this, the main issue for the Italian banking system is evaluating whether these changes are enough to bring the Italian financial system to the same level of efficiency as other developed countries. Our chapter casts some doubts on the effectiveness of these changes.

First, as we have mentioned above, the Italian banking system charges high prices to customers. Second, although the consolidation process has increased the efficiency of banks and competition in their traditional activities, the level of efficiency in non-traditional activities, such as corporate finance, investment banking and portfolio management, has not improved. Third, we have observed an increase in operating efficiency, but not a rise in the functional efficiency of Italian banks (Silipo, 2009), especially in the South of Italy (*Mezzogiorno*), where the functional distance between banks and the local economy is bigger and plays an important role in the development of the area (Alessandrini *et al.*, 2005).

Investment management companies: structure and effects on savings allocation

It is reasonable to think that the cross-ownership characterizing Italian banks is related to the high costs for customers. Also, the Italian financial system is unique not only because of cross-ownership, but also because of the nature and behaviour of the investment management companies (IMCs). The majority of IMCs are controlled by insurance or banking groups. This contributes not only to raising barriers against foreign and internal competitors and exploiting revenue positions, but also to subordinating IMCs to the strategies chosen by their owners, by affecting their organizational autonomy and potential innovation process.

Moreover, mergers and acquisitions in recent years have not increased efficiency in the asset management industry. As a consequence of this, a number of facts can be observed, such as the coexistence of IMCs with different and independent strategies, but belonging to the same parent company (see the Eurizon and Fideuram case), the presence of many small and medium-sized IMCs controlled by a unique owner (see the case involving many IMCs related to banking groups or popular banks), the merger of IMCs with a different degree of specialization, but belonging to a new consolidated banking group and so on (Messori, 2010b).

Today, more than 90 per cent of asset management products are distributed through banking channels and, as a consequence of the IMCs' ownership, the asset management industry has contributed 11.1 per cent to the earnings margin (*margine di intermediazione*) in a sample of fourteen Italian banking groups, according to an Associazione bancaria Italiana survey (2007). The existence of cross-ownership between financial institutions and IMCs allows banks to earn on a savings perspective, a *cross income*, recovering potential dissipation of profits because of lower competition in traditional activities.

Although it is difficult to estimate the consequences of IMCs' ownership for savings allocation in Italy, some indicators show the inefficiency of IMCs in the allocation of Italian households' savings.

A first indicator of this inefficiency is related to the savings allocation among different types of funds. As an example, Italian equity funds boosted their performance in 2000, during the 'Bubble Burst'. Furthermore, over the period 1999–2000, Italian underwriters of equity funds invested significantly in markets (Nasdaq 100 and European markets) that were suffering the greatest losses. On the other hand, a large proportion of underwriters did not invest in equity funds over the period 2001–2, when equity markets performed poorly. Similarly, they did not invest in the following years, 2003–6, when equity markets performed better, losing in turn any gain they could have made during this period. On the other hand, the net collection of bond funds was positive from 1998 on. This means, according to Messori (2010a), that Italian savers invested their money in bond and liquidity funds during the period of the last stock exchange boom.

There are many causes of this inefficient savings allocation. The first comes from the supply side: Italian banks' increasing financial need led them to increase the net issue of bonds and to exploit IMCs as a distribution channel to place their products in the market.

A second cause comes from the demand side. The Bank of Italy's survey on Italian households' wealth and income (2008) shows that Italian families are not well informed about financial services available in the market. About one-third of them are not able to read an account statement; more than half are not able to understand the importance of the diversification of investments and two-thirds are not able to distinguish the degree of risk related to bonds and stocks (see Visco, 2010). However, in addition to this lack of knowledge among investors, there is the increasing complexity of financial products, which increases the degree of asymmetric information between buyers and sellers and allows banks and IMCs to easily affect buyers' decisions.

Empirical evidence (Mediobanca, 2007; Barucci, 2007; Petrella, 2006) shows that over the last decade Italian investment funds performed badly. In particular, they exhibited lower levels of performance than their benchmarks, especially in the case of bond funds. Barucci (2007) shows that over the period 2004–6, investment funds in Italy had a negative alpha value (performance net of distribution costs), despite a better gross performance than their benchmarks. In other words, distribution costs for IMCs decreased efficiency to a lesser extent than that of their benchmarks. In fact, comparing TER (*total expense ratio*) of Italian funds with that of European funds, the Italian TER seems to be higher than the European average. Further, Barucci (2007) shows the existence of a reverse relationship between extra performance and the level of bank fees. Distribution costs are crucial for savings allocation: Italy is second in European countries in terms of distribution costs, despite a level of production cost slightly lower than the European average.

Moreover, the financial crisis negatively affected the asset management industry. In fact, from 2006 to 2009, the wealth of the Italian asset management industry suffered heavy outflows and losses were greater for Italian investment funds compared with foreign funds: the ratio between the wealth of Italian and foreign funds reduced significantly from 2000 to 2010 (Messori, 2010a). Because of this, the Italian asset management sector has been reshaped and power transferred from Italian funds to foreign funds.

The scenario looks worse if we take into account that IMCs have replaced institutional investors (pension funds, insurance companies) in the Italian financial market because of their historical weakness. Nevertheless, the lack of well-performing institutional investors and the inefficient savings allocation of IMCs did not allow the exploitation of the high saving propensity and the high net financial wealth of Italian households in order to cope with the Italian economy's decline in the last two decades.

In this respect, it is crucial to investigate the efficiency of the Italian banks in savings allocation. The analysis of the functional efficiency of the Italian banking system is beyond the scope of this study (for further details, see Silipo, 2009). We can only look at whether Italian banks play the role of *social accountant* (Stiglitz and Weiss, 1988) efficiently, as in this case, the economy should be characterized by a banking system supporting the production process and innovation.

A first index of banking support for the production system is the ratio between banking loans provided to the private sector and deposits. In 1997, this ratio was 100 in the Eurozone and 105 in Italy. Ten years later the same index was about 177 in Italy, against 120 as the European average (see Messori, 2010b). Although this evidence might be due to the contraction of savings in Italy over the same period, data on loans/GDP ratio seem to confirm the existence of wide banking support for the production system. In fact, the ratio between banking loans to the private sector and GDP has registered a steady increase since 1997, and shown the same tendency, although at a lower rate, since the financial crisis (see Panetta and Signoretti, 2010).

We can conclude that loans growth over the last decade cannot be associated with a recovery in the Italian economy. Of course, there are many reasons for Italy's economic decline. Insufficient innovation, poor public sector performance, and inadequate development of and performance by the financial sector are some of them.[2] This chapter has only investigated whether the inefficient allocation of bank loans or their inadequate allocation to more innovative investments can be considered as one of the causes of that decline. Strictly speaking, despite the Italian banks' good support for the production system, the slow speed of the Italian economy raises the question of whether the banking system has been selecting and implementing effectively investment projects boosting growth or whether it has just used households' savings to finance less remunerative investments.

Concluding remarks

The Italian banking system was been involved in an intense regulation process in the 1990s which led to a substantial restructuring of the banking sector. In our study, we have evaluated the effect of this change on savings allocation and efficiency of the banking system. There are two main conclusions to be drawn from our study.

First, the level of competition and efficiency in the Italian banking system appears to be far from that of more financially developed countries, despite the competitive pressure because of the liberalization of banking counters. This may be due to the higher cost of services charged by Italian banks with respect to the European average.

Second, cross-ownership among banks is not the only distortive factor characterizing the Italian financial system. Other factors are the behaviour and the nature of the investment management companies, which are fully controlled by the Italian banks. This negatively affects the efficiency of IMCs in the allocation of households' wealth, raises barriers to internal and foreign competitors, gives the chance to exploit revenue positions and finally, subordinates IMCs to the strategies chosen by their owners, which affects their innovation processes.

Finally, we argue that the high level of competition in the banking industry has increased the propensity to lend money but has not raised the banks' functional efficiency, which would allow selecting and implementing more profitable investment projects, and then boosting Italian economic growth.

Notes

1 A classic paper on this topic is Berger *et al.* (2004).
2 These sources of decline are analysed, for example, in Toniolo (2004) and Messori and Silipo (2012).

Bibliography

Agostino, M. R., Leonida, L. and Trivieri, F. (2005). Profits persistence and ownership: evidence from the Italian banking sector. *Applied Economics*, 37, 1615–21.

Alessandrini, P., Croci, M. and Zazzaro, A. (2005). The geography of banking power: the role of functional distance. *Banca Nazionale del Lavoro Quarterly Review*, 235, 129–67.

Angelini, P. and Cetorelli, N. (2003). The effects of regulatory reform on competition in the banking industry. *Journal of Money, Credit, and Banking*, 35, 663–84.

Bain, J. (1965). *Barriers to New Competition*. Harvard, MA: Harvard University Press.

Barucci, E. (2007). *Raccolta e performance dei fondi comuni di investimento in Italia*. Assogestioni Working Paper 2007/1 November.

Beltratti, A. (2008). *Gestione finanziaria e consulenza: mercato e integrazione verticale*. Assogestioni Working Paper 2008/3 May.

Berger, A. N. (2000). *The Integration of the Financial Services Industry: Where Are the Efficiencies?* Finance and Economics Discussion Series 2000–36, Board of Governors of the Federal Reserve System (U.S.).

Berger, A. N., Demirguc-Kunt, A., Levine, R. and Haubrich, J. G. (2004). Bank concentration and competition: an evolution in the making. *Journal of Money, Credit and Banking*, 36 (3), 433–51.

Berger, A. N., DeYoung, R. and Gregory, F. U. (2001). Efficiency barriers to the consolidation of the European financial services industry. *European Financial Management*, 7, 117–30.

Cerasi, V., Chizzolini, B. and Ivaldi, M. (2009). *The Impact of Mergers on the Degree of Competition in the Banking Industry*. Discussion paper, Dipartimento di Economia, Università Bocconi.

Coccorese, P. (2002). *Competition Among Dominant Firms in Concentrated Markets: Evidence from the Italian Banking Industry*. CSEF Working Paper 89, Università di Salerno.

Financial Stability Board (2011). *Peer Review of Italy*. Review Report. Available online at www.financialstabilityboard.org/wp-content/uploads/r_110207b.pdf (accessed 15 January 2015).

Focarelli, D. and Panetta, F. (2003). Are mergers beneficial to consumers? Evidence from the Italian market for bank deposits. *American Economic Review*, 93, 1152–72.

Guiso, L., Sapienza, P. and Zingales, L. (2006). *The Cost of Banking Regulation*, CEPR Discussion Paper 5864.

Inzerillo, U. and Messori, M. (2000). Le privatizzazioni bancarie in Italia, in De Nardis, S. (ed.), *Le privatizzazioni italiane*. Bologna: Il Mulino, pp. 119–190.

Mediobanca (2007). *Interim Report*. Available online at www.mediobanca.it/en/investor-relations/bilanci/financial-reports.html (accessed 15 January 2015).

Messori, M. (2001). La concentrazione del settore bancario: effetti sulla competitività e sugli assetti proprietari. *Quaderni CEIS*, 151, 1–65.

Messori, M. (2002). Consolidation, ownership structure and efficiency in the Italian banking system. *BNL Quarterly Review*, 221, 177–217.

Messori, M. (2004). *The Consolidation of the Italian Banking System: Effects on Competitiveness and Ownership Structure*. Discussion paper, Università di Roma Tor Vergata.

Messori, M. (2010a). I problemi del settore italiano del risparmio gestito. Typescript.

Messori, M. (2010b). Nota sull'evoluzione del risparmio gestito nel mercato finanziario italiano. Typescript.

Messori, M. and Silipo, D. B. (2012). *Quale sviluppo dell'economia italiana cinquant'anni dopo*. Milan: EGEA.

Mueller, D. C. (1977). The persistence of profits above the norm. *Economica*, 44, 369–80.

Panetta, F. and Signoretti, F. M. (2010). *Domanda e offerta di credito in Italia durante la crisi finanziaria*. Banca d'Italia – Questioni di Economia e Finanza, 63.

Petrella, G. (2006). Option bid-ask spread and scalping risk: Evidence from a covered warrants market. *Journal of Futures Markets*, 26 (9), 843–67.

Sapienza, P. (2002). The effects of banking mergers an loan contracts. *Journal of Finance*, 57 (1), 329–67.

Silipo, D. B. (2009). *The Banks and the Italian Economy*. Berlin: Physica-Verlag.

Spaventa, L. (2008). *Il risparmio delle famiglie in fuga dai fondi comuni d'investimento*. Assogestioni Working Paper 2008/2 May.

Stiglitz, J. E. and Weiss, A. (1988). *Banks as Social Accountants and Screening Devices for the Allocation of Credit*. NBER Working Paper No. W2710.

Toniolo, G. (2004). L'Italia verso il declino economico? Ipotesi e congetture in una prospettiva secolare. *Rivista italiana degli economisti*, 1, 29–46.

Trivieri, F. (2007). Does cross-ownership affect competition? Evidence from the Italian banking industry. *Journal of International Financial Markets, Institutions and Money*, 17 (1), 79–101.

Visco, I. (2010). *Financial Education in the Aftermath of the Financial Crisis*. Special Address to the OECD–Bank of Italy Symposium on Financial Literacy, 'Improving financial education efficiency', Rome, 9 June.

PART V

Memories

25

CINEMA AND PUBLIC MEMORY

Paolo Jedlowski

Introduction

Film-making has been, and still is, one of the most important cultural industries in Italy. Its aim is to provide products for mass entertainment; however, from the period after the Second World War, the Italian film industry has often felt to also have a sort of social mandate to accomplish. Characterized by a strong realism-oriented approach, it produced entertainment films, but also contributed to depicting Italy to Italians, telling stories in which they mirrored, identified and also criticized themselves.

In particular, some films contributed to developing stories and images of the past, thereby giving shape to what could be defined as the *public memory* of the country, that is the different ways in which some events of the collective past have been selected as meaningful ones, staged, played and publicly discussed. This chapter focuses on these films.

Their analysis will fulfil two needs: on the one hand, it will allow us to cast an eye over one of the most important fields of Italian cultural production, even though within the time frame of the last thirty years and with only some specific films taken into consideration. On the other, it will provide a way to address an important issue: the relationship of Italians with their past.[1]

Nostalgia

An optimal starting point could be *Cinema Paradiso* (original title: *Nuovo cinema Paradiso*) by Giuseppe Tornatore, a film from 1988. It is an interesting film for both the above-mentioned aims, insofar as it deals with the history of cinema and public memory.

As for the history, *Cinema Paradiso* won the best foreign language film Oscar in 1990. Between 1948 and 1975, Italian film-makers had been awarded the Oscar for this category nine times with films by Vittorio De Sica, Federico Fellini and Elio Petri, but when Tornatore was awarded the Oscar it had not happened for fifteen years. It was not by chance. Between the mid-seventies and the late eighties, the Italian film industry went through a severe crisis. Its golden age was during the fifties: in 1955, over 800 million tickets were sold (on average, each Italian citizen went to the cinema 16 times in that year). However, in 1980 the number of tickets sold decreased to 240 million, and in 1990 to 90 million. The largest market share was represented by American films. After 1990, the number of tickets sold reached over 100 million a year, and

American supremacy was challenged again by several Italian films, and also some European films: Italy, along with France and Germany is one of the European Union countries with the highest number of circulating films produced elsewhere. Of course, the context has changed: cinema is no longer the main storytelling vehicle in Italy, and elsewhere. Film-watching habits have changed (people tend to watch films more at home on TV than in cinemas) and dependency on TV is significant in many respects. Cinema no longer plays the key role as a form of entertainment and in the collective imagination that it did in its golden age; but its crisis has been a transformation phase, not its own end.

As for public memory, the film by Tornatore explicitly discusses it. It is actually about nostalgia: memory as a regret for something lost. The film tells the story of a film director who comes back to the village of his childhood and recalls the old cinema which fascinated him as a child. He feels regret for his childhood, for 1950s Italy and for cinema itself. The memories of the main character help the audience understand how cinematographic images are carved in our memory and how going to the cinema is part of our history. In the same year, also *Splendor* by Ettore Scola was released; 'Splendor' was the name of a little town's cinema and the plot of the film is based on its history during its glory years until its closing down, at the end of the seventies. Both films were permeated by nostalgia for some earlier stages of the country's modernization, when Italians were perhaps more able to dream.

Nostalgia is a specific nuance of memory. Over the last thirty years, it increasingly became a leitmotif in international film-making (and perhaps the success of *Cinema Paradiso* abroad is also due to its ability to sense this mood). In Italy, such a theme was expressed differently from how it was in other countries. It is not much evident in Tornatore's film, but it is in *Splendor*, where nostalgia for old-time cinema is not only the regret for something lost, but a criticism of the deficiencies of the present.

This way of depicting nostalgia had been even more explicit in another film by Scola released a few years before: *We All Loved Each Other So Much* (*C'eravamo tanto amati*, 1974). The film deals with a piece of the history of Italy from the *Resistenza* (the Italian resistance movement against Nazism and Fascism which took place between 1943 and 1945) until the early seventies, recounted through the memories of three friends who had been comrades during the partisan struggle. The rhythm and style of narration (the alternation between black-and-white and colour, the soundtrack, some soft-focus effects, etc.) evoke a kind of nostalgia in the audience. In a sense, it is a vague nostalgia, for the fact that life flows on and time goes by; the time of passions worn down by disillusionment. Yet, there is a more definite nostalgia: that for the *Resistenza* and the hopes it carried with it. These hopes have been frustrated. In their final conversation, at the time of narration, the three friends regretfully complain: 'We thought we could change the world, but the world changed us.' Nostalgia is flanked by disillusionment. The ideals that once motivated their actions have been lost, but it was the characters who first betrayed them, at least in part. What the film leads the viewer to wonder is: how could this occur?

The *Resistenza* had been a sort of founding myth for Republican Italy for a long time. Scola does not neglect the myth, but he does not use it to legitimate the present. The film evokes in the audience a nostalgia combined with a thoughtful, critical attitude. It does not encourage either the glorification of the past, or regret for the same. Notoriously, the object of nostalgia is often embellished by the feeling embedded in it: yet, reflective nostalgia does not yield to this temptation, at least not totally: it leads us to meditate, investigate and reconsider history (Boym, 2001).

We cannot affirm that Italian society, as a whole, is particularly attentive to history. Perhaps, in a comparative perspective, Italy is more attentive than other countries (after all, Italian philosophical culture, upon which generations of teachers have been educated, is the historicism of Benedetto Croce). However, in Italians' approach to the past, many deficiencies, removals, deformations and silences are present. A part of Italian cinema has strongly opposed such attitudes. Scola is a particularly emblematic example, even if this attitude is quite common among other film-makers.

For this reason among others it is not appropriate to talk about nostalgia films in Italy like those of other countries (Morreale, 2009). We do not mean that the sentiment of nostalgia is alien to the Italian culture. Rural Italy, Italy of small provincial towns, Italy in its first stages of industrial modernization are often idealized in common discourses. However, cinema has not often indulged in this kind of idealization. Also in *Amarcord* (1974) by Federico Fellini, sometimes regarded as a sort of forerunner of nostalgia films, the description of the social world of a small town is more grotesque than amiable. Not even British heritage cinema (Higson, 1996), with its ability to stage – and in some ways glorify – the national past, has proper counterparts in Italy. As Derek Duncan wrote, in the *heritage movies* 'the past offers at least the illusion of a better way of life' (Duncan, 2000: 152). In Italian films, on the other hand, usually 'there is no mechanism through which to render the past a more habitable place than the present'.

This does not imply that there are no Italian nostalgia films, but they are too limited in number to be considered as mainstream. In any case, they are nostalgia films to a limited extent only; they are, more or less overtly, political films in which an indulgent memory is required to legitimate certain values of the present. An explanatory example is *Time for Loving* (*Sapore di mare*), released in 1982 and directed by Carlo Vanzina. It is a comedy for a very wide audience, which successfully became a blockbuster film (*Sapore di Mare 2* was released immediately after the first film). The film starts with a voice off informing the audience that the story is set about twenty years earlier. Since it is an early eighties film, the story starts at the beginning of the sixties in summer, at a seaside resort. The sixties setting is confirmed by the recurrent presence of famous songs of that period in the soundtrack (the title of the film itself recalls a sixties song: *Sapore di sale*). A group of young people have a good time with jokes, swims, excursions and summer love affairs. Each topic is dealt with under the shade of mockery (the leading character is a TV comic actor and the screenplay develops in the manner of a sequence of comic gags); however, the use of the camera, the voice off and the soundtrack induce the audience to follow the narration with indulgent eyes and attitude. *We were naive*, the film seems to suggest, *but we were young and we were united*. And this is what we are longing for.

Indeed, the adolescents described in the film are not particularly agreeable and they have two interests only: sex and money. Sex is only hinted at, very macho, and never practised. Money becomes the criterion of evaluation for everything. Were the young people of the sixties like these? Surely not. These were the years of family beach holidays, of course, but also the period when the family started to be criticized. Gender relationships were changing and sexual liberation was about to begin. The youth counterculture which would lead to the breakout of the 1968 protest movement was developing. The songs young people listened to were not only the commercial hits included in the film's soundtrack. And economic success was not necessarily considered as a value. The young people of the sixties were far from being those depicted in the film. Those in the film look rather like some Italian adults living in the eighties, when the film was released: the kind of Italians who turned their back on social commitment, much more like the characters of the 'culture of narcissism' described by Christopher Lasch (1979) in America. Thus, the film establishes a sort of continuity between the present with this kind of Italians and the sixties, thus bypassing twenty years: a retrospective projection cancelling history.

This film and its sequel are the most appropriate examples of the transposition of American postmodern nostalgia films to Italy. They take inspiration from *American Graffiti*, *Grease* or, even more, the TV sitcom *Happy Days*. Postmodern nostalgia films are overtly anti-historical.

The philosophy behind them is the commercialization of vintage. Nostalgia serves to promote generational identities, depriving the concept of generation of any historical feature beyond its determination as a community of consumers. In Italy, this kind of nostalgia film has another function: repressing the years when Italy was shaken by the social movements referred to as '*Sessantotto*' ('Sixty-eight').

Memories of the *Sessantotto*

We are, thus, getting closer to a fundamental feature of Italian public memory: it is a divided and contradictory memory, permeated by recurring conflicts. Some are willing to remember what is repressed by others. And this is particularly true as for the *Sessantotto*.

What we are concerned with here is not exactly the year 1968. This was in Italy – as well as in Europe – the year of the most serious youth protests, school occupations and demonstrations. But in Italy, youth movements involved wide sectors of society and lasted almost until the end of the seventies. They were characterized by two stages: the first was more spontaneous, creative and anti-authoritarian; the second was more politicized and characterized by the hegemony of a Marxist-Leninist ideology over the movement as a whole.

The first stage was the hardest to recollect, at least in film-making, and for a time it seemed it could be depicted only through its absence, as in several early films by Gabriele Salvatores (who later achieved worldwide success with *Mediterraneo* in 1991). Recently *The Dreamers* (2003) by Bernardo Bertolucci succeeded in grasping some of its nuances. *The Dreamers* is set in Paris, but it catches a spirit detectable anywhere in Europe: a less politicized and strongly cultural 1968, characterized by audacious explorations, emancipations, sexual discoveries and the challenge to any taboo. And a cinephile attitude as well. The passion for cinema of the three characters, which is gracefully depicted by Bertolucci, was also shared in Italy by a generation defined as 'natural-born cinephile' (Ortoleva, 1993).

The most comprehensive attempt to present the *Sessantotto* was *The Best of Youth* (*La meglio gioventù*) by Marco Tullio Giordana. The film, lasting over three hours, was released in 2003 and was immediately after screened on TV in two episodes broadcast at prime time. It met with great success among audiences in other countries too. It stretches over more than thirty years of history, from 1966 until the present. With respect to the *Sessantotto*, the most significant narrative options are basically two. The first option consists in setting its starting point in 1966 with the flood in Florence, when young people were brought together to provide help and rescue the books from flooded libraries: it was a rehearsal for a generation that finds a sense of accomplishment in commitment to the community. The second is focusing on anti-psychiatry (very significant in Italy, indeed), to describe the spirit of youth movements of that time. The leading character of the film, in fact, becomes a psychiatrist after having naively helped, along with his brother at the beginning of the story, a mentally ill woman to leave the mental hospital where she had been shut up. Once a doctor, he fights to restore the dignity of mentally ill people and to foster their social inclusion, opposing psychiatric institutions both from a scientific and political perspective. It is a narrative choice which – despite its obvious partiality – allows the recall of some emblematic aspects of passions, motivations and ideals of the young people of those years. When his wife is seduced by the revolutionary armed struggle later in the story (an aspect of the second stage of the Italian *Sessantotto* which will be dealt with later), he helps to have her arrested. But the film does not end with a sense of disillusion. In the final scenes, the nephew of the main character leaves for a coming-of-age trip to Europe, like the one happily made by his uncle at the beginning of the story. He receives his uncle's legacy: it is a new beginning.

Gian Piero Brunetta, the most authoritative historian of the Italian cinema, wrote: '*The Best of Youth* is an important film covering more than thirty years of our history without any moralism, didactic claims or pre-cooked or warmed-up truths. It does so without any nostalgia or embellishment, . . . delivering a small story which can be received and recognized as common heritage for everyone' (Brunetta, 2004: 451). It is a great film, indeed, which can be compared to the German feature film series *Heimat* by Edgar Reitz (1984, 1992 and 2004), even though on a smaller scale: an attempt to reconcile everyday memory with history. It should, however, be noted that, in an effort to account for the reasons its characters have for remembering '1968', the film gives little attention to those who do not recognize themselves in those movements. And the eighties – the toughest for those identifying themselves in that period, because they were characterized by an almost totally opposite atmosphere – are practically absent from the whole time frame (Manzoli, 2012).

'Years of Lead'

As for the second stage of the *Sessantotto*, those years have been very often defined as the 'years of lead' in public discourses. This phrase is borrowed from the title of a film by the German film-maker Margarethe von Trotta (*Die Bleierne Zeit*, 1981), based on the history of the Baader-Meinhof terrorist organization in Germany, and referred to the Italian context immediately after the 1968 student protest movements. This context was generated, on the one hand, by the decision of some small extra-parliamentary left-wing organizations, the *Brigate Rosse* (Red Brigades) in particular, to start an armed struggle against the state through a series of terrorist attacks peaking in 1978 with the kidnapping and assassination of Aldo Moro, the then president of the *Democrazia Cristiana* (the Christian Democratic Party). On the other hand, it was generated by the 'strategy of tension' brought about by neo-Fascist organizations whose aim was to spread panic among the population and to foster the establishment of an authoritarian regime; historically, neo-Fascist terrorism was the first to appear on the scene with the bombing of a bank in Milan, in 1969.

Actually, the seventies saw considerable changes in Italian society. Salaries and consumption levels increased, the rights of workers were strengthened and an excellent national health service was established; higher education increased considerably; society became more secularized; family law radically changed. Referring to those years as the 'years of lead' could cast a shadow over all this, but it is also useful to consider together two forms of terrorism which were very different from each other. The Red Brigades killed state officials, journalists and reformist politicians. Neo-Fascists committed indiscriminate massacres. They were two equally odious forms of terrorism, but also far from being symmetrical in their aims and methods. The memory of left-wing terrorism was widely reviewed and reformulated, and cinema provided a considerable contribution to that. The same cannot be affirmed, until recent years, for right-wing terrorism (Uva, 2007).

Among the films dealing with left-wing terrorism, in the period immediately after the 'years of lead', the most famous is perhaps *To Strike at the Heart* (*Colpire al cuore*, 1983) by Gianni Amelio. The plot revolves around the relationship between a fifty-year-old university professor (played by Jean-Louis Trintignant) and his fifteen-year-old son. The son finds out that his father regularly sees a young terrorist, a student of his, and his girlfriend. He realizes his father's incapacity to step back from the couple and watches him when he helps the woman to escape after her partner has died as a result of a gunfight with the police. The son then reports the woman and his father to the police and has them arrested.

Francesco Rosi in *Three Brothers* (*Tre fratelli*, 1981) had already clearly denounced the fault of those who, acting ambiguously, did not side with 'either the State or the Red Brigades' in the seventies. Amelio issued an even more bitter denunciation of the connivance and responsibilities of a part of the Italian intelligentsia. But the relationship between the armed struggle and the large social movements of the early seventies is very difficult to review. Left-wing terrorism – although involving a very limited number of militants – originated from those movements and this urges all those who participated in them to self-criticism. For many it was a shocking admission, as Nanni Moretti – a film-maker who directed his first films in those years and who would achieve huge success afterwards – emphasized in an interview: 'Discovering, at the end of the seventies that the Red Brigades were not Martians working for the secret services, that was indeed a shock. They were people who had been members of the FGCI [the Italian communist youth federation], of the Catholic left-wing movement and of the extra-parliamentary left-wing movement' (quoted in Uva, 2007: 61).

We should acknowledge that Italian cinema has never concealed such a collective responsibility and that it was able to 'work through' it in a sort of trajectory which seems to end with the recent *Good Morning Night* (*Buongiorno Notte*, 2003) by Marco Bellocchio. The story of *Good Morning Night* is based on the kidnapping and murder of Aldo Moro by the Red Brigades in 1978. After a reconstruction of the cultural background of the members of the revolutionary armed organizations, rooted in the legacy of the partisan fight against Nazi-Fascism, but which also implied the refusal of the democratic choices made by the Italian Communist Party, the film ends up showing a small group of people whose ideology makes them completely blind to reality. Red Brigade members are perfectly and tragically unable to interpret what is happening outside the prison where they have confined themselves when they imprisoned Moro. A prison from which, with the licence of imagination, the only one to get out is Moro himself, depicted in the final shot alive and walking free.

Right-wing terrorism was much less discussed, as has already been pointed out. Once again it was Marco Tullio Giordana who tried to give an account of it in his latest film *Piazza Fontana: The Italian Conspiracy* (*Romanzo di una strage*, 2012). The film is based on the massacre at the bank premises of Piazza Fontana, Milan, in 1969. This was the first episode of the 'strategy of tension'. After the bombing in Milan, several other terrorist attacks were carried out: the bombing of Piazza della Loggia, Brescia, in 1974 and the Bologna massacre at the central station in 1980 were among the most notorious events. Trials left few doubts that these attacks had been planned by neo-Fascist organizations, allegedly with the involvement of sections of the secret services and military hierarchies, which actively contributed to the side-tracking of investigations. But, unlike left-wing terrorist organizations, in no case has the truth about the perpetrators of these crimes ever definitively been found out.

Giordana's film is based on the bombing of 12 December 1969 and the subsequent investigations carried out by the police into left-wing organizations which led to the death of the anarchist Giuseppe Pinelli during an interrogation. It then tells of the subsequent campaign led by left-wing extra-parliamentary organizations against the police officer in charge of the investigations which ended up with his assassination by some members of the radical left, three years later. Finally, it reconstructs the side-tracking of the investigations by the state's high officers and suggests well-reasoned hypotheses about the guilt of some elements of the Italian secret services and the connivance of some politicians.

Giordana attempts to reconstruct a shared national memory, thereby restoring the dignity of the victims on both sides (the painful memory of Pinelli's death is juxtaposed with respect for the police officer who was subsequently killed), without renouncing the denunciation of those who developed subversive plots. The film achieved great success with audiences (in the first week, it came in fifth at the box office, an extraordinary result considering it was not a light entertainment product). All newspapers wrote about it. Film reconstructions of the period of terrorism in Italy are often very different and contrasting (Foot 2009; Cento Bull 2010), but the film finally succeeded in placing 'black' terrorism and the alleged support for it at the centre of public attention.

Across generations

The course of public memory is inconstant. The sequence of the subjects under the spotlight does not follow the chronology of the events to which reference is made. So, in recent decades, the memory of controversial events of the relatively recent past is flanked by the reconstruction of earlier events, as in the case of the Holocaust (Gaetani, 2006; Minuz, 2010).

After several years of silence, the memory of the persecution and extermination of millions of Jews and of the responsibilities that Italians had for that, had emerged in public discourses from the seventies on. Cinema had strongly participated in this 're-emergence of the repressed'. *The Garden of the Finzi-Contini* (*Il giardino dei Finzi Contini*), a 1970 film by De Sica, is one of the first and most famous examples. Indeed, the problem was to convey this memory to subsequent generations and somehow to further develop the representation of the events of that time. Both issues are dealt with by the film *Facing Windows* (*La finestra di fronte*, 1993) by Ferzan Özpetek (a Turkish director naturalized in Italy). The main characters of the film, a man and a woman seeking the past, in an attempt to help an old man suffering from amnesia, discover the story of homosexual love frustrated by the deportation of the beloved to a concentration camp.

Dealing with the deportation of homosexuals is the expression of the ability to expand the memory of the Holocaust which has characterized the whole panorama of the European cinema over the last few years, denying what some people (such as Robin, 2003), have defined as a 'saturation' of the theme. The main problem is, however, avoiding stereotypes, which could generate indifference in the younger generation. Roberto Benigni brilliantly addressed the issue with *Life is Beautiful* (*La vita è bella*, 1997).

Despite some criticisms, the film was awarded three Oscars. In Italy, it was the greatest financial success ever and it is still shown to school students. The choice made by Benigni and by the scriptwriter Vincenzo Cerami was to tell about the deportation of Jews in a fairy-tale style: a daring choice which was, however, able to overcome the audience's resistance. Cinema has contributed to making the Holocaust the 'cultural trauma' (Alexander *et al.*, 2004) par excellence of European history. Benigni's film in Italy contributed to maintaining it as such, as much as *Schindler's List* (1993) by Spielberg.

It is true, however, that the memory of Fascism is still hard to address in Italy. The same is even more true for the memory of colonialism (see Chapter 28 in this volume). The only Italian film since the post-war period explicitly dealing with the memory of colonialism is *Time to Kill* (*Tempo di uccidere*, 1989) by Giuliano Montaldo, based on the novel *The Short Cut* by Ennio Flaiano. *The Battle of Algiers* (*La battaglia di Algeri*) by Gillo Pontecorvo should also be mentioned, but it focused on French colonialism. When foreign films dealt with Italian colonialism, they were not shown in Italy: *The Lion of the Desert* (1979), a big-budget international film recounting the events of the Libyan Resistance movement and of its old leader, Omar al-Mukhtar, who was executed by hanging by the Italians, was screened throughout the world, but it was not distributed in Italy. The re-emergence of the repressed colonial past still seems too risky and able to divide, rather than unite the country (Labanca, 2005).

In fact, a line of a famous Neapolitan song says: '*Scurdammoce o passato!*' (Let's forget the past!): this is the most common attitude in Italian society in public discourses about the most controversial events of the past. Despite this attitude and although it keeps some taboos, it seems that contemporary Italian cinema really wishes to create a coherent picture of the past. A good example might be the spectacular film *Baarìa* (2009) by Tornatore, an overview of the twentieth century from its beginning until the recent past. This film is driven by the pleasure of narration, but it is also strongly interested in relationships across the generations. At the end of the film, the main character, as a child, reappears almost magically: we are in the present and he is walking among the ruins of the house where viewers know he spent his life. Among these ruins, he finds a piece of jewellery which he, as an adult, had given to his daughter. This is an astonishing narrative invention, completely unrealistic, but able to arouse the desire to reappropriate one's past for one's own future, almost through shock.

An even more ambitious film is *We Believed* (*Noi credevamo*, 2010) by Mario Martone, a film distributed on the occasion of the celebrations for the 150th anniversary of the unification of Italy. The plot is based on the story of three friends who participate in the struggle for the country's unification starting from the late 1820s; it is not easy to follow, since it requires a good knowledge of the history of Italy, rather than providing it (see Chapter 26 in this volume). The film is more tragic than celebratory: the pronoun 'we' in the title, implying a national community, is an object of nostalgia which has actually never become true; and the verb 'to believe' in the past form implies the hope of thinking that something is possible, even if this hope is retrospectively overburdened with deceits. In fact, the film raises more questions than it provides reassurance on national identity. Its great success in cinemas testifies to a desire – shared by a large proportion of the public – to reassess history.

Memories of the present

The revival of Italian cinema after the crisis of the seventies and eighties has taken place in the light of a restored narrative strength. Scriptwriters have become key players again. The aspect that has been revived is a careful, although critical look at reality (Zagarrio, 2006), a feature that had always been distinctive of Italian cinema tradition.

The review of some aspects of the past is part of this reality-focused approach. But, for many recent Italian films, reference to a *memory of the present* could also be made: the explicit attempt to cast an eye on current events to fix them for a future memory.

A typical example of such an approach is *The Yes Man* (*Il portaborse*, 1991) by Daniele Luchetti. The film portrays a cynical minister and his speech-writer. The arrogance of power combined with intrigues and corruption is embodied in the character of the politician. His subordinate, initially seduced by the minister's character, can no longer bear how his dignity is trampled and citizens are cheated. The practice of 'vote of exchange', the share-out of public resources among political parties, and the unlawful funding arrangements are revealed to the speech-writer in the behind-the-scenes activities of the corridors of power, leaving him astonished; the film does not generically hint at these aspects, but it explains them thoroughly. In his letter of resignation, despite the huge benefits of the job, the speech-writer accuses the minister of acting like a cruel feudal lord. In a TV speech, the minister makes use of his subordinate's words, pretending to act as a champion of the fight against corruption.

In the film, the minister's role was played by Nanni Moretti. He is 'the most successful Italian filmmaker of the last two decades, in terms of consistency, quality and intelligent business practice' (Marrone, 2004: 239). He is a film-maker, actor and producer: after the international success of *Dear Diary* (*Caro Diario*, 1993, which won the Palme d'Or in Cannes), Moretti became perhaps the most highly esteemed Italian film-maker abroad. In 2006 he made *The Caiman* (*Il Caimano*, 2006). It is the most critical film on Berlusconi and 'berlusconism' made in Italy. In the fictional story, a secondary film-maker tries to make a film on contemporary Italy; in the 'film inside the film' a tycoon, who looks like Berlusconi, appears in a scene in which money falls on him from the sky. It is as if Moretti were asking the audience: 'Don't you ever ask where the money Berlusconi has used to develop his empire comes from?' And later on in the story, in the last scene shot by the fictional film-maker, the tycoon incites his supporters to attack the magistrates; the riots breaking out outside the Court are the apocalyptic prophecy of a justiceless regime. This seems to be a second question addressed to the audience: 'Aren't you aware of what is happening?'

Civil tension also covers other themes. As for the invasive presence of organized crime, the most sensational success of recent years was *Gomorrah* (*Gomorra*, 2008, awarded Best European Film of the year by the European Film Academy) by Matteo Garrone, based on a novel by Roberto Saviano. Paolo Sorrentino focuses on the collusion between politics and the mafia in his film *Il divo* (2008), a disquieting reconstruction of the career of one of the leading characters of the Italian political landscape, Giulio Andreotti (played by the greatest contemporary actor in Italy, Toni Servillo). Giulio Manfredonia in *Qualunquemente* (2011) places focus on the same relationships in a ravaged suburban setting through a grotesque, although efficient approach. The title is an untranslatable word ('whichever-ly'), invented by the comedian Antonio Albanese to parody the jargon of some unscrupulous and scarcely educated political representatives.

Andrea Molaioli in *The Jewel* (*Il gioiellino*, 2011) reconstructs and examines Parmalat's financial crash in the late nineties. Parmalat was one of the leading companies in the food industry in Italy: its bankruptcy preceded the recent financial crises in the United States and Europe. Several other films discuss the transformation of the economic landscape; and several deal with migration flows to Italy since the nineties. Sometimes the results are excellent, as in the case of *Letters from the Sahara* (*Lettere dal Sahara*, 2006) by Vittorio De Seta, and *Terraferma* (2011) by Emanuele Crialese. Before *Terraferma*, the story of the arrival of African migrants, Crialese had filmed *The Golden Door* (*Nuovomondo*, 2006), the story of a family of Sicilian emigrants to the USA. The topic of immigration is hence associated with the memory of Italian emigrants of the early twentieth century. It is the same attitude shown by Gianni Amelio, who in *Lamerica* (1994) deals with the arrival of Albanian migrants in Italy, and in *The Way We Laughed* (*Così ridevano*, 1998) reactivates the memory of migration flows from Italy's rural south to the industrial north in the years of the post-war economic boom. Crialese's and Amelio's films oppose racism against immigrants, which is widespread in today's Italy. These are films which do not express a common sentiment; they rather tend to contest it.

Conclusions

In conclusion, issue-oriented cinema in Italy, that principally under discussion here, is not the expression of the most widespread contemporary culture in Italy; it is rather its 'counterpoint'. It belongs to Italian culture, criticizing it at the same time, thereby offsetting predominant trends.

With some exceptions, this kind of cinema hardly competes with American blockbusters and more commercial Italian films. Its audience is neither limited, nor numerous. It is composed of adult, well-educated and mainly metropolitan cinemagoers. Assuming that Italy is currently experiencing a sort of 'subcultural hegemony' (Panarari, 2010), produced above all by TV and high-circulation magazines, this kind of Italian film-making industry seems to contrast this hegemony by expressing the collective memory of social groups which do not surrender unawareness.

These films – through the ways people watch them and the issues they raise – shape new spaces of mediation between people's memories and what the whole of society is willing to represent. This cinema, therefore, has an impact on the way public memory is addressed. The latter being neither a static, nor a homogeneous whole, harbours different stances, interpretations and selections of significant past events. In recent decades, historical memory in Italy has repressed some past events several times, but it has also tried to bring to light the repressed past; it has voiced conflicting views of the past, but it also attempted to build a common memory. Cinema has participated in these processes acting both as an indicator and as a key player.

Note

1 For a comprehensive history of Italian cinema, see Sorlin (1996) and Brunetta (2003). As for the definition of public memory, we take it to mean 'the memory of the public sphere, a discursive space within society where different collective memories confront each other' (Jedlowski, 2005: 40; see also Rampazi and Tota, 2007; Perra, 2010): it does not correspond to institutional memory, but to the set of discourses, newspaper articles, TV programmes, films, novels and other cultural products spreading images and interpretations of the past which are publicly accessible.

Bibliography

Alexander, J. C., Eyerman, R., Giesen, B., Smelser, N. J. and Sztompa, P. (2004). *Cultural Trauma and Collective Identity*. Berkeley, CA: University of California Press.

Boym, S. (2001). Ipocondria del cuore: nostalgia, storia e memoria. In F. Modrzejewski and M. Sznajderman (eds.), *Nostalgia. Saggi sul rimpianto del comunismo* (pp. 1–88). Milan: Bruno Mondadori.

Brunetta, G. P. (2003). *Guida alla storia del cinema italiano*. Turin: Einaudi.

Brunetta, G. P. (2004). *Cent'anni di cinema italiano. 2. Dal 1945 ai giorni nostri*. Rome-Bari: Laterza.

Cento Bull, A. (2010). The legacy of the strategy of tension and the armed conflict in a context of (non) reconciliation. In A. Mammone and G. A. Veltri (eds.), *Italy Today* (pp. 101–13). Oxford: Routledge.

Duncan, D. (2000). Good morning Babilonia. In J. Forbes and S. Street (eds.), *European Cinema. An Introduction* (pp. 145–56). New York: Palgrave.

Foot, J. (2009). *Italy's Divided Memory*. London: Palgrave Macmillan.

Gaetani, C. (2006). *Il cinema e la Shoah*. Genoa: Le Mani.

Higson, A. (1996). The heritage film and British cinema. In A. Higson (ed.), *Dissolving Views: Key Writings on British Cinema* (pp. 232–48). London: Cassel.

Jedlowski, P. (2005). Media e memoria. Costruzione sociale del passato e mezzi di comuncazione di massa. In M. Rampazi and A. L. Tota (eds.), *Il linguaggio del passato* (pp. 31–43). Roma: Carocci.

Labanca, N. (2005). History and memory of Italian colonialism today. In J. Andall and D. Duncan (eds.), *Italian Colonialism: Legacy and Memory* (pp. 29–46). Oxford: Peter Lang.

Lasch, C. (1979). *The Culture of Narcissism*. New York: Norton.

Manzoli, G. (2012). La rappresentazione degli anni ottanta nel cinema italiano contemporaneo. In P. Matera and C. Uva (eds.), *Anni ottanta: quando tutto cominciò* (pp. 193–215). Soveria Mannelli: Rubbettino.

Marrone, G. (2004). The new Italian cinema. In E. Ezra (ed.), *European Cinema* (pp. 233–49). Oxford: Oxford University Press.

Minuz, A. (2010). *La Shoah e la cultura visuale. Cinema, memoria, spazio pubblico*. Rome: Bulzoni.

Morreale, E. (2009). *L'invenzione della nostalgia. Il vintage nel cinema italiano e dintorni*. Rome: Donzelli.

Ortoleva, P. (1993). Naturalmente cinefili: il '68 al cinema. In G. P. Brunetta (ed.), *Storia del cinema mondiale*, vol. I, 1, *L'Europa: miti, luoghi, divi* (pp. 935–52). Turin: Einaudi.

Panarari, M. (2010). *L'egemonia sottoculturale. L'Italia da Gramsci al gossip*. Turin: Einaudi.

Perra, E. (2010). *Conflicts of Memory*. Oxford: Peter Lang.

Rampazi, M. and Tota, A. L. (eds.) (2007). *La memoria pubblica*. Turin: UTET.

Robin, R. (2003). *La mémoire saturée*. Paris: Stock.

Sorlin, P. (1996). *Italian National Cinema 1896–1996*. London and New York: Routledge.

Uva, C. (2007). *Schermi di piombo. Il terrorismo nel cinema italiano*. Soveria Mannelli: Rubbettino.

Zagarrio, V. (ed.) (2006). *La meglio gioventù*. Venice: Marsilio.

26

THE RISORGIMENTO IN CONTEMPORARY ITALY

History, politics and memory during the national jubilees (1911–1961–2011)

Annarita Gori

The Risorgimento: a shared myth?

In 2011, Italy celebrated its national jubilee. It was the third time that the country was called to confront its past, the complex process of nation-building and, as on the previous anniversaries, to deal with the issue famously highlighted by the liberal politician Massimo D'Azeglio: 'Italy is made; now the Italians must be made'. The meanings underlying these three celebrations allow us to reflect on the different ways in which the past history of the country was used by the ruling classes to build a common sense of identity; and to underline how this process developed throughout the century. Jubilees are considered here not only as an anniversary, but also as a 'procedure employed by national state and by specific politic cultures to define themselves, and with the ways in which the politics of memory, legitimization strategies, languages of political communication and commemorative machineries have served as channel liable to persuade and to penetrate society' (Baioni, 2011: 399). These commemorations, in fact, were important occasions for reflection for politics and civil society, and for social scientists as well: in addition to being a celebratory moment, they were also significant events which encouraged reflection on Italian national identity and the relationship between politics, memory and the Risorgimento.

The Risorgimento is a crucial period in Italian history: it marks the foundation of Italy as a united nation, but it is also the defining moment for some problematic divisions that have characterized the country: masses vs. elites; South vs. North; monarchy vs. republic, etc. For these reasons, the Risorgimento, its uses and its interpretations, will be the focus of this chapter: analysing the myth of the Risorgimento through the lens of the jubilees will help shed light on some basic problems of Italian history of the last 150 years, such as national identity in dispute between political parties and local belonging, historical revisionism, the persistence of divisions and the relationship with the national anniversaries of other countries.

The historiographical debate on the Risorgimento has developed in parallel with the different phases of the study of its myth and its relationship to the idea of nation: the debate began with the codification and the active promotion of the study of the Risorgimento by the state in the Giolitti era; the subject of the Risorgimento enjoyed increasing interest until the first national jubilee and a subsequent decrease because of the new centrality given in the collective imagination to the *Resistenza* as the founding act of the Italian state; and, more recently, the debate has benefited from the revival of studies on this period in the last ten years, characterized by the attention paid to new trends in cultural history (Riall, 2007; Isnenghi and Cecchinato, 2008; Ginsborg, 2007), a revaluation of the concept of 'masses' as opposed to that of class, and an analysis of the celebrations of the Italian Risorgimento in a European context (Baioni *et al.*, 2012). The new focus on the Risorgimento, however, has also been accompanied by a wave of historical revisionism that has led to an oversimplified, and sometimes misleading, reading of the events and characters of national unification (Del Bocca, 2003; Di Fiore, 2007; Aprile, 2010). The most disruptive change in the last jubilee seems due to those political forces – especially the Lega Nord (Northern League) and the Neo-Bourbons – that have shifted the focus of the debate from ideological to territorial divisions, encouraging a dangerous combination of revisionism and revanchist policies.

This wave of revisionism and the rejection of the Risorgimento have spread beyond the field of historiography; this phenomenon is indeed also the result of the changing attitude of political parties towards the Risorgimento, especially those excluded from the official organization of the celebrations. In 1911, Republicans, Socialists and Catholics never called into question the process of national unification; instead, they proclaimed themselves the real heirs of the Risorgimento ideals, an attitude confirmed and developed further by the Communist Party in 1961. The situation was quite the reverse, in 2011: with a new political class, the focus of dispute had completely shifted; in fact, what was under attack from the secessionist parties – some of them, such as Northern League, part of the government that organized the celebrations – was no longer the interpretation or the appropriation of the Risorgimento, but the historical event itself. The most evident symptom of this change is that the most strenuous defenders of the memory of the Risorgimento were no longer the political parties, including some of those in the government, but the President of the Republic Giorgio Napolitano (2012) and his predecessor Carlo Azeglio Ciampi (2012), the chairman of the *Comitato dei Garanti* for the *Centocinquantenario*.

However, this does not imply a lack of national belonging among the population; on the contrary, the sense of belonging has been proved by the thousands of people who participated in the celebrations and the myriad initiatives organized at a local level that resembled the diffuse character and extreme localism of the celebrations of 1911.

1911: the triumph of the Savoy dynasty and the 'double fiftieth'

In 1911, Italy celebrated its first anniversary through a variety of events that involved a number of cities, each of which often had its own Risorgimento Day (Gentile, 1997: 20; Franco, 2002: 41–2). The existence of independent exhibitions highlighted the fragmentation of the Italian process of nation-building through an effective representation of the myth of the Risorgimento as consisting of several local stories (Brice, 2010: 48). Such fragmentation led to an original 'Italian way' in national celebrations, which found its most important realization in the Jubilee Exhibitions. These in fact were divided into three between Turin, Rome, and later on Florence.

This choice ensured that each of the three cities, which at different times during the Risorgimento had been the capitals of the Kingdom of Italy, represented a specific aspect of the Italian national character. Turin, the industrial capital, hosted the Labour Fair (Tobia, 2003); Florence, in line with its stereotype of 'the cradle of art' dating back to the nineteenth century, organized a portrait exhibition in Palazzo Vecchio (Gori, 2011); finally, Rome, the new capital and the symbol of long-awaited Italian unity, hosted various exhibitions: one of modern art, the 'Mostra delle Regioni' in Piazza d'Armi, and one specially dedicated to the Risorgimento in the Vittoriano.

According to the organizers, the 1911 exhibitions had a twofold aim. On the one hand, they were to be 'a testimony and, in some ways, even a challenge to all those foreigners and compatriots still doubtful' (Caracciolo, 1980: 39) of the role that in the previous two decades Italy had taken up as a newly born economic and industrial power. On the other, the exhibitions were to transmit to the Italian people a strong feeling of unity founded on the Risorgimento and its mythology. However, the supposed unity that the organizers and the liberal ruling class alike wanted to show was quite an abstract notion to say the least. The most evident example of Italy's national fragmentation and of its divided memory is the Vittoriano itself, the monument built for King Victor Emmanuel II that was inaugurated on 4 June 1911 and hosted the Risorgimento exhibition. In all its strength and majesty, the Roman monument represented the upholder of national unity, but it lacked any depiction of the nation, merely sublimated by sixteen statues representing the regions and located in the porch (Porciani, 1993: 400; Tobia, 1998). It is also possible to interpret the Vittoriano as the ultimate celebration of the Italian royal house, in the context of a kind of *patriotic pedagogy* connected to quite a conciliatory view of the Savoy dynasty as the leading force behind the Risorgimento (Brice, 1998). In fact, in 1911 the liberal ruling class proposed a symbolic representation of the Risorgimento

> essentially based on the assimilation of the different versions of the national myth common during the Risorgimento, from that of Mazzini to that of Garibaldi. The Liberal state transformed them all into integral parts of its national myth, after removing all elements that contrasted ideologically with its own political ideals.
>
> *(Gentile, 1997: 17)*

The idea of a national 'pacification' was the common theme around which the commemoration at the Campidoglio on 27 March 1911 was organized. During this event, the President of the Senate Giuseppe Manfredi remembered how, also thanks to 'heroic attempts', Italy had managed to resurrect itself under the aegis of the 'long-lasting glories of the Savoy dynasty, whose work for the redemption of Italy is like an unassailable citadel'. Manfredi went on to say that 'the royal house is now identified with the people' and that 'the people's devotion to the Savoy dynasty was [firstly] a feeling, a matter of principle. But nowadays it is a tradition.'[1] In truth, a large part of the population felt excluded from the official celebrations and did not share the feelings of patriotism transmitted there. It is for these reasons that in the Italian case it would be more correct to talk about 'jubilees' in the plural. There are numerous explanations for such a definition. First, one could argue that the birth and expansion of veterans' association, and thereafter of political movements, contributed to a broader reflection of one's historical roots and of the so-called *democratic* Risorgimento. Second, the years that immediately preceded 1911 saw a plethora of anniversaries related to the leading figures and historical events of Risorgimento. On these occasions, all those people far from the liberal ruling class had started to try new modalities of celebration, even making themselves more visible on the urban scene.

Those who celebrated the 'other Jubilee' were in fact the leading figures of the democratic Risorgimento and of the new popular parties. If nationalist leaders and the intellectuals of the journal *La Voce*, such as Giuseppe Prezzolini, had denounced the discrepancy between the official celebrations and the country's real state, talking about a 'sad year', the Socialists went as far as coining the expression 'double Jubilee'.

In the daily newspaper *L'Avanti!*, Claudio Treves (1911) explicitly spoke of 'two fiftieth anniversaries': one for the middle class and one for the people still struggling for their rights. 'The enduring state of wretchedness and social degradation prevented the proletarian masses from feeling active participants in the life of the nation, and therefore from identifying with the mythologies of the Risorgimento.' Similarly, the Republican Party, fiercely opposed to the Savoy-oriented celebrations, organized a counter-ceremony at the statue of Garibaldi at the Janiculum in Rome. The Republicans proposed themselves as the only true interpreters of the spirit of the Risorgimento, rejecting the monarchy that for them had 'usurped' the patriotic celebrations.

Equally clear was the stance of the Catholics, whose newspaper *L'Unità Cattolica* – which for many years came out draped in black as a sign of protest against the breach of Porta Pia – spoke of 'a year of mourning'. The papacy, while still prohibiting Catholics from participating in political life, saw the fiftieth anniversary as an occasion for emphasizing the existence of a Christian patriotism, presumably more attentive to the values of the people. The opposition of Catholics to the jubilee celebrations never took the form of street demonstrations, but was instead characterized by intellectual protests carried out through newspapers, brochures and pamphlets, such as one by Florentine Catholic students (Editorial, 1911). In it, one could read:

> We could feel how the true soul of the people was absent from that formal official parade . . . A prayer to God sprang from our young hearts: may God, thanks to the sacrifice and heroism of our martyrs, eradicate this old political Italy, otherwise destined to a never-ending slavery.

In conclusion, it seems that the idea of the nation and the public use of the Risorgimento were defined through the mediation of different political ideologies and territorial affiliations. All this did not lead to a weakening of patriotism and patriotic feelings, but to their reformulation. It engendered a critique not of national unity itself, but of the liberal state and the patriotism of its ruling class.

Between the Risorgimento and the *Resistenza*: the celebration of 'Italia '61'

Fifty years later, Italy was again to take stock of its national status and of the maturity of an identity shared by the whole of the population. Turin was chosen as a 'showcase' of a new Italy, a bridge between past and future (Merolla, 2004; Pace *et al.*, 2005). This kind of representation was developed along two different lines: the first, linked to the role of the city in Italy's economic and social growth, was embodied in the futuristic buildings of the International Exhibition of Work; the second, focusing on history and politics, took the form of the Mostra delle Regioni (Exhibition of the Regions), and the Historical Exhibition of Italian Unity.

In this last case, the organizing committee strongly underlined the meaningful connection between the Risorgimento and the anti-Fascist *Resistenza* (on anti-Fascism today, see Chapter 27 in this volume), as evident in the twentieth pavilion of the Mostra delle Regioni dedicated to the long unification process and, above all, in the Historical Exibition located in Palazzo Carignano (Bouchard, 2005), the building that had been home to the first Italian parliament. Here, in fact, the liberation from Nazi-Fascism, to which the last room (significantly called *Echi risorgimentali nella Resistenza*) was devoted, was represented as a 'Second Risorgimento' (Traniello, 1997), since – as was explained in the catalogue of the exhibition – '[thanks to the *Resistenza*], the Risorgimento truly ended. Because of all this, today's Italy can freely celebrate its first hundred years of unity, as the Fathers of the Risorgimento had envisioned' (Luraghi, 1961).[2]

The association of the Risorgimento and the *Resistenza* should also serve as a historical catalyst to keep together a still very fragmented country, in a moment marked by deep socio-economic and political transformations: the imbalances due to the economic boom and the internal migrations; the abandonment of the *conventio ad excludendum* towards the Italian left parties, which characterized most of their political existence in the post-war period; and finally, the neo-Fascist reprisals that started after the demonstrations in Genoa of June 1960. By connecting the Risorgimento to the *Resistenza* in a state-funded exhibition (Ballone, 1997: 415; Crainz, 1986), it was therefore possible to see a way out of that contradictory 'institutional silence/testimonial emphasis' and from the so-called 'long winters of the *Resistenza*' (Santomassimo, 1994) which had characterized the previous years – dominated by centrist political movements.

That said, nevertheless, the public use of the Risorgimento – and, in parallel with that, the use of the *Resistenza* – does not seem to having been a linear process shared by the whole of the political arena. On the contrary, it was at the centre of deep struggles – like what had happened in 1911. On top of that lay the paradox that, whereas the 1911 jubilee had had a very strong secularist – if not anticlerical – orientation, that of 1961 was organized by the Christian Democrats. These counted among their ranks the men in charge of the events, such as the MP Giuseppe Pella – who acted as president of the Italy '61 Committee – and the mayor of Turin.[3] In 1961, as in 1911, Catholics deprecated the behaviour of the old liberal ruling class, presenting themselves as the upholders of 'true' national unity. Such unity had only been completed now that the Christian Democrats – after decades of mistakes on the part of the liberals – had restored both the Church and the state as the basis of the Italian national character.

The closeness between Italy and the Vatican in terms of practices of memory, and in the commemoration of the Risorgimento, comes out very clearly when analysing some of the public statements of the leading figures of the time. If the President of the Republic Giovanni Gronchi ended his speech to the Chambers on 25 March 1961 during the Centenary Commemoration with a call to God to make a more prosperous and peaceful Italy, the Archbishop of Genoa, Cardinal Giuseppe Siri – in his pastoral letter for Easter 1961 – asked Catholics to

> celebrate the centenary of the unification of Italy, praying to God for the sake of 'our' country. A prayer that has to do with the consolidation of the ever more perfect unity in the civil organization and moral behaviour, in the fraternal relationship between all the citizens united under the Catholic tradition.[4]

At the same time, as had happened fifty years earlier, the left-wing parties again utilized the theme of the double centenary, declaring themselves as the only true interpreters of national memory. Using the linkages established with the Risorgimento – which had become evident during the first free elections of 1948, when the image of Garibaldi was the emblem of the *Fronte Democratico Popolare* – and considering themselves as the moral heirs of the Resistance movement, these parties fiercely opposed how the Christian Democrats utilized the national memory on the public scene.

In the daily newspaper *L'Avanti!* the socialist parliamentarian Cesare Marini (1961) wrote:

> The ruling class has so far given quite a conciliatory reading of the Risorgimento. National pride and the ambition of different sectors of society could thus be satisfied. The Risorgimento is a bit of everything: it is Victor Emmanuel for the monarchists,

> Mazzini for the Republicans, Cavour for the Liberals, Garibaldi for the Democrats and the secularists. The Catholics are missing, and former priests cannot speak on their behalf. Yet, there are the organizers themselves who – with their 'omnipresence' – are taking a sort of revenge for their previous 'absence'.

In *L'Unità* too, the journalist and political scientist Saverio Vertone (1961) openly spoke of 'Italia '61' as 'something between a great advertising campaign of Fiat neo-capitalism and a joyful and conventional patriotic masquerade: a sort of big "Risorgimento show"'. Also, the Communist leader Palmiro Togliatti (1961) complained about the improper use of the Risorgimento in the celebrations, but despite all the misinterpretations of the jubilee, he noted that 'the people and the workers – as well as the Communist activists – are consciously and with great enthusiasm taking part in the celebrations'.

The popular feelings recorded by Togliatti were not accepted by many historians and intellectuals close to the leftist parties (Baris, 2012: 219). According to them, the centenary exhibitions – even though promoting a critical re-reading of the Risorgimento and having become an occasion for intellectual debate – were not so appealing in terms of historical commemorations. The Italian Marxist historian Ernesto Ragionieri (1964) explicitly spoke of the *Fine del Risorgimento*, whereas the historian and journalist Vittorio De Caprariis (1961) in *Il Mondo* complained about the crisis of the myth of the Risorgimento: 'the celebrations were marked by a sort of coldness and formality on the part of those who should have been its leading figures, especially the young, who felt that past as remote history'.

It is then possible to agree with Massimo Baioni (2011: 411), who recently argued that

> Italia '61 seemed to be at one and the same time the heyday and the twilight of the celebration of the myth of the Risorgimento. Through its modernization, Italy had entered an epoch that required languages, symbols and memorial practices even further removed from this country's traditional framework of patriotic and national myth.

2011: a 'controversial' jubilee

'See you in 2011': it was with this slogan, depicted on large placards, that 'Italia '61' ended. Fifty years later, Italy again celebrated its history and, one more time, opened a debate about the Risorgimento and its public use in the middle of a political crisis that started in the mid-1990s, whose weakening effects obviously impacted on the celebrations of the 150th anniversary.

Unlike the previous two jubilees, in 2011, no law was introduced to prepare an organic plan of events and raise funds; in 2007, the centre-left government established some agencies, such as a *Comitato interministeriale* (Interministerial Committee), a *Unità tecnica di missione della presidenza del consiglio* (Technical Mission Unit of the Prime Minister's Office) and a *Comitato dei garanti* (Guarantee Committee). In particular, the problems encountered in the four years preceding 2011 are due to the lack of overview of the event because of the economic difficulties linked to the global crisis, but also to the attitude of some Italian parties that, through the *Comitato interministeriale* chaired by the Minister for Culture Sandro Bondi, demanded that the celebration take into account 'the limits and flaws of unification, in particular the so-called Southern Question'.[5] The members of *Comitato dei garanti*, and especially the president Carlo Azeglio Ciampi, fought from the beginning against an indiscriminate and instrumental historical revisionism; nonetheless, especially in 2009, in the Committee there was an evident 'fear that this political and cultural mindset, fuelled in particular by the Northern League, might have such a negative impact on the celebrations, that there was the risk of their "derailment"' (Fiocco,

2012: 192). This supposed derailment did not come about, but the controversy sparked by the Lega Nord and the general climate of uncertainty about the celebrations led to some significant consequences: first, the regional exhibition, initially planned to continue the tradition started in 1911, was not organized; second, several members of the committee resigned because of the apathy of the government (Galli Della Loggia, 2009). In 2010, in fact, in addition to Carlo Azeglio Ciampi, Gustavo Zagrebelsky, Ludina Barzini, Marta Boneschi, Ugo Gregoretti and the writer Dacia Maraini also withdrew from the committee; Maraini said to the *Corriere della Sera*:

> The committee has been hollowed out from the inside . . . we were ignored; we were nothing more than a fig leaf, while someone was trying to promote a 'revisionist' reading of the Risorgimento in line with the ideology of the League.
>
> *(Carioti, 2010)*

This uncertainty also impacted on the overall planning of the anniversary, which, except for a set of heterogeneous exhibitions scheduled in Turin from March to November 2011 and evocatively called 'Experience 150', did not have any great event, as opposed to the previous anniversaries in 1911 and 1961.

The historical Expo called '*Fare gli Italiani*' was conceived by Walter Barberis and Giovanni De Luna, and aimed to

> display a hundred and fifty years of national history, investigating the modalities and results of the project through which Italians were 'made'. It does so by looking at their capacity to absorb the various fractures that traversed our national history in terms of society, politics, economy, ideology and culture.
>
> *(Barberis and De Luna, 2011: 11)*

Italian history, also in order to answer recent critiques based on federalist and separatist ideas, was conceived precisely as the union of a set of fractures: city/countryside, North/South, emigration/immigration; these were then displayed to visitors through fourteen different blocks (e.g. the Church, wars, factories, mafia, consumerism, etc.).

The exhibition was sufficiently successful to be extended to November 2012. At the same time, it was also criticized for the ways in which it presented the Risorgimento. The first room of the exhibition, dedicated to the men and women of the Risorgimento – represented through busts lit up in turn from which one could hear these men and women's most famous sayings – seemed 'an expedient thanks to which the curators got rid of a problem that was difficult to handle more than anything else' (Bertolotti, 2012: 105).

Did, then, 2011 see an 'end of the Risorgimento', as foreseen fifty years earlier? Not at all. In 2011 the Museum of the Risorgimento in Turin was reopened, now under the direction of Umberto Levra. In the museum, this historical period is represented not only in a national perspective, but with several references to European history too; furthermore the Risorgimento, from 2005 onwards, became a real 'hot topic' among politicians, journalists and historians. The most discussed topic in newspapers, as well as at conferences and in several monographs, was how the Risorgimento produced on the one hand a kind of nationalist-populist 'neopatriotism' – think, for example, of how in 2011 Garibaldi was the protagonist of an advertising campaign for an Italian telephone company – while fostering, on the other hand, a federalist revisionism which projected contemporary issues and problems onto the past.

This was underlined some time before by historian Alberto Mario Banti (2010) in *La Repubblica*:

> The trivialisation of historical figures and events, which politicians are now evoking as if these people were supporters and forerunners of a given political project or party, is very far from the historical analysis that is being brought about by researchers. Researchers utilize today's Italy not as a final aim [of their interpretation] but as a starting point.[6]

This struggle, and the contrasts between different political opinions, reached its peak around 17 March 2011. At its core was the debate on the legitimacy of proclaiming a special national holiday only for 2011 to celebrate Italian unification. With regards to the national celebrations, the leader of Südtiroler Volkspartei and President of the Autonomous Province of Bozen, Luis Durnwalder, during the councillors' meeting of 7 February 2011, argued that the province was not to take part in the celebrations of 17 March. A few days later, in response to a request for clarification, Durnwalder replied on the province's website:

> You know that in 1918 the region of Südtirol was annexed to Italy against the wish of the population. We had a great deal of suffering under Fascism because of the assimilation politics pursued by the regime. But we only wanted to maintain our own culture. So, do you honestly think we should celebrate something? I fully respect others' feelings, but I demand the same respect for all those citizens who do not want to celebrate.[7]

Also in the North, an anti-celebration stance was taken by the Lega Nord (see also Chapter 17 in this volume). This case is more complex than the Südtirol Volkspartei: first of all because the Lega was a party in government in 2011; second, because that same year, the party headed by Umberto Bossi faced local government elections; these were critical to strengthening its hegemony over the territory, but came at a moment when opinion polls already predicted a dramatic loss of votes for the party (Spagnolo, 2012). The decision by Lega Nord ministers to vote against turning 17 March into a bank holiday was therefore not surprising: in this way, the Lega made a strong statement of identity, choosing 'to distinguish itself from the allies in an explicit and direct way; highlighting, once again, its hostility to the Italian unification process and brandishing the flag of the party of the North' (Diamanti, 2011). Furthermore, the Lega did not organize its own federalist demonstrations, as happened in the South with the Neo-Bourbons; this probably reflected an identity dilemma: while rejecting the idea of unity, the party could still take advantage of the jubilee by trying to put forward its own interpretation of the Risorgimento, which underlined the pivotal role played by the North and by proposing a kind of 'Lega version' of the ideas and figure of Carlo Cattaneo. Probably, the absence of large pro-federalist events was also linked to the 'stagnation' of the federalist process, which had lost part of its initial momentum. Nevertheless, even though the Lega did not organize any large demonstrations, it continued to campaign against the jubilee in its newspaper, significantly entitled *La Padania*. On 17 March, the Lega Nord, published a special seven-page issue dedicated to the hundred-and-fiftieth anniversary significantly entitled 'Let's celebrate a farewell to parasites. United in Federalism.' In it – besides news about several towns in Padania that refused to celebrate – was an article by Diego Scalvini (2011) calling for the advent of a 'new Risorgimento, able to erase the original sin of centralism and that will acknowledge historical territorial identities. . . . A problematic historical truth, expunged from textbooks and relegated to the dark corners of a few bookshops.'[8]

This said, it would be unfair to confine the critique of the Risorgimento, and of its public usage, to Northern Italy and its regional politics. In fact, in parallel with the Northern League's articles and the declarations of members of linguistic minorities, new and rather nonconformist essays also emerged. These were mainly by radical Catholics and neo-Bourbonists, and focused on a revisionist re-reading of the Risorgimento. Such feelings of Southern *revenge*, together with the denunciation of the 'crimes' perpetrated by the House of Savoy, and of the waste of the riches of the Kingdom of the Two Sicilies, are probably the most significant themes of this now extensive literature. Furthermore, all this is being amplified by new neo-Bourbonic and independentist movements such as Insieme per la rinascita, Neoborbonici, V.a.n.t.o. and Rdsin.

These groups gave voice to a feeling of discontent and revanchism that had existed for a long time in Southern Italy, and that resulted in a strongly divided memory of the Risorgimento and the emergence of a large and diverse number of political cultures with various local roots. In order to legitimate themselves and gain consensus, they used and reworked in a revisionist manner the history of the unification of the country, focusing in particular on 'the events [which] happened during '59–'61 that caused the disappearance of various state and regional entities, especially the collapse of the Kingdom of the Two Sicilies' (De Lorenzo, 2013: 9). Although primarily rooted in political extremism, especially on the far right, in recent years neo-Bourbonism lost its connotation of an informal movement of public opinion, taking a more overtly political form which led to the 'birth of many small parties of Southerners, which were established in the hope of picking up some "protest" votes in the context of the current economic crisis and the loss of credibility of the traditional national parties'. However, in light of their dismal election results and their inability to develop a credible platform, these networks continue to propose as their strong point the public use of history 'which took extreme forms as the *Centocinquantenario* drew near, with the open rejection of the official celebrations, the proposal of their own calendar of celebrations and a large presence in the field of popularized history' (Montaldo, 2012: 106).

Works such as those cited in the introduction to this chapter – the most famous exponent of which is the journalist Pino Aprile, the renowned author of the trilogy *Terroni, Giù al sud* and *Mai più terroni* – contain allegations against the process of Italian unification and tortuous theories about the economic decline of the Kingdom of the Two Sicilies, ahistorically described as a third economic power in nineteenth-century Europe. Such theories demonstrate how this 'so-called anti-Risorgimento "historical revision" is as replete with indisputable statements and indignant tones, as it is lacking in studies that prove the former and justify the latter' (Lupo, 2011: 3). This new wave of revisionist thinking, and its connections with political movements, was evident during the three days of *Malaunità: Controcelebrazioni dell'Unità di Italia*, which took place in Naples between 15 and 17 March 2011. The event was named after the collected volume *Malaunità*, edited by Aprile, Del Boca, Di Fiore, Guarini and others. Not only was the book presented in Naples, but there also took place a 'libertarian' flash mob in Piazza dei Martiri, a public commemoration of the fallen Southern patriots and an intercessory prayer in the church of San Ferdinando. The public reading of the names of soldiers, bandits and émigrés, followed by a parade carrying the old Bourbon flag and a votive candle, produced a sort of syncretism with Catholic rites, as if a new 'civil religion' was being born.

As we have mentioned, however, the awareness that our process of unification is not a collectively shared memory should not be too alarming. It is true that during 'the *Centocinquantenario* a wave of revanchist revisionism spread across Italy, leading to what has been defined as a "history of Italy à la carte" in which each political subject has chosen its own version of national identity, grafting it onto an ever-different origin and erasing the distance between past and present' (Catastini *et al.* 2012: 184); however, the phenomenon, despite the intensification due to the media, never brought about a large and potentially subversive movement, but was rather confined to posturing. The number of people who participated in the jubilee, both in the North and the South, seemed to prove that, albeit a bit hazy and in different ways than in previous jubilees, the sense of identity still stands.

Notes

1 The speech by Joseph Manfredi is quoted as attached document in the article by Luca Tedesco (2011).

2 The choice of dedicating a room to the Resistance and not to the Lateran Treaty was stigmatized by the MSI (see La conciliazione e la guerra '15–'18 bandite dalla Mostra di Italia '61, *Il Secolo d'Italia*, 25 May 1961).

3 In connection with the role played by the DC as organizer of the celebrations, the Italian historian Emilio Gentile (1997: 357–8) argued how 'the national myth appeared as a leading player in the Italian political arena, although in the context of a performance which – at a symbolic level – resulted in a self-glorification of the ruling party more than in the celebration of national unification'.

4 Pastorale del Card. Siri per l'Unità d'Italia, *Il Popolo*, 18 (86).

5 Considerazioni in merito alle linee programmatiche del Governo per la celebrazione dei 150 anni dell'Unità d'italia del 5 ottobre 2009. Available online at www.italiaunita150.it (accessed 14 January 2015).

6 See also the intense and prolonged debate as a consequence of his comments on the 'national-populist' show of Roberto Benigni at the Sanremo music festival (Benigni e 'Fratelli d'Italia', dubbi su una lezione di storia, *Il Manifesto*, 20 February 2011).

7 Available online at www.provinz.bz.it/land/landesregierung/durnwalder/chat/chat_i.aspx?Pg=6 (accessed 14 January 2015). On this web page are also some enthusiastic comments, mostly in German, by inhabitants of the province of Bozen.

8 See also the voting declarations on a law on the celebrations of 150 years of Italian unification by the regional councillors of the Lega Nord in Lombardy on 22 February 2011 in part available on YouTube.

Bibliography

Aprile, P. (2010). *Terroni!, Giù al sud*. Milan: Piemme.

Aprile, P., Del Bocca, L., Di Fiore, G., Guarini, R., Patruno, L., Schifano, J.-N. and Napoli, E. (2011). *Malaunità. 1861–2011 centocinquat'anni portati male*. Naples: Spazio Creativo.

Baioni, M. (2011). Anniversaries and the public uses of the Risorgimento in twentieth-century Italy. *Journal of Modern European History*, 9 (3), 397–414.

Baioni, M. (2012). Considerazioni a margine di un anniversario controverso. *Passato e Presente*, 30 (86): 83–93.

Baioni, M., Conti, F. and Ridolfi, R. (2012). *Celebrare la nazione. Grandi anniversari e memorie pubbliche nella società contemporanea*. Milan: Silvana Editoriale.

Ballone, A. (1997). La Resistenza. In M. Isnenghi (ed.), *I luoghi della memoria* (pp. 403–38). Rome-Bari: Laterza.

Banti, A. M. (2010). Il Risorgimento non è un mito. *La Repubblica*, 16 November: 58–9.

Barberis, W. and De Luna, G. (2011). *Fare gli italiani, 1861–2011: Una mostra per i 150 anni della storia d'Italia*. Milan: Silvana.

Baris, T. (2012). La Resistenza e il Risorgimento nelle celebrazioni dell'Italia Unita nel periodo repubblicano (1961–2006). *Ricerche Storiche*, 42 (2), 211–30.

Bertolotti, M. (2012). Fare gli italiani. 150 anni in mostra. *Passato e Presente*, 30 (86), 95–105.

Bouchard, N. (2005). Italia '61: The Commemorations for the Centenary of Unification in the First Capital of the Italian State. *Romance Studies*, 23 (2), 117–29.

Brice, C. (1998). *Monumentalité publique et politique à Rome: le Vittoriano*. Rome: École française de Rome.

Brice, C. (2010). Il 1911 in Italia. Convergenza di poteri, frazionamento di rappresentazioni. *Memoria e Ricerca*, 13 (34), 47–62.

Caracciolo, A. (1980). Il 'fatale' millenovecentoundici. In G. Piantoni (ed.), *Roma 1911* (pp. 39–44). Rome: De Luca.

Carioti, A. (2010). Tensioni tra i garanti dell'Unità d'Italia. Dimissioni, appelli, proteste. *Corriere della Sera*, 23 April: 45.
Catastini, F., Mineccia, F. and Spagnolo, C. (2012). Centocinquanta: storia d'Italia à la carte. *Ricerche Storiche*, 42 (2), 183–8.
Ciampi, C. A. (2012). *Non è il paese che sognavo. Taccuino laico per i 150 anni dell'Unità d'Italia*. Milan: il Saggiatore.
Crainz, G. (1986). La 'legittimazione' della Resistenza. In M. Argentieri (ed.), *Fascismo e antifascismo negli anni della Repubblica* (pp. 62–97). Milan: FrancoAngeli.
De Caprariis, V. (1961). Senza eredi?, *Il Mondo*, 28 March: 1.
De Lorenzo, R. (2013). *Borbonia Felix*. Rome: Salerno.
Del Bocca, L. (2003). *Indietro Savoia! Storia controcorrente del Risorgimento*. Casale Monferrato: Controstoria.
Di Fiore, G. (2007). *Controstoria dell'unità di Italia: fatti e misfatti del Risorgimento*. Milan: Rizzoli.
Diamanti, I. (2011). Una festa da celebrare sottovoce. *La Repubblica*, 21 February: 1.
Editorial (1911). L'anno giubilare. *Italia Nova*, June: 2.
Fiocco, G. (2012). La sindrome del declino: note sulle celebrazioni del 2011. *Ricerche Storiche*, 42 (2), 189–210.
Franco, R. (2002). *Le Italie degli Italiani. Le celebrazioni del 1911*. Badia Fiesolana: EUI Press.
Galli Della Loggia, E. (2009). Noi italiani senza memoria. *Corriere della Sera*, 20 July: 1, 10.
Gentile, E. (1997). *La grande Italia*. Milan: Mondadori.
Ginsborg, P. (ed.) (2007). *Storia d'Italia. Annali 22. Il Risorgimento*. Turin: Einaudi.
Gori, A. (2011). Una regione in Mostra. In L. Berti (ed.), *Arezzo e la Toscana nel regno d'Italia (1861–1946)* (pp. 265–80). Arezzo: Società storica aretina.
Isabella, M. (2012). Rethinking Italy's nation-building 150 years afterwards: the new Risorgimento historiography. *Past and Present*, 217 (1), 247–68.
Isnenghi, M. and Cecchinato, E. (eds.) (2008). *Fare l'Italia: unità e disunità nel Risorgimento*. Turin: UTET.
Lupo, S. (2011). *L'unificazione italiana. Mezzogiorno, rivoluzione, guerra civile*. Rome: Donzelli.
Luraghi, R. (1961). L'ordinamento della mostra. In Comitato Italia '61 (ed.), *Italia '61. Celebrazioni del Centenario dell'Unità d'Italia* (pp. 229–92). Turin: Tip. ILTE.
Marini, P. C. (1961). Per sanare il bilancio di cent'anni l'inno di Mameli non basta. *L'Avanti!*, 4 April: 6.
Merolla, M. (2004). *Italia '61. I media celebrano il Centenario della Nazione*. Milan: FrancoAngeli.
Montaldo, S. (2012). La 'fossa comune' del Museo Lombroso e il 'lager' di Fenestrelle: il centocinquantenario dei neoborbonici. *Passato e Presente*, 30 (87), 106–18.
Napolitano, G. (2012). *Una e indivisibile: riflessioni sui 150 anni della nostra Italia*. Milan: Rizzoli.
Pace, S., Chiorino, C. and Rosso, M. (eds.) (2005). *Italia '61. Identità e miti nelle celebrazioni per il centenario dell'Unità d'Italia*. Turin: Allemandi.
Porciani, I. (1993). *Stato e nazione: l'immagine debole dell'Italia*. In S. Soldani and G. Turi (eds.), *Fare gli Italiani* (pp. 385–428). Bologna: Il Mulino.
Ragionieri, E. (1964). Fine del 'Risorgimento'? *Studi Storici*, 5 (4), 3–40.
Riall, L. (2007). *Garibaldi: Invention of a Hero*. New Haven, CT: Yale University Press.
Santomassimo, G. (1994). I lunghi inverni della Resistenza 1945–1955. *In/formazione*, 25–6, 5–8.
Scalvini, D. (2011). Un nuovo Risorgimento sconfigga il centralismo. *La Padania*, 17 March: 10.
Spagnolo, C. (2012). Fine dello Stato? Appunti sulle celebrazioni del centocinquantenario dell'Unità d'Italia. *Ricerche storiche*, 42 (2), 273–310.
Tedesco, L. (2011). Roma 1911 e la disfida dei Cinquantenari. *Storicamente*, 7. Available online at www.storicamente.org/01_fonti/tedesco_roma_1911.htm (accessed 13 January 2015).
Tobia, B. (1998). *L'Altare della Patria*. Bologna: Il Mulino.
Tobia, B. (2003). Il Giubileo della Patria: Roma e Torino nel 1911. In U. Levra and R. Roccia (eds.), *Le Esposizioni torinesi 1805–1911* (pp. 145–74). Turin: Einaudi.
Togliatti, P. (1961). Il centenario dell'Unità. *L'Unità*, 26 March: 1.
Traniello, F. (1997). Sulla definizione di Resistenza come 'secondo Risorgimento'. In C. Franceschini and G. Monina (eds.), *Le idee costituzionali della Resistenza* (pp. 17–25). Rome: Presidenza del Consiglio dei ministri.
Treves, C. (1911). I due cinquantenari. *L'Avanti!*, 27 March: 2.
Vertone, S. (1961). L'odierna inaugurazione di Italia '61 in un clima da fiera sabauda e clericale. *L'Unità*, 6 May: 6.

27

THE 'SPACES' OF ANTI-FASCISM IN ITALY TODAY

Philip Cooke

Introduction

At an early stage in the 2013 election process Beppe Grillo, the leader of the Five-Star Movement, got into hot water over his views on Fascism and anti-Fascism. Grillo and other politicians had gathered at the Viminal Palace in Rome in order to officially 'deposit' the symbols of the parties they represented. This process allows for symbols to be checked to establish whether they are misleading or, indeed, inflammatory. Before submitting his symbol, Grillo got into conversation with Simone Di Stefano, the Roman leader of Casapound – initially a social centre founded on neo-Fascist principles, but which had mutated into a political party and was contesting the election throughout Italy. At the election Casapound would go on to win almost 48,000 votes (0.14 per cent of the electorate) and no seats in the Chamber of Deputies. Grillo's Five-Star Movement did, as we know, a lot better. Between mouthfuls (Grillo was constantly eating during the campaign, or so it seemed) the two discovered they had a great deal in common. At a certain point, Di Stefano asked the crunch question: 'Are you anti-Fascist?' Grillo's response was not – as befits a skilled politician – an unequivocal yes or no, but instead he used the phrase 'L'antifascismo non mi compete,' which can be variously translated into English as 'It's not my responsibility,' 'It doesn't come under my jurisdiction,' or more literally 'It doesn't lie within my competence.'[1] It is not productive to submit Grillo's chosen expression to minute textual exegesis. Suffice it to say that the exchange between Grillo and Di Stefano provoked a debate (one of many) which would run throughout the course of the election, and beyond. Much of the debate was rather sterile, focussing on the 'yes' or 'no' issue which Grillo's words attempted to circumvent. In one of many intriguing developments, the bronze monument in Parma dedicated to the partisan hero Guido Picelli was covered in pro-Grillo graffiti: 'You are just a communist like Bersani. Viva Grillo!' According to the director of a documentary film on Picelli this was a double outrage to the partisan's memory. While the graffiti was bad enough, the suggestion that he was a 'communist like the secretary of the PD' was arguably a greater insult.[2]

After the election, the issue appeared to die down for a bit, until 25 April, the official date of the Liberation of the city of Milan from the Nazis and the Fascists at the end of the Second

World War, and a national 'anti-Fascist' holiday. The 25 April has become the subject of much speculation in recent years, with calls from some Berlusconian quarters for it to no longer be a national holiday provoking outrage. Indeed, when Berlusconi first came to power in 1994, the 25 April celebrations became a demonstration against him and all he represented. But, if anything, Grillo provoked more indignation than Berlusconi (usually at his villa in Sardinia) has ever done, by releasing a spectacular tirade on his blog.[3] Entitled 'The 25 April is dead', Grillo provided some very compelling reasons as to why this should be the case in Italy today:

> In the nomination of a member of the Bilderberg group to be president of the Council of Ministers 25 April is dead.
>
> In the big belly laugh of the P2 member Berlusconi being in Parliament 25 April is dead.
>
> In the destruction of the tapes of the conversations between Mancino and Napolitano 25 April is dead. . . .
>
> In the failed election of Rodotà 25 April is dead.
>
> In the resurrection of Amato, the treasurer of Bottino Craxi,[4] 25 April is dead. . . .
>
> In the million and a half young Italians who have emigrated in these recent years because there's no work 25 April is dead.
>
> In the indifference of too many Italians who will soon have a nasty wake-up call 25 April is dead.
>
> Today let's avoid talking about it, celebrating it; let's keep silent out of respect for the dead.
>
> If the partisans came back amongst us, they would start crying.

What Grillo was saying was arguably clear enough – the hopes, aspirations and desires of the partisans had not been realized. Italy was in a mess and, in the circumstances, celebrating 25 April seemed hardly justified. Quite what the political motives were behind this statement was another matter. The satirist Michele Serra approved with customary irony in his ever acute opinion column in *La Repubblica*. According to Serra, this was the first 'left-wing thing' (*cosa di sinistra*) which Grillo had uttered: 'We had never realized that 25 April and anti-Fascism were so dear to his heart' (26 April 2013). Serra grasped the apparent paradox, but felt it was an important sign of an acceptance of an ideological standpoint from an individual without politics. Equally, Grillo's words were taken in many circles to be yet another insult flung at the Resistance and anti-Fascism in general. At Monte Sole, near Bologna, the site of the largest Nazi massacre of civilians in Western Europe, an 89-year-old former partisan muttered that if someone was half-dead, it was Grillo, and not 25 April (*La Repubblica* [Bologna], 26 April 2013).[5] Rather more importantly, when the new speaker in the Chamber of Deputies, Laura Boldrini, gave her opening speech, the mention of the Resistance and anti-Fascism brought the chamber to its feet.[6] That the new speaker was erroneously believed to be the daughter of one of Italy's best-known partisans, Arrigo Boldrini, only further contributed to the apparent relaunch of anti-Fascism in the chamber and, naturally enough, further opprobrium towards Grillo.

The debate raised a number of relevant (and some irrelevant) issues. Some of these related strictly to Grillo and the ideology of the Five-Star Movement. On a wider level the polemic encouraged observers to reflect on the place of anti-Fascism in Italian politics, political culture and society, and of the role of the past in present-day Italy. Discussions of the relevance or otherwise of anti-Fascism are far from new, and this certainly explains why Grillo, whose movement is all about novelty, innovation, difference and distance, should have wished not to identify the Five-Star Movement with it. The perception that the 'anti-Fascist paradigm' – which had been firmly established after the tumultuous events of July 1960[7] – was dissolving in some way can, however, be traced back to the 1980s (see also Gallerano, 1986; Baldassare, 1986; Ganapini, 1986; Pecchioli, 1985; Tranfaglia, 1985).

This was a period of ascendancy for Bettino Craxi and his PSI, which was characterized, amongst other things, by an attack on anti-Fascism and the memory of the Resistance in general. In an important article published in 1986, Nicola Gallerano effectively demonstrated the shift in the socialist left by comparing the editorials of the journal *Mondoperaio* from 25 April 1975 and 25 April 1985. In the first, Federico Coen described the celebration of the Resistance 'not as a formal rite, but a political fact'. Against the 'renewed virulence of the neo-Fascist infection' the Resistance was an 'obligatory point of reference'. In Gallerano's own words Coen's editorial was representative of a

> way of referring to the Resistance and to anti-Fascism which was common to the entire left, including of course an element of ritual: it expressed effectively the *continuity* and the transformative potential of a collective feeling, strongly unitary in nature and potentially hegemonic. It would be consecrated on a symbolic level in 1978 with the election of Sandro Pertini as the President of the Republic.
>
> *(Gallerano, 1986: 109–10)*

By 1985, however, Ruggero Guarini would argue that anti-Fascism had a negative side to it. It had carried out the job of underlining 'the frequently tenuous similarities' between the various political forces and, as a consequence downplayed their 'frequently profound differences'. By this he was explicitly referring to the differences between the PCI and the PSI, the emphasis of which was a central pillar of Craxi's political strategy. Guarini continued, in a key section, by suggesting that the binary oppositional formula 'Fascism/anti-Fascism' was less important than the 'totalitarianism/democracy' antithesis. Communism and Fascism, in other words, had some shared characteristics, particularly when it came to their refusal of 'modernity'. Italian Socialist politics under Craxi were, by extension, 'modern'. These ideas were taken up by another socialist thinker, Lucio Colletti, who wrote in the pages of the *Corriere della Sera* that if 'democracy cannot but be anti-Fascist, the opposite is not always true'. The political erosion of the 'anti-Fascist paradigm' in the 1980s coincided with developments in the historiographical field which saw major changes in the way that anti-Fascism (and Fascism) were interpreted, with the major figures in the debate being Renzo De Felice in Italy and François Furet in France, the latter arguing that anti-Fascism was a 'Trojan Horse', designed to permit the entry of Soviet Communism into Western Europe.[8]

The validity of anti-Fascism became a central theme of discussions in the mid-1990s when the fiftieth anniversary of the Resistance coincided with the collapse of those parties which had formed the 'constitutional arch' of the First Republic. In this period, De Felice was joined by the likes of Ernesto Galli della Loggia, who in his influential *La morte della patria* (1996) went even further by arguing that the anti-Fascist paradigm had never really existed, or was not as strong as was commonly believed to be the case. This view conflicted sharply with the sophisticated analysis provided by De Luna and Revelli (1995). The debate continued into the new millennium with Sergio Luzzatto publishing a strong condemnation of widespread revisionist tendencies in his 2004 book *La crisi dell'antifascismo* (see also Collotti, 2000; De Bernardi and Ferrari, 2004; Lupo, 2004; Mammone, 2006; Rapini, 2005; Rapone, 2000; Rogari, 2006;

Santomassimo, 2003 and 2004). As I write, Luzzatto's adherence to anti-Fascism is now itself under fire as he has published a book (Luzzatto, 2013; Cooke, 2014) which examines, from a critical perspective, the brief partisan career of Primo Levi – arguably the greatest icon of Italian anti-Fascism.

It is clear, then, that the question of the contemporary relevance of anti-Fascism is one which has been frequently posed. In this chapter I will concentrate, as far as possible, on recent discussions, focusing on areas or 'spaces' of Italian life and society where anti-Fascism is still present. I take it as a given that Fascism is still at large in Italian society (see Chapter 28 in this volume).

The political parties

Traditionally anti-Fascism was the preserve of the political parties which emerged from the ruins of the Second World War and formed the constitutional arch (on this topic, see, above all, Pavone, 1995, which contains the most influential analysis of the presence of Fascism and anti-Fascism in the Italian Republic up to the late 1950s; see also Permoli, 1960 and, among others, Amendola, 1994; Lepre, 1997; Quazza, 1990; on Catholic anti-Fascism, see Malavasi, 1982). But after 1989, the *tangentopoli* scandals and much else besides, those traditional parties were either wiped out or sought new identities and, as a consequence, new ideas. The announcement that the PCI was to change direction was, most significantly, made by Achille Occhetto at a meeting with former partisans at Porta Lame in Bologna. As I have argued elsewhere (Cooke, 2011), the PCI's attachment to the Resistance tradition was never quite as unequivocal as was generally perceived. What then of the new party's (by which I mean the current PD) views on the Resistance and anti-Fascism?

The new PD came into being in 2007, under the leadership of Walter Veltroni. Senior party figures were asked to draw up a 'manifesto of values', which was issued in early 2008. As soon as the document was released, it was noted by many that there were no explicit references in it to the Resistance and anti-Fascism. Sensing a problem, Veltroni wrote a letter to Alfredo Reichlin (who had been involved in the Resistance movement in Rome) and other members of the commission which had drawn up the manifesto. The 'perplexities' over the absence were, Veltroni stated in his letter, easy to explain. The values (of anti-Fascism and the Resistance) were, quite simply, a given:

> part of us, of our history and identity . . . The Resistance, the principles which gave it life and supported it, are part of the fundamental and natural patrimony of the Democratic Party . . . It is in the Resistance that the roots of our Republic are to be found. It is thanks to that civil and moral rebirth that Italy found freedom again . . . It is there, in that time and in those choices, that we find the values of 'constitutional patriotism' invoked by President Giorgio Napolitano.[9]

Veltroni finished his letter by stating that the reference to the values of anti-Fascism had the potential to 'unite, and not divide, the country' and for all these reasons he felt that there should be a more explicit reference to them in the PD document. Veltroni's letter was well crafted, and certainly seems to have calmed the nerves of those members who were troubled by the lacuna. But it does reveal a problem. Despite his claims that anti-Fascism was, according to Veltroni, an unquestionable pillar of the party's identity, the very fact that he had to remind the commission of this indicates that there was a *perception* of some ambivalence. This ambivalence has become clearer as time has passed. While it is clear that anti-Fascism has never been jettisoned completely from the PD's ever-shifting identity, its attachment to it is now, more than ever, more ritual then real. A search of the party's website throws up a few press articles, sundry organized events, but nothing which could be even loosely described as a theoretical document containing the word 'anti-Fascism'. After the resignation of Pierluigi Bersani, who made ritual references to anti-Fascism throughout his leadership of the PD, Fabrizio Barca announced his desire to stand for election as the party's new leader. Barca is the son of Luciano Barca, a communist intellectual and one-time editor of the communist daily *l'Unità*, who died in November 2012. Despite his pedigree, however, Fabrizio Barca's policy statement of April 2013, 'A new party for good government', only mentioned Fascism once (in relation to the reform of the 'public machine'), and anti-Fascism did not figure.

In the 1980s the Italian Socialist Party and its leader Bettino Craxi were, as we discussed above, one of the principal actors in the dismantling of the 'anti-Fascist paradigm'. The current leader of the new Italian Socialist Party is Riccardo Nencini. The press archive of the party's website reveals that in 2009 Nencini wrote a letter of support to Giuliano Vassalli, the constitutionalist, who had organized a conference to protest against Bill n.1360 (aimed at creating an 'Order of the Tricolour' open to all war veterans irrespective of which side they fought on). At the party congress the previous year Maria Grazia Caligaris (a regional councillor in Sardinia) made a speech which included the indignant cry:

> The other word which is no longer pronounced is anti-Fascism! And in Sardinia the President, who was elected by the people did not support the celebrations of 25 April!!!!! The Governors lack democratic culture, discredit the institutions, but buy the paper founded by Antonio Gramsci.[10]

So, therefore, some evidence of some anti-Fascist feeling amongst the new socialists. But, as it currently stands, the party's statute and its 'manifesto of values' contain no references to anti-Fascism. In fairness, the page dedicated to the history of the party describes how in 1943 the then PSIUP (the Socialist Party of Proletarian Unity) was largely composed of 'influential personalities of the anti-Fascist left' (but only Sandro Pertini gets a mention). Much more space is, predictably, given to the figure of Bettino Craxi, whose 'Socialist Gospel' of 1978 was, so we are told, inspired by the thought of Proudhon and Carlo Rosselli. As many veteran socialists pointed out at the time, Rosselli would have been turning in his grave in Florence, if he heard that his ideas had been appropriated by the man who, more than any politician of the institutional left, was responsible for the massacre of the spirit of anti-Fascism in Italy. What remains of the old PSI is, therefore, essentially the PSI of Craxi, and not of Pertini, Nenni, nor for that matter of Filippo Turati or Giacomo Matteotti.

It is a relatively easy, if slightly painful task, to expose the now tenuous adherence to anti-Fascism on the part of what remains of the traditional parties of the Italian Left (with the exception of *Rifondazione Comunista* – see below). What it more interesting is not perhaps the shift away from anti-Fascism, but a general abandonment of the *past* in Italian politics (see Chapter 25 in this volume). Throughout the First Republic the symbols, rituals and language of politics were deeply embedded in Italian history from the Unification onwards. Legitimization was sought by reference to history. The past, or at least large elements of it, has now passed.

One party, however, can always be relied upon to keep the flame. *Rifondazione Comunista* (RC), a section of the old PCI which could not go along with Occhetto's change in direction after 1989, maintains a strict adherence to the values of anti-Fascism and the Resistance. The party has, in Bianca Bracci Torsi (herself a former partisan) a senior party member who is responsible for anti-Fascism at a national level. There are regional and city representatives and the party is particularly committed to spreading the message to its young members. Following an enquiry to RC's press office I received a lengthy and detailed email describing the extent of the party's activities in this area. It is worth quoting an extract:

> The opposition to Fascism in all its forms . . . has always been one of the founding principles of the Party of Communist Refoundation, together with the constitution, which gathered the legacy of those struggles. The Resistance to Fascism, from its first appearance to its end, and the war of liberation against the Republic of Salò and the Nazi occupiers are not for us glorious pages of a history which has passed and should be celebrated, but a daily commitment against a possible move backwards, in Italy and Europe, to dark times which are once again favoured by an epochal crisis of that form of capitalism which in the different forms of Fascism has always found its closest ally. What is needed is a rediscovery of an awareness of the past, of the courage and steadfastness of those times, and an understanding of the present.

Inevitably statements such as this strike a chord with those people who are sympathetic to the Resistance and anti-Fascism. But like it or not, those people are a small minority in Italy today. RC, which was part of the 'Civil Revolution' alliance in the 2013 elections, obtained no seats in the Chamber of Deputies or the Senate.

Youth and the social centres

Since the institutional left has, by and large, abandoned any real sense of adherence to anti-Fascism, who, if anyone, has taken up its mantle? In the main, allegiance to anti-Fascism (or what is described as anti-Fascism) now resides within the complex and fractured galaxy which is represented by the ultra-left, many of whom reside in the 'social centres' of Italy's cities. These groups have embraced modern methods of communication, notably Facebook. In a way this reveals they have caught up with the neo-Fascists, whose Web presence, particularly in the 1990s, was far better organized than their opponents. 'Antifascismo Militante Italiano' (AMI), for example, was established in February 2011 'with the aim of spreading ANTIFA culture (which must be distinguished from a generic anti-Fascist culture)'. Its Facebook page describes its fundamental ideals – elimination of the European Union and the single currency, a cultural revolution of the entire people 'which for years has believed in capitalism', state ownership of major companies, the elimination of the banking system and of xenophobic and nationalist culture. In a message to this author, representatives of AMI further explained what they stand for:

> Phil, we will reply to you on Facebook so that all messages are public. AMI above all is not a movement, or a collective or a committee. It is not formal at all. It's simply a page which encourages militant anti-Fascism through direct action. And since there is nothing formal about us, there are no direct links with any anti-Fascist organization. AMI is simply a way of understanding anti-Fascism which counters institutional 'do-gooding' anti-Fascism. We promote direct anti-Fascist acts with the sole objective of destroying and preventing any Fascist act with all the means available to us.

Florence, if the Web is anything to go by, would appear to be a magnet for these types of new anti-Fascist organizations. On its website the 'Brigades of Active Solidarity' describe their attitude to anti-Fascism in the following way:

> We believe that the struggle against fascism did not conclude with the Liberation and the Resistance, but that there is an urgent need to fight against every reappearance of Fascism (*rigurgito fascista*), which sadly we note grows every day, above all in a moment of crisis such as this in which xenophobic hatred and the desire for order risk spreading to wide sections of society. We are convinced that the memory of the Resistance should not be reduced to a mere monument, but is the starting point for a daily antifascism.[11]

As was the case with traditional anti-Fascism, these new militant anti-Fascists honour their fallen heroes. The most celebrated of them is Davide Cesare or 'Dax', who was an anti-Fascist member of the ORSO (Officina della Resistenza Sociale – Social Resistance Workshop). Dax was attacked on 16 March 2003 after a night out in the Porta Ticinese area of Milan, well known for its left-wing bars, and stabbed to death. According to an article in English, one of Dax's friends was stabbed outside Milan's central station in December 2012, in a clear indication that Fascist violence was not over. The tenth anniversary of Dax's death saw a large demonstration in Milan, with police estimating 5,000 demonstrators, and the demonstrators themselves 10,000. According to the author(s) of 'Milan's Black Night' the demonstration showed that

> Davide's struggle, not just against fascism but also capitalism, continues today despite all violent attempts to subdue it. Indeed, perhaps it is the turnout on Saturday of not only antifascists but of working class militants from a wide range of struggles that still gives meaning to the slogan: 'Dax lives'.[12]

The demonstration for Dax culminated on the Sunday with 'People's Sports for Dax'. And perhaps one of the more interesting developments within the social centres is the development of sporting associations and facilities which promote 'anti-Fascist values'. In the main what is on offer is combat sports designed to provide a powerful blend of 'training and activism'. Martial arts, boxing (and indeed mountain-climbing) are traditionally seen as right-wing sports, with gyms as recruitment centres, so the idea is to offer access to training in these disciplines in order to counter this tendency. According to a recent Web article on 'Italy's anti-Fascist gyms and boxing clubs', from which the above quotations were taken, the history of these organizations began with the opening in Turin in October 2001 of the Palestra Popolare AntiFa Boxe within the Askatasuna social centre. There are similar facilities in Florence (the Palestra Popolare San Pietrino, part of the nExt Emerson social centre), which offers boxing, contemporary dance, aikido and t'ai chi, Milan, Bologna, Palermo (the Antifa Boxe), Cosenza and many others. In January 2012 the 'first popular sports network meeting' took place in Ancona.[13]

The Constitution

The Italian constitution is a text which still enjoys the status, indeed almost mystical aura, of a sacred document. The Constitution was drafted during the period of anti-Fascist unity after the Second World War. While the Constitution itself continues to be seen as generically anti-Fascist, there are specific clauses (and laws) which are often the subject of discussion. Of these the most significant is the XIIth *disposizione transitoria* (transitional provision), which bans 'the reorganization, in any form' of the Fascist party. Clause XII inspired the 1952 Scelba law, and other laws brought in over the years. Unsurprisingly, there have been a number of recent attempts to have Clause XII removed from the Constitution, and just as many initiatives to defend and promote it. In March 2011, for example, a group of PdL senators presented a *disegno di legge costituzionale* (bill) which would have abrogated the clause. The promoter of the bill was Cristiano

De Eccher and it was signed by Francesco Bevilacqua, Achille Totano, Fabrizio De Stefano (all members of the PdL) and Egidio Digilio (of the Fli).[14] The text of the bill, written in the standard impenetrable language which characterizes such documents, argued that if the clause was 'transitory', then historical circumstances had changed, and it was now time to 'close a chapter which has no reason to remain open and, in addition, to reduce those spaces of special legislation which, in any case, hardly correspond to a full realization of the principle of liberty'.

In September 2011 two Neapolitan artists contributed in an innovative and interesting way to the debate on neo-Fascism and the application of the Constitution. Sebastiano Deva and Walter Picardi arranged for a giant poster to be placed on view in a street in the centre of Naples. The poster contained the image of the carved head of Mussolini which is to be found at his tomb in his birthplace of Predappio. Above it, in large letters, was the slogan *Nessuna Luce Mio Duce* (No Light My Duce), and to its right the invitation to viewers to consult the Facebook page *Cripta Mussolini*. The two artists were participating in an art exhibition known as 'Campania Senses' which was due to open later that month at the Museum of Contemporary Art in Casoria. As they explained, the idea behind the poster and their exhibit was to request the closure to the public of Mussolini's crypt, a place of pilgrimage 'in complete contempt of the fundamental dispositions of the Italian constitution'. The artists had themselves visited the crypt in the month of August, where they had met 'parents who brought their children to do the Fascist salute, adults, old people, boys and girls. The remains of the Duce, unfortunately, represent a potent attraction for people . . . who exalt Fascist culture'. The Facebook page was designed so that visitors could leave their comments on the issue, in order to create a collection of 'anti-Fascist thoughts' which would be turned into a book and placed in the crypt in Predappio itself in 2012. The exhibition at Casoria was a reproduction of the crypt in a claustrophobic environment in which participants would 'experience the black heart which is still beating in the history of our country today' (*La Repubblica*, 13 September 2011). Needless to say, Mussolini's crypt is still open to the public, and Predappio continues to attract a large number of visitors. A pilgrimage there is still an essential rite of contemporary neo-Fascist culture.

The partisan associations

Of the various partisan organizations established during or shortly after the Second World War, the largest is the ANPI (Associazione nazionale partigiani d'Italia). For years the association's president was the communist senator and partisan leader from Ravenna, Arrigo Boldrini. As time passed, the ANPI leadership began to address the issue of what would happen to the organization once its membership eventually dwindled to a few ex-combatants aged 90 or above. At the 2001 congress held at Abano Terme (near Padua), a motion was put forward by some partisans, including Massimo Rendina from Rome, which asked for a change in the ANPI statute to permit young people to join the organization. The motion was vigorously opposed by Boldrini, who argued that the organization would lose its identity if membership was opened up to those who had not actively participated in the Resistance. Boldrini, who was in his mid-80s at the time, slapped the table in irritation. At one point Rendina himself gave an impassioned speech, saying that a choice had to be made between a change in identity and death. He was privately backed up by Giovanni Pesce, the Milanese partisan who had become something of an icon for protesting students in the late 1960s. There was certainly a feeling at this congress amongst the more left-leaning participants that changes were going to happen within an organization which, for a variety of reasons, had never really managed to connect with the younger generations (an exception being during the 1970s). By the next congress, in 2006, Boldrini's failing health meant that he was no longer capable of continuing as president. He was elected honorary president, and replaced by the Genoese Raimondo Ricci, who allowed a change in the ANPI statute which opened the doors of the association to non-partisans. Article 23, which details who can join the association, now contains a paragraph stating that

> in addition membership is open to . . . those who share the patrimony of ideas, the values and the aims of the ANPI and who intend to contribute, in their role as anti-Fascists . . . to the preservation, care of and diffusion of the knowledge of the events and values that the Resistance passed on to the new generations as a founding element of the Republic, of the Constitution and the European Union . . . an essential part of the patrimony of the country.[15]

Not much had changed in the language used by the ANPI, but the decision to allow in non-partisan members was a significant one. At the 2011 congress, held in Turin, it was reported that membership had risen from 95,000 in 2008 to 131,000. Ricci ascribed these healthy numbers to the 'authoritarian turn' under Berlusconi which had shown itself in the 'continuous attacks on the Constitution, considered by the premier as an obstacle or impediment to the business of governing' (*La Repubblica*, 24 March 2011).

Another novel development at the 2011 ANPI conference was the fact that the opening speech was made a woman, Marisa Ombra, who argued that

> the partisans are not dying . . . [the young] will be the new ANPI: we are trying to approach the young people so that they can become the new ruling class of the association. The new partisans are the women, the students, all those Italians who with their generosity, passion and enthusiasm are erecting a wall against those people who are undermining rights and the civil way of life.

Conclusion

Anti-Fascism is by no means dead and in the above discussion I have tried to give some examples of where it is currently 'located'. What is clear, however, is that these different anti-Fascist strands are disparate and very rarely coordinated to create something organic. This lack of cohesion is perhaps best exemplified by a recent example from the city of Florence, which can certainly claim a distinguished anti-Fascist past – it was the home of the Rosselli brothers, of the partisan insurrection of August 1944, of Piero Calamandrei, of the journal *Il ponte*, of Tristano 'Pippo' Codignola, and of Angiolo Gracci, amongst many others.[16] In early March 2013 Florentine members of various ANTIFA groups organized a counter-demonstration to protest against the march in memory of the victims of the *foibe*. The ANPI were involved in the discussions and arrangements in what appeared, on the face of it, to be an exemplary illustration of cooperation between the old and the new in anti-Fascism. Things did not turn out as hoped. Before the march began the 88-year-old former partisan Silvano Sarti was harangued by a woman who was not yet thirty: 'Oi, Sarti, off you go. Go and throw them out of this march. We'd said no party flags, but above all no PD flags. Shame on them. They're in with the Fascists.' What had happened, albeit rather unexpectedly, was that two representatives of the PD, Marta Torcini and Maria Teresa Focardi (the daughters of partisans as it turned out) had decided to participate and brought along their party flags with the intention of waving them in the streets of Florence, along with those of the anarchists and the young members of the social centres. Members of the left-wing trade union the CGIL were also there, as were thirty members of SEL (Left Ecology Freedom). Discussions became more and more animated with the two PD women at the centre of a growing storm. Insults flew ('You're not going anywhere with that flag'; 'The PD is the party that runs Florence and lets the Fascists take to the streets') which were countered with the accusation, 'You say you're anti-Fascists, but you're just like them.'[17] At one point a young man tried to set light to one of the PD flags. Eventually, the march began with the ANPI trailing 100 metres behind those of the social centres, which left an awkward gap in the procession. When it came to the representatives of the CGIL and the PD to start walking, they were stopped. In protest, the members of the SEL refused to march. Anti-Fascist unity, if ever it had existed in the twentieth century, was clearly going to be difficult to achieve in the twenty-first.

Notes

1 The video of the encounter can be viewed on YouTube and a number of other websites.

2 Giancarlo Bocchi on the Facebook page of *Il Ribelle. Guido Picelli un eroe scomodo*. Monuments to the Resistance and to anti-Fascism are, of course, an important part of the landscape (see Galmozzi, 1986), although there are few new ones to speak of.

3 For the full text see www.beppegrillo.it/2013/04/il_25_aprile_e_morto.html (accessed 14 February 2014).

4 Bottino is not Craxi's real first name, which is Bettino. This is a play on words: *bottino* means 'booty'.

5 Monte Sole is now a park with an efficient visitor centre which deals with busloads of school trips – including schoolchildren from Germany. The massacre is the subject of Giorgio Diritti's film *L'uomo che verrà* (2009).

6 The speech can be viewed on YouTube via a search for '*Laura Boldrini discorso di insediamento*'.

7 It was in June and July 1960 when an anti-Fascist movement inspired by former partisans brought down a coalition government which included the neo-Fascist MSI. These events paved the way for the period of centre-left governments in Italy. On 1960, see Cooke (2000a).

8 The bibliography on De Felice is huge. For the most succinct statement of his view, in the form of an interview with Pasquale Chessa, see De Felice (1995). For an attempt at a rebuttal, see Pistillo (1998). More generally on the reception of De Felice's work, see Fiorentino (2002). Furet's most popular work on the subject is his 1983 book, translated into English in 1999.

9 The letter can be found at www.festademocratica.it (accessed 14 February 2014) under the title '*I principi della resistenza e dell'antifascismo parte del PD*'.

10 www.partitosocialista.it/site/artId__764/307/DesktopDefault.aspx (accessed 14 February 2014).

11 http://brigatesolidarietaattiva.blogspot.co.uk/2012/12/bsa-toscana-firenze-e-antifascista.html (accessed 14 February 2014).

12 All information from http://strugglesinitaly.wordpress.com/2013/03/17/daxlives/ (accessed 14 February 2014).

13 See http://strugglesinitaly.wordpress.com/2013/04/29/en-an-overview-of-italys-anti-fascist-gyms-and-boxing-clubs/ (accessed 14 February 2014).

14 The full text of the bill, which contains many moments of unintended hilarity, is available online at www.senato.it/leg/16/BGT/Schede_v3/Ddliter/36662.htm (accessed 14 February 2014).

15 The statute can be consulted on most websites in the ANPI network. See, for example, www.anpigiovaniudine.org/node/205 (accessed 14 February 2014).

16 Gracci (partisan name 'Gracco') was the focal point of Florentine extra-institutional Resistance memory. His death in 2004 was seen by many as a decisive moment in the decline of the anti-Fascist spirit in the city. On Gracci's 'Resistenza continua' social movement, see Cooke (2000b).

17 http://firenze.repubblica.it/cronaca/2013/03/10/news/antagonisti_purgano_il_corteo_antifascista_via_pd_sel_e_cgil_dalla_manifestazione-54242926/ (accessed 14 February 2014). For further discussion, see www.selfirenze.org/content/sel-e-pd-non-abbassano-le-loro-bandiere-lantifascismo-%C3%A8-una-cosa-seria-e-patrimonio-fondante (accessed 14 February 2014).

Bibliography

Amendola, G. (1994). *Intervista sull'antifascismo*. Bari: Laterza.

Baldassare, A. (1986). La costruzione del paradigma antifascista e la Costituzione repubblicana. *Problemi del socialismo*, 7, 11–33.

Collotti, E. (ed.) (2000). *Fascismo e antifascismo: rimozioni, revisioni, negazioni*. Rome-Bari: Laterza.
Cooke, P. (2000a). *Luglio 1960: Tambroni e la repressione fallita*. Milan: Teti.
Cooke, P. (2000b). The Resistance continues: a social movement in the 1970s. *Modern Italy*, 5 (2), 161–73.
Cooke, P. (2011). *The Legacy of the Italian Resistance*. New York: Palgrave Macmillan.
Cooke, P. (2014). Primo Levi partigiano. *Il mestiere dello storico*, VI(2), 59–63.
De Bernardi, A. and Ferrari, P. (eds.) (2004). *Antifascismo e identità europea*. Rome: Carocci
De Felice, R. (1995). *Rosso e nero*. Milan: Baldini and Castoldi.
De Luna, G. and Revelli, M. (1995). *Fascismo, antifascismo. Le idee, le identità*. Florence: La Nuova Italia.
Fiorentino, F. (2002). Bibliografia di e su Renzo De Felice. In L. Goglia and R. Moro (eds.), *Renzo De Felice. Studi e testimonianze* (pp. 333–506). Rome: Edizioni di Storia e Letteratura.
Furet, F. (1983). *Le passé d'une illusion: Essai sur l'idée communiste au XXe siècle*. Paris: Laffont/Calmann-Lévy. (English translation by Deborah Furet: *The Passing of an Illusion: The Idea of Communism in the Twentieth Century*. Chicago: University of Chicago Press, 1999).
Gallerano, N. (1986). Critica e crisi del paradigma antifascista. *Problemi del socialismo*, 7, 106–33.
Galli Della Loggia, E. (1996). *La morte della patria: la crisi dell'idea di nazione tra Resistenza, antifascismo e Repubblica*. Rome-Bari: Laterza.
Galmozzi, L. (1986). *Monumenti alla libertà. Antifascismo, Resistenza e pace nei monumenti italiani dal 1945 al 1985*. Milan: La Pietra.
Ganapini, L. (1986). Antifascismo tricolore e antifascismo di classe. *Problemi del socialismo*, 7, 98–105.
Lepre, A. (1997). *L'anticomunismo e l'antifascismo in Italia*. Bologna: il Mulino.
Lupo, S. (2004). Antifascismo, anticomunismo e anti-antifascismo nell'Italia repubblicana. In A. De Bernardi and P. Ferrari (eds.), *Antifascismo e identità europea* (pp. 365–78). Rome: Carocci.
Luzzatto, S. (2004). *La crisi dell'antifascismo*. Turin: Einaudi.
Luzzatto, S. (2013). *Partigia*. Milan: Mondadori.
Malavasi, G. (1982). *L'antifascismo cattolico. Il movimento guelfo d'azione*. Rome: Lavoro.
Mammone, A. (2006). A daily revision of the past: Fascism, anti-Fascism, and memory in contemporary Italy. *Modern Italy*, 11 (2), 211–26.
Pavone, C. (1995). *Alle origini della repubblica: scritti su fascismo, antifascismo e continuità dello stato*. Turin: Bollati Boringhieri.
Pecchioli, U. (1985). Perché si è riaperto il dibattito su fascismo e antifascismo. *Rinascita*, 8, 8–9.
Permoli, P. (ed.) (1960). *Lezioni sull'antifascismo*. Rome-Bari: Laterza
Pistillo, M. (1998). *Fascismo – Antifascismo – Resistenza. Mussolini – Gramsci. 'La guerra civile 1943–1945' di Renzo De Felice*. Manduria: Lacaita.
Quazza, G. (1990). L'antifascismo nella storia italiana del Novecento. *Italia contemporanea*, 178, 5–16.
Rapini, A. (2005). *Antifascismo e cittadinanza. Giovani, identità e memorie nell'Italia repubblicana*. Bologna: Bononia University Press.
Rapone, L. (2000). Antifascismo e storia d'Italia. In E. Collotti (ed.), *Fascismo e antifascismo: rimozioni, revisioni, negazioni* (pp. 219–40). Rome-Bari: Laterza.
Rogari, S. (2006). *Antifascismo, Resistenza, Costituzione*. Milan: FrancoAngeli.
Santomassimo, G. (2003). La memoria pubblica dell'antifascismo. In F. Lussana and G. Marramao (eds.), *L'Italia repubblicana nella crisi degli anni settanta* (pp. 137–71). Soveria Mannelli: Rubbettino.
Santomassimo, G. (2004). *Antifascismo e dintorni*. Rome: Manifestolibri.
Tranfaglia, N. (1985). L'antifascismo non è alle nostre spalle. *Rinascita*, 11, 8–9.

28

ITALY'S COLONIAL PAST

Roberta Pergher

In August 2012, a number of news outlets—including the *New York Times* and the BBC—reported on the inauguration in a village near Rome of a mausoleum and memorial park to Fascist Field Marshal Rodolfo Graziani.[1] The honoree certainly had plenty of "achievements" to his name. In the early 1930s he fought the resistance in Italy's Libyan colonies by imprisoning 100,000 civilians in concentration camps in the Sirte desert. About 40 percent of the internees perished (Rochat, 1981). In the war against Ethiopia in 1935–6, Graziani employed poison gas and later brutally repressed any form of opposition, ordering for instance the massacre of the estimated 2,000 inhabitants of the Debre Libanos convent (Campbell, 2010: 318). Until his death in 1955, he never expressed the slightest remorse.

Despite this lamentable record, considerable public funds were made available for his memorialization.[2] Local authorities (as well as wider circles of politicians on the right) were happy to foster the memory of a war criminal, brushing off criticism with the contention that he had fought for the glory of the fatherland. Their attitude revealed the degree to which the Fascist past, including the regime's crimes, has now been condoned in Italy (Mammone, 2006). Critical responses to the memorial—from blogs to demonstrations to the monument's defilement—aimed for their part to restore that anti-Fascist consensus on which the Republic of Italy had been founded. Both sides, however, couched their reactions in similar terms, in the sense that they were exclusively about Fascism.[3] There was little attempt to grapple with the history of Italian colonialism and the African experience under Italian rule.[4]

That colonial history had begun soon after Italian unification and lasted well over sixty years. In the second half of the nineteenth century, conscious that other European powers had already occupied the world's most valuable regions, a number of Italian businessmen and politicians clamored for colonies. A less powerful faction opposed expansion, believing that Italy's millions of emigrants represented its most precious resource overseas (Choate, 2008). Still the "scramble for Africa" was on, and many felt that for Italy to be seen as a European player, it needed a share in the action.

In the early 1880s, the Kingdom of Italy set up outposts in the Red Sea ports of Assab and Massawa. The occupation of the hinterland in the following years brought the establishment of the colony of Eritrea. In 1888, Italy claimed Somalia. However, the desire to expand further and colonize Ethiopia fared less well and ended in military defeat in 1896. The famed loss at Adwa compounded the disappointment of 1881, when France had forcibly imposed a protectorate over Tunisia, long considered by Italy to be its de facto possession. Humiliation over these missed opportunities lingered until the invasion of Libya in 1911. The success of the campaign in 1912 added the two colonies of Tripolitania and Cyrenaica as well as the Dodecanese Islands, extending Italy's presence in the Mediterranean.

After World War I, with the Fascists in power, Italy continued the push for expansion, though with visions of a different kind of empire. While in the liberal period colonial holdings were pursued mainly for commercial exploitation and political status, the Fascists envisioned a demographic colonialism that would provide land to a toiling Italian settler population. After the invasion of Ethiopia in 1935, this vision came to define expectations and policies and found early expression in a state-sponsored settlement program in Libya. Yet the Fascist expansionist zeal, in an uneasy alliance with a rapidly expanding Nazi Germany, eventually led to total defeat in World War II and the loss of all colonies.

A number of characteristics are immediately apparent from this short survey. The first is that, in comparison with other European powers, the Italian colonial project began late, ended early, and was geographically limited. Second, the most significant episodes of Italy's colonial rule took place under Fascism and ended with Fascism, and it is thus not surprising that the Fascist past and its legacy have often stolen the spotlight from the colonial experience as such. Third, Italy was forcibly deprived of its colonies in the aftermath of World War II, and therefore never experienced a concerted phase of decolonization. It thus did not face the concurrent intellectual and moral imperatives to adjust its self-perception and relationship to the world. The result is that, even though Italy does indeed have a significant colonial past, public awareness has been fragmentary at best, and often overshadowed by debates about Fascism. Historiography too, as we will see, for a long time neglected Italy's ventures overseas. But alongside the public sphere and historical scholarship, there is a third realm where "knowledge" of the colonial past is retained—namely in the form of personal memories of those who lived through it. After brief discussions of the public and then scholarly arenas, this contribution will turn to those personal memories, arguing that historians can make much greater use of them than they have, and in that way extend to the wider public a realistic but intelligible account of how ordinary Italians became caught up in colonial violence and domination.

★

Scholars have criticized the public's neglect of the colonial past as a form of "colonial amnesia" (Triulzi, 2006). Even so, every few years the colonial past returns to claim the front pages. June 2009 saw Colonel Mu'ammer al-Gaddafi's first visit to Italy.[5] He arrived at Rome's airport dressed in full military regalia and bearing on his chest a 1931 photograph of Libyan resistance fighter Omar Mukhtar. The photo showed Mukhtar in chains after his capture by the Italians and shortly before his execution. (This was in advance of a Rome meeting that was meant to strengthen relations between Italy and Libya.) In this context, the resurgence of past colonial crimes in the news served as a foil against which to deride the antics of a colorful dictator and highlight not Italy's past crimes but its current amends in the form of financial aid and commercial investment in Libya. Yet Italy was not just making amends; it was gaining access to lucrative oil and natural gas reserves. And it was paying its former colony to detain and deport African migrants seeking passage to Italy, effectively outsourcing the repression of unwanted immigration (De Cesari, 2012).

Four years previously, in April 2005, another "eruption" of Italy's colonial history had taken place, this time relating to the return of the Axum stele—war booty from Italy's Ethiopian campaign in the late 1930s—from Rome's Piazza di Porta Capena to Ethiopia.[6] Even though its restitution was promised in a 1947 peace agreement, the stele had remained in Rome for nearly 60 years because of delays and obstructions on Italy's part (Acquarelli, 2010). Press coverage in 2005 presented a benevolent Italy conscientiously effecting the restoration despite the great difficulty of transporting an artistic treasure, despite concerns that an unstable political situation in Ethiopia might endanger the stele, and despite the fact that much of Italy's "own" art remained dispersed in museums and collections around the world.

If colonial echoes thus periodically reverberate in the public arena, they do so in very particular ways that occlude and distort the history of Italy's colonial rule (Baratieri, 2009). For one thing, the echoes are intense but short-lived. As many scholars have pointed out, because of Italy's abrupt and enforced decolonization, there has never been a sustained societal engagement and thus no means by which to address the colonial past at more than surface level (Labanca, 2004). A second important but often overlooked point, however, is the one already made above, namely that colonial issues have been for the most part subsumed under the Fascist experience. As we have seen in the case of Field Marshal Graziani, the specific questions of colonial rule are often lost behind point-scoring in relation to post-Fascist politicking. Moreover, because the colonies could be treated as an excrescence of Fascist rule rather than as part and parcel of Italian history and thus a continuing responsibility of the new Republic, there has been little sense of a colonial legacy even where we might expect it. For instance, the 2008 agreement between Libya and Italy[7] included a highly publicized provision to police migration across the Mediterranean. This provision might well have reminded us of Italian colonialism's demographic program, which in 1938 and 1939 involved the migration of thousands of Italians to Libya, with the intention of eventually settling half a million Italians on the Libyan shore and two million in East Africa. And yet in the response to immigrants in Italy today there is little to no memory of the Fascist promise of an *Africa Italiana* hosting millions of Italians.[8]

Finally, it is not least because of Fascism's claim to be a far lesser evil to Nazism (Ben-Ghiat, 2004) that Italy has come to understand itself as a benign power, a claim that has often been extended to the realm of its colonial politics. The postwar United Nations War Crimes Commission reports had provided early authentication of Italy's colonial atrocities (the use of concentration camps and gas in warfare) and a number of serious scholarly publications appearing in the 1970s made it impossible to deny these crimes, but the notion that the Italians had been *brava gente*, "good people," in the colonies, and in every other context, has prevailed (Bidussa, 1994; Del Boca, 2005; Focardi, 2013). According to this view, Italy had only acted like every other European power in Africa, indeed more benignly and self-effacingly so, and today it is in any case offering gestures of reconciliation, eager to assist and educate its former colonies.

★

If we turn from public discourse to scholarship, it is not hard to find historical works that seek to overturn the public's benign complacency. In the postwar years, work on the colonies by Italian historians tended to take one of two forms. On the one hand, there were the inevitable apologetic and celebratory accounts, most prominent among them a monumental study of Italy's colonial "achievements" commissioned by the Foreign Ministry in the 1950s to show what excellent colonizers the Italians had been and how they had been slighted by postwar peace agreements depriving them of their colonial possessions (Morone, 2010). On the other hand, there were the lonely exponents of conscientious scrutiny and attendant condemnation, most notably Angelo Del Boca, whose work can still be read with profit today. An early critic of the notion of the *brava gente*, Del Boca decried the actions of the regime and its functionaries. Yet in generally depicting Italian settlers, workers, and even soldiers as either duped or plainly exploited by the regime, he in fact unwittingly reinforced the very notion he was seeking to critique, reinforcing the contrast between bad regime and good people.

The political upheavals of the early 1990s in Italy and in Europe as a whole offered room to rethink Italy's historical legacy, including its participation in European imperialism. When scholarship on the colonies experienced a revival in the 1990s, it was no doubt also prompted by (though initially not necessarily in conversation with) the rise of postcolonial studies. Moreover, shocked by the xenophobic reaction to immigration, many scholars felt impelled to delve into the precedents of Italian racism.[9] But once again it was new currents in the scholarship on Fascism that colored depictions of the colonial past. In 1992 the "First Republic" collapsed and with it the already weakened anti-Fascist consensus (as outlined by Philip Cooke in Chapter 27 in this volume). With Mussolini's Italy now openly painted in more rosy colors in some quarters, many historians felt called upon to prove just how repressive and brutal the Fascists had been. And the colonies offered a natural arena to do so.

However much it has been subordinated to debates about Fascism, there is no doubt that this recent slate of work has given us a clearer sense of the political and institutional dimensions of Italy's colonial past, of gender and race relations in the colonies and the homeland, and the cross fertilization between Italian culture and the nation's colonial endeavors. Some recent studies have also interwoven Italy's colonial and postcolonial history with an eye toward immigration today (Lombardi-Diop and Romeo, 2012; Mellino, 2006). Contemporary fiction by authors from the former colonies is raising awareness of colonialism in ways that can engage audiences more deeply than straight historical work ever can (Polezzi, 2007; Jedlowski, 2012). As a result we now have a much fuller account of what Italian colonialism was like—brutal, exploitative, involving various interest groups, garnering a modicum of enthusiasm from below, and thus in its basic contours not unlike other colonialisms (Labanca, 2002).

Many exponents of this recent wave of colonial historiography have been outraged by the lack of public awareness of the crimes Italy committed in Africa and the lack of postcolonial sentiment still today. Yet there is nothing particularly Italian about these silences and evasions. All active empires share the conviction of being "good empires," morally superior to all others, and it is the legacy of all fallen empires that their descendants seem unable to relinquish this illusion fully—though the particular national myths and silences vary. It is true that the Germans, who underwent a similar colonial trajectory to Italy's, seem to outdo everyone in condemning their colonial past through government action, scholarship, and public debate, as evidenced by the 2004 apology for the Herero genocide perpetrated by Germany in Namibia, but then the Germans have had plenty of practice in "coming to terms" with their past. Britain too succeeded in decolonizing its public discourse to an incomparably greater degree than Italy, but it also easily accommodates positive assessments of its empire by reputable scholars. In the case of Italy, the fact that colonial rule was also Fascist rule has set definite limits to the degree to which scholarship today can celebrate the country's "benign" mission in Africa. There are simply no equivalents of a Niall Fergusson in Italy today. And while the topic of colonialism does not receive appropriate attention in the Italian history school curriculum, Italy's government has not (yet) legislated the teaching of a positive imperial past, as happened in France in 2005.[10]

Thus in Italy as elsewhere, scholars, armed with a sense of the historian's moral responsibility as custodian of national memory, have often condemned what they see as a self-serving and politicized whitewash of the past. And in Italy as elsewhere, despite historians' claims to objectivity and scientific standards, they have often failed to convince the public. Indeed, they find themselves accused of blind spots of their own, and of only telling a negative story that has nothing to offer the nation. It seems that rendering the colonial past plausible and accessible involves more than just persuading people that atrocities occurred. It means making intelligible how it was that ordinary Italians saw meaning in the colonial project and how they came to engage in brutal exploitation, even murderous violence. Above all, it means focusing on how participants made sense of their quotidian involvement in a colonial enterprise that seems so entirely illegitimate and problematic today.

★

So far I have largely avoided using the term "memory," even though, in contemporary scholarship on the past's representation in the present, the vocabulary of memory and associated terms such as amnesia, repression, trauma, and so forth are the norm.[11] The reason for avoiding the term is that "memory" functions at best as a rather imprecise and overworked metaphor for the processes of public communication through which the past is described, re-enacted, and refracted by people who often have no direct recollection of the events in question. It is questionable whether the social knowledge of the past can be adequately conveyed as "memory," particularly when that knowledge is made up of a thousand different perceptions and judgments, which seem to go far beyond the act of recall. In the colonial context, I thus prefer to reserve the term for the dwindling number of people still alive who in one way or another played a direct part in Italy's colonial activities. We might add to this number those no longer alive who wrote their memoirs or whose experiences have been recorded in oral history collections. Of course, such private memories do not constitute some kind of "pure" storage of the past, untainted by subsequent public discourse. As is now generally understood, we tend to recall the past not as we originally experienced it, but as we last told it (Bridge and Paller, 2012). Our telling and retelling is influenced by the wider cultural context, and with each new instance of recall, a new contextual layer is laid down in memory. Public narratives and mood thus seep into personal memory. Yet I will argue that the personal narratives of former colonialists—as well as those of their former subjects—are not just sediment formed from the swirling currents of public discourse. While they are often complex and hard to read—the entanglement of Fascism and colonialism in settler narratives, for example, is even more intractable than in public and scholarly discourse—they nevertheless contain crucial experiences and evaluations that may help us think through the specificities of Italy's colonial past. As an example of what can be recovered from such memories, the remainder of this chapter focuses on the experience and postwar narratives of former Italian settlers in the colonies.

One of the central themes that emerges from oral history interviews conducted in 2004 with Italians who had resided in Libya[12] and from published recollections of Italians in East Africa is the colonists' memory of their own hard work, with associated narratives about economic ambitions, lack of alternatives, and, most importantly, broken dreams. Accounts from workers, soldiers, and settlers in Libya and East Africa speak of deprivation and hardship, not only during war and rebellion, but also afterwards, when Italians purportedly controlled the territory and began to settle and exploit its resources. The recollection of hardship is directly tied to the perception that, as my interviewee Samuele Turrini relayed to me, in the colonies, "there was nothing." In such recollections, the Italians turned desert landscapes into blooming gardens and modern cities thanks to their ingenuity, stamina, patience, and more than anything, plain hard work (Labanca, 2001; Taddia, 1988). In almost all memories, the colonists' sweat and toil is presented as a legitimation for having participated in the colonial enterprise and as an investment that warranted—but never delivered—a reward.

Africa represented a great hope also because of the lack of alternatives. For Carlo Lo Cascio the luckiest were those who got land in Sicily—a much better prospect than going to the colonies. Afra Rinaldi remembered the family's new Libyan farmstead as "all sand," but, nonetheless, an improvement on their life on the Italian peninsula. Earlier, scores of Italians had availed themselves of the opportunity to emigrate; now with new restrictions in place both in receiving countries and within Italy itself, emigration was no longer possible. Settlers spoke of Africa as their "American" opportunity, perceiving their relocation as part of a long-standing family and community history of migration rather than as beholden to the regime's expansionist aspirations. Many Italians who went to Africa—not only temporary workers but also those expected to settle permanently—were hoping to make a "fortune" in order to return to their homes in Italy and live a better life there. While implicitly acknowledging their readiness to exploit the colonies, they were explicitly emphasizing the temporary character of their presence there, an emphasis admittedly designed to diminish their "guilt" as colonizers, but one that also spoke of their world and what had made sense to them.

Historian Nicola Labanca, too, finds in such oral histories not straightforward "nostalgia" but a lot of talk of sacrifice and suffering (Labanca *et al.*, 2000). To be sure, many who were forcibly removed in the postwar period from what had become their homes bemoaned what they had lost. But what strikes one again and again is that Italy's former colonists tend to regret rather what they had never gained. Colonial riches were for many an unfulfilled "promise"—measured against their sense of what colonialism should have delivered.

Many former colonists talk about going to Africa with great hopes, nourished by regime propaganda but also by a broader sense of the golden opportunities that imperialism bestows. Luigi Montelli went to Africa on his brother's assurance that he would become the estate "manager." His imagination was fed by a common perception of what it meant to be a "colonizer," and he fancied himself the facsimile of a British overseer commanding a large estate in Africa. For Montelli, the British colonizer was a model to be emulated, but according to the regime it was an exemplar to be shunned. Enrico Nadini told of one family that came to Libya with the "wrong ideas." Husband and wife had fallen on hard times in Italy and dreamt of an African comeback. Soon enough they were sent back to Italy because they were not interested in hard work but "wanted to command like the English in Kenya." Nadini here echoed what the settlement agencies' archival documents testify repeatedly: that Fascist colonialism conceived itself as different, independent of native labor, built on the sweat and muscle of Italian families; and that from the regime's standpoint, many Italians proved themselves unfit because of unrealistic expectations. Then, as now, highlighting the peculiarities of Italian colonialism was meant to justify the enterprise. Then, as now, other colonialisms served as a foil against which to fantasize about one's own achievements and legitimacy.

Alongside hard work and broken dreams, a second abiding theme in settler memories relates to the tension between the presence of an authoritarian government and the sense of liberty that the colonies indulged. Many went to the colonies with high expectations and enthusiasm for the "African adventure" and the possibilities for self-realization it afforded (Taddia, 1988). This was partly because of a shared sense that imperialism entitles, gives freedoms, bestows mastery. At the same time, Italians, even those in Africa, were living under a dictatorship. Turrini noted that there was "maximum liberty" in the colony "in spite of Fascism." Francesco Amilon said there was "more elasticity" in the colony, "more," that is, in comparison with Italy. Interviewees time and again felt the need to comment on the regime's authoritarianism, even if only to dismiss its influence in Africa. And yet, the authoritarian control was real, not only for the native populations, who were subjected to very different treatment, to exploitation and outright violence. Soldiers, laborers, and settlers talk about how their days were structured, how they were directed in the most basic tasks, how they sought to circumvent rules and prohibitions time and again, and how, when they were caught, punishments were severe, sometimes even entailing repatriation to Italy.

These remarks provide a bridge to a third cluster of memories, concerning the native populations. Settlers like to talk of shared human hardship and claim that in the long run amicable and equitable relations were necessary and even desirable. For instance, settlers who moved to Libya in the late 1930s recall their good intentions in treating the Arab population on an "equal" basis. Apparently, these good intentions were even state-sanctioned. Carlo Lo Cascio remembered that during the passage to Libya settlers were taught the concept of "*sua-sua*": Arabs and Italians were "*sua-sua*," the same, in their own ways. Such recollections are certainly shaped by the desire to purge the image of Italians as evil colonizers and salvage the legacy of their former presence in Libya. Yet, while I would not dispute the possibility of friendship between individual Italians and Arabs in Libya, such talk of "equality" cannot disguise the systemic inequality and oppression.

The reality of oppression stood in contrast to the particular vision of the settlement program. Of course, there were also large estates with native labor, but for the settlement of thousands of Italians, the idea was one of a self-contained and segregated Italian society. Fascist settlement agents specifically forbade the creation of a traditional white colonial ruling class. Italian farmers under contract in Libya were not allowed to hire indigenous labor, even if paid out of their own pockets. Settlers were not supposed to take on the persona of a dominating, lordly colonialist. Instead, they were called upon to master and appropriate the land with their own sweat. Agricultural settlement, hard labor, and ownership of the soil were regarded as indispensable for permanently and unmistakably establishing Italian claims to sovereignty. Yet this vision never truly came to fruition.

While several interviewees seemed to recall a society where "for us they didn't exist," the colonies depended heavily on native labor. Rinaldi told of how Arabs had prepared the land and thus upon her family's arrival in Libya in November 1938 they did not have to work until the sowing season a few months later. Lo Cascio remembered the 40 native workers his family employed, without mentioning, and conceivably without knowing, that the state contract forbade the hiring of native labor. Turrini spoke of his father's involvement in road construction, where each crew consisted of one Italian engineer, one Italian assistant, one Italian builder, and 400–500 Arab workers. And yet these stories did not seem to unsettle the triumphant narrative of *Italian* labor transforming the colony.

Montelli, the most critical of my conversation partners regarding the settlement plan, asserted that "it had not been right to take the land from the Libyans," but added that "*we* worked the land," implying that the Libyans had not. Such comments are, of course, informed by perceptions of the "proper" use of natural resources. It is the talk of the modernization and valorization drive enacted by colonizers the world over. But when he referred to the appropriation of the land, Montelli said "*they* took the best land," meaning, presumably, "they" the Fascists or the colonial higher-ups. Also Lo Cascio, in mentioning disputes with the Arabs over the land, said that "*they*", the Fascists, "muscled in on Arab territory." Here, the dictatorship, or the presence of an authoritarian colonial government, provided some absolution to the negative reality of one's own involvement in colonial matters.

When Italians do talk about conquest, war, and the violence perpetrated against Africans, they do so in a straightforward, matter-of-fact way. Soldiers talk of hard-fought battles, the massacres of enemy soldiers, the use of gas (Taddia, 1988), openly admitting the war crimes denied by the Italian government into the 1990s. The war stories are told as if there had been no good guys or bad guys, only combatants—never mind that only their side had defied the

Geneva Conventions. Field Marshal Graziani, for instance, was remembered by several of my interviewees as ruling with an "iron fist." Rather than denying or hiding atrocities, they talked about them without my asking, as part of the historical narrative, as they progressed through time in recollecting the Italian presence in Africa. Here as elsewhere, the problem is not so much that former colonists defend their involvement in colonialism, but rather that they do not even see why they would need to. They rarely recognize the lack of legitimacy of the enterprise as a whole, its brutality and arbitrariness. They talk of their own difficulties in life, of illness and death, of tragedies, and even of occasional happiness, but they do not see themselves as perpetrators. Rather, they cast themselves as victims.

It is worth pointing out that although I have here highlighted Italian memories, African recollections represent an indispensable element in the reconstruction of Italy's colonial past and the recognition of its legacy today. Yet even the remembrances of Africans do not provide an easy route into accuracy. Several scholars have for instance shown how the memory of the colonized can sometimes reinforce the image of the *italiani brava gente* (Doumanis, 1997). This is the case in Eritrea, where the conflict with Ethiopia has given rise to a representation of the Eritrean askari in the Italian army, and by extension the Italians, as modernizers and nation-builders (Palma, 2007; Triulzi, 2006; Iyob, 2005).

★

On one level, then, the colonists simply reproduce the same kinds of memory moves that we know from public discourse, with Fascism serving as overlay and alibi. My interviewees rarely reflected on colonialism per se because their memories related not just to a colonial but also to a Fascist past. This entanglement of Fascism and colonialism in private memory has had paradoxical effects. On the one hand, the fact that in Italian public discourse there is room for a positive assessment of Fascism has helped to create space for positive private memories of the Fascist enterprise in Africa (Pergher, 2012). Indeed, the colonial sphere has become a particular showcase for Fascism's modernizing and civilizing potential. On the other hand, the fact that the settlers themselves were domineered and often chose to work against official rules served in their minds to distance them from the regime and thus absolve them of the state's harshest actions against the colonized. Fascism here functions as the convenient culprit in addressing colonial injustices. In other words, the colonists seem to enjoy a double helping of defense mechanism by having their cake and eating it too: "Because it was us, Fascism could not have been so bad; and because Fascism was in charge, it really was not us."

Yet if these accounts seem to be offering the same mixture of inconsistent viewpoints, rationalizations, and apologias, on a deeper level they do present a way of transcending the *brava gente* narrative and reaching an understanding of involvement that at least admits the reality of violence. For one thing, we have plainly seen that the everyday was embedded in structures of expropriation and exploitation. For another, many settlers have memories or knowledge of violence. For all the rosy colors, the unvarnished nature of colonial rule is not hard to expose to the light.

Moreover, if we read between the lines to get at the assumptions and experiences that shaped their perceptions and behavior, we can see that they acted in ways that made sense and seemed normal, and at the same time that they were not "innocent" or somehow outside the structures of exploitation. Above all, the colonists were informed by a general sense of colonialism as a system that conferred advantages and entitlements, a system legitimated by an alleged European superiority in cultural, biological, and technological terms. This undergirded their expectations at the time and continued to inform their assessment thereafter. Because the colonists' frame of reference was often an implicit understanding of European colonial practice—either as model or lesson—their narratives help to place the Italian colonial past in the much broader story of Italy's, Europe's, and Africa's past.

Even so, the colonists were also underdogs. The experience of poverty at home and of migration as the only way out was another crucial part of their mental universe. They were used to the notion that leaving was the key to self-improvement. Moreover the settlers' world was one in which powerful entities—the regime, but also the family, the neighbors, and the military unit—shoved you around. Uncovering this universe of experiences and expectations helps us better locate Italian colonialism in the past, but it also offers us a sense of the various contexts that frame judgment and perception today.

The argument here then is that, listened to attentively, personal memories so often dismissed as rose-tinted or even whitewashed can indeed enable us to enrich the "public memory" of Italy's colonial past and thus succeed where critical scholarship has often failed. For one, the complexity presented in these individual accounts forces us to discard the simplistic duality of "good people" and their opposite. These accounts show recognizably human individuals operating within a particular system where being "good"—which required stepping outside the moral imperatives of that system—was an exception, not the norm. No one who conformed to this system was doing "good," but neither did the failure to challenge a system engineered to meet open defiance with harsh repercussions make people uniformly "evil." Moreover, the same individuals might find themselves performing very different roles at different times. There is no reason to believe that the family man entertaining cordial relations with the native population was not the same one who participated in the massacres of Addis Ababa, when following the attack on Viceroy Graziani in 1937 not only the military but also civilians were given free rein to subdue the city's population.

On an even broader level, the personal memories are also useful in comprehending and locating contemporary responses to postcolonial questions. Through their narratives we discover that colonists' expectations and justification had drawn on a whole repertoire of experiences and preconceptions—relating to European imperialism, fascination with Africa and the Orient, the legacy of overseas migration, also to experiences of poverty and marginalization, and to popular ideas of how to get by and how to make a fortune, and more. This rich archive of norms and common sense is revealing not least because parts of it continue to shape attitudes today. But even where the colonists' own mental horizons are not our own, uncovering them helps us to recognize the meta-level at which such judgments are formed. In public debates, this kind of broader context is seldom addressed explicitly. Colonial issues, when they emerge, are discussed in narrow terms, and rarely do we explore the quiet connections that are made when the colonial past actually "erupts" in the news. I refer to that repertoire of understandings, prejudices, attitudes, and assumptions that is constructed through schooling, the cursory reading of papers, the leisurely enjoyment of a novel or a film, and discussions with friends and acquaintances, and that in some way or another is shaped by and reflects on the colonial past. Judgments about the colonial past, we realize, are embedded in an extensive body of opinions concerning Africa more broadly, immigration in Italy today, Italy's role in the world, what it is to be "modern," "civilized," and "developed," and so on. Harder to define and dissect, this postcolonial imagination (albeit rarely informed by the sensibility of postcolonial scholarship) undoubtedly acts as a broader and deeper repository of opinions about what Italy's colonial past might mean and how it might matter. The more aware we can be of this broader context, the more we can truly locate and explicate the significance of Italy's colonial experience for the present. And the more we as scholars can make the public aware of the assumptions and experiences that lie below the surface, the more we can encourage a taking of responsibility in the present for that colonial past.

Notes

1 Gaia Pianigiani, "Village's tribute reignites a debate about Italy's Fascist past," *New York Times*, 29 August 2012: A6. "Italy memorial to Fascist hero Graziani sparks row," *BBC*, 15 August 2012. Available online at www.bbc.co.uk/news/world-europe-19267099 (accessed 30 December 2013).

2 In April 2013, under the new regional governor Nicola Zingaretti, public funds were cut and the municipality accused of misappropriating funds allocated for the creation of a park and a monument to the unknown soldier. See "Svolta ad Affile, Zingaretti annuncia: 'Stop ai fondi per il mausoleo di Graziani,'" *La Repubblica*, 22 April 2013. Available online at http://roma.repubblica.it/cronaca/2013/04/22/news/affile_zingaretti_stop_ai_fondi_per_il_mausoleo_di_graziani-57227641/ (accessed 15 January 2015).

3 For a discussion of the continuing presence of Fascism and anti-Fascism in public discourse in Italy today, see Chapter 27 by Philip Cooke in this volume.

4 For a discussion of Italy's "obliterations" of the colonial past, see the interview with historian Alessandro Triulzi. Davide Banfi, "Triulzi: 'Graziani non va celebrato. Troppe amnesie sull'Italia coloniale,'" *La Repubblica*, 5 October 2012. Available online at http://roma.repubblica.it/cronaca/2012/10/05/news/triulzi_graziani_non_va_celebrato_troppe_amnesie_sull_italia_coloniale-43922288 (accessed 15 January 2015).

5 "Gheddafi a Roma con l'eroe anti-coloniale: 'Ma quella pagina ormai è passata,'" *La Repubblica*, 10 June 2009. Available online at www.repubblica.it/2009/06/sezioni/esteri/gheddafi-italia/gheddafi-visita/gheddafi-visita.html (accessed 15 January 2015).

6 "La stele di Axum torna a casa, al via il trasporto in Etiopia," *La Repubblica*, 18 April 2005. Available online at www.repubblica.it/2005/d/sezioni/cronaca/stele/stele/stele.html (accessed 15 January 2015).

7 The agreement was signed in Benghazi on 30 August 2008.

8 Much more present in public discussions of immigration and racism in Italy today is Italians' own experience of mass emigration during the nineteenth and early twentieth century. A key publication aimed at a broad readership was Gian Antonio Stella, *L'orda. Quando gli albanesi eravamo noi* (Milan: Rizzoli, 2003).

9 Drawing a direct link between popular racism in the 1990s and colonial racism was anthropologist Paola Tabet's study of racial prejudice among Italian schoolchildren in *La pelle giusta* (Turin: Einaudi, 1997). Also *La Menzogna della Razza. Documenti e immagini del razzismo e dell'antisemitismo fascista* (Bologna: Grafis, 1994) edited by the Centro Furio Jesi and published in conjunction with an exhibition took contemporary racism in Italy as an incentive to revisit the past.

10 Art. 4 of Law n. 2005–158 from 23 February 2005 required that schoolteachers highlight the "positive role of the French presence overseas." Following the intervention of President Jacques Chirac in early 2006 the law was modified and Art. 4 repealed.

11 For a discussion of public memory in cinema and filmic representation of the past, see Chapter 25 by Paolo Jedlowski in this volume, which also addresses the near absence of the colonial past in Italian film.

12 In 2004 I conducted 12 separate interviews with 14 former settlers in Libya who now reside in Italy. I have changed the names of my interviewees to protect their privacy.

Bibliography

Acquarelli, L. (2010). Sua altezza imperiale. L'obelisco di Axum tra dimenticanza e camouflage storico. *Zapruder*, 23, 58–73.

Baratieri, D. (2009). *Memories and Silences Haunted by Fascism: Italian Colonialism, MCMXXX–MCMLX*. New York: Peter Lang.

Ben-Ghiat, R. (2004). A Lesser Evil? Italian Fascism in/and the Totalitarian Equation. In H. Dubiel and G. Motzkin (eds.), *The Lesser Evil. Moral Approaches to Genocide Practices* (pp. 137–53). New York: Routledge.

Bidussa, D. (1994). *Il mito del bravo italiano*. Milan: il Saggiatore.

Bridge, D. J. and Paller, K. A. (2012). Neural correlates of reactivation and retrieval-induced distortion. *The Journal of Neuroscience*, 32 (35), 12144–51.

Campbell, I. (2010). *The Plot to Kill Graziani. The Attempted Assassination of Mussolini's Viceroy*. Addis Ababa: Addis Ababa University Press.

Choate, M. (2008). *Emigrant Nation. The Making of Italy Abroad.* Cambridge, MA: Harvard University Press.

De Cesari, C. (2012). The paradoxes of colonial reparation: foreclosing memory and the 2008 Italy–Libya Friendship Treaty. *Memory Studies*, 5 (3), 316–26.

Del Boca, A. (2005). *Italiani, brava gente? Un mito duro a morire.* Vicenza: Neri Pozza.

Doumanis, N. (1997). *Myth and Memory in the Mediterranean: Remembering Fascism's Empire.* New York: Macmillan.

Focardi, F. (2013). *Il cattivo tedesco e il bravo italiano. La rimozione delle colpe della seconda guerra mondiale.* Rome-Bari: Laterza.

Iyob, R. (2005). From Mal d'Africa to Mal d'Europa? The Ties that Bind. In J. Andall and D. Duncan (eds.), *Italian Colonialism: Legacy and Memory* (pp. 255–82). Oxford: Peter Lang.

Jedlowski, P. (2012). Public Memories in Italy: Contemporary Narratives about the Italian Colonial Past. In I. Capeloa Gil and A. Martins (eds.), *Plots of War. Modern Narratives of Conflict* (pp. 32–9). Boston, MA: De Gruyter.

Labanca, N. (2001). *Posti al sole. Diari e memorie di vita e di lavoro dalle colonie d'Africa.* Rovereto: Edizioni Osiride.

Labanca, N. (2002). *Oltremare: storia dell' espansione coloniale italiana.* Bologna: Il Mulino.

Labanca, N. (2004). Colonial rule, colonial repression and war crimes in the Italian colonies. *Journal of Modern Italian Studies*, 9 (3), 300–13.

Labanca, N., Marchi, A. and Pescio, C. (2000). *Memorie d'oltremare: Prato, Italia, Africa.* Florence: Giunti.

Lombardi-Diop, C. and Romeo, C. (2012). *Postcolonial Italy: Challenging National Homogeneity.* New York: Palgrave Macmillan.

Mammone, A. (2006). A daily revision of the past: Fascism, anti-fascism, and memory in contemporary Italy. *Modern Italy*, 11 (2), 211–26.

Mellino, M. (2006). Italy and Postcolonial Studies. *Interventions: International Journal of Postcolonial Studies*, 8 (3), 461–71.

Morone, A. M. (2010). I custodi della memoria. Il comitato per la documentazione dell'opera dell'Italia in Africa. *Zapruder*, 23, 25–38.

Palma, S. (2007). Il ritorno di miti e memorie coloniali: l'epopea degli ascari eritrei nell'Italia postcoloniale. *Afriche e Orienti*, 9, 57–79.

Pergher, R. (2012). The Consent of Memory. Recovering Fascist–Settler Relations in Libya. In G. Albanese and R. Pergher (eds.), *In the Society of Fascists: Acclamation, Acquiescence and Agency* (pp. 169–88). New York: Palgrave Macmillan.

Polezzi, L. (2007). "Mal d'Africa" and Its Memory: Heroes and Anti-heroes in Pre- and Postwar Readings of the Italian Presence in Africa. In D. Hipkins and G. Plain (eds.), *War-torn Tales: Literature, Film and Gender in the Aftermath of World War II* (pp. 39–64). Oxford: Peter Lang.

Rochat, G. (1981). La repressione della resistenza in Cirenaica, 1927–1931. In E. Santarelli, G. Rochat, R. Rainero, and L. Goglia (eds.), *Omar al-Mukhtar e la riconquista fascista della Libia.* Milan: Marzorati.

Taddia, I. (1988). *La memoria dell'Impero: autobiografie d'Africa Orientale.* Manduria: P. Lacaita.

Triulzi, A. (2006). Displacing the colonial event. *Interventions: International Journal of Postcolonial Studies*, 8 (3), 430–43.

INDEX

Note: Page numbers in *italic* refer to *tables*. Page numbers in **bold** refer to **figures**. Page numbers followed by 'n' refer to notes.